MONEY AND EMPLOYMENT

Paul Davidson (May 1987)
(*photograph by Louise Davidson*)

Money and Employment

The Collected Writings of Paul Davidson, Volume 1

Paul Davidson
Edited by Louise Davidson

NEW YORK UNIVERSITY PRESS
Washington Square, New York

First published in the U.S.A. in 1991
by NEW YORK UNIVERSITY PRESS
Washington Square
New York, N.Y. 10003

Printed in Great Britain

Library of Congress Cataloging-in-Publication Data
Davidson, Paul.
    Money and employment/Paul Davidson: edited by Louise Davidson.
    p.   cm.— (The collected writings of Paul Davidson: v. 1)
    Includes bibliographical references and index.
    ISBN 0–8147–1835–3
    1. Money.   2. Employment (Economic theory).   3. Keynesian
economics.   I. Davidson, Louise.   II. Title.   III. Series:
Davidson. Paul.   Essays.   Selections: v. 1.
HB119.D37A25   vol. 1
[HG229]
330 s—dc20
[331]   90–45973
                                                              CIP

Contents

Acknowledgements

We wish to acknowledge the following journals and publishers for permission to reprint the articles that appear in these two volumes:

Canadian Journal of Economics and Political Science; Southern Economic Journal; Public Finance; Economic Journal; American Economic Review; Review of Economics and Statistics; Oxford Economic Papers; Johns Hopkins University Press; University of Colorado Press; *Econometrica; Land Economics; Highway Research Record*; University of New Mexico Press; Oxford University Press; *Journal of Political Economy; The Annals*; Ballinger Publishing Co.; *Economic Inquiry*; Brookings Institution; University of Pennsylvania Press; Cambridge University Press; Institute for Energy Studies; *Challenge Magazine; Economie Appliquée; Journal of Post Keynesian Economics; Economies et Sociétés; Nebraska Journal of Economics and Business; The Public Interest; Kredit und Kapital*; McGraw Hill Publishing Co.; *Journal of Economic Literature*; Macmillan, London; *Eastern Economic Journal; The New Leader; Quarterly Review of Economics and Business; Thames Papers in Political Economy*; Edward Elgar Publishing Co.; *Cambridge Journal of Economics*.

Introduction to Volumes of the Collected Writings of Paul Davidson

Although I have been a 'professional economist' for more than three decades, I still believe, and hope, that my most creative work lies ahead. Nevertheless, at this stage, there apparently was some desire for a collection – one single set of volumes – where most of my important professional writings (other than books) would be gathered. The result has been these two volumes entitled *Money, Employment, and Resources*. This title succinctly summarizes those broadly defined areas of economic policy where I have concentrated my attention.

My career as an economist began rather later than usual. I had graduated at Brooklyn College in 1950 with majors in Chemistry and Biology, and never took a course in economics during my undergraduate years. I went on to graduate training in Biochemistry at the University of Pennsylvania from 1950 to 1952, easily completing most of my courses while working as an instructor in Biochemistry at the Medical and Dental Schools. I decided to do a Ph.D. thesis regarding DNA (this was before the discovery of the 'double helix'). Although I had enjoyed my teaching duties I quickly lost interest in biochemical research and withdrew from the programme. Not knowing what I would 'do for a living', I returned to New York and enrolled at City University for a business programme to prepare me for the world of commerce. While there I had to take a course in basic economics. As a biochemist trained in the questions of experimental design and statistical inference, I was appalled by the misuse of empirical data by economists. It was then that I decided that this was a field where I could both make a mark for myself and a contribution to society and the economics profession.

After military service on a biochemical research team, I completed my M.B.A. programme. I then enrolled in the graduate economics programme at the University of Pennsylvania where I came under the influence of Sidney Weintraub. He was just completing his masterpiece *An Approach to the Theory of Income Distribution*. Sidney became the dominating influence in my early career as I worked on my doctoral dissertation, 'Theories of Relative Shares'.[1] This explains my early interest in macroeconomics, and especially income distribution. My first published article, 'A Clarification of the Ricardian Rent Share' (Chapter 1, Volume 2) was in this area. Although Weintraub had an important influence on my thinking over the years, we collaborated only on one published paper,

'Money as Cause and Effect' (Chapter 9, Volume 1) and one unpublished paper, 'Theory of Monetary Policy under Wage Inflation' (Chapter 10, Volume 1).

1 MONEY, INFLATION, INCOME DISTRIBUTION AND EXPECTATIONS

The connection between inflation, income distribution, and money was only vaguely perceived by Weintraub in those days. His discussion of the Keynes's Finance Motive Notes seemed oddly disjointed when combined with Sidney's masterful exposition of the aggregate supply–demand interdependence of Keynes's *General Theory*. It was not until I 'cracked the nut' of Keynes's Finance Motive analysis and showed my results to Roy Harrod (who happened to be visiting Pennsylvania at the time), that I got a glimmer of the true role of money in the Keynesian Revolution. Harrod was very enthusiastic about my paper and sent it on to the editor of the Oxford Economics Papers with his recommendation. With characteristic English reserve, Harrod wrote to me from Christ Church on 27 May 1964 indicating that he believed the editor 'to be favourabiy disposed to it'.

It was the publication of my 'Keynes's Finance Motive' which provided me with the confidence to strike out on my own in attempting to integrate monetary analysis into Keynes's revolutionary general theory. Accordingly, I have made this article the lead chapter of the first volume.

The third chapter in volume 1, entitled 'Money, Portfolio Balance, Capital Accumulation and Economic Growth', was written in 1965 and submitted to *Econometrica* in March 1966. The paper was a criticism of Tobin's 1965 *Econometrica* 'money and growth' model; it also presented an alternative approach to money and capital accumulation more in tune with Keynes's *General Theory*. My alternative to Tobin's 1965 accumulation analysis involved utilizing the ratio of the spot market to the forward market price for capital, i.e. the market price of existing real capital relative to the cost of producing new capital, as the relevant 'invisible hand' ratio directing the entrepreneurial determination of the rate of investment or disinvestment in real capital. This ratio is, of course, the equivalent of the famous q-ratio that Tobin was to discover in 1968.

The story of this paper's history from submission until its publication may have a moral for fledgling economists just beginning their career. Nine months after submission, on 6 January 1967, the editor of *Econometrica* sent back two referees' reports. He indicated that 'Both referees have found much in the paper of merit, but both feel that it falls short of being publishable in its present form . . . [because it] is not precise enough in its analytic content.' The editor encouragingly indicated that he would be 'very willing to consider a revision that would be more analytic in character'. Both referees noted the lack of analytical precision. One referee specifically stated his displeasure at the paper's 'essayistic and non-analytical character'.

Although this submitted manuscript utilized the same supply and demand diagrams as the published paper, it was devoid of any algebraic expressions. This absence of equations was apparently the basis for the referees' 'non-analytical' characterization. I revised the paper by merely introducing a simple algebraic equation in the text just before the verbal description of each supply or demand relationship that was discussed – a total of fourteen equational additions. Otherwise, the textual exposition remained virtually unchanged.

On 13 April 1967, the editor informed me that this revised version of the manuscript was accepted for publication. I was overjoyed, and hoped the paper would appear with a rejoinder from Tobin. I thought a response from such an eminent economist – even if very critical (which I could not conceive as possible) – would be extremely useful. The paper was published in the April 1968 issue without any comment from Tobin. Although I still think this was one of my best papers, and even though it appeared in a very prestigious journal, it apparently failed to create any stir in the profession. I decided that it would be necessary to write a book which would tie all my thoughts on money and employment together in a bundle that could not be overlooked. That book, which was written during my stay at Cambridge University in 1970–1, was *Money and the Real World*.

My visit to Cambridge was one of the most productive investments of my life. I gained tremendously from the almost daily interactions with Basil Moore[2] (who was also visiting), as well as less frequent, but still fruitful, discussions with Nicky Kaldor, Richard Kahn, Michael Posner and Ken Galbraith (also visiting).

Most important was my relationship with Joan Robinson. We immediately embarked on heated discussions regarding drafts of various chapters of my manuscript on *Money and the Real World*. She was clearly unhappy with my arguments regarding the Cambridge post-Keynesian approach. I remember her being particularly distressed with my criticisms of Kaldor's neo-Pasinetti theorem (see my 'Demand and Supply of Securities' paper – Chapter 4, Volume 1).[3] After a few weeks of such discussions, she finally refused to speak to me about my work.

Nevertheless, almost every morning when I arrived at my office at the Faculty building on Sidgwick Avenue, I would find a blank sheet of paper with a handwritten question on the top. Joan was setting me an essay to write. I diligently wrote my answer and when she went up for morning coffee, I would place the paper on her desk. After lunch I would find the paper back on my desk with her easily recognizable scrawl indicating why the various points I had made were either wrong-headed or just plain wrong.

I learned a tremendous amount from these daily essay exercises – and, although she did not admit it at the time, I believe so did Joan Robinson. For in the years following my visit to Cambridge, I would often receive notes from her indicating when she especially liked a published paper of mine. For example, on 3 July 1978 she wrote about my paper 'Money and General Equilibrium' (Chapter 12, Volume 1) which was published in the French journal *Economie Appliquée* (produced by the Institut des Sciences Mathématiques et Economiques Appliquée, or ISMEA): 'I much enjoyed your piece in ISMEA. I hope you will put the same points where they will be read in the USA.' And on 13 September 1978 regarding my paper 'Why Money Matters' (Chapter 13, Volume 1), Joan wrote: 'I like your piece about "crowding out". This ought to settle the matter.'

My friendship with John Hicks began after we met at the International Economics Association's Conference on 'The Microfoundations of Macroeconomics' in 1975 at S'Agora in Spain, where neoclassical Keynesians, monetarists, general equilibrium theorists, and the emerging group of what was to be called Post Keynesians met. All the participants apparently agreed that the meeting was a failure. Hicks recognized this in his introduction to the final meeting of this conference where he stated that 'our discussions had so far not done what we had set out to do. We had met to discuss a rather central issue in economics; but it had been shown that economists were not in a good state to discuss central issues . . . we were each shooting off on our own paths, and we were lucky if we could keep in sight even our closest neighbour.'[4]

Nevertheless, Hicks told me after he heard my 'Discussion of Leijonhufuvd's Social Consequences of Inflation' (Chapter 4, Volume 2) that he believed that his views on the microfoundations of macroeconomics were closer to mine than to anyone else's at this conference.

After this S'Agora conference, Hicks and I started to correspond and I believed I had some impact on his changing view regarding the importance of ISLM.[5] In our continuing correspondence and at several meetings in London and at his home in Blockley during these years, Sir John provided me with some very useful insights – which though difficult to specify, no doubt had an influence on my developing thought, especially in regard to time, liquidity, contracts and expectations. On 13 February 1983, he wrote to me regarding my 'Rational Expectations: A Fallacious Foundation' paper (Chapter 12, Volume 2): 'I do like it very much. I have never been through that RE literature; you know that I don't have proper access to journals; but I had just enough to be put off by the smell of it. You have now *rationalized* my suspicions, and have shown me that I have missed my chance, of labelling my own point of view as *non-ergodic*. One needs a name like that to ram a point home.'

2 RESOURCE ECONOMICS

My interest in resource economics developed from a brief interlude in my academic career in 1960–1, when, because of my low salary at Rutgers University and the needs of my growing family, I took a position as the Assistant Director of the Economics Division of the Continental Oil Company (Conoco). At Conoco, I headed a small group of staff economists who were primarily involved in providing economic projections and evaluating investment projects for the Management Executive Committee of the corporation. The experience of participating in managerial decisions of a large corporation, even though it was in a staff rather than line position, was invaluable in clarifying in my mind the fundamental flaws of the neoclassical theory of entrepreneurial expectation formation and decision-making. My 1963 article, 'Public Policy Problems of the Domestic Crude Oil Industry' (Chapter 22, Volume 2), represents the distillation of analytical arguments that I developed in order to try to affect the decision-making of management at Conoco and the positions they should take relative to the new economic policy approach of President Kennedy.[6] This 'Domestic Crude' paper was apparently quite well regarded in the profession. Several well-known scholars in the field, for example, A. F. Kahn, M. A. Adelman and R. H. Heflebower, initiated some further 'correspondence' discussion with me.

One of these kind people – I never found out which one – recommended my name to Allen Kneese of Resources for the Future as a potential principal investigator on the demand for water recreational activities. (Apparently, they did not believe in the age-old adage 'Oil and water do not mix'!) Kneese and RFF provided a grant for me to do a study of 'The Social Value of Water Recreational Facilities . . .' (Chapter 34, Volume 2). The success of this initial study brought forth new invitations to take on additional 'resource' analysis, for instance, involving 'Recreational Use of TVA' (Chapter 37, Volume 2) and 'Scenic Enhancement of Highways' (Chapters 35 and 38, Volume 2). A further massive study of two national recreation surveys for the US Bureau of Outdoor Recreation resulted in a book entitled, *The Demand and Supply for Outdoor Recreation* (Washington: Government Printing Office, 1968).

In 1973, with the OPEC embargo, the question of crude oil and energy was again on the nation's mind. Art Okun contacted me and asked me to do a study regarding President Nixon's Project Independence for Brookings. At approximately the same time, people at the Ford Foundation's Energy Policy Project requested a study regarding incentives and the oil industry. Our studies for Ford and Brookings are 'The Relations of Economic Rent and Price Incentives to Oil and Gas Supplies' (Chapter 24, Volume 2) and 'Oil: Its Time Allocation and Project Independence' (Chapter 25, Volume 2).[7]

During the 1970s, the 'energy problem' was continually on the public's mind. Between 1973 and 1979, I was asked to testify nineteen times before various Congressional Committees on some aspect of this problem. As an example of the type of prepared statement which I would submit before being cross-examined by Congressional members, I have included testimony presented to the House Ways and Means Committee in 1975 (Chapter 39, Volume 2). I decided to include this sample of my Congressional testimonies in order to provide the reader with some idea of the arguments I thought, at the time, could be developed from our professional studies that would be persuasive to policy-makers – and to provide some predictions which I hoped might contribute to new legislation. I leave it to the reader to judge, from hindsight, how persuasive my arguments and how accurate my forecasts, were.

In a similar vein, I have also included written testimony prepared for the Federal Communications Commission[8] in 1978 (Chapter 40, Volume 2) as well as a speech given to Savings and Loan Examiners in 1980 (Chapter 41, Volume 2). These last two papers are offered to the reader as illustrations of how I tried to carry my professional analysis over to the arena of actual policy decision-making.

3 A NOTE ON THE COVERAGE OF THESE VOLUMES

These volumes contain some ninety pieces – several that were never published – which I have written over the years. Within each part (e.g. money, macroeconomic employment, income distribution and inflation, etc.) the papers are usually presented in terms of their chronological order. Occasionally, however, this ordering procedure has not been followed. If, for example, two papers dealt with the same topic, even if they were written years apart, they are presented together here. For example, 'More on the Aggregate Supply Function' (Chapter 31, Volume 1) published in 1962 is followed by 'The Aggregate Supply Function' (Chapter 32, Volume 1) published in 1987.

In any collection of papers, there is always the question of repetition. Journal articles have to be constructed as 'stand alone' pieces able to provide the reader with background analytical framework as well as the particular focus of the paper. An author cannot assume that the reader is familiar with the author's earlier writings or his analytical framework – especially if the author is striving for an innovative approach to the problem at hand rather than relying on the old clichés of the orthodox mainstream of the profession. Hence there is bound to be some textual overlap in papers discussing topics in the same or closely related areas. How should one deal with such duplication?

In these volumes two typical cases of repetition tended to occur. Sometimes, an earlier paper's analysis was incorporated, without significant change, into a latter, larger essay. In such cases, only the later paper is presented, while a note is added citing the existence of the earlier paper. For example, 'Monetary Theory and Policy in a Global Context With a large International Debt' (Chapter 21, Volume 2) incorporates 'A Modest Set of Proposals for Resolving the International Debt Crisis', *Journal of Post Keynesian Economics, 10,* Winter 1987–8, and hence the latter was not included in these volumes.

A more difficult problem arises when two manuscripts share, and therefore discuss, the same analytical base. In such cases there is bound to be some expositional duplication in the body of each paper, if both are in the collection. On the other hand, there may be significant differences in many aspects as each paper investigates different facets of the issues involved. Here some arbitrary judgement is necessary in deciding the degree of repetition. If it was felt that a particular section of one paper was in all its significant aspects almost identical and that no important side comments or implications would be lost, the section was deleted from one of the papers with an explanatory note that the analysis of that section could be found in the other cited paper.

By this method, it is hoped that the most severely repetitious portions of this collection of writings have been removed, protecting the reader's precious time, without severely limiting those who wish to trace how, and if, my ideas evolved over time. Nevertheless, many readers will still find some text passages that appear to them to be very similar to other paragraphs already read. There can be no way to avoid this situation completely without severely disrupting the flow of the argument in each paper and its particular implications.

Finally, a word about omissions from this collection other than those due to textual overlap. The normal book review in a professional journal of 750 to 1000 words is, I believe, much too short for the reader to learn anything in depth regarding the analytical approach of the reviewer. Consequently, journal length book reviews have not been included, although review articles have.

I hope that the readers of these volumes will obtain some sense of the enthusiasm with which I worked out the analysis of the problems undertaken in these essays and the pleasure I received. I have always considered the conclusions tentative, and have always been open to additional arguments. Over the years, I have had many stimulating discussions with professional colleagues and friends as well as many of my students. It is impossible to list all who have, each in their own way, contributed to my understanding of economics. Perhaps these volumes should be dedicated to them.

Notes

1. I successfully defended my Ph.D. thesis in August 1958, just a few days after the birth of my daughter Diane. I was awarded my Ph.D. degree from the University in February 1959. The dissertation was published as *Theories of Aggregate Income Distribution* (Rutgers University Press, 1960).
2. These discussions, although much less frequent in recent years, are still always a delight.
3. In 17 August 1973 letter, Joan came as close to apologizing as she could when she wrote, 'however, I agree with you that Nicky's NeoPasinetti theorem is no good. I regret that I tried to rationalize it in my *Heresies.*' Nevertheless she still felt the need to provide some admonishment and added that she had not written to me about 'your book because I was put out at your making me say the exact opposite of what I had been teaching for 30 years, see, in particular, page 125'.
4. Quoted in *The Microfoundations of Macroeconomics*, edited by G. C. Harcourt (London: Macmillan, 1977), p. 373.
5. See Hicks's 'ISLM: An Explanation', *Journal of Post Keynesian Economics, 3*, Winter 1980–1. See also footnote 9, p. ix, of Hicks's 1977 book, *Economic Perspectives*, where he indicates that my spot–forward market analysis may be more in line with 'parts of the *General Theory*' than his own reliance on the spot (Monday morning) transactions approach.
6. Although I do not believe I was very successful in changing Conoco's strategies, I apparently impressed the President of the firm sufficiently that he asked me to help write his public speeches – which were, in those days, numerous.
7. Most of the recreational and energy studies were done on the basis of contract research. As the Principal Investigator on these projects I was able to finance graduate students, as research assistants, who were then listed as co-authors on these publications. (Professors F. Gerard Adams who was also a co-author on the recreational studies was recruited to help with the utilization of the latest computer techniques of the time. Professor Lawrence Falk, who had worked for a major oil company, was recruited as a co-author for his knowledge of the data of the oil industry and some practical aspects of industry decision making.)
8. During the period 1968 to 1978, I was a consultant for the Western Union Corporation. During this period I was responsible for the development of econometric studies of the various price, income, and cross-elasticities which affect the various types of electronic communication that this public utility provided. These studies were the basis upon which rates structured by the company and approved by the Federal Communications Commission and the various State regulatory agencies. I presented the original economic analysis and the supporting detailed econometric estimations for the record in Docket 16258 (1968) of the FCC.

Part I
Money

1 Keynes's Finance Motive*

In *The General Theory*, Keynes distinguishes between three motives for holding cash '(i) the transactions-motive, i.e. the need of cash for the current transaction of personal and business exchanges; (ii) the precautionary-motive, i.e. the desire for security as to the future cash equivalent of a certain proportion of total resources; and (iii) the speculative-motive, i.e. the object of securing profit from knowing better than the market what the future will bring forth' (Keynes, 1936, p. 170). Keynes recognized that 'money held for each of these three purposes forms, nevertheless, a single pool, which the holder is under no necessity to segregate into three watertight compartments' (ibid., p. 195); however, he did suggest that these three categories formed an exhaustive set and that all other reasons for holding money (e.g. the income motive or the business motive) are merely subcategories of these three major divisions (ibid., pp. 194–200). According to Keynes, the quantity of money demanded for transactions and precautionary purposes 'is not very sensitive to changes in the rate of interest' (ibid., p. 171); rather it 'is mainly a resultant of the general activity of the economic system and of the level of money-income' (ibid., p. 196); the quantity of money demanded for speculative purposes, on the other hand, responds to 'changes in the rate of interest as given by changes in the prices of bonds and debts of various maturities' (ibid., p. 197). Although Keynes did not actually use the terms in *The General Theory*, the money held to satisfy the first two motives is usually called active balances, while money held for speculative purposes is customarily referred to as idle balances.

In reply to Ohlin's (1937) lengthy criticism of his position, in a 1937 review and restatement of his ideas, Keynes introduced a new and some-what novel purpose for demanding money, namely, *the finance motive* (1937a). Keynes argues that if the level of investment was unchanged, then the money held to 'finance' new investments was a constant amount and could therefore be lumped under a subcategory of the transactions motive, where capital goods transactions are involved. In other words, entrepreneurs typically hold some cash balances to assure themselves that they will be able to carry out investment plans. These balances can be looked upon as transactions balances, since given the marginal efficiency of capital schedule, the rate of interest, and the consumption function, there will be a unique level of investment demand for any given level of output, i.e. for

* *Oxford Economic Papers* (17 March 1965).
The author is grateful to C.F. Carter, Miles Fleming, Sir Roy F. Harrod, Helen Raffel, Eugene Smolensky, Sidney Weintraub, and Charles R. Whittlesey for helpful comments at various stages.

any given output level, there will be a certain volume of planned investment transactions for which transactions balances will be maintained.

'But', Keynes argued, 'if decisions to invest are (e.g.) increasing, the
extra finance involved will constitute an additional demand for money'
(1937a, p. 247). Thus, according to Keynes, the finance motive was an
important additional component of the aggregate money-demand function
when the decision to change the level of investment occurred. For example, if the marginal efficiency of capital schedule were to shift outwards
because of improved profits expectations, then for any given level of
output and rate of interest, entrepreneurs would desire to engage in more
investment transactions than before; consequently when the marginal
efficiency of capital function shifts, it gives rise to an additional demand for
cash balances (cf. Robinson, 1952, pp. 20–2).

To clarify the essence of the finance motive, and to indicate why it is not
properly taken into account in the discussion of the transactions motive,
Keynes wrote:

> It follows that, if the liquidity-preferences of the public (as distinct from
> the entrepreneurial investors) and of the banks are unchanged, an excess
> in the finance required by current ex-ante output (it is not necessary to
> write 'investment', since the same is true of *any* output which has to be
> planned ahead) over the finance released by current ex-post output will
> lead to a rise in the rate of interest; and a decrease will lead to a fall. I
> should not have previously overlooked this point, since it is the coping-
> stone of the liquidity theory of the rate of interest. I allowed, it is true,
> for the effect of an increase in *actual* activity on the demand for money.
> But I did not allow for the effect of an increase in *planned* activity, which
> is superimposed on the former . . . Just as an increase in actual activity
> must (as I have always explained) raise the rate of interest unless either
> the banks or the rest of the public become more willing to release cash,
> so (as I now add) an increase in planned activity must have a similar,
> superimposed influence. (1937b, p. 667)

Considering that Keynes felt that the finance motive was the coping stone
of his liquidity preference theory, it is surprising to see that the concept has
practically disappeared from the literature.[1]

There was, however, a very clear practical illustration of this point
offered by Keynes about a year later when his attention was devoted to the
imminent rearmament programme and the prospect of war. In a letter
printed in the 18 April 1939 edition of the London *Times*, Keynes elucidated his reasoning still further. The immediate question was how to
finance the pending additional government expenditures for rearmament.
Keynes argued that 'If an attempt is made to borrow them [the savings
which will result from the increased production of non-consumption (war)

goods] before they exist, as the Treasury have done once or twice lately, a stringency in the money market must result, since, pending the expenditure, the liquid resources acquired by the Treasury must be at the expense of the normal liquid resources of the banks and of the public.' In other words, an increase in planned governmental expenditures will normally result in an increase in the aggregate demand for money function, even before the expenditures are undertaken.

Is the finance motive really as significant as Keynes believed? And if it is, why has it been given short shrift and almost vanished by neglect in the post-Keynesian literature? The rest of this paper will be devoted to answering these questions. We will show that the almost ubiquitous adoption of a strained and somewhat distorted variant of the Keynesian system resulted in the omission of the finance motive *and* the incorrect specification of the transactions demand for money function. As a consequence of these imperfections in the model, a needless theoretical controversy about the independence of the real and monetary subsectors developed[2] which has led subsequent work into many blind avenues, for, as will be argued below, the finance motive provides the link to demonstrate that the aggregate demand for money function is *not* independent of events in the real sector. Thus an unnecessary polarization has occurred to beguile some, and bedevil others, more interested in comprehending Keynes's own thought.

1 THE FINANCE MOTIVE

Most writers have simply ignored the finance motive[3] by popularizing, in the name of Keynes, a macroeconomic system which made it easy to completely abrogate the finance motive. This system, which is pedagogically centred about the familiar 45-degree diagram[4] (Figure 1.1), and which (by definition) prevents the analysis of non-equilibrium positions (i.e. positions off the 45-degree line), has achieved such popularity that it is, if not unfair, impossible, at this date, to associate it with any one economist. Consequently, in what follows, the writings of Hansen have been chosen merely as a familiar example and should not be interpreted as suggesting that Professor Hansen is either the sole or even the primary source of the error.

According to Hansen, the demand for transactions balances function, L_t, shows 'the *desired* volume of active or "transactions" cash balances at various levels of income Y' (1949, p. 61). Thus Hansen writes the demand for transactions balances as

$$L_t = kY \tag{1.1}$$

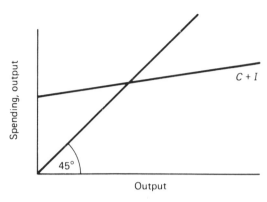

Figure 1.1

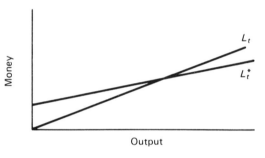

Figure 1.2

where k is a constant. He thereupon plots the function as the straight line L_t emanating from the origin (Figure 1.2). The implication of Hansen's diagram is that the demand for transactions balances is a function of the 45-degree line (i.e. the output identity line). In other words, Hansen has made the quantity of money demanded for transactions purposes a function of the actual level of output at each level of output.

Once we go back to Keynes, however, it is clear that in his writings on the finance motive, the quantity of money demanded for transactions balances is not directly related to output, rather it is associated with planned or expected spending propensities, i.e. it is a function of the aggregate demand for goods (the $C + I$ line in Figure 1.1), which, in turn, is a function of the level of output. The quantity of money demanded, therefore, is only indirectly related to the level of output via the aggregate demand function. In other words, Keynes's transactions-demand concept is functionally related to, in the simplest case, the summation of the consumption function and the investment-demand function. If we assume that the quantity of money demanded for transactions balances is equal to some fraction of the aggregate demand for goods at each level of output, then the transactions-demand-for-money function would be drawn as L_t^* rather than L_t in Figure 1.2 (since it is related to the $C + I$ line rather than the 45-degree line in Figure 1.1).[5]

Much more is involved here than merely a geometric misrepresentation of the demand for transactions balances, for it now becomes obvious that the relationship between the quantity of money demanded for transactions and the level of output is a 'function of a function', rather than a simple direct relationship. Thus, to trace out the change in the quantity of transactions money demanded for a given change in output it is necessary to obtain the change in the quantity demanded of transactions balances for a given change in aggregate demand *and* the change in aggregate demand for a given change in output.[6] In other words, the change in the quantity of money demanded for transactions purposes depends not only on changes in output, but also on the relationship of the change in the level of aggregate demand with a change in output (e.g. given the level of investment, on the marginal propensity to consume). Furthermore, given the customary payments period in the economy, it follows that if consumers and/or investors decide to spend more at any given level of income (an upward shift in the aggregate demand function), then there will be an increase in the demand for money for the purchase of goods *at each level of output* (an upward shift on the L_t^* function).

Let us summarize symbolically the argument as developed so far. The demand for transactions balances should be written as

$$L_t^* = \alpha C + \beta I \tag{1.2}$$

where α and β are constants ($0 \leqslant \alpha \leqslant 1; 0 \leqslant \beta \leqslant 1$) whose magnitudes depend primarily on the frequency of payments and the overlapping of payments and receipts in the system, and C and I are the real consumption and investment functions respectively. Assuming linear functions merely for algebraic simplicity, the consumption function may be written as

$$C = a_1 + b_1 Y \tag{1.3}$$

where a_1 is a constant ($\geqslant 0$) and b_1 is the marginal propensity to consume. The investment-demand function, on a linear conception, is:

$$I = a_2 - b_2 i \tag{1.4}$$

where a_2 and b_2 are constants, and i is the rate of interest. Combining equations (1.3) and (1.4) into (1.2) we obtain

$$L_t^* = \alpha a_1 + \beta a_2 + \alpha b_1 Y - \beta b_2 i. \tag{1.5}$$

If we assume a constant rate of interest (which is implicit in the usual 45-degree diagram), then the fourth term on the right-hand side of equation (1.5) is a constant; thus, equation (1.5) appears to be similar to Hansen's equation (1.1) except that the function does not emanate from the origin.

There is, however, a significant analytical difference between equations (1.1) and (1.5). In Hansen's system, the parameter k of equation (1.1) depends only on the customary length of the payments period in the economy, and consequently, the equation is entirely independent of the behavioural parameters of the real sector (equations (1.3) and (1.4)). Thus, as long as the conventional payments period is unchanged, the magnitude of k is fixed and therefore Hansen's transactions demand for money function is stable – even if the parameters of the aggregate demand-function change. On the other hand, equation (1.5) shows that some of the parameters (the a's and the b's) are common to both the transactions demand for money function *and* the real consumption- and investment-demand functions. Thus, according to equation (1.5), even if the payments period is unchanged (i.e. α and β are constant), any change in either the investment demand or the consumption functions will result in a shift of the entire transactions demand for money schedule; or as Keynes noted, any 'increase in planned activity' will result in an increased demand for money *at each level of output*. Accordingly, any change in the parameters of the aggregate-demand function (contrary to Hansen's system) will result in a shift in the L_t^* function. The demand for money function is *not* independent of changes in the real sector.

It is the shift in the L_t^* function induced by a change in spending propensities that Keynes was describing when he discussed the finance motive.[7] Whenever there is a shift in the aggregate-demand function, there will be a concomitant shift in the demand for money schedule. Consequently, when there is an increase in planned investment, for example, the equilibrium quantity of money demanded will ultimately increase for two reasons: (i) a shift in the L_t^* function (i.e. the finance motive), and (ii) a movement along the new L_t^* function as output increases and induces further spending via the multiplier. It is the shift in the L_t^* function which puts additional pressure on the rate of interest.[8]

Thus, every upward shift of the aggregate-demand function (the $C + I$ line in Figure 1.1) implies the prevalence of a 'finance motive' as spending units switch over from one money-demand function to a higher one. Once this change has occurred, spending units will maintain larger transactions balances than before *at each level of output*. At that point the dynamic finance motive merges with the static concept of the transactions motive. The finance motive thus evolves as one of the dynamic elements in the static Keynesian model (Robinson, 1952, pp. 80–7); its major contribution is in macroeconomic path analysis rather than in comparative statics.

2 IMPLICATIONS OF THE ANALYSIS

It is useful to distil three important implications of the analysis before further elaborating on it. These are:

1. Since the demand for money function is not as stable as Hansen's formulation implies (i.e. it varies every time the aggregate-demand function shifts), and since it does not emanate from the origin, *even if the rate of interest is a constant*, there is no reason to expect a constant relationship between the demand for money for transactions purposes and the level of output. In other words, and in the language of monetary theorists, we should *not* expect the income velocity of money to be constant. The recognition of the 'finance motive' concept prepares us for some clearer understanding of monetary phenomena.

For example, Friedman, recognizing that the income velocity of money is a demand-oriented phenomenon, has attempted to estimate the income elasticity of demand for money. He has found that observed short-run variations in income velocity imply an income elasticity less than unity, whereas secular evidence indicates an elasticity which exceeds unity (Friedman, 1959, pp. 328–30). In a novel (and perhaps somewhat forced) explanation, Friedman tries to reconcile these conflicting short-run and secular estimates of elasticity by imputing differences between 'permanent' income and prices and measured income and prices (ibid., pp. 334–8). Our finance motive analysis, however, suggests a much simpler explanation which is entirely consistent with Friedman's short-run and secular estimates. If the short-run demand for transactions-balances function has a positive intercept and is either a straight line or concave to the abscissa, then:

$$\frac{dL_t^*}{dY} < \frac{L_t^*}{Y}.$$

It therefore follows that the income elasticity of demand for transactions balances will be less than unity along the entire function.[9] In other words, given the normal aggregate consumption and investment functions and the rate of interest, we would expect Friedman to find out that as the economy moved toward equilibrium, short-run movements in output will be accompanied by less than proportional changes in the quantity of money demanded by spending units.

Observed secular changes in the quantity of money demanded, on the other hand, are most likely the result of viewing particular demand points on different L_t^* functions as the latter shifts through time in response to changes in the parameters of the system. The 'income elasticity' calculated from observations which cut across short-run L_t^* functions will obviously be larger in magnitude than the elasticity measured along any one L_t^* function and might easily result in estimates which exceed unity. This secular 'elasticity' measurement, however, has little or no relationship to the usual concept of income elasticity which assumes a given preference scheme (i.e. given behavioural parameters).

2. A shift in *any* component of the aggregate demand for money function will induce a concomitant shift in the transaction demand for money function. Thus, when Keynes linked the finance motive with changes in the decision to invest, he was, as he readily admitted, discussing 'only a special case' of the finance motive [10] (1937a, p. 247).

Generally speaking, the finance motive will be involved whenever the aggregate demand function is changed. For example, if we add a government spending function (assuming, for the moment, no change in the $C + I$ line in Figure 1.1) then we would have to shift up the L_t^* function (in Figure 1.2) to include government's demand for transactions balances. Furthermore, to the extent that the quantity of money demanded per dollar of consumption is different from the quantity demanded per dollar of planned investment (i.e. $\alpha \neq \beta$) or planned government spending (or planned foreigners' purchases for that matter), then the total demand for transactions balances will depend upon the composition of aggregate demand (at each level of output), while the latter, in turn, will depend at least in part on the distribution of income (cf. Keynes, 1936, p. 201). To illustrate, if income is redistributed from spending units which have high liquidity needs to units which have lower liquidity needs to carry out a given volume of planned expenditures, then even with the same level of aggregate demand for goods, the quantity of money demanded will be reduced. For example, to the extent that consumers have less leeway in matching their receipts to their obligations (because of less flexible consumer credit institutions), consumers may require higher balances per dollar of planned expenditures than business firms.[11] Thus, the composition of aggregate demand as well as the level of output may be an important determinant of the demand for cash balances.

At the level of public policy, as well as correct theory, it thus appears that once the L_t^* function is related to the components of the aggregate demand function rather than to the 45-degree line, some important insights appear. For example, if the economy is initially at some output level, say Y_1, and if the government decides to increase its purchases of new goods and services by x dollars (on the assumption that the supply of money is unchanged), the magnitude of the impact on the rate of interest at the original Y_1 level (as well as at any other Y level) will depend on whether the government 'finances' the increased expenditure by borrowing or by taxation[12] (this was noted earlier in the revealing quotation from Keynes regarding war finance). This suggests that even before an expansionary activity occurs, a planned increase in government spending will affect the money market through the demand for new balances to finance and fund the projected outlay. Assuming investment demand to be relatively inelastic to changes in the rate of interest, the magnitude of the impact on the money market will be greater if the government borrows rather than increases taxes to finance the expenditure, since borrowing will result in the addition of the government component to the aggregate demand function; while financing via income taxes, for example, will reduce the consumption component while elevating the government component. Thus, in the latter case, we should not expect the aggregate demand curve to be elevated as much as in the former case: the shift in the L_t^* function will be less with taxation than with borrowing. (Hansen's L_t function, on the other hand, portends a complete absence of impact on the money market until after the increase in economic activity actually occurs.)[13]

3. If the demand for transactions balances is related to the aggregate demand function, then a straight-line L_t function which emanates from the origin belongs to the world of Say's Law – a world where the aggregate demand function coincides with the 45-degree line,[14] i.e. a world where the aggregate demand function is linear and homogeneous with respect to output. In such a world, however, 'money is but a veil' and there exists a dichotomy between the real and monetary sectors so that there can be no monetary obstacle to full employment for the real and monetary factors are completely independent[15] (cf. Hicks, 1957, pp. 282–3). Once, however, it is recognized that the demand for transactions balances is a function of aggregate demand, which, in turn, *is not homogeneous with respect to output*, then the demand for money function is not homogeneous with respect to output. It therefore follows that the system cannot be dichotomized into independent monetary and real subsets since the scale of activity is an important determinant of the level of aggregate demand and, therefore, of the quantity of money demanded. (Certainly, Keynes believed that the analytical separation of the real and monetary sectors was wrong (1936, p. 293)).

3 THE FINANCE MOTIVE AND THE INTERDEPENDENCE OF THE REAL AND MONETARY SECTORS

The inappropriateness of attempting to dichotomize the system into independent real and monetary subsets can be clarified by utilizing the more general Hicksian *IS–LM* framework where both the rate of interest and the level of output are simultaneously determined, rather than relying on the 45-degree diagram which assumes a constant rate of interest. The *IS–LM* system has the advantage of showing both the real sector and the monetary sector on the same diagram; consequently, interdependence can be visually observed if when one function shifts, the other is concomitantly displaced.

In Hicks's system (1937), the basic determinants of the *IS*-function are the marginal efficiency of capital schedule and the aggregate consumption

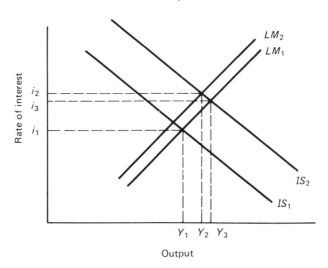

Figure 1.3

function, while the *LM*-function is based on the money demand and supply functions. The *IS*-function may be derived by combining equations (1.3) and (1.4) with the output identity $Y \equiv C + I$:

$$Y = a_1 + b_1 Y + a_2 - b_2 i, \tag{1.6}$$

or

$$Y = \left(\frac{1}{1 - b_1}\right)(a_1 + a_2 - b_2 i). \tag{1.7}$$

Equation (1.7) is the *IS* function; it traces out all the values of output and the rate of interest which are compatible with the investment demand and consumption functions. In Figure 1.3 it is plotted as the downward sloping IS_1 line, since as the rate of interest declines, according to equation (1.7), the level of output will rise.

The demand for money equation can be derived by adding the speculative and precautionary demand functions to the demand for transactions-balances function. Since we are only interested in the implications of the finance motive, i.e. of shifts in the transactions-demand function, we do not have to specify the form of the precautionary and speculative demand functions, we may merely assume them as given and constant (or varying directly with the transactions demand function). Thus the demand for money function can be derived from equation (1.5) as:

$$L = \alpha a_1 + \beta a_2 + \alpha b_1 Y - \beta b_2 i + \sigma, \tag{1.8}$$

where L is the total demand for money, and σ stands for the unspecified precautionary and speculative demand functions.

Given an exogenously determined supply of money, $\bar{m}$, and letting the demand for money equal the supply of money, we obtain the LM function as:

$$i = \frac{a_2}{b_2} + \left(\frac{\alpha}{\beta b_2}\right)(a_1 + b_1 Y) - \frac{1}{\beta b_2}\bar{m} + \frac{1}{\beta b_2}\sigma \qquad (1.9)$$

Thus, given α and β, and the a's and the b's, once outside of the liquidity trap, the LM function is plotted as upward sloping (see LM_1 in Figure 1.3) since, as Y increases, the rate of interest rises. The values of i and Y which satisfy both (1.7) and (1.9) simultaneously are revealed as the equilibrium rate of interest and the equilibrium level of output of the system (i_1 and Y_1 in Figure 1.3).

The interdependence of the money market (equation (1.9)) on the real sector (equation (1.7)) is now easily demonstrated. For example, suppose an outward shift of the investment demand function (equation (1.3)) is posited. In other words, assume a_2 increases. It follows from equation (1.7) that at each rate of interest, the Y ordinate of the IS function will increase by an amount equal to the change in a_2 multiplied by $1/(1 - b_1)$; this means simply that the IS function moves outward to IS_2 in Figure 1.3. Observe that whereas in Hansen's system, the *LM function would remain unchanged when the IS curve shifts* (Hansen, 1949, pp. 77–80), it can be seen from equation (1.9) that when a_2 increases, the i ordinate of the LM function will increase by an amount equal to the change in a_2 multiplied by $(1/b_2)$ at each output level. Thus, the whole LM function shifts upward to LM_2 in Figure 1.3, so that the new equilibrium level of output and rate of interest (Y_2 and i_2, respectively) are higher than before.[16] In a similar manner, equivalent simultaneous shifts in the IS and LM functions can be demonstrated whenever any of the parameters of the consumption or investment demand functions change.

The inevitable conclusion is that the system cannot be dichotomized into independent real and monetary subsets; consequently, it is not correct to separate monetary economics from real economics as has often been done.[17] It is important to note that the interdependence of the real and monetary sectors does not require the fine theoretical point (which may have little practical significance) of a real balance effect (cf. (Patinkin, 1956, pp. 105–15), (Modigliani, 1963, pp. 83–4, 88), (Hicks, 1957, pp. 282–5)). That so much controversy about the possible independence of the real and monetary sectors has appeared in the post-Keynesian literature is surprising in view of Keynes's warning that the 'division of Economics between the Theory of Value and Distribution on the one hand and the Theory of Money on the other hand is, I think, a false division' (Keynes,

1936, p. 293). Had the interconnection between the finance motive, the transactions motive, and the aggregate-demand function been understood originally, much of this barren controversy could have been avoided.[18]

Once the finance motive concept is understood, it is easy to demonstrate the correctness of Keynes's *obiter dictum* that an overdraft system is an 'ideal system for mitigating the effects on the banking system of an increased demand for ex-ante finance' (1937b, p. 669). For example, if there is an outward shift of the *IS* function from IS_1 to IS_2 as profit expectations rise, and if the resulting increase in demand for cash to finance the additional investment plans can be furnished by overdrafts, then the supply schedule of money will increase *pari passu* with the increase in the demand for money function. Consequently, the *LM* function will not shift; rather it will remain firm as LM_1 so that the equilibrium level of output will expand to Y_3 while the equilibrium rate of interest increases only to i_3 (Figure 1.3). Consequently, as Keynes noted, 'to the extent that the overdraft system is employed and unused overdrafts ignored by the banking system, there is no superimposed pressure resulting from planned activity over and above the pressure resulting from actual activity. In this event the transition from a lower to a higher scale of activity may be accomplished with less pressure on the demand for liquidity and the rate of interest' (ibid.).

4 THE ROLE OF PRODUCTIVITY AND THRIFT: A DIGRESSION

With the aid of Figure 1.3, it is now easy to demonstrate that much of the controversy between Robertson and Keynes on the role of productivity and thrift in determining the rate of interest is mainly a semantic confusion between movements along the demand schedule for money and shifts in the schedule.[19] An increase in the productivity (i.e. expected profitability) of capital would induce an outward shift in the *IS* curve (from IS_1 to IS_2 in Figure 1.3) and, as we have already argued, a concomitant shift in the demand for money schedule so that given the supply of money, the *LM* curve is elevated from LM_1 to LM_2. Since LM_2 lies above LM_1, Robertson was correct when he argued that an increase in productivity will raise the rate of interest (*at each level of output*) as the demand for money function shifts (cf. Robertson, 1948, pp. 10–12). On the other hand, Keynes was correct when he stressed that, given the supply of money, the increase in the equilibrium quantity of money demanded (due to the finance motive shifting the L_t^* function 'superimposed' upon a movement along the L_t^* schedule as output increased) caused the equilibrium rate of interest to rise from i_1 to i_2 (e.g. Keynes, 1937a p. 247). Since Keynes was discussing a movement from one equilibrium rate of interest to another, he stressed changes in spending propensities and output as the producer of changes in the equilibrium quantity of money demanded and in the rate of interest; whereas Robertson was essentially viewing the impact of changes in 'productivity' on the entire demand for money schedule.

The discussion of the role of thrift was enshrouded in the same confusion. An increase in thrift (i.e. a downward shift of the consumption function) would result in an inward movement of the *IS* function (say from IS_2 to IS_1) and a reduction in the demand for money schedule, so that the *LM* curve would be depressed (say from LM_2 to LM_1). Here again, we can see that Robertson, in arguing that an increase in thrift lowers the rate of interest (at each level of output), is emphasizing the shift in the entire demand for money schedule, while Keynes stressed the fall in the equilibrium rate of interest from i_2 to i_1, which resulted from a decline in the equilibrium quantity of money demanded as spending propensities and output fell (Keynes, 1936, pp. 98, 183–5, 372).

5 SOME CONCLUDING REMARKS

From the argument above it seems to follow that the disappearance of the finance motive from the post-Keynesian literature has led to some omissions and some confusions, making for wrong theoretical constructions and an inadequate understanding of certain policy implications of money supplies in a growing economy where 'finance' must be provided or deflationary pressures emerge via the rate of interest.

It is provocative to speculate briefly on this aspect for the theory of growth. For example, Gurley and Shaw argue that the growth of non-monetary intermediaries will reduce the growth in the demand for money by spending units, and consequently 'reduces the required growth of the money stock' necessary for a policy of expansion (1960, p. 228). Furthermore, Gurley and Shaw claim that 'a favorable climate for the growth of non-monetary intermediaries is one in which there is an expansion of national output based primarily on private expenditures . . . that are financed to a great degree by external means' (ibid.), since such circumstances will induce the expansion of financial intermediaries and ultimately lower the demand for money.

Gurley and Shaw's thesis can be made more specific by using our Figure 1.3. If when the marginal efficiency of capital increases so that the *IS* schedule shifts from IS_1 to IS_2, in the absence of either an overdraft system, or financial intermediaries, or specific action by the Monetary Authority, the supply of money would be unchanged, and the new equilibrium levels will be i_2 and Y_2. *If* financial intermediaries are in the system and *if* they are induced to expand their activities *pari passu* as output expands, then the ultimate equilibrium level of output will be higher than Y_2 and the rate of interest will be lower than i_2 (say, Y_3 and i_3 in Figure 1.3). This movement from the original equilibrium values of Y_1 and i_1, to Y_3 and i_3 can be looked upon as occurring in two stages. In the first instance, the outward shift of the *IS* function has increased the demand for money function as planned spending increases. The resulting increase in economic activity, if Gurley and Shaw are correct, simulates the growth of non-monetary intermediaries who are able to reduce the liquidity needs of spending units for any level of planned expenditures by rearranging the overlap of payments and receipts via the sale of financial assets of high liquidity. Thus, in the second stage, the demand for money function is reduced as the intermediaries grow. The final result on the demand for money function depends upon the magnitude of these two countervailing forces. As a first approximation, we may assume that they just neutralize each other, so that despite the constancy of the money supply the relevant *LM* function may be LM_1 instead of LM_2. Thus, Gurley and Shaw's system of non-monetary intermediaries suggests a somewhat different, and perhaps more difficult, path than Keynes's overdraft system for avoiding shortage of liquidity as plans for expansion are made.[20]

On the theoretical plane, the omission of the finance motive has led to an undue concern with dichotomized models and has resulted in ignoring one strand of thought (e.g. Davidson and Smolensky, 1964; Weintraub, 1958; 1961) which suggests that any such effort is, in effect, returning us to Say's Law and barter models, almost a perversion of what should have been learned from Keynes. Small wonder then that many 'Keynesian' models proclaim unemployment an attribute almost solely to rigidities in the wage structure. On the other hand, recognition of the finance motive reveals almost another 'liquidity trap'; this one will restrain expansion in the economy as consumption and investment plans are prepared in advance of actual expenditures unless the Monetary Authority is alert to this phenomenon and have taken appropriate measures to alleviate the strain. As Keynes cogently argues, the development of the analytical concept of the finance motive highlights the fact that

> the banks hold the key position in the transition from a lower to a higher scale of activity. If they refuse to relax (i.e. to provide additional finance), the growing congestion of the short-term loan market or the new issue market, as the case may be, will inhibit the improvement, no matter how thrifty the public purpose (sic) to be out of their future income. On the other hand, there will always be *exactly* enough ex-post saving to take up the ex-post investment and so release the finance which the latter had been previously employing. *The investment market can become congested through shortage of cash. It can never become congested through shortage of saving. This is the most fundamental of my conclusions within this field.* (Keynes, 1937b, pp. 668–9, italics added)

It is at this level that the finance motive deserves more attention and investigation than it has received. For theory to neglect any relationship which can be important, cannot help but close either avenue of investigation. Our analysis has already indicated that the finance motive can be used to shed new insights into the income velocity of money, the income elasticity of demand for money, macroeconomic path analysis and economic expansion, and the relationship of the real and monetary sectors. Other problems in monetary theory may prove tractable once the 'finance motive' is better understood.

APPENDIX[21]

In the traditional (e.g. Hansen's) formulation, the demand for transactions (L_t) [and precautionary (L_p)] balances are usually taken as a linear function of the level of output,

$$L_t + L_p = kY \tag{A1.10}$$

while the speculative demand function (L_s) is assumed to be inversely related to the rate of interest (outside the liquidity trap). If, for algebraic simplicity, we assume a linear relationship, then the speculative demand for money balances can be written as:

$$L_s = \lambda_1 - \lambda_2 i, \quad \text{for } i > i_0 \tag{A1.11}$$

where i_0 is the liquidity trap value of i. Combining equations (A1.10) and (A1.11) with an exogenously determined money supply, $\bar{m}$, the traditional *LM* function can be written as

$$i = \frac{\lambda_1 - \bar{m}}{\lambda_2} + \left(\frac{k}{\lambda_2}\right) Y. \tag{A1.12}$$

Equation (A1.12) is traditionally interpreted as indicating the rate of interest in the money market which will bring the total demand for money into equilibrium with the total supply of money for any given level of output.

The equilibrium level of output for the economy is obtained by solving equations (1.6) and (A1.12) simultaneously as

$$Y^* = \frac{\lambda_2 (a_1 + a_2) + (\bar{m} - \lambda_1)b_2}{\lambda_2(1 - b_1) + kb_2} \tag{A1.13}$$

while the equilibrium rate of interest is

$$i^* = \frac{k(a_1 + a_2 + (\lambda_1 - \bar{m})(1 - b_1)}{\lambda_2(1 - b_1) + kb_2} \tag{A1.14}$$

With the finance motive system stressed in this paper, on the other hand, the transactions (and precautionary) demand for money is related to the aggregate demand function, i.e.

$$L_t + L_p = \alpha C + \beta I. \tag{A1.15}$$

Substituting the consumption and investment demand functions (equations (1.3) and (1.4)) into equation (A1.15) yields

$$L_t + L_p = \alpha \, (a_1 + b_1 Y) + \beta \, (a_2 - b_2 i). \tag{A1.16}$$

Combining equation (A1.16) with equation (A1.11) and equating the sum to the exogenously determined supply of money, the *LM* function can be written as

$$i = \frac{\alpha a_1 + \beta a_2 + \lambda_1 - \bar{m}}{\beta b_2 + \lambda_2} + \frac{\alpha b_1}{\beta b_2 + \lambda_2} Y. \tag{A1.17}$$

Solving equations (1.6) and (A1.17) simultaneously, the equilibrium level of output in this system is given by

$$Y^* = \frac{\lambda_2 \, (a_1 + a_2) + (m - \lambda_1) b_2 - (\alpha - \beta) a_1 b_2}{\lambda_2 (1 - b_1) + \beta b_2 + (\alpha - \beta) b_1 b_2} \tag{A1.18}$$

while the equilibrium rate of interest for the entire system is

$$i^* = \frac{\alpha a_1 + \beta a_2 + (\lambda_1 - \bar{m})(1 - b_1) + (\alpha - \beta) a_2 b_1}{\lambda_2 (1 - b_1) + \beta b_2 + (\alpha - \beta) b_1 b_2}. \tag{A1.19}$$

A comparison of equations (A1.13) and (A1.18) shows that, if, *and only if* $\alpha = \beta = k$, then the equilibrium level of output in both the traditional and finance motive systems will be identical. This result can be interpreted with the help of Figure 1.A1.

If, as we have argued in this paper, the demand for transactions balances is a function of the aggregate demand for goods, then when IS_1 shifts to IS_2 (in Figure 1.A1), the LM_1 function shifts to LM_2, and the equilibrium values for Y and i rise from Y_1 to Y_2 and i_1 to i_2, respectively. The locus of equilibrium points which will be derived for given shifts in the *IS* and *LM* functions is given by the dashed line in Figure 1.A1, and would be algebraically represented by equation (A1.12). This implies, however, that the traditional interpretation of equation (A1.12) is incorrect. This equation does not show the rate of interest in the money market which brings the demand for money into equilibrium with the supply of money *for any level of output*; rather, if $\alpha = \beta = k$, equation (A1.12) indicates the various combinations of rates of interest and output levels which will bring about simultaneous equilibrium in both the commodity and money markets, given specified changes in the real behavioural parameters of the aggregate demand function.

On the other hand, in the more realistic case where $\alpha \neq \beta \neq k$, the equilibrium level of employment of the traditional system as derived via equation (A1.13) will be different from the result obtained via (A1.18), once the finance motive is recognized. Consequently, when $\alpha \neq \beta$, the traditional approach tends to suggest that for a given shift in *IS*, the resulting equilibrium level of output (say Y_3 in Figure 1.3) will differ from the resulting equilibrium level of output (say Y_2 in Figure 1.3) which would occur, if the transactions demand is related to the aggregate demand function rather than to the level of output.[22]

Consequently, only in the case where $\alpha = \beta = k$, can the traditional algebraic formulation of the *LM* function be salvaged by reinterpreting it ·as a sort of

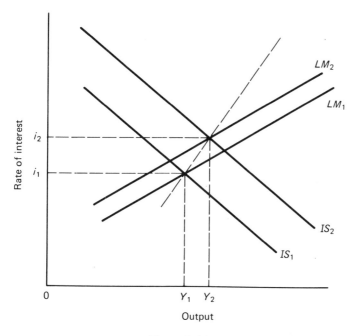

Figure 1.A1

long-run growth path which results from shifting short-run *IS* and *LM* functions. (This analogy to the microconcepts of short-run and long-run curves is admittedly somewhat forced, but it may help clarify my position to some readers.)

In the more general (and more realistic case) where $\alpha \neq \beta$, the traditional formulation does *not* correctly describe the equilibrium expansion path of the system, and should, therefore, be discarded.

Notes

1. Only a few 'Keynesians' even discuss it (e.g. Robinson, 1952, pp. 20–2, 80–7; Weintraub, 1958, p. 135).
2. For an example of a popular post-Keynesian model showing this independence of subsectors, see (Modigliani, 1944). For a discussion of some aspects of the dichotomization of the real and monetary sectors, see (Patinkin, 1956, pp. 105–15, 454–9).
3. Tsiang is an important exception in that he discusses the finance motive before discarding it as unimportant. Tsiang argues (as did Keynes) that all transactions must be financed. Tsiang, however, then jumps to the incorrect conclusion that the '"finance" and transactions demand for money . . . are really the same thing' (Tsiang, 1956, p. 547). Thus, Tsiang implies that Keynes's coping-stone is really a redundancy.
4. Had an alternative geometrical apparatus using aggregate supply and demand

functions (as developed by Weintraub (1958, Ch. 2) been adopted, the omission of the finance motive and the incorrect specification of the transactions demand for money function would probably not have occurred. With Weintraub's scheme, it would have been obvious, I believe, to relate the demand for money schedule with the demand for goods function.

5. Keynes, of course, recognized that the demand for transactions balances was not only related to the aggregate demand function, but also via 'the business motive' to the parameters of the aggregate supply function (i.e. to the price of inputs, production functions, degree of industry integration, and the degree of monopoly) (Keynes, 1936, pp. 195–6). To make the following analysis comparable to the usual post-Keynesian treatments of liquidity preference, however, we shall make the explicit assumption (which is implicit in the works of others) that, either (1) there is no change in the aggregate supply function, or (2) any change in the quantity of money demanded for 'the business motive' occurs only *pari passu* with changes in the aggregate demand function. Accordingly, we can focus our attention entirely on aggregate demand.

6. Symbolically this can be stated as

$$\frac{dL_t^*}{dY} = \frac{dL_t^*}{dD} \cdot \frac{dD}{dY}$$

where D is aggregate demand.

7. In the case of war finance, discussed by Keynes in 1939, what was involved was an increase in the government component of aggregate demand which was to be financed by borrowing before the actual spending occurred.

8. As we will show below, it was this aspect that led D. H. Robertson to utter the triumphal note that Keynes has at last restored productivity 'to something like its rightful place in governing the rate of interest from the side of demand' (Robertson, 1938, p. 317).

9. Letting E_m represent the income elasticity of demand for money, the elasticity can be defined as

$$E_m \equiv \left(\frac{dL_t^*}{dY}\right)\left(\frac{Y}{L_t}\right).$$

It follows therefore that the income elasticity of demand for money is greater than (equal to, less than) unity, when (dL_t^*/dY) is greater than (equal to, less than) L_t^*/Y.

Keynes believed that the income velocity was not constant, and furthermore, he suggested that the elasticity of demand for money would normally be less than unity at less than full employment (1936, pp. 304–6, also see pp. 201, 299).

10. Keynes's justification for linking the finance motive to changes in planned investment was his belief that planned investment is 'subject to special fluctuations of its own' (1937a p. 247). In his discussion of war finance, however, Keynes was generalizing the finance motive to other components of aggregate demand.

11. In a recent article, Miles Fleming (1964) carefully analyses the implications of business firms changing their timing of payments via the use of trade credit.

12. In either case, of course, the equilibrium rate of interest and the equilibrium level of output will rise.

13. Hahn, in a similar case, noted that the traditional liquidity preference theory 'predicts that the rate of interest will remain constant' when, for example, the (original) Y_1 level is a disequilibrium level; that is, when '*ex ante S* < *ex ante I*'

or, more generally stated, if aggregate demand exceeds aggregate supply at the disequilibrium level of Y_1 (Hahn, 1955, p. 62). On the other hand, Hahn claims that the loanable funds approach correctly indicates that there will be a rise in the rate of interest *at the Y_1 level* when aggregate demand rises above aggregate supply. Consequently, Hahn attempts to correct the traditional liquidity preference approach to this disequilibrium situation by introducing the demand for finance via a 'subtransactions' mechanism among investors, holders of cash, and producers of capital goods, as people attempt 'to substitute bonds for capital goods' (ibid., p. 63).

Nevertheless, Hahn is not entirely happy with his amended version of liquidity preference and he concludes that his 'period analysis is highly artificial . . . This probably means that L.F. [loanable funds] as here formulated is more than L.P. [liquidity preference], since *we will never be able to find a time when the rate of interest is independent of the demand for "finance"'* (ibid., p. 64, italics added).

Under the interpretation of the finance motive given in this paper, there is no reason to resort to Hahn's 'highly artificial' period analysis. We are always dealing with a situation involving an aggregate demand level for each level of output – even in the example cited by Hahn. Thus when aggregate demand is increased above aggregate supply *at a given level of output*, if the finance motive is then correctly introduced, the liquidity preference approach will demonstrate that the rate of interest must increase, even at the original (disequilibrium) level of output – for there is a need for more money to enforce the increased demand for goods.

Finally, it should be noted that the analysis presented in this paper firmly supports Hahn's assertion that the rate of interest is never independent of the demand for 'finance'.

14. The case where the aggregate demand function is a straight line emanating from the origin at an angle other than 45 degrees is a trivial case, since the only solution to the system occurs at a zero level of output.

15. In a world of Say's Law (e.g. a Robinson Crusoe economy), value theory can, of course, be treated independently of monetary theory.

16. Since normally $b_2 > 1$, while $1 - b_1 < 1$, a change in a_2 will have a larger impact on the *IS* function (1.7) than on the *LM* equation (1.9), that is the *IS* curve will shift more than the *LM* curve so that the new intersect will always be to the north-east of the original intersection.

In Hansen's traditional system, since the *LM* curve is not displaced, the new equilibrium level of output and rate of interest is Y_3 and i_3 respectively.

For completeness, it should be pointed out that the traditional (e.g. Hansen's) algebraic formulation of the *LM* function can, given a restrictive and highly unrealistic assumption, be resuscitated by reinterpreting it as representing the loci of equilibrium points (a sort of long-run equilibrium path) traced out as *both* the short-run *IS* and *LM* functions shift in response to changes in the parameters of the spending propensities. In the following Appendix, it is demonstrated that if, *and only if* $\alpha = \beta$ (that is, if the additional quantity of transactions money demanded for an additional dollar of planned consumption is *always* equal to the additional quantity of transactions money demanded for an additional dollar of planned investment spending, or planned government, or planned foreigners' purchases), then a money sector function based on equation (1.3) being written in the traditional algebraic form of $L = kY + \sigma$ (where $k = \alpha = \beta$) describes an equilibrium path which cuts across shifting *LM* curves, when the latter are displaced as a result of shifts in the *IS* function.

(I am extremely grateful to Sir Roy F. Harrod for bringing this possibility initially to my attention, and to Helen Raffel for providing me with a basic mathematical proof for clarifying this point.)

17. It can be shown that value theory provides the logical underpinnings for macroeconomic and monetary theory (Davidson and Smolensky, 1964, Ch. 9–13) (Weintraub, 1958, Ch. 2, 8).

18. Weintraub has criticized the common Keynesian models which he calls 'Classical Keynesianism', for reverting, in the name of Keynes, to barter concepts where, for example, price level phenomena have no real effects (Weintraub, 1961).

19. Since we have demonstrated that the economy cannot be divided into independent real and monetary subsets, it should not be surprising to find that the 'real' variables of productivity and thrift have an impact on the monetary sector.

20. Although an analysis of international liquidity problems with planned expansion of world trade is beyond the scope of this paper, it would appear that Keynes's 'Bancor' plan envisaged a different path for solving international liquidity problems (via liquidity supply creating aspects, including overdrafts) than the development of international non-monetary intermediaries such as the IMF and IBRD.

In a paper entitled 'Plan to Increase International Monetary Liquidity' (to be published by the Joint Economic Committee), Sir Roy Harrod proposes a system of automatic annual increases in 'drawing rights' by members of the IMF. Under his plan, current drawing rights plus additional annual increments would automatically become an inseparable part of the member's deposit, and could be used at the member's own discretion at any time. Harrod further proposes that 'deposits at the IMF should constitute what may be called international legal tender'. Harrod presents forceful arguments to show why such a plan will overcome the already serious problem of international liquidity shortage, and would also provide necessary additional liquidity for future expansion of international trade.

Conceptually, Harrod's proposal has some properties similar to an overdraft system, except that Harrod would not have any interest charges for the use of these additional drawing rights (overdrafts), nor would he require individual members to pay the fund back for the drawing rights used. His plan would allow the supply of international liquidity to increase *pari passu* with increased demand for liquidity resulting from the necessity of financing planned expansion of world trade, and would convert the IMF from a non-monetary intermediary to an institution performing a liquidity creating supply function.

21. This Appendix is based on a mathematical proof provided for me by Helen Raffel. Any errors occurring in the interpretation of this proof are mine alone.

22. A similar comparison of equations (A1.14) and (A1.19) indicates that when $\alpha = \beta = k$ the equilibrium rate of interest is the same in the two systems, but when $\alpha \neq \beta \neq k$, the equilibrium rate of interest differs in the two systems.

References

Davidson, P. and Smolensky, E. (1964) *Aggregate Supply and Demand Analysis*, New York.

Fleming, M. (1964) 'The Timing of Payments and the Demand for Money', *Economica*, 31 May, pp. 132–57.

Friedman, M. (1959) 'The Demand for Money: Some Theoretical and Empirical

Results', *Journal of Political Economy*, 67 (August), pp. 327–51.

Gurley, J. G. and Shaw, E. S. (1960) *Money in a Theory of Finance*, Washington.

Hahn, F. H. (1955) 'The Rate of Interest and General Equilibrium Analysis', *Economic Journal*, 65 (March), pp. 52–66.

Hansen, A. (1949) *Monetary Theory and Fiscal Policy*, New York.

Hicks, J. R. (1937) 'Mr Keynes and the "classics": A Suggested Interpretation', *Econometrica*, 5 (April), pp. 147–59.

Hicks, J. R. (1957) 'A Rehabilitation of "Classical" Economics?', *Economic Journal*, 67 (June) pp. 278–89.

Keynes, J. M. (1936) *The General Theory of Employment, Interest, and Money*, New York.

Keynes, J. M. (1937a) 'Alternative Theories of the Rate of Interest', *Economic Journal*, 47 (June), pp. 241–52.

Keynes, J. M. (1937b) 'The Ex-ante Theory of the Rate of Interest', *Economic Journal*, 47 (December), pp. 663–9.

Modigliani, F. (1944) 'Liquidity Preference and the Theory of Interest and Money', *Econometrica*, 12 (1944), pp. 45–88; reprinted in *Readings in Monetary Theory*, New York, 1951, pp. 186–239.

Modigliani, F. (1963) 'The Monetary Mechanism and Its Interaction with Real Phenomena', *Review of Economics and Statistics*, 45, (February, suppl.) pp. 79–107.

Ohlin, B. (1937) 'Some Notes on the Stockhom Theory of Savings and Investments II', *Economic Journal*, 47 (June) pp. 221–40.

Patinkin, D. (1956) *Money, Interest, and Prices*, Evanston.

Robertson, D. H. (1938) 'Mr Keynes and "Finance"', *Economic Journal*, 48 (June) pp. 314–18.

Robertson, D. H. (1948) *Essays on Monetary Theory*, London.

Robinson, J. (1952) *The Rate of Interest and Other Essays*, London.

Tsiang, S. C. (1956) 'Liquidity Preference and Loanable Funds Theories, Multiplier and Velocity Analyses: A Synthesis', *American Economic Review*, 46 (September), pp. 540–64.

Weintraub, S. (1958) *An Approach to the Theory of Income Distribution*, Philadelphia.

Weintraub, S. (1960) 'The Keynesian Theory of Inflation: The Two Faces of Janus?', *International Economic Review*, 1 (May), pp. 143–55.

Weintraub, S. (1961) *Classical Keynesianism, Monetary Theory, and the Price Level*, Philadelphia.

2 The Importance of the Demand for Finance*

In his criticism of my finance motive analysis, Horwich (1966) has made an assumption which is fundamentally different from the one underlying my analytical model as well as Keynes's own writings. Moreover, the Hicksian *IS–LM* apparatus is also based on the Keynes–Davidson (hereafter referred to as K–D) assumption.

Horwich has presented two separate cases: (1) the fixity of output case, involves an exogenous increase in the investment demand function which does not alter the equilibrium level of output (y) (ibid., pp. 242–5) and (2) an increase in investment demand leads to an increase in output which may or may not be accompanied by an increase in commodity prices.

1 THE FIXITY OF OUTPUT CASE

The first two paragraphs of Horwich's 'reinterpretation' of my argument is entirely consistent with the K–D analysis of the finance motive. Underlying the K–D approach is the simple proposition that, in economics, *demand has always connoted want plus the ability to pay*. Thus, the increased demand for capital goods, in a monetary economy, requires additional cash for finance and therefore firms must sell either existing debt securities held in their portfolio or sell new debt securities.[1] If the liquidity preference of the rest of the community and the supply of money is unchanged, then the rate of interest will rise as the price of securities declines, even before there is any change in the level of income.

In terms of the concepts of active (M_1) and idle (M_2) balances, sales of securities by firms result in the transfer of M_2 balances from the rest of society (or the creation of new money by the banks) to M_1 balances of firms who will need the *finance* for the increased *planned* investment transactions (cf. Robinson, 1952, p. 21). Horwich argues, however, that the transferred balances from the rest of society to the investing firms remain as M_2 balances *until* they are actually expended by the firms and received as additional current income by the factors of production in the capital goods industries (Horwich, 1966, p. 245). This implies that firms can *never* hold (or increase) active balances even when they are holding cash to pay for the planned current transactions of business exchanges (and are not holding the cash primarily to speculate on changes in the price of securities).

* *Oxford Economic Papers*, July 1967.

This view is symptomatic of the fundamental difference between Horwich and the K–D approach. Horwich (1966, pp. 243, 245) has assumed that the demand for M_1 balances is dependent only (primarily?) on the level of output, y. Since the sale of securities by the firms does not, by itself, provide additional output or income for the firms, then Horwich is forced to argue that the funds held by the firms to finance the additional planned investment transactions cannot, by definition, be active balances. As long as the output parameter, y, is unchanged (by assumption), any initial shift in the total demand for money function (L) must, in Horwich's system, be temporary and the L curve must be restored to its original position. It is this restoration of the L curve to its original position which distinguishes Horwich from the K–D approach.

Even in *The General Theory*, the transactions motive involved 'the need of cash for the current *transaction* of personal and *business* exchanges' (Keynes, 1936, p. 170, italics mine). Thus, if there is an increase in planned business transactions (at a given y level), there will be, *ceteris paribus*, an increase in the demand for M_1 balances.[2] In a monetary economy, any increase in the demand for goods implies not only an increase in wants but also, and this cannot be stressed too much, an increase in the ability to pay. *In a monetary economy, an increase in the ability to pay means an increase in active balances.* This is the essence of the K–D analysis of finance.

The demand for transactions balances depends primarily on planned transactions, and only to the extent that planned expenditure is a stable function of y will M_1 vary directly with y. In his *Trade Cycle*, Hicks noted that this simple K–D supposition underlies the *IS–LM* interpretation of the Keynesian system, when he wrote:

> The demand for money, Keynes held, can be divided into two parts: in the first place *there is a demand for money to finance current transactions*, and in the second place there is a demand for money to act as a liquid reserve. *The amount of money required for the first purpose will depend, in the main, upon the volume transactions in money terms, and this will vary closely with money income* (the Y of our diagram). (Hicks, 1950, p. 140. Italics mine)

The main purpose of my finance motive paper was to show that if the demand for transactions balances is made a direct function of planned transactions rather than of output or income (as has often been done), then when exogenous changes in the real behavioural functions are introduced, the analysis would provide significant new insights on macroeconomic path analysis, income velocity, and the interdependence of the real monetary sectors. Horwich evades the fundamental issue of whether transactions demand depends on planned transactions or actual output. He apparently does not recognize that planned aggregate expenditure is not necessarily identical, or even equal, to aggregate output. It is this lack of awareness of the difference between planned transactions and actual output which leads Horwich astray – even in his own analysis.[3]

Horwich argues that when the investment demand function increases, the firms' demand for finance instantaneously shifts out the total demand for money curve, L (drawn on the assumption of a given y level), as firms sell securities to obtain larger balances while the y level is (by assumption) unchanged and neither the stock of money nor the commodity price level is altered. Since the aggregate demand for commodities has increased, the ratio of total cash balances to aggregate demand (which now exceeds aggregate supply) must (by hypothesis) be lower than before. Horwich interprets this lower ratio of total cash balances to aggregate demand as implying a lower Marshallian k, and thus he infers 'the demand for real balances, is lowered', i.e. L shifts back to its original position, so that 'on net firms have accordingly shifted from existing securities into goods, the demand *schedule* for money remaining constant'[4] (Horwich, 1966, p. 244).

According to Horwich, 'the direct effect' of this restoring shift in L is to increase commodity prices which, in turn, reduces the supply schedule of money in real terms. It should be clear, therefore, that the restoration of L to its original position in Horwich's scheme is not the result of a change in commodity prices but the *cause* of the price increase. (If, however, prices rise then the demand for real active balances should increase, if real expenditures are to be maintained.)

It is this restoration of the L function to its original position which the K–D approach omits. But this second shift is only a figment of Horwich's own assumption. If L is assumed to be a stable function of y, and if y is assumed unchanged, then *obviously* the L function must be restored to its original position. If planned transactions and not y is the primary independent variable, however, then the second shift of the L function to its original position would occur (at the original y level) only if the increase in investment demand was a one-shot increment. In the one-shot case, the demand for active balances rises with the increase in investment demand. When the one-time transactions are completed, the demand for goods and therefore the demand for M_1 balances will be restored to their original level. If, however, the exogenous increase in investment demand is a permanent one, then the demand for goods *and* active balances would be permanently above its original position (at this initial y level), and, of course, the original y cannot be restored as the equilibrium output level unless the demand for goods, and therefore for active balances, has decreased elsewhere in the economy (cf. Robinson, 1952, p. 21; Keynes, 1937b, p. 667).

Horwich has, however, restored the initial y as the equilibrium level by virtue of his second shift to the L function. This restored equilibrium of aggregate demand and supply at a constant output (supply) level can occur, *ceteris paribus*, if the increase in investment demand was of a one-shot nature. Horwich, trapped by his fixity of output assertion and the assumption that L is a stable function of y, can present a consistent analysis only if he implicitly assumes that the increment in investment was a single-dose type. In that case, however, his results are completely compatible with the K–D approach; the apparent difference lies in the fact that K–D were analysing a permanent change in investment.

2 CREDIT RATIONING

If institutional barriers constrain the rise in interest rates which would be associated with the increased demand for finance at the original y level (assuming the money market cleared before the increase in demand for finance), then credit rationing occurs, and individual firms are prevented from making their 'wants' for additional goods effective in the market by their inability to borrow cash balances. Queueing for finance, *even at the initial y level*, is a readily understandable phenomenon only under the K–D approach for it highlights

> in what sense a heavy demand for investment can exhaust the market and be held up by the lack of financial facilities on reasonable terms. *It is, to an important extent, the 'financial' facilities which regulate the pace of new investment.* Some people find it a paradox that, up to the point of full employment, no amount of actual investment, however great, can exhaust and exceed the supply of savings . . . If this is found paradoxical, it is because it is confused with the fact that *too great a press of uncompleted investment decisions is quite capable of exhausting the available finance*, if the banking system is unwilling to increase the supply of money and the supply from existing holders is inelastic. It is the supply of available finance which, in practice, holds up from time to time the onrush of 'new issues'. But if the banking system chooses to make the finance available and the investment projected by the new issues actually takes place, the appropriate level of incomes will be generated out of which there will necessarily remain over an amount of saving exactly sufficient to take care of the new investment. *The control of finance is, indeed, a potent, though sometimes dangerous, method for regulating the rate of investment* (though much more potent when used as a curb than as a stimulus). (Keynes, 1937a, p. 248. Italics mine)

Of course, if there was some queueing initially (before the increase in the demand for finance), then the length of the queue will increase as planned transactions rise as a result of entrepreneurs attempting to finance more investment projects than before.

Once the fundamental K–D notion that the demand for transactions balances is primarily a function of planned transactions[5] ($C + I$ in the simplest case) rather than y, then it is inevitable that a shift in the *IS* curve will induce a shift in the *LM* curve, and one of the basic causes of interdependence between the real and monetary sectors can be demonstrated.

3   THE VARIABLE OUTPUT CASE

Horwich never analyses the variable output case. He merely argues that the second (restoring) shift of *L* will, if prices are stable, be exactly offset by the fact that 'since *L* is a positive function of output, the increase in *y* draws the schedule back towards the right' (1966, p. 246) so that the leftward and rightward movements just cancel each other. (Horwich asserts that these movements *just* offset each other; he does not prove it.)

If, however, *L* is a function of planned expenditures, i.e. $L = f_1 (C + I)$, while $C + I = f_2(y)$ then, of course, contrary to Horwich's result, a change in the investment demand function will alter the relationship of *L* with *y* at every *y* level. Nothing that Horwich can present will disapprove this logical result and its implication that the *LM* function will shift with every change in real expenditure behaviour.

4   THE MECHANICS OF FINANCE

I am unable to comprehend the discussion of the financial mechanism which Horwich ascribes to my analysis (1966, pp. 249–50). Accordingly, I can only briefly summarize what I believe is the K–D view on the mechanics of finance.

The K–D point is that if there is an increase in planned transactions, then the demand for finance will increase the demand for M_1 balances at each *y* level over what it would have been. In the simplest case (corresponding to the traditional 45° diagram), this implies that when there is a shift in the $C + I$ line due to a change in *I*, then the demand for M_1 balances (at the y_1 level) increases as firms typically go to the short-term loan market for additional financing. If there is no constraint on the money supply (as is the usual assumption in the simple multiplier analysis), then the quantity of money will rise concomitantly with the increase in demand for balances to finance the additional investment expenditures,[6] while, for the moment, *y* remains unaltered. As the funds are dispensed and output in the investment goods industries expands, wage and non-wage incomes rise. This rise in incomes induces a further increase in planned *C* (by hypothesis) leading to an increase in the quantity of M_1 balances demanded by households in order to finance these additional consumption transactions.[7] (If the quantity of consumer goods demanded is to rise, then households must have increased their ability to pay.) The households will obtain the additional active balances either from their increased money-income receipts, or by selling debt securities (consumer credit).

Accordingly, after the first round, y is higher by an amount equal to the increase in investment, but the system is not in equilibrium since the demand for consumer goods now exceeds the current output of consumer goods. If households use consumer credit to 'finance' their additional expenditures, it is the household sector which now obtains the additional finance. If, however, consumers finance their planned additional transactions from current income receipts, then the business sector will find that the amount of M_1 balances remaining at the current interest rate will not be sufficient to finance all the necessary business exchanges. In the absence of changes in trade credit or the money supply, therefore, firms may induce the transfer of M_2 balances into active balances by selling additional new (or old) securities to households. This stage-by-stage process of finance can be envisaged as recurring until a new equilibrium level of output is reached. At that point, finance becomes a 'revolving fund' where the repayment of some short-term loans makes available financing for other short-term loans.

Thus, the Keynesian argument that 'if investment is proceeding at a steady rate, the finance (or the commitments to finance) required can be supplied from a revolving fund of a more or less constant amount' (Keynes, 1937a, p. 247, also 1937b, p. 666) – which Horwich ridicules (1966, p. 248) – is a statement about an equilibrium position. When the system is out of equilibrium then the pool of finance may not be large enough for all demands being made upon it, and some of it may be diverted to any sector of the economy where demand for M_1 balances is rising, leaving less of the pool available for financing entrepreneurs.

In equilibrium, in a two-sector model, a positive rate of net investment implies that the aggregate planned net debtor position of firms is growing *pari passu* with the planned net creditor position of households. This may be accomplished by firms either (i) selling old or new securities to households (the age of the security is irrelevant), or (ii) increasing the claims of households on firms by retaining earnings. In disequilibrium, on the other hand, when – to use Horwich's poor choice of language – investment is in excess of savings (1966, p. 250), then, at a given interest rate, the planned increase in firms' net debtor position exceeds the planned increase in the households' net credit position.[8]

5   *EX ANTE* SAVINGS AND FINANCE

Horwich attempts to revive the pre-Keynesian emphasis of savings as the precursor of finance when he concludes that an exogenous increase in consumption (i.e. a shift in the consumption function) can be financed 'by simply reducing *ex ante* savings' without any 'net effect on the demand for money schedule' (ibid., p. 251) at a given level of y.

With an exogenous increase in consumption, households need additional M_1 balances which *cannot* be obtained from *ex ante* savings. These M_1 balances will be obtained by households either (1) via a concomitant shift in the speculative demand function, (2) or a change in the quantity of speculative balances held induced by a change in the rate of interest, or, (3) a change in the quantity of money. *None of these alternatives involves* ex ante *savings* per se. Alternative (1) merely implies that an exogenous increase in consumption will leave financial markets unaffected only if there is, *pari passu*, a decrease in 'liquidity preference proper' (and not a concomitant change in *ex ante* savings which, by definition, must just offset changes in *ex ante* consumption out of any income level). As Keynes argued, 'it is only through its influence on current liquidity preferences that ex-ante savings can come into the picture' (1937b, p. 667).

Horwich does not present any reason to expect offsetting movements in the speculative demand for money and the demand to finance exogenous increases in consumption transactions. (After all, it is not inconsistent to suggest that households may change their consumption behaviour while maintaining their bull–bear position.) In the absence of fortuitous offsetting changes in consumption behaviour and speculative demand, an increase in planned consumption spending *will* alter the total demand for money function. As Keynes forcefully argued: 'If there is no change in the liquidity position, the public can save ex-ante and ex-post and ex-anything-else until they are blue in the face, without alleviating the problem in the least – unless, indeed, the result of their efforts is to lower the scale of activity to what it was before' (1937b, p. 668).

The essence of the Keynesian position is that the demand for cash for 'savings' is the demand for a store of value. This demand for money is the 'liquidity preference proper'. Of course, it is perfectly proper to introduce a wealth effect in the demand for money as a store of value. Thus one could specify the total demand for money as $D_m = f_1 (T, i_c, i_e, W)$ where T is planned transactions and represents the demand for active balances, while i_c is the current rate of interest, i_e is the expected rate of interest, and W is the stock of wealth of the public. The last three variables are relevant to the portfolio balance decision, i.e. the demand for money as a store of value (as a form of savings). Given i_c and i_e, the demand for speculative balances D_s, can be written as $D_s = \gamma W$, where $\gamma \geq 0$. In the usual Keynesian liquidity preference analysis it is often implicitly assumed that $\gamma = 0$. Nevertheless, whether $\gamma = 0$ or not is not relevant to Horwich's point which is that an *exogenous increase* in C will cause either a *decrease* in γ, or, of course, a change in expectations about the future rate of interest. Horwich gives no reason why the public should prefer to hold less of its wealth in the form of money, i.e. why there should be an *exactly* offsetting movement in the speculative demand for money. Nor does he suggest why an exogenous change in C should affect expectations about the future rate of interest relative to the present rate of interest. He merely *asserts* that there can be a diversion of 'balances going into (a) securities *or* (b) hoards' (1966, p. 251). Simply stated, therefore, Horwich's position should be that if there is an exogenous increase in C, this may be financed by a concomitant shift in the demand for speculative balances, *if*, for example, there is a simultaneous decrease in the wealth effect on liquidity preference proper. Accordingly, the quantity of idle balances demanded at any rate of interest will be less than before the exogenous change in C. This has nothing to do with the *ex ante* savings function, it merely implies that, for some unexplained reason, Horwich assumes that the public wishes to hold less of its total stock of wealth in the form of money when there is an exogenous increase in consumption. To deny the possibility of such an outcome would be foolish; on the other hand, to hypothesize, without any explanation, exactly offsetting changes in consumption and liquidity preference proper and to ascribe the latter change to the *ex ante* savings function is an infelicitous mode of expression which is more likely to obfuscate than to clarify.

6 CONCLUSION

The K–D finance motive analysis indicates that if there is an exogenous change in aggregate demand at a given y level, then, equilibrium of the demand and supply of money will require a higher interest rate even at the same y level. Contrary to Horwich's scheme, therefore, the *LM* curve will shift when there is a shift in the *IS* function. This, after all, is the coping-stone of Keynes's liquidity preference theory (1937b, p. 667).

Notes

1. The new debt securities will often be short-term notes and even overdrafts can be used to finance the actual construction of new capital goods. After the construction is finished, the investment will be funded in the long-term capital market and the short-term notes redeemed. (Cf. Robinson, 1952, p. 21; Keynes, 1937b, p. 664.)

   For simplicity, the possibility of equity financing is omitted from this discussion.
2. In his initial development of the finance motive, Keynes indicated that finance balances 'may be regarded as lying half-way, so to speak, between active and inactive balances' (Keynes, 1937a, p. 247). By this, I believe Keynes meant that when there was a shift in the aggregate demand function, there was a shift, by spending units, from one money demand function to another (cf. Davidson,

1965, p. 53). By the time Keynes refined the finance motive concept, the demand to finance changes in planned expenditures was wholly incorporated in the active balance concept (Keynes, 1937b, p. 668).

Robinson has argued that the holding of cash by entrepreneurs for some large scale purchase of goods should be classified as part of the *active* circulation (1952, p. 15).

3. Horwich confuses the $C + I \equiv y$ accounting identity with the $C + I = y$ equilibrium condition. In disequilibrium when $C + I \neq y$, it is essential to distinguish as to whether L is a function of $C + I$ or of y. The K–D approach contributes something to our understanding of macropath analyses, while Horwich's system, which does not recognize that $C + I \neq y$, can not provide such insights.

4. Apparently Horwich defines the Marshallian k as the ratio of the total money supply to the aggregate demand for goods, rather than, as more commonly represented, the fraction of national output which is held as active cash balances. In a disequilibrium situation these definitions will yield different results. Under the usual definition, k would rise rather than (as Horwich claims) fall when aggregate demand and therefore M_1 increases (cf. Robinson, 1952, p. 22).

5. With the word 'transactions' appearing on both sides of the verbalized form of the demand for transactions balances function, it is difficult for me to comprehend why Horwich and others insist on using the level of output y as a first approximation for planned transaction, unless they desire to constrain their discussion only to the equilibrium position and are not interested in path analysis.

6. This assumes no change in real expenditure behaviour or liquidity preferences of the rest of the community.

7. These induced additional consumption expenditures are, of course, what lead to a multiplier that is greater than unity.

8. In disequilibrium the banks may play a particularly key role for if they increase the quantity of money in order to finance the investment plans, then expansion can occur with the banks looking after that part of the real wealth of the economy which, for the moment, the public does not wish to hold directly (cf. Kahn, 1954, pp. 237–8).

References

Davidson, P. (1965), 'Keynes's Finance Motive', *Oxford Economic Papers*, 17, March, pp. 47–65.

Hicks, J. R. (1950), *A Contribution to the Theory of the Trade Cycle* (Oxford).

Horwich, G. (1966), 'Keynes's Finance Motive: Comment', *Oxford Economic Papers*, 18, July, pp. 242–51.

Kahn, R. F. (1954), 'Some Notes on Liquidity Preference', *Manchester School*, 22, September, pp. 229–57.

Keynes, J. M. (1936) *The General Theory of Employment, Interest, and Money* (New York).

Keynes, J. M. (1937a) 'Alternative Theories of the Rate of Interest', *Economic Journal*, 47, June, pp. 241–52.

Keynes, J. M. (1937b) 'The Ex-ante Theory of the Rate of Interest', Economic Journal, 47, December pp. 663–9.

Robinson, J. (1952), *The Rate of Interest and Other Essays* (London).

3 Money, Portfolio Balance, Capital Accumulation, and Economic Growth*

Most growth models, whether they be of the Keynesian-Kaldor, Harrodian, or Solow–Swan type, ignore or at least minimize the role of the money supply in the process of accumulation and growth. In general, real factors rather than monetary phenomena are emphasized. There has been little success in developing a theory of capital accumulation and growth which unites Keynesian marginal efficiency and liquidity preference concepts. Instead, full employment is often made a precondition of the analysis.

Tobin has, at least, attempted to study the relationship between money and growth but his system is defective since it omits the construction of a demand for capital schedule by entrepreneurs that can be formulated independently of the savings propensity and portfolio decisions of households. (An independent investment demand function – the essence of the static Keynesian system – is often omitted in growth analysis.) This paper shows Tobin's model is applicable only to nonmonetary Say's Law economies, and attempts to remedy the defects of such an analysis.

In a modern monetary, market-oriented economy, full employment is likely to be neither automatic nor a position of stable equilibrium (as Phillips curves imply a highly unstable full employment price level). To assume full employment as a precondition is to remove the problem of the role of the money supply in the process of accumulation and growth from the real world. This paper presents an analysis which allows the examination of the role of money within the context of a Keynesian system permitting independent savings, investment and liquidity preference functions. It does not make full employment a precondition of the model.

Professor Tobin, (1965), has emphasized the role of money in the process of capital accumulation and economic growth. Since most 'Keynesian' growth models ignore the monetary requirements for accumulation,[1] To-

* *Econometrica*, 36 (April 1968). The author is indebted to M. Fleming, L. R. Klein, E. Smolensky, and S. Weintraub for many helpful comments on an earlier draft and to his colleagues who commented on a draft which was presented at a Rutgers Research Seminar in the autumn of 1966.

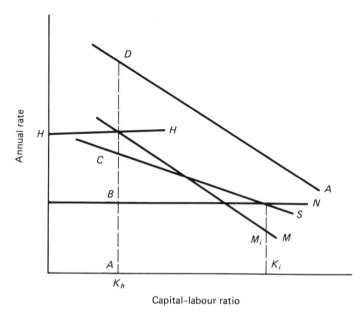

Figure 3.1

bin's emphasis on the relationship between money and growth (which is closer in spirit to Keynes's *Treatise* than to his *General Theory*) deserves close study.

In essence, Tobin's argument is based on the fact that balanced growth at full employment requires the stock of capital to increase at the same rate as the natural rate of growth of the effective labour force, which Tobin assumes constant. Tobin's work is, therefore, directed towards uncovering the adjusting mechanism in both nonmonetary and monetary economies that will lead to this form of balanced growth.

1 TOBIN'S MODEL

1.1 The Conditions of Balanced Growth

Tobin's basic diagram (Figure 3.1) relates readily recognizable concepts while employing rather unusual and unfamiliar units. The *A* curve represents the average annual output per unit of capital – or the output–capital ratio – while the *M* curve is the marginal annual product of capital. Since the production function is assumed to be linear and homogeneous, the average and marginal products of capital depend only on the ratio of capital to labour, which is plotted along the abscissa.

On the same diagram, the *S* function is derived from the savings behaviour out of disposable incomes of households (ibid., pp. 667–8). Hence, the vertical distance between the *A* curve and the *S* curve at each capital–labour (*K–N*) ratio represents the amount of the average product of capital that households desire to divert to consumption uses. The distance between the abscissa and the *S* curve, therefore, indicates the amount of the average product of capital that is available for non-consumption purposes, if household consumption demands are met and if the existing capital stock is actually employed. Tobin, however, prefers to interpret the vertical distance between the abscissa and the *S* curve as showing 'the amount of net savings and investment per year, per unit of existing capital stock. Therefore, it tells how fast the capital stock is growing. In Harrod's terminology, this is the "warranted rate of growth" of the capital stock'[2] (ibid., p. 674). Although this is not essential to the Tobin model, the *S* curve, in Figure 3.1, is so drawn that its height is always at the same constant proportion of the *A* curve. This reflects the common assertion of most growth models that the average propensity to save is invariant with respect to income (e.g. Harrod, 1959, p. 454).

Tobin's interpretation of the vertical height of the *S* curve as the 'warranted rate of growth of capital' is valid only if (1) both the existing capital stock and the labour force are fully employed at each point of time, and if (2) net investment goods are the only alternative to consumption goods, i.e. if there are no purchases of goods by governments or foreigners. Whether conditions (1) and (2) are met or not, it should be clear that the vertical distance to the *S* curve merely indicates the amount of non-consumption aggregate demand which must be forthcoming to make it profitable to fully utilize the existing stock of capital and labour force at the point of time. This may, or may not, be equivalent to the warranted rate of growth in the capital stock, since only under the highly restrictive assumptions of (a) full employment, and (b) no wearing out of capital in a two-sector economy will this vertical gap depict the actual rate of capital accumulation.

Having recognized these restrictive provisos implicit in Tobin's interpretation of the height of the *S* curve, let us continue to follow the mechanics of his system. In Figure 3.1. Tobin introduces a constant natural rate of growth of the labour force as a horizontal line *N*. Arguing that the *S* curve reflects the 'warranted' investment demand of the system (rather than the necessary non-consumption demand to insure full employment output), Tobin asserts that if the warranted rate of capital accumulation exceeds the natural rate of growth of labour, i.e. if the *S* curve lies above the *N* line at a given *K–N* level, then, assuming full employment of both factors, capital deepening will occur as the rate of capital growth increases more rapidly than the labour force. The economy will move out along the *X* axis. (Of course, the economy would move inward if the 'warranted investment' was less than the natural rate of growth of labour.) Accordingly, when the capital intensity is k_i, Tobin's warranted investment demand allows capital and labour to grow at the same rate and therefore 'the equilibrium capital intensity is k_i' (Tobin, 1965, p. 674). If each factor is being paid its marginal product, then the annual rent per unit of capital in equilibrium will be M_i. According to Tobin, therefore, 'the rate of return on capital, in long-run equilibrium, is a result of the interaction of "productivity" and "thrift", or of technology and time preference' (ibid.).

It should be clear, however, that, since Tobin's S curve merely reflects the level of non-consumption demand that must be forthcoming to fully employ the existing stock of capital, rather than net investment demand directly, Tobin's model will not determine the actual rate of capital accumulation uniquely, unless it is assumed that (1) there are no government or foreign sectors, and (2) Say's Law prevails, i.e. there is always full employment.

It is true that Tobin develops this diagram for a non-monetary, two-sector economy (where full employment and Say's Law must apply), but he then utilizes the implications of this figure for the analysis of a monetary economy (where Say's Law doesn't apply) by introducing the concept of portfolio balance. Of course, this is scarcely an accident in view of his concentration upon the concern with these matters in his work of recent years (Tobin, 1955; 1958; 1961).

1.2 Portfolio Balance and Tobin's Monetary Growth Model

The decision of an individual as to how much of his income to consume in the current period and how much to postpone for the future depends on his time preference.[3] This decision was assumed by Keynes under the propensity to consume. Once the present consumption decision is made, however, an individual is faced with the second decision as to 'what form he will hold the command over future consumption which he has reserved' (Keynes, 1936, p. 166). This second question is the one which Tobin has called portfolio balance.

In a non-monetary model possessing only a single reproducible capital asset, Tobin argues that there can be neither a separation of the investment and savings act nor portfolio choices (other than vintage choices) (Tobin, 1965, p. 672). It is the introduction of monetary assets which permits (1) the separation of the investment from the saving decision and (2) portfolio choices for individuals, although for a closed economy as a whole, no such portfolio choice exists. Consequently in a non-monetary, closed economy, household decisions to save for future consumption, if they are executed, must automatically increase the stock of capital. In a monetary economy, however, this is no longer necessarily true, for households may decide to increase their wealth holdings in the form of money and, as long as there are other economic units such as business firms, banks, or governments willing to provide additional funds either by drawing down their cash balances or increasing the supply of money, the increased wealth holdings by households does not automatically augment society's wealth. This was, of course, a fundamental tenet of Keynesian economics, i.e. there is an essential difference between monetary and non-monetary economies and, therefore, there is a dichotomy of analysis for the two worlds, but in a monetary economy, a dichotomy between the real and monetary sectors is simply evanescent! (cf. Keynes, 1936, p. 293; Davidson and Smolensky, 1964a, pp. 198–204; 1964b; Robinson, 1963, pp. 70–2.)

Despite Tobin's emphasis on the need to analyse portfolio balance decisions (which is, of course, more in the spirit of Keynes's *Treatise*), there are three surprising aspects in his neo-Keynesian growth model: (1) the exclusion of uncertainty, expectational phenomena, and private debt in a model of a monetary economy which emphasizes the growth of the capital stock and money supply; (2) the absence of a separate investment demand function (separate, that is, from the savings function of households); and (3) neglect of the importance of the demand for money for transactions and finance purposes (Tobin, 1965, p. 679). Tobin simply assumes market clearance at full employment in a world of perfect certainty.

The absence of uncertainty and expectations about the future yield of real capital (ibid., p. 673–4) and future prices (ibid., p. 676) and the absence of placements (i.e. titles to debts or shares) in his model, requires Tobin to posit a strange form of money – one which pays interest if you hold on to it – in order to have a portfolio choice at all. Tobin has ignored his earlier caution that 'if cash is to have any part in the composition of . . . [portfolio] balances, it must be because of expectations or fears of loss on other assets' (Tobin, 1958, p. 66).

In a world of certainty, money holdings serve no purpose and have no place (Tobin, 1961, p. 26). Consequently, the savings decision will still determine investment; increments to wealth will be held only in the form of real assets which have a positive yield. Since Tobin, at least initially, introduces portfolio balance decisions and an assumption of constant prices, his money must have an exogenously determined positive yield for the public to hold it at all. This strange institutional arrangement of paying interest for holding money in a world with a 'money-void', allows money to enter portfolios. Paradoxically, Tobin fails to note that once money serves as a store of value, the saving decision of households no longer determines the level of real investment. The desire to accumulate wealth by households does not require society to increase its stock of real assets for 'there is always an alternative to the ownership of real capital-assets, namely the ownership of money and debt' (Keynes, 1936, p. 212).

Thus the introduction of money into the model immediately severs the connection between the determinants of the savings decision and the determinants of the investment decision. It is at this point that Tobin requires, and yet fails, to introduce into his model an explicit investment demand function based on entrepreneurial expectations of profit. Rather Tobin lets ex-ante savings determine the level of investment[4] – except in the non-equilibrium impasse (which he attributes to Harrod) where investors insist upon a minimum rate of return above the yield savers will accept.[5]

Tobin has portfolio decisions determine the disposition of savings between the two alternative stores of value – money and real wealth. (There are no placements in his model!) Thus, given the propensity to save, the only demand for capital goods in Tobin's system is a demand for real wealth as a store of value by savers! If there are positive supplies of both money and capital goods, then, in portfolio balance equilibrium, the yield on each must be equal. Since the institutionally determined yield on money is given, then, according to Tobin, capital must be demanded until its certain return (as given by the M curve in Figure 3.1) is equal to the certain yield on money. Thus, given the savings propensity, in the simplest Tobin model, if the institutionally determined yield on money is equal to M_i (in Figure 3.1), then the long-run equilibrium rate of accumulation will be established; otherwise, an impasse will occur in the sense that the savings behaviour of the community is inconsistent with the rate of capital accumulation that will bring the yield on capital into equality with the yield on money. Under these circumstances, unless the savings propensity can be changed, the Tobin model cannot reach an equilibrium position (Tobin, 1965, pp. 676–8).

Tobin's analysis implies that entrepreneurs are, in long-run equilibrium, obliged to accumulate at a rate determined by the savings behaviour of the public. This is clearly contrary to the spirit of Keynesian analysis where the rate of accumulation depends on the desire of entrepreneurs to invest and not on savers' propensities (cf. Kaldor, 1960, pp. 226–32; Robinson, 1963, p. 83).

Although Tobin recognizes that savers and investors can have different motivations that may ultimately end in an impasse (Tobin, 1965, p. 675), he questions the relevance of post-Keynesian growth models that 'separate the investment decision from savings behavior' (ibid.). In his model, Tobin emphasizes primarily 'the forms of saving and wealth rather than their total amounts' (ibid., p. 676). In other words, Tobin's analysis assumes that the level of output (and therefore savings) is given and predetermined at any point of time. To analyse the role of money in a model where the full employment level is predestined, and future events are known with absolute certainty, is like *Hamlet* without the melancholy prince.

What is lacking from Tobin's system is an attack on the problem of the simultaneous determination of the total size of savings (and output) and the forms that the savings magnitude will take. One of the essential elements necessary for this concomitant determination is the introduction and construction of an explicit demand for capital goods by entrepreneurs (investors) that can be formulated independently of the savings propensity and the portfolio decisions of households. As we will argue below, placements are a much more preferable store of value than capital goods. The latter are demanded primarily to obtain the future flow of capital services in production in the expectation of making profits, rather than being demanded as a store of value *per se*.

The serious limitations of the Tobin model and its apparent non-Keynesian espousal of Say's Law are enough to invite a reconsideration of the problem of the monetary requirements for accumulation and growth in a monetary, market-oriented economy that does not automatically maintain full employment. This is the important topic that Tobin has opened for view.

2 ECONOMIC GROWTH IN A MONETARY ECONOMY

2.1 The Demand for Capital

Recently, Witte (1963) has revived an exposition of the aggregate investment function that can be modified and usefully employed here (also see Clower, 1954). A firm desires capital for its expected profit stream over time. What is actually desired by the firm is the services of capital goods. To obtain these services, firms normally need to acquire the use of capital goods. Thus, according to Witte, the firm's demand for the flow of capital services leads to a demand for a stock of capital goods, and, for any given set of circumstances, there will be an optimal size of capital stock for each firm. Consequently, the aggregate demand for capital goods (where the demand is really for the services of capital which is functionally related to the stock of capital) is derived from the summation of the demand curves of all firms. Thus, following Witte, in Figure 3.2a, a demand curve is derived (for a given set of profit expectations and the rate of interest) that relates the 'quantity of the capital good desired to be held to the market price of the capital goods' (Witte, 1963, p. 445). This stock demand curve for capital, D_k, in Figure 3.2a includes the Wicksteedian reservation demand of capital owners at each moment of time. This demand function can be stated as

$$D_k = f_1 (p_k, i, \phi, E) \tag{3.1}$$

where D_k is the stock demand for capital, p_k is the market price of capital goods, i is the rate of interest, ϕ is a set of profit expectations, E is the

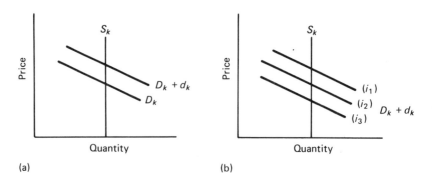

Figure 3.2a, b

number of entrepreneurial investors who can obtain finance for their demand for capital goods, and $f'_{1pk} < 0, f'_{1i} < 0, f'_{1\phi} > 0, f'_{1E} > 0$.

The stock supply schedule for capital goods (S_k) can be drawn as vertical in Figure 3.2a, since stock supply is the aggregate of existing capital goods inherited from the past. Thus, at any point of time,

$$S_k = \alpha_k \tag{3.2}$$

where S_k is the stock supply of capital and α_k is a predetermined constant at any instant of time.

If there was no production or depreciation of capital goods (e.g. in a pure exchange economy), then, of course, the resulting market price would be whatever is necessary to divide up the stock without remainder among demanders. For a production economy, however, flow considerations must be added to the stock analysis of capital. Flow demand for capital is due to the depreciation per unit of time of the existing stock. For simplicity we will assume that depreciation is a (small) fraction n of the existing stock of capital per unit of time. Hence, the flow demand for capital is

$$d_k = nS_k = n\alpha_k \tag{3.3}$$

where d_k is flow demand (depreciation) and $0 < n < 1$.

Combining equations (3.1) and (3.3) yields the total market demand for capital

$$D_k + d_k = f_1 (p_k, i, \phi, E) + n\alpha_k \tag{3.4}$$

which, because of our simplifying assumption about the rate of depreciation, implies that the market demand curve, $D_k + d_k$ is parallel and to the right of the stock demand curve in Figure 3.2a. The horizontal difference between the two curves represents depreciation.

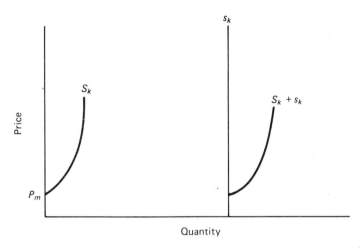

Figure 3.3

The flow supply schedule of capital goods indicates the output quantities which will be offered on the market by the capital goods industry at alternative expected market prices, i.e.,

$$s_k = f_2(p_k) \equiv I_g \tag{3.5}$$

where s_k is flow supply of capital, and I_g is gross investment. This schedule, like all supply schedules, will, in a purely competitive environment, merely reflect rising marginal costs because of diminishing returns due to fixed plant and equipment in the investment goods industry, i.e. $f'_{2pk} > 0$. The flow supply curve, s_k, is represented in Figure 3.3. There is a minimum flow supply price, p_m in Figure 3.3, which is the shut-down price for the industry. If the market price falls below p_m, then no flow supply offering will be made as capital goods producers find that shutting down involves smaller losses than producing for market.

The market supply situation can be obtained by laterally summing the stock and flow supply schedules (Figure 3.3), i.e. by combining equations (3.2) and (3.5) to obtain

$$S_k + s_k = \alpha_k + f_2(p_k). \tag{3.6}$$

The horizontal difference between the stock supply schedule and the flow supply curve in Figure 3.3 represents the gross output of the investment goods industry that will be forthcoming at any given market price in a given period of time.

Combining the market demand function $(D_k + d_k)$ with the market supply function $(S_k + s_k)$ in Figure 3.4, it can be shown that at a market price of p_1, the capital goods market will clear, i.e.

Money

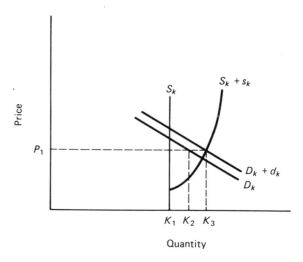

Figure 3.4

$$(D_k + d_k) - (S_k + s_k) = 0. \tag{3.7}$$

According to Figure 3.4, at the market price of p_1, the gross output of the investment goods industry will be $k_3 - k_1$, while depreciation equals $k_3 - k_2$. The value of net investment $(p_k I_n)$ is equal to the difference between the flow supply quantity and the flow demand quantity multiplied by the market price, i.e.

$$p_k I_n = p_k(s_k - d_k). \tag{3.8}$$

In Figure 3.4, net investment output equals $k_2 - k_1$. The growth of capital during the period will be $(k_2 - k_1)/k_1$.

Any increase in the stock demand for capital goods will, *ceteris paribus*, raise the market price and consequently lead to an increased flow of output of capital goods, as the producers of investment goods attempt to maximize profits by producing where marginal costs equal market price.

Investors determine the stock quantity of capital goods they desire by computing the present value of the expected future earnings of the future flow of productive services of the stock of capital and comparing it to the current market price of capital goods. Consequently, it is the expectations of investors about future profits relative to the current rate of discount and their ability to obtain finance – in order to execute this demand – which determines the position of the stock demand curve, and given rate of depreciation, the market demand curve in Figure 3.2a.

For any given set of expectations about the prospective money yield of capital, a higher rate of interest implies a higher rate of discount, and therefore, a leftward shift in the stock demand for capital schedule in Figure 3.2a. Thus, given entrepreneurial expectations and the rate of depreciation, there is a different demand for capital schedule for every possible rate of interest (Figure 3.2b) (cf. Keynes, 1930a, pp. 202–3). Given expectations of entrepreneurial investors, the rate of interest, the existing stock of capital, and its rate of depreciation, a market price for capital will be determined. If this price exceeds the minimum flow supply price of capital goods, p_m, new gross investment will be undertaken. The resulting rate of capital accumulation will depend on the rate of capital depreciation and the elasticity of supply in the capital goods industries (Clower, 1954). Thus, as Keynes pointed out, 'A fall in the rate of interest stimulates the production of capital goods not because it decreases their costs of production but because it increases their demand price' (Keynes, 1930a, p. 211).

Contrary to Tobin's position, therefore, the rate of capital accumulation in a monetary economy is not solely determined by either the savings or portfolio decisions of households; rather the growth of the capital stock depends on entrepreneurial expectations of profits from the future flow of capital services, the rate of interest and the ability to obtain finance, the rate of capital depreciation, and the supply elasticity of the capital goods industries. It is the demand by the users of capital assets in combination with the profit maximizing decisions of the suppliers of capital goods which, according to Lerner, determine the schedule of the marginal efficiency of capital[6] (Lerner, 1944, p. 334). It is only Tobin's implicit assumption that *ex ante* investment must equal the *ex ante* savings level at full employment which allows Tobin to ignore these latter aspects in his system. Once we admit the inapplicability of Say's Law in a monetary economy, these aspects of entrepreneurial expectations, finance, wearing out, and supply elasticities become essential elements in understanding accumulation and growth phenomena.

To assume full employment is to sweep all the problems of short-run equilibrium adjustments behind the scenes. In the real world of monetary economies, full employment is not automatic and short-run adjustments in the level of effective demand and the rate of capital accumulation are not independent phenomena. Would anyone deny that the rate of capital accumulation in the United States was affected by the 'Great Depression'? To postulate that automatic short-run adjustments leading to full employment occur instantly behind the scenes is to remove the problem of the role of money in the process of growth from the problems of the real world!

2.2 A Digression on the Stationary State

As long as net investment is positive, the stock of capital will increase each period. If there is no change in the stock demand schedule for capital over

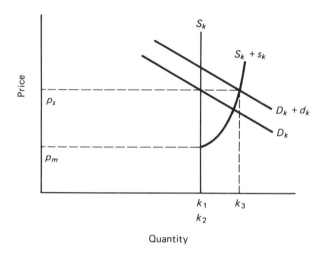

Figure 3.5

time – that is, if there is no change in profit expectations (ϕ), the rate of
interest (i), or the number of entrepreneurial investors (E) – then ultimately a stationary state will be reached where the gross output of the
capital goods industry equals the rate of depreciation of the capital stock.
Such a situation is represented in Figure 3.5. This stationary state is, of
course, completely compatible with a less than full employment effective
demand level.

At the stationary state price of p_s in Figure 3.5, there is no capital
accumulation. As long as the market price exceeds p_s, however, net
investment is undertaken. If the market price is less than p_s but greater
than p_m, net investment is negative while gross investment is positive. At a
market price below p_m, gross investment falls to zero and the rate of
decline in the capital stock is equal to the rate of depreciation.

Since the interest rate is constrained to positive values, the ultimate
source of continual capital accumulation for a profit-maximizing, market-
oriented, monetary economy lies in investors believing in the continuous
growth of profit opportunities over time ($\Delta \phi > 0$). Profit expectations
depend primarily on the expected value productivity of capital services
over time. There is no natural law of diminishing value productivity over
time as long as either new consumer goods can be continually introduced,
or the income elasticity of demand for all existing goods equals unity, or
the population and their total purchasing power grows at least as rapidly as
output, or some combination of these factors. Consequently, there is no
a priori reason to believe in the inevitability of the stationary state.

2.3   The Influence of Portfolio Balance

How then do non-consumption (savings) and portfolio decisions enter into this model? As Keynes pointed out the consumption (and therefore, the saving decision) and the investment decisions are wholly related to current economic activity. The portfolio decision by individuals, on the other hand, relates 'to the whole block of their existing wealth. Indeed, since the current increment is but a trifling portion of the block of existing wealth, it is but a minor element in it' (Keynes, 1936, p. 141); i.e. the level of current investment is of secondary importance in the portfolio balance decision and vice versa. Moreover, the motivations of savers and investors are different.[7]

What savers are interested in is protecting, and possibly increasing, the value of their wealth holdings for the future. Since there are only two types of instruments that link the uncertain economic future with the present – durable equipment and monetary claims (i.e. financial assets including money) (Keynes, 1936, pp. 145–6, 212) – savers must store their value in one or both of these instruments. Savers are not primarily interested in capital goods for the same reasons that investors are, i.e. for the future flow of services to be derived from the capital goods; rather savers are merely interested in the title to the capital goods as a store of value. Investors, on the other hand, are not primarily interested in the title to capital; what is relevant to them is the marginal supply price per unit of the service of the factor of capital. (Similarly, entrepreneurs do not care whether they own their own labour force (slaves) or allow others to hold title to the factor called labour; what is relevant is the marginal supply price of labour services.)

Although the value of the future productivity of a capital good ordinarily exceeds its carrying costs over its useful life, its liquidity premium is negligible (cf. ibid., ch. 17). Consequently, if the saver expects to convert his store of value into future consumption goods in a different time pattern than the stream of anticipated earnings over the life of the capital asset, he will, at some point of time, have to search for a buyer of that asset. The saver knows that in selling the capital good, he may have to disrupt its future production (and therefore reduce its yield) and incur delivery costs, if he must physically dismantle and transport the equipment to the buyer as part of the terms of sale. Moreover, since real capital assets are normally large, indivisible physical units, the saver may be required to search out a buyer of the whole unit in a future period, even if he desires only to increase his consumption in that period by some amount smaller than the expected value of the whole physical asset. The smaller the unit of asset, therefore, the greater its saleability is likely to be. Thus, as Makower and Marschak have shown, sales of large units 'not only increase the dispersion of future yields, but also reduce their actuarial values' (1938, p. 279). Since the saver is interested in maximizing his store of value, it is clear that if the saver can sell, with a minimum of search costs for a buyer and without disrupting productivity and incurring delivery costs, the title to either the entire asset or to some fraction of the asset as the saver's needs arise, then he will, *ceteris paribus*, be better off. Consequently, the development of placements, i.e. equity and loan securities, have allowed savers to store value over time in small readily saleable asset units, with a minimum of delivery costs and no lost production. This development has, however, further severed the connection between the demand for capital decision (control of the services of the factor) and the portfolio balance decision (ownership of the factor) (cf. Keynes, 1936, p. 150).

Since savers are interested in titles to wealth only as a store of value, while investors desire the flow of productive services from capital goods, portfolio balance decisions and investment decisions will depend on different price level. The latter depends on the market demand price relative to the maximum flow supply price of capital goods, while the former depends on the price of securities – and there is no important direct relationship other than the interest rate mechanism between these different price levels (Keynes, 1930a, p. 249).

Given the stock of capital and its rate of depreciation, for the level of investment to change either the stock demand schedule for capital or the flow supply schedule for investment goods must change.[8] For the saver's portfolio balance decision, however, what is relevant is the comparison of the yield on money to the yield on placements. Accordingly, it is the market price of placements, rather than the market price for capital goods, that is the applicable price level for portfolio decisions.

At any point of time, there is a given stock of securities; therefore, the stock supply schedule of placements (S_p^1) facing the public is perfectly inelastic (Figure 3.6) (cf. Scitovsky, 1964, pp. 15, 19–20). Increases in the supply of equity or loan securities will depend primarily on entrepreneurial demands for capital goods and their necessity to externally finance that demand. Business firms can usually finance replacement investment entirely from depreciation allowances. Accordingly, it is only the net change in the stock of capital goods that must find additional financing, and since a portion of this net change may be internally financed by the firm, it is only to the extent that the firm uses external sources of finance that the supply schedule of placements will shift outwards as capital accumulates.[9] Hence the stock supply schedule of securities is likely to shift even less in each time period than the stock supply schedule of capital goods.

Our unit of measurement of the quantity of placements is in terms of the income per period to which the ownership of a placement constitutes an absolutely certain claim (cf. Turvey, 1960, p. 21). The use of a certainty income claim unit of measure means that, for our purposes, we may ignore

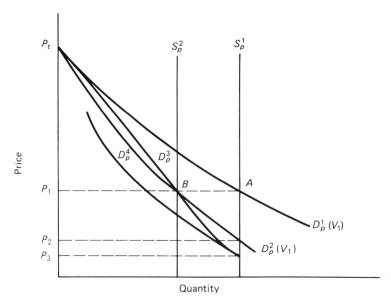

Figure 3.6

the differences between types of placements. Each bond, preferred stock, or common share would be measured, for example, as a claim for $1 of certain income in the form of interest or dividends per period. Thus, if ownership of one common share (as usually measured) involved a probability of only 0.5 of a $1 income claim per period, then, using the probability statement as a weighting device, two shares would, in this example, equal one placement unit in our model. Thus, in Figure 3.6, the quantity of placements is measured in units of certainty dollar income claims.[10] Accordingly, 'the rate of interest' is inversely related to the price of placements.

The stock supply of placements available to the general public (savers) at a point in time is equal to all previously issued placements which exist (a_p) less those placements presently held by the banking system (a_p^h), where this latter quantity will be taken as exogenous to our model. Thus

$$S_p = a_p - a_p^h = a_p^s \tag{3.9}$$

where S_p is the stock supply of placements offered to the public, and a_p^s is the effective quantity of securities at hand at any point of time.

The flow supply of placements offered to the public per unit of time is given by

$$S_p = f_3 (p_k, I_n, g, h, p_p) \tag{3.10}$$

where g is the fraction of the cost of net investment output (I_n) that is externally financed, h is that fraction of long-term external finance that is provided by the banking system, and p_p is the market price of placements. If g and h are taken as exogenous while the cost of net investment is defined as $p_k (s_k - d_k)$, then (3.10) may be specified as

$$s_p = \frac{(1 - \bar{h})(\bar{g})[p_k(s_k - d_k)]}{P_p} \tag{3.11}$$

Given any level of net investment that must be financed via a new placement issue to the public, the quantity of placements (measured in income claim units) that must be sold to fund this level of investment declines as the market placement price increases; i.e. the flow supply curve with respect to p_p is a rectangular hyperbola.

The market supply of placements is obtained by summing equations (3.9) and (3.11):

$$S_p + s_p = a_p^s + \frac{(1 - \bar{h})(\bar{g})[p_k(s_k - d_k)]}{P_p} \tag{3.12}$$

Since both $\bar{g}$ and $\bar{h}$ are likely to be less than unity, while $d_k > 0$, placement flow supply is normally considered to be much less important than flow supply considerations in the capital goods market, i.e. $(s_p/S_p) \ll (s_k/S_k)$. Indeed, s_p is normally such a 'trifling element' in the block of existing placements, that as a first approximation it is often assumed that the short-run supply of placements is completely dominated by its stock characteristics. In essence, the supply is then predetermined and can be represented by the vertical curve in Figure 3.6. Specifically if $(1 - \bar{h})(\bar{g})[p_k(s_k - d_k)]$ is negligible (e.g. if $h = 1$, or $g = 0$, or $[p_k(s_k - d_k)] \approx 0$), then

$$S_p + s_p = a_p^s. \tag{3.13}$$

The fact that the net investment term $p_k(s_k - d_k)$ appears in the market placement supply equation (3.12) does indicate, however, that the total supply of placements available to the public is not completely independent of the demand for capital goods. Though the excess flow demand for capital ($s_k - d_k$) may, therefore, react on the price of placements (and the price of placements on the demand for capital via the rate of interest), the existence of g and h as exogenous variables suggests that capital goods demand and the supply of placements are independent 'at least in the sense that any degree, positive or negative, of the one is compatible in appropriate circumstances with any degree, positive or negative of the other' (Keynes, 1930a, p. 145). Consequently, for certain aspects of single-period analysis that are discussed in this section, supply aspects of placements will be treated as a stock concept. From p. 63 on, however, the flow supply of placements will be added to the analysis to obtain generalizations on the rate of capital accumulation under various hypotheses about the concurrent actions of the banking system and the magnitudes of g and h.

The demand for placements by the public requires savers to decide how much of their wealth to keep in the form of obligations of firms or titles to capital and how much in the form of bank deposits (money) (cf. Robinson, 1956, pp. 233–4). It is at this point that the portfolio balance decision becomes relevant. For if we assume that savers expect the future price of consumption goods to be the same as the present price (or at least no higher than their carrying cost so that savers do not store their wealth in inventories of consumer goods), then money and placements are the only forms in which savers will want to store wealth. The disposition of savers to store value between money and securities will depend upon the expected return on each. At any instant, of course, the current return on securities is inversely related to the current placement price level. The expected returns on securities, however, depend on the expected future price level of securities. For if a change in security prices is expected, then a capital gain or loss will be anticipated. The return on money, on the other hand, is the convenience yield of being able to meet obligations when they come due, and this will be related to the expected volume of transactions between income payment periods – the transactions and finance motives (Davidson, 1965) – plus the ability to make purchases of securities if their future price is expected to fall at a per annum rate which exceeds the rate of interest (Keynes, 1936, p. 202).

Because these expectations of future placement prices are uncertain, the individual will attempt to manage his store of wealth in the most efficient way while being subject to two types of risks: (1) an income risk, and (2) a capital risk (Kahn, 1954, p. 240). If the individual keeps all his wealth in the form of money, he loses future income but keeps his real wealth intact. If he holds securities, he gains future income but risks loss of real wealth. In an uncertain world, both risks are vexatious and an individual will divide his wealth at the margin into money and securities depending on his disposition to bear income risks and capital risks (cf. Davidson and Smolensky, 1964a, p. 83; Tobin, 1958). At each security price level, and for each possible portfolio division, individuals will appraise the probability of these risks differently and the wealth holding public will divide itself into two groups – the bulls, who demand securities, and the bears, who sell them. Consequently, the savers' demand schedule for securities (e.g., D_p^1 in Figure 3.6) can be derived, given the public's expectations about the future, their present portfolio situation, and their aversion to income risks and capital risks. This demand function includes a Wicksteedian reservation demand by the bulls.

The public demands placements solely as a store of value so that the market demand function is entirely a stock demand, i.e.

$$D_p = f_4(p_p, \bar{R}, \lambda, \beta, \gamma, e, V) \tag{3.14}$$

where D_p is the market demand for placements at a point of time, p_p is the market price of placements, $\bar{R}$ is the 'certain' income claim per placement ($\bar{R} = \$1$ because of our unit measure of placements), λ is a set of expectations about the rate of change of future placement prices, β and γ represent the public's aversion to income risk and capital risk respectively, e represents the number of savers and the distribution of savings among them, and V is the magnitude of the public's total store of value at any point of time. V is defined as the total money balances held by savers as a store of value (M_2) plus the total market value of placements held by the public. We will follow the normal practice of assuming e is unchanged in our model (cf. Brechling, 1957, p. 191; Weintraub, 1958, p. 156).

Given β, γ, and V, for any given expectation λ_1, the market demand curve – e.g. $D_p^1 (V_1)$ in Figure 3.6 – will be downward sloping; i.e. $f'_{4p_p} < 0$, since as the price declines the expected capital gain from purchasing a placement increases, while the (income) opportunity cost of holding money balances as a store of value increases. Hence the public will want to substitute placements for money holdings as the price of securities declines. The demand curve in Figure 3.6 is depicted as intersecting the price axis at p_t, indicating that at that 'high' price the quantity of placements demanded equals zero as the risk of capital loss becomes so great, while the opportunity cost of holding money is negligible. This is the traditional Keynesian liquidity trap, where every member of the public is a complete 'bear' since that price 'leaves more to fear than to hope, and offers, at the same time, a running yield which is only sufficient to offset a very small measure of fear' (Keynes, 1936, p. 202).

If, for example, individuals should increase their desire to avoid capital risks (and/or increase their estimate of the probability of a capital loss in the future), that is, if they should become more bearish at any placement price level (e.g. γ increases), then the savers' demand schedule for securities should shift downward from $D_p^1 (V_1)$ to $D_p^2 (V_1)$ in Figure 3.6; i.e. $f'_{4\gamma} < 0$. This implies that the public wishes to hold less of its wealth in the forms of titles to capital and more in the form of currency or bank deposits.[11] If the supply of placements is constant and if V is unchanged, then the price of securities will fall from p_1 to p_2. Since the total value of placements declines as p_p falls, V will decline, reducing the demand for placements, i.e. $f'_{4v} > 0$. In Figure 3.6, however, the shift from $D_p^1 (V_1)$ to $D_p^2 (V_1)$ was due only to an increase in bearishness, with V unchanged at V_1. The resulting market demand curve when both the change in bearishness and the change in V are accounted for will be D_p^3 in Figure 3.6. At any price below p_1, $\Delta V < 0$ and therefore the quantity of placements demanded will be less than the quantity demand on the unchanged V demand curve, D_p^2 (V_1), while at any price above p_1, the demand quantities will be greater. The horizontal difference between D_p^3 and D_p^2 at any price will depend on the magnitude of the marginal propensity (j) to demand placements when V changes because of a change in the market price of placements, given the expectations about future security prices. The magnitude of j is a measure of a wealth effect, due to changes in placement prices, on the demand for placements (cf. Brechling, 1957, p. 191). If $j = 0$, then D_p^3 and D_p^2 would coincide. The often mentioned 'locked-in' effect due to a security price fall implies that $j \approx 0$, at least for prices below the initial price p_1. In any case, the market price declines (from p_1 to p_3) and the expected real return on loan and equity securities will have risen until in equilibrium the actual portfolio mix of households (which is, by hypothesis, unchanged) is the desired one. (Of course, this will raise the rate of interest and therefore lower the demand for capital goods – in the traditional Keynesian manner.) It is the flexibility of the market price of placements that permits each household unit to hold as many placements as it desires and to alter its portfolio as often as it desires, while in the aggregate the public holds exactly the quantity of placements and money that is made available to it.

This decline in the price of placements can be offset by the commercial banks or the Monetary Authority purchasing securities and simultaneously creating bank deposits for households. In this latter case, the price of securities will not fall as much as in the former (and it may remain unchanged or even rise) as banks reduce the effective supply of securities available to the public (i.e. a_p^b increases), while households increase their holdings of money and decrease their holdings of placements (cf. Keynes, 1930a, p. 142). If the banking system adopts this latter course, then the ultimate effect on the rate of interest and therefore on the demand for capital goods will be different than if the stock of money was kept constant. For example, in Figure 3.6, we can assume that after the market price has declined to p_3, the banks buy securities on the open market, shifting S_p to the left. If the banks could purchase all the placements at the market price of p_3, then there would be no change in V (only a change in the composition of the public's portfolio holdings); and the public would be moved up a demand curve based on a constant $V(D_p^4$ in Figure 3.6). Open market purchases, however, involve bidding up the price of placements and thus altering the magnitude of V at each price. Accordingly, the public will move up the varying $V(D_p^3)$ curve, and the supply schedule must be shifted to the S_p^2 line to restore p_1. Comparing points A and B on Figure 3.6, we note that, *mutatis mutandis*, the actual portfolio holdings of the public have shifted from placements towards money as the banking system has satisfied the bearish sentiment of the public and prevented the rate of interest from rising. Although the public has shifted out of titles to capital goods, the community need not alter its holdings of real capital goods at all.

In summary, in an economy where the major form of money is bank deposits, portfolio decisions in combination with the operations of the banking system will determine what proportion of the community's total of real wealth is owned by households and what proportion is owned or looked after by the banking system (cf. Kahn, 1954, pp. 237–8). Portfolio decisions, except to the extent that they affect the rate of interest via the usual liquidity preference relationships, will have no direct effect on the demand for investment goods. Thus portfolio balance can affect the rate of accumulation only via the interest rate or some other impact via ϕ or E on the demand for capital goods. It is this question of the impact of portfolio decisions on the demand for capital via ϕ or E to which we now turn.

2.4   Security Price Levels and Second Hand Placements, and the Rate of Investment

At any point of time, firms will have a demand for a stock of capital that will depend on the discounted expected flow of future income resulting from the utilization of the services of capital, relative to the acquisition cost of these services. Thus, for alternative acquisition costs, there will be different quantities of capital demanded. Given the stock of capital and its depreciation rate, there will be a market price based on market demand. As we have already pointed out, if this market price exceeds the minimum flow supply price of capital, new capital goods will appear on the market; i.e. gross investment will be positive. Given the rate of depreciation and the market demand price above the minimum flow supply price, the annual rate of capital accumulation will be more rapid, as the supply conditions in the capital goods industry are more elastic.

Each planning period, therefore, the firm will decide, on the basis of a present value calculation based on (a) its profit expectations, (b) the rate of interest, and (c) the current market price of capital assets, whether its current stock of capital is optimal. If the firm believes it has too much capital then it may sell some of its stock. If it has too little it may either (a) buy second hand capital or (b) order new investment goods. Of course, if the market price for capital goods is below the minimum flow supply price, no new investment goods will be produced. If above, new capital goods will be produced. All this has been discussed above.

Entrepreneurs, however, may have an alternative market – the organized securities market dealing in second hand titles to capital goods – that can sometimes be used to gain control of the future services of capital. As

Keynes pointed out, because of the absence of any precise knowledge of the prospective yield of any long-lived assets, the daily re-evaluations of equities on the organized exchanges are based on a tacitly agreed upon convention, i.e. the existing market value of equities are 'uniquely *correct* in relation to our existing knowledge' and the market value 'will only change in proportion to changes in this knowledge' (Keynes, 1936, p. 152). Thus, a saver who holds equities as a store of value 'need not lose his sleep merely because he has not any notion what his investment will be worth ten years hence' (ibid., p. 153). It is not surprising therefore that (a) since equity-holding savers are typically individuals who do not manage or have any knowledge (or even interest) in the long-run prospective yield of the capital assets that they legally own, and (b) since market valuations are a result of a convention established on 'the mass psychology of a large number of ignorant individuals' (ibid., p. 154), the price of equities at any point of time need bear little relationship to entrepreneurial views of future profit opportunities.

Thus, if the price of equities is depressed (because, perhaps, households have increased their preference for money *vis-à-vis* titles to capital goods due to a pessimistic view of the future price of equities or a change in risk preference – i.e. either λ, β, or γ have changed), it may be possible to buy titles to capital goods at a price below the flow supply price of capital (e.g. market value is less than replacement value). Then individual firms can obtain control of the flow of services from the existing capital stock more cheaply by stock takeovers (mergers, amalgamations, etc.) than by purchasing either second hand assets directly or buying newly produced equipment.[12] Since this will reduce the number of independent demanders of capital goods (E in equation (3.1)), it may retard the rate of capital formation for the society by reducing the demand in the capital goods market (cf. ibid., p. 151).

Alternatively, if equity prices are high relative to the market demand price for capital (so that market value exceeds replacement value) because households' view of the future indicates little risk of capital loss and a high probability of large capital gains if equities are purchased now, then entrepreneurs will always find it cheaper to buy new equipment than attempt to gain control over the flow of services from existing capital via the purchases of second hand equities. Moreover, as Keynes indicated, when equity prices are high 'there is an inducement to spend on a new project what may seem an extravagant sum, if it can be floated off on the stock exchange at an immediate profit' (ibid.). Thus, potential entrepreneurial investors may find their ability to finance the demand for capital goods easier (increasing E in equation (3.1)) in a period of high equity prices either because households wish to reduce their holdings of idle balances, or the high prices of common stocks relative to their dividend yields imply that firms can retain profits – that is withhold cash balances from households (cf. Keynes, 1930b, p. 195) – or that banks are willing to provide additional bank deposits to a previously unsatisfied fringe of entrepreneurial borrowers as investment is undertaken. Accordingly, although there may be no direct relationship between portfolio balance decisions that depend upon household expectations of the future price of securities[13] and the capital demand decisions of firms that depend upon future expected profitability of capital services and the rate of interest, there may be some interaction via either financing ability or the ability to take over second hand real assets via merger. The actual rate of production of new investment goods will always depend upon (a) the existence of a discrepancy between the market demand price of capital and the minimum flow supply price of capital and (b) the supply elasticity of the capital goods industries. Thus, though there may be a link between the security market and the market for capital goods, there is also 'many a slip 'twixt the cup and the lip'.

Keynes used 'the term *speculation* for the activity of forecasting the psychology of the [placement] market, and the term *enterprise* for the activity of forecasting the prospective yield of assets over their whole life' (Keynes, 1936, p. 158). Placement market activity is, for the most part, independent of both investment activity and the rate at which new securities are being floated; i.e. $\bar{g} (1 - \bar{h}) [p_k(s_k - d_k)]$ is likely to be exceedingly small relative to the total number of transactions occurring in the securities market. Organized placement market activity, based as it is primarily on second-hand transactions and not new issues, depends almost entirely on people's views about how rich they are likely to be in the future; i.e. $\Delta\lambda$ is likely to be much more important than s_p in affecting security prices. As Keynes noted, the value of equities will often appear quite absurd to 'a rational observer from the outside' (Keynes, 1930b, p. 360), for 'the vast majority of those who are concerned with the buying and selling of securities know almost nothing whatever about what they are doing' (Keynes, 1930b, p. 361), while the professional speculator is normally interested only in taking advantage of the expected misguided views of the crowd (Keynes, 1936, pp. 154–8).

If savers should take a rosier view of the future and therefore accept a lower present return on a store of equity wealth for the promise (hope? expectation?) of higher future returns than the entrepreneurial view of the prospective yield of a capital asset, then stock prices can rise almost without limit (as long as bullishness persists) and without directly altering the demand for capital goods except by making finance more readily available to investors. In the limiting case, where investors see no new profitable opportunities while savers maintain their rosy view of future placement prices, placement prices can increase, the rate of interest will decline, while the demand for capital will remain virtually unchanged.

If, on the other hand, savers should require a higher present return on equities, perhaps because the future looks worse to them than it does to the entrepreneurs, then security prices will fall while the flow of new capital goods will not be affected except if (a) the price of titles to capital falls below the flow supply price of capital, (b) firms find their ability to obtain finance reduced as individuals increase their preference for money in their portfolios, and the supply of money remains unaltered so that entrepreneurial demands for capital are aborted by higher interest charges and/or credit rationing (reducing E in equation (3.1)), and (c) the decrease in security prices colours entrepreneurial views about future profit yields of capital goods (reducing ϕ in equation (3.1)).

The only unequivocal link between portfolio balance behaviour and the demand for capital goods by investors is via the usual Keynesian interest rate mechanism. Nevertheless, the introduction of an exogenous money creating banking system allows investors to make investment decisions that can be incompatible with the public's portfolio preferences at the current rate of interest. If the investors can obtain finance, then the market price of placements will be the adjusting mechanism that will bring the savers' portfolio balance decisions into harmony with the investment projects undertaken. In a monetary economy, it is finance that provides the energy fuel that permits the investment tail to wag the portfolio balance dog.

2.5 Finance and Capital Accumulation

It is now possible to use our model to suggest the mechanism that relates the path of capital accumulation to the supply of money. At this stage we can no longer ignore the flow supply aspects of placements.

Assume initially a stationary state economy. The market price for capital goods is p_s. New capital goods (financed internally via the business sector's depreciation reserves) are merely replacing capital as it wears out in each period of time. Assuming no change in λ, the demand and supply curves for placements are fixed and can be represented as D_p^1 and S_p in Figure 3.7a. The price of placements is unchanged at a price of p_1 as the placement market clears in each period for as many periods as the economy remains in the stationary state. Now let us postulate an increase in the demand for capital by investors due to an exogenous improvement in profit expectations at the beginning of period t. This will lead to an increase in the demand for capital goods, provided the additional demand can be financed (cf. Keynes, 1930b, p. 149) (for as we always teach in courses in micro-economics, demand for any commodity implies *want plus the ability to pay*). Thus there will be an increase in net investment, $\Delta(s_k - d_k) > 0$.

Since the previous level of capital demand was being adequately financed, there must have been sufficient transaction cash balances in the system to maintain the initial level of consumption and gross investment transactions. With the improved profit expectations, however, there will be

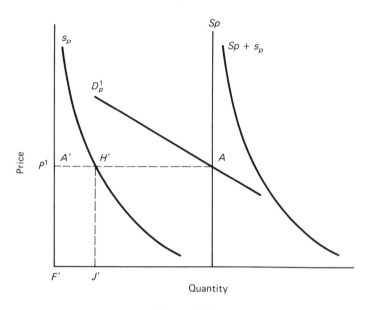

Figure 3.7a

an additional demand for money to finance the additional demand for
capital even at the initial income level (Davidson, 1965). Thus some firms
will, *ceteris paribus*, require additional cash balances to buy net investment
goods. They may engage an investment banker (or a promoter) who, after
convincing himself of the correctness of the investors' expectations, will
borrow funds from a commercial bank on a short-term loan to finance the
increased demand for investment goods. (Of course, particularly in the
case of financing increments in working capital, the firms may borrow
directly from the banks.)

Accordingly, if the entire increase in the cost of investment is borrowed
on short-term credit from the banks, then, *ceteris paribus*, the quantity of
money is increased:

$$\Delta M = \Delta C, \tag{3.15}$$

where ΔC is the increase in cost (market value) of the output of the
investment goods industries when net investment increases ($\Delta I_n > 0$).

These newly created funds will be used by the firms to make payments
that ultimately become income to owners of factors engaged in the capital
goods industry. There will be, therefore, an increase in the money balances
of households *pari passu* with the growth in investment expenditures;
hence the real wealth of the community (but not that part directly owned by
the household sector) and savers' money balances increase simultaneously.[14]

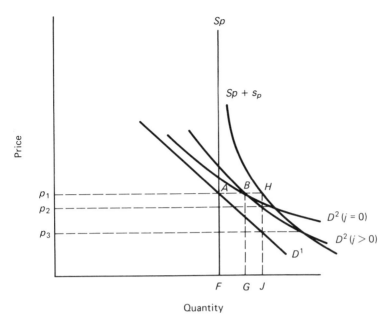

Figure 3.7b

Some households that were previously in portfolio balance now find their real income and their money holdings have increased. They will, of course, increase their planned consumption expenditures and consequently hold some of the additional money for transactions purposes. The remainder becomes household savings and the households must decide in what form to store wealth. (This process continues over other households as the multiplier – and income velocity – process works itself out.) Accordingly, at the end of the process, some of the new money has been absorbed permanently into active balances (ΔM_1) and the remainder is idle balances (ΔM_2). This increase in M_2 increases V and induces a rightward shift in the placement demand curve in Figure 3.7b from D^1. The magnitude of the wealth effect on the demand for placements when the idle balances of savers is exogenously altered is measured by m, the marginal propensity to demand placements as M_2 changes. If $m = 1$, which is the usual assumption underlying the traditional speculative demand curve for money (cf. Brechling, 1957, pp. 195–6), then, given λ, the demand curve for placements will be shifted out from point A to point B at the p_1 price. This shift from point A to B is indicative of an increase in demand at p_1 that is just sufficient to absorb a volume of new placements (at a price of p_1 per unit) so that purchases equal ΔM_2; i.e. $FABG = \Delta M_2$ in Figure 3.7b. At any price below p_1, the total value of the public's initial holdings of placements will decline and hence there is another wealth effect on the demand for placements such that if $j > 0$, the shift in the placement demand curve will not be sufficient to purchase ΔM_2 worth of additional placements even if $m = 1$. Similarly if $j > 0$ at any price level above p_1, the demand for additional placements will exceed ΔM_2. If, on the other hand, $j = 0$ – i.e. a change in the total market value of the public's initial stock of placements does not, in itself, affect the demand for placements, so there is no second wealth effect – then, at any price, the increase in demand will involve additional purchases that just equal ΔM_2. The curves D^2 $(j = 0)$ and D^2 $(j > 0)$ in Figure 3.7b represent these two possible cases. The D^2 $(j = 0)$ curve will have a rectangular hyperbolic relationship with respect to D^1.

The number of placements that must be floated to completely fund any given increase in the cost of investment (ΔC) varies inversely with the market price of placements. If, for example, $g = 1$ and $h = 0$, then, given ΔC, the flow supply curve of placements is the rectangular hyperbola s_p in Figure 3.7a where $F'A'H'J' = \Delta C$. The total market supply curve in the period can be represented by $S_p + s_p$ in Figure 3.7a. By placing the market supply curve $S_p + s_p$ onto Figure 3.7b we can readily see what will happen to the market price of securities. Since $\Delta M_2 < \Delta M = \Delta C$, therefore $FABG$ $(= \Delta M_2)$ must be less than $FAHJ$ $(= \Delta C)$. Consequently, the new market supply curve, at the p_1 market price, must lie to the right of the new market demand curve. If $j = 0$, then the new market demand curve is hyperbolically related to the downward sloping D^1 curve. Since the new supply curve has the same rectangular hyperbola relationship to the vertical S_p curve, the new intersection must occur at some lower market price, p_2. Of course, if $j > 0$ then the intersection will occur at even a lower market price, p_3. The revenue from the sale of new placements at the market clearing price will be sufficient to pay off the outstanding short-term bank loans.

Thus if householders do not alter their expectations about the future price level of placements, and if their feelings about income and capital risk have not altered, and if the commercial banks or the Monetary Authority does not purchase some of the additional securities, then the rate of return on securities must rise (security prices fall) in order to induce households to alter the relative portfolio holdings from money towards securities.

In summary, given the expectation of the community, if the rate of return on securities is to be kept constant or reduced as the level of economic activity expands with an increase in net investment, and if all the titles to the increment in net investment are to be held by the public (rather than the banks), then the quantity of money will, in general, have to increase by an amount that exceeds the increased cost of investment; i.e. ΔM must be $> \Delta C$.

The rate of increase in M in each period which would be necessary to keep the rate of interest constant, when net investment is increasing and expectations about the rate of change of future placement prices is unchanged, will depend upon (1) the magnitudes of g and h, (2) the marginal propensity to increase M_1 as transactions increase, and (3) m – the marginal propensity to buy placements with changes in M_2. If $g = 1$, $h = 0$, $m = 1$, and if M_1 is always proportional to commodity transactions, while the latter is proportional to real output (so that, for example, there is no change in the degree of industrial integration), and if the capital–output ratio is a constant, then the required proportionate increase in the money supply that will keep the rate of interest unchanged is equal to the proportionate increase in capital goods that is forthcoming. If all these conditions are fulfilled, then the demand for placements will increase at the same pace as the supply of placements. If these conditions are not met, – unless there are exactly offsetting influences – the rate of increase in M, which will leave interest rates unaltered, will not be equal to the rate of growth of capital goods.[15]

Since in our example above, $\Delta I_t > 0$, the equilibrium level of economic activity in period t will be greater than in $t - 1$, and the economy will depart from the stationary state. The funds that were obtained by floating the new issue in period t are used to retire the short-term bank loan and, therefore, are available at the banks to finance the same level of net investment in the $t + 1$ period as in the t period.

The veracity of Keynes's dictum that 'if investment is proceeding at a steady rate, finance . . . [is] a revolving fund of a more or less constant amount' (Keynes, 1937a, p. 247) is readily demonstrable. If in $t + 1$, $\Delta I = 0$, then the firms have no difficulty in financing the same level of net investment as in the t period via short-term bank borrowing. Again, the increase in capital stock will result in a simultaneous increase in household balances – but, if $\Delta I = 0$, then $\Delta Y = 0$. Consequently, there is no need for households to increase their M_1 holdings and all the increment in their money holdings are initially M_2. If $m = 1$, this shifts the demand for placements out sufficiently to absorb, at the current market price, enough new placements to fund the entire short-term borrowing. In such a situation, the planned net debtor position of firms has increased *pari passu* with the planned net creditor position of households (at the current rate of interest). Obviously, finance is a revolving fund that need not be augmented even if net investment is positive as long as net investment and the rate of economic activity are unchanged from period to period (and expectations are unaltered). Of course, a constant positive level of net investment each period implies a declining rate of capital growth and economic stagnation as the level of economic activity remains unchanged.

If, on the other hand, we posit another improvement in profit expectations in $t + 1$, so that there is an additional demand for money to finance an increment in net investment, and if the banks provide these additional balances via short-term credit expansion, then at the higher $t + 1$ equilibrium level of output, the additional money (net of additional active balances) held as a store of value will not shift the placement demand curve sufficiently, even if $m = 1$, to float the entire new issue at the current market price (i.e. $\Delta M_2 < \Delta M = \Delta C$). Consequently, if the rate of interest is to be kept unchanged when $g = 1$ and $h = 0$, again we note that ΔM must be greater than ΔC.

We might inquire what would have happened in $t + 1$ if the banks refused to expand the money supply, i.e. $M_{t+1} = M_t$, as firms attempted to increase their demand for capital goods because of improved profit expectations. (For ease of exposition we ignore the net investment that can be financed from the revolving fund and concentrate only on the increments in net investment and finance.) If additional finance is to be obtained, then some households must be induced to give up some of their portfolio money holdings in exchange for securities. Hence the market price must initially fall (rate of interest must rise) to encourage households to substitute placements for money in their desired portfolios (cf. Gurley and Shaw, 1955, p. 525). As the additional investment projects are carried out, economic activity increases and additional money is absorbed into active balances, leaving less money permanently available for portfolio balance. Consequently, the demand for securities at any price level is reduced, and, of course, the equilibrium level of output will be lower and the rate of interest higher than if the supply of money had expanded in pace with the additional investment demand.

Every actual increase in the level of investment will, if the money supply is unchanged and $g > 0$, increase the quantity of placements and reduce the quantity of money available as a store of value; therefore, placement prices will decline. The greater the increase in net investment demanded per unit of time, the greater the quantity of active balances demanded, and therefore, the greater the reduction in M_2 balances. Thus, the greater the growth in demand for net investment, *ceteris paribus*, the greater the decrease in demand and increase in supply of placements, and therefore, the greater the decline in placement prices (the more rapid the rise in interest rates). This lack of finance will ultimately limit the rate of capital accumulation as another 'liquidity trap' restrains expansion[16] since 'a heavy demand for investment can exhaust the market and be held up by the lack of financial facilities on reasonable terms. It is, to an important extent, the financial facilities which regulate the *pace* of new investment [at less than full employment] . . . too great a press of uncompleted investment decisions is quite capable of exhausting available finance, if the banking system is unwilling to increase the supply of money' (Keynes, 1937a, p. 248).

Thus, in any expansion, as Keynes argued:

the banks hold the key position in the transition from a lower to a higher scale of activity. If they refuse to relax [i.e., to provide additional finance], the growing congestion of the short term loan market or the new issue market, as the case may be, will inhibit the improvement, no matter how thrifty the public purpose to be out of their future income. On the other hand, there will always be *exactly* enough ex-post saving to take up the ex-post investment and so release the finance which the latter has been previously employing. *The investment market can become congested through a shortage of cash. It can never become congested through a shortage of saving* [or savers not *wanting* to own the titles to the real wealth (at some reduced placement price level) that has been produced]. *This is the most fundamental of my conclusions within this field.* (Keynes, 1937b, pp. 668–9; italics mine)

It should be apparent, therefore, that if growth is to be sustained, the money supply must increase as output rises. In an uncertain world, however, where expectations are volatile and unpredictable (rather than the given datum assumed in our model), the relationship between the required increase in the money supply and the increase in real wealth is much too complex to be handled by any simple rule. Money clearly matters in the process of economic growth in a monetary economy, but a simple rule can be no substitute for wise management of the money supply (cf. Keynes, 1930a, ch. 15).

2.6 Finance, Capital Accumulation, and Public Policy

Our mechanism has emphasized that for increases in capital demand to be effective, firms must be able to obtain additional finance. Thus, for a steady rate of capital accumulation and growth to occur, the banking system and the Monetary Authority must play an essential role by providing the initial funds on terms which investors deem attractive[17] (cf. Keynes, 1930b, p. 149; Gurley and Shaw, 1955). It is at the level of financing investment projects that the money supply plays an essential role in stimulating economic growth in a monetized market economy, and not at the level of portfolio balances. Keynes wrote a long time ago that 'the rate at which the world's wealth has accumulated has been far more variable than habits of thrift have been' (Keynes, 1930b, p. 149). To this dictum we may add 'or habits of portfolio balance'. If we can expand Keynes's Treatise analogy, we might note that the Seven Wonders of the World were not built by either habits of thrift or portfolio balance; rather they were the result of the desire for personal capital monuments by kings and other important personages plus these people's ability to obtain finance in order to command the necessary real resources. (Of course, a respected government – or a feared one – has no difficulty in finding a means of finance (cf. Robinson, 1956, p. 276, n. 1).) Once the active decision to increase the real wealth of the world in this form was implemented all that the ancient households could do was to adjust their savings and portfolios in the light of the variables that were left open to them.

Most Keynesian growth models have (erroneously) ignored the monetary requirements for growth.[18] Professor Tobin has, at least, attempted to show that monetary factors are of primary importance in growth. Unfortunately, he ties money supply requirements too closely to portfolio balances and not sufficiently to the requirements of finance where it belongs.

In modern money economies with a developed banking system, there is normally a continual fringe of unsatisfied borrowers. Banks often restrict credit in the sense that 'the amount lent to any individual . . . [is] governed not solely by the security and the rate of interest offered, but also by reference to the borrowers' purposes and his standing with the bank as a valuable or influential client' (Keynes, 1930b, p. 365). It is this restriction on credit (limiting E in equation (3.1)) that limits the rate of accumulation as often as a high rate of interest.

The policy implication of this analysis is that since capital accumulation primarily depends upon (1) investors' views of the future (ϕ), (2) the ability of firms to obtain finance (E) and the rate of interest (i), and (3) supply conditions in the capital goods industries (s_k), and since (1) and (3) are not normally under public policy control, then the money supply should be controlled so as to make finance as easy as possible until full employment at any point of time is reached.

At full employment the rate of capital accumulation will depend only on its expected profitability (ϕ), and the elasticity of supply of the capital goods industries (s_k). If this should result in a rate of accumulation that exceeds the natural rate of growth in the labour force, then ultimately, in a free market, money and real wages and prices will rise, forcing savers (particularly bondholding rentiers) to reduce real consumption – forced savings – and allowing some further expansion in investment goods industries and a higher level of full employment with a greater labour force participation rate (which implies that there is nothing 'natural' about the natural rate of growth of the labour force)[19] (Davidson and Smolensky, 1964a, pp. 170–1; 1964b).

The accompanying inflation and its income redistribution will have undesirable social effects. The real income and wealth of bond-holding savers will be reduced; this will alter the views as to the probabilities attached to income and capital risks of portfolio holdings, which will feed back onto security price levels. Moreover, entrepreneurs may build inflationary expectations into their future income stream calculations, thereby raising the demand for capital via ϕ (Davidson and Smolensky, 1964a, p. 203). Finally, the Monetary Authority is unlikely to continue to allow easy financing under such circumstances. In the absence of an integrated monetary, fiscal, and incomes policy for full employment, therefore, the output of the investment goods industries ought ultimately to slow down because of the shortage of finance.

If, on the other hand, the economy is in a position where the demand price for capital brings forth an increase in the stock of capital (where the rate of capital accumulation is still less than the long run rate of growth in the labour force), then unless the capital–labour ratio can decline over time, the threat of surplus labour and depression will tend to appear. In these circumstances, only the socialization or subsidization of investment or other non-consumption demands, or reductions in the rate of growth of the effective labour force (e.g. a reduction in the work week) can maintain full employment.

In a market-oriented economy, there is no automatic market mechanism which will adjust the rate of capital accumulation to the rate of increase in the effective labour force. The most that can be said is that, given technology, given the distribution of income, given the expectations of entrepreneurs, and given the liquidity preference of the public, there may be an attainable rate of interest which will bring the warranted rate of growth of capital into equality with the natural rate of growth of the labour force (cf. Harrod, 1952, pp. 129–69). If such an optimum rate exists, then the Monetary Authority should orient its policy to obtaining and maintaining this optimum or natural rate of interest.[20] Thus in an economy of steady growth, the supply of money would have to be continually expanded, and as I have shown elsewhere, unless this additional finance is supplied in advance of the actual expansion, the economy may be restrained by almost another 'liquidity trap' (Davidson, 1965, p. 62), this time by virtue of the fact that the shortage of finance may choke off investment, rather than the fear of capital loss precipitating the liquidity crisis.

Notes

1. It is not too difficult to understand why many of the students of Keynes (who was primarily a monetary theorist) have tended to ignore the role of money in the analysis of growth. In part it is due, as Harrod has noted, to the fact that Keynesians 'base themselves largely, if not exclusively on his *General Theory*, which is taken to have superseded the *Treatise on Money* . . . But there is much of value in the *Treatise . . . Econometrica* (1968). It is a paradox that the man whose world-wide fame during most of his life-time arose from his specific contributions to monetary theory, which were rich and varied, should be studied mainly in one of his books which contains little about money as such' (Harrod, 1963, p. 412). In a conversation (May, 1965). Harrod suggested three reasons why Keynesians did not stress the role of money: (1) in the depression, cheap money alone could not bring about an expansion, (2) during the war, there was direct control over aggregate demand plus a desire to keep interest costs on the increasing debt as low as possible, so that cheap money policies were automatically advocated; inflation was fought by voluntary agreements

between labour unions and the government and food subsidies kept the cost of living down; and (3) by 1951, the balance of payments and the Korean inflation required tight money policies. Consequently, considerations other than those of growth and capital accumulation were of primary importance in monetary affairs since the writings of *The General Theory*; thus, the English students of Keynes, at least, believed that there was not much purpose in advocating monetary policies to stimulate growth.

With Keynesian growth theorists emphasizing only the real (supply) aspects of growth, study of the financial requirements for growth have been left to essentially non-Keynesian scholars, such as members of the Chicago school (e.g. Friedman and Schwartz, 1963), and others such as Gurley and Shaw (1955, 1960).

2. For Harrod, however, the warranted rate of growth in the capital stock is related to his capital requirements concept which is defined as 'that addition to capital goods in any period which producers regard as ideally suited to the output which they are undertaking in that period' (1952, p. 260; cf. 1948), i.e. warranted rate of growth of capital reflects entrepreneurial *ex-ante* investment desires. In Tobin's model, however, it reflects the *ex-ante* savings propensity. As indicated below. Tobin does not have an independent investment demand function and there can be no underemployment equilibrium in his model, since he implicitly assumes that *ex-ante* investment equals *ex-ante* savings.

3. There is a tendency for modern model-builders to assign more precision to this process of time preference than either the neoclassicists or Keynes would have. Does the rational economic man have a precise plan for future consumption or is he merely altering his consumption time pattern in some vague way? Keynes argued that 'an act of individual savings means – so to speak – a decision not to have dinner to-day . . . But it does *not* necessitate a decision to have dinner or to buy a pair of boots a week hence or a year hence or to consume any specific thing at any specific date' (Keynes, 1936, p. 210).

4. Kaldor, on the other hand, has insisted that it is the investment, rather than the savings propensity, that is 'the ultimate stuff and substance which *make* societies progressive' (1960, p. 228).

5. The Harrod impasse occurs, according to Tobin, when investors desire a minimum return per unit of capital of HH (in Figure 3.1), and therefore they would tolerate a maximum $K–N$ ratio of k_k. For k_h to be an equilibrium capital intensity, *ex ante* investment per unit of capital would have to be the distance AB, while *ex ante* consumption is CD. Hence, there will be a deflationary gap of BC. In Tobin's words this is an 'impasse' because in his model, in the absence of other non-consumption demand, the savings behaviour assumed in the S curve would prevent the establishment of any equilibrium and the economy would plunge towards a zero level of output.

6. This way of viewing the investment decision does have an advantage in more closely identifying the question of the elasticity of the marginal efficiency schedule to the rate of accumulation. The elasticity of the marginal efficiency schedule will, for a given change in the rate of interest, affect the magnitude of the shift in the market demand schedule for capital. The actual change in investment goods output will depend on the supply elasticity in the capital goods industry as well. (See Keynes, 1936, p. 334).

7. For simplicity in the analysis that follows, we will completely identify the saving (store of value) function with households, and the investing (flow of future capital services) function with business firms.

8. Thus Tobin's assumption that the 'value of money in terms of goods is fixed'

(1965, p. 676), is incompatible with changes in the level of investment due to changes in the stock demand for capital.

9. In 1965, for example, capital consumption allowances plus undistributed corporate profits was approximately 80 per cent of gross private domestic investment in the United States.

10. Of course, an increase in the probability of receiving an income claim would have the same effect as increases in 'short sales' in the securities market. It may be viewed as an increase in effective supply. We shall ignore these problems in the following analysis since their introduction would make the analysis more complicated without altering the major conclusions.

11. This increase in bearishness may result from the fact that rapidly fluctuating stock prices may increase the public's uncertainty about the future and therefore increase their expectation of capital risk. On the other hand, steadily increasing stock prices may reduce the public's expectation of capital loss and therefore increase their bullishness. Thus, changes in portfolio balance decisions may be the result of the rapidity and the trend in changing security prices, rather than their current effective yield (cf. Harrod, 1952, p. 252).

12. This is particularly likely to occur if poor management of a firm has caused savers to have a pessimistic view about its future earning ability. Thus, a stock takeover by an efficient management may improve the 'productivity' of the capital goods of the firm that has been swallowed up. (Also control of the first firm's assets may come without even buying a majority of the outstanding stock).

13. If the future price of consumer durables is expected to increase, then households may increase their purchases of durables until the marginal carrying costs of the additional goods equal the expected decline in the commodity purchasing power of money.

14. For simplicity of exposition, we will, at this point, ignore the possibility of retained profits by the capital producing firms. To the extent that some profits are retained, internal finance in the business sector is possible.

15. Thus, the justification of Tobin's conclusion that in equilibrium 'money and capital must grow at the same rate' (Tobin, 1965, p. 679) requires a host of heroic assumptions which were not specified in his model.

16. For an analysis of this new type of liquidity trap using the Hicksian *IS–LM* model, see (Davidson, 1965, p. 62).

17. An investment project will appear attractive to entrepreneurs if the expected return to capital less interest charges is large. Thus, profits per unit of capital may, from the investors' view, rise, even if the marginal product of capital is declining, if interest charges to the firm are falling more rapidly than the marginal product. In this sense, interest is merely a transfer of income between entrepreneurs who wish to command resources and savers who have a store of purchasing power.

18. There are a few exceptions where the importance of money is at least mentioned, e.g. (Robinson, 1956; Tobin, 1965; Weintraub, 1966). It is interesting to note that the father of modern growth theory, Harrod, had an important article on 'The Expansion of Credit in an Advancing Economy' as early as 1934 (reprinted in Harrod, 1952).

19. Given leisure-income preferences, and the rate of growth of population, the natural rate of growth of the labour force is market determined.

20. This optimum rate of interest is not a welfare growth optimum. It merely 'causes the propensity to invest to be at a level that gives full, but no more than full employment' (Harrod, 1963, pp. 406–7) at each point of time. It has little

or nothing to do with what 'people wish in relation to present and future consumption' (Harrod, 1964, p. 906).

References

Brechling, F. P. R. (1957), 'A Note on Bond-holding and the Liquidity Preference Theory of Interest', *Review of Economic Studies*, 24, pp. 190–7.
Clower, R. W. (1954), 'An Investigation into the Dynamics of Investment', *American Economic Review*, 44 (March), pp. 64–81.
Davidson, P. (1965), 'Keynes's Finance Motive', *Oxford Economic Papers*, 17 (1965), pp. 47–65 (Chapter 1 in this volume)
Davidson, P. and E. Smolensky (1964a), *Aggregate Supply and Demand Analysis* (New York).
Davidson, P. and E. Smolensky (1964b), 'Modigliani on the Interaction of Real and Monetary Phenomena', *Review of Economics and Statistics*, (November), 46 pp. 429–31.
Friedman, M. and A. J. Schwartz (1963), 'Money and Business Cycles', *Review of Economics and Statistics*, 45 (February, suppl.), pp. 32–78.
Gurley, J. G. and E. S. Shaw (1955), 'Financial Aspects of Economic Development', *American Economic Review*, 45 (September), pp. 515–38.
Gurley, J. G. and E. S. Shaw (1960), *Money in a Theory of Finance* (Washington).
Harrod, R. F. (1948), *Towards a Dynamic Economics* (London).
Harrod, R. F. (1952), *Economic Essays* (New York).
Harrod, R. F. (1959), 'Domar and Dynamic Economics', *Economic Journal*, 69 (September), pp. 451–64.
Harrod, R. F. (1963), 'Themes in Dynamic Theory', *Economic Journal*, 73 (September), pp. 401–21.
Harrod, R. F. (1964), 'Are Monetary and Fiscal Policies Enough?' *Economic Journal*, 74 (December), pp. 903–15.
Kahn, R. F. (1954), 'Some Notes on Liquidity Preference', *Manchester School*, 22 (September), pp. 229–57.
Kaldor, N. (1960), *Essays on Economic Stability and Growth* (London).
Keynes, J. M. (1930a), *A Treatise on Money*, Vol. I (London).
Keynes, J. M. (1930b), *A Treatise on Money*, Vol. II (London).
Keynes, J. M. (1936), *The General Theory of Employment, Interest, and Money* (New York).
Keynes, J. M. (1937a), 'Alternative Theories of the Rate of Interest', *Economic Journal*, 47 (June), pp. 241–52.
Keynes, J. M. (1937b), 'The Ex-ante Theory of the Rate of Interest', *Economic Journal*, 47 (December), pp. 663–9.
Lerner, A. P. (1944), *The Economics of Control* (New York).
Makower, H. and J. Marschak (1938), 'Assets, Prices, and Monetary Theory', *Economica*, 5 (August), pp. 261–88.
Robinson, J. (1963), *Essays in the Theory of Economic Growth* (London).
Robinson, J. (1956), *The Accumulation of Capital* (London).
Scitovsky, T. (1964), *Papers on Welfare and Growth* (London).
Tobin, J. (1955), 'A Dynamic Aggregative Model', *Journal of Political Economy*, 63 (April), pp. 103–15.
Tobin, J. (1958), 'Liquidity Preference As a Behavior Towards Risk', *Review of Economic Studies*, 25 (February), pp. 65–86.

Tobin, J. (1961), 'Money, Capital and Other Stores of Value', *American Economic Review Papers & Proceedings*, 51 (May), pp. 26–37.

Tobin, J. (1965), 'Money and Economic Growth', *Econometrica*, 33 (October), pp. 671–84.

Turvey, R. (1960), *Interest Rates and Asset Prices* (London).

Weintraub, S. (1958), *An Approach to the Theory of Income Distribution* (Philadelphia).

Weintraub, S. (1966), *A Keynesian Theory of Employment, Growth and Income Distribution* (Philadelphia).

Witte, J. G. (1963), 'The Microfoundations of the Social Investment Function', *Journal of Political Economy*, 71 (October), pp. 441–56.

4 The Demand and Supply of Securities and Economic Growth and Its Implications for the Kaldor–Pasinetti Versus Samuelson–Modigliani Controversy*

The Keynesian revolution is usually thought to have begun with *The General Theory of Employment, Interest, and Money* (Klein, 1966, p. ix; Harrod, 1951, p. 462). According to Keynes's biographer, however, *The General Theory* emerges from Keynes's attempt to simplify the intricate analysis of his *Treatise on Money* (Harrod, 1951, p. 437). It is the *Treatise* (hereafter referred to as TM) rather than *The General Theory* (hereafter GT) which is Keynes's 'most mature work', 'the work of a lifetime', and the one where the student will 'get the best picture of his [Keynes's] total contribution to economics' (ibid., p. 403).

Admittedly, Keynes's fundamental 'law' on effective demand is developed extensively only in the GT, and one can readily agree with Klein that 'the revolution was solely the development of the theory of effective demand' (1966, p. 56). Nevertheless, it may be argued that the liquidity preference theory of 1936 represents a retrogressive movement from the monetary analysis of the TM, where, in the latter, Keynes's 'views about all the details of the complex subject of money are . . . to be found' (Harrod, 1951, p. 403). As Sir Roy has lamented, 'it is a paradox that the man whose world-wide fame during most of his lifetime arose from his specific contributions to monetary theory, which were rich and varied, should be studied mainly in one of his books which contains little about money as such' (Harrod, 1963, p. 442).

It is also a sorry fact that in the post-Keynesian literature the role of money in the growth models has too often been ignored. Moreover, the relationship between money and growth is likely to continue to be misunderstood so long as modern Keynesian monetary analysis is based solely

* This article appeared in the *American Economic Review* (1968). The author is grateful to M. Fleming, E. Smolensky and S. Weintraub for comments on an earlier draft.

on Keynes's 1936 work. The essence of growth is dynamic change, and Harrod has pointed out that 'the *Treatise* is more dynamic than the latter volume' (Harrod, 1951, p. 433). In the TM, we only 'get an analysis of the economy when it is out of equilibrium and in a state of movement' (ibid., p. 457). Robinson (1951, p. 56) and Klein also note that the TM emphasis is on movement and dynamics (1966, p. 28). It is my belief, therefore, that a more solid advance in understanding of the money–securities–economic growth nexus can be made by judiciously mixing elements of Keynes's 1930 monetary analysis with his 1936 classic approach to the principles of effective demand.

Some of the confusion which hitherto has prevented the combining of the analysis of the TM with the concepts of the GT can be eliminated by some recourse to microeconomic concepts. For example, the Marshallian stability conditions, at any given output level, can be identified with the earlier work, while the Walrasian stability conditions, at any given supply price, can be the interpretative key to the later volume. If, in the TM, one substitutes the Marshallian concept of demand price for the term 'investment', and supply price for 'savings', the terminological turmoil arising from Keynes's discussion of the inequality of savings and investment is readily resolved. Thus, to recall the argument of the TM, when investment exceeds (is less than) savings – i.e. the demand price, D_p, exceeds (is less than) the supply price, S_p, which includes normal profits at a given level of output, Q_1, as in Figure 4.1a – then, in the market period, transactions occur at the demand price of p_1. This results in windfall profits (losses) as revenues exceed (fall short of) normal supply requirements. The invisible

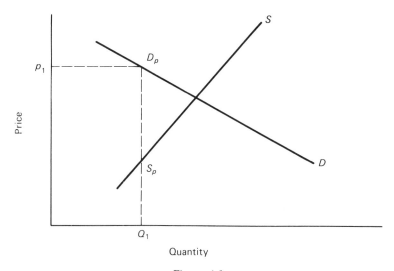

Figure 4.1a

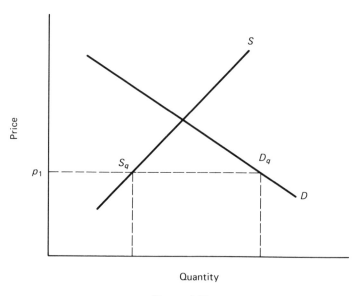

Figure 4.1b

hand of the market-place, operating via these windfall profits (losses) encourages entrepreneurs to expand (contract) output and employment. It is the analysis of the factors which lead to a discrepancy between D_p and S_p which brings about the dynamic change in prices and subsequently output in the TM.

In the GT, on the other hand, Walrasian stability conditions are implicitly utilized. If *ex ante* investment exceeds (is less than) *ex ante* savings, then the demand quantity, D_q, exceeds (is less than) the supply quantity, S_q, at the given supply price of p_1, as in Figure 4.1b. Market transactions occur at the price of p_1, and the demand quantity of D_q is sold, while production is equal to the supply quantity, S_q, as inventories are drawn down. Entrepreneurs, reacting to the involuntary reduction (increase) in inventories caused by the invisible hand, are induced to expand (contract) output (cf. Samuelson, 1964a, pp. 223–4; Harrod, 1951, p. 456). Since in this latter case, the market price is equal to the supply price – which is easily translated into wage units – for the given level of output and employment, there can be no windfall profit or loss on current production. Consequently, actual savings must always equal actual investment as unplanned inventory changes play the role which windfall profits did in the TM.[1]

With the GT, however, a more subtle change in view is imparted through the adoption of the Walrasian conditions than merely the simple transfer in concept from demand and supply prices to demand and supply quantities.[2] Perhaps due to the persuasion of the friendly coterie surrounding Keynes at Cambridge, the 1936 volume is geared primarily to the establishment of a stable equilibrium with less concern for the forces promoting dynamic movement (Harrod, 1951, p. 457; Robinson, 1951, p. 56). Subsequent mathematical formulation of the Keynesian model has accentuated the tendency to suppress the earlier features of dynamism in their concentration on the simultaneous solution of the equations of the system. The equilibrium position rather than the mechanism of change has become the characteristic post-Keynesian analysis.

If Harrod is correct in arguing that Keynes had concluded that his critics 'simply failed to grasp' (Harrod, 1951, p. 435) the complexities of the 1930 analysis, then it is reasonable to believe that the GT was the result of a search for a 'simplification' (ibid., p. 437). If the main breakdown in communication between Keynes and others was on the principle of effective demand, then it is not surprising that although 'money enters into the economic scheme in an essential and peculiar manner, [Keynes purposely fitted] technical monetary detail . . . into the background'[3] (Keynes, 1936, p. vii).

If Keynes's real contribution was 'to show that if savings are not offset by legitimate investment outlets, failure to generate a high level of employment will follow' (Keynes, 1937a, p. 81), then in winning the battle of Say's Law in his 1936 volume, Keynes may have underplayed the complexities of monetary market phenomena through an oversimplified monetary analysis.

Actually, Ohlin, with D. H. Robertson always (for company) in pursuit, was quick to seize upon the deficiencies of the truncated monetary analysis of the GT (Ohlin, 1937; Robertson, 1938). Under their hammering, Keynes was forced to retreat and confess the incompleteness of his work in a series of exchanges in the *Economic Journal* (1937a, b). As Keynes had already developed a more powerful and complete monetary analysis in his TM, however, he was immediately able to moderate his liquidity preference argument to encompass the needs of finance, and thereby enjoin his critics with what he characterized as the 'coping-stone of the liquidity theory' (1937b, p. 667). In essence, Keynes was merely restoring the theory of bearishness and the demand for capital goods as elaborated in the TM into consistency and orderliness with his liquidity preference apparatus.[4]

Rather than a coping stone, Keynes's 1937 finance motive discussion is the Rosetta Stone which makes possible the deciphering of the ancient TM hieroglyphics into modern post-Keynesian terminology. In attempting to analyse the role of money in the real, non-golden-age, world of economic growth, I have become even more aware of the defects of the truncated monetary approach of the GT as against the perspicacity and elaboration of the TM's analysis of the interrelations of commodity and security markets, and the roles played by the various financial institutions which

Keynes tends to dismiss as mere 'technical detail' in the GT. Since the TM is an analysis of 'an economy on the move', while the latter volume emphasizes static equilibrium,[5] much insight can be derived by restructuring the bearishness concepts of the TM with the more widely used classificatory scheme of the GT.

Given the deliberate ensconcement of detailed monetary analysis in the GT, it is not surprising that, thirty years after the Great Depression, the efficacy of monetary policy in promoting economic growth has been viewed, as Professor Samuelson points out, with scepticism by a significant portion of the academic 'Keynesian' majority of the economics establishment (see 1964b, pp. 341–42). Elsewhere I have already made some attempt at providing a simple model of capital accumulation (Davidson, 1968) which blends the stock and flow elements in the demand and supply of (1) real capital, (2) money, and (3) securities (which are essential features of the analytical structure of the TM) with the more familiar principles and concepts of effective demand developed in the GT. Within such a framework it is possible to provide more perspective on the interplay among the organized security exchanges, corporate financing policy, investment bankers, and the banking system in channeling the financial funds necessary for capital accumulation. Regrettably this is an analysis which is virtually ignored in most 'analytical' post-Keynesian models. That Keynes did not wish to ignore the financial market institutions is evident from the inclusion of chapter 12 in GT. Nevertheless, he considered these aspects a 'digression' which was 'on a different level of abstraction from most of this book' (Keynes, 1936, p. 149). While the literary content of this chapter gets high marks for brilliance, and the reader is struck by many telling phrases, the analytic portion is slim. No wonder discussions of financial institutions and their impact on the economy have flowed primarily from the pens of non-Keynesian scholars.

Now that over three decades have past, it is due time that Keynesian economists were weaned from the mollycoddling liquid of liquidity preference and imbibed in the stronger distillations of the TM, including its real 'non-golden' age disequilibrium approach to dynamic change.

1 THE TWO CAMBRIDGES DEBATE

In the time remaining, I should like to suggest a few of the general elements of a theory of security markets and apply it to a controversy which has recently engaged the scholars of Cambridge, England, and Cambridge, Massachusetts. In any complete macromodel, the real capital market can be developed in terms of stock and flow relationships which show that the growth in the stock of real capital depends primarily on entrepreneurial expectations of profits from the future flow of capital services, the rate of discount, the ability of entrepreneurs to obtain finance, the rate of capital depreciation, and the supply elasticity of the capital goods producing industries (see Davidson, 1968). Because of space limitations in this paper, however, real investment will be taken as exogenously determined.

In our model, an analysis of household portfolio decision-making based on the bearishness concepts of the TM and its relationship to corporate financing policies can be introduced to indicate that at least one aspect of the two-Cambridges debate – the Samuelson–Modigliani Anti-Pasinetti Theorem versus Kaldor's Neo-Pasinetti Theorem – is really a storm in a teacup. This aspect of the altercation could have been avoided had both parties followed the TM approach which insists that the savings decision of households is not only independent of the investment decision of firms, but household savings decisions are, as a first approximation, independent of portfolio balance (or bearishness) decisions. As Keynes emphasized: 'Although these [savings and bearishness] factors react on one another . . . [they] are independent in the sense that any degree, positive or negative, of the one is compatible in appropriate attendant circumstances with any degree, positive or negative, of the other' (Keynes, 1930, vol. 1, p. 145, also see pp. 141, 147).

The particular point in the two-Cambridges controversy which I will discuss involves the fact that Pasinetti developed a growth model which demonstrates 'the irrelevance of workers' propensity to save . . . (while uncovering) the absolutely strategic importance for the whole system of the decisions to save of just one group of individuals: the capitalists' (Pasinetti, 1962, p. 274). Samuelson and Modigliani demonstrate, however, that if the savings propensity of worker households ($s\hat{w}$) is high enough, the workers end up doing all the accumulation, as the capitalists' households share of total wealth approaches zero (Samuelson and Modigliani, 1966, pp. 275–7). Accordingly, the Samuelson and Modigliani proof, which they call the 'Duality Theorem' but which Kaldor labels the 'Anti-Pasinetti Theorem', appears to severely restrict the generality of the Cambridge, England, growth analysis. Consequently, Kaldor found it necessary to offer in rebuttal, a 'Neo-Pasinetti Theorem', which presents some seminal ideas about the demand for securities in the context of economic growth.[6]

Essentially, Kaldor attempts to associate the net acquisition of financial assets by the personal (household) sector with net personal savings and the availability of finance for business investment. In Kaldor's words:

net savings out of income sets up a demand for securities, [and] net dis-savings out of income (= net consumption out of capital or capital gains) sets up a supply of securities. There is also a net supply of new securities issued by the corporate sector. Since, in the securities market, prices will tend to a level at which the total (non-speculative) supply and

demand for securities are equal, there must be some mechanism to
ensure that the [consumption] spending out of capital (or capital gains)
just balances the savings out of income *less* any new securities issued by
corporations.[7] (Kaldor, 1966, p. 316).

Since Kaldor is discussing long-run golden age equilibrium, the balancing mechanism to which he alludes cannot be the level of output (Y)
which by hypothesis is growing at the full employment rate over time.
Instead, given the savings propensities, Kaldor suggests that – for any
given volume of new issues by corporations – it is the level of security
prices which equilibrates not only the demand and supply of securities but
also the sum of net personal savings of households plus corporate retained
profits with net investment in the system (ibid., p. 318).

The essence of Kaldor's position is given in the statement that 'the net
savings of the personal sector (available for investment by the business
sector) will depend, not only on the savings propensities of individuals, but
on the policies of the corporations towards new issues. In the absence of
new issues the level of security prices will be established at the point at
which the purchases of securities by the savers will be just balanced by the
sale of securities by the dis-savers, making the net savings of the personal
sector zero' (ibid.).

If accepted at face value, Kaldor's statement is truly a surprising *volte-
face* Keynesian theory, especially since it is a Keynesian of Kaldor's stature
who appears to be implying that given the distribution of income, given the
level of net investment (I), and given the corporate new issue policy, the
level of security prices (i.e. the rate of interest) will cause aggregate
personal consumption to just fill the gap between the full employment level
of output and investment spending. After all these years of verbal duels,
acrimony, and clarification, Kaldor's analysis suggests that the rate of
interest is the mechanism which ensures that effective demand is always
maintained at the full employment level.[8] Kaldor, in his attempt to defend
Pasinetti's neo-Keynesian analysis from the American neoclassical assault,
has unwittingly reinstated the *deus ex machina* of the neoclassical system –
the rate of interest – as the balancing mechanism, not only for maintaining
equilibrium in the securities market, but also for ensuring a level of
effective demand always ample to secure full employment.[9]

Fortunately for Keynesian economics, Kaldor's own analysis does not
require this neoclassical mechanism once it is recalled that Keynes recognized – insisted really – that the household savings decision is distinct from
the household portfolio balance or bearishness decision (Keynes, 1930,
vol. 1, p. 141). In fact if the terms portfolio, portfolio balance, and change
in portfolios, respectively, are substituted for the words net savings,
savings, and net savings when they appear in that order in the preceding

quotation from Kaldor, then Kaldor's revised statement is simply a perceptive elaboration on Keynes, with some incisive implications on how traditional Keynesian mechanisms will restore equilibrium, with or without full employment as a precondition.

2   THE BASIC RELATIONSHIPS

The public's demand for securities (or placements) can be conceptualized as a stock demand for a store of value (ibid., vol. 1, pp. 141–3, 248–51) and this can be written as

$$D_p = f_1(p,\lambda,\beta,\gamma,e,V) \tag{4.1}$$

where D_p is the market demand for placements at any point in time, p denotes the market price of securities, λ is a set of expectations about the rate of change of future security prices, β and γ represent the public's aversion to income and capital risk, respectively, while e represents the number of wealth owners and the distribution of wealth among them, and V stands for the magnitude of the public's total store of value at any point of time. V is defined as the total of money balances held by savers as a store of value[10] (M_2) plus the total market value of placements held by the public at any point of time. This stock demand for placements, D_p, includes the Wicksteedian reservation demand for securities by the 'bulls'. Given λ, β, γ, e, and V, a demand curve for placements can be drawn as downward sloping $D_1 D_1'$ in Figure 4.2, i.e. $f_{1p}' < 0$, since as the price declines, the expected capital gain from purchasing a security increases, while the (income) opportunity cost of holding money balances as a store of value increases. Hence the public will want to substitute placements for money holdings as the price of securities declines. Furthermore, every act of actual personal savings implies an increment in V and consequently an outward shift of the $D_1 D_1'$ curve (i.e. $f_{1v}' > 0$) in Figure 4.2. In line with his argument of a quarter century ago, Kaldor refers to this relationship between the demand for placements and changes in V as the nonspeculative demand for securities (see Kaldor, 1960, pp. 42, 48). In the terminology of the TM, on the other hand, this shift in the demand curve for securities would be an increase in bullishness.

At any point in time, a given stock of outstanding securities exists as inherited from the past. Accordingly, the stock supply schedule of placements facing the public (S_p) is perfectly inelastic (in Figure 4.2 and 4.3), that is

$$S_p = \alpha \tag{4.2}$$

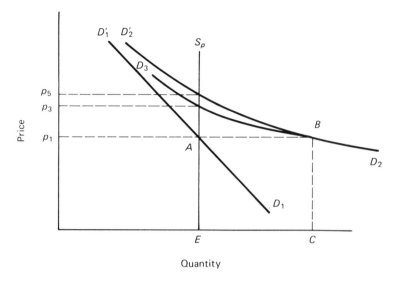

Figure 4.2

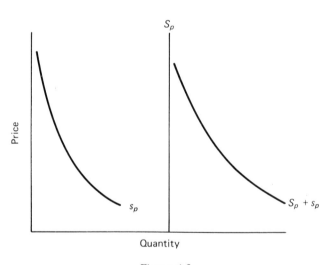

Figure 4.3

where α is a predetermined constant. If there are no new securities issued by corporations, then an equilibrium price of p_1 will be established.

The unit of measurement of the quantity of placements runs in terms of the income per period to which ownership of a placement constitutes an absolutely certain claim (cf. Turvey, 1960, p. 21). The use of a 'certainty-income-claim' unit of measure signifies that, for our immediate purposes, we may ignore the varieties in market types of placements. Accordingly, 'the rate of interest' is inversely related to the price of securities.[11]

Increases in the quantity of placements supplied will functionally depend on the entrepreneurial demand for investment goods and their demand for external finance to underwrite the investment. The flow supply schedule of placements can be specified

$$s_p = (igK)/p \tag{4.3}$$

where s_p designates the flow-supply of placements, and where, following Kaldor's symbols, i reveals the fraction of the firms' current investment (denoted by gK, where K = capital, g = growth rate) which corporations decide to externally finance via the issue of new securities to the public (cf. Kaldor, 1966, p. 317). Given i, g, and K, the flow supply schedule (s_p) with respect to the placement price, p, in any time period constitutes a rectangular hyperbola (see Figure 4.3).[12] The market supply schedule of placements in any period is obtained by summating equations (4.2) and (4.3); thus

$$S_p + s_p = \alpha + (igK)/p \tag{4.4}$$

The market supply curve, $S_p + s_p$, is the lateral summation of the stock-and-flow-supply curves in Figure 4.3

3   KALDOR'S NEO-PASINETTI THEME

Returning to Kaldor's argument, maintenance of equilibrium in the securities market requires that any increase in the demand for placements must equal the quantity of new issues supplied by corporations, plus the liquidation of securities by shareholders wanting to obtain active money balances to finance consumption out of capital gains. Thus Kaldor writes the equilibrium condition as

$$s_w W = cG + igK \tag{4.5}$$

where s_w is the wage earners' marginal propensity to save, W is the wage bill, and c is the fraction of capital gains (G) which stockholders wish to consume (ibid.).

At this stage, Kaldor is effectively assuming no savings out of profit distributions (ibid., p. 316) so that all capitalist savings is done by the firm. Most importantly, Kaldor states that

as far as my own ideas are concerned, I have always regarded the high savings propensity out of profits as something which attaches to the nature of business income, and not the wealth (or other peculiarities) of the individuals who own property [sic]. It is the enterprise, not the particular body of individuals owning it at any one time, which finds it necessary in a dynamic world of increasing returns, to plough back a proportion of the profits as a kind of prior charge on earnings . . . This is because (i) continued expansion cannot be ensured . . . unless *some proportion* of the finance required for expansion comes from internal sources . . . Hence the high savings propensity attaches to profits as such, not to capitalists as such. (ibid., p. 310).

No wonder Kaldor and Pasinetti believe in the 'absolute strategic' importance of the capitalists' propensity to save in the process of growth. This so-called 'capitalists' propensity to save' is primarily a measure of corporate investment policy and the availability of finance rather than the savings behaviour of particular households. Even the Cambridge, Massachusetts, neoclassicists cannot deny the 'strategic' importance of actual investment expenditures on economic growth. Kaldor and Pasinetti are merely reminding us of the essentiality of finance in carrying out investment plans (cf. Davidson, 1965; 1967).

Despite this evidence which suggests that the two-Cambridges controversy may simply be a result of a semantic confusion involving savings and investment propensities and the finance motive, let us continue to examine the Neo-Pasinetti Theorem for its implications on the demand and supply of securities in the context of economic growth by utilizing the stock demand and stock-flow supply schedules developed above. Considerations of these in some detail will clarify the Neo-Pasinetti Theorem and free Kaldor from the necessity of restoring the rate of interest to its neoclassical role.

The equilibrium condition expressed in equation (4.5) tacitly posits that all savings out of wages will be utilized to increase the demand for placements in personal portfolios; and further, that there will be no increase in the demand for speculative money holdings as a store of wealth. Substantially the argument entails that there is a marginal propensity to purchase placements (k) out of personal savings which is assumed to equal unity.[13] If k does equal one, the marginal propensity to hold speculative balances as wealth increases is zero.[14] (cf. Brechling, 1957, pp. 195–6; Davidson, 1968).

3.1 When No New Securities Are Issued

Given the level of investment, and the distribution of income between wages and profits, and the household savings propensities assumed by Kaldor in his Neo-Pasinetti Theorem, then if $k = 1$, the demand curve for placements will shift from point A to point B at the initial price of p_1 in Figure 4.2. This shift from A to B is indicative of an increase in demand which is just sufficient to absorb (at a price of p_1 per unit) a value of additional placements equal to the personal savings out of wages; that is in Figure 4.2, $ABCE$ must equal $s_w W$, if $k = 1$.

Since k is assumed equal to unity, the area of the rectangle obtained by taking the horizontal difference between the initial $D_1 D_1'$ and the new $D_2 D_2'$ curve and multiplying it by the ordinate height of the price level, for any price, will always equal total savings out of wages.[15] Thus, the $D_2 D_2'$ curve will have a hyperbolic relationship with respect to $D_1 D_1'$; if consumption out of capital gains is precluded (that is, if $c = 0$ in equation (4.5)). If no new securities are issued, then the price of placements would rise until p_5 in Figure 4.2. This higher price level would induce the public to hold the same quantity of securities in their portfolio as initially even though the state of bullishness had risen (i.e. the demand for placements has increased) because of savings out of wages (or in Kaldor's terminology because of an increase in non-speculative demand).

Actually, Kaldor has assumed that $c \neq 0$ and consequently, that shareholders may be eager to liquidate some of their securities to finance consumption out of capital gains equal to cG. A value of $c > 0$ presumes a sort of 'real-placement-balance' effect analogous to the Pigou–Patinkin 'real balance' effect. This implies that at any price above the initial p_1 price, the 'reservation' demand for securities is contracted somewhat which, in turn means that there is a marginal propensity to demand placements (j), whenever there is a change in the price of placements, which is negative[16] (i.e. $j < 0$). If $j < 0$, then the portion of the $D_2 D_2'$ curve above p_1 does not wholly convey the magnitude of the aggregate demand for placements since the reduction in reservation demand will mean that the quantity demanded at any price will fall short of that shown on the $D_2 D_2'$ curve (for the latter is drawn on the hypothesis that $j = 0$).

The point is that curve $D_2 B D_3$ depicts the stock demand for placements at any point of time when there is some positive consumption out of capital gains. Hence when $k = 1$, and $j < 0$, the increase in placement prices will only mount to p_3 as the net increase in bullishness of the public is somewhat repressed compared to when $k = 1$ and $j = 0$.

If we posit a less than full employment initial equilibrium state, then this additional consumption (out of capital gains) will lead, of course, to an uplift in economic activity and a multiple increase in output (as embodied in the traditional multiplier analysis). A new equilibrium output level will be established where the sum total of personal savings out of wages will be enlarged as employment and the wage bill expands, while capitalists spend in excess of their dividend income (as assumed by Kaldor) and thereby reduce savings out of profits. Money income, real output, and employment will be augmented.

If, on the other hand, we start with the neo-Keynesian assumption of an initial given full employment equilibrium, then the increase in security prices when $j < 0$ induces an increase in aggregate consumption and consequently an increase in aggregate demand. The upshot is the familiar concept of an 'inflationary gap' (or an 'inflationary barrier' in Mrs Robinson's terminology (1963, p. 13)). This involves an initial disequilibrium between investment and savings (an essential element in the fundamental equations of TM) and with a free market, the Pasinetti model would require the market price to increase to the higher demand price which would yield increased profit margins, a result which is identical to the formation of (windfall) profits in the TM.[17] Under the inflationary gap approach of the post-1936 Keynesian Revolution, the adjusting mechanism in a free market requires that money wages and therefore supply prices rise, forcing fixed income groups (particularly bond-holding savers) to cut their real consumption demand because of a reduction in real income. The consequent 'forced savings' of rentiers will restore equilibrium in the commodity market by squeezing net capitalist personal savings to a level equal to net investment minus the sum of savings out of wages plus retained profits. (In the Pasinetti model, of course, the forced savings of rentiers will be augmented by the forced savings of workers as the real wage declines with an increase in demand price.)

Thus, the level of output will be the instrument (at less than full employment) for equating net personal and corporate savings with net investment, while the wage–price mechanism and the existence of fixed money income contracts will ensure the equilibrium of net savings and investment at full employment (cf. Davidson and Smolensky, 1964a, ch. 11; 1964b; Weintraub, 1958, ch. 6).

On this argument it becomes apparent that even in a Kaldor–Pasinetti world, the price of placements (i.e. rate of interest) will not affect the total of personal savings directly (except for Kaldor's assumed real-placement-balance effect); rather it will have its impact directly on the portfolio balance decision. With $k = 1$, $j = 0$ and no new issues forthcoming then there will be no actual change in the portfolio holdings of the public; as the price of securities rises to p_5 households will be induced to hold the same quantity of securities when their bullishness has increased. Alternatively with $j < 0$, when $k = 1$, then the price of securities need rise only to p_3 to reflect the lesser intensity in bullishness on the part of the public as they continue to hold the same quantity of securities.

Of course, it might be argued that instead of assuming an initial equilibrium level of employment, the comparable case for the Neo-Pasinetti Theorem should begin by positing that corporate savings plus wage-earner household savings exceed, at the initial employment level, the exogenously determined level of investment. In this latter case, especially if $c = 0$, the demand price for goods will be less than the supply price. This will result in windfall losses (i.e. less than normal profits) in the TM or lower profit margins in the Kaldor–Pasinetti model (or involuntary inventory accumulations in the GT), which should induce profit maximizing entrepreneurs to contract output, thereby lowering the total wage bill until savings and investment are equal. Of course, if, following Kaldor, we assume $c > 0$, then the magnitude of the contraction necessary to bring about equilibrium in the goods market would be somewhat less.

Without protracting this analysis further by handling other possible cases, we can state that it does not really matter whether equilibrium in the goods market is initially assumed or not, for it is the level of output and/or the wage-price mechanism and the existence of fixed money contracts which are the primary mechanisms for bringing aggregate supply and demand (i.e. savings and investment) into equilibrium in modern market-oriented economies.

3.2 External Finance Via New Public Issues

The analysis for the situation when corporations issue new securities to the public can be readily obtained by combining, in Figure 4.4, the combined stock-flow supply analysis in Figure 4.3 with the demand analysis of Figure 4.2. For simplicity assume a given level of savings out of wages. If $k = 1$, then, as we have already demonstrated, the demand curve shifts from $D_1 D_1'$ to $D_2 D_2'$ if $j = 0$ (or to $D_2 B D_3$ if $j < 0$ at prices above p_1) in Figure 4.4. If the amount of external finance required equals total savings out of wages, that is if $iI = s_w W$, then the increase in the demand for placements at the initial price of p_1 (diagrammatically, a shift from A to B in Figure 4.4) will be just sufficient to absorb all the newly issued securities. Accordingly, the market supply schedule of securities, $S_p + s_{p1}$, will be a rectangular hyperbola which passes through point B and the increase in the quantity of securities supplied at p_1 will just counter-balance and neutralize the increase in bullishness as households add to the quantity of securities they possess in their portfolios.

If external finance requirements are less than savings out of wages, i.e. if $iI < s_w W$, and if $k = 1$, then the rectangular hyperbola market supply curve, $S_p + s_{p2}$, will locate to the left of point B. Accordingly, if $j < 0$, then the equilibrium price will rise to p_2 (or p_4 if $j = 0$) as the augmentation in household bullishness is not blocked by a large enough increase in the offering of new issues to maintain the initial price of p_1. The market price rises only enough to entice the more bullish (wage-earning) households to increase the portfolio holdings of securities by an amount equal to the quantity of new issues. Of course, with increased consumption out of capital gains, aggregate demand rises as before and therefore either

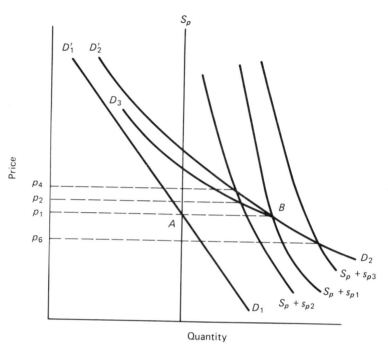

Figure 4.4

changes in economic activity (at less than full employment) or alternatively wage–price inflation will carry total net personal savings into harmony with net investment less corporate retained profits.

If the amount of external finance demanded by firms exceeded savings out of wages, i.e. $iI > s_w W$, then the market supply schedule of placements, $S_p + s_{p3}$, would be a rectangular hyperbola lying to the right of point B. This means that firms attempt to float new issues in excess of the increase in bullishness at the initial p_1 price level. Accordingly, if $j = 0$ below p_1 then the placement price level declines to p_6 in order to stimulate households to add to their holdings of securities. In this last situation, one might not expect any change in aggregate consumption since $j = 0$ (by assumption). The lower price of placements, however, signifies a higher rate of interest which in turn could lower the attractiveness of investment by reducing present value estimates, which ultimately could result in a cutback in output until the savings–investment equilibrium is achieved at a lower employment level with lower investment and less savings out of wages. If $iI > s_w W$, therefore, full employment may not be able to be maintained as business firms find they can obtain the desired external finance only at higher interest costs. Of course, all this abstracts from monetary policy specifically designed to curtail interest rates to lower levels when employment declines (and an assumed exogenous I).

4 SUMMARY

The analysis has shown that given the savings propensities of the various income classes and given $k \leq 1$, then the price of placements will alter until the household sector absorbs into its portfolio all the securities offered to it. The change in placement prices (and therefore in the rate of interest) does not in itself affect the total of personal savings or the distribution of savings between workers and capitalists. Given different degrees of bearishness between workers and capitalist households, the price of placements will alter the distribution of securities between them. It is only Kaldor's assumption of a real balance effect for placements when their price increases (that is, a posited negative j) which modifies the savings behaviour of capitalists' households.

Nevertheless, it is either changes in output (at less than full employment) or inflationary changes in wages and prices at full employment which constitutes the prime channels for working the appropriate changes in the level of personal savings to bring it into equilibrium with the exogenously determined level of investment. The flexibility of the market price of placements merely permits each household unit to hold as many placements as it desires, and to shift its portfolio holdings around as often as desired, while in the aggregate, the personal sector holds exactly the quantity of securities which is allocated to it. The rate of growth, on the other hand, is determined in a modern economy by the investment decisions (of business firms) which can be actually financed and carried out within the monetary and resource constraints of society.

Notes

1. Keynes attempted to justify the change in emphasis from windfall profits to unintended inventory changes as being more realistic (Keynes, 1936, p. 51, n. 1).
2. Modern neo-Keynesians, despite similarities in their growth models, are deriving their analysis from different Keynesian sources. Kaldor (1954) and Pasinetti (1962) are utilizing Marshallian D_p and S_p conditions with market transactions occurring D_p (at full employment). Since Kaldor essentially utilizes demand prices as the market-clearing mechanism in his growth model, he can say 'I am not sure where "marginal productivity" comes into all this' (Kaldor, 1954, p. 100). Productivity is relevant for the supply price and not the demand price. Joan Robinson, on the other hand, is emphasizing the supply price aspect of Walrasian conditions in her analysis of the rate of profit in economic growth (1963, pp. 10ff). Thus, despite many similarities in the Kaldor–Pasinetti and Robinsonian Cambridge varients of growth models, there remain important differences. For example, the Robinson analysis is much more involved with the relationship of technology, the money wage, and profit margins (the degree of monopoly) to 'normal' (i.e. supply) price (e.g. ibid., pp. 7, 10, 17, 29, 36–37,

41, 45, 47, 70–74, 77–78, 120–21). These items are virtually ignored in Kaldor--Pasinetti type growth models.

3. This evaluation of the relationship between the TM and GT finds support in Klein's remark that the liquidity preference theory was not an essential element of the GT: 'It merely rounds out the theory and makes it complete . . . Keynes . . . remarked that, as it actually happened, he first conceived of the savings–investment equation [i.e. the excess demand equation] as the determinant of the level of output. This left him without a theory of interest; so he then developed the liquidity preference theory' (Klein, 1966, p. 43).

4. Cf. Harrod's comments on Keynes's 'remarkable' consistency in the development of his theories (1951, pp. 467ff).

5. This is especially true when comparing the money market analysis of the two books. The stock approach to money of the GT makes the securities market appear to be in continuous static equilibrium. Observed security prices, on the other hand, are normally disequilibrium ones. The reader might engage in an interesting exercise if he tried to unravel the meaning of the four possible bull and bear markets which Keynes analyses on pp. 252–4 of Volume I of the TM. (Hint: Disequilibrium is the essence in understanding the analysis of these bull and bear markets.) Moreover, if it was recognized by 'Keynesians' that the money market may not always clear (as *The General Theory* leads one to believe), i.e. that there is a 'fringe of unsatisfied borrowers' (Keynes, 1930, vol. 11, p. 365), then some of the controversy over whether the monetary authority should control solely the rate of interest (which does not necessarily clear the market) or whether they should control primarily the money supply itself could be clarified. If the object is to affect aggregate demand, and if the interest rate does not clear the market, the money supply is the more strategic policy variable for the monetary authorities.

6. As note 3 suggests, Kaldor is deriving his analysis primarily from concepts of the TM. Consequently, it should not be surprising that Kaldor ultimately attempts to analyse the demand and supply of securities – an analysis which is specifically developed in the TM, but which is only implicit in the GT emphasis in the demand and supply of money. For some unexplained reason Samuelson and Modigliani (1966) ignore Kaldor's analysis in their reply. It should be apparent that Kaldor–Pasinetti are presenting a model based solely on the demand price approach of the TM (at full employment, while Samuelson–Modigliani are offering a neoclassical productivity model based solely on supply price at full employment. Since productivity is not a determinant of demand price, once one recognizes Kaldor's demand price orientation, it is easy to understand why he exclaims, 'I am not sure where "marginal productivity" comes in on all this' (1954, p. 100). Samuelson–Modigliani, on the other hand, make productivity the essence of their system by emphasizing supply price.

7. This must be regarded as an extension of views expressed over 28 years ago in Kaldor's analysis of 'Speculation and Economic Stability'. In that article, Kaldor argued that the price of bonds and shares are 'largely determined' by speculative influences (1960, pp. 42–4).

8. Samuelson has, in a more jocular moment, referred to Jean Baptiste Kaldor (1964b, p. 345). While I think this is scarcely appropriate, in the light of Kaldor's constant emphasis on full employment policy, there would be some point to the indictment if Kaldor really believed that the rate of interest induces consumption to fill the deflationary gap.

9. This unintended result – if Kaldor's argument were valid – would do much to

justify a witticism uttered some years ago by D. H. Robertson when he wrote: 'Now as I have often pointed out to my students, some of whom have been brought up in sporting circles, high-brow opinion is like a hunted hare; if you stand in the same place, or nearly the same place, it can be relied upon to come round to you in a circle' (1956, p. 81).

10. In the TM, Keynes associates money held as a store of value with saving deposits. Even in the GT, money-time deposits are included by Keynes in his definition of money (1936, p. 167, n. 1), a definition which places Keynes much closer in spirit to Professor Friedman than to most 'Keynesian' monetary theorists.

11. Of course, an increase in the probability of receiving an income claim would have the same effect as increases in 'short sales' in the securities market. It may be viewed as an increase in effective supply. We shall ignore these problems in the following analysis since their introduction would make the analysis more complicated without altering the major conclusions.

12. Kaldor would associate the non-speculative supply of securities (1966, p. 317) with our flow-supply schedule (see 1960, p. 42).

13. This is the same assumption Kaldor employed 28 years ago (1966, p. 45, no. 1).

14. Although Kaldor's analysis makes no specific mention of the money supply, it is implicit that the money supply increases by an amount equal to $s_w W$. Initially therefore workers' savings accrue to them entirely as idle balances. Since Kaldor assumes the marginal propensity to hold speculative balances is zero, the demand for placements curve shifts outwards as described below. It should be noted that Keynes believed that $0 < k < 1$, since 'the inactive demand for liquidity partly depends on the aggregate of wealth' (Keynes, 1937b, p. 668).

15. More generally, the area of the appropriate rectangle will always be equal to k times savings out of wages, no matter what the value of k.

16. At prices below p_1, on the other hand, the oft-mentioned 'locked-in' due to a security price fall implies that $j \approx 0$. Kaldor's association of changes in consumption of capitalists with capital gains rather than capital losses tends to suggest he tacitly believes that $j = 0$ for prices below the initial price level.

17. In fact, Pasinetti's stability analysis involves a differential equation (1962, p. 275) which analyses the same factor (i.e. I–S) which leads to dynamic changes in the fundamental equations of the TM (Keynes, 1930, vol. 1, pp. 135–7).

References

Brechling, F. P. R. (1957), 'A Note on Bond-holding and the Liquidity Preference Theory of Interest', *Revue of Economic Studies*, pp. 190–7.

Davidson, P. (1965), 'Keynes's Finance Motive', *Oxford Economic Papers* (March), pp. 47–65.

Davidson, P. (1967), 'The Importance of the Demand for Finance', *Oxford Economic Papers* (July), pp. 245–53.

Davidson, P. (1968), 'Money, Portfolio Balance, Capital Accumulation, and Economic Growth', *Econometrica*, (April).

Davidson, P. and E. Smolensky (1964a), *Aggregate Supply and Demand Analysis* (New York).

Davidson, P. and E. Smolensky (1964b), 'Modigliani on the Interaction of Real and Monetary Phenomena', *Revue of Economics and Statistics* (November), pp. 429–31.

Harrod, R. F. (1951), *The Life of John Maynard Keynes* (London).

Harrod, R. F. (1963), 'Themes in Dynamic Theory', *Economic Journal* (September), pp. 401–21.

Kaldor, N. (1954), 'Alternative Theories of Distribution', *Revue of Economic Studies*, pp. 83–100.

Kaldor, N. (1960), 'Speculation and Economic Stability', *Revue of Economic Studies*, 1939, reprinted in *Essays on Economic Stability and Growth* (1960). All references are to the reprinted essay.

Kaldor, N. (1966), 'Marginal Productivity and the Macroeconomic Theories of Distribution', *Revue of Economic Studies*, pp. 309–19.

Keynes, J. M. (1930), *A Treatise on Money* (London, 1930).

Keynes, J. M. (1936), *The General Theory of Employment, Interest and Money* (New York, 1936).

Keynes, J. M. (1937a), 'Alternative Theories of the Rate of Interest', *Economic Journal* (June), pp. 241–52.

Keynes, J. M. (1937b), 'The Ex-ante Theory of the Rate of Interest', *Economic Journal* (December), pp. 663–9.

Klein, L. R. (1966), *The Keynesian Revolution*, 2nd edn (New York).

Ohlin, B. (1937), 'Some Notes on the Stockholm Theory of Savings and Investment II', *Economic Journal* (June), pp. 221–40.

Pasinetti, L. L. (1962), 'Rate of Profit and Income Distribution in Relation to the Rate of Economic Growth', *Revue of Economic Studies* 1962, pp. 267–79.

Robertson, D. H. (1938), 'Mr Keynes and "Finance"', *Economic Journal* (June), pp. 314–18.

Robertson, D. H. (1956), *Economic Commentaries* (London).

Robinson, J. (1951), *Collected Economic Papers*, Vol. I (New York).

Robinson, J. (1963), *Essays in the Theory of Economic Growth* (London).

Samuelson, P. A. (1964a), *Economics*, 6th edn (New York).

Samuelson, P. A. (1964b), 'A Brief Survey of Post Keynesian Developments', in *Keynes's General Theory Reports of Three Decades*, ed. by R. Lekachman (New York).

Samuelson, P. A. and F. Modigliani (1966), 'The Pasinetti Paradox in Neoclassical and More General Models', *Revue of Economic Studies* (October), pp. 269–302 and 'Reply to Pasinetti and Robinson', pp. 321–30.

Turvey, R. (1960), *Interest Rates and Asset Prices* (London).

Weintraub, S. (1958), *An Approach to the Theory of Income Distribution* (Philadelphia).

5 The Role of Monetary Policy in Overall Economic Policy*

1 INTRODUCTION

Any objective inquiry into improving the economic effects of the monetary policy of a central bank should begin with (1) a statement of objectives of such policy and (2) a discussion of means that can achieve these goals.

The four most often mentioned practical goals of monetary policy are:

(1) To prevent inflation;
(2) To encourage full employment;
(3) To encourage sustained rapid economic growth;
(4) To counteract balance-of-payments deficits.

In framing these objectives I have deliberately worded objectives no. 1 and no. 4 in negative or obstructive formats, while no. 2 and no. 3 utilize more positive wording. My rationale for this is to emphasize that active pursuit of objectives no. 1 and/or no. 4 by traditional monetary methods will normally obstruct the achievements of objectives no. 2 and no. 3. Accordingly, it is my view that monetary policy should be oriented solely towards achieving full employment and economic growth. This does not mean, of course, that monetary policy should operate in a vacuum. Nor does it mean that money and monetary policy cannot have some impact on the general price level or the balance of payments.

What I wish to recommend is the coordination of monetary and fiscal policy with an incomes and foreign trade price policy so that the four objectives listed above can be approached simultaneously. Mere coordination of monetary and fiscal policy, while a step in the right direction, will not be the administrative panacea for reaching these objectives under present institutions – even if accurate forecasts of future events could be achieved.

Although discretionary control over the money supply is essential if we are to obtain full employment and sustained economic growth, any attempt to utilize changes in the money supply as the primary tool to restrict

* Statement to the Subcommittee on Domestic Finance: Committee on Banking and Currency – House of Representatives, US Congress, December 1968.

general price increases or to cure balance-of-payments deficits will, under our present market-oriented system, insure unemployment while severely hampering growth.

2 FULL EMPLOYMENT AND ECONOMIC GROWTH

Full employment and economic growth with their promise of unprecedented prosperity, could presently provide a higher standard of living for all Americans. Full employment and growth could mean the rapid elimination of poverty in the United States. Full employment and growth could bring about increased social stability as group antagonisms diminish with rising income levels. Full employment and growth could improve our position in the cold war not only by strengthening our defences, while simultaneously increasing our aid to the uncommitted countries, but it would also demonstrate to the world the vitality of a market economy in providing for the economic and social advancement of its citizens and its friends. With all these obvious advantages that accrue to a fully employed economy, surely full employment and economic growth must be the primary economic goals of our society.

Yet, except for the military escalation in Vietnam, operating in tandem with the 1964 tax cut, American economic policy-makers, Republicans and Democrats, cabinet members and central bankers alike have, for more than a decade, pursued a course designed to prevent the achievement of full employment. The policy-makers, of course, are not malevolent but they have been trapped in a conflict of goals which dilutes our fervour for maximum output.

Several years ago, Secretary of Labour Willard Wirtz posed the problem very graphically when he said: 'You sometimes get the feeling, sitting where I do that there is a shell game going on in the discussion of this particular [unemployment] problem, and that the shells are marked "inflation", "unbalanced budget", and "unfavourable trade balance". . . every suggestion which is made to advance the purpose of full employment is met by one or another of these arguments, and very often by all three.'

Why do we participate in such a game, the outcome of which cheats us out of full employment and rapid growth? The game goes on and on because the winners (and the game is rigged so that we know who the winners will be) outvote the losers at the polls. But majority rule ought not to be tyranny. Majority rule is neither right nor proper here because we have failed to guarantee an inalienable right to the minority – the right to a job and a respectable level of income. Up to now we have failed to create an economic environment in which democratic rule yields the optimum result within a monetary, *market*-oriented economy. Such an economic environment can be created, however, with an appropriate battery of monetary, fiscal, and income policies. Until such coordinated policies are developed, this shell game will continue and as the late President Kennedy lamented, we will continue to content 'ourselves with pious statements about the wastes of our human resources'.

Ever since the 1930s, economists have realized that recessions can be avoided and full employment can be achieved by fiscal policies such as tax cuts or increased governmental spending and/or expansion in the money supply. Moreover, if the economy begins from a position of less than full employment, policies that stimulate increased economic activity simultaneously reduce unemployment, and stimulate investment and growth; for one of the most important messages of the 'Keynesian' Revolution in economics was the complementarity of consumption and investment in recession. Thus we learned that it is possible to have more butter, more plant and equipment, and more guns, too, if only we had the courage to pursue certain fiscal and monetary policies.

Although there continues to be a debate among economists as to whether, as the Chicago school succinctly asserts, 'money matters', that is, a questioning of the relative efficacy of expansionary fiscal compared to monetary policies, most economists now agree that expansion of *market* aggregate demand is a requirement for continuous full employment and economic growth in peacetime. What has been often overlooked in this professional controversy over whether 'money matters', is that an increase in market demand means not merely an increase in wants but also an increase in the ability to pay for goods and services. An increase in the ability to pay, in a modern market-oriented, monetary economy, must involve an increase in the supply of money *before* the increased demand can be made operational in the market-place. This fundamental notion that an easy-money policy is a *pre*-requisite to expansion and growth is, as I have tried to demonstrate in a number of articles (Davidson, 1965; 1967; 1968), an essential concept necessary to the understanding of the mechanism underlying the traditional Keynesian policy prescriptions for economic expansion.

As John Maynard Keynes wrote more than 30 years ago:

The banks hold the key in the transition from a lower to higher scale of activity . . . The investment market can become congested through a shortage of cash. It can never become congested through a shortage of savings. This is the most fundamental of my conclusions in this field. (Keynes, 1937b, pp. 668–9)

Or again:

A heavy demand for investment can exhaust the market and be held up by the lack of financial facilities on reasonable terms. It is, to an important extent, the 'financial' facilities which regulate the *pace* of new investments . . . too great a press of uncompleted investment decisions is quite capable of exhausting the available finance, if the banking system is unwilling to increase the supply of money . . . The control of finance is, indeed, a potent, though sometimes dangerous, method for regulating the rate of investment (though much more potent when used as a curb than as a stimulus). (Keynes, 1937a, p. 248)

Easy-money policies are a necessary but not a sufficient condition for stimulating economic growth. If the desire for new investment goods is weak because of poor profit opportunities, then easily obtainable finance will not, by itself, do the trick. If, on the other hand, the desire for investment is strong among businessmen, the banking system and the monetary authority can play an essential role in providing funds on terms which the investors deem attractive. It is at the level of financing investment projects that the money supply plays an essential role in stimulating economic growth in a monetized market economy, once the investment desire is present in the economy.

Fiscal policy, on the other hand, may develop latent investment demand either by increasing profit opportunities by augmenting consumer or government demands in the market-place or by increasing after-tax profits on existing market demands by use of subsidies, tax credits, or profit-tax cuts. Nevertheless, unless investors can obtain funds, they cannot place orders for additional investment goods no matter what level of profits are expected to be earned on the potential investments. Since in modern, money economies with a developed banking system, the money market may not 'clear'; that is, there may be an unsatisfied fringe of borrowers (particularly when business is active), aggregate demand may be deficient merely because there is a shortage of money. Accordingly, *fiscal policy may be a necessary, but it is not by itself a sufficient condition for full employment and economic growth.* In a monetary economy, it is finance (i.e. increases in the money supply) which provides the energy fuel that permits the investment tail to wag the gross national product dog.

It is obvious, therefore, that the necessary and sufficient conditions for full employment require the coordination of fiscal and monetary policy. To the extent that H.R. 11 has as one of its major objectives 'to improve the coordination of monetary, fiscal, and economic policy', it must be warmly supported.

Nevertheless, coordination of monetary and fiscal policy is not the panacea for our economic problems. In the absence of a coordinated 'incomes policy' to prevent inflation and a foreign trade policy to correct balance-of-payments deficits, a coordinated fiscal and monetary policy may be required to deal with these latter issues – a task which they are not equipped to efficiently handle.

Accordingly, before providing my conclusions on H.R. 11's detailed recommendations for coordination, I should like to discuss the inflation and balance-of-payments questions.

3 INFLATION

The 1964 tax cut was the first major measure taken by Congress for the expressed purpose of expanding aggregate market demand in order to move towards full employment. This action plus the subsequent military expenditure expansion as hostilities in Vietnam increased brought the United States close to full employment and rapid economic growth for the first time in more than a decade. But with this achievement came the usual corollary of a free market economy – rising prices.

No one is against full employment *per se*. Moreover, if one begins in a recessionary period, full employment and rapid economic growth are complementary objectives which simultaneously can be achieved by a judicious mix of proper monetary and fiscal policy. It is the increasing inflationary effects as unemployment declines which constitute a basic conflict and which induce policy-makers to adopt measures designed to restrain aggregate demand, and hence hopefully restrict price increases by creating slackness in labour and product markets.

This fear of inflation is not new; however, the fear of massive unemployment which was generated in the Great Depression, as well as the hot and cold wars which followed, overrode the objections to inflation and made possible the expansionist policies in the 1940s and early 1950s. But almost a third of a century has passed since the Great Depression and for many citizens these terrible years are as remote as the ravages of the Civil War. Continuing inflation in the 1940s and the early 1950s increased our fear of rising prices, while the continuing prosperity has dulled, for most white urban workers at least, the fear of unemployment. At the present time, inflation and not unemployment appears to be the most likely source of economic dislocation, although it is my firm belief that much of the riots of the urban ghetto community and the problems of the rural poor reflect the continuing unemployment and underemployment problems in those sectors of the economy. A truly fully employed economy would not only raise the level of real income for the entire community, but it would open up job opportunities for members of many minority groups, so that, in general, the average level of real income of these minorities would rise more rapidly than the national average.

Under present institutional arrangements, however, the rate of inflation that would accompany sustained full employment would severely damage (1) the real income of those citizens on relatively fixed money incomes, the so-called rentier groups – the retired, the disabled, unemployed, widows, orphans, mothers with abandoned children, and even some white collar workers, certain government employees such as policemen, teachers, etc., and (2) the real wealth of middle- and upper-income groups who held their wealth in the form of savings accounts, bonds, and other fixed sum obligations. Moreover, even organized labour would find inflation galling in that it would mean that collectively gained money-wage advances turned out not to be as sizeable an increase in economic welfare as they would have been with stable prices. Management, on the other hand, might find the increased truculence of labour (both organized and unorganized) under sustained full employment exceedingly difficult to deal with. The inflationary pressures would also create problems in export markets and encourage foreigners to compete domestically.

The resulting political winds, which were correctly foreseen 25 years ago by Kalecki, have produced a 'political trade cycle', where, as the level of unemployment declines and prices rise, rentier and other interests combine to pressure government to return to the orthodox policy of cutting down budget deficits and restrictive monetary policies. Thus it is not surprising that first the Federal Reserve Board, and later the administration began to advocate restrictive policies *before* full employment had been reached, much less sustained. These restrictive policies, whether coordinated or not, ultimately place the major burden of fighting inflation often on those citizens least capable of bearing it – a group which may be called the LIFO workers – the *last* hired *in* prosperity, the *first out* in recession. This group includes young people just entering the labour force, unskilled workers primarily located in ghetto areas, and even older workers nearing retirement ages (unless protected by seniority rules). Equity, it seems to me, requires that we redistribute this burden more broadly.

Of course, it is not irrational for the rentier and other groups to bring political pressure to stop inflation since they can suffer absolute (or at least relative) economic losses as prices rise. Though they may favour full employment and economic growth in the abstract they are forced by their economic self-interest to push for the only anti-inflationary policies available – restrictive monetary and/or fiscal policies. As a consequence, no matter under whom or how well monetary and fiscal policies are coordinated, we will be unable, *for political reasons*, to achieve full employment and sustained economic growth until a viable economic policy designed to sever the existing connection between rapidly rising prices and low levels of unemployment is introduced *and* coordinated with monetary and fiscal policies.

In order to understand what general type of policy is required, it is essential to define explicitly some basic economic concepts and principles. Although economists have at times demonstrated excessive taxonomic dexterity in categorizing 'causes' of inflation, we can avoid many semantic problems by taking recourse to a few simple economic concepts.

It is neither rising prices of *non-reproducible goods* such as rare paintings or sculptures, nor the prices of securities listed on the New York Stock Exchange, nor even the prices of reproducible non-consumer goods like aircraft carriers, which are the main focus of public concern in discussions of inflation. Inflation becomes a major cause of public interest *only* when it is the market prices of *reproducible goods* that bulk significantly large in consumers' budgets that are continuously increasing. Keeping this pragmatic view of the public concern about inflation in mind, the problem can be readily analysed by concentrating on what economists call the 'flow-supply price of goods', where the latter is defined as that price 'which is sufficient and just sufficient to make it worthwhile for people to set themselves to produce the aggregate amount' (Marshall, 1950, p. 373) of output. Our emphasis on supply prices should not be interpreted as supporting the myopic view that demand factors cannot affect price; nevertheless, if the supply price for any given quantity of reproducible goods does *not* alter, then no matter how far the market price may be momentarily displaced from that supply price, the price of future output will subsequently return.[1]

Supply prices can increase for three main reasons: (1) diminishing returns, (2) increasing profit margins, and (3) increasing money wages (relative to productivity increments).[2]

For more than a century, economists have taught that every expansion of output and employment will normally involve increasing costs and increasing supply prices because of the law of diminishing returns. Diminishing returns, it is held, is inevitable – even if all labour and capital inputs in the production process were equally efficient – because of the scarcity of some input such as raw materials or managerial talent. Actually, however, economic expansion will lead to increasing costs (and prices) not only because of the classical law of diminishing returns but also because labour and capital inputs are really not equally efficient. Expansion of output in our economy often involves the hiring of less-skilled workers, and the utilization of older, less efficient standby equipment and therefore adds to diminishing returns. Thus, as long as unemployment is declining, diminishing returns inflation will be an inevitable and unavoidable consequence of further expansion.

The severity of diminishing returns inflation will vary with the level of unemployment. When the rate of unemployment is high (say about 5 per cent), idle capacity will exist in most firms, so that diminishing returns are likely to be relatively unimportant. As full employment is approached, however, an increasing number of firms will experience increasing costs, and diminishing returns inflation will become more important. Although in the short run diminishing returns inflation is an inevitable consequence of every expansion in employment, in the long run, improvements in technology, government-sponsored training and educational programmes, and increases in capital equipment per worker can offset this price rise.

The second type of inflation will occur when businessmen (particularly in our more concentrated industries) come to believe that the market demand for their product has changed sufficiently so that it is possible for them to increase the mark-up of prices relative to costs. If managers in many industries increase their profit margins, we will experience a profits inflation as the supply or offer prices rise.

Third, every increase in money-wage rates which is not offset by productivity increases will increase costs, and if profit margins are maintained, increase supply prices. Consequently, we can expect that increases in money-wages induce price increases. This phenomenon is often referred to as wage-price inflation. Since as unemployment levels decline it is easier for workers to obtain (collectively and individually) more liberal wage increases, we may expect wage inflation to become more pronounced as employment rises; although wage inflation can occur even without expansion, if labour is able to secure increases which exceed productivity increments.

Historically, rises in the price level have been due to some combination of these three inflationary forces. Thus, changes in the price level are ultimately related to changes in money wage rates, changes in profit margins, and diminishing returns.

Every significant expansion in economic activity will induce some price increases because of diminishing returns. With rising prices, workers will, at a minimum, seek cost-of-living wage increases. Moreover, as pools of unemployment dry up, workers will be more impenitent in their total wage demands. Managers will be more willing to grant wage increases in a rising market, for they are more certain that they will be able to pass the higher labour costs on in higher prices. Also, management will find that as they hire more workers to meet the rising demands for their products, the cost of searching out and training the remaining unemployed will increase; consequently, they will often attempt to bid away workers from other employers rather than to recruit from the remaining unemployed. In addition, if management believes that the growth in demand is sufficiently strong they will increase profit margins and increase the inflationary tendency. Finally, legislators may find that the legal minimum wage becomes substandard as inflation occurs, and therefore, in a humanitarian spirit, they may raise the legal minimum. All these factors feed back on each other to create mounting wage-price pressures for as long as the economic expansion is permitted to continue.

Since the rate of diminishing returns, the rate of increase in money–wage rates, and changes in profit margins are normally closely related to decreasing unemployment levels, our present anti-inflationary policies are oriented to maintain a sufficiently high unemployment rate to control the impact of changes in these factors on price levels. Any monetary and/or fiscal policy aimed at preventing *all* price increases before full employment is reached, can be successful only if they perpetuate sufficient unemployment. All expansions in economic activity, whether they are initiated by increasing government's demands for goods and services or by an increase in demand by the private sector tend to bring about some price increases.

It should be obvious, however, that any increase in aggregate demand would induce changes in the supply price of reproducible goods, if there is no change in the money wage rate (relative to productivity) or gross profit margins, *only to the extent that diminishing returns are present*. Moreover, this diminishing returns associated price rise would be a once-and-for-all rise associated with increasing real costs of expansion due to lower productivity. Installation of new equipment and training programmes would help offset any price rise due to this aspect.

If, on the other hand, there is an increase in money wages in excess of productivity, *whether demand is unchanged or not*, the resulting supply price will be higher except if gross profit margins decreased proportionately. Similarly, increases in gross profit margins can induce price increases. Consequently, in the real world of changing levels of aggregate demand (usually at less than full employment) an *incomes policy* which controls both the money wage and profit margins will provide more stability in the purchasing power of money than a policy which permits 'free' collective bargaining and unrestricted pricing practices.

Although some economists have attacked such a policy as undesirable because it would not permit markets to allocate resources optimally, I believe that such a criticism is for all practical purposes irrelevant. First of all, these critics implicitly assume that present resource markets are efficient allocators. There is, however, evidence that indicates that existing labour markets are not very good allocators under existing free collective bargaining arrangements (Weintraub, 1963, ch. 5). More importantly, resource allocation merely requires changes in relative prices and not in the general price level. Different variants of income policy have been suggested which would permit these relative price changes while restricting a general price increase (Lerner, 1967; Weintraub, 1963, ch. 6).

Secondly, any possible loss in social welfare due to possible resource misallocation, in our economy, will be small relative to the welfare loss resulting from our continuing failure to maintain full employment and growth. As long as there are several million unemployed who are willing and able to work, I think that an economy that continuously utilizes these resources is less wasteful than a system which requires millions to be perpetually 'on the dole' (a system which ultimately must foster social antagonisms) in order to maintain reasonable price stability via monetary and fiscal policies alone.

In sum, *there is no monetary or fiscal policy which can provide sufficient conditions to insure price stability, without wrecking any chance of sustaining full employment and economic growth.* Hence there is an urgent need to develop a viable incomes policy.

An incomes policy obviously requires that the public interest be taken into account at the wage bargaining table and when management is making its pricing decisions. This policy must be considered a necessary supplement to monetary and fiscal policies which would *guarantee* continuous full employment. In return for this guarantee of full employment and optimum production levels, labour would be required to restrict its wage demands to, at most, rises in productivity, while business must hold profit margins constant.

The administrative details of implementing such a policy could take a variety of forms. The British, for example, have established restrictions on wage, salaries, and dividend increases. A National Board for Prices and Incomes was established which can require notifications of increases in prices and pay and can legally delay implementation of these increases if the board finds them unjustifiable and if voluntary compliance to holding the price–pay levels cannot be obtained. In a larger economy, such as ours, we may prefer a somewhat different arrangement than that adopted by the British. In any event, collective bargaining or pricing decisions which do not take the public interest into account should no longer be tolerated.

If, in fact, we could go even further and keep both money wages and gross margins constant, then with technological progress, price levels would decline. This would allow all consumers, including rentiers, to share in the gains of technology. This ideal variant of an income policy (which is less likely to be politically acceptable) would provide the greatest degree of fairness; for as long as some groups in society have their income fixed in money terms, then equity should require that all remuneration be somewhat fixed in money terms.

The desirability of instituting a full employment policy in coordination with an incomes policy is clear. The problem is to find a political leader who will advocate these policies which will be, at least initially, unpopular. (Many people might find themselves liking the results of such a policy, once they got over the shock of it.) Who will come forth to demand a simultaneous full employment and an incomes policy? Is there anyone in our society who will provide the political impetus that will convince most of us to pay this required tariff to sustain full employment?

Obviously no one has yet appeared on the political scene. No one will speak against the status quo and for the LIFO workers (who are usually the young, the uneducated, the migrants, and the members of minority groups, who are often disenfranchised by race, age, education, and residential requirements). Many 'liberal' groups are not ready to admit that unions ought to be restrained in the public interest, while 'conservatives' do not desire to see managerial pricing decisions limited by the public interest.

4   BALANCE-OF-PAYMENTS DEFICITS

I have held the payments problem for last for two reasons: (1) the magnitude of the payments problem for the United States is small in comparison to the previously discussed subjects; and (2) it is my personal belief that the United States should not allow foreigners to control its domestic economic policies; accordingly, methods for dealing with payments deficit should have a relatively lower priority.

The traditional monetary policy approach for eliminating a payments deficit is tight money – a policy specifically aimed at (1) staunching net short-term capital outflows, and simultaneously (2) inducing slack demand at home, thus encouraging industries with exportable products to search for new markets abroad, while domestic demand for imports declines. If such a policy is successful, although our balance-of-payments position will improve, the recessionary effects make it socially undesirable.

An increase in exports relative to imports is the obvious cure for a payments deficit. This can be accomplished without creating unemployment (or even devaluation) via an alteration in the domestic price level relative to the foreign price level. A prominent English economist, Sir Roy Harrod (1965), has recently shown that an incomes policy could not only be used to control the price level at home, but it could be used simultaneously to alter the export price level relative to import prices in order to improve the balance of payments. Hence, it would appear that an incomes policy could be designed concomitantly to prevent inflation and eliminate payments deficits, thus freeing monetary and fiscal policy to concentrate on achieving full employment and growth. Moreover, the utilization of an incomes policy, which allows export prices to alter slowly relative to import prices, would tend to eliminate the need to alter exchange rates and thus reduce the possible capital gains incentive for speculation against so-called 'key currencies'.

5   CONCLUSIONS AND RECOMMENDATIONS

Having developed my position at length, I believe I can now succinctly present my major conclusions and recommendations to the committee.

(1) A coordinated monetary, fiscal, and incomes policy should be a major objective of economic policy-makers. Since fiscal policy and incomes policy are, by their very nature, likely to reside in the executive branch of the government, it seems practical to give responsibility for coordinating monetary policy with these other policies to the administration.

To disperse power over these various policies would be almost to guarantee that economic policies would, at times, be at cross purposes. It is obvious that the brake on an automobile is a check on the accelerator, but no one seriously suggests that one passenger in the car should work the accelerator and another the brake pedal. By analogy, we cannot afford separate passengers to operate monetary, fiscal, and other economic policies independently.

Nevertheless, it is of limited value to coordinate control of the brake and accelerator pedals only, while the steering wheel of money wages and profit margins are left to be driven by an 'invisible hand'. As long as unbridled wage and price decisions are permitted, disastrous crashes can be avoided only by utilizing the brake pedal almost continuously and/or constraining the accelerator pedal to permit very slow forward movements.

(2) The major instrument of monetary policy should be the money supply and its prime target should be to provide sufficient finance to bring the unemployment rate down, say to 3 per cent or less.

As long as money markets do not automatically 'clear', the expected rate of return (adjusted for risk) on new investment projects can be significantly greater than the rate of interest. Consequently, a reduction in the rate of interest may not stimulate additional investment purchases as credit rationing limits the number of entrepreneurs who can obtain finance in order to make operational their demand for capital goods. Furthermore, when there is an unsatisfied fringe of borrowers there is no way of knowing whether those investments projects which are being financed are more productive than those projects which cannot obtain funds. Consequently, control over interest rates rather than over the supply of money may result in misallocating resources in the investment goods industries. The monetary authority must, therefore, exercise its role via primarily the money supply and not rely on interest rate changes alone to do the job.

(3) Although monetary, fiscal, and incomes policies should be coordinated, it must be recognized that the first two should be oriented primarily to achieving full employment and growth and should not be concerned with price level problems *per se*. An incomes policy, on the other hand, should have primary responsibility for controlling our domestic price level and its relationship to import prices.

(4) If rapid economic growth is to be sustained, the money supply must increase in anticipation of the output growth. In an uncertain world, where expectations are volatile and often unpredictable, the relationship between the required increase in the money supply and the increase in the economy's wealth is much too complex to be handled by any simple rule. Money clearly matters in the process of economic growth in a monetary economy, but a simple rule can be no substitute for wise management of the money supply.

Accordingly, the money managers cannot fix their gaze to any one statistical index – although they should always keep global statistics such as the unemployment rate and the rate of growth of gross national product in view. Nevertheless, disaggregative statistics on unemployment rates for particular groups and regional gross product growth must also be utilized in suggesting a desirable coordinated fiscal, monetary and incomes policy. Price indexes, for reasons I have already elaborated on, should be of secondary importance for the money managers.

(5) Although it would be possible to achieve monetary policy solely via open market operations (as long as the public owned a significant amount of government bonds), I see little reason for restricting the Fed solely to this tool. If the objectives are clearly recognized, then the Fed ought to be given as much flexibility as possible in choosing the method of achieving these objectives, since no two particular cases will be identical in all respects.

(6) Reducing the number of members of the Federal Reserve Board should not necessarily be an objective. What is desired is better educated members who understand the interrelationships of monetary, fiscal, and incomes policies, not fewer members. I do not believe it is essential that members need know the intricacies and mechanics of the banking system any more than members of the Council of Economic Advisors need know the labyrinthine relationships among governmental bureaux.

(7) If monetary policy is coordinated with the other economic policies of the administration then I see no merit in having the Fed making separate reports – separate from *The Economic Report of the President* – to Congress. If monetary policy is left uncoordinated, then a requirement for separate quarterly reports by the Fed not only has little merit, but such a requirement might be detrimental if it opened the Federal Reserve Board to more political pressure to pursue, what I have labelled above, 'political trade cycle' policies.

(8) Coordination would necessarily involve representatives of the Treasury and CEA at open market committee meetings, and, I would hope, these representatives would be participants and not merely interested onlookers.

(9) As far as appraisal of the structure of the Federal Reserve is concerned. I believe that it follows from my strong advocacy of coordination that (a) the Chairman of the Board's term be coterminous with the President of the United States, and (b) since the Federal Reserve is an instrument of the public and not of the member banks, there is no necessity to maintain the fiction of private ownership. Accordingly, the Federal Reserve bank stock should be retired.

(10) Since a central bank by its very nature as the monetary authority does not need a cushion of 'undistributed profits', I see no reason why the Federal Reserve should not pay all its earnings over to the Treasury, while funds to operate the System would be appropriated by normal legislative means. Certainly, if the Chairman of the Federal Reserve had to submit a budget request to the President – as does the Secretary of the Treasury and the Chairman of the CEA – coordination of policy would be facilitated.

(11) The term of members of the Federal Reserve Board depends, in

part, on what individuals are likely to be appointed as members. If members are to be selected primarily from the banking community and are expected to return to this sector after a single term, then I believe the longer the term the better, for a long term frees the members from having their own future economic self-interest affect their decisions. If, on the other hand, one anticipates selecting them from the academic field – such as is now done for CEA members – then a term similar to Cabinet members seems desirable if coordination is going to be efficiently accomplished. In any case the choice of five years rather than, say, four years, as H.R. 11 provides, strikes me as strangely incongruous with political realities.

(12) It follows from my analysis in section 3 above, that the Federal Reserve's policies of the last three years have been socially undesirable. The continued rise in the consumer price level during the past few years is indicative of the failure of monetary policy to contain the inflationary pressures, while the continued high unemployment rate in the ghettos must, at least in part, be associated with these policies. Ultimately, policy-makers must recognize that labour and management in our system share responsibility with the monetary and fiscal authorities for the maintenance of price level stability, full employment, and economic growth. An incomes policy is an essential consort to a sound monetary policy. Until this notion is accepted, modern market-oriented systems such as ours will continue to follow erratic paths of economic growth.

Notes

1. If only non-reproducible goods such as works of arts by dead artists were rising, no major public policy problem would arise. This latter case would be an example of a pure demand–price inflation and could readily be analysed primarily by concentrating on changes in demand factors.
2. If imports are an important component of the output of most reproducible goods, then rising import prices can affect the flow supply price. For the United States, I do not believe this is a significant problem and hence I have omitted it from the discussion.

References

Davidson, P. (1965), 'Keynes's Finance Motive', *Oxford Economic Papers*, 17 (March), pp. 47–65.
Davidson, P. (1967), 'The Importance of the Demand for Finance', *Oxford Economic Papers*, 19 (July), pp. 245–53.
Davidson, P. (1968), 'Money, Portfolio Balance, Capital Accumulation, and

Economic Growth', *Econometrica*, 36 (April), pp. 291–321 (chapter 3 in this volume).

Harrod, R. F. (1965), *Reforming the World's Money* (London).

Keynes, J. M. (1937a), 'Alternative Theories of the Rate of Interest', *Economic Journal*, 47 (June), pp. 663–9.

Keynes, J. M. (1937b), 'The Ex-Ante Theory of the Rate of Interest', *Economic Journal*, 47 (December), pp. 663–9.

Lerner, A. P. (1967), 'Employment Theory and Employment Policy', *American Economic Review Papers and Proceedings*, 57 (1967), pp. 1–18.

Marshall, A. (1950), *Principles of Economics*, 8th edn (New York).

Weintraub, S. (1963), *Some Aspects of Wage Theory and Policy* (Philadelphia).

6 Discussion Paper: 'Money in Britain, 1959–69'*

Any discussion of the growth of monetary and financial institutions can focus on at least four different, but not necessarily independent, aspects. These are:

1. The efficiency of financial institutions' operations: This is primarily a technical question, a sort of production function problem involving laws of returns.

2. Equity considerations: For example, is the growth and evolution of financial institutions related to price discrimination against certain borrowers or submarket borrowers? Do bankers make overly large profits for performing a public service for which they have a semi-monopolistic franchise?

3. Monetary effects on the real domestic sector and the international sector. For example, how does the growth of financial institutions affect aggregate output levels? The Radcliffe Report suggests two possible mechanisms through which monetary changes operate on the real sector. These are (a) the interest incentive effect which recognizes that changes in the rate of discount will change the present value of any given income stream and therefore alter the demand price for capital goods, and (b) the general liquidity effect, or what I would call the availability of finance effect. The Radcliffe Report, in my opinion, tends to downplay the importance of the quantity of bank money in this latter effect by rolling it into the portmanteau concept of the 'whole liquidity position of the economy'. This view seems, at times, almost to disregard the fact that borrowers must have bank money if they are to make their demand-price calculations of investment projects operational in the capital goods markets. Since the ability of businessmen significantly to increase their demand for investment goods by arranging for increased clearings of debts outside the banking system is, in the short period, extremely limited, any increase in the availability of bank money to markets where there is an 'unsatisfied fringe of borrowers' will result in a significant increase in the demand for goods.

4. Resource allocation: The differential growth and evolution of financial institutions will affect the allocation of resources not only between employ-

* This paper appeared in *Money in Britain, 1959–69*, ed. D. R. Croome and H. G. Johnson (Oxford University Press, 1970).

ment and unemployment, but also between the consumption and investment sectors, and among industries in each sector.

In the traditional course in monetary economics, the money market is
often assumed to operate as a 'perfect market'. Under such a view, all
potential borrowers have equal access to the market, and given the supply
of funds, it is the borrowers with the highest expectations of profits who
gain the necessary claims to bid for real resources.

In the real world, however, the financial industry is a highly structured,
segregated, and oligopolistic community. Certain borrowers are likely to
be discriminated against, although the magnitude of discrimination may
well be different in periods of slack demand than in periods of high demand
for credit. Legal, institutional, and customary factors including such things
as accounting rules, safety rules on portfolio composition, etc. tend to
perpetuate this discrimination which not only gives rise to some of the
equity questions suggested in item 2 but also alters the allocation of
resources from what it would be in a perfect market.

Another way of viewing this aspect could be developed as follows. In the
absence of financial institutions each income receiving unit would have to
plough its savings into tangible goods, and resource allocation would
largely depend on the unit's view of what physical goods were a good store
of value. With growth of financial institutions, a mechanism is provided
which permits (but does not require) the efficient transfer of command of
real resources from economic units that wish to spend less than income to
units that wish to spend more. Nevertheless, it should be made clear that
such a system does not guarantee that the abstaining households will be
able to command, in the future, as many resources as they relinquish at the
present time. Nor does it require that those who abstain gain title to the
increment of real wealth which such abstinence permits.

Moreover, if abstinence exceeds the desire of other units to spend in
excess of their income, the services of the real resources will be wasted,
while if the excess spending of these latter units exceeds abstinence when
resources are already fully employed, financial institutions can permit
some units to outbid others for resources so that some units may have
involuntarily to relinquish command over real resources. These questions
of voluntary and forced abstinence, the ownership of real wealth, and the
ability to make economic provision for the future raise questions about
equity of a different type than those in item 2 above.

I wish now to comment on five topics raised by Mr Clark in his extremely
interesting paper. My comments will be primarily concerned with items 2
and 3 above.

1. Mr Clark indicates that monetary controls in the 1960s have been
continually tightening while the trend of the pre-Radcliffe 1950s was that of
monetary ease. This difference in trend should, *ceteris paribus*, exacerbate

commercial bank policies of discriminating between types of borrowers. To the extent that this discrimination leaves large submarkets with little or no access to credit, but with large potential profits if finance can be made available, there is an incentive for either maverick bankers or outsiders to attempt to service these potentially lucrative submarkets. Custom and tradition being as strong as it is in the UK, it is not surprising that the presence of these potentially profitable submarkets has encouraged the establishment of new financial institutions, which can take advantage of arbitrage between the quoted costs of borrowing from the clearing banks and the bid prices of the borrowers discriminated against.

Nevertheless this type of arbitrage behaviour cannot go on forever without the traditional sources of credit taking some steps to avoid the complete loss of these discriminated markets, partly because these older institutions hope to salvage some segment of these submarkets for the future when credit conditions ease. Thus the rate spread on loans and overdrafts above bank rate will rise to discourage others from borrowing at the clearing banks in order to relend to one of the disadvantaged borrowers.

Furthermore, the clearing banks can stake out a claim on these discriminated submarkets by forming subsidiaries, whereas they would break the rules of the 'money game' if they were to expand into these markets through a department of the parent bank. For example, Clark suggests that if a subsidiary buys equities, it has not violated the rule against participation in equities by clearing banks. Moreover, by the establishment of a subsidiary, overhead costs are separated from the parent operation, allowing more flexibility in the pricing and bilateral bargaining on loan transactions than might be allowed by the accounting practices of the more conventional parent organization.

2. The widespread use of the overdraft in the UK as compared to the fixed loan approach of the US commercial banks shifts some of the risks of illiquidity from the business firms to the banks. Thus firms need less precautionary balances if they have unused overdraft facilities, while banks need larger precautionary balances. To the extent that there are economies of scale in the demand for precautionary balances, the overdraft system makes a more efficient use of funds for any given quantity of money than the fixed loan system, as far as society is concerned. Even so, from the viewpoint of the banks it means that, at any point of time, less can be lent out at interest. Since the production of bank money involves no real resources, it is not obvious that this efficiency improves welfare, except for the fact that, in my opinion, central bankers tend to pursue the wrong social objectives. Thus, the overdraft system permits the economy to expand further, for any given credit squeeze, than the fixed loan system. Given the bank rate, however, the clearing banks are bearing the entire

cost of providing this more efficient use of funds and it is therefore not surprising to find Mr Clark indicating that the tight monetary policy is pushing the clearing banks into preferring fixed loans to overdrafts. In addition, Clark's suggestion of regularizing compensating balances as a feature of bank loans would further push the costs of maintaining precautionary balances onto the borrowers. In a world of uncertainty, the need for precautionary balances is a necessary adjunct of a viable monetary system, but whether the banks or the borrowers should pay the costs is, at least partly, a question of equity.

If there are no tacit agreements among financial institutions, competition for inputs may raise their price and therefore ultimately increase the price of output. This is particularly likely to occur if the existing market price does not clear the market of borrowers. If the total money supply in the system is fixed by the central bank then higher rates on funds flowing into the various financial institutions merely increase the economic rents paid to the depositors. (Of course, to the extent that different rates on deposits are paid by different financial institutions, this will affect the flow of funds from one institution to another.)

Economic units keep funds in current accounts for the usual liquidity preference motives. The use of such a repository is appealing to the individual because of the negligible cost of converting from this store of value to the medium of exchange; hence it should not be necessary to pay owners of these funds in order to encourage them to maintain their current accounts. In fact, one can view the account balance as a payment to the bank for providing an asset which can serve the dual functions of money without cost and with maximum safety from loss, fire, or theft.

If, however, banks simultaneously provide an interest-bearing bank account form which, though legally requiring seven days notice, in practice permits one to move from the store of value to the medium of exchange on demand without cost, then as long as the interest payment exceeds the convenience of cheque writing (as opposed to travelling to the bank and standing in a queue to obtain the medium of exchange), the inconvenience costs of converting from store of value to medium of exchange for deposit accounts has been overcome and the deposit account becomes a superior store of value. As Clark notes, rising interest rates on deposit accounts have produced movement in this direction. If it was not for uncertainty as to when specific payments were to become due and to legal restrictions as to who may have deposit accounts, the transfer from current accounts to deposit accounts would probably be considerably greater than the banks have so far experienced.

This will, of course, have sharp effects on bank earnings and the level of economic rents paid to depositors. It is not surprising, therefore, to find that such a potential adverse impact on bank earnings in this oligopolistic industry encourages tacit agreements on input prices. Of course, if the oligopoly power in the industry is too diffuse for informal agreements to bind all the producers, then, as in the US, government regulation may be necessary to prevent impairments to the liquidity of some financial institutions, as funds flow from one financial institution to another in response to changing competitive input price offers.

3. The growth of the Eurodollar market has, at least for the US, required the Monetary Authority to tighten the monetary screw even further than otherwise in order to achieve the slackness in the domestic goods markets which the Federal Reserve believed was essential for combating inflation. Regardless of the merits or otherwise of the Federal Reserve's policy, the existence of a parallel market such as the Eurodollar market, while not unduly hampering the Fed's ability to raise the prime rate, did severely constrain its ability to limit the growth in the credit supply. As long as any system of fixed exchange rates remains, therefore, the existence of such large 'parallel' markets can, as Clark notes, hamper the Monetary Authority's ability to affect real output via what Radcliffe called the general liquidity effect.

Moreover, I would agree with Clark that the existence of such markets *need not* imply the transmission of high interest rates from one country to another. If such apparent transmission occurs it is probably due to deliberate central bank policy attempting to change the nation's balance of payments by affecting the international lending balance rather than policy aimed directly at either the trade balance or the existing exchange rate. Accordingly I would blame deliberate policy rather than 'the world hunger for capital', as Clark suggests, as the mechanism of high interest rate transmission.

4. The requirement that local authorities must behave as if they were merely another borrower in the private sector, while the national government's borrowing is (unless the masochistic views of politicians and central bankers interfere) supported by the central bank, is, as far as I am concerned, an archaic anomaly of the Dark Ages in economic thinking. Coordination of all governmental borrowing and taxation is such an obviously desirable social objective that I am at a loss to explain why more progress has not been made in this area. If it is in the social interest for local governments to command real resources, then the transfer of claims for resources should be effected in the most expeditious manner without, as a matter of equity, leaving a large perpetual burden of financial claims on the future.

5. The reduction in the number of clearing banks since the Radcliffe Report, even if stimulated by production economies of scale, must result in an even tighter oligopolistic structure than before, particularly if foreign and overseas banks do not compete for, or at least do not solicit, domestic

loans. As the number of members of such an oligopolistic system declines, the probability increases that their individual views on what 'good' banking practices are will be similar, so that tacit agreements will more readily arise even when they are not even recognized as such by the parties involved. Furthermore, increased public scrutiny of the remaining clearing banks assures that no one bank – at least under the aegis of the parent firm – behaves unconventionally. Simultaneously, the reduction in numbers will make it easier for bankers to discourage their customers from seeking alternative sellers, lowering the effective cross-elasticity of demand among the remaining banks. Under such circumstances, the equity questions become more important and may require continual surveillance of bank charges by the National Prices and Incomes Board.

A study of Professor Almarin Phillips reported in the *Federal Reserve Bulletin* (July 1967) showed that after adjusting for loan size, bank size, geographical region, and time (which was a proxy for monetary policy and interest rate levels), there is a significant association between the rate charged on loans by banks, and banking concentration. If this relationship carries over to the UK, then the merging of the clearing banks should, *ceteris paribus*, increase borrowing costs. This would ultimately involve questions of equity between the borrowers and the banks which is a particularly difficult problem if there still remains a fringe of unsatisfied borrowers. The central bank can still maintain control over aggregate demand for any given set of circumstances (unless we are in a liquidity trap) by altering the quantity of credit.

Competition between the clearing banks and other financial intermediaries is, as Clark points out, quite a separate question. Nevertheless, since different financial institutions cultivate different submarkets, such competition will lead to both a reallocation of resources depending on which borrowers ultimately receive the funds and a possible redistribution of bank discrimination practices.

7 Money and the Real World*

'Money,' Hicks has declared, 'is defined by its functions . . . "money is what money does,"' (1967, p. 1). Harrod notes that 'Money is a social phenomenon, and many of its current features depend on what people think it is or ought to be' (1969, p. x). 'Money,' Scitovsky adds, 'is a difficult concept to define, partly because it fulfils not one but three functions, each of them providing a criterion of moneyness . . . those of a unit of account, a medium of exchange, and a store of value' (1969, p. 1).

While economists have probably spilled more printers' ink over the topic of money than any other, and while monetary theory impinges on almost every other conceivable branch of economic analysis, confusion over the meaning and nature of money continues to plague the economics profession. Pre-Keynesian neoclassical economists tended to emphasize the medium of exchange aspect of money, as the early quantity theorists stressed a strict relationship between the money aggregate and transactions (or income). In a neoclassical world of perfect certainty and perfect markets, with a Walrasian auctioneer assuring simultaneous equilibrium at a given point of time, it would, of course, be irrational to hold money as a store of value as long as other assets provided a certain positive yield (Samuelson, 1947, pp. 122–4). In the absence of uncertainty, neoclassical theory had no room for the store of value function in its definition of money; nor would money play any more important role than peanuts in a neoclassical world. The *tâtonnement* process implies that no transactions occur until equilibrium is attained (i.e. recontracting is essential); hence, anyone holding money either during the auction or till the next market period is irrational. Why hold money if it is really not needed for transactions, since in equilibrium goods trade for goods, and since the present and the future value of all economic goods can be determined (at least in a probability sense) with complete certainty?[1] The essential nature of money is disregarded in all Walrasian general equilibrium systems since there is no asset whose liquidity premium exceeds its carrying cost.[2] As Hahn has recently admitted '*the Walrasian economy that we have been considering*, although one where the auctioneer regulates the terms at which goods shall exchange, *is essentially one of barter*' (1970, p. 3).

* *The Economic Journal*, March 1972. The author is extremely grateful for the many helpful comments of Sidney Weintraub, Basil J. Moore, Jan Kregel and Miles Fleming on earlier drafts of this paper. This paper evolved from an ongoing study on *Money and the Real World* which is being supported by a grant from the Rutgers University Research Council. The results of this study were published by Macmillan (1972).

Keynes was the first important economist bluntly to accuse the neoclassical view of the nature of money as foolish. Keynes wrote:

> Money, it is well known, serves two principal purposes . . . it facilitates exchanges . . . In the second place, it is a store of wealth. So we are told, without a smile on the face. But in the world of the classical economy, what an insane use to which to put it! For it is a recognised characteristic of money as a store of wealth that it is barren . . . Why should anyone outside a lunatic asylum wish to use money as a store of wealth? (1947, p. 186–7)

His answer to this rhetorical question was clear and unequivocal: 'our desire to hold money as a store of wealth is a barometer of the degree of our distrust of our own calculations and conventions concerning the future . . . the possession of actual money lulls our disquietude' (ibid., p. 187). Distrust? Disquietude? These are states of mind which are impossible in a world of certainty.

It is in the Keynesian world where

> expectations are liable to disappointment and expectations concerning the future affect what we do today . . . that the peculiar properties of money as a link between the present and the future must enter. . . . Money, in its significant attributes, is above all a subtle device for linking the present to the future. (Keynes, 1936, pp. 293–4)

This link can exist only if there is a continuity over time of contractual commitments denominated in money units. It is the synchronous existence of money and money contracts over an uncertain future which is the basis of a monetary system whose maxim is *'Money buys goods and goods buy money; but goods do not buy goods'* (Clower, 1969, pp. 207–8).

Despite the victory of the Keynesian Revolution for many practical short-run employment policies, subsequent developments in monetary theory by Patinkin, Friedman, Tobin and others have regressed on this crucial aspect of uncertainty. These modern monetary theorists, some who have been labelled neoclassical, some Keynesian, but all right of centre, have ignored Keynes's insistence that certain propositions were so uncertain in principle as to be incapable of having any numerical value; and they have instead substituted the concept of quantifiable, predictable risk for uncertainty.[3] At the same time, these modern monetary theorists have swung with the Keynesian pendulum towards emphasizing the extreme opposite view of the primary function of money from that which the pre-Keynesian neoclassicists held. For these monetary theorists it is, paradoxically, the store of wealth function of money which is highlighted in their models of complete certainty. Thus, for example, Tobin declares,

'The crucial property of "money" in this role is being a store of value' (1968, p. 833), as he emphasizes asset choice or portfolio balance among a menu of assets all with *certain* yields. Friedman defines money as 'anything that serves the function of providing a *temporary abode for general purchasing power*' (1968, p. 186), while simultaneously assuming that in equilibrium there is no uncertainty since all 'permanent' anticipated real values are unchanged during the period under analysis, i.e. all changes are foreseen from the beginning (Friedman, 1970, p. 223; also see Friedman, 1971, pp. 326–9).

Similarly, the well-known real balance effect of Patinkin's model is based on the store of value aspect of money. The flexibility of money wages and prices, which is essential to the generation of a real balance effect and the equilibrium position, requires certainty conditions (Patinkin, 1965, p. 275) and therefore removes the need for money as a store of value.[4] Patinkin succinctly epitomizes the modern monetarist view of money being concerned 'with the *utility of holding money*, not with that of *spending* it. This is the concept implicit in all cash-balance approaches to the quantity theory of money; and it is the one that will be followed explicitly here' (ibid., p. 79). Furthermore, Patinkin continues

> our concern . . . is with the demand for money that would exist even if there were perfect certainty with respect to future prices and interest. Uncertainty does play a role in the analysis, but only uncertainty with respect to the timing of payments. Thus one by-product of the following argument is the demonstration that dynamic or uncertain price and/or interest expectations are not a *sine qua non* of a positive demand for money . . . The general approach of the following argument is in the Keynesian spirit of analysing the demand for this asset as one component of an optimally chosen portfolio of many assets. (ibid., pp. 80–1)

But how can an analysis of portfolio decisions which irretrievably dispenses with uncertainty and faulty expectations – as does much of what passes for advanced monetary theory in the current literature, be in the 'spirit of Keynes'? The music of this lively if mislabelled 'Keynesian' gavotte which emphasizes portfolio balance in a world of certainty may be the melody to which most modern monetarists trot, but surely it is not attuned to Keynes's majestic monetary dirge for Say's Law. It is only in a world of uncertainty and disappointment that money comes into its own as a necessary mechanism for deferring decisions; money has its niche only when we feel queasy about undertaking any actions which will commit our claims on resources on to a path which can only be altered, if future events require this, at very high costs (if at all).

Recognition of this desire to avoid the commitment of claims on resources provides the insight necessary to describe the social institutions associated with money as well as the elemental and peculiar properties which are necessary to fulfil the two equally important functions of money, namely, a generally accepted medium of exchange, and a store of value in a modern, monetary, market-oriented, but uncertain world.

These necessary properties of anything which will fulfil the functional definition of money are:

(1) a zero (or negligible) elasticity of productivity, so that if individuals, uncertain about the future, want to defer additional commitments of resources, their increased demand for money as a mode for postponing action will not encourage entrepreneurs to employ additional resources in the production of additional quantities of the money commodity;

(2) a zero (or negligible) elasticity of substitution, so that if individuals want to preserve additional options for action for the future, the increase in the price of money induced by an increase in the demand for money as a store of value does not divert people into substituting other assets, which have high elasticities of productivity, as a store of value. Hence the demand for a store of value, in an uncertain world, does not generate the demand to commit resources. Thus the virtuous interaction between supply of resources and the demand for resources which is succinctly expressed via Say's Law is broken;

(3) the cost of transferring money from the medium of exchange function to the store of value function or vice versa must be zero (or negligible) so that individuals do not find it expensive to defer decisions or to change their minds. Minimizing their transactions costs requires the existence of at least two economic institutions: (a) offer and debt contracts denominated in money units and (b) legal enforcement of such contracts. An additional contribution to the minimizing of such transactions costs is the presence of an institution, namely a clearing system, which permits using private debts in the settlement of transactions as long as it is expected that the private debt can be promptly converted into the form of money which is enforceable in the discharge of contracts.

In sum then, in an uncertain world, a monetary system is associated with at least two and usually three institutions – namely, contracts, enforcement and clearing. The thing which becomes the money commodity will have two properties, a zero (or negligible) elasticity of productivity and a zero (or negligible) elasticity of substitution between it and any other good which has a high elasticity of productivity.

It is a failure by many able but wrong-headed economists to comprehend

Money

the importance of these three institutions and two properties which are peculiar to money in a monetary economy, which has led to the shunting of much of modern monetary analysis on to a wrong line.

Any model of a monetary, market-oriented economy which attempts to provide insights about the real world should have the following characteristics:

(1) Decision-making by firms and households who are fully aware that human judgement is fallible.
(2) The existence of contractual agreements, enforceable by acceptable legal institutions, which permit the sharing of some of the burdens of uncertainty between the contracting parties.
(3) Different degrees of organization of spot and future markets for all sorts of real goods and financial assets. In many cases, either only a spot or a future market exists for a particular item because of difficulties of organizing a market in a world of incomplete information; and even in markets which do exist, there may be significant and increasing transactions, search and information costs.
(4) Money buys goods in these markets, and goods can buy money, but except for some relatively small – but not necessarily unimportant – markets, goods never buy goods.[5] As an immediate corollary to this condition it follows that demand involves want plus the ability to pay and therefore financial conditions can affect real markets.
(5) The various institutions which develop in organizing a market can affect the price path in the market as it reacts to a disequilibrium situation.
(6) There is a generally available clearing mechanism for private debts which permits the existence of a fractional reserve banking system. There are also non-bank financial institutions which, because they lack a generally available clearing mechanism independent of the banking system, cannot create a medium of exchange. Nevertheless, these financial intermediaries can affect financial flows and hence market demands.
(7) There is 'confidence' in the monetary and financial system.

Thus the main characteristics of a real world monetary economy are Uncertainty, Fallibility, Covenants, Institutions, Commerce, Finance and Trust. These are the Seven Wonders on which the Modern World is based. Simultaneously, these are the sources of the outstanding faults of a modern monetary, free market economy, namely 'its failure to provide for full employment and its arbitrary and inequitable distribution of wealth and incomes' (Keynes, 1936, p. 372).

1 THE NATURE AND IMPORTANCE OF MONEY

Hicks has observed that although 'monetary theory is less abstract than most economic theory, it cannot avoid a relation to reality' (1967, p. 156). Yet, much of the current literature on monetary theory, based on Walrasian general equilibrium foundations (to which Professor Hicks has provided much impetus), is unrealistic. In the real world, money is not created like the manna from heaven of a Patinkinesque world or dropped by helicopter as in Friedman's construction. In the real world, money 'comes into existence along with debts, which are contracts for deferred payment, and Price-lists, which are offers of contracts for sale or purchase' (Keynes, 1930, p. 3). Contracts are therefore essential to the phenomenon of money, and the existence of institutions which can enforce the discharge of contractual commitments for future action are essential in providing trust in the future operation of the monetary system. Thus, the existence of institutions, normally operating under the aegis of the state, provides assurances of the continuity between the present and the future which is necessary if one is going to hold money as a store of value. It is with the development of such state-sponsored institutions that the government appropriated to itself the right to define what is the unit of account and what *thing* should answer that definition. Thus the state 'claimed the right to not only enforce the dictionary but also to write the dictionary' (ibid., p. 5). Only if the community loses confidence in the ability of state institutions to enforce *contracts*, does the monetary system break down, and the community reverts to barter practices. For a developed interdependent economy where production takes time and contractual commitments for the hiring of resources must occur some time before everyone can possibly know how valuable the outcome will be, barter practices are so wasteful of resources, and so costly, that most members of society will cling to any ray of hope in the government's ability to enforce contracts in the future. Hence most communities reveal a preference to use even a crippled monetary system rather than revert to barter. It is only when the situation has deteriorated to such an extent that everyone is completely uncertain of the meaning of contractual commitments, that a catastrophic breach in the continuity of the system is inevitable. Such a catastrophe, by wiping out all existing contracts simultaneously, provides a foundation for developing a new monetary unit of account which can be utilized in denominating new contractual commitments.

Thus, as Keynes insisted so many years ago, money and contracts are intimately and inevitably related. Money as a numeraire is *not* merely a device to help the neoclassical economist specify the relationship among diverse goods – it is not merely a lowest common denominator. The very institution of money as a unit of account immediately gives rise to at least two types of contracts – contracts which offer to provide goods and services in exchange for money (i.e. offers to buy money via the production and delivery of goods at some moment of time after the offer is made) and offers to provide money for goods (i.e. offers to deliver money at some point of time after the offer is made). If money was simply a neoclassical numeraire, then goods could buy goods without the intermediation of money. 'The numeraire is not money; it is not even a partial money; it is not even assumed that it is used by the traders themselves as a unit of account. It is no more than a unit of account which the observing economist is using for his own purpose of explaining to himself what the traders are doing' (Hicks, 1967, p. 3).

It is the synchronous existence of money as a unit of account and the presence of 'offer contracts' and 'debt contracts' which are denominated in money units which forms the core of a modern monetary production economy. Money is and must be the thing which is ubiquitously involved on one side or the other of all contracts if these contracts are to be enforceable in a viable monetary system. Money is that thing that by delivery discharges contractual obligations. Money can function as the medium of exchange only because it is a general tenet of the community that acceptance of the monetary intermediary as a temporary abode of general purchasing power involves no risks (only uncertainties), since the state will enforce enactment of all future offer contracts which may be entered into, in terms of the unit of account.

In a world of uncertainty where production takes time, the existence of money contracts permits the sharing of the burdens of uncertainties between the contracting parties whenever resources are to be committed to produce a flow of goods for a delivery date in the future. Such contractual commitment (e.g. hire contracts and forward contracts) are, by definition, tied to the flow-supply price. Ultimately, underlying the flow-supply price is the relationship between the money-wage rate and productivity phenomena. If individuals are to utilize money as a temporary abode either because they expect to accept delivery of reproducible goods in the very near future, or because they desire a vehicle for transferring immediate command of resources to the more remote and indefinite future, then these economic units must have *confidence* that no matter how far the current spot price for any producible good may be momentarily displaced by spot market conditions, the market price for the good will not be above some expected level at a future date.

As long as the flow-supply prices are expected to be sticky,[6] coherent and continuous, each individual 'knows' he can, at any time, accept a contract offering future producible goods at a delivered money price which does not differ significantly from today's flow-supply price. Moreover, in an economy where production is going on, sticky flow-supply prices imply relatively stable forward prices of producible goods since the latter will never exceed (and will normally equal) the flow-supply prices associated with the same delivery dates.[7] Since these forward prices reflect the best current expectations of the spot prices at the future delivery dates (Working, 1966, pp. 446–7), they are the best estimates of the *future* costs of buying such goods either by currently accepting a contract for forward delivery or by waiting until the future date to buy them spot. Hence, the current set of forward prices (and therefore flow-supply prices) are the best measures of the purchasing power of money at any future date; they are the prices individuals will use in calculating the *real* balances they wish to hold. Ultimately, then, in a viable monetary–production–specialization economy, expectation of sticky money wages combined with the public's belief in the sanctity of contracts for future performance encourages the public to accept, as a temporary abode of purchasing power, either the thing the state terms as money, or any private debt contract for which there is a clearing mechanism and for which there is public confidence in the ability of any individual to convert it immediately into legal money without costs.[8]

Any economy which uses such a medium of exchange has a tremendous advantage over a similarly endowed hypothetical economy which permitted only barter transactions – for the cost of anticipating the needs of trading partners and then searching out such partners greatly exceeds the resources used in bringing buyers and sellers together in a money economy. It is only the presumed existence of the costless Walrasian auctioneer which permits general equilibrium models to reach a Walrasian equilibrium solution (Hicks, 1967, pp. 6–7). The assumption of zero transactions costs, Hicks reminds us, 'is hopelessly misleading when our subject is money. Even the simplest exchanges are in fact attended by some costs. The reason why a well-organized market is more efficient than a badly organized market . . . is that in the well-organized market the cost of making transactions is lower'[9] (1967, p. 6).

The desire on the part of rational economic men to minimize all costs – including transaction costs – leads to the discovery that while the introduction of a medium of exchange reduces transaction costs over a barter system, the process of clearing titles to money rather than taking delivery of the intermediary commodity itself can lower transaction costs even further.

Bank money is, of course, simply evidence of a private debt contract, but the discovery of the efficiency of 'clearing', that is the realization that some forms of private debt can be used in settlement of the overlapping myriad of private contracts, immensely increased the efficiency of the monetary system. Three conditions are necessary in order for such a private debt to operate as a medium of exchange:

(1) the private debt must be denominated in terms of the monetary unit;

(2) a clearing institution for these private debts must be developed; and
(3) assurance that uncleared debts are convertible at a known parity into the legally enforceable medium of exchange.

The development of an institution to clear specific types of private debts and an institution to prevent the misuse of these private debt facilities not only permits but assures – because of the lower costs of transactions – that these private debts will replace state enforced legal money as the main medium of exchange in most transactions. Thus any form of private debt can become a medium of exchange if institutions are created which permit increases in clearings while preventing misapplication of these private debt facilities. What prevents other kinds of private debt (e.g. trade credit, commercial paper) from becoming part of the medium of exchange is either the absence of a specific clearing institution that deals in the specific type of debt under consideration, or if such an institution exists its facilities are not available for most of the transactors in the community.[10] Thus, for example, the ability of businessmen to enlarge their demand for the hire purchase of capital goods by arranging for increased clearings of debts outside the banking system is, in the short run, extremely limited, and hence financial constraints on investment demand may restrict investment purchases even when the present value of additional capital goods greatly exceeds the flow-supply price of these goods. Thus the lack of a sufficient quantity of the medium of exchange can restrain the economy even when there are owners of idle resources who would be willing to enter into offer contracts at the going money-wage rate.

What permits money to possess purchasing power is, ultimately, its intimate relationship to 'offer contracts' in general and contracts involving labour offers specifically. Thus it is the money-wage rate, that is the number of units of the money-of-account which labour is willing to buy for a given unit of effort, which is the anchor upon which the price level of all producible goods is fastened. It is the fact that changes in the quantity of money are inevitably tied to changes in the stock of existing contracts, and that the offer price for a contractual commitment for the forward delivery of all reproducible goods is, *when money buys goods*, constrained by money flow-supply prices whose principal component is ultimately the money-wage rate, that causes changes in the quantity of money, changes in the level of employment of resources, changes in the money-wage rate and changes in the price level to be inevitably interrelated.

It is only in the Walrasian general equilibrium world where the quantity of money is (a) conceived to be independent of the level of contracts[11] and (b) provided to the community like manna from heaven, that the general equilibrium theorist finds no secure anchor for the level of absolute prices which are indeterminate in his system. Having cut the connections between money, labour offer contracts and flow-supply prices, these modern Walrasians conclude that the level of prices is whatever it is expected to be, for if it were not, money holders would, with the cooperation of the ubiquitous Walrasian auctioneer, simply bid up or down the price level until the purchasing power of money was at the level they wanted it to be, while resource utilization (full employment) would be unaffected[12] (cf. Patinkin, 1965, pp. 44–5; Hicks, 1967, pp. 9–10; Tobin, 1955, p. 105).

In the real world, money is among the most ancient of man's institutions. Barter economies are more likely to be the figments of economists' minds than the handmaiden of human transactors. A description of activity in a barter system may be useful as a benchmark for observing the effects of money on the system, but the results of such comparative anatomy should never be taken seriously as indicative of real world alternatives. The barter transactions implicit in the Walrasian approach can only be meaningful as an analysis of the immediate exchange of pre-existing goods. The majority of important transactions in a modern mass production economy, however, involve the contractual commitment of resources for the production of goods and services to be delivered at a future date. Modern neoclassical monetarists, finding that the real world does not possess perfect certainty, or a fixed quantity of labour hirings, or flexible wages and prices, or the ability to recontract of their theoretical framework, 'resemble Euclidean geometers in a non-Euclidean world who, discovering that in experience straight lines apparently parallel often meet, rebuke the lines for not keeping straight – as the only remedy for the unfortunate collisions which are occurring' (Keynes, 1936, p. 16).

2   MONEY, FINANCIAL INSTITUTIONS, AND ECONOMIC GROWTH – AN OVERVIEW

In the absence of a money with the requisite zero elasticities, each income-receiving unit would have to plough its savings into commodities, for without such a money the decision of what reproducible thing to buy with the thing being sold cannot be postponed. In such a mythical neoclassical economy, income-receiving units must store value in those physical goods which they believe are most 'productive'. Even if decision-making units are ignorant about the future they must 'override and ignore this ignorance' (Shackle, 1967, p. 290). Say's Law prevails, and the allocation of resources between consumption and capital goods will depend entirely on the savings propensities of the income-receiving units.

With the existence of a non-reproducible money and appropriate financial institutions for clearing, a mechanism is provided which permits (but does not require) the efficient transfer of current command over resources (as long as resource offer contracts are denominated in terms of money) from economic units that wish to spend less than their income to those units that wish to spend more. Moreover, the existence of a clearing system which permits private debt to discharge contracts makes it possible for those who want to spend more than their income to obtain immediate claims on resources, while those who wish to spend less do not have to surrender their immediate claims. Such a system, however, does not guarantee that the abstaining economic units will be able to obtain command, in the future, over as much of the services of resources as they have decided not to use at the present time. Nor does it require that those who abstain gain title to the increment of real wealth which such abstinence permits.

If abstinence exceeds the desire of other units to spend in excess of their income, and if savings can be stored in a form which does not require resource utilization, i.e. the item which is utilized as a store of value has a zero elasticity of productivity, then the potential services of some real resources will be wasted as their offer contracts are not accepted. If, on the other hand, the aggregate desire to spend exceeds abstinence when resources are already fully employed, then the creation of additional units of the medium of exchange by financial institutions can permit some decision-makers to outbid others in accepting resource offer contracts; as a consequence, some income recipients may be forced to relinquish command over real resources involuntarily. These questions of voluntary and forced abstinence, the ownership of titles to real wealth, and the ability to make economic provision for the future are fundamental aspects of the problem of economic growth.

Since the creation of private debt by financial institutions does not by itself require the use of resources, jobs are not created merely by the process of increasing certain forms of private debt such as bank money. Job creation will depend on what the increment in bank money is used for. The immediate (first round) purpose will, of course, depend on why individuals were willing to go into debt. If individuals desired more money either to hold as a store of value or to demand other things that have a zero elasticity of productivity (e.g. titles or other non-monetary forms of private debt), then this increment of money is immediately enmeshed in the 'financial circulation'[13] and though it may change hands from time to time it will not create jobs unless it moves (in a subsequent round) into the 'industrial circulation' where it will be used to accept offer contracts for new production.[14]

If, on the other hand, the initial user of the increment of bank money desired it to *increase* his acceptances of offer contracts for new goods and services – the finance motive for demanding money – then new jobs will be created on the first round and on subsequent rounds as portions of the increment of money remain in the 'industrial circulation' as the income generating multiplier process works its way through the economy. The increment of money that remains in the industrial circulation is often referred to as 'active balances' to distinguish it from the money in the financial circulation which is somewhat misleadingly labelled as 'idle balances' since the latter nomenclature suggests a zero velocity. Financial balances may still change hands while remaining in the financial circulation if individuals alter their bear position, while the community maintains its position.

In a monetary economy, many financial non-bank intermediaries evolve which provide links between the financial and industrial circulation. These non-bank financial intermediaries can affect the level of aggregate demand either by removing the medium of exchange from the bear hoards of abstaining households or by borrowing newly created money from commercial banks, and then making these funds available to economic units who want to accept offer contracts for new goods and services in excess of their current incomes.

These non-financial intermediaries are able to extract the medium of exchange either from bear hoards, and/or directly from commercial banks by providing a store of value in the form of a debt contract which promises

(1) a greater yield than money;
(2) greater confidence in the reliability of the intermediary to meet its obligation when it comes due than the confidence that would be generated by the debt contract of the economic unit which wishes to spend in excess of its income;
(3) greater confidence in the future parity between the intermediary's debt and the medium of exchange (if conversion is required before the maturity date of the debt contract) than is expected from other securities and
(4) very low transactions costs in converting the non-bank intermediary debt into the medium of exchange at any date in the future.

The difference between the liabilities of non-bank financial intermediaries and commercial bank liabilities is that clearing institutions exist for the latter which permit them to be a perfect substitute for legal money both as a medium of exchange and as a store of value, while no such similarly accessible clearing institution exists for the former. Hence liabilities of non-bank financial intermediaries, while being a good substitute for money as a store of value, cannot be used in settlement of an obligation. As a consequence there will always be some transaction costs involved in converting non-bank financial intermediary liabilities which are used as a store of value into the medium of exchange – a cost which does not exist for legal money or bank money.

In sum then, therefore, the difference between non-bank financial intermediary liabilities and commercial bank liabilities is that although both are evidence of private debt, only the latter can be generally used to discharge a contract. Accordingly, given the stock of money, increases in non-bank financial intermediaries' liabilities can raise aggregate demand for new goods and services only to the extent that (a) they replace existing legal money or commercial bank liabilities in the bear hoards of economic units and (b) these balances which are released from bear hoards are channelled to potential buyers who have the want, but without these channels of finance would not have the ability, to accept the offer contracts that are available in the market place.

Any increase in commercial bank liabilities, on the other hand, because of the existence of clearing institutions, provides either an additional store of value or an additional medium to settle debts and contracts – a costless option for the holder. To the extent that these bank debts are made to potential buyers of additional goods and services, aggregate demand is, of course, expanded.

As long as full employment is a social objective, and as long as a 'work requirement' is a condition for earning income for propertyless households so that full employment becomes a humanitarian as well as an economic objective, then monetary policy should always be geared to increasing the supply of money available to all potential buyers of producible goods who are willing to spend in excess of their income, as long as the point of effective demand is less than full employment. If, and only if, effective demand exceeds full employment volume, then monetary policy should, as a matter of fairness, become restrictive in order to thwart potential buyers who have preferential access to bank facilities from forcing abstinence on other income recipients, whose monetary income is relatively fixed and who do not have similar ease of access to bank credit.

A simple rule for expanding the money supply will not permit the efficient operation of such a monetary policy because exogenous changes in the desired portfolio composition between money and other financial assets will alter the quantity of money available to the industrial circulation; and, in a monetary economy, only money can buy goods, and goods can buy money. Any 'shortage' of money from the industrial circulation can be viewed as either frustrating potential buyers from obtaining goods, or preventing sellers from finding takers for their offer contracts.

Notes

1. The introduction of production into a Walrasian model requires that all future prices of all possible quantities that could be bought or sold be known with certainty; otherwise, production involves an irreducible uncertainty since there must be a current contractual commitment to hire resources to produce products which will be available to the market at some future date.
2. See Keynes's definition of a non-monetary economy (1936, p. 239).
3. Risk can, *via* probability statements, be reduced to a certainty; uncertainty

cannot. Modern monetarists fail to detect this crucial difference. Keynes, on the other hand, insisted that uncertainty was the sole intelligible reason for holding money, and by uncertainty he meant that there 'was no scientific basis on which to form any capable probability whatever. We simply do not know' (Keynes, 1947, pp. 184–5). Thus, true uncertainty, in the Knight–Keynes sense, does not obey the mathematical laws of probability. Keynes, who spent a substantial part of his early years studying and analysing the concept of Probability, believed that certain propositions (or events) were incapable of possessing a measurable value in terms of probability statements or decision weights (Harrod, 1951, pp. 653–4). Nowadays, Shackle comes closest to expressing the Keynesian view when he indicates that uncertainty involves doubt or disbelief of all conceivable outcomes; the complete set of subjectively determined eventualities need not have decision weights that sum to unity or any particular total. Nor is it necessary when changing decision weight for one eventuality or recognizing the possibility of a new and different outcome to alter the weights of the other events (Shackle, 1955, pp. 9–10).

4. Patinkin permits uncertainty to enter the front door *via* the assumption that during the 'period' the individual is uncertain as to when he receives payments or is required to make payments, while simultaneously kicking uncertainty out of the back door by asserting synchronization of payments, by the end of the period, in equilibrium (e.g. Patinkin, 1965, pp. 14, 80).

5. Goods should be interpreted as including financial assets as well as real commodities and services. In some markets such as organized exchanges, assets may clear against assets, without resort to money as a medium of exchange (cf. Clower, 1969, pp. 207–8).

6. Sticky flow-supply prices means that the annual rate of change in the money-wage rate relative to the rate of change in productivity is expected to be comparatively small.

7. By definition the price that buyers are offering to pay for forward delivery can never exceed the flow-supply price since the latter is the money-price required to call forth the exertion necessary to produce any given amount of the commodity for any given delivery date (cf. Kaldor, 1960, pp. 34–5). If, for example, the public suddenly changes its views about the rate of inflation in future flow-supply prices and if people act on the basis of such anticipations, they would immediately bid up the current spot price of all durables *and* they would place additional orders for forward delivery (of producible goods) at the current flow-supply price associated with the greater production flow. In other words, changes in the expected rate of inflation of producible goods will affect the current spot prices of all assets and the marginal efficiency of capital goods (cf. Keynes, 1936, pp. 142–3, 231), while the resulting forward price of output will *not* exceed the current flow-supply price associated with the induced greater effective demand.

8. 'In other words, expectation of a relative stickiness of wages in terms of money is a corollary of the excess of liquidity-premium over carrying-costs being greater for money than for any other asset' (Keynes, 1936, p. 238).

9. What Hicks fails to realize is that, in an uncertain world, there will only be an accidental matching of buyers and sellers in any spot market at any point of time – no matter how well organized. Thus, unless there is a residual buyer or seller who is willing to step in and make a market whenever one side or the other of market temporarily falls away, the spot price can fluctuate violently. Such fluctuations are incompatible with individuals' desires to hold such items as a store of value.

10. Of course, some forms of private debt may discharge commitments for small closed subsets of transactors within the community via a clearing mechanism, if there is a large number of continuous offsetting flows of goods and debts traded restricted to this subsector, e.g. stock market clearings. Nevertheless this private debt is not generally acceptable and therefore is not money.
11. Since recontracting is not only permitted but is required for Walrasian equilibrium to occur.
12. Thus many modern neoclassicists are in essence providing a bootstrap theory of the price level of goods in place of a bootstrap theory of the price level of bonds.
13. Since organized security exchanges develop institutions which permit the 'clearing' of securities for securities among a close set of transactors, the stock of money involved in circulating financial balances is kept to a minimum and the volume of such 'active' balances will be relatively independent of the activity involved in the churning of the security portion of individual portfolios. Nevertheless, since certain financial institutions maintain money balances in order to 'make a market' in securities, it is possible that the quantity of money needed to maintain such markets may rise slightly with expansion of the securities market (especially with geographical distance between transactors).
14. It may move into the industrial circulation by improving financial conditions and/or reducing interest rates and thereby inducing entrepreneurs to increase their demand for fixed capital, or by increasing the demand for delivery of working capital goods thereby calling for additional supplies.

References

Clower, R. W. (1969), 'A Reconsideration of the Microfoundations of Monetary Theory', *Western Economic Journal*, 6, 1967, reprinted in *Monetary Theory*, ed. by R. W. Clower (Middlesex, 1969). All references are to the reprint.

Friedman, M. (1968), *Dollars and Deficits* (New Jersey).

Friedman, M. (1970), 'A Theoretical Framework for Monetary Analyses', *Journal of Political Economy*, 78.

Friedman, M. (1971), 'A Monetary Theory of Nominal Income', *Journal of Political Economy*, 79.

Hahn, F. (1970),'Some Adjustment Problems', *Econometrica*, 38.

Harrod, R. F. (1951), *The Life of John Maynard Keynes* (London).

Harrod, R. F. (1969), *Money* (London).

Hicks, J. R. (1967), *Critical Essays in Monetary Theory* (Oxford).

Kaldor, N. (1960), 'Speculation and Economic Activity', *Review of Economic Studies*, 1939, reprinted in *Essays on Economic Stability and Growth*, ed. by N. Kaldor (London, 1960). All references are to the reprint.

Keynes, J. M. (1930), *A Treatise on Money*, Vol. I (London).

Keynes, J. M. (1936), *The General Theory of Employment, Interest, and Money* (London).

Keynes, J. M. (1947), 'The General Theory of Employment', *Quarterly Journal of Economics*, 51, 1937, reprinted in *The New Economics*, ed. by S. E. Harris (Boston). All references are to the reprint.

Patinkin, D. (1965), *Money, Interest, and Prices*, 2nd edn (New York).

Samuelson, P. A. (1947), *Foundations of Economic Analysis* (Cambridge).

Scitovsky, T. (1969), *Money and the Balance of Payments* (Chicago).
Shackle, G. L. S. (1955), *Uncertainty in Economics* (Cambridge).
Shackle, G. L. S. (1967), *The Years of High Theory* (Cambridge).
Tobin, J. (1955), 'A Dynamic Aggregative Model', *Journal of Political Economy*, 63.
Tobin, J. (1968), 'Notes on Optimal Growth', *Journal of Political Economy*, 76.
Working, H. (1966), 'New Concepts Concerning Futures Markets and Prices', *American Economic Review Papers and Proceedings*, 52.

8 A Keynesian View of Friedman's Theoretical Framework for Monetary Analysis*

Despite Friedman's numerous trenchant confrontations with 'Keynesians', he has never compared his analytical framework with the 'Theory of a Monetary Economy' developed by Keynes. The purpose of this paper is, therefore, to enumerate a few of the more fundamental conceptual differences between the monetary analysis of Keynes and that of Friedman. Keynes's analysis involves (1) the concept of uncertainty in the Knight–Keynes sense, (2) the inapplicability of a Walrasian system to a real world production economy where false trades occur, and (3) the essential properties of money which follow from the existence of uncertainty. This paper shows that recognition of these conceptual differences leads to significantly different specification of the demand for money and its supply aspects in the Keynesian system compared with Friedman's theoretical framework.

In response to some critics, Professor Friedman has elaborated and made more explicit his views on 'A Theoretical Framework for Monetary Analysis', a framework which he claims 'almost all economists would accept' (Friedman, 1970a, p. 234). Undoubtedly, this new presentation will evoke wide praise and attention; and the obvious future influence of Friedman's theoretical framework on economic thinking makes a critical examination of certain key elements and assertions of his analysis important. Before the dialogue becomes immersed in a critical discussion of the many fine analytical points raised by Friedman, it is essential to begin with a statement of some of the fundamental conceptual differences between the analytical monetary structure developed by Keynes and the model presented by Friedman, for despite Friedman's numerous trenchant confrontations with 'Keynesians', he has never compared his analytical

* This article was first published in *Journal of Political Economy* in 1972. It was later reprinted with slight addendum in 1974. R. J. Gordon (ed.), *Milton Friedman: Monetary Framework. A Debate with His Critics* (Chicago: University of Chicago Press, 1974).

I am grateful for helpful comments from M. Fleming, J. A. Kregel, B. J. Moore, and S. Weintraub. This paper evolves from a study on *Money and the Real World* which was supported by a grant from the Rutgers University Research Council.

framework with the 'Theory of a Monetary Economy' developed by Keynes.

Friedman's claim that his discussion of 'The Keynesian Challenge to the Quantity Theory' (ibid., pp. 206–17) 'does not misrepresent the body of his [Keynes's] analysis' (ibid., p. 210), even though a 'qualification' is neglected, is simply not true. Since Friedman has declared that a 'fair-minded reader' can be misled by Tobin's criticism of a model labelled Friedmanian but which 'ignores large parts of our argument' (Friedman, 1970b, p. 320), and since Friedman has asserted that Tobin has given a 'completely erroneous' impression via a 'straw man . . . a non-Friedmanian Friedman model that produces its effects by a myopic concentration on a single element out of a complex mosaic' (ibid., p. 327), fair play suggests that Friedman should not have attacked a straw-man version of the Keynesian system which others have, in the name of Keynes, erected, nor should he have ignored several important chapters in Keynes's *General Theory*.[1]

This is not the place either to put forth a complete Keynesian theoretical framework for analysing the role of money in the real world or to engage in a debate as to what Keynes 'really' meant;[2] space will permit only an enumeration of a few of what I believe are the more fundamental conceptual differences between Keynes's 'Theory of a Monetary Economy' and Friedman's framework. These distinctions can be readily viewed by focusing upon three aspects of Friedman's theoretical framework – namely, omissions, misspecifications, and false assertions about the nature of Keynes's model.

From the Keynesian view, the basic factors Friedman omits are:

1. The essence of uncertainty, in the Knightian sense (Keynes, 1936, p. 148, n. 1; pp. 293–4), so that decisions involving contractual commitments for future performance and payment are made by individuals who recognize that all anticipations cannot, and often will not, be realized.

2. The existence of particular market institutions, organizations, and constraints (for example, money contracts, the legal system, money, and sticky money-wage rates) which exist only because uncertainty is present (Keynes 1930, ch. 1; 1936, ch. 17). (Other institutions, such as the Walrasian auctioneer and flexible money-wages and prices, are not applicable, even as a logical construct to define the norm or trend around which the real world monetary-production economy fluctuates, as long as plans can be, and are, disappointed. Thus these institutions cannot be used to close logically the Keynesian system; they are logically inadmissible to the Keynesian model.)

3. The existence of money which, in an uncertain world, has a dual function – namely, a medium of exchange and a store of value. In a *modern*

monetary, production, specialization economy, money has two essential properties, namely (a) a zero (or negligible) elasticity of production and (b) a zero (or negligible) elasticity of substitution between money and any other good which has a high elasticity of production.[3] These two properties are necessary if an object is to possess liquidity (Keynes 1936, p. 241, n. 1). The existence of a money possessing these properties underlies Keynes's basic propositions that (a) as a purely theoretical matter, if there is uncertainty in a monetary, production economy, a long-run equilibrium position characterized by full employment of labour need not exist (ibid., pp. 30, 191, 235–6); (b) stickiness of the money-wage rate is necessary if money is to play its peculiar role in such an economy (ibid., pp. 238–9); and (c) if wages and prices are flexible, 'the quantity of money is, indeed, nugatory in the long period' (ibid., p. 191).[4]

In Friedman's framework, since *all expectations* are realized (Friedman 1970a, p. 223), and therefore there is no uncertainty, these essential properties are unimportant, since in such a world a rational economic man would never hold money for precautionary purposes (nor would there be any speculative motive, if, in fact, all men's expectations about the future rate of interest were always realized). If the future is uncertain, the quantity of money will be an important policy variable only if there is a *variety* of opinion about the perfidious future (Keynes, 1936, p. 172); if there is a variety of expectations, then some people's plans must be disappointed.

Within the Friedman framework, a Keynesian view would suggest misspecification of:

4. The demand function for money and the supply processes for altering the money supply.

Finally, from a Keynesian view, at least two of Friedman's assertions about Keynes's model are incompatible with the *General Theory*, specifically:

5. Keynes assumed that before full employment all adjustments to changes in demand take place via quantity changes (Friedman 1970a, pp. 209–10).

6. The price analysis underlying Keynes's model is 'arbitrary' and has 'no underpinning in economic theory' (ibid., p. 222).

1 KEYNES VERSUS FRIEDMAN ON THE PRICE LEVEL

Friedman's discussion of Keynes's view about prices ignores large parts of Keynes's argument as he developed it in chapters 20 and 21 of *The General Theory*. For example, Friedman (1970a, pp. 209–10) states, 'Keynes explored this penetrating insight by carrying it to the extreme: *all adjustment in quantity, none in price.* He qualified this statement *by assuming it to apply only to conditions of underemployment'* (italics added).

Even a cursory reading of chapters 20 and 21 of *The General Theory* would show that, in Keynes's view, money prices as well as output tended to vary with changes in demand, in the short run, at less than full employment. In these chapters, Keynes develops various elasticity concepts, such as the elasticity of output e_o, the elasticity of money prices e_p, and the elasticity of money wages e_w, which represent proportionate changes in the various variables for a given proportionate change in effective demand. The change in money prices for any given relative change in demand is given by the formula, $e_p = 1 - e_o - (1 - e_w)$ (Keynes, 1936, p. 285). Thus, unless $e_o = 1$ and $e_w = 0$, prices will show some change for any given change in demand. Indeed, throughout *The General Theory*, Keynes maintained that at less than full employment an 'increase in effective demand will, generally speaking, spend itself partly in increasing the quantity of employment and partly in raising the level of prices' (ibid., p. 296).

Therefore, Friedman is in error when he suggests that Keynes used a 'rigid price assumption' which is 'arbitrary. It is entirely a *deus ex machina* with no underpinning in economic theory' (Friedman 1970a, p. 222). Keynes's 'Theory of Prices' (Keynes, 1936, ch. 21) was, of course, firmly based on those 'homely and intelligible' theoretical concepts 'the conditions of supply and demand; and in particular, changes in marginal cost and the elasticity of short-period supply' (ibid., p. 292). One of the explicit objectives of *The General Theory* was 'to bring the theory of prices as a whole back to close contact with the theory of value' (ibid., p. 293). Keynes skilfully constructed the elasticities of output, wages, and prices from traditional price theory concepts.[5] Empirical estimates of these elasticities (see Weintraub and Habibagahi, 1971) would go a long way toward answering some of the questions on the adjustment process which Friedman raises in the concluding section of his paper (Friedman 1970a, p. 234). Unfortunately, such elasticity concepts are not specified at all in Friedman's framework; therefore, before economists rush off to heed Friedman's request for 'a more subtle examination of the record . . . to disentangle what is systematic from what is random and erratic' (ibid., p. 235), it is essential that the relevant theoretical constructs to be estimated from the record be agreed upon.

Unlike Keynes, Friedman (ibid., p. 222) bases his quantity theory approach to price-level phenomena on the Walrasian equations. Although the Walrasian system may have a long history in the economic literature, and therefore Friedman's approach is not open to the charge of blatant arbitrariness which Friedman (ibid.) levels against Keynes,[6] the theoretical foundation underlying the Walrasian equations is, from a Keynesian point of view, not applicable to any analysis of a monetary production economy (Keynes, 1963, pp. 8–9; Clower, 1965; Jaffé, 1967, pp. 9–13; Hahn, 1970, p. 3; 1971, p. 417).

2   THE CRUX OF THE MONEY MATTER: UNCERTAINTY, CONTRACTS, AND THE MONEY-WAGE RATE

What Friedman and so many other modern monetarists have failed to grasp is that Keynes utilized a 'wage unit' and postulated the stickiness of the money-wage rate not simply, as Friedman (1970a, p. 220) claims, logically to close the system or to rationalize wage rigidity because 'something had to be brought in from the outside to fix the price level; it might as well be institutional wage rigidity' (ibid., p. 209); rather Keynes (1936, p. 239) was attempting to deal with a vital logical condition for a viable monetary system, as well as an obvious fact of life.

In a world of uncertainty where production takes time, the existence of money contracts permits the sharing of the burdens of uncertainty between the contracting parties whenever resources are to be committed to produce a flow of goods for a delivery date in the future. Such contractual commitments (for example, hire contracts and forward-offer, or supply, contracts) are, by definition, tied to such flow-supply concepts as the flow-supply price. Ultimately, underlying the flow-supply price is the relationship between money-wage rates and productivity phenomena. If individuals are to utilize money as a temporary abode of purchasing power, either because they expect to accept delivery of a reproducible good in the very near future or because they desire a vehicle for transferring purchasing power to the more remote and indefinite future, then these economic units must have *confidence* that no matter how far the current spot price for any reproducible good may be momentarily displaced by spot market conditions,[7] the market price for the good will be at some anticipated level at a future date.[8] As long as the flow-supply price is sticky (that is, the annual rate of change in the money-wage rate relative to productivity is small), individuals 'know' they can, whenever they desire, accept a contract offering the good at a delivered money price *not* significantly different from today's money flow-supply price, at a future date. Accordingly, the existence of money as an asset with negligible carrying costs, stickiness in the money-wage rate, and the availability of contracting in money terms for performance at future dates permits individuals, at any moment of time, to delay decisions which would necessitate exercising their currently earned claims on resources.

Keynes was not using a handy institutional rigidity which was due to a friction or a readily correctable imperfection in the labour market to close his system. A 'perfect' labour market with flexible prices would be incompatible with a system where there are contracts, and money is used as a store of value, except under the most stable conditions of demand and supply where all prices remained basically unchanged over time.[9] If the number of units of money which labour is willing to buy for a given unit of effort, the money-wage rate, fluctuates rapidly every time there is a small change in demand, there will be no asset whose liquidity premium always exceeds its carrying costs[10] (a situation which Keynes (1936, p. 239) notes is the 'best definition' for a 'non-monetary economy'). *'The importance of money essentially flows from its being a link between the present and the future'* (ibid., p. 293), and this link can exist only if there is a continuity over time in contractual commitments in money units. The synchronous existence of money and money contracts over the uncertain future where change is inevitable *and* unpredictable is the basis of a monetary system whose maxim is: *'Money buys goods and goods buy money; but goods do not buy goods'* (Clower, 1969).

In a neoclassical world of perfect certainty and perfect markets, with a Walrasian auctioneer assuring simultaneous equilibrium at a given point of time, it would of course be foolish to hold money as a store of value as long as other assets provided a certain positive yield (Samuelson, 1947, pp. 122–4). In the absence of uncertainty, neoclassical theory has room neither for contracts nor for the store-of-value function of money. Some modern theorists – finding the real world does not possess either the perfect certainty, flexible wages and prices, complete absence of disappointment, or the ability to recontract characteristics of their theoretical norms – 'resemble Euclidean geometers, in a non-Euclidean world who, discovering that in experience straight lines apparently parallel often meet, rebuke the lines for not keeping straight – as the only remedy for the unfortunate collisions which are occurring' (Keynes, 1936, p. 16).

Keynes's challenge to the quantity theory as a useful analytical tool is significantly different from the 'Keynesian Challenge to the Quantity Theory' which Friedman (1970a, pp. 206–17) presents. Keynes was the first important economist to accuse bluntly the neoclassical view of the nature of money as foolish. Keynes (1947, pp. 186–7) wrote: 'Money, it is well known, serves two principal purposes . . . it facilitates exchanges . . . In the second place, it is a store of wealth. So we are told, without a smile on the face. But in the world of the classical economy, what an insane use to which to put it! For it is a recognized characteristic of money as a store of wealth that it is barren . . . Why should anyone outside a lunatic asylum wish to use money as a store of wealth?'

His answer to this rhetorical question was clear and unequivocal (ibid., p. 187): 'Our desire to hold money as a store of wealth is a barometer of the degree of our distrust of our own calculations and conventions concerning the future . . . The possession of actual money lulls our disquietude.' Distrust? Disquietude? These are states of mind[11] impossible in a

world of certainty (that is, even in a world where the sum of the probabilities equals unity).

All Walrasian general equilibrium models imply worlds of certainty. The
tâtonnement process, which is essential to the establishment of equilibrium
and implies no transactions occur until equilibrium is attained (that is,
recontracting is essential),[12] implies that anyone holding money either at
any point in the auction or till the next market period is demented or at
least economically irrational. Why hold money if it is not needed for
transactions, since in equilibrium goods trade for goods, and since the
present and future values of all economic goods can be determined, at least
in a probability sense, with complete certainty? The essential nature of
money is disregarded in the Walrasian system, as no asset exists whose
liquidity premium always exceeds its carrying costs (Davidson, 1969,
p. 319). As Hahn (1970, p. 3) has recently admitted, '*The Walrasian
economy* that we have been considering, although one where the auctioneer regulates the terms at which goods shall exchange, *is essentially one of
barter*' (italics added).

Friedman (1970a, p. 222) explicitly states that his quantity theory of
money relies upon and is 'summarized in the Walrasian equations of
general equilibrium'. He acknowledges that in long-run equilibrium in his
view 'all anticipations are realized . . . [and that he regards] the long-run
equilibrium as determined by the earlier quantity theory plus the Walrasian equations of general equilibrium' (ibid., p. 223). It is difficult to
understand, therefore, from a Keynesian point of view, why the resources
of so many economists have been wasted on Walrasian models[13] in general,
and quantity theory models in particular, where the latter make a fetish
about the importance of the rate of growth of the quantity of money. If the
Walrasian equations – which describe a barter economy, an economy
where 'money can play no essential role' (Hahn, 1971, p. 417) – is the
logical norm or trend around which Friedman believes the actual world
fluctuates, then the quantity of money is indeed nugatory.

It is the fact that money is a means of deferring decisions about the use of
claims on resources which underlies Keynes's objection to Say's Law. In a
world of uncertainty, he who hesitates to spend his current claims is saved
to make a decision another day. A decision to save, in Keynes's view, is not
a decision to 'consume any specified thing at any specified date' (Keynes,
1936, p. 210). Above all, individual savings decisions in a modern *monetary*
economy do not involve the current purchase of newly produced consumer
durables in order to obtain a stream of utility over time, as Friedman has
often implied. Instead, the decision to save merely requires the individual
to decide whether to hold his claims in immediate liquid command
(money) or to part with command and leave it to spot market conditions at
a future date to determine on what terms he can convert this deferred
command back into immediate command (ibid., p. 166).[14] Consequently,

as long as the spot markets for 'titles' to real capital goods are better organized than the spot markets for the hire purchase of reproducible capital goods, economic units will choose titles rather than demand real capital as a vehicle for transferring purchasing power over time (see Davidson, 1968, pp. 302–4; Davidson, 1969, pp. 302–4). Thus, as the discussion of portfolio changes in the next section will explain, exogenous changes in the money supply will *not* directly spill over into changes in the demand for reproducible durables.

In sum, in an uncertain world, income earners will often be temporarily satiated or completely occupied with their recently purchased economic goods, or even preoccupied with non-economic affairs, and thus may be currently unable or unwilling to predict what specific goods they will need at specific dates in the future; they may feel queasy about undertaking any contractual actions which will commit current earned claims on resources onto a path which can be altered, if future events prove necessary, only at very high costs, if at all. Recognition of this motivation to save in order to avoid the commitment of claims on resources provided Keynes the insight necessary to describe the social institutions associated with money, as well as the essential properties of anything which will fulfil the two equally important functions of money – namely, a generally accepted medium of exchange, and a store of value in a *modern, monetary, production-oriented, but uncertain world*.

The vital properties of anything which will fulfil the functional requirements of money are:

1. A zero (or negligible) elasticity of production, so that if individuals, uncertain about the future, want to defer additional commitments of resources, their increased demand for money as a mode for postponing action will not encourage entrepreneurs to employ additional resources in the production of additional quantities of the money commodity.
2. A zero (or negligible) elasticity of substitution between money and any other asset which has a *high* elasticity of production, so that if individuals want to preserve additional options for action for the future, the increase in the price of money induced by an increase in the demand for money as a store of value does not divert people into substituting other assets, which have high elasticities of production, as a store of value. Hence, because of these elasticities, the demand for a store of value in the form of money in an uncertain world does not generate the demand to commit resources and the virtuous interaction between supply of resources and the demand for resources, succinctly expressed via Say's Law, is broken.
3. The cost of transferring money from the medium-of-exchange function to the store-of-value function, or vice versa, must be zero (or negligible) so that individuals do not find it expensive to defer decisions or to

change their minds. Minimizing their transactions costs requires the existence of at least two economic institutions: (a) offer and debt contracts denominated in money units, and (b) legal enforcement of such contracts. An additional contribution to the minimizing of such transactions costs is the presence of an institution – namely, a clearing system – which permits using private debt contracts in the settlement of transactions as long as it is expected that the private debt can be promptly converted into the form of money which is enforceable in the discharge of contracts.

Thus, the main characteristic of a real world monetary economy are Uncertainty, Fallibility, Covenants, Institutions, Commerce, Finance, and Trust. These are the Seven Wonders on which the *Modern* World is based.

3   THE DEMAND AND SUPPLY OF MONEY

A Keynesian view of Friedman's theoretical framework would suggest that Friedman's demand function for money is misspecified, while some important aspects of the supply of money in a modern bank-money economy suffer from benign neglect.

The various forms of the demand-for-money function which relate the quantity of money demanded to income (Friedman, 1970a, eq. (6), (12)) are an acceptable first approximation for the correct demand-for-money relationship only if the problem being analysed assumes there is *no change* in the aggregate demand for goods, but only a change in the quantity of goods demanded. Although Keynes (1936, p. 199) specified a similar demand-for-money function in one section of his *General Theory* as a 'safe first approximation', Ohlin (1937) was quick to point out the deficiencies of such a demand function for money. Keynes (1937, p. 667) was forced to admit that this form of the demand for money was misspecified:[15] 'I allowed, it is true, for the effect of an increase in *actual* activity on the demand for money. But I did not allow for the effect of an increase in *planned* activity, which is superimposed on the former.'

Keynes then retreated to his much more carefully detailed *Treatise* analysis of the demand for money, and as I have shown elsewhere, this properly specified demand – which includes the finance motive – has important ramifications for observed differences between the short-run and long-run income elasticity of demand for money (Davidson, 1965, pp. 53–5, the interdependence of the real and monetary sectors (ibid., pp. 57–60), and the path of economic expansion (ibid., pp 61–2). Thus, from a Keynesian point of view, Friedman's demand function for money which omits *planned* expenditures as a specific independent variable can lead to wrong theoretical constructs and policy implications.[16]

On the supply side, the essential characteristic of a zero elasticity of production immediately determines the market supply behaviour of producers of the money commodity in a bank money economy. Thus if one is to specify properly how changes in the supply of money come about, he must relate them to the relevant banking institutions and operations which bring forth money, even though the elasticity of production is zero. In the real world, Keynes (1930, p. 3) reminds us at the very beginning of his *Treatise on Money*, money 'comes into existence along with debts, which are contracts for deferred payment and . . . offers of contracts for sale or purchase', that is, the supply of money, and debt and production-offer contracts are intimately and inevitably related. From a Keynesian viewpoint, money does not enter the system like manna from heaven, or dropped from the sky via a helicopter, or from the application of additional resources to the production of the money commodity. The supply of money in a modern economy can increase only via two distinct processes – both of which are related to contracts. It is these processes and not the shadows on the cave wall[17] of the banking institutions through which these processes operate which are the focal point of the Keynesian view about the supply of money.[18]

In the first case, which may be called the income-generating finance process, an increased desire to buy more reproducible goods per period – the finance motive – induces individuals, firms, governments, or foreigners to enter into additional debt contracts with the banking system. If these contracts are accepted by the banking system, then additional private debts of banks are issued and used to accept additional offer contracts of producers and workers.

In the second method, the portfolio-change process, the banking system removes assets which have a negligible elasticity of production (specifically securities) from the wealth holdings of the general public by offering private bank-debt contracts as an alternate store of value at a rate of exchange which members of the public find very favourable.[19]

In the income-generating finance process, increased desire for the hire purchase of capital goods (or even consumer durables), exports purchases by foreigners, or government expenditures by legislators can provoke money demanders (money holders) to initiate the process which produces an increase in the quantity of money, as long as banks are willing to make additional bank-debt contracts available under the rules of the game (and, of course, it is in the self-interest of each banker to do so). This endogenous increase in the money supply is initially used to accept additional offer contracts (as long as some resources are idle). Depending on the supply elasticities of the various industries stimulated, and therefore the aforementioned elasticities of Keynes's price formula, changes in real income and/or prices will be observed to follow (with varying time-lags) this endogenous change in the money supply.

In the portfolio-change process, on the other hand, changes in the money supply are immediately used by the general public as a substitute for securities as a vehicle for transferring purchasing power to the indefinite uncertain future. If both money and securities have zero or negligible elasticities of production, and if they are very good substitutes for each other as store of value while they exhibit very low elasticities of substitution with respect to all other goods which have high elasticities of production, then the exogenous increase in quantity of money via this process will not directly stimulate any additional demand for resource use. Thus, exogenous increases in the money supply due to open-market operations initiated by the Monetary Authority can increase the demand for resource-using reproducible capital goods only via the usual Keynesian effect of lowering the discount rate used by firms to evaluate the expected stream of future quasi-rents from potential investment projects, or by reducing the amount of credit rationing to a previously unsatisfied fringe of borrowers (or, perhaps even by altering long-term expectations of quasi-rents).

Friedman and other monetarists, however, suggest that exogenous increases in the money supply, via open-market operations for example, may not only operate via the traditional Keynesian interest rate mechanism on the demand for hire purchase of real capital goods, but will also increase, *pari passu*, the demand for household durables. The increased demand for consumer durables is due to (1) a real balance or wealth effect and/or (2) a portfolio-balance effect. This latter effect, it is claimed, is a result of economic units finding that the proportion of their portfolio which they hold as money is excessive, and therefore they display an infinite (or very high) elasticity of substitution between money and *resource-using reproducible durables* as components of their portfolios (Friedman and Schwartz, 1963, pp. 60–1; Moore, 1968, p. 228). Keynes (1936, pp. 93, 319), of course, recognized that windfall capital gains (due to the open-market operations) could affect the propensity to consume durables and non-durables, although there is little evidence to suggest this plays a major role in increasing the demand for consumer durables. On the other hand, Keynes would reject the implications of the portfolio-balance effect, namely the notion that resource-using reproducible durables are a good substitute for money as a component of one's portfolio – for this would violate one of the essential properties of money. Thus, another fundamental conceptual difference between Keynes on the one hand, and Friedman and the portfolio-balance monetarists on the other, is the magnitude of the elasticity of substitution between money (and financial assets) and *resource-using reproducible durables* as vehicles for transferring purchasing power to the uncertain future.[20]

The low elasticity of substitution between financial assets including money and reproducible durable goods requires two necessary conditions: (1) the money-wage be sticky so that the liquidity premium of money exceeds its carrying cost, while the contractual obligations underlying the securities are safe stores of value (see Keynes, 1936, p. 207; Davidson, 1969, pp. 317–18); and (2) as I have demonstrated elsewhere, the existence of uncertainty and significantly greater transaction and carrying costs associated with the spot market for the hire purchase of physical goods relative to the costs associated with the spot market for titles to physical goods (Davidson, 1968, p. 303; 1969, p. 302–3). The lower the transactions and carrying costs in the spot market for 'titles', the larger the elasticity of substitution between money and securities. Simultaneously, the lower these costs which are associated with money and securities, the closer to zero the elasticity of substitution between these financial assets and reproducible physical goods. (As long as money-wage rates are sticky!)

Hence, in the Keynesian system, changes in the quantity of money occurring via the income-generating finance process will be associated with, to use Friedman's symbols, changes in y, while changes in money due to the portfolio-change process will be directly associated with changes in k. Thus not only do changes in the quantity of money matter, when viewed through Keynesian glasses, but what brings about these changes is also important.

4 EPILOGUE

In sum, a view through Keynesian glasses highlights certain characteristics – uncertainty, sticky money-wage rates, contracts, carrying and transactions costs, zero elasticities of production and substitution for money – which interact to make a monetary economy function quite differently from one described by the Walrasian general equilibrium analysis which ultimately underlies Friedman's theoretical construct. In a Keynesian world, contracts and a sticky money-wage rate are essential to the viability and stability of an economic system. As Keynes (1936, p. 269) observed: 'The chief result of . . . [a flexible money-wage] policy would be to cause a great instability of prices, so violent perhaps as to make business calculations futile in an economic society functioning after the manner in which we live. To suppose that a flexible wage policy is a right and proper adjunct of a system which on the whole is one of laissez-faire, is the opposite of the truth.'

Thus it is obvious that Keynes's conclusions are significantly different from those which Friedman derives from his framework. In this paper, I have tried to explain what I believe are some of the conceptual differences which bring about these contrasting views. A fruitful further exchange of ideas will be enhanced, if, in his rejoinder, Friedman devotes some space to:

(a) indicating why his framework, which assumes a completely exogenous money supply (Friedman, 1971, p. 329) is preferable to a Keynesian analysis which, when the finance motive and elasticity properties of money are included, permits money-supply changes to be endogenous under certain circumstances and exogenous under others;

(b) indicating why he prefers to describe the long-run norm or trend about which the actual world fluctuates via a system of Walrasian equations since this mathematical system will describe a unique norm only if there are no false trades and no disappointments while, in the real world, disappointment and false transactions are a recognized fact of life (and are taken into account in Keynes's system);

(c) indicating why a framework which determines the price level by imposing an exogenous money supply onto a logical construct of a non-monetary economy (the Walrasian equations) is preferable to Keynes's 'Theory of Prices', which makes the money price level of the flow of output dependent on the Marshallian concepts of demand and flow-supply prices;

(d) indicating why he prefers a framework which never deals specifically with the finance motive and instead buries it in a portmanteau variable (as if the fact that businessmen often obtain financial contractual commitments from banks before ordering investment goods is a relatively unimportant factor in the demand for money) rather than adopting the Keynesian demand for money which specifically accounts for the demand for finance (and which also specifies the precautionary motive as the basic reason for the demand for money as a store of value).

A positive response by Professor Friedman on these aspects will lead to further discoveries and a shift of view on both sides in response to difficulties and objections. If, on the other hand, Friedman avoids these issues and instead protests that I have either misinterpreted Keynes, or utilized some uncoordinate, shrewd (or wrong) side comments of Keynes which are peripheral to Keynes's 'Theory of a Monetary Economy', then it will be up to fair-minded readers to judge for themselves whether Keynes's writings on the essential properties of money, the theory of prices, the finance motive, uncertainty and the precautionary motive, etc., are trivial or whether they do add up to a fundamentally different paradigm involving significantly different conclusions. Ultimately, I am sure, time rather than controversy will separate the true from the false.

Notes

1. Specifically chaps. 12, 17, 20, and 21. Unfortunately, Friedman is guilty of the same fault he attributes to Tobin, namely, that although he 'looks at everything through different glasses . . . he [Friedman] takes it for granted that we [all

economists] wear the same glasses he does' (Friedman 1970b, p. 322). Without polling all economists, it is impossible to find out how many hold theoretical views about money which differ significantly from those currently presented by Friedman and many so-called Keynesians. I would suggest that Keynes, Shackle, Clower, R. F. Kahn, Champernowne, Harrod, Minsky, Hines, J. Robinson, Kaldor, Weintraub, and I are only a few of those who have, in print, viewed monetary phenomena through different coloured glasses than Friedman offers in his current article.

2. In this symposium, I can only highlight some aspects which I believe to be critical to Keynes's theory. I am working on a monograph, *Money and the Real World* (to be published by Macmillan) which will develop and set forth Keynes's entire analytical framework of *The General Theory* and the *Treatise on Money* and its implications for modern economic growth theory.

3. 'A zero elasticity [of production and of substitution] is a more stringent condition than is necessarily required' (Keynes 1936, p. 236, n. 1). Those who do not believe that Keynes said these elasticities are essential properties of money should look in the index to *The General Theory* under 'Money – its essential properties', where references are made to (1) the entire chap. 17 entitled, 'The Essential Properties of Interest and Money', and to (2) page 293 where these properties are specifically linked to disappointed expectations. (I will leave it to the economic historians to resolve whether these properties were associated with wampum or cowrie shells; and if not, whether these trinkets actually performed the dual functions of money. Certainly, both Friedman's framework – which explicitly states that the supply of money depends 'critically' on banking factors (Friedman 1970a, p. 208) – and Keynes's model are developed to deal primarily with bank-money economies where these elasticities are relevant. Whether either framework would deal with 'wampum economies' where there were no well-organized spot markets for securities, and therefore no speculative motive, is an interesting digression, but it should not distract from the basic issues of this symposium – namely, the differences of the two frameworks for analysing modern monetary economies.)

4. Friedman 'summarily' dismisses propositions (a) and (b) as already having been proved false while ignoring proposition (c) altogether (Friedman 1970a, p. 206). The rejection of propositions (a) and (b) depend either on defining equilibrium as synonymous with market clearing instead of in the usual sense of the term that nothing changes in the system (Davidson 1967, pp. 563–4), or by assuming some variant of a Pigou effect based on expectation of future money-wage and price changes in a world where *all* expectations are realized. If, however, Friedman had analysed the concept of money by its essential properties within a framework where expectations can be disappointed, he would have noted that a dismissal of propositions *a* and *b* is unwarranted.

5. Some may say that Keynes's price formula is a mere truism (derived from the definition of the Marshallian short-period supply price schedule) and that such elasticities by themselves are empty empirically and theoretically, since they involve the pure arithmetic of adding up all the components that make up the general price level. But how else can one proceed intellectually, unless one accounts for all the components of the price level? The function of a theoretical framework then is to explain the relationships between all the various components after they have been specifically identified, to indicate which components are active and which are passive, to suggest under what conditions components will change endogenously and when they will change exogenously. For example, in Keynes's model, observed changes in money wages could be either a response to change in demand if $e_w > 0$, or it could be a result of the social and political struggle to alter the relative money wage structure (Keynes, 1936, pp.

13–14); consequently money-wage changes may be partly exogenous. Thus, Keynes recognized that 'if there are strong social or political forces causing spontaneous changes in the money-rates of efficiency wages, the control of the price level may pass beyond the power of the banking system' (Keynes, 1930, p. 351), a result which is impossible in the Friedman framework in which money wages are completely endogenous!

6. Although Friedman's assertion about the lack of theoretical underpinning is not applicable to Keynes's analytical framework, it is pertinent to the 'neo-classical synthesis' framework developed by many American 'Keynesians'. Friedman indicates his indebtedness to Leijonhufvud's (1968) 'brilliant book' and then he disregards the main thesis of this book, namely, that there is a world of difference between the monetary economics of Keynes and that of the American 'Keynesians'. Keynes (1936, p. 32) would reject the assumption that the price level was determined outside the system, a postulate Friedman (1970a, p. 220) claims is a logical necessity in Keynes's analysis.

7. Since Friedman (1970a, p. 199) insists that the income version of the quantity theory completely excludes transactions involving existing assets, and since it is the income version which he propounds, therefore he has rejected analysing spot prices – the only prices in the real world which might promptly change with respect to every change in demand, since these market prices are not directly related to flow-supply elasticity concepts. Thus Friedman has excluded from his analysis the main type of real world markets for which his flexible-price assumption might have some relevance.

8. In a world of uncertainty, the forward price (which can never exceed the flow-supply price) (Kaldor, 1960, p. 35) is the best estimate of the spot price at the future date (Working, 1962, pp. 446–7). Thus, if production is occurring and if the flow-supply prices of goods (that is, money-wage costs plus profit margins) are sticky, then they are reliable estimates of future costs of buying such goods either spot or forward; and therefore, the flow-supply prices are, in Friedman's language, the set of prices used in the calculation to determine the desired real quantity of money at any future date (see Friedman, 1970a, p. 194).

9. Friedman may claim that flexibility need not imply instability as long as demand and supply functions are relatively stable over time, for then the money wage can be theoretically flexible as long as in the actual world it is really sticky. If this is Friedman's position, there is little conflict between him and Keynes about the desirability of sticky money wages (although if, in the real world, either money wages get unstuck or involuntary unemployment occurs, Keynes and Friedman would recommend different policies to restore full-employment stability). Nevertheless, Friedman would require the further assumption that labour demand relative to labour supply (adjusted for pro-ductivity) is actually stable over time, but as indicated below (see n. 13), the existence of 'false transactions' in the real world alters the parameters of any Walrasian system and thereby alters the demand and supply functions and the set of equilibrium prices. Thus, in the real world of uncertainty and false trades, it is unlikely that the demand and supply of labour in a Walrasian system which describes the trend of the actual world will be stable over any length of time.

10. As a supplement to a sticky-money wage policy, Keynes (1936, p. 270) suggested that the authorities permit fluctuating (*not flexible*) exchange rates in order to maintain external equilibrium and prevent conditions in the foreign sector from jeopardizing the domestic economy. This policy is consistent with

Keynes's views on the undesirability of flexibility in an uncertain world; Keynes was advocating that the authorities permit slow wavelike fluctuations (perhaps a crawling peg or controlled small annual rates of change?) rather than either adhering to a rigid parity policy (Keynes, 1936, p. 339) or withdrawing from the exchange markets and permitting prompt changes in exchange rates to occur in response to every change, ephemeral or otherwise, in the foreign sector. *In an uncertain world*, there will only be an accidental matching of buyers and sellers in any exchange market at any point of time – no matter how well organized. Thus, unless there is an institution – a residual buyer and seller – willing to step in and make a market whenever one side or the other temporarily falls away, the exchange rate can vary violently. Such mercurial movements would add additional uncertainty in undertaking any long-term international contractual commitments or in using foreign currencies as a temporary abode of purchasing power by multinational corporations. Hence, if foreign exchange markets do not have institutions which limit the day-to-day rate at which parities can alter, the additional uncertainty in the foreign sector would reduce the offers and acceptances of supply contracts for forward delivery and payment with foreigners and this would create unemployment and disruption in the foreign sector.

11. These states of mind emphasize the precautionary motive, and not the speculative motive, as the fundamental reason for demanding money as a store of value under uncertainty (see Keynes, 1936, pp. 170–2; and n. 15 below). Friedman, on the other hand, implies that Keynes thought that the speculative motive was the only reason for demanding money because of uncertainty and therefore Friedman puts great emphasis on 'absolute liquidity preference', that is, a highly elastic speculative demand function as 'the key element' in the Keynesian system (Friedman, 1970a, pp. 212–15). This total absorption in the shape of the speculative demand function may correctly characterize some 'Keynesian' models which produce their effects by a myopic concentration on a single element out of a complex mosaic, but it is not a complete or accurate representation of Keynes's view on the demand for money as a store of value in an uncertain world.

12. In his analysis of the Walrasian system, Jaffé (1967, p. 12) has underscored the fact that a production economy provides a 'complication' for the system which can only be resolved by a complete 'abandonment of reality'. If some production occurs in response to non-equilibrium prices (and I assume Friedman would not deny that this does occur in the actual world) then the effect of such 'false transactions' is to change the parameters of the system and thereby assure that 'whatever equilibrium the market converges to – if it converges at all – must be different from the equilibrium that would result if there were no change in the original parameters' (Jaffé, 1967, p. 9). This 'complication' can be avoided, according to Jaffé (ibid., p. 14), if it is assumed that all production and consumption plans are always realized. This assumption is, of course, explicitly utilized by Friedman (1970a, p. 223), but the use of such an assumption is, as Jaffé (1967, p. 14) has stated, simply an ingenious means for 'contriving market models to elucidate mathematical systems instead of developing mathematical models to elucidate market systems'.

If false transactions and disappointments are, in the actual world, continuously occurring and thereby inducing continuous changes in the parameters of any Walrasian system which purports to be representative of the long-run trend of the real world, then the resulting Walrasian system, if there is one, would fluctuate around the path of the actual world and not vice versa. It is as if every time air friction caused a falling body to fall at less than $\frac{1}{2} gt^2$ in the real world, the value of the gravitational constant for the perfect vacuum case would change!

This is, of course, precisely why Keynes (1963) indicated it was necessary to develop a 'Theory of a Monetary Economy' which differed substantially from the framework of a 'Real-exchange Economy'. He stressed that the differences between a 'Monetary Economy' and a 'Real-exchange Economy' had been greatly underestimated and that the "machinery of thought" of the latter (in modern parlance, the Walrasian equational system) leads economists to erroneous conclusions; the belief that it is easy to adapt the conclusions of the latter 'to the real world of Monetary Economics is a mistake. It is extraordinarily difficult to make the adaptation, and perhaps impossible without the aid of a developed theory of Monetary Economics' (Keynes, 1963, pp. 8–9).

13. One theorist who has engaged in such activities admitted that 'there is something scandalous in the spectacle of so many people refining the analysis of economic states which they give no reason to suppose will ever, or have ever, come about. . . . It must now, I fear, be admitted that the study of the Walrasian "grouping" [sic] or tatonnement process has not been very fruitful' (Hahn, 1970, pp. 1–2). It is indeed an astonishing intellectual achievement to be able to utilize a framework which assumes a grouping process to obtain equilibrium and simultaneously assumes perfect knowledge about all future markets!

14. In the absence of well-organized spot markets for durables with elasticities similar to money, Keynes (1936, p. 171) believed 'liquidity preference due to the precautionary motive would be greatly increased, whereas the existence of an organized market gives an opportunity for wide fluctuations in liquidity preference due to the speculative motive'. The existence of spot securities markets permits a speculative motive to interact with the basic precautionary motive. Hence, for Keynes, any event which creates uncertainty – for example, large increases in the money supply or, alternatively, rapidly falling money wages and prices (with a constant nominal money supply) – will affect the demand for money via the precautionary reason, speculative reason, or both; therefore, if such events increase the precautionary demand, they may have little effect on the rate of interest even if the speculative demand is not very elastic (see Keynes, 1936, p. 172). Thus Friedman's discussion of a 'Keynesian' system which virtually ignores the precautionary motive and instead emphasizes "absolute liquidity preference" in the form of a highly elastic speculative demand is a straw man, a non-Keynes Keynesian model, a perversion of Keynes's own views about liquidity preference.

15. Friedman (1971) presents a new and 'superior' way for specifying the demand-for-money function and closing his theoretical system. In this new version, Friedman has adopted, after years of debate and acrimony, the demand function for money specified on page 199 of Keynes's *General Theory*. Unfortunately, this is the function which Keynes in his finance motive analysis was quick to recognize as misspecified and as such distracting economists' attention from the important role of money. Despite Friedman's recent conversion to Keynes's view about the demand for money, this latest paper (Friedman, 1971) is still deficient from a Keynesian view for it relies on (a) a Fisherian distinction between real and monetary rates of interest which Keynes (1936, pp. 142–3) properly rejected as confusing the effect of inflationary expectations on the marginal efficiency of capital for an effect on the rate of interest; (b) an assumption that all 'permanent' anticipated real values are unchanged during the period under analysis – that is, anticipations about nominal income, real growth, and the real rate of interest are either predetermined or exogenous and

these anticipations are 'firmly held' so that, in essence all changes in the variables are foreseen from the beginning (inconsistent with Keynes's conception of uncertainty) – and (c) the assumptions that the money supply 'can be regarded as completely exogenous' and that the income elasticity of demand for money is unity (both assumptions are incompatible with Keynes's finance motive analysis) (Davidson, 1965).

Even in Friedman's hands, his new 'superior' monetary theory crumbles into a dichotomized model where the unknowns of the real sector (real consumption, investment, income, the realized real rate of interest) are determined by a self-contained subset of equations independent of the quantity of money – so that in Friedman's latest version the quantity of money is indeed nugatory! (In fairness, it should be pointed out that Friedman rejects the dichotomy of the real and monetary sectors implied in his analysis and regards the marrying of the real variables with his nominal analysis as 'unfinished business'; he admits that he 'has nothing to say directly about the division of changes in nominal income between prices and quantity'. Since Keynes's model does make the monetary sector an integral and inseparable part of the real sector, in a world of uncertainty, and since Keynes does discuss the division of changes in effective demand between prices and quantities, why not return to Keynes's original analysis?)

16. Of course, one cannot literally accuse Friedman of omitting anything from his demand-for-money function (Friedman, 1970a, eq. (7)), since this equation contains a portmanteau variable which is a proxy for all things that might conceivably affect the demand for money. Nevertheless, nowhere in his framework does Friedman specifically deal with the finance demand for money; and even his use of the symbol u for the portmanteau variable at the end of his equation (7) implies that Friedman views this variable as similar to an error term which results from the interaction of a very large number of independent factors, each of which have a very small effect on the dependent variable. Keynes, on the other hand, believed that the finance motive was 'the coping stone' of his liquidity theory.

17. Namely, the observed movements of high-powered money, deposits, and currency.

18. Since Friedman defines money as including demand deposits *and* time deposits – both evidence of debt on the part of banks – he can hardly deny that the processes which change the volume of these private debt contracts are the primary mechanisms for changing the money supply in a modern economy.

19. Both the income-generating finance process and the portfolio process can be reversed to alter the supply of money. If, for example, the public wishes to reduce its demand for reproducible goods, it may use some of its monetary claims to extinguish existing debts to the banking system. If the banks then do not utilize the portfolio-change process to replace the money being turned into the banking system, then the money supply available to the general public will decline as the demand for money declines.

20. If consumer durables are conceived as good substitutes for money as a component of households' portfolios, it must be because consumer durables provide the service of liquidity similar to money. Such durables could conceivably provide a store of liquidity services only if there are spot markets for consumer durables available at future dates which will permit the holder to convert consumer durables back into the medium of exchange *and* the costs of transacting in such markets are not more than the cost of transacting in 'titles' to such reproducible durables. (See Davidson 1968, 1969, for a further discussion of why these conditions will not be met.)

References

Clower, R. W. (1965), 'The Keynesian Counter-Revolution: A Theoretical Appraisal', in *The Theory of Interest Rates*, edited by F. H. Hahn and F. Brechling (London: Macmillan).

Clower, R. W. (1969), 'A Reconsideration of the Microfoundations of Monetary Theory', in *Monetary Theory*, edited by R. W. Clower (Harmondsworth: Penguin). (Original in *Western Economic Journal* 6 (December 1967), pp. 1–8.)

Davidson, P. (1965), 'Keynes's Finance Motive', *Oxford Economic Papers*, 17 (March), pp. 47–65 (chapter 1 in this volume).

Davidson, P. (1967), 'A Keynesian View of Patinkin's Theory of Employment', *Economic Journal*, 77 (September), pp. 559–78.

Davidson, P. (1968), 'Money, Portfolio Balance, Capital Accumulation, and Economic Growth', *Econometrica*, 36 (April), pp. 291–321 (chapter 3 in this volume).

Davidson, P. (1969), 'A Keynesian View of the Relationship Between Accumulation, Money and the Money-Wage Rate', *Economic Journal*, 79 (June), pp. 300–23.

Friedman, M. (1970a), 'A Theoretical Framework for Monetary Analysis', J.P.E. 78 (March/April), pp. 193–238.

Friedman, M. (1970b), 'Comment on Tobin', Q.J.E. 84 (May), pp. 318–27.

Friedman, M. (1971), 'A Monetary Theory of Nominal Income', J.P.E. 79 (March/April), pp. 323–37.

Friedman, M. and A. Schwartz J. (1963), 'Money and Business Cycles', *Rev. Econ. and Statis.*, 45 (suppl.; February), pp. 32–64.

Hahn, F. H. (1970), 'Some Adjustment Problems', *Econometrica* 38 (January), pp. 1–17.

Hahn, F. H. (1971), 'Equilibrium with Transactions Costs', *Econometrica*, 39 (May), pp. 417–40.

Jaffé, W. (1967), 'Walras' Theory of *Tâtonnement*: A Critique of Recent Interpretations', JPE, 75 (February), pp. 1–19.

Kaldor, N. (1960), 'Speculation and Economic Stability', in *Essays on Economic Stability and Growth*, by N. Kaldor (London: Duckworth). (Original in *Rev. Econ. Studies.* 6, (1939), pp. 1–27.)

Keynes, J. M. (1930), *A Treatise on Money*. (London: Macmillan).

Keynes, J. M. (1936), *The General Theory of Employment, Interest and Money* (New York: Harcourt Brace).

Keynes, J. M. (1937), 'The Ex-ante Theory of the Rate of Interest', *Econ. J.*, 49 (December), pp. 663–9.

Keynes, J. M. (1947), 'The General Theory', QJE, 51 (February 1937), pp. 209–23. (Reprinted in *The New Economics*, edited by S. E. Harris New York: Knopf, 1947.)

Keynes, J. M. (1963), 'On the Theory of a Monetary Economy', *Nebraska J. Econ. and Bus.*, 2 (Autumn), pp. 7–9. (Original in *Festschrift für A. Spiethoff*. Munich: Duncker & Humblot, 1933.)

Leijonhufvud, A. (1968), *On Keynesian Economics and the Economics of Keynes* (London: Oxford).

Moore, B. J. (1968), *An Introduction to the Theory of Finance* (New York: Free Press).

Ohlin, B. (1937), 'Some Notes on the Stockholm Theory of Savings and Investment II', *Econ. J.*, 47 (June), pp. 221–40.

Samuelson, P. A. (1947), *Foundations of Economic Analysis* (Cambridge, Mass.: Harvard Univ. Press).

Weintraub, S. and A. Habibagahi (1971), 'Keynes and the Quantity Theory Elasticities', *Nebraska J. Econ. and Bus.*, 10 (Spring), pp. 13–25.

Working, H. (1962), 'New Concepts Concerning Future Markets and Prices', AER, 52 (June), pp. 431–60.

9 Money as Cause and Effect*

A recurring theme in the long evolution of monetary theory is the dispute whether changes in (bank) money supplies play a causal part in influencing economic phenomena or whether their variations are an effect of economic activity, overcoming the obstacles of barter in an interdependent production economy. The view of money as causal represents a Currency School legacy, descending from Lord Overstone and the charter revision of the Bank of England in the 1840s. Money, viewed as an effect, constituted the core of the 'real-bills' Banking Principle doctrine espoused at the time by William Tooke. Precursors abound as Marget's (1938) careful documentation reveals.

A reconsideration of certain aspects of the causal attributes of money supply is particularly appropriate in a model in which money-wages are determined outside a market *tâtonnement* system, either institutionally negotiable via collective bargaining or implemented by government decree as in Nixon's and Heath's Phase I and Phase II economic policies. Despite obvious facts about the determination of money-wage rates, macromodels still maintain the fiction that money-wage rates are merely 'another' price, determined in the market-place as another endogenous variable, unaffected by the confrontation of big labour and big business.

The model presented below embodies the economically realistic position that money-wages are determined independently of market *tâtonnements*. Undoubtedly, even for those who dispute its factual relevance – an empirical rather than an *a priori* issue – the case is worth exploration because of certain novel implications for monetary theory and policy.

1 CAUSALITY AND STATISTICAL LEADS

Professor Friedman has often claimed that the 'leads' and 'lags' between money supply changes and other series disclose money as both cause and effect of the other series. In short, money supply variations are classed as causes or effects depending on whether the turning points in money supplies come before or after changes in prices, output flows and employment.

Of course, the assignment of causal status by pinpointing time series dates is perilous.[1] Puzzles arise over the accuracy of data, over events in

* *Economic Journal* (December 1973). This chapter was coauthored with Sidney Weintraub.

between if quarterly data are used, over erratic patterns where money leads one series and not another. Further, when 'leads' and 'lags' vary from a low of one month to a high of 26 months (Friedman, 1972, p. 15) the whole art of dating becomes tenuous. If the underlying economic structure was rigid, and extraneous elements did not intervene, 'leads' or 'lags' would always be of the same duration; scientific extraction for valid prediction would follow. But when calendar 'leads' and 'lags' are fitful, there is the awkward possibility that 'extraneous' events rather than changes in the money supply are the causes affecting prices and other economic phenomena. Assigning a causal status to money as the key to stabilization could then cause mischief.

Above all, imputing causality by interpreting the fluctuations in the time series suffers crucially from the overlooking of various *anticipations* which can induce a deceptive statistical lead of a money supply series over the GNP series.[2] For example, if businessmen expect an increase in sales some months hence, and begin a phased programme of increased equipment installation and inventory expansion, they are likely to borrow in advance of the event. With orders in hand, their capital goods suppliers are also likely to borrow (or obtain a line of credit) to guarantee their working capital needs, *even before extra capital goods are produced*. If the Monetary Authority acquiesces by providing the finance required, then the statistical series will show the money supply increase as *preceding* the output increase. To the casual chart reader the money growth may appear to cause the investment upturn and the wider multiplier ramifications. Such statistical interpretation overlooks the causal impetus residing in the preparatory business actions; unlike Keynes (1937) who construed the finance-motive as embracing an advance monetary demand for increased transactions balances.[3] A naïve interpretation of distributed lag regression analysis may suggest 'unidirectional causality', from money to prices and output (Sims, 1972); a further thought should, in this case, assign causal significance to the prior business decisions fostering subsequent output growth and culminating in larger money supplies to serve as Adam Smith's 'wheel of commerce'.

If, on the other hand, the Monetary Authority refuses to expand the money supply despite the higher demand for finance, then the rate of interest will rise if, as Keynes noted, 'the liquidity-preferences of the public (as distinct from the entrepreneurial investors) and of the banks are unchanged' (1937, p. 667). If the entrepreneurial investors are successful in obtaining finance at a higher rate of interest by drawing off 'speculative' money balances, then some increase in output will follow (although somewhat less, *ceteris paribus*, than if the money supply increased and the interest rate level were unchanged). If the ensuing decline in asset prices in security markets induces the Monetary Authority to intervene to maintain 'orderliness' in these capital markets, the statistical series may show the money supply series lagging behind output growth, and the chart-reader might then correctly interpret the causality as going from *planned* output growth to money supplies. Hence, if favourable expectations induce an output expansion, the resulting leads or lags in money supply and GNP data will depend on the reactions of the Monetary Authority and the banking system to entrepreneurs' increased demand for finance.[4] Unidirectional causality cannot be determined merely by viewing the leads and lags in time series data.

Of course, in executing its mandate the Monetary Authority can, by means of open market operations, initiate a change in the supply of money, even if entrepreneurial intentions are unchanged. In the ensuing portfolio reshuffle, the banking system absorbs from the public assets which have a negligible elasticity of production – namely securities – by offering bank money on attractive terms as an alternative store of wealth. The lower interest rates and easier money availability can enlarge the demand for resource-using reproducible goods, stimulating an output flow through the familiar Keynesian mechanism involving the schedule of marginal efficiency of capital and the multiplier. Granted some investment sensitivity to lower interest rates and easier availability of money, the exogenous increase in the money supply may justifiably be described as having *caused* the later increase in output.

Considering the diversity of circumstances, chart reading, like calculating a coefficient of correlation, provides an inconclusive guide to what caused what. Observed lags of an output series behind a money supply series may be due either to an anticipatory income-generating finance process, where planned output growth causes an increase in the money supply, or to a portfolio change process where a planned increase in the money supply by the central bank causes an increase in demand; consequently, leads and lags in statistical series are poor indicators of the direction of cause and effect.

2 MONETARIST EVALUATION

In his several attempts at refining monetary theory, involving a metamorphosis from Old to New Quantity Theory, Friedman has repeatedly insisted that changes in the money supply cause changes in money income, after a variable time lag.[5] In familiar symbols with $MV = PT$ in the Old Theory, the direction of causation was from M to P; in the New Quantity Theory with $MV = Y$ (where Y = money income) it is from M to Y. Friedman has even calculated a money income elasticity, estimating that a 1 per cent money variation (on his M_2 definition) creates about a 1.8 per cent steady state ('permanent') money income increase. In assigning policy significance to these calculations, Friedman, and the monetarists, are propounding what amounts to a causal Currency Principle despite their disclaimers that money supply variations also appear as *effects* of economic conditions.

Friedman has also attached a major reservation to his doctrines which severely limits the significance of his monetarism: but unfortunately, this critical qualification has failed to attract the attention that it deserves.

The New Quantity Theory is more tautologous than the Old. In the older income-velocity version ($MV = PT$) more money could affect *either* P, T, or V. In the new theory ($MV = Y$), only Y or V can be affected. In as much as Friedman regards V as a function solely of a set of variables, none of which can depend on the money supply, the direct impact of changes in money supply is after a time lag, not at all on V but entirely on Y. The separate impacts on P and Q where $Y = PQ$, are thus consolidated, never isolated.

This has some far-reaching implications: if Y alone is affected by changes in M in a time series showing positive association between changes of $M(t)$ and $Y(t)$, *the Modern Quantity Theory is devoid of a theory of inflation* despite some airy confident assertions about the dominance of money influences on the price level in the 'long run' (of indeterminate calendar time). Money income alone is affected by short-run money supply variations; how much of the money increase runs in the form of price movements, and how much in output and employment, is left obscure.

It makes a vast difference for policy if the prime monetary effect in the short run – in which we all expect still to live – is on output (and employment) rather than upon prices. We welcome more output if this can be fostered through the portfolio reshuffles accompanying new money supplies: but as a rule we deplore any associated inflationary phenomena.

Analytically, the inconclusiveness in monetarist doctrine can be described as follows:

$$\Delta M_t \rightarrow \Delta Y_{t+} = (Q\Delta P + P\Delta Q)_{t+} \quad \text{(approximately)} \qquad (9.1)$$

$$\frac{\Delta M_t}{M} \rightarrow \frac{\Delta Y_{t+}}{Y} = \left(\frac{\Delta Q}{Q} + \frac{\Delta P}{P} \right)_{t+} \quad \text{(approximately)} \qquad (9.2)$$

Monetary injections occur at date (t) and money income increases at a future later date ($t+$). Clearly, price movements and output movements need not be simultaneous. But Friedman does not distinguish between the separable ΔP and ΔQ components.

Until ΔP and ΔQ are separately accounted for the monetarists are bereft of a theory of the effect on the price level of increases in the money supply. In conditions of unemployment, or in a growth context where the effective labour force is growing unevenly, increased money supply may cause output expansion rather than inflation. If the price level is determined outside the monetary sector, by money-wage movements, an abnormal money growth may be the prelude to a downturn of output, if the price level has risen even more. Significantly, there may be no simple rule how to expand the money supply so as to maintain steady output–employment growth.

Friedman has been explicit in acknowledging that the New Quantity Theory has indeed stumbled over the separable price and output variation (e.g. 1971, pp. 330, 337). But the significance of this admission for policy[6] has become submerged in formal debates over side issues such as the predictive efficiency relevance of monetarist and 'Keynesian' models. The vital distinction between price effects and output effects has been overlooked despite its central importance. Examination of the inconclusiveness of matters embodied in equations (9.1) and (9.2) is overdue. We shall now suggest a more detailed theory of money, distinguishing effects on price and on output.

3 GENERAL EQUILIBRIUM MODELS

The assumption in modern mathematical general equilibrium models that the labour market clears, with the real wage equating the demand and supply of labour begs an important question in that the money wage is wholly neglected, as though Keynes never wrote on the subject (cf. Weintraub and Weintraub, 1972).

In terms of Walrasian demand and supply equations the underlying argument is that output, resource allocation, and income division are generated by real processes, modified possibly by Pigou real balance effects in recognizing the influence of money supply. Implicitly this 'real-economy' theorizing assumes a barter economy, where agreements to exchange are reconciled, with money having a passive clearing influence on consummated market transactions already determined. Money's influence is inevitably confined to affecting the price level, whose absolute height is a matter of indifference since all real phenomena are separately determined.

Friedman, for one, acknowledges the Walrasian foundation in describing the real phenomena of relative output, prices, and incomes. A 'natural' rate of unemployment is also generated by the Walrasian equations. The Old Quantity Theory of the price level in a Fisher or Cambridge cash-balance form is the result. Despite its elegance, the New Theory thus constitutes a tautologous arithmetical appendage to the static equilibrium model. To be sure, the New Theory has more meaning in a growing economy – or one moving from lesser to fuller employment – where output is envisaged as a variable, with one Walrasian equilibrium transformed into another. For output changes, therefore, the New Theory contains a dynamic mechanism for explaining money income growth.

The fictional Walrasian world, where money is superimposed only *after* all the real elements are resolved, presents an impediment to a serious theory of money. The assumptions underlying his equations set up Walrasian producers and consumers free of uncertainty and sure of their tastes, resource productivity, and market conduct. Overall, the models are static, with no yesterday or tomorrow. Interconnected market events are tied in a timeless setting where market information is universally possessed and 'all transactions are carried out at a single date' (Hahn, 1971, p. 417).

Inevitably, in a model cut off from the yesterdays and the uncertainty created by a history still to be made, money is entirely redundant. 'Money can play no essential role' (ibid, p. 417) in bridging the interval between the time of income receipt and expenditure, or to accumulate 'as a temporary abode of purchasing power', or to serve as a short- or longer-run asset. Under full certainty, with all transactions carried out at a single date, it is clearly irrational to hold, as a store of value, money rather than interest-bearing assets timed to mature at the desired expenditure date.

Although some 'Keynesians' have also embraced the general equilibrium model in the mistaken opinion that it is compatible with Keynes's arguments, the one crucial hypothesis that vitiates the Walrasian-type analysis is its stipulation that the labour market must clear, with labour-demand determined by marginal productivity and labour supply governed by real wage considerations (see Weintraub and Weintraub, 1972). For this imposes full employment by assumption. Money can then affect only the price level: money-wage levels, in the model, are a by-product.

Curiously, the old and new Walrasian theorists never specifically inquire how any *one* absolute price may emerge as the common numéraire to which other prices are adapted. The unique importance of the price of labour – the money-wage – is not acknowledged. In treating the money-wage as simply one price in general equilibrium theory, the question of whether the mode of money-wage determination makes any difference is not even raised.

But, suppose the money-wage is determined not in the market-place but around a bargaining table and that as a result of union contracts negotiated in the recent past, money-wage schedules are set up and actually prevail for a *future* contract period, say of three years. Surely, the search for an endogenous market theory of money-wage determination is then both futile and incongruous; it would be more accurate to argue, in this sequence, that as money-wages are determined *outside* the theoretical market system over the forthcoming three-year interval, it must follow that prices will, in the circumstances, adjust to money wages, rather than the converse. Even simultaneous determination of wages and prices would be precluded once *money* wages were already settled outside the demand–supply equations of a Walrasian system. Only real wages would remain to be resolved endogenously.

General equilibrium theorists in their attachment to implausible models of a real economy have, unfortunately, refrained from exploring this situation even as a hypothetical case. They have argued that relative prices, with money-wage rates being 'merely' one price, are ground out mechanistically by solving the equations. Not surprisingly, therefore, money variations can, at the most, only modify the absolute price level in this full employment mutually interdependent demand–supply system.

Basically, for monetary theory, the crucial omission by the general equilibrium theorists has been the effects of changes over time, and the uncertainty attached to them. These are the phenomena that push money and contracts to the front as human institutions devised to mitigate some of the bad results of uncertainty in a world where production takes time. The wage contract is undoubtedly the most ubiquitous agreement of all. If it were constantly revised and recontracted, production would be inhibited in a decentralized market economy. The assumption of continuous labour market clearing may imply a contradiction for this model – as Keynes suspected in abandoning the prescription of lower money-wages for alleviating unemployment.

Recently, Arrow and Hahn have confirmed the view that in general equilibrium models money cannot play an essential role. They have stated 'in a world with a past as well as future in which contracts are made in terms of money, no equilibrium may exist' (1971, p. 361) and 'if a serious monetary theory comes to be written, the fact that contracts are written in terms of money will be of considerable importance' (ibid., p. 357). This recognition represents an important step forward, but leaves us far short of even a *tentative* 'serious monetary theory' to replace the past confidence in general equilibrium analysis.

Thus, if 'money matters', its importance may depend on the level of money-wages determined in labour contracts. For price level stability it is vain to believe that money-wages can be freely flexible as simply one price among many. The money-wage level, as a price entering practically all cost functions and the greater part of consumer demand functions, cannot be left free to move without this affecting practically *all* prices, and thus employment through the demand for money. A change in this 'one' price, in the simultaneous system, affects *all* prices in a way scarcely true of any other input or any other income; it cannot be attributed to merely the importance of a rise in the price of peanuts. (To sympathetic interpreters, this view of the pivotal position of the money-wage rate was, of course, the essential element in Keynes's attack on Say's Law and the Old Quantity Theory.)

When, on the other hand, the money-wage level is taken as mainly an exogenous variable, it may still have endogenous elements operating on it either through past wage, price, or employment events, or future anticipation about these variables. It is safe to assume that the precise level of the money-wage rate is *not* bargained in the competitive market-place in the same way as is the price of peanuts. As a result, the equation system of general equilibrium theory must be changed to allow the possibility of an equilibrium which fails to clear the labour market. Within the matrix of supply equations, money-wage costs of production are obviously determinate, especially in the simple set of equations involving fixed production coefficients. Given profit margins and/or monopoly mark-ups, with labour as the sole variable factor – the simple Keynesian case – the money-price level is now determined.

In this view, a money increase influences output levels if, and only if, it effects a 'portfolio adjustment' which, in turn, induces an increase in aggregate demand. Towards the price level, money plays a more passive role though it may exert *some* causal effect on prices, through the increases in output levels because productivity may alter as output and employment expand. Over time, however, this effect is likely to be negligible, and may go in either direction depending on the balance between the static tendency to diminishing returns and the dynamic effects of technological advance.

4 A QUASI-MATHEMATICAL STATEMENT

A general equilibrium set of equations including the demand and supply of money would now be lengthy. It would have to cover financial sectors, and intermediate products with monopoly, international flows, and growth factors. Introducing realistic elements such as the divisibility of outputs and input agents, advertising and cultural influences on demand, and varying degrees of monopoly, would add to its intricacy. Finally, to allow for the complete set of equations it would have to cover the full complex of current and future markets. All this elaboration would be lengthy and inevitably incomplete and contentious. A detailed equational statement thus belongs to the future, and to a weighty tome.

Nevertheless, just for pedagogical purposes, we will indicate some of the changes needed in the simplest Walrasian model. With fixed coefficients, and assuming fully integrated output in each of the firms comprising an industry, we can write:

$$\left(\frac{w}{A} + U + \mu \right)_i = P_i \tag{9.3}$$

where:

w = average money wage
A = average labour productivity

U = unit user cost, involving depreciation through use
μ = other unit costs, such as taxes, interest charges, rents, etc, plus unit profit margin

for the ith firm (or industry). In (9.3) unit costs appear on the left, and are equated to price. More concisely:

$$(kw/A)_i = P_i \tag{9.4}$$

where k is a (potentially variable) mark-up over unit labour costs in the firm (or industry).

Equation (9.4) is true in each firm and each industry. Generalizing for the economy we can write:

$$P = kw/A \tag{9.5}$$

In (9.5) the general wage cost mark-up formula appears as some weighted aggregate of individual industry (or firm under monopoly) product prices. The k-term now denotes the average economy-wide mark-up of prices over unit labour costs, or the reciprocal of the wage share. A variety of studies reveals k to be remarkably constant in Gross Business Product data in which the concept of the market price level has bearing, although there may be a secular trend, as shown by Godley and Nordhaus (1972).

Thus Walrasian supply equations can be written as in (9.3), culminating in (9.5). In the Walrasian system, too, consumer market demand equations, derived from individual demand functions, can be written as:

$$D_1 = D(P_1, P_2, \ldots P_n, Y) \tag{9.6}$$

In (9.6), the Ps represent individual prices and Y denotes income, money income for our purposes. Aggregating in macroeconomic fashion for the closed system:

$$Y = PQ \tag{9.7}$$

where Q = output volume.

Also, since $A = Q/N$, where N = employment, as by (9.5) and (9.7) $Y = kwN$ (9.6) may be written as:

$$D_1 = D(P_1, P_2, \ldots P_n, kwN) \tag{9.8}$$

Examining (9.8) we see the macroeconomic interdependence of demand and cost equations: a change in k, w, or N is capable of (1) shifting unit costs, and thus the price level, and (2) affecting the demand equations. If N

and k are given, then the (average) money wage emerges as the unique price level parameter without recourse to, or even mention of, money supplies! If employment is a variable (perhaps because money supply varies) the price level depends on variations in average productivity as the level of effective demand varies, as well as on money-wages.

5 THE WAGE AS NUMÉRAIRE

A price dimension in absolute terms is given thus by the height of w, the average money-wage. A change in the money-wage will change both the cost and the consumer demand function, and thus the various prices and the price level. The money-wage, especially if it is resolved not via a market *tâtonnement* but at the bargaining tables or by government decree, is inherently the *numéraire par excellence* in the modern economy. A change upwards in w exerts simultaneously a 'cost push' and, in consumer markets where wage and salary compensation explain nearly 90 per cent of consumption purchases, a 'demand-pull'.

In a more extended analysis the question arises, of course, of whether a change in *any* price is not as vital as a change in money wages in a mutually interdependent system. The difference between the wage levels and other prices is, however, more one of kind than one of degree. Interest charges, and perhaps taxes, are the only other cost elements whose variations directly affect practically *all* costs. Quantitatively, however, the wage cost is far more significant than either of these charges. Even in the non-integrated model, inputs of unfinished materials are rarely likely to have the universality or the quantitative importance of money wages, except in an open economy (such as the British) highly dependent on some imports of materials and foods.

On this view of the economic process, the price level becomes resolved once the money-wage is given. At the present time k may be taken as an empirical constant – it has as a matter of stylized fact been constant for about 70 years. In a more detailed exposition it might be conceived as evolving from the play of market power, in that forces of competition or monopoly determine its magnitude and thereby determine income shares.

6 A THEORY IN A CLOCK-TIME SETTING

We return now to the original theme of depicting the causal incidence of changes in money supplies, isolating the separable price and output changes. This is the basic problem which Friedman has left as 'unfinished business' (1971, p. 330).

There is a grain of truth in the wisecrack that time was invented to

prevent everything from happening at once. Consider, as did Dennis
Robertson, a 'slice of time' between t_0 and t_1, for example between July (t_0)
and August (t_1). An intermediate date is labelled t_+.

We suppose a definite variation in the money supply (M_0) to occur at t_0 as
a result of monetary policy. Starting with $M_0 = \bar{M}$ on 30 June, we enlarge
$\bar{M}$ to $M_0 + \Delta M$ on 1 July. Thereafter, we trace the price level (P),
employment (N) and output (Q) over the $t_0 \rightarrow t_1$ interval. There is disequilibrium at t_0, but by t_1, in the absence of any new shock, a new equilibrium
state may emerge.[7]

Dennis Robertson described money as constantly 'on the wing', rather
than 'sitting'. Monetary analysis should retain the flavour of his image, in
contrast to the 'sitting' image of the modern portfolio approach which is
more apt in a non-flow, final equilibrium setting. Our model is designed
also to illustrate how changes in money holding impinge on the variables of
the real sector, and the feedback of these variables on the desired demand
for money. Monetary and real sectors are thereby interrelated.

The sequence runs in terms of *nominal* money balances. This is appropriate if we wish to analyse how variations in nominal money supplies
affect the economy. In as much as the price level is an explicit variable in
our argument, the nominal-money demand function may be translated into
real terms so that our procedures merge ultimately with that of Friedman.[8]

As a provisional simplification it is assumed that the money increment
(ΔM) provided by the central bank at t_0 is transmitted directly to the public
either via new loans, or by acquiring second-hand debt contracts from the
public via the spot market for such securities. Thus we render irrelevant
the vast literature on the money supply-reserve balance multiplier according to which the central bank initially affects reserve balances, and after a
time lag, the money supply (either M_1 or M_2).[9]

7 A SIMPLIFIED AUTONOMOUS MONEY SUPPLY MODEL

The analysis can be formalized in a structural equation system (which from
initial data traces out the new economic aggregates until they are disturbed
by new shocks).

By hypothesis, given the price level, aggregate output, and interest rates
for the period just closed, economic agents desire to hold money balances
(M^*) at the t_0 date equal to:

$$M^*_{t_0} = f_1 (P_{t_0}, Q_{t_0}, r_{t_0}, \bar{B}, \bar{P}_e, \bar{r}_e) \tag{9.9}$$

Thus the demand for money depends on current money income (P_{t_0}, Q_{t_0})
and current interest rates (r_{t_0}), bond holdings (B) and currently held

expectations of price levels (P_e) and interest rates (r_e).[10] The bar over a symbol indicates that the variable is exogenous.

We now introduce an autonomous change in the supply of money by the Monetary Authority, acting on information of past events, some predictions on the near-future outlook and coloured by its ideological policy rules. The key variables are those of equation (9.9). Thus

$$\Delta M^s = M^s_{t+} - M^s_{t_0} \tag{9.10}$$

where superscript s denotes the *planned* money-supply aggregate to be implemented by the central bank policy decision.

Since the Monetary Authority can alter the money supply by dealing in debt contracts on organized spot markets it can cause the effective rate of interest (i.e. the spot price of financial assets) to adjust instantaneously to the change in the money supply. Thus, at each instant of time between t_0 and t_1, as the money supply varies the rate of interest may take on different values unless the public's demand for money is simultaneously shifting. Ignoring possible money-demand *shifts* at each point of time, the quantity of desired money balances changes in response to movements in interest rates so that

$$M^*_{t_0} \to {}_{t_1} = f_2 \left(P_{t_0}, Q_{t_0}, r'_{t_0} \to {}_{t_1} \right) \tag{9.11}$$

where the $M^*_{t_0} \to {}_{t_1}$ and $r'_{t_0} \to {}_{t_1}$ notation denotes an incomplete equilibrium (i.e. disequilibrium) process.

Between t_0 and t_1, we assume exogenous new wage bargains implemented immediately, increasing money wages from w_{t_0} to w_{t_1}. The wage change can be described as an exogenous shock superimposed on the exogenous money-supply change.

Assuming the degree of monopoly unchanged $(k_{t_0} = k_{t_1})$, and assuming a given increase in average labour productivity from A_{t_0} to A_{t_1}, the entrepreneurs stipulate, via the wage cost mark-up considerations of equation (9.5), the price level (P_{t_1}) which they would be willing to accept for any level Q_{t_1} of output to be offered to the market. The immediate change in the offer-supply price level associated with output flow in the period t_1 is

$$P'_{t_1} - P_{t_0} = f_3 \left(w_{t_1} - w_{t_0}, A_{t_1} - A_{t_0}, k_t \right) \tag{9.12}$$

In equation (9.12), P'_{t_1}, denotes the new price level accompanying the new money-wage (and new supply of money). If the contractual money-wage increment exceeds the productivity increment, then entrepreneurs, assessing higher production costs for any flow of output, will lift their offer prices.

In the modern mass production economy, production costs are normally incurred, and paid, prior to receiving sales revenue; the costs represent a working capital investment of entrepreneurs. If current production flow costs duplicate the preceding period, the proceeds from past sales could exactly finance the current working capital costs.[11] If, however, wage increases raise production costs, *then even unchanged production schedules* will require more working capital in money terms. Accordingly, entrepreneurs will increase their short-term borrowings from the banks, to coincide with the Monetary Authority's hypothetical increase of the money supply. The increase in money which is necessary because of higher wages is thereby quickly drawn into the income stream.

Assume, initially, that entrepreneurs maintain the production flow. The increase in money necessary to cover the higher working capital requirements may be more than, equal to, or less than, the autonomous increase in money provided by the Monetary Authority. If the finance demand for increased working capital needs exceeds ΔM^s, interest rates will rise ($r'_{t_0 \to t_1} > r_{t_0}$), and the inflationary wage increase, despite the monetary expansion, will *cause* tight money even if the output flow remains unchanged. At the higher interest rates, however, production will be constrained so that the money-supply increment will fail to sustain the Q_{t_0} output (and employment) at the new price level.

If, on the other hand, the money-supply increase exceeds the additional working capital requirements imposed by the higher production costs, the rate of interest will decline through a 'portfolio shuffle' as the central bank exchanges money with the public for bonds through open market operations. The resulting fall in interest rates may stimulate higher investment outlays, so that some portion of the exogenous increase in the money supply can admittedly *cause* an enlargement of aggregate demand.

Finally, if the exogenous increase in the money supply just equals the additional working capital requirements for the t_0 production flow, then interest rates will be unchanged and, *ceteris paribus*, $Q_{t_1} = Q_{t_0}$. (Of course, these cases abstract from autonomous changes in entrepreneurial and consumer expectations, and any resultant change in transactions demand and/or liquidity preference.)

Labour productivity in t_1 will usually differ from productivity in t_0. In the static competitive case, more output is associated with diminishing returns. In real life, changes in technology and/or increases in the capital stock will improve labour productivity, so that $A_{t_1} > A_{t_0}$. This can cushion the impact of money-wage increases in costs and price levels.

The desired equilibrium demand for money at the terminal date will emerge as

$$M^*_{t_1} = f_4 (P_{t_1}, Q_{t_1}, r_{t_1}, \bar{B}, \bar{P}_e, \bar{r}_e) \tag{9.13}$$

If output is unchanged, $r_{t_1} = r_{t_0}$. If the change in the money supply exceeds the change in money-wages relative to productivity, then $r_{t_1} < r_{t_0}$. Hence, changes in the money-wage *numéraire* relative to productivity require equal changes in the money supply, if money is to remain 'neutral' with respect to output. Prices, however, will be higher by the excess of average money-wage change over the productivity change.

In the event of a lesser increase in money supplies, *ceteris paribus*, the monetary policy will *be restrictive* with respect to output, even though prices will still increase: a higher increase in money supply will be *expansionary* with respect to output.

Beyond the finance demand for money for transactions purposes, if the non-transactions demand for money (however it may be compartmentalized into speculative, convenience, or precautionary demands) is affected by the pace of changes in M, P, or Q, then there will be further effects on interest rates. Normally, changes in the M, P, Q variables are indeed almost certain to alter expectations and the desired money-demand function.

8   AN EVALUATION OF MONEY AS CAUSE AND EFFECT

The dynamics of the model originate in the movements of money-supply and money-wage rates which, over time, induce price, output, and interest-rate responses. Once the change in money-wages occurs, part of the money-supply increment is deflected to support the higher price level. If the non-transactions demand for money also alters, there are then new effects on interest rates.

Output variations will depend on that part of monetary expansion which is not siphoned off to sustain rising prices. That is, only that part thus left over from support of $Q\Delta P$ (and any non-transactions demands) is available to depress interest rates (stimulate spot security prices) and to transmit a stimulus to economic activity. A condition for a monetary stimulus to output is, therefore, that the increase in money supply must be more than enough to sustain the price rise, plus any increased speculative and precautionary demand for money.

The system is recursive. Once money-wages rise (unless offset by increases in productivity), there is a direct *causal* influence on the price level: the money-wage rise nudges prices upwards. Only by providing just enough new money merely to hold output constant, with prices thus increased, can the Monetary Authority claim not to exert any influence on the economy. More money, in the 'sustaining' case, is properly interpreted as being an *effect* of the higher price level, required to stabilize the real Q, N, and r variables.

In the *stimulating* or *constrictive* cases where $Q_{t_1} \gtrless Q_{t_0}$, money *primarily influences output*, in the normal case. To the extent that output variations affect productivity, if the policy is output stimulating with increased productivity rising with increased production the money expansion can be interpreted as stimulating output and as restraining prices. If, on the other hand, falling productivity accompanies expansion, monetary expansion will stimulate output *and* raise prices. If productivity is unaffected so are prices unaffected. Corresponding relations can be traced for the case of a constrictive policy.

Changes in the money supply always affect output except in the production sustaining case. They may have some effect on price levels if labour productivity varies either way with output. So long as the money-wages are determined around a bargaining table, monetary policy can have only limited control over the price level.[12]

In the literature about the Phillips curve, higher output and higher employment tighten labour markets and result in higher wage settlements, so that indirectly, money supply can after all affect the price level. But note, what is decisive is not the level of output, nor the amount of money, nor the movement in interest rates, nor (as a rule), the movement in labour productivity either way but the magnitude of the money-wage rise. The money-wage thus remains the crucial and causal price level variable, so long as productivity and the degree of monopoly do not change substantially from year to year. In the long run, the productivity variations tend to lower prices or at least to restrain the price-raising effects of wage rises.

9 THE COMPLEXITY OF MONETARY THEORY

Our step-by-step account of the effects of disequilibrium suggests some of the complexities of monetary policy, which the Monetary Authority must have in mind in juggling with the many economic variables.[13]

A rise in money-wages will almost always induce an increase in money supply unless, for some reason, the central bank hopes that a constrictive policy will restrain money-wage rises. In recent years, such hopes have been proved delusory.

Ordinarily, if wage increments exceed productivity, and if there is excessive unemployment, more money will have to be provided merely to maintain recent production levels. Public pressure to ameliorate unemployment is likely to prevent a seriously constrictive policy; with the labour force growing an expansion in money supply will, sooner or later, become unavoidable. To satisfy the public concern to curb unemployment, the immediate growth in money supply will have to exceed that allowed by any 'normal' rule.

In sum, where social and political attitudes determine the money-wage exogenously, low levels of unemployment are also likely to be insisted on. So long as the price level, for the most part, is set by wage bargains which are beyond the control of the central bank, the Monetary Authority, at best, can ensure ample supplies of money to remove the financial impediments to full employment and growth. It is ill-equipped, however, to exert any effective control over price levels.

For the real phenomena of growth and full employment, monetary policy does remain decisive. With respect to inflation, in an exogenous wage economy, it is nowadays impotent. It could regain its former eminence but only if it were allowed to make inroads on money-wages at a cost in unemployment and human misery which would at present be considered unacceptable to modern *democratic* societies. In such societies, some form of incomes policy might be the only effective means for accomplishing price level stability.

Notes

1. The identification of correlation with causation violates careful econometric usage and evades the profound cognitive issues. Apparently this confusion is being perpetuated by students of the monetarists' school (e.g. Sims, 1972).
2. Cf. J. Tobin (1970) and M. Friedman's reply (1970).
3. For a full discussion of the integration of the finance motive into the *IS–LM* apparatus, see Davidson, 1965, and Davidson, 1972, ch. 7.
4. The role of financial intermediaries who 'make' security markets is also important. For a detailed analysis of the impact of the 'finance' demand on security markets and institutions, see Davidson, 1972, ch. 13.
5. For example, in his newest 'superior' theoretical model Friedman notes that the money supply 'can be regarded as completely exogenous' (1971, p. 329).
6. This aspect has been dealt with at length in Weintraub and Habebagahi (1971).
7. Our procedure thus differs from much modern work. Friedman, for example, emphasizes the *desired* money demand: effectually, his theoretical system is always in equilibrium, responding almost instantaneously to money-supply variations. This is the only intelligible interpretation of his statement that money is 'a temporary abode of purchasing power'. As an abode it is being held 'at home', temporarily, to be sure. But as it is in its abode it is not being shuffled about in transactions. If all individuals (or the full economy) are holding the 'desired' real balances, then nothing is really happening in the economy: there are neither flows of money moving toward any individual, or flowing out from him. Indubitably, the concentration on 'desired' money holdings stresses established equilibrium portfolios where individuals are content to hold the prevailing 'right' nominal money balances.
8. Cf. W. Smith who has pointed out that it is not imperative to write the desired money demand function in terms of real balances (1970, p. 774).
9. As most of this literature frequently employs a linear lag relationship of $\Delta M = m\Delta R$, where ΔR refers to the increment of reserve balances, some expository verbosity is eliminated. In our model, we assume that the central bank deals directly with buyers and sellers of debt in financial markets.

10. For expositional simplicity at this stage, we are assuming that planned expenditures during the interval are a function of current money income. The interest rate, r, may be interpreted as some average level of rates; equity prices would have to be stipulated in a more thorough account of the process.

11. Some of last period's sales receipts will be used to pay off last period's short-term bank loans which were used to finance some of last period's investment in working capital. These same sums are, therefore, available to finance a similar investment in working capital this period.

12. A reservation extends to our hypothesis of a constant k or wage share in Business Gross Product. Empirically, for stable economies such as the US, UK, Canada, etc., this assumption appears warranted. If, however, excess money emissions accompanied a flight from currency – hyper-inflation – and important changes in relative shares, then this part of the argument would have to be modified.

13. In our analysis we have ignored the possibility that wage increments may affect price and interest rate expectations. To the extent that the new wage increments increase inflationary expectations there will be some disgorging of money balances on (1) real goods which were planned to be purchased in the near future and where the additional carrying costs are less than the expected increase in supply price till the date of planned purchase and (2) financial assets, if any, whose future spot price net of carrying costs is expected to keep pace with inflation. To the extent, however, that inflationary expectations raise expectations of higher interest rates in the future, the speculative demand for cash balances will increase, thereby at least partially offsetting the disgorging of cash holdings due to expected increases in the supply prices of reproducible goods.

References

Arrow, K. J. and F. H. Hahn (1971) *General Competitive Analysis* (San Francisco: Holden-Day).

Davidson, P. (1965), 'Keynes's Finance Motive', *Oxford Economic Papers*, 17 (March), pp. 47–65.

Davidson, P. (1968), 'Money, Portfolio Balance, Capital Accumulation and Economic Growth', *Econometrica*, 36 (April), pp. 291–321.

Davidson, P. (1969), 'A Keynesian View of the Relationship Between Accumulation, Money, and the Money Wage Rate', *Economic Journal* (June), pp. 300–23.

Davidson, P. (1972), *Money and the Real World* (London: Macmillan).

Friedman, M. (1970), 'Comment on Tobin', *Quarterly Journal of Economics*, 84 (May), pp. 318–27.

Friedman, M. (1971), 'A Monetary Theory of Nominal Income', *Journal of Political Economy*, 79 (March–April), pp. 323–37.

Friedman, M. (1972) 'Have Fiscal–Monetary Policies Failed?' *American Economic Review*, Papers and Proceedings, 62 (May), pp. 11–18.

Friedman, M. and A. J. Schwartz (1963), 'Money and Business Cycles', *Review of Economics and Statistics Suppl.*, 45 (February), pp. 32–64.

Godley, W. A. and W. D. Nordhaus (1972), 'Pricing in the Trade Cycle', *Economic Journal* (September), pp. 853–82.

Hahn, F. H. (1971) 'Equilibrium with Transactions Costs', *Econometrica*, 39 (May), pp. 417–38.

Keynes, J. M. (1936), *The General Theory of Employment, Interest and Money* (New York: Harcourt, Brace).

Keynes, J. M. (1937) 'The Ex-ante Theory of the Rate of Interest', *Economic Journal* (December), pp. 663–9.

Marget, A. (1938), *The Theory of Prices* (New York: Prentice-Hall).

Sims, C. H. (1972) 'Money Income and Causality', *American Economic Review*, 62 (September), pp. 540–52.

Smith, W. L. (1970), 'On Some Current Issues in Monetary Economics: An Interpretation', *Journal of Economic Literature*, 18 (September), pp. 767–82.

Tobin, J. (1970), 'Money and Income: Post Hoc Ergo Propter Hoc?' *Quarterly Journal of Economics*, 84 (May), pp. 301–17.

Weintraub, S. and A. Habebagahi (1971) 'Keynes and the Quantity Theory Elasticities', *Nebraska Journal of Economics and Business*, 10 (Spring), pp. 13–25.

Weintraub, S. and E. R. Weintraub (1972) 'The Full Employment Model: A Critique', *Kyklos*, 25, Fasc. I.

10 The Theory of Monetary Policy Under Wage Inflation*

Central bankers are a maligned lot. They are castigated for creating too much money and inflation, chided for too little money and unemployment, denounced as too committed to fixed exchange rates in the past, and flayed for being too receptive to floating exchange rates now. Judging from the brickbats they do practically everything wrong. Their wisdom is held in such low esteem that Professor Friedman would supplant them by a low-level clerk – of undoubted integrity to be sure – acting under strict instructions to augment the money supply by an abiding rule of 3 (or 4 or 5) per cent per annum. Discretion would be superseded; an inexorable rule would be mandated.

Fealty to the fixed percentage rule, we are assured, would be conducive to a stable economy, immune to inflation and verging on full employment. The economy would only be afflicted by a (vague) 'natural' amount of unemployment.

Paradoxically, despite its professions to the contrary, the Friedman version of monetarism is rooted in the belief that 'money does *not* matter': it matters only when the money supply (M) alters at an erratic pace. A steady M-trend (write M_1, M_2, or M_3) would provide an anchor of economic stability. Deft intercession by the monetary authority, long regarded as a counterweight to other sources of economic instability, is excoriated as being the root cause of our erratic economic record.

While steady money growth is often elevated to the status of a unique maxim for economic virtue, the serious message contains two injunctions: steadiness *and* (say) 4 per cent. Despite some unguarded exaggeration of the persistence principle, nobody can contend that steadfastness at 100 per cent per week would ensure stability!

Thus the monetarist prescription is a two-part rule: steadiness and 4 (or 3 or 5) per cent. The 4 per cent feature relies on a computation of the 'normal' historical growth path, statistically processed, at constant prices.

The 4 per cent aspect is thus identified as compatible with 'normal' (?) 'natural' (?) non-inflationary growth. The terms 'normal' and 'natural', are undoubtedly evasive, as if affairs in the economic universe were indepen-

---

* This chapter, written with Sidney Weintraub in 1974, has not previously been published. For perspective, it may be remarked that this is conceived as a sequel to our article on 'Money as Cause and Effect'. (Chapter 9 in this volume).

dent of human actions; they are a throwback to the ancient concepts of the 'natural order'. However, for one subsequent analysis the vague terms will remain unchallenged: we ourselves will be guilty of using the imprecise concept of 'full employment'.

Our purpose will be to question both the steadiness and the 4 per cent rule. The 4 per cent rule rests on Friedman's theory that inflation is monetary in origin.[1] If this is toppled then the 4 per cent aspect must lose its appeal. Further, if the inflation rate is unsteady, and the natural growth rate deviates from the rigid Friedman estimates, there can be scope for relaxing the steadiness principle.

On our interpretation, therefore, it is too early to eliminate the Federal Reserve, or central bankers generally, hereafter referred to as the Monetary Authority (or MA). The proper exercise of their judgement can enhance economic well-being. While they may err, and maintain us short of full employment, fealty to a rigid and sacrosanct monetary rule, resembling the gold standard ritual up to the world-wide depression of the 1930s, can be a prescription for a new débâcle.

Besides providing an alternate set of monetary prescription, our analysis can be envisaged as a contingency plan, or fallback position, once the monetarist theory is implemented and found wanting. Inexorably, the subsequent restoration of the MA would replicate existing central banks, with one major omission: less confusion about the price level consequences of their actions, through an awareness that money plays a less significant part than they have suspected, and that inflation can only be exorcised through incomes policy, rather than monetary manoeuvres. Some minor qualification of this view will be offered below though; in the main, it withstands qualification.

Our own theory of inflation places money-wages relative to labour productivity in centre-stage, relieving the MA of culpability, in the usual course of economic events, for fuelling the upward price trend by heavy money emissions. Obviously, we are not talking of hyperinflation and a complete structural break-down.[2] In mind is the persistent erosion of the value of money in the Western world over the last 40 years, where disproportionate movements of money-wages relative to labour productivity have been instrumental in engendering the cumulative price trend. In no way has it been a case of the MA running the printing presses in conditions of full employment to pay government bills.[3] (More will be said on this later.)

In passing, it should be noted that the proponents of the view that 'all inflations involve an excess emission of money', have failed notoriously to provide an account of the theory of *money*-wages, and the appropriate trend of money-wages (and salaries) that is consonant with price-level stability.

1   AN INITIAL STATE OF HARMONY (THOUGH NOT BLISS)

Initially, we can visualize a state of equilibrium harmony, as Joan Robinson might term it.[4] Producers in the period just closed have produced
exactly the right volume of goods. Consumers have cleverly equated
marginal rates of substitution to relative product prices. There is a price
level (P), output (Q), employment (N), and some unemployment (U).
Further, an average money-wage (w) and the average labour productivity
(A). (Of course, $A=Q/N$.) Further, the money supply (M), and interest
rates (r).

Producers are content with their decisions while the unemployed accept
their lot, with only mild grumbling so that political tensions are absent.
Though it may not be exactly a world of bliss to elate J. B. Clark, it also
lacks the revolutionary ferment discerned by Karl Marx.

To be sure, in this harmonious state the demand for *desired-money*
balances, $M^*=M$, the supply money.

2   THE LIQUIDITY EQUATION

Money is a creature of uncertainty. The demand for it is compounded out
of ignorance of some present phenomena and vagueness of the dimensions
of future events even when their direction is reasonably predictable. In a
perfectly certain world, such as an economy which never changed, and was
never expected to change, the demand for money would dwindle to zero.
A study of a money economy must acknowledge the ubiquitousness of
uncertainty.[5] The desired money balances that individuals wish to hold
can, nevertheless, be specified as a (malleable) function of some major
economic variables.

The demand for money, or liquidity as Keynes described it, can thus be
written as:

$$M^* = f(P^*, Q^*, N^*, U^*, r^*, B^*) \tag{10.1}$$

In (10.1), the one new term, B, denotes the stock of wealth, represented as
a rule by a complex of financial assets, such as bonds, stocks, promissory
notes and perhaps savings accounts, where these are not pre-empted in M.
The asterisks are intended to convey that what matters are not only near
past but also *future* estimates of the magnitudes of the variable; changed
expectations of the future, or an altered view of the evolution of the
economy, can affect the immediate demand for money.

3   MORE MONEY FOR GROWING OUTPUT

At date t_0, glancing back at the t_{-1} intervals just closed, the MA must act to fix M for the $t_0 \to t_1$ intervals. Perhaps $t_0 \to t_1$ is a calendar month (though we shall find it easier to visualize annual magnitudes).

On Keynes's 'multiplier' principle of consumption and investment inter-dependence, it is known that:

$$Q = Q(I), \text{ with } I = I(r), \tag{10.2}$$

where I denotes *real* investment.

Suppose the monetary authority is disturbed over the size of unemploy-ment, and also aware that future technical progress will raise average productivity, while the labour force grows. The maximum *output* growth on normal work-week patterns would thus be:

$$\max \frac{\Delta Q}{Q} = \frac{\Delta A}{A} + \frac{\Delta N}{N} + \frac{\Delta U}{U} , \text{ for } t_0 \to t_1 \text{ interval} \tag{10.3a}$$

In (10.3) ΔU will actually be a decrement if the unemployed are absorbed; it entails, however, a positive addition to the employed labour force.

Monetary policy is thus confronted with a decision for abetting $\Delta Q/Q$, and thus in acting out its mandate on its best surmise of concrete size of the relations

$$\partial A/\partial m \text{ or } EQS \equiv m\partial Q/Q\partial m, \text{ for } t_0 \to t_1. \tag{10.3b}$$

where m is the marginal product of labour and EQS is, obviously, the elasticity of output to the money supply.

If in (10.3a) (annual) productivity growth is 3 per cent, while the labour force grows by 1 per cent and unemployment falls by 1 per cent, on rigid Quantity Theory strictures, a 5 per cent money expansion would be appropriate if inflation was precluded, with $\Delta P = 0$.

The argument would have intuitive appeal: to underwrite $\Delta N/N$, a proportionate $\Delta M/M$ would be warranted. Similarly, to absorb the unem-ployed; because of previous unemployment compensation, a moderated money response might be justified.

With respect to $\Delta A/A$, or the growing affluence, more perspicacity is required. To finance more output, even at constant prices, a proportionate money increase will be needed (construct Quantity reasoning). Further-more, with higher real incomes, individuals will ordinarily desire larger real money-balances.

How much more? This will depend then on the functional dependency of liquidity to real income.[6] While the real demand for money requires some overcompensation by the MA because of affluence, inventory theorizing suggests that some cash economies are possible at higher real income aggregates.[7]

In the present state of obscurity on the exact shape of the M^* function, the rigid Quantity Theory proportionality thesis might be tentatively invoked, with the MA exercising some 'feel' over ameliorating, explosive, or volatile elements with a stochastic base.

3.1 The Rationale for a Non-steady $\Delta M/M$ Path

Leaving aside the delicate issues raised by affluence and by inventory considerations, even if it were wholly free of fears of inflation the MA might often be well advised to abandon a steady $\Delta M/M$ path. For if any of the terms in (10.3) altered, by bulges in technical progress, or bumps in labour force growth, or breaks in the unemployment rate, then the $\Delta M/M$ ratio would also have to alter – or constitute a source of instability.

Steady money growth would only be appropriate if the various components of (10.3) aggregated to the same percentage outcome year after year. A steady monetary increment, for example, might be disastrous for an underdeveloped economy experiencing an *un*steady annual productivity advance. Likewise, the steady M-path would be suspect for an affluent economy that somehow got mired in a depression, or achieved a miraculous technological breakthrough.

Similarly, sudden and sharp breaks in the demand for real balances could render the steady $(\Delta M/M)$ rule a stultifying obeisance to a ritual despite its dour economic consequences. Keynes remarked that if people wanted more green cheese, an efficient economy would produce more green cheese.[8] If they want more pocket money, the central bank would be derelict if it failed to provide it: money wanted for mere cash holdings could hardly cause inflation.

3.2 The Interest Rate

In (10.3a, 10.3b), in striving to facilitate an enlarged output flow, the MA would operate on the money supply; in practice this would entail changes in r, culminating in effects in the I-sector. A lower r, however, would probably add to the demand for cash balances, as a related speculative–precautionary money-balance effect.[9] This, too, would probably commend a ΔM enlargement in amount in excess of rigid Quantity Theory precepts.

For later reference we write the familiar (income) Equation of Exchange, where the strict Quantity Theory presumes $V=\bar{V}$. Thus:

$$M\bar{V} = PQ \qquad\qquad (10.4)$$

MA judgement in implementing monetary policy, even in a non-inflationary world where $P = \bar{P}$, requires an estimate of $(V + \Delta V)/V$ projected over the future, with $\Delta V/V$ generally presumed 'small'.

It is in respect to ΔV that mechanistic Quantity Theory reasoning dissolves. For if $V = \bar{V}$, to sustain a $(\Delta A/A)$ 5 per cent expansion would impel an enlargement of $(\Delta M/M) = 5$ per cent. Yet earlier (10.2) it was averred that to secure leverage over Q, I, a function of r, had to expand. For monetary policy and output theory, what is thus important is the elasticity of the $I(r)$ function, and M^* with respect to interest rates. Herein lies the key to ΔV, given $P = \bar{P}$.

The relevant elasticities for some modifications are thus:

$$E_{qI} = (I\Delta Q/Q\Delta I) > 0 \tag{10.5a}$$

$$E_{Ir} = (r\Delta I/I\Delta n) < 0 \tag{10.5b}$$

$$E_{Mr} = (r\Delta M^*/M^*\Delta r) < 0 \tag{10.5c}$$

Neglecting signs, the smaller E_{Mr} the smaller the augmentation to lower r. In so far as E_{Ir} is too large, I will be sensitive to minor reductions in r. With a large multiplier, E_{qI} will permit restoration of full employment.

3.3 An Alternate Inflation Analysis

The monetarists gear their theory of monetary policy to the premise that money supplies are the villain causing inflation. Our theory of inflation absolves the MA of complicity for our price level instability. Essentially, it alleges that money-wage (and salary) excesses are critical in the P-ascent. In consumer markets, the money-wage is a key parameter capable of lifting both costs curves and demand curves: 'cost-push' and 'demand-pull' inflation possess a simultaneous origin:

For subsequent reference we write the basic Wage-Cost Mark-Up (WCM) price level relations as follows:

$$\text{WCM: } PQ = kwN \text{ so that } P = kw/A. \tag{10.6}$$

In (10.6) k = the average mark-up of prices over unit labour costs (w/A); it is also equivalent to the reciprocal of the wage share (PQ/wN), where PQ = Gross Business Product, or the output of the enterprise sector of the economy in which the market price level concept is germane.[10] A perusal of data for the US and Western economies suggests the validity of the hypothesis $k = \bar{k}$ over the long trend and year to year.[11] (If 'near-constancy' did not prevail we would witness frequent revolutions in income division.)

Causation in (10.6) runs from right to left: to control P, $\Delta w/w$ mus[t] largely conform to $\Delta A/A$. (w = Employee Compensation, or wages and salaries, in national income accounts.)

From (10.4) and (10.6):

$$MV = Y \text{ and } Y = PQ \tag{10.7a}$$

$$\frac{\Delta M}{M} + \frac{\Delta V}{V} = \frac{\Delta P}{P} + \frac{\Delta Q}{Q} \quad \text{(omitting } (\overset{\Delta}{\Delta M \Delta V}/MV) \text{ and} \tag{10.7b}$$
$$(\Delta Q \Delta P/PQ))$$

$$\frac{\Delta P}{P} = \frac{\Delta w}{w} + \frac{\Delta k}{k} - \frac{\Delta A}{A} \quad \text{(omitting } (\Delta w \Delta k/ka) \text{ and} \tag{10.7c}$$
$$(-\Delta A \Delta P/PA))$$

Taking $\Delta k = 0 = \Delta V$, at least initially further simplification is possible.

3.4 The Appropriate Increase in the Money Supply

Assuming $V = 0$, it follows from (7b) that:

$$(\Delta M/M) = (\Delta P/P) + (\Delta Q/Q) \tag{10.8}$$

Earlier, holding $(\Delta P/P) = 0$:

$$(\Delta M/M) = (\Delta Q/Q). \tag{10.3a}$$

From (10.8), with $(\Delta P/P)$ governed by (10.6) or (10.7c), on mechanistic Quantity Theory reasoning, maximum output growth requires that the money supply expand by an amount ample to sustain $\Delta P/P$ plus an extra money sum to push $\Delta Q/Q$ on to full employment.[12]

3.5 A Causal Classification of Monetary Policy

Merely to *sustain* the Q-level is apparently essential to provide enough money to compensate for the price level increase. Thus ΔM can be decomposed into two portions, one part essential merely to maintain Q whenever $\Delta P > 0$, with the residual imparting some expansive ΔQ and ΔN effect.

Thus, interpreting Δ's as involving changes over time:

$$\Delta Q = f(\Delta M - \Delta P) = f(\Delta M, \Delta w, \Delta A) \tag{10.9}$$

From (10.9), monetary policy can be classified as:

Stimulating or *Expansive*: $(\Delta M/M) > (\Delta P/P)$ (10.10a)

Neutral or *Sustaining*: $(\Delta M/M) = (\Delta P/P)$ (10.10b)

Recessionary or *Constrictive*: $(\Delta M/M) < (\Delta P/P)$. (10.10c)

In (10.9) ΔM can alter ΔQ causally so long as $(\Delta M/M) \lessgtr (\Delta P/P)$. In (10.10a), which suggests an initial $U > 0$ and $\Delta A > 0$, over time with $(\Delta M/M) > (\Delta P/P)$ monetary policy is stimulating: 'more money matters', as conducive to higher Q- levels.

In the neutral case, monetary policy lacks causal influence: $\Delta M/M$ merely maintains Q. The money posture would be neutral in respect of Q even though the ΔM statistic looked large.

In the *constrictive* case where the monetary effort fails to match $\Delta P/P$, the MA could be charged with fostering unemployment by its (relatively) niggardly actions regardless of the absolute size of ΔM.

Some sample values may lend concreteness to the analysis. For example, suppose P rose in t_1 by 10 per cent because of a $((\Delta w/w) - (\Delta A/A) = .1)$ while full employment output growth is put at 6 per cent. On a mechanistic analysis a $(\Delta M/M) < 16$ per cent would be constrictive, despite the fact that the $(\Delta M/M)$ augmentation was large, maybe 10 per cent, compared to the past trend. Conversely, if $(\Delta A/A)$ promised at most to be 6 per cent, with $\Delta P/P > 0$, a $(\Delta M/M) > 6$ per cent would contribute to some 'overheating', probably an unsustainable expansion in the I-sector and some pressure on consumer prices, because of the structural distortion, and bursting out into a profit inflation.

We put the full employment case aside for, apart from its failure to distinguish wage inflation, the monetarist explanation would be apt for the profit inflation contingency.

3.6 The Influence of Monetary Policy on the Price Level

From (10.6), and the general tenor of this analysis, monetary policy cannot determine the course of P. Thus, on our analysis, the MA is generally falsely accused of complicity in causing inflation. Despite the chronic denunciation of the MA by economists, more blame could be attached to the 'rising aspirations' of income recipients for a fast growth in money-incomes, under the delusion that it would signify a commensurate real income gain.[13]

Inflation, then, is conceived at the bargaining table, in the agreement between big labour and big business. It can only be aborted there by voluntary restraint or coercive government policy.[14]

We can now qualify the doctrine that the MA is unable to influence *P*. For it has an *indirect* influence of indeterminate magnitude. Contrary to the monetarist view, it lacks a *direct* impact on *P*.

Suppose the MA pursued what we have characterized as a *neutral* money posture in a period of unemployment. Or that it embarked on a *constrictive* policy intending to force $(\Delta U/U) > 0$.

Conceivably, as unemployment grew, there might be some wage restraint. Either unions would accept smaller pay settlements, or there might be some relaxation of wage rates reached previously.

The implications are alarming: by increasing *U*, monetary policy can curb *w*. Note, however, that the necessary flow must fall on *w*, with *U* serving only as a means towards the end.

Nevertheless, historically labour has pointed to unemployment as a rationale for raising the wage ante, appealing to purchasing power doctrines for high employment. If the pitch is successful, the upshot will be more unemployment and a further *P*-advance.

Thus if:

$$(\partial w/\partial U)\,(dU/dM) > 0, \text{ then } (\Delta P/\Delta U) < 0. \tag{10.11}$$

Overlooking the 'purchasing power' situation, according to (10.11) the MA may restrain *P*, but indirectly.

Besides the ambiguity of the restraining effect, the duration of ΔU may be protracted. A heavy cost toll in human suffering and output loss may be attached to the programme.

3.7 Productivity Impacts

Another indirect channel through which monetary policy may exert some *P*-incidence is via effects on ΔA resulting from stimulating or retarding *Q*.

The outcome may go either way. On the static laws of returns, a cutback in *Q* and *N* should raise *A*, and thus lower *P*. In a dynamic context, however, by choking *Q* and deferring some *I*-activity, the monetary clamp will retard the ΔI lift on ΔA.

3.8 Variation in Velocity: The Friedman Calculations

Our estimates of the impact of *M* on *Q* have been mechanistic, positing the false assumption of $\Delta V = 0$.

An *a priori* account of potential sources of fluctuations in ΔV must go to the roots of M^*. Liquidity preference, under the various $\pm\ P, Q$ combinations invites consideration of at least nine cases. Thus:

Many of the cases have important historical parallels while illustrating the diversity of macroeconomic phenomena. To unravel the separate instances, much of the argument would be tedious in describing 'possi-

Table 10.1   The ΔP and ΔQ Matrix

ΔP \ ΔQ	+	0	−
+	Growth under inflation	Zero growth and Inflation	Stagflation
0	Real growth	No growth	Output recession
−	Growth and price deflation	No growth price deflation	Depression

bilities'. Fortunately, Professor Friedman's calculations allow us to short-cut the exposition.[15] He has computed an elasticity of money incomes, quantifying the ultimate enlargement of money income emanating from a relative increase in the money supply (on his definition of money which need not be in question here). Thus:[16]

$$EYM = (M\Delta Y/Y\Delta M) = 1.82 \tag{10.12}$$

That is with $\Delta M/M = 1$ per cent, after allowing for time lags, $(\Delta Y/Y) = 1.8$ per cent.

Friedman envisages (10.12) as expressing the causality of money for money income. For our purposes, by extracting the portion of ΔM that serves merely to sustain ΔP, we can estimate the extent to which the money augmentation will affect Q.

Built into the Friedman formula are estimates of V, or of the demand for money as Q and P vary. Projecting E_{ym} forward for predictive purposes, there is an implicit hypothesis that money velocity relationships will, in the future, conform to those prevalent in the past. This may be so; only time will tell. The confidence that Friedman has placed in it, in a way, elevates it, if not to the status of a 'constraint', at least to what he calls an impressive 'regularity' in monetary experience.

From the Friedman elasticity and earlier formulae, we can write:

$$(\Delta Q/Q) = [(A'wk)/(Aw'k')][E_{ym}(\Delta M/M) + 1] - 1, \tag{10.13a}$$

where $A' = A + \Delta A$, $k' = k + \Delta k$, $w' = w + \Delta w$.

If $k = k'$ (for some simplification), then merely to hold $Q = \bar{Q}$ the money increase would have to be:

$$\frac{\Delta M}{M} = \frac{Aw' - A'w}{A' W(EYM)} \tag{10.13b}$$

with $EYM = 1.84$, and starting with index numbers of $100 = A = w$, if $A' = w'$, the money supply need not increase. With $w' > A'$, then (13b) yields the necessary $(\Delta M/M)$ magnitude.

3.9   The Friedman Puzzle

Friedman has observed that the magnitude of the respective $Q\Delta P$ and $P\Delta Q$ effects of ΔM are indeterminate. That is:

$$(\Delta M/M) = 1.82\ (\Delta Y/Y) = (\Delta P/P) + (\Delta Q/Q) \qquad (10.7b)$$

While EYM is estimated at 1.8, vagueness surrounds its distribution between $\Delta P/P$ and $\Delta Q/Q$. In later writings he concludes that in the 'short period' $\Delta Q = 0$, so that the effect of $\Delta M/M$ must be wholly on P. Over time, as $\Delta Q > 0$, the P- effect dims while the Q- effect mounts.[17]

Our version of events yields different results: the ΔP moves depend on the $\Delta w/\Delta A$ relationship. Thereupon, ΔQ depends on whether the ΔM advance is stimulating, neutral, or constrictive.

It is with respect to the time path of ΔQ, that lags, expectations, uncertainty, and dynamic consideration affect the analysis. We return to the issues below.

4   MONETARY POLICY AND INTEREST RATES

In its grand designs, monetary policy is dedicated to P and Q (or N or U) objectives. The MA may pursue the goals fitfully, boldly, or guardedly. In tight money episodes, it generally succeeds too well in fostering unemployment; it fares ignominiously against inflation – to judge by a 40-year history.

Other objectives generally assume a secondary place. There is a subsidiary concern with r, spurred by the thought of maintaining an 'orderly' market for government bonds or for the placement of industrial securities.

It was noted earlier that in pursuit of Q-objectives, the MA would usually affect I by its ΔM actions. Practically, however, the MA may be unable – or reluctant – to drive r low enough – or to raise it high enough – to achieve its Q objectives.

In a deep depression, where r is already low, under the 'absolute' liquidity preferences of Keynes, the MA may be powerless to depress r further and thus, to stimulate Q through I. This would provide the shining hour for fiscal policy.

In other instances the MA may recoil from forcing $\Delta r < 0$. Foreign exchange considerations may, for example, intrude: more on this below.

Conceivably, the MA may fear that dragging r downward too quickly will encourage bond market speculation, carrying r below the MA target. Normal financing may be deranged; if the consensus opinion is that r will shortly tumble, long-term borrowing will be postponed with some subsequent congestion in new flotations.

Bond market expectations can thus limit the freedom of action of the MA in speedily pursuing its goal. It may also be an argument for decisive MA actions, rather than trifling with ΔM changes towards ΔQ and ΔN goals. But boldness must be tempered by the vagaries of ΔV.

In tight money circumstances the Δr rise will plummet bond prices, threatening the solvency of financial institutions. A 'credit crunch', or severe tight money episodes (such as in 1968) have been ignited by the illusion by the Fed that its monetary adamancy would subdue inflation.

MA trepidation of a credit crunch must, in our view, be marked as a plus: MA wariness has generally averted a Q and N débâcle. Strong money antidotes inevitably fail to prevent inflation while accentuating the unemployment predicament.

It is a persuasive surmise, in reading the history of Federal Reserve policy, that only the intuitive fear of chaos in financial markets has averted more serious recessions, while alarm over inflation from monetary relaxation in periods of recovery has aborted the ascent to full employment. Thus we fluctuate around Q-levels always short of full employment while reporting unmitigated failure in stemming the inflation tide. The one arrow of monetary action directed against the two targets of P and Q, scores depressing hits on the latter despite careful aim at the former. The record reveals the sorry P-outcome.

5 AN OPEN ECONOMY

In the open economy the MA has also had to assess the effects in exchange rates and the foreign balance, including trade and capital flows often alerted by war scares, taxation, and speculative fever feeding upon a variety of hopes and fears. To curb capital outflows, the MA has often restricted ΔM, to elevate r despite a high U level. Keynes, for these reasons, favoured abandoning fixed exchange rates, or subjecting capital movements to controls so as not to impair domestic full employment objectives.[18]

Domestically, a capital exodus would be offset by monetary expansion; capital inflows would be sterilized. Floating exchange rates, including a 'dirty' float managed for domestic exigencies would also be justified. Here, however, the reaction of the world economy would enter prominently in the application of policy.

It would be futile at this place to try to unravel all the complexities of the open economy. The paramount conclusion, however, would be that in-

flows of funds deemed too large for the proper ΔQ tempo would compe[
offsetting sterilization. Outflows would have to be replaced, to underwrite
full employment.

Issues of inflation need not enter, especially under an effective incomes
policy maintaining a suitable balance of w to A. Price level concern can
then be discarded.

Floating exchange rates can obviously facilitate the ΔQ task of the MA.
The really serious issue, however, would concern the instability engen-
dered in export–import industries, including occasional entrants into either
category, through exchange rate fluctuations. But this involves the frequency and amplitude of exchange rate variation. One way or the other,
through fixed or variable exchange rates, the importance of full employment is too great to be left to international chance. MA judgement and
prescience are at a premium in open economies, that is, in actual economies today.

Exchange floats which affect the price of imports can menace the
domestic price level. By sufficient control over money incomes, P-stability
can still be established. Rising import prices entail some retardation in ΔA,
requiring annual pay increases below *domestic* productivity gains to maintain P-balance.

6   THE TROUBLESOME LAGS

Lags between ΔM and ΔY occupy nearly centre stage in monetarist
analyses. We now consider aspects of the delayed time sequences in
applying our own views of the P and Q evolution. In suggesting that their
significance has been exaggerated, we may note that Friedman has estimated their delay as covering one to 36 months behind initial monetary
causes. None the less, while stressing the lag thesis to question past
monetary policy, he has advocated 'spending M pace'. Hence, considering
other sources of economic instability the 'lags' cannot be regarded even by
him as unduly serious from a policy standpoint.

6.1   Some Theory of Lags[19]

The matter of lags invites some philosophic conjecture.

If the lags are so short that the response is instantaneous, clearly there is
no problem: press the button and hear the buzzer ring, instantaneously, as
far as we can detect. Largely, it will be argued that there is practically no
lag with respect to Δw and ΔP, so that lags here hardly enter the discussion.

On longer lags, if we press the button now and it won't ring for five years
or more, there are questions of whether, when that date arrives, we want it

to ring. In any event, no sound is emitted till then; it hardly hurts – or helps – until the five years elapse. If it may ring at an inopportune time, and we are able to redress it before it happens, again there is no serious problem. Considering that fiscal policy can be invoked as an offset to monetary policy, 'long lags' need not be so troublesome so long as fiscal policy operates with reasonable dispatch.

What are the long lags? Not w or P, on our theory. If it is a long time before monetary policy affects Q, this cannot be a serious matter. For employment cannot get 'overly' full. If ΔQ grows too quickly, a sharp turn of the monetary screw can be effective expeditiously, as has often been observed in the housing market at the onslaught of tight money.

So the lags of ΔM on either ΔQ or ΔP are not at all worrisome. It may be surmised that the theory of 'long and unpredictable lags' has been a bogey invented to instil fears of inflation in the minds of the MA, to warn them that what they do now will have inescapable effects at some unknown date in the future. Hence, they had better be very cautious before throwing our economy fairly permanently out of kilter – a responsibility that few are willing to assume lightly. The bogey of lags is thus a counsel of fear, that some terrible consequences will emerge at a date uncertain in time.

To repeat, however, long lags of ΔM on Q are doubtful, and certainly not dangerous, especially if what is entailed is monetary easing to stimulate Q and N towards maximum output and full employment.

Long lags, generally with baneful consequences, would be something to fear only if there were neither early future recognition symptoms, or if there were no effective antidotes. Neither of these conditions are present with respect to Q, while the fear psychosis with respect to P is utterly suspect.

We conclude that the story of lags as an impediment to monetary policy, warranting a steady rule, is a hairy tale designed to forestall remitting monetary efforts to accomplish full employment on the grounds that the actions would predestine inflation. With the latter argument faulty, and the former plea to inaction insubstantial, the lag emphasis is an exaggerated bit of voodoo to abide monetary do-nothingness in the one area where it can contribute positively, namely with respect to Q and N.

The ΔP lags, by and large, with respect to changes in w are notoriously short. Often the ink was scarcely dry on new contracts between unions and management in steel, cars, electrical machinery, or in construction industries, before prices erupted. The price hike sometimes preceded, sometimes followed, or was announced simultaneously, with the union–management bargain. Lags at the first stage, in the industry subject to agreement, are frequently negligible.

Considering the minor perturbations in the annual data on k, the insignificance of serious lags of the effects of Δw on ΔP appears confirmed.

Obviously, a wage boost and price hike in steel, say, may take some time for the full effects to filter through the economy. But this would cover a few months rather than a few years. Lags scarcely jeopardize our theory of the price level: they seem sufficiently short as to encourage benign neglect, for theory or policy.

Even if they were of longer duration, they ought not to be troublesome for the MA struggling to deflect Q to a targeted level. For if the price advance is foreordained by the wage pressure, and is only more slowly seeping through the economy in a Leontief chain, for ΔM to support the $\Delta P/P$ plus $\Delta Q/Q$ combination, the ΔM augmentation would have to surpass the amounts necessary for merely a ΔQ expansion itself. Ultimately, a greater $\Delta M/M$ variation would be imperative as the full chain of prices responded.

Considering our inflationary age, it is mainly a theoretical exercise to dwell on a price deflation sequence.

Our policy conclusion requires scant amendment in contemplation of lags, so far as P-tendencies go. Standing at date t_0 and looking ahead, on the basis of known wage contracts and estimates of those forthcoming, some estimates of the $(\Delta w/\Delta A)$ ratio and thus the $(\Delta P/P)$ outbreak, must be formulated. To prevent any erosion of Q (or N), a $\Delta M/M$ emission must be prepared with allowance for ΔV according to the best understanding currently available.

6.2   Q-lags

How quickly Q and N levels respond to stimulating ΔM variations is more complex and obscure, depending on historical circumstances.

The speed and sensitivity of I to r will depend on: (1) the economy-wide state of plant capacity compared to normal operations; (2) the degree of confidence attached to output forecasts; (3) the credit standards applied in bank lending; (4) any tax breaks conducive to haste or delay in I; (5) the nature of new drawing board technology; (6) the speed with which MA actions are translated into easier bank credit availability. Finally, (7) international phenomena, including speculative foreign exchange phenomena.

Considering the list, it is hardly surprising that a unique answer on the time lag between ΔM and ΔQ eludes us.

Still, all is not lost for monetary policy despite ignorance of the precise $\Delta M \rightarrow \Delta Q$ reaction time. For if the reaction time is a full year from the date of an MA emisssion ΔM, procrastination can consign the economy to an unnecessary long bout of unemployment. Yet the results are by no means fatal: a long lag only means that full employment is deferred. We have had much experience with such phenomena. To shorten the time lag the MA can assure the enterprise sector of the availability of funds until U hits some reasonable level.

Fast reaction times amount to the absence of lags; policy errors are likely to be less costly. If Q responded very quickly, full employment could be accomplished in a flash; ΔV would be learned without pains.

Emphasis on 'long' lags is largely a counsel to do nothing. How long? How serious? If effects are serious then policies with shorter lags must be devised rather than using the 'long-lag' thesis as a reason to wash our hands of any effort at a more rational policy. Actually, Friedman's 'long lags' are merely a result of what we regard as an optical illusion, namely, associating 'later' inflation with 'earlier' money supply growth.

The reluctance of the MA to provide assurance that ample funds will be available for full employment is almost wholly attributable to its preoccupation with inflation. The complication caused by 'long lags' is of a pseudo-nature that would vanish if inflation were banished by the applicability of an effective incomes policy. Lags seem more difficult in expounding the policy problem on the mistaken monetarist P-theory, rather than comprising a serious obstacle to full employment engineered by sufficient measurements in the money supply.

By moving faster than the business community is prepared to implement I-plans, the MA may speed them into action. Of course, some I-programmes may be ill-conceived, but error is also part of the attraction process in an uncertain world, where the effects of I-decisions are imperfectly foreseen. Judgements on which projects will really be able to pay their way are never accurate, even apart from pressures of the lack of funds to finance projects.

Our conclusion then is that the theory of lags as applied to the $\Delta Q/Q$ response to $\Delta M/M$ variations is overdrawn and a bogey to rationalize inaction. Some of the empirical calculations of lags in $(\Delta Y/Y)$ to $(\Delta M/M)$ are, in our view, mirages attributable to the assigning of causal responsibility for inflation to money emissions. On our own belief that this inflation theory is simply an error, the long lag obstacles connote a specious objection to the use of MA directions to use monetary measures for full employment. Even granting them some validity, they would not comprise a serious objection to the use of monetary policy to reduce unemployment so long as incomes failed to rise, for then inflation would be precluded beyond some insignificant P-wriggles.

So long as inflation is arrested or overbid by incomes policy, $(\Delta M/M)$ accretions in the usual range, of 10 per cent per annum or less, *can hardly do any harm*, regardless of the length of the lags. For employment cannot be overly full. If $(\Delta M/M)$ seems to approach the 'overheating' stage, the policy can be reversed – without any serious or permanent damage to the economy.

7   A STEADY RATE OF MONEY INCREASE

Lags may thus be a bogey erected by alarmist thinking to instil monetary caution. The great danger is that because of a deluded belief that their actions affect the *P*-course, the MA will keep $(\Delta M/M)$ too low, and condemn the economy to a frequent performance short of full employment.

It remains to consider the argument for steady accretions to the money supply, say of 4 per cent per annum under the Friedman presumption.

Clearly, 4 (or 5) per cent limitation would be ample for the historical trend of Q. But it would be likely to mire the economy in frequent recession, and depression, unless wage movements were compatible with a stable price level, implying annual *average* wage (and salary) increments of about 3 to 4 per cent in conformity with per capita productivity advances.

Friedman, in all this, has simply reversed causation; he merely assumes that money-wages will behave properly so long as $\Delta M/M$ is geared only to $\Delta Q/Q$. For over a decade now this assumption has simply been invalid. Thus the 4 (or 5) per cent rule is a presumption for unemployment or recession unless an incomes policy stabilized the wage-salary trend. Can the steadiness rule then survive?

Standing at the date t_0, the MA would have to evaluate the projected $(\Delta w/\Delta A)$ relation and its implications for P. Thereupon, merely to *maintain* Q, the $(\Delta M/M)$ emission would have to be large enough to cover the price level advance. Ominous implications for the steadiness rule are implicit. The rule would have to be relaxed whenever the pace of w/A altered so as to menace a steady P. Unless some regularity was brought to the wage–productivity nexus, monetary policy will have to be more fitful, and generally showing higher rates of change than Friedman contemplates.

A steady M-growth, when P revealed a steady rise, would impart instability in Q, deflecting it from potential maximum $(\Delta Q/A)$. Inexorably, as the monetarist ritual compelled obedience to the steadiness rule, concern with the Q and N shortfall would countenance the abandonment of the steady M path for a more meaningful Q ascent and V descent.

We would thus have no quarrel with the steady-M rule if inflation were precluded by an effective incomes voluntary or mandatory policy. But the rule of 4 per cent could be disastrous for N, without contributing a better P outcome, if the past explosive wage behaviour is repeated in the future. Likewise, unless the $(\Delta w/\Delta A)$ variations are 'steady', any steady-M rule will obstruct the march to maximum w and minimum U.

Friedman's 4 per cent rule is predicated on the belief that wages, and thus the price level, would be accommodating along a flat trend so that real growth would occur steadily by 4 per cent. But if the premise of P-stability is shattered, there can be little virtue in a policy of a steady M if it forced an unsatisfactory Q path, with excess unemployment and wage-induced inflation.

8   CHANGES IN LIQUIDITY PREFERENCE

Our own presumption for monetary policy, not unlike the Friedman monetarist exposition, has been mechanistic, indicating the correct ΔM to cover the normal ΔQ path, and to stimulate Q once inflation has set in. It is as if V never changes, either absolutely or percentage-wise. (The latter is assumed by Friedman.)

Yet there can be bouts of liquidity demand, as when some trepidation prevails so that people want to hold more cash and demand deposits instead of savings accounts, bonds, etc. Likewise, there can be occasions of liquidity disgorging, with individuals and firms wanting to hold lower money stocks. The MA could thereupon curtail new emissions of money.

The MA would also have to keep its eye peeled on capital inflows and outflows, to prevent derangement of the domestic economy.

Ultimately, to sense the changes in money demand that are unrelated to transaction needs at changed P or Q levels requires an uncanny prescience. It cannot be a mechanical calculation based on past data extrapolated painlessly to future conduct. Judgement at the MA conclave can never be in plentiful supply; perfect judgement can only be acknowledged *ex post*. Mechanical rules might narrow the area of human error, but they can never cope successfully with non-mechanistic human circumstances.

9   A RECEIPE FOR MONETARY POLICY

It may be useful to consolidate our thoughts on monetary policy.

Standing at any point in time, with an irrevocable past and looking towards an impenetrable future, the MA would first have to assess the prospective P development which, in our view, is almost wholly independent of the MA actions. Secondly, there is the possible maximum ΔQ expansion.

The P development would assume priority for it is likely to continue to be more erratic than the *potential* Q-path.

Depending on the speed of any ΔQ advance, allowing for lags as best it can, the MA would have to reach a verdict on its ΔM expansion. If it calculates for the annual period in prospect, and prefers a 'steady' monthly money accretion, it can issue a time profile to plot its strategy to those delegated with executing the ΔM instructions. If it desires to concentrate the ΔM expansion within a few days (or weeks), before the ΔQ flow can gather momentum, the likelihood is that there will be some money market instability, with r descending as the market absorbs the extra funds, and then recovering to an intermediate point as the funds are absorbed into the income stream for transactions financing.

On the assumption of proportionate wage-productivity behaviour, so that inflation is eliminated as a threat, we could largely concur in the

Friedman 4 per cent rule. Where the unemployment rate is unduly high, a greater money augmentation would be justified.

Where the money-wage advance promises to be excessive, the MA must make $(\Delta M/M)$ at least large enough to compensate for the price move, or face the prospect of a recessionary downturn in Q, and a greater descent in N in the light of productivity gains. MA timidity because of fears of inflation will only compound inflation with the frustrations of unemployment.

In an environment of wage–price upheavals, the MA is likely to reveal an excess of prudence in the comfortable rationalization that it is guarding the economy against the unfavourable price outcome. Hence with its belief in a monetary original sin for inflation, the MA is likely to prove more culpable in causing unemployment.

On this assessment, what the monetarists require to buttress their monetary prescriptions is a feasible incomes policy. Then it should be possible to implement the 4 per cent rule with almost complete fidelity. Until that time is reached the MA will have to render a judgement on the w/A course and the P-trend and impute a proper weight in deciding its money emissions.

With the price level protected through Incomes Policy, the only de-murrer challenging the 4 per cent steadiness rule would be in instances of liquidity crises, involving extra money-demand, or if money holdings are being disgorged. Further, there will be the need to contain foreign inflows or outflows of funds. The latter are likely to be sufficiently common as to require more than an obedient clerk abiding a fixed money rule, occupying the office of the MA.

10 CONCLUSIONS

In that happy day when inflation is exorcised, by the invocation of an Incomes Policy, we could, for the most part, endorse the 4 per cent rule, and the steadiness aspect of it. In the non-inflationary world, the necessary monetary actions can be minimal, executed perhaps by a clerk following routine instruction. Yet any liquidity bouts will have to be skilfully hand-led, requiring judgement, insight, and actions transcending routine instruc-tion.

In the inflationary system that seems destined to remain with us because of our failure to design an operationally feasible incomes policy, it is too early to dismiss central bankers and to dismember their decision-making processes. The central bank fears of inflation will undoubtedly prevent us from realizing a steady diet of full employment output. Replacing them by the routine clerk following the 4 per cent steadiness rule would, however, probably wreak more unemployment havoc than restoring the old gold standard at the 1900 price of gold.

Notes

1. This scarcely requires documentation. See, e.g. 'A Theoretical Framework for Monetary Analysis', *Journal of Political Economy* (March–April 1970), p. 195. Or: 'Inflation is always and everywhere a monetary phenomenon . . .', in 'What Price Guideposts', George Shultz and Robert Aliber (eds), *Guidelines, Informal Controls, and the Market Place* (Chicago: University of Chicago Press, 1966), p. 18.
2. Even in hyperinflation the process would *not* continue unless money incomes, wages and salaries particularly, kept mounting. Ms Robinson, for example, points out that in the great German inflation wages were adjusted hourly, according to a 'cost-of-living' index! She observes that the importance of this facet was neglected by Bresclani–Turroni, in his book on the *Economics of Inflation*. See her pithy review article, *Economic Journal*, (1938), p. 510.
3. On the persistent refusal of economists to apprehend the wage-price events, and modify their Quantity Theory or Monetarist preconceptions, see the lament of Peter Wiles, 'Cost Inflation and the State of Economic Theory', *Economic Journal* (June 1973).
4. Joan Robinson, *The Accumulation of Capital* (London: Macmillan, 1956).
5. This position is developed as the central thesis in Paul Davidson, *Money and the Real World* (London: Macmillan, 1974). Also see F. Knight, *Risk, Uncertainty and Profit* (New York: Houghton Mifflin, 1921).
6. See Milton Friedman, *The Optimum Quantity of Money, and Other Essays* (Chicago: Aldine, 1969), chapter 1. Also Keynes 'The Ex Ante Theory of the Rate of Interest', *Economic Journal*, 1937.
8. General Theory, *The General Theory of Employment, Interest and Money* (London: Macmillan, p. 235)
9. Cf. J. M. Keynes, *The General Theory of Employment, Interest, and Money* (London, 1936).
10. See Sidney Weintraub, *A General Theory of the Price Level* (Philadelphia: Chilton Book Co., 1959).
11. Cf. John Hoiton, *International Comparisons of Money Velocity and Wage Mark-Ups* (New York: Augustus Kelley, 1968).
12. S. Weintraub and Hamid Habebazaki, 'Money Supplies and Price–Output Indeterminateness', *Journal of Economic Issues* (June 1972). Reprinted in *Keynes and the Monetarists*. (New Brunswick, Rutgers University Press, 1973).
13. For an outline of a market-oriented incomes policy, cf. Henry Wallich and Sidney Weintraub, 'A Tax Based on Incomes Policy', *Journal of Economic Issues* (June 1971). (Reprinted in, *Keynes and the Monetarists*) (New Brunswick, Rutgers University Press, 1973).
14. Cf. A. J. Brown, *The Great Inflation* (Oxford, Oxford University Press, 1955).
15. M. Friedman, *Optimum Quantity of Money*, (Chicago, Aldine Publishing, 1969).
16. His calculation assumes that, $\Delta V/V$, rather than V, is constant. Thus:

$$\text{As } MV = Y, \therefore \ \frac{\Delta V}{V} + \frac{\Delta M}{M} = \frac{\Delta Y}{Y} \cdot \text{As } \frac{M\Delta Y}{Y\Delta M} = 1 + \frac{M\Delta V}{V\Delta M} \ ,$$

it follows that $\quad \dfrac{M\Delta V}{V\Delta M} = .82.$

17. See M. Friedman 'A Theoretical Framework For Monetary Analysis' in *Milton*

Friedman's Monetary Framework, ed by R. G. Gordon (Chicago, University of Chicago Press, 1974).

18. Cf. J. M. Keynes, *Treatise on Money* (London, 1930).
19. See Keynes, *Treatise on Money* (London, Macmillan, 1930) vol. 2, p. 223–224 on the bismuth-magnesia cycle.

11 Discussion of Papers on the Keynesian Model

In reading these three papers I was struck by the complete absence of Keynes's analysis in modern Keynesian models – at least as presented by such eminent Keynesians as Tobin, Eisner and Clower–Leijonhufvud (hereafter C–L).[1] I would like to suggest that Keynes's concepts were never part of the intellectual tool-kit of most American Keynesians and that therefore it is not surprising that American Keynesians are virtually bankrupt when it comes to offering advice to the Ford administration on alleviating the problems of inflation and recession simultaneously.

C–L were not the first but they were the most successful at forcing our profession into realizing that there is at least a paradigm's worth of difference between the economics of Keynes and Keynesian economics. Keynes's principle message in both his *Treatise* and *General Theory* was that there is no way, except by coincidence (dare I say by double coincidence), that a real world free market price system could coordinate or prereconcile plans of all economic agents in a production economy.

Tobin's model, except for one small concept, the q ratio, completely ignores Keynes's analytical framework. This is not as surprising as it might appear! In both his opening and concluding paragraphs, Tobin indicates that Keynes was a failure as a theorist; if this is so, then Tobin has reason to steer clear of Keynes's theoretical constructs. But is it true?

Tobin states that Keynes could not prove the existence of underemployment equilibrium. But as I pointed out in a 1967 *EJ* article on Patinkin's system, the view that Keynes provided only a disequilibrium model comes from living in a Walrasian rather than a Marshallian paradigm. In the former, equilibrium is defined as synonymous with market clearing or the prereconciliation of buyers' and sellers' plans by the price system. Hence in a Walrasian world, unless workers' supply plans are reconciled with employers' hiring decisions in the labour market, the system, *by definition*, is not in equilibrium. Walrasian theory defines away the problem of underemployment equilibrium but that does not, despite Tobin's contention to the contrary, prove the case. Definition is not proof!

For Marshall and Keynes, on the other hand, there is a conceptual distinction between market clearing and market equilibrium; Patinkin himself recognized this distinction on p. 643 of the 2nd edition of his book when he noted that equilibrium 'means in the usual sense of the term that nothing tends to change in the system'. In a Keynes–Marshall world, clearing is a sufficient but it is *not a necessary* condition for equilibrium.

Thus equilibrium or the absence of change is possible without market clearing in both the Marshall–Keynes world and the real world!

As Keynes's 1937 Lecture Notes indicate (reprinted in Vol. XIV of his *Collected Works*, pp. 179–83), Keynes had no doubt that his model was applicable to a world of underemployment equilibrium (in the Marshallian sense where nothing tends to change in the system) as well as a world where things are changing. Apropos of Tobin's view of Keynes's model as one of disequilibrium, Keynes noted that other economists who 'lay the whole emphasis and find the whole explanation in the *differences* between effective demand and income and they are so convinced that this is the right course that they do not notice that in my treatment this is not so' (ibid., p. 181). Equation 2.1.1 of Tobin's model relies on a difference between 'E' (aggregate effective demand) and 'Y' (actual real income) to explain changes in the rate of production.

Keynes compared the neoclassical economists to Euclidean Geometers in a non-Euclidean world who discover 'in experience that straight lines apparently parallel often meet, rebuke the lines for not keeping straight as the only remedy for the unfortunate collisions which are occurring' (*The General Theory*, 1936, p. 16). In my view, C–L, Tobin, and Eisner are modern day Euclideans, who attempt to perform conceptual experiments in a Walrasian world and apply the resulting remedies to a non-Walrasian real world. C–L go so far as to suggest that the basic question for modern theorists is 'whether we can conceive of an economy that is *completely* characterized by equilibrium relations of the kind identified by Walras' and then see if we can interpret actual experience as bearing a family resemblance to the Walrasian construct. C–L build an ingenious mythical neo-Walrasian exchange economy – which has no concept of time and no production and hence no forward contracting for labour services.

When faced with policy problems, however, American Keynesians really do not have sufficient faith in the logic of their neo-Walrasian parables. Stronger spirits at Chicago, Providence, Pittsburgh and Rochester are capable of adopting a hypothetical world remote from experience, as though it was the world of experience and then living in it consistently. For Keynesians like Tobin, Eisner, and C–L, however, common sense cannot help breaking in – with injury to their logical consistency.

C–L urges us to 'jettison' some of the assumptions of standard neo-Walrasian theory, especially the one that no false trading occurs at non-equilibrium prices; and then re-examine this Walrasian world. C–L are inviting us to throw out the Walrasian baby while still examining the remaining bathwater for telltale rings.

Eisner in essence follows C–L advice. He recognizes that workers and employers operate continually on plans that are going to be disappointed, i.e. they false trade, but Eisner still clings to a Walrasian framework. Hence Eisner must introduce all sorts of *ad hoc* elasticity constraints, improperly behaved functions, intertemporal market failures, etc. to achieve the crashes that he knows are occurring in actual experience; while ignoring the fact that false trading in the labour market means that the parameters of the system are continually changing and hence the real world cannot achieve the state of bliss underlying his Walrasian model.

Eisner admits that money is more important than peanuts – a statement which is incompatible with a Walrasian world, for as Arrow and Hahn have demonstrated, in such a world 'money can play no essential role'. Eisner has the common sense to recognize that there is something special about money but he is trapped by his Walrasian myopia to argue that money is not omnipotent, that in principle its supply and demand equations are not different from those for peanuts. Here Eisner has clearly ignored at least one-twenty-fourth of Keynes's *General Theory*, a chapter which is essential for monetary theorists trying to understand Keynes's monetary theory. This chapter is entitled 'The Essential Properties of Interest and Money'. In this chapter Keynes clearly specified two essential or necessary elasticity properties for *liquidity* in a Keynes world. These properties distinguish money and liquid assets from peanuts, and as Keynes emphasized, 'The attribute of "liquidity" is by no means independent of the presence of these two characteristics' (*The General Theory*, p. 244).

If Tobin is going to insist that Theory with a capital T must be confined to a neo-Walrasian (Euclidean) world, where parallel lines can't crash, then Tobin must concede that in this Alice in Walrasland world a private market economy will, if it approaches equilibrium without government interference, attain full employment. Squirm as he may, Tobin cannot avoid that definitional conclusion unless he engages in the most crass *ad hoc* theorizing.

Moreover, Tobin is incorrect when he follows Friedman in claiming that Keynes deviated from Marshall in reversing the relative speeds of adjustment of price and quantity. Even Leijonhufvud, who was the first to state that the 'revolutionary element' in *The General Theory* was the reversal of these speeds of adjustment, has now recanted and joins Patinkin and myself in arguing:

> It is *not* correct to attribute to Keynes a general reversion of the Marshallian ranking of relative price and quantity adjustment velocities . . . (Although) most recent writings on Keynes' theory including my own insist on examining it from a Walrasian prospective . . . Keynes was, of course, a price theoretical Marshallian . . . and ignoring this fact will simply not do. (A. Leijonhufvud, 'Keynes' Employment Function', *Hist. of Pol. Econ.*, VI (1974), p. 169).

At only one point does Tobin pick up and then, in my view, incorrectly define a critical Keynes concept that has been previously virtually ignored in the Keynesian literature. This is Tobin's *q*-ratio which he defines as the ratio of the market valuation of equities to replacement costs. But a close reading of chapters 11, 17 and the revealing Appendix to chapter 14 of *The General Theory*, where Keynes deals at great length with the demand and supply prices of capital goods plus the theory of spot and forward markets for capital goods of his *Treatise*, shows that Tobin's q-ratio is defined in Keynes's model as the ratio of the spot price of existing capital goods (and not equities) compared to the forward price (or replacement) price of capital goods. If q is properly defined, then when $q>1$ in Keynes's system, capital goods markets are in a state of *backwardation* and the production of capital goods is positive. If $q<1$, then a *contango* exists, capital goods are redundant and gross investment is zero.

Time is a device which prevents everything from happening at once and production takes time. Thus time is essential to Keynes's paradigm, while in the Walrasian world all transactions are agreed upon at once before anything occurs. With the introduction of backwardation and contango concepts in the Keynes model, however, forward contracting becomes an essential aspect of the economic process as it moves over time. In Keynes's model and in the real world, producers abhor what neo-Walrasian theorists love – namely recontracting. Seriatim forward contracting through time is the most important human institution yet devised for controlling the uncertain future. In fact one could look upon the private institution of catenated forward contracts as the way a free enterprise production economy attempts to assure wage and price controls and stability over time. It is not surprising, therefore, when the duration of private contracts begins to be shortened to less than the production gestation period, that the stability of a production economy is threatened and a search for a social contract to bolster the institution of private contracts is needed.

Tobin insists in presenting a model which he labels the Walras–Keynes–Phillips (WKP) model. Three stranger bedfellows I cannot imagine. Even Tobin recognizes the incompatibilities involved in this bed as he observes that 'Keynes would scorn equation (2.3.1)' of the WKP model which embodies the 'adaptive expectations hypothesis' (I have already indicated Keynes would scorn equation 2.1.1 by quoting from Keynes's 1937 lecture notes; and in a moment I will indicate why Keynes would scorn the remaining equation 2.2.2 of the WKP model – So I would like to ask Tobin, where is Keynes in the WKP model?).

Keynes wrote a whole chapter on 'Expectations as Determining Output and Employment' and yet Keynesian models not only ignore Keynes's views on expectations as if he never wrote on the subject, but they adapt the cuckoo world approach of adaptive expectations which as Tobin recognizes is incompatible with Keynes's analysis. (The adaptive expectations hypothesis implies that even though false trading occurs, and hence the parameters of the system are altered, expectations zero in on an unchanged, stable, and unique real equilibrium path. This is an illogical situation.) No wonder Tobin ends up by creating a problem for Keynes when Tobin declares 'Keynes's choice of adjustment mechanisms is a crucial element of his theory'. As Patinkin, I and Leijonhufvud (not to mention the English Keynesians) have declared, the relative speeds of adjustment were *never* crucial to Keynes's paradigm analysis; it only appears as a problem in bastardized Walras–Keynes models.

Having bastardized and bowdlerized Keynes's model till it is neither internally consistent nor relevant to the real world, American Keynesians should not be taken seriously for policy prescriptions. For example, using equation 2.2.1, Tobin declares: 'Prices begin to decline because Y_1 (the actual level of real income) is less than Y^* (full employment).' As Gerry Ford might say, 'if only it were so.'

Keynes was not only human but he was fallible. His writings are not without error. But like the other truly great economists – Smith, Ricardo, Marx, Marshall – he had that element of genius which permits the modelling of the real world directly. Keynes, the monetary theorist, did not begin his analysis by studying a world without money and then imagine why in certain circumstances 'money' should be invented. Keynes adopted the view that what must be modelled from the very beginning is a real world production economy and not how a barter economy behaves when money is imposed on it. He explicitly stated, 'Money plays a part on its own' – while in a Walrasian world money can play no essential role. Keynes insisted money 'affects motives and decisions . . . so that the course of events cannot be predicted either in the long period or in the short without a knowledge of the behaviour of money between the first state and the last'. In other words, Money Matters.

In conclusion, the American economics profession has never examined Keynes's original paradigm. Instead American Keynesians contrive macro market models to elucidate a mathematical system, instead of developing mathematical models to elucidate real world market systems.

True progress in science is made by standing on the shoulders of geniuses who went before. Unfortunately, our most eminent American Keynesians are building edifices while standing on the hunchback of a French bell-ringer, rather than on the strong shoulders of the Bursar of King's College, Cambridge.

Note

1. R. Clower and A. Leijonhufvud, 'The Coordination of Economic Activity: A Keynesian Perspective', *AER Papers and Proceedings*, 65 (May) 1975, pp. 182–8; R. Eisner, 'The Keynesian Revolution Reconsidered', *AER Papers and Proceedings*, 65 (May), 1975, pp. 189–94; J. Tobin, 'Keynesian Models of Recession and Depression', *AER Papers and Proceedings*, 65 (May), 1975, pp. 195–202.

12 Money and General Equilibrium*

In order to have a meaningful discussion of whether the concept of money can be given a meaningful role in any general equilibrium theory, it is essential to explain specifically what is meant by 'money' and what is meant by a 'general equilibrium' (hereafter GE) system. Much of the confusion in professional discussions occurs because these terms are often used differently by different economists – and unfortunately even by the same economist to mean different things at different times and places.

1 MONEY

Modern monetarists mistakenly believe that the use of illustrative examples of money can provide a definition of a concept; hence, modern monetary theory abounds with so-called 'definitions' of M_1, M_2, M_3 . . ., M_7 which are exemplifications rather than explanations. Imagine the confusion and chaos that would occur if astronomers defined 'planets' by using the name of specific heavenly bodies (how would you tell a planet from a moon?), or even worse if some chemists defined the term 'molecule' in terms of specific inorganic salts, while a second group included specific inorganic acids with the salts, and a third group included inorganic bases, etc.

Scientific communication and progress can only occur when definitions are cast not in terms of specific illustrations but are formulated in terms of *essential* features and properties. Then, if a specific item possesses these essential properties and features, it is an example of the defined thing no matter how strange this may appear to the layman, e.g. a whale is a mammal, not a fish, or bamboo shoots are grass, not trees.

In this spirit of scientific definition, I shall insist that the concept of money in existence in a modern production, market-oriented economy involves two fundamental, concomitant features. These features, in turn, require two necessary properties. Money is that thing which by delivery permits economic agents to discharge obligations that are the result of spot and/or forward contracts. Thus the first definitional feature is that *money is the means of contractual settlement*. Money is also capable of acting as a vehicle to move generalized (non-specific) purchasing power over time, i.e. the second feature involves *money as a one-way* (present to future) *time machine*.[1]

* *Economie Appliquée*, 4 (1977).

In modern monetary economies, this second feature which is known as liquidity, is possessed in various degree by some, but not all, durables. Since any durable besides money *cannot* (by definition) be used as a means of settlement of future contractual obligations, in order for a specific durable to be a vehicle for moving generalized purchasing power over time, it must be readily resaleable at any time in a well-organized orderly *spot* market. The degree of liquidity associated with any durable is a measure of its capability as a 'liquidity time machine' and that depends on the degree of organization of its spot market.

The means of contractual settlement or payment feature of money, on the other hand, is *not* possessed by any other durable except money. If some 'liquidity time machine' was suddenly to also possess this means of settlement feature (or to lose it) at that moment the durable would become (would no longer be) money. Thus, for example when in the 1930s the US Supreme Court upheld the abrogation of the gold clause in business contracts, gold was no longer money in the United States – even though it may have retained a degree of liquidity to the extent it was saleable for money in spot markets.

It therefore follows that exemplifications of money in any economy (e.g. M_1, M_2, etc.) can only be identified in relationship to the existing law of contracts in the particular economic system under observation and the market organization and institutional arrangements which permit contracting in money terms over short (the initial instant or today) and longer periods of calendar time. Obviously, therefore, some monetarists have abused the concept of money in their extended 'definitions' which include corporate securities, bonds, etc. (e.g. M_3, M_4, etc.) for they have improperly identified the time machine aspect as the essential feature of money and have basically ignored the means of contractual settlement feature – while the latter is the essence of anything which deserves the title of money.

Money plays an essential and peculiar role only when contractual obligations span a significant length of calendar time. If the economic system being studied only permits *spot* transactions, i.e. contracts which require payments at the immediate instant, then even if its members utilize a convenient medium of account (the numéraire) and/or exchange, such a numéraire is *not* money in the full sense of the term. Spot transaction economies (which are equivalent to Hicks's flexprice economies (see Davidson, 1978, ch. 16) have, as Keynes insisted, 'scarcely emerged from the stage of barter' (Keynes, 1930, p. 3). In other words, a world in which economic activity never involves contracts for payment at specified future dates that are weeks, months or even years in the future is an economy in which both the settlement concept of money and its related notion of liquidity are vacuous.

Money only matters in a world – our world – where there are multitudinous catenated forward contracts in money terms. In such an economy it is necessary that there be some continuity as to what will be the thing which by delivery settles the resulting obligations. The existence of market institutions which permit (and encourage) contracting for future payment creates the need for money and liquidity.[2] This is an essential aspect affecting the performance of all real world market-oriented monetary economies where the activity of production requires the passage of calendar time. Any economic model which ignores these time-related monetary contractual obligations and associated liquidity concerns will be a misleading guide to practical affairs; and any economists who use such a defective model will be deserving recipients of the businessman's traditional scoff, 'They have never had to meet a payroll!'

The attribute of liquidity requires that money possess certain 'essential properties', namely, a zero (or negligible) elasticity of production and a zero (or negligible) elasticity of substitution.[3] (Since I have developed this 'essential' elasticities property theme at great length elsewhere (Davidson, 1978, ch. 6, 9), it will be assumed in what follows that the reader is familiar with that analysis.)

Arrow and Hahn in their monumental study of general equilibrium analysis have recognized that money, contracts and time are inevitably and intimately related. If money matters then the 'terms in which contracts are made matter. In particular, if money is the good in terms of which contracts are made, then the price of goods in terms of money are of special significance. This is not the case if we consider an economy without a past and without a future' (Arrow and Hahn, 1971, p. 356).

This crucial theme, which was the foundation of Keynes's monetary equilibrium analysis, has been developed at length in my *Money and the Real World*, especially in the second edition when the Arrow and Hahn conclusion that 'If a serious monetary theory comes to be written, the fact that contracts are indeed made in terms of money will be of considerable importance' (ibid., p. 357) and, therefore, in 'a world with a past as well as a future and in which contracts are made in terms of money, no [general] equilibrium may exist' (ibid., p. 367) is put in perspective. This motif is basic to the examination of what economists mean by the concept of GE and its relationship to money.

2 GENERAL EQUILIBRIUM

Despite the pervasive use of the term GE in the professional literature, a search for a unique unchanging definition to be shared by all proponents can prove difficult if not futile. Until recently, Walras's Law, i.e. the simultaneous clearing of all markets, was thought by most to be *sine qua non* property of GE. Recently, however, some have claimed that 'general Equilibrium will *not* be considered as bearing a necessary relationship to theories of Walras' (Weintraub, 1977, p. 2) and, by extension one assumes no necessary relationship to Walras's Law. Thus in recent years a plethora of different interpretations of GE have been developed – some apparently only tenuously related to its original Walras's Law meaning – as GE proponents were confronted by the logical inadequacies of the original Walrasian theory to provide a well-formed microfoundation for macro-economic theory which deals with production, money, and expectations about an uncertain future.

Confusion persists, however, even amongst those who still adhere to the Walrasian foundation of GE. Some believe that Walrasian equilibrium was applicable to the short-run (Patinkin, 1965, p. 50) others have insisted that it represented only a long-run norm (Friedman, 1974, p. 48, 150).

In his admirable survey of *General Equilibrium Systems*, Bent Hansen has recognized that the 'nature of equilibrium has not always been clear to the economists who used the concept' (1970, p. 3). Hansen suggests that equilibrium has been defined differently by different economists:

> The most common definition of equilibrium is equality of demand and supply. A market is said to be in equilibrium if the quantity in demand is equal to the quantity in supply. An alternative definition states that demand price and supply price must be equal . . . These definitions or, rather, conditions of equilibrium, thus presume some law of motion for prices and quantities. A third definition of equilibrium . . . states that equilibrium prevails if all plans and expectations of all economic subjects are fulfilled so that, at given data, no economic subject feels inclined to revise his plans or expectations. This definition of equilibrium obviously calls for laws of motion governing the revisions of plans and expectations. (ibid.)

Despite these differences in definition of equilibrium and the laws of motion involved, it is normally believed that the simultaneous clearing of *all* markets is a necessary and sufficient condition for GE (Barro and Grossman, 1971, p. 88) – a result which Patinkin summarized via *Walras's Law* (1965, p. 35). Of course, if Walras's Law is a necessary condition for equilibrium, then Keynes's *General Theory* which demonstrated the possibility of less than full employment equilibrium (when the labour market does not clear) would be a contradiction in terms. Those who maintain the importance of Walras's Law therefore have concluded either 'Keynesian economics is the economics of unemployment *dis*equilibrium' (ibid., pp. 337–8), or else Keynes's claim was the boast of a charlatan theoretician, i.e. if Walras's Law holds, Keynes's contribution to equilibrium theory was either ill conceived or negligible.

In 1939, Hicks had proclaimed:

I believe I have had the fortune to come upon a method of analysis which is applicable to a wide variety of economic problems . . . The method of General Equilibrium . . . was specially designed to exhibit the economic system as a whole . . . [with this method] we shall thus be able to see just why it is that Mr. Keynes reaches different results from earlier economists on crucial matters of social policy . . . (Hicks, 1939, pp. 1–4)

Thus, Hicks encouraged a line of development of macromonetary theory which was carried through to fruition by Lange and Patinkin.

Initially, it was assumed that Walrasian theory and GE were synonymous. The research programme initiated by Hicks was, starting with a fully articulated preference schedule of economic agents and initial endowments, to demonstrate that there existed an equilibrium price vector which could prereconcile the independent desires of all agents, and to demonstrate that this equilibrium was unique and stable. The formal theory of GE turned out to be, for economists, exceedingly difficult but by early 1960s most economists believed that Patinkin had finally resolved Hicks's 1939 inquiry as to why Keynes reached different results from orthodox theory.

2.1 Patinkin's Model and Walras's Law

Patinkin has probably done as much as any other economist to propagate the notion that GE models can provide a proper microfoundation for macroeconomics and thereby permits the integration of monetary and macrotheory within the framework of a market-clearing GE system. Of course, had Patinkin successfully done what he claimed, there would be no need for this symposium on 'Money and General Equilibrium' for the problem would have been resolved more than two decades ago. The existence of this symposium implicitly recognizes that economic theory was shunted onto a wrong track by Hicks and Patinkin. Hence, it will be useful to look at Patinkin's model to see where he went wrong.

Basic to Patinkin's model is his view of equilibrium which he characterizes as 'only at the price E_n – where the amount of excess demand is zero, where, that is, the amount people want to buy is equal to the amount people want to sell – can equilibrium prevail' (Patinkin, 1965, p. 11). Moreover

The corresponding concept of equilibrium in the market as a whole . . . is defined as the existence of equilibrium in the market for each and every good. A set of prices which brings the market as a whole into equilibrium will be called an equilibrium set . . . The term 'equilibrium prices' must also be expressed or tacitly qualified by the phrase 'at a given array of initial endowments.' . . . In equilibrium, the amount of excess supply in each commodity market is, by definition, zero. Hence the amount of excess demand for money must also be zero. Thus . . . it suffices to show that this set of prices establishes equilibrium in each of the commodity markets alone. This relationship, which is a particular form of what is known as Walras' Law, is basic to the following analysis. (ibid., p. 35)

Since Walras's Law requires that the existence of excess supply in one market involves excess demand in one or more other markets, Patinkin has made market clearing synonymous with GE. Furthermore, by imposing 'well behaved' demand and supply functions (the latter is vertical at the full employment level (ibid., pp. 209–11) and a law of motion via the *tâtonnement* pricing system and the gross substitutability of all excess demands, Patinkin assures existence, uniqueness, and stability of the equilibrium solution of his model.

Patinkin claims his equilibrium is short run, an equilibrium which exists only on the Monday of a Hicksian week; long-run equilibrium would require the same short-run solution to prevail week after week[4] (ibid., p. 50).

Patinkin's model involves economic agents who, possessing perfect certainty as to future prices and interest rates, engage solely in spot transactions for all commodities on the Monday of a marketing period. All trades are at the equilibrium price vector which makes trading plans reconcilable, i.e. no false trades. Since such a spot market economy is essentially a barter system, how could Patinkin claim he had integrated money into this GE non-monetary economy?

In true Alice in Walrasland fashion, Patinkin claims to develop a demand for money function in this timeless perfectly certain GE world by imposing a stochastic payments process. In this payments process, the date of settlement of all contractual obligations for goods[5] ordered on Monday is not part of the terms of the contract. Instead the settlement is determined by a lottery during the marketing period so that there is *uncertainty* as to the hour of actual settlement (i.e. the probability of having to make payment at X hours is < 1) although all payments must be made before the following Monday (ibid., p. 82). It is the risky, but statistically predictable, timing of payments which is, in Patinkin's world, the fundamental *and only* reason for a demand for money.

Patinkin deserves kudos for having recognized that the demand for money is essentially related to uncertainty, the passage of time, and the need to discharge contractual obligations at a future date *and* that no GE system could provide a role for money without all these aspects. Unfortunately, Patinkin's solution via a stochastic payments process still need not generate a demand for money by the public during the marketing week. Since the actual hour of payment is statistically determinable in Patinkin's scheme, the risk of default is insurable and all economic agents could buy *and* pay for insurance against default 'on the spot' on Monday morning. Hence, in equilibrium, all Monday morning markets (including the insurance markets) will clear. The public can make all payments spot so that no money need be demanded by the public for payments during the rest of the marketing week.

What Patinkin and others did not fully comprehend is that Walras's Law assures that since goods essentially trade for goods, money as conceptualized in section 1 above can never play a unique role in the system. Only by introducing the most artificial and contrived devices (e.g. a stochastic payment scheme) can a system based on Walras's Law obtain what appears to be a role for money, but even such *ad hoc* theorizing can, with further analysis, usually be shown to violate some logical relationship. In Keynes's world – the real world – money plays a unique role because of its properties and features. In such an economy an excess demand for money does *not* require an excess flow supply in another market, or vice versa; Walras's Law does not apply for there is no automatic market mechanism to assure simultaneous market clearing at full employment in a monetary production economy.

Although Hicks's *Value and Capital* did encourage general equilibrium theorists into a delusive search for reconciling their system of analysis with a macrotheory involving money, production, prices and employment, in recent years Hicks has been warning that GE concepts were logically inadequate to deal with such a monetary equilibrium system. Hicks now insists that 'the use of a [general] equilibrium concept is a signal that time, in some respects at least, has been put on one side' (1976, p. 140). Keynes's monetary framework required an 'in [calendar] time' approach which recognized 'the irreversibility of time . . . that past and future are different' (ibid., pp. 135–6). This lack of recognition of Keynes's 'in time' monetary analysis meant, according to Hicks:

> The 'Keynesian revolution' went off at half-cock. The [general] equilibrists did not know that they were beaten . . . they thought that what Keynes had said could be absorbed into their equilibrium system; all that was needed was the scope of their equilibrium system should be extended. As we know, there has been a lot of extension, a vast amount of extension; what I am saying is that it has never quite got to the point . . . to look over my own work, since 1935, and to show how some aspects of the struggle, and the muddle, are reflected in it . . . I have found myself facing the issue, and (very often) being baffled by it.
>
> I begin (as I am sure you will want to begin) with the old ISLM (or SILL) diagram . . . I must say that diagram is now much less popular with me than I think it still is with many other people. It reduces *The General Theory* to equilibrium economics; it is not really *in* time. (ibid., pp. 140–1)

Hicks's *Value and Capital* provided the impetus for shunting economics onto a wrong line of inquiry while the development of the intellectually challenging but difficult mathematical techniques of GE made those economists who had invested so much effort into their mastery anxious to display their use in resolving the issue raised by Hicks. Part of the problem, however, was due to the fact that prior to *Value and Capital* the concept of equilibrium as used by Marshall, Keynes, etc. (and as still used by some economists today) did not require simultaneous market clearing as a necessary condition. Even in Patinkin's *Money, Interest and Prices* we find equilibrium being utilized in two senses. Although market clearing is synonymous with GE throughout most of his volume, in Appendix K Patinkin admonishes Keynes for not meaning equilibrium 'in the usual sense of the term that nothing tends to change in the system' (1965, p. 643). Elsewhere I have demostrated that market clearing may be a sufficient, but it is not a necessary condition for equilibrium as defined by Patinkin in Appendix K; hence underemployment equilibrium can exist, and be unique and stable, without the need to involve Walras's Law (Davidson, 1967).

Keynes had declared that his *General Theory* was 'Chiefly concerned with the behaviour of the economic system as a whole . . . [where] the actual level of output and employment depends not on the capacity to produce or on the pre-existing level of income, but on the current decisions to produce which depend in turn on current decisions to invest and on present expectations of current and prospective consumption' (Keynes, 1936, pp. xxxii–iii). Although such a claim obviously means that neither Walras's Law nor Say's Principle (see *infra*) is applicable, since Keynes maintained the assumption of (Marshallian) income maximizing entrepreneurs (ibid., p. 53), Patinkin and others assumed Keynes was logically inconsistent in claiming to have developed an underemployment equilibrium. What was not recognized at the time was that Marshallian microtheory was logically distinct and different from Walrasian microtheory (Patinkin, 1976). In Keynes's Marshallian framework there are three features which permit equilibrium in the sense of nothing changing in the system, without market clearing. These are (a) aggregate demand and/or supply functions for goods and therefore for labour are formulated in a different manner than in the traditional Walrasian GE (e.g. Patinkin's) model[6] and/or (b) the Gross Substitution Theorem is not universally applicable throughout the system and/or (c) the elasticity of expectations is zero (or negligible).[7] In any economy where features (a), (b), or (c) are applicable either separately or in combination (see Davidson, 1967; 1978, ch. 9, 16), the pricing system does not automatically reconcile the desires of all agents within the physical limits of the system. Thus, equilibrium in the sense of Walras's Law need not exist, although equilibrium is the sense of a maintained state (as defined in Patinkin's Appendix K) can persist. Moreover, if in such an economy, equilibrium in the sense of all markets clearing simultaneously occurs, it is the result of coincidence and not due to a deliberate and automatic market mechanism.

The crux of Keynes's underemployment equilibrium analysis involves Chapter 17 of his *General Theory* where money, time-related monetary contracts, liquidity preference phenomena and the interrelations between the real and financial subsectors are fully developed. From this chapter it is obvious that features (b) and (c) are, in some sense, the most distinctive differences between Keynes's framework and the GE system. Nevertheless, because of the difficulty and obscurity of Chapter 17, its message has been ignored. Instead, feature (a) was developed by Clower (based on Chapters 2 and 8 of *The General Theory*) to demonstrate that 'Keynesian economics is price theory without Walras's Law' (Clower, 1965, p. 124).

2.2 Clower's Revolution Against Walras's Law

In 1965, Clower, unhappy with the GE research programme 'launched by Hicks in 1937 and now being carried forward with such vigor by Patinkin' (1965, p. 103) counter-attacked to protect Keynes from charges of theoretical incompetence or even quackery. Clower attempted to get 'what looked like Keynesian results' (Hahn and Brechling, 1969, p. 304) from a GE model, i.e. Hicks–Walrasian microtheory by introducing income-constrained demand curves via the dual-decision hypothesis. This hypothesis provided a different formulation for demand curves and hence, except in conditions of full employment, did not satisfy Walras's Law (Clower, 1965, p. 111). Thus Clower could achieve what appeared to be an underemployment solution where Walras's Law was clearly inapplicable – while the level of employment and prices need not change in the system. Clower stated that the dual-decision hypothesis demonstrated how 'effective excess demand may be insufficient to induce price adjustment, despite the obvious sufficiency of notional excess demand [to achieve full employment]' (ibid., p. 123).

In essence, Clower's analysis assumes that since households do not know for certain the monetary values of the sale of the labour (factor) services during the period they will be purchasing goods, their consumption expenditures are constrained by their realized current income receipts rather than their desired (full employment) income receipts. Hence when workers do not sell all the labour they desire (an excess supply of labour) their demand for goods is constrained so that there is no excess demand for goods and Walras's Law is inapplicable.[8]

For Clower (and later Leijonhufvud), the problem of unemployment was that there is no market mechanism, in a monetary economy, to coordinate full employment hiring decisions with the full employment purchasing decisions which would then be forthcoming. Apparently, in a

Clower construction, if only entrepreneurs would hire the full employment level of workers, then notional and actual income receipts of households would be equal and therefore actual spending would equal desired (notional) demand at full employment. Hence there would be no insufficiency of *current* effective demand for the products of these workers; Walras's Law would apply and full employment equilibrium would be maintained.

Clower insisted that although he could not find any evidence in Keynes's writings to indicate that Keynes utilized the dual-decision hypothesis, Keynes either had this 'hypothesis at the back of his mind, or most of the *General Theory* is nonsense' (Clower, 1965, p. 120).

Unfortunately Clower's construction, although it seems to achieve 'Keynesian results' does not get to the essence of the underemployment problem of monetary economies. In a monetary, production, market-oriented economy, even if entrepreneurs hire the full employment level of workers, there can be an insufficiency of aggregate effective demand, when all the goods currently produced cannot be profitably sold at any price-money wage level. It is the prospect of possible insufficient effective demand at full employment which clearly differentiates Keynes's analysis of a monetary economy from either a GE system or Clower's model. The possibility of insufficiency of effective demand at any level of employment in Keynes's system is a result of his definition of money and its essential properties, where money 'cannot be readily produced; – labour cannot be turned on at will by entrepreneurs to produce money' (Keynes, 1936, p. 230), nor is any other producible good a gross substitute for money as either a means of setting contractual obligations or as a time machine (see Davidson, 1978, ch. 9). Since all Walras's Law systems and even Clower's model ultimately require the gross substitutability of excess demand, such models are incapable of introducing money into their framework. To oversimplify and paraphrase Clower, *Keynes's economics is Marshallian price theory without the gross substitution theorem, Walras's Law or even Say's Principle as fundamental conventions*.

Clower's model is ultimately an inadequate representation of Keynes's framework for two reasons. First, money is not explicitly introduced into Clower's model. (Clower incorrectly claims that 'a model with income and without money could be called Keynesian' (Hahn and Brechling, 1965, p. 305)). Secondly Clower mistakenly asserts that *Say's Principle*, when 'no transactor consciously *plans* to purchase units of any commodity without at the same time *planning* to finance the purchase either from profit receipts or from the sale of units of some other commodity . . . may be regarded as a fundamental convention of economic science' (Clower, 1965, p. 116). If the commodities and profit receipts referred to in Say's Principle are a result of the production (using labour services) process, then Clower is mistaken about the fundamental nature of Say's Principle.

Money

It is not the income constrained demand curves which ultimately distinguish monetary economies from GE systems (for Clower has demonstrated how income constraints can be introduced into non-monetary GE models), rather it is the existence of money, that peculiar thing defined in section 1, that makes the difference. Keynes emphasized that the theory he wished to develop involved

> an economy in which money plays a part on its own and affects motives and decisions and is, in short, one of the operative factors in the situation, so that the course of events cannot be predicted, either in the long period or in the short, without a knowledge of the behaviour of money between the first state and the last. And it is this which we ought to mean when we speak of a *monetary economy*. (Keynes, 1936, pp. 408–9)

Thus contrary to Clower's first claim, Keynes specifically denied that his analysis could be represented without explicitly introducing a specific and unique role for money.

One of the most important sufficient conditions for demonstrating both the uniqueness and stability of a GE solution is the gross substitutability of excess demands (Arrow and Hahn, 1971, pp. 15, 215, 305). It is not an exaggeration, therefore, to state that Walras's Law models specifically, and axiomatic (Walrasian) value models (which most economists believe is *the only* microtheory) in general, have traditionally utilized some price mechanism or law of motion which assumes the gross substitutability of all excess demand to achieve equilibrium. Since Walras's Law asserts that 'in any disequilibrium situation, there is always an element of excess demand working directly on the price system to affect prevailing elements of excess supply' (Clower, 1965, p. 121), to the extent that GE systems are identified with solving the problem of reconciling all conditional intentions of economic agents within the productive capacity of the economy, gross substitutability is a basic building block. Ultimately, this means that in a GE model the only thing acceptable today in exchange for today's (or even tomorrow's) products is, in effect, other of today's products (or the present value of tomorrow's products in terms of today's products). Thus an excess of demand in one of today's markets implies an excess of supply in another of today's markets.

In a monetary economy, however, the existence of money which can purchase today's goods *or* tomorrow's goods but which exists outside the list of products that can be produced today or tomorrow (by the application of labour) destroys the universality of Walras's Law *and* Say's Principle and gives money a fundamental and peculiar role in the system. Thus a monetary economy operates differently from either a GE system or a Clower construction.

It is, as Shackle emphasized a decade ago, because

money is that institution which permits *deferment* of specialized fully detailed choice . . . And when exchanges are mediated by money, which exists, and can be increased in existing quantity, with virtually no use of productive resources, and which is not desired for its own sake but, in the last resort, only because it will exchange for other things . . . is the identical equality broken between the total of expected [or even realized] production earnings and the total of intended expenditures. (Shackle, 1967, pp. 91–3)

Since the real world moves through calendar time towards an uncertain (and unknowable) future, man has created the institution of money which alleviates the need for fully detailed and specific choice at the 'initial instant'. Because of the peculiar properties of this money, neither Walras's Law nor Say's Principle is applicable to a monetary economy.

Say's Principle, for example, is violated whenever the federal government plans to finance the purchase of newly produced goods with newly created money (whose elasticity of production is zero) obtained by selling bonds to the banking system. In such a transaction, the government has consciously and with impunity violated Say's Principle by planning to buy commodities without using the sales receipts of producible commodities to finance the purchase. In fact, in a Keynes framework, many autonomous expenditures, whether by the public or the government, are initially financed via the creation of money in violation of Say's Principle (cf. Davidson, 1978, pp. 270–80, ch. 13, 16). The expansionary effects of deficit spending are, in large measure, due to the willingness of governments to violate Say's Principle!

Clower originally avoided this obvious problem of how can non-income induced spending be financed, by (i) concentrating primarily on the aggregate demand of households where it is assumed all expenditures are, in the aggregate, constrained by actual income and (ii) by assuming that actual payment for the sale of labour (factor) services precedes *in time* the purchase of all goods so that the latter are constrained by the former. Implicit in all this is that actual expenditures in the goods markets are not only constrained, but also induced by income, i.e. there is no autonomous spending.

If, however, factor payments must precede product purchases, how can entrepreneurs pay for their hired labour when they have not yet sold the goods? To resolve this chicken–egg dilemma, Clower, in a 1969 revision of his paper, inserted a long paragraph (Clower, 1969, p. 289) to describe the market organization and financing mechanism of his model. In this passage, Clower, apparently unwittingly, violates Say's Principle in order to start the trading process in motion.

Clower states that a central marketing authority assures that no purchase order 'is "validated" unless it is offset by a sale order that has *already* been executed' (ibid., italics added). But Clower states:

> It is implicit in this entire line of argument that at some "initial" stage in the evolution of market trading arrangement, the market authority advances a nominal quantity of *book* credit to one or more transactors to set the trading process in motion (without such initial advances no sales order could ever be executed since no purchase order would ever be validated). (Clower, 1969, p. 289)

Hence the starting purchase orders are validated by an advance of credit, not by the sales of producible commodities. This means that at the beginning of trade (each Monday morning of the Hicksian week) Say's Principle is inapplicable. Moreover as long as, in the aggregate, the outstanding volume of debts are never completely extinguished (as in the real world) then Say's Principle is never universally operative. (Patinkin, and by implication Clower, avoids this inoperative aspect of Say's Principle by assuming all bonds are redeemed on the last hour of the marketing period within a single trading week – as if refinancing debt positions or even perpetual bonds are unimportant phenomena.[9)]

In sum, the existence of money with its peculiar elasticity properties and its related contractual institutions (and not simply income-constrained demand curves) means that Walras's Law and Say's Principle have as much relevance to a monetary economy as Euclidean propositions regarding parallel lines have to a non-Euclidean world. Keynes compared classical economists to Euclidean geometers in a non-Euclidean world who, observing that 'straight lines apparently parallel often meet, rebuke the lines for not keeping straight – as the only remedy for the unfortunate collisions' (Keynes, 1936, p. 16). Similarly, GE economists who insist that flexible wages and prices alone, because of gross substitution and Walras's Law, assure the existence of a stable and unique full employment equilibrium are utilizing non-monetary propositions to prescribe remedies for the problems of a monetary economy. (This is also true for those who use Say's Principle.)

Instead of continuing to develop such non-monetary models in the delusive hope of ultimately being able to provide comprehension and counsel for the monetary economy in which we live, economists should follow Keynes's metaphorical research programme: 'Yet, in truth, there is no remedy except to throw over the axiom of parallels and to work out a non-Euclidean geometry. Something similar is required today in economics' (ibid.).

If we are to understand how a monetary economy operates we must throw out the assumption of gross substitutability of all excess demands,

Walras's Law and Say's Principle as fundamental conventions for analysing a monetary economy.

Although Clower's income-constrained demand curves can explain the problem of why a GE system will not automatically return to full employment once it is in a recession, it cannot explain why a full employment level of production once achieved may not be able to be maintained. In a monetary economy, it is the peculiar properties of money, in a world where the future is uncertain that is the fundamental cause of unemployment. What a monetary economy permits, which a barter economy and general equilibrium system does not, is the existence of one or more time machines – money and other liquid assets – which can transfer purchasing power over time for future goods and future liabilities without absorbing significant current productive resources into the production of these wonderful time machines.

This does not denigrate the importance of Clower's attempt at an *ad hoc* revision of GE systems to achieve 'Keynesian results'. Nevertheless, such specific case modification as the dual-decision hypothesis is suggestive of a degenerate research programme à la Lakatos where novel facts and anomalies (unemployment) are explained at the cost of decreasing analytical content and continual *ad hoc* hedging of theories.[10] Clower's 1965 work was an invaluable contribution forcing economists (a) to reassess the Walrasian GE framework and (b) to recognize that Keynes's results need not be relegated to the position of a disequilibrium anomaly. Within a decade after Clower's initial attack on the GE research programme, it was obvious that a number of macroeconomic issues could not even be phrased in the timeless, perfect informative Walrasian framework of Patinkin or Arrow–Debreu. Accordingly, even though as late as 1971 Arrow and Hahn could still define an equilibrium as having the 'usual meaning' in economic theory in that it involved

> a set of prices and production and consumption allocations such that each firm maximizes profits at the given prices, each household maximizes utilities at the given price and with the income implied by those prices and its initial holdings of asset and profit shares, and aggregate consumption is feasible in not exceeding the sum of aggregate production and initial endowments (Arrow and Hahn, 1971, p. 107)

equilibrium notions were already beginning to proliferate in the literature. Following Clower's lead, many economists attempted *ad hoc* modifications of GE systems in the false hope that Keynes's analysis did not 'preclude our search for more sophisticated Arrow-Debreu type systems that are consistent with unemployment' (Weintraub, 1977, p. 2). As a consequence, the current literature bristles with concepts such as 'momentary equilibria', 'temporary equilibria', 'Keynesian equilibria', and even 'a sequence of momentary equilibria', as economists realize that 'the simple stories of general competitive analysis must be recast drastically in order to model the concerns of macrotheorists' (ibid., p. 11). To one who has no vested interest in the research programme of GE that has developed since 1937, it appears that current GE researchers have refused to accept the findings of others that 'The General Equilibrium Model is Incomplete and Not Adequate for the Reconciliation of Micro and Macroeconomic theory' (Shubik, 1975). Instead GE theorists have exhibited a blind faith that if they continue to develop multitudinous and idiosyncratic *ad hoc* modifications of their systems, an intelligent model where money can play a unique role will be developed. Let us briefly examine an example of one recent attempt at *ad hoc* modifications of GE systems to achieve Keynesian results and a role for money.

2.3 Grandmont's ad hoc Modifications of GE

Grandmont and a number of his colleagues have attempted to demonstrate that the Keynesian concept of unemployment can be explained in GE models which explicitly deal with calendar time, money, and very inelastic price expectations (Grandmont and Laroque, 1976; Grandmont and Younès, 1972). In their explanation of 'Temporary Keynesian Equilibria' the typical Grandmont *et al.* model has the following features (e.g. Grandmont and Laroque, 1976, p. 54):

(1) the absence of any financial system (no borrowing and no spot market for selling or reselling securities);

(2) non-storable consumption goods are the only producible items (no capital goods). It therefore follows that the only buyers of goods are consumers and hence all spending is induced (and constrained) by income. Thus there is no autonomous spending and implicitly all goods purchases follow Say's Principle;

(3) fiat money is the only store of value and the only thing that can be carried over from one period to the next;

(4) all transactions take place in spot markets, but some markets are assumed to adjust via price changes, while others are assumed to adjust via quantity changes.

In reality, feature (4) means that Grandmont *et al.* are merely applying the techniques of GE analysis to the now largely discredited neoclassical synthesis findings that price rigidities are the sole cause of unemployment (ibid., p. 53). By adopting Hicks's 'fixprice' system, Grandmont demonstrates that a 'temporary competitive equilibrium' can exist due to downward rigidity of money-wages (or price) and a zero or negligible price elasticity expectations so that excess supply in the labour market (or the product market) does not alter entrepreneurial hiring and production plans for future periods[11] (ibid., p. 54). In sum, Grandmont *et al.* achieve temporary Keynesian equilibrium with unemployment by making rigid money-wages and/or monopolistic competition (fixprices) 'a central feature of the Keynesian model',[12] (ibid., p. 53). This state can be maintained if current results do not affect future plans.

Although Grandmont's results are achieved by assuming *ad hoc* restraints on the typical GE law of motion (price adjustment), features (2) and (3) above are worthy of note for they introduce into the system (without acknowledgement) Keynes's essential elasticity properties of money. Grandmont's money has a zero elasticity of production (since it is fiat, while all producibles are assumed non-storeable) and a zero elasticity of substitution since it is the only store of value available. Nevertheless, Grandmont's framework still is not a model of a monetary economy in the sense of section 1 for the analysis is limited to a world of spot transactions with no contracts in money terms over time.

In sum, Grandmont gets a 'Keynesian' underemployment solution because of downward wage and price rigidities – a result the neoclassical synthesis achieved decades ago and which led Patinkin to label Keynes's theory as disequilibrium economics. Keynes would not deny the existence and importance of monopoly power and money wage rigidities, but Keynes argued that a reduction in money wages (or prices) would not, *ceteris paribus*, have a direct tendency to increase employment (Keynes, 1936, pp. 260–2). For Keynes it was the existence of money and not monopoly power which invalidates Walras's Law for a real world monetary economy.

3   WHAT SHOULD WE MEAN BY GE?

Although Grandmont *et al.* have introduced some essential monetary properties into their models, their systems remain faulty for they rely on *ad hoc* constraints to the fundamental GE price adjustment process to achieve 'temporary' equilibrium while they do not emphasize the role of money. None of the GE researchers seems to realize that the schism between GE and monetary analysis is as deep and irreparable as the difference between Euclidean and non-Euclidean geometry, and that as I have already indicated the fundamental conditions or axioms of GE analysis must be thrown out, if monetary equilibrium is to be analysed.

Whether the resulting monetary equilibrium system analysis should still be labelled GE is partly a semantic problem. (Would it be rational to call geometry without the axiom of parallels Euclidean?) The intellectual auxiliary baggage of gross substitution, Walras's Law, Say's Principle, optimality of reconciled choices of all agents via the price system, etc. are so closely identified with the concept of general equilibrium, while this paraphernalia is so incompatible with a monetary economy that to apply the term GE to a monetary equilibrium system would seem to me to be a semantic travesty. Semantic confusion can only result from throwing out the intellectual baggage of GE, while retaining the label.

Others, however, while recognizing the recent failures of GE theory to provide a microfoundation for macroeconomies are not yet ready to throw out their (non-monetary) systems and/or the GE nomenclature. Weintraub argues, for example, that although an Arrow–Debreu world is based on a full-employment assumption and is therefore logically incompatible with underemployment equilibrium; such an incompatibility 'ought not to preclude our search for perhaps more sophisticated Arrow–Debreu type systems that are consistent with unemployment' (Weintraub, 1977, p. 2). But the full employment assumption is inevitably related to Walras's Law! Thus to avoid this Walras's Law stigma, Weintraub states that GE should 'not be considered as bearing a necessary relationship to the theories of Walras; *a general equilibrium model is simply some specification of states of the world and a set of rules that structure the manner in which those states change over time*' (ibid.). To me such a definition throws away the baby of GE while keeping the bathwater.

One pre-eminent worker in the field of GE spent his inaugural lecture at Cambridge University trying to explain the *Notion of Equilibrium in Economics*. Hahn uses the Arrow–Debreu paradigm as the touchstone concept because '(1) it is precise, complete and unambiguous, (2) it has been much maltreated by both friend and foe . . . [and] because it so happens that all serious work which is now proceeding to recast the equilibrium notion is being undertaken by those who have been most active in building the [Arrow–Debreu] paradigm in the first place and who consequently understand it' (Hahn, 1973, p. 3). Thus Professor Hahn recognizes that the Arrow–Debreu general equilibrium system, although precise and unambiguous, is also defective and needs recasting and he, like Weintraub, believes the resulting system can still be called a GE. It is, however, precisely when it comes to the role of money that the GE deficiencies are most obvious and, I reiterate, if the role of money is to be properly identified, the recast analysis will bear so little resemblance to the traditional GE concept, that it will be a mockery to maintain the GE nomenclature.

At the risk of some repetition of our earlier argument, let us follow Hahn's lead and proceed by starting with the precise and unambiguous concept that any GE system involves the existence of a stable and unique market clearing solution to the problem of prereconciling *all* conditional intentions of *all* economic agents in the system when each agent is operating under rational interdependent choices of action in the light of informed reason – the information having to include the choices made by others at the same point in calendar time as the agent. Any such GE system must be able to demonstrate that existing markets can achieve such prereconciliation by establishing a set of prices which (a) gathers all information including information on conditional intentions of all agents for each point of time, (b) converts this information into knowledge and (c) delivers that knowledge to all economic agents equally and simultaneously. Thus the GE concept *assumes* in its most rigid form that there are no false trades; i.e. no transactions which provide misleading information about the conditional intentions of others; or in its weak format that even if transactions occur at false (or non-equilibrium) prices they do not either (i) mislead economic agents about the 'true' nature of the economic system or (ii) alter the 'true' nature of the system or (iii) prevent the time trajectory of the economy from converging towards the equilibrium state.

As Hahn has already noted in this touchstone GE system 'money can play no essential role' (Hahn, 1971, p. 417). In fact such an equational system can be utilized only in the negative sense of demonstrating why the real world 'economy cannot be in this state' (Hahn, 1973, p. 14). Thus the Arrow–Debreu system 'must relinquish the claim of providing necessary descriptions of terminal states of economic processes' (ibid., p. 16). In other words, even in the longest of long run, the equations of a Walrasian, or Arrow–Debreu world will never describe the norm or trend towards which the real economy is groping![13]

More specifically Hahn notes that what should be required of any equilibrium notion is that 'it should reflect the sequential character of actual economies . . . in an *essential* way. This in turn requires that information processes and costs, transactions and transactions costs and also expectations and uncertainty be explicitly and essentially included in the equilibrium notion. This is what the Arrow–Debreu construction does not do' (ibid.).

But as soon as conditions of a sequence of time and uncertainty are pressed on the system, GE concepts simply will not do! For example, Perroux argues that as soon as information is unequal among all economic agents, as it must be in an uncertain world where all agents do not have equal access to information and some information may be unknowable when the future does *not* yet exist, then 'general equilibrium is no longer constructable, nor mathematically formalisable' (Perroux, 1973, p. 267). Attempting to reduce uncertainty to a Markov process, a tree of events, or subjective probabilities so that a decision strategy can be decided once and for all at the initial instant is an 'ingenious procedure for formally constructing an equilibrium but it does not tackle the problem of uncertainty' (ibid., p. 273). Once it is recognized that all agents do not and can never know the true states of the world, then even this probability construction collapses (Arrow and Hahn, 1971, p. 126).

Despite the millions of man hours economists have already spent in a vain search for a monetary GE theory that can deal with uncertainty (in the sense of the unknowable), calendar time, prices, production, money and employment, many still hope that such a theory can be developed. Hahn believes that the technique of GE can be salvaged if the concept of equilibrium is redefined such that 'an economy is in equilibrium when it generates messages which do not cause agents to change the theories they hold or the policies they pursue' (Hahn, 1971, p. 25). Thus agents are still assumed to have responses conditional on the actions of others, and the price system can reconcile these responses as the market provides information to all agents, but this definition of equilibrium Hahn suggested 'implies *almost* the missing traditional complement that markets are cleared . . . short enough and rare enough episodes of uncleared markets would on my definition be consistent with equilibrium' (ibid., p. 26–7).

Hahn, therefore, permits equilibrium to exist even if Walras's Law is violated as long as the actions of agents are not 'systematically and persistently inconsistent' (ibid., p. 28). It is gratifying to know that inconsistencies can be ignored as long as they are sufficiently uncommon and random occurences so that they can be neglected; but that is hardly the solution to the problem at hand (cf. Clower, 1965, p. 113). The Great Depression and the recent world-wide experiences of stagflation cannot be dismissed so readily.

Hahn admits that his concept of equilibrium is 'not at all clear' and is an 'ill-specified hypothesis' (Hahn, 1973, p. 26). Hahn has avoided the essential question as to whether we can analyse a monetary economy with a conceptual system which does not provide a special role for money.

4 CONCLUSION

Traditional General Equilibrium axioms and laws are incompatible with a monetary system. GE concepts involve non-monetary systems; such systems cannot be recast to give money an essential role without losing their non-monetary essence. Thus to speak of monetary GE models is a contradiction in terms.

The concept of money in the full sense of section 1 can only be developed in a monetary equilibrium model which rejects Walrasian microtheory for Marshallian price analysis. In his *Treatise* and *General Theory* Keynes developed such a monetary model in which the concepts of time, uncertainty, catenated spot and forward contracts, market organizations, institutions and money play fundamental roles affecting the behaviour of economic agents. I have elaborated and developed this model in my *Money and the Real World* (Davidson, 1978). This analytical framework rules out many of the basic GE propositions and consequently a monetary model functions quite differently from one described via the techniques and laws of GE.

If GE economists continue to recast their models often enough, they may, by accident, ultimately rediscover Keynes's great wheel of money mechanism – but the resulting model will bear as much resemblance to what is commonly understood as GE systems as non-Euclidean geometry does to Euclidean systems.

Notes

1. Thus we are affirming Keynes's Treatise Classification of Money which is 'that by delivery of which debt-contracts and price-contracts are *discharged* and in the shape of which a store of General Purchasing Power is held' (Keynes, 1930, p. 3).
2. 'It is, however, interesting to consider how far those characteristics of money as we know it . . . are bound up with money being the standard in which debts and wages are usually fixed . . . The convenience of holding assets in the same standard as that which future liabilities may fall due . . . is obvious' (Keynes, 1936, pp. 236–7).
3. 'The attribute of "liquidity" is by no means independent of these two characteristics. For it is unlikely that an asset, of which the supply can be easily increased or the desire for which can be easily diverted by a change in relative price will possess the attribute of "liquidity" in the minds of owners of wealth' (Keynes, 1936, p. 241 nl).
4. Monetarists, however, claim this is a *long-run* GE position and not a description of the actual state of the economy (Friedman, 1974, pp. 44, 48, 150–1).
5. Borrowing via bonds, on the other hand, can only take place on Monday morning and *all* bond redemptions are 'fixed for the last hour of the week' (Patinkin, 1965, p. 81). Debt obligations are, therefore, completely certain *and* are never carried over from one week to the next.
6. As I have demonstrated elsewhere, Patinkin did not correctly introduce the aggregate supply function (and hence the demand for labour) into his model (Clower, 1969, pp. 565–75) and hence did not correctly analyse a Keynes world in which equilibrium can occur without Walras's Law. In 1976, Patinkin admitted his analysis of Keynes's aggregate supply function was wrong (1976, p. 91, n. 12) and he attempted to provide a new formulation for the aggregate supply function. Unfortunately Patinkin's 1976 supply analysis was still faulty and a further correction is forthcoming (1977). Nevertheless, I still believe that Patinkin's specific aggregate supply of goods and demand for labour, and the similar analysis in GE system in general are logically inadequate and incorrect.
7. If for example current expectations are disappointed but the elasticity of expectations is zero (so that there is no substitutability between present and future goods) then nothing tends to change in the system.
8. Actually Clower's dual decision hypothesis is similar to Keynes's analysis of the classical doctrine of 'supply creates its own demand'. For Keynes this doctrine meant that the aggregate demand function, $f(N)$, and aggregate supply function, $\phi(N)$, were 'equal for *all* values of N, i.e. for all levels of output and employment, and that when there is an increase in $Z(=\phi(N))$ corresponding to

an increase in N, $D(= f(N))$ necessarily increases by the same amount as Z' (Keynes, 1936, pp. 25–6). In other words if $f(N) = \phi(N)$ then if firms hire less than the full employment level of workers, income will be constrained and aggregate demand will equal supply at less than full employment. Thus, any level of income can be an equilibrium one if $f(N)$ and $\phi(N)$ are equal for all levels of N, i.e. there 'is an infinite range of [equilibrium] values all equally admissible' (ibid., p. 26). Thus if firms hire initially the full employment level of output and if $f(N) = \phi(N)$, then there would be no shortage of effective demand, i.e. there is 'no obstacle to full employment' (ibid.).

9. Since the major borrowers in the modern economy are business firms and governments who (normally) have a perpetual life, they may never retire their outstanding debt. In fact, bankruptcies occur when borrowers are unable to refinance their obligations, and if such debtors are large organizations these can create monetary crises for the economy (e.g. Penn-Central Railroad in 1966, Lockheed in 1970, and New York City in 1975 in the US). For a further discussion of the importance of financing 'positions' in a monetary economy, see (Davidson, 1978, ch. 16).

10. Grossman has demonstrated the *ad hoc* nature of Clower's Keynesian general equilibrium system (1972, pp. 29–30).

11. As I have shown elsewhere (Davidson, 1978, ch. 16) a zero elasticity of expectations is the basis of Keynes's Static (no change) Model 1b.

12. In a similar model, Grandmont *et al.* demonstrated a maintained equilibrium state can occur 'only if traders are willing to hold as an asset (in the long run) the existing stock of money' (1972, p. 356). But such 'long run' holding of money would be economically irrational! (Cf. Shackle quote on p. 207).

13. Thus Friedman's claim that his monetary theory is based on a long-run set of Walrasian equations is logically incorrect (Friedman *et al.*, 1974, pp. 44, 150). The Arrow–Debreu (Walrasian) system is not a harmless 'as if' assumption since it is logically incompatible with other assumptions which are necessary in macromodels of monetary, production economies where money plays a unique and important role, i.e. where money really matters!

References

Arrow, K. J. and F. H. Hahn (1971), *General Competitive Analysis* (San Francisco: Holden-Day).

Barro, R. J. and H. I. Grossman (1971), 'A General Disequilibrium Model of Income and Employment', *Amer. Econ. Rev.*, 61, pp. 82–93.

Clower R. W. (1965), 'The Keynesian Counterrevolution: A Theoretical Appraisal', in *The Theory of Interest Rates*, ed by F. H. Hahn and F. P. R. Brechling (London: Macmillan).

Clower, R. W. (1969), 'The Keynesian Counterrevolution: A Theoretical Appraisal', in *Monetary Theory*, ed by R. W. Clower (Harmondsworth: Penguin).

Davidson, P. (1967), 'A Keynesian View of Patinkin's Theory of Employment', *Econ. Jour.*, 77, pp. 559–78.

Davidson, P. (1978), *Money and the Real World*, 2nd edn. (London: Macmillan).

Friedman, M. *et al.* (1974), *Milton Friedman's Monetary Framework: A Debate with His Critics* (Chicago: University of Chicago Press).

Grandmont, J. M. and G. Laroque (1976), 'On Temporary Keynesian Equilibria', *Rev. of Econ. Stud.*, 43, pp. 53–67.

Grandmont, J. M. and Younès, G. 'On the Role of Money and the Existence of Monetary Equilibrium', *Rev. of Econ. Stud.*, 39, pp. 355–72.

Grossman, H. I. (1972), 'Was Keynes a "Keynesian"? A Review Article,' *Jour. Econ. Lit.*, 10, pp. 26–30.

Hahn, F. H. (1971), 'Equilibrium with Transactions Costs', *Econometrica*, 39, pp. 417–40.

Hahn, F. H. (1973), *On the Notion of Equilibrium in Economics* (Cambridge: Cambridge University Press).

Hahn, F. H. and F. Brechling (1965), *The Theory of Interest Rates* (London: Macmillan).

Hansen, B. (1970), *General Equilibrium Systems* (New York: McGraw-Hill).

Hicks J. R. (1939), *Value and Capital* (London: Oxford University Press).

Hicks, J. R. (1976), 'Some Questions of Time in Economics', in *Evolution Welfare and Time in Economics*, ed by A. M. Tang *et al.* (Lexington: Heath Books).

Keynes, J. R. (1930), *Treatise on Money*, Vol. I, (London: Macmillan).

Keynes, J. R. (1936), *The General Theory of Employment Interest and Money* (New York: Harcourt), reprinted as Vol. VII of *The Collected Works of J. M. Keynes*; references are to the reprint.

Keynes, J. R. (1973), *The Collected Works of John Maynard Keynes, XIII* (London: Macmillan).

Leijonhufvud, A. (1974), 'Varieties of Price Theory: What Microfoundations for Macrotheory?', UCLA Discussion Paper, Los Angeles.

Patinkin, D. (1965), *Money Interest and Prices*, 2nd edn (New York: Harper & Row).

Patinkin, D. (1976), 'Keynes' Monetary Theory', *Hist. of Pol. Econ.*, 8, pp. 1–150.

Patinkin, D. (1977), 'Keynes' Aggregate Supply Function: A Correction', *Hist. of Pol. Econ.*

Perroux, F. (1973), 'The Economic Agent, Equilibrium, and the Choice of Formalisation', *Economie appliquée*, pp. 249–85.

Shackle, G. L. S. (1967), *The Years of High Theory* (Cambridge: Cambridge University Press).

Shubik, M. (1975), 'The General Equilibrium Model is Incomplete and Not Adequate for the Reconciliation of Micro and Macroeconomic Theory', *Kyklos*, 28, pp. 545–73.

Weintraub, E. R. (1977), 'The Microfoundations of Macroeconomics: A Critical Survey', *Jour. Econ. Lit.*, 15, pp. 1–23.

13 Why Money Matters: Lessons from a Half-century of Monetary Theory*

Years ago, Dennis Robertson (1956, p. 81) uttered the following witticism about economic doctrine: 'Now, as I have often pointed out to my students, some of whom have been brought up in sporting circles, high-brow opinion is like a hunted hare; if you stand in the same place, or nearly the same place, it can be relied upon to come round to you in a circle.'

In the past half-century, the role, importance, and functions of money in the economy have been the 'hunted hare' in monetary theory. The first section of this paper presents a brief historical prospective. The second section provides an example of the periodic recurrence of themes in monetary theory by showing that one of the most vociferous controversies of the late 1970s involving the 'crowding out' effect had actually been debated and resolved forty years ago by Keynes. The third section summarizes some fundamental aspects of monetary theory that, like the hunted hare, are coming round to the forefront again in order to explain why money matters.

1 A BRIEF HISTORICAL PROSPECTIVE

Half a century ago the quantity theory of money, especially the convenient pedagogical form of the equation of exchange developed by Fisher (1911), reigned supreme in the United States. In England, Marshall and Pigou had popularized the Cambridge cash balance approach. In his 1923 *Tract on Monetary Reform*, Keynes (1971, p. 60) insisted that the quantity theory is 'fundamental . . . [and] not open to question. Nevertheless, it is often misstated and misrepresented' – a statement that is just as true today as it was a half-century ago. In Keynes's *Tract* (1971, p. 63 n), 'exposition follows the general lines of Professor Pigou . . . and of Dr. Marshall rather than the more familiar analysis of Professor Irving Fisher'. Keynes's version of the quantity theory differed significantly from Fisher's in that Keynes emphasized (1) a behavioural demand for money rather than a more mechanical velocity concept; and (2) this demand for money (and

* *Journal of Post Keynesian Economics*, 1 (1978).

goods) could not be considered, in an analysis of the real world, entirely independent of the supply of money. In a perceptive passage Keynes (1971, p. 65) argued that the quantity theory 'has often been expounded on the further assumption that a *mere* change in the quantity of money can not affect k [velocity] . . . that is to say, in mathematical parlance, that n [the quantity of money] is an *independent variable* . . . Now "in the long run" this is probably true.'

Then Keynes continued: 'But this *long run* is a misleading guide to current affairs. *In the long run* we are all dead. Economists set themselves too easy, too useless a task if in tempestuous seasons they can only tell us that when the storm is long past the ocean is flat again.'

In actual experience Keynes (ibid., pp. 65–7) insisted that changes in the money supply could affect either velocity or income or both; moreover, in certain circumstances changes in income induced changes in the money supply. Starting from this general view of the quantity theory, which asserts that none of the variables in the cash balance equation can be assumed to be independent in the mathematical sense, Keynes went on to develop a monetary framework in the *Treatise* and *The General Theory* which Harrod (1969, p. 151) has characterized as 'a study in depth of a magisterial quality not matched in the present century'.

Keynes, of course, was pre-eminently a monetary theorist. Throughout his life Keynes was a firm believer in the importance of money and a passionate advocate of monetary reform, both domestically and internationally. Keynes's criticisms of most quantity theorists involved their use of simplifying and tacit assumptions as to what variables are taken as independent so as to provide a unique and unindirectional cause-and-effect relationship running from money to either prices or money incomes.

In this respect it is enlightening to compare the views of Keynes and Friedman on the role and relationship of money to the economic system. In a 1933 article entitled 'A Monetary Theory of Production', Keynes insisted that what should be modelled from the very beginning is the operation of a real world monetary production economy, not a barter system upon which money is superimposed. In Keynes's words (1973, pp. 408–9):

An economy which uses money but uses it merely as a neutral link between transactions in real things and real assets and does not allow it to enter into motives or decisions might be called – for want of a better name – *a real exchange economy*. The theory which I desiderate would deal . . . with an economy in which money plays as part of its own and affects motives and decisions and is, in short, one of the operative factors in the situation, so that the course of events cannot be predicted either in the long period or in the short, without a knowledge of the behavior of money between the first state and the last. And it is this which we ought to mean when we speak of a monetary economy.

Thus Keynes specifically rejected the idea that money was neutral in either the short or the long run. Once money enters, real relations are different. For Keynes the real and monetary subsectors were not independent. Unfortunately, such an analytical bifurcation is inherent in Hicks's pathbreaking 1937 article and is explicitly claimed as a virtue in Modigliani's 1944 article (p. 190), which purports to explain Keynes's liquidity preference theory of money. These 'Keynesian' articles, which established the *IS–LM* framework as the basis for the Keynesian neoclassical-synthesis approach, are not compatible with Keynes's analysis. To Keynes, if not the Keynesians, *money matters*!

Milton Friedman, on the other hand, continually proclaims the importance of money while he misuses and abuses the quantity theory (in Keynes's sense) by presuming which variables are independent and what the direction of causality is. In his 'Theoretical Framework for Monetary Analysis', Friedman explains (1974, p. 27):

> We have accepted the quantity theory presumption . . . that changes in the quantity of money as such *in the long run* have a negligible effect on real income so that nonmonetary forces are 'all that matter' for changes in real income over decades and money 'does not matter' . . . I regard the description of our position as 'money is all that matters for changes in *nominal* income and for *short-run* changes in real income' as an exaggeration but one that gives the right flavor of our conclusions.

Thus, for Friedman and modern quantity theorists, the real income level is in the long run independent of the money supply, while long-run changes in nominal income are caused by changes in M and not vice versa. In the short run in which we live, on the other hand, the modern quantity theory, as Friedman admits (1974, p. 50), 'does not specify anything about the division of a change in nominal income between prices and output'. Thus the modern quantity theory, according to Friedman, is devoid of any short-run theory of inflation. Moreover, in Friedman's view (1977, p. 470), the attainment of this long-run position by the economy 'may take a long chronological time . . . time to be measured by quinquennia or decades, not years'. If monetary theory can only provide anti-inflation policy guidelines for such a long run, then we are all truly dead!

To return to our historical prospective, by 1924 Keynes had already embarked on the draft of a new book which began the long metamorphosis of his quantity theory into his *Treatise of Money* and *General Theory*, which provided a monetary framework for a production economy that took account of the complex interdependencies involving money, markets, time, prices, contracts, money wages, expectations, output, and employment. Keynes's technical monetary analysis is developed in the lucid but somewhat solemn tones of the eminent professional monetary theorist in his *Treatise on Money*, which Harrod (1951, pp. 402–3) has described as follows: 'This great work embodied Keynes's gathered learning and wisdom on the subject of money which was preeminently his own special field . . . it was the work of a lifetime.'

When Keynes realized that his critics simply failed to grasp the complexities of the *Treatise* analysis, he provided *The General Theory* as a jarring simplification which forced direct attention to the fact that there is no automatic market mechanism that reconciles the plans of all buyers and sellers at the full employment level of output. In developing *The General Theory*'s simplification and clarification of the principle of effective demand that determines the scale of output and employment, Keynes (1936, p. vii) noted that , while 'money enters into the economic scheme in an essential and peculiar manner, technical monetary detail falls into the background'. Since these technical details have been dealt with at great length in his *Treatise*, Keynes's willingness to suppress these complications to make this point is understandable, although from hindsight it is regrettable. Unfortunately, this deliberate concealment of monetary technicalities in *The General Theory* was coincidentally followed in time by the introduction of the highly mathematical framework of general equilibrium (GE) analysis where, although it was not initially recognized, money could logically play no essential role. Thus, economists attempting to understand the revolutionary aspects of Keynes's system were (as we shall see) tempted by claims of the developers of GE analysis to use this new tool to compare the pre-Keynesian system with Keynes's *General Theory* (while ignoring the monetary aspects of the *Treatise*). This led many so-called Keynesians to develop in the 1940s and 1950s a neoclassical framework in which money was unimportant.

As early as 1937, while Keynes was still attempting to refine his new concepts (e.g. adding the finance motive to the demand for money) as a result of an exchange of ideas between Ohlin (1937) and Keynes (1973, pp. 201–23), Hicks was publishing a 'potted version'[1] of what he believed to be Keynes's central argument. Hicks's truncated view of the Keynesian system, however, started a retrograde movement of modification and alteration of the new concepts forged by Keynes. By the 1950s the mutant 'Keynesian' neoclassical synthesis was sufficiently entrenched in the orthodox macroeconomic literature for some economists to begin to warn that what had been propagated as *the* Keynesian theory of output and employment was a perversion of Keynes's own views about the real sector.[2] These warnings went practically unnoticed and unheeded – at least till Leijonhufvud's volume in 1968 – so that currently the analytical concepts used in macroeconomic writings emanating from some bastions of American 'Keynesianism' are in conflict with Keynes' own grand design.

Accordingly, while Keynes's own analysis provided the impetus for a precipitous decline in the popularity of Fisher's quantity theory approach between the 1930s and 1950s, Keynes's own monetary views held the spotlight only for the brief decade of the thirties. After the Second World War, Keynes's theory followed Fisher's into near-oblivion, while a bastardized and bowdlerized version of Keynesianism in which money hardly mattered dominated the field for almost two decades. As it was analytically refined over time, this neoclassical-synthesis Keynesianism became so devoid of content for real world monetary problems that by 1956 it was a relatively simple matter for Milton Friedman to revive (after more than two decades) Fisher's quantity theory in modern garb and demonstrate its superiority over the then dominant neoclassical-synthesis Keynesian school of thought. The popularity of Friedman's monetarist theory, however, peaked at the beginning of the 1970s as a resurgence of Keynes's original monetary analysis, combined with economic events, has re-exposed its glaring defects.

As late as the mid-1960s, however – except, perhaps, in the writings of Shackle, Kahn, Clower, Minsky, Weintraub, and Davidson – few if any monetary theorists had focused on the fact that 'Keynesian' monetary theory was a perverted caricature of Keynes's own view on money. Even Leijonhufvud, who had centred attention on the difference between 'Keynesian economics and the economics of Keynes' in his famous book subtitled *A Study in Monetary Theory*, did not understand what Keynes's original monetary framework involved. In his 1968 book (p. 52) Leijonhufvud claimed that 'in the Keynesian macrosystem the Marshallian ranking of price and quantity adjustment speeds is reversed . . . The "revolutionary" element in *The General Theory* can perhaps not be stated in simpler terms.' This misconception of the difference between Keynes and earlier monetary theorists was immediately adapted by Friedman (1974, p. 16 n. 7) as the basis for his revival of the quantity theory. By 1974, however, Leijonhufvud (p. 169) had recognized his mistakes and admitted that 'it is *not* correct to attribute to Keynes a general reversal of the Marshallian ranking of relative price and quantity adjustments'. Leijonhufvud (1974, pp. 164–5) has finally recognized that 'most of the recent writings on Keynes's theory, including my own, insist on analyzing it in a Walrasian perspective . . . But Keynes was, of course, a price theoretical Marshallian, and . . . ignoring this fact simply will not do.'

Leijonhufvud's rediscovery of Keynes's price theory is not an isolated 'hunted hare' incident. Some eminent economists (including two Nobel Prize winners) have travelled Robertson's full cycle of high-brow opinion and in the last few years have recognized that a serious monetary theory can be developed only by restoring Keynes's basic building blocks.

Perhaps the strongest example of this cycle is illustrated in the following statements of J. R. Hicks, the first published in 1939, the second in 1976. In 1939 (pp. 1–4) Hicks exclaimed:

I believe I have had the fortune to come upon a method of analysis which is applicable to a wide variety of economic problems . . . The method of General Equilibrium . . . was specially designed to exhibit the economic system as a whole . . . [with this method] we shall thus be able to see just why it is that Mr. Keynes reaches different results from earlier economists on crucial matters of social policy.

Thus, Hicks encouraged a line of development of macromonetary theory that was carried through to fruition by Lange and Patinkin. In 1976, however, Hicks had recognized that 'the use of a [general] equilibrium concept is a signal that time, in some respect at least, has been put on one side' (p. 140), while Keynes's monetary framework required an 'in [calendar] time' approach that recognized 'the irreversibility of time . . . that past and future are different' (pp. 135–6). This lack of perception of Keynes's 'in time' monetary analysis by neoclassical Keynesians meant, according to Hicks (1976, pp. 140–1):

The 'Keynesian revolution' went off at half-cock. The [general] equilibrists did not know that they were beaten . . . they thought that what Keynes had said could be absorbed into their equilibrium system; all that was needed was the scope of their equilibrium system should be extended. As we know, there has been a lot of extension, a vast amount of extension; what I am saying is that it has never quite got to the point . . . to look over my own work, since 1935, and to show how some aspects of the struggle, and the muddle, are reflected in it . . . I have found myself facing the issue, and (very often) being baffled by it.

I begin (as I am sure you will want to begin) with the old ISLM (or SILL) diagram . . . I must say that diagram is now much less popular with me than I think it still is with many other people. It reduces *The General Theory* to equilibrium economics; it is not really *in* time.

Hicks then suggests that general equilibrium analysis, with its focus on steady-state economics, shunted economics onto a wrong line for more than two decades. Hicks (1976, pp. 142–3) declares: 'I shall not say much about steady state economics . . . it is my own opinion that it has been rather a curse . . . it has encouraged economists to waste their time upon constructions that are often of great intellectual complexity but which are so much out of time, and out of history, as to be practically futile and misleading.' Thus Hicks has rediscovered the faults of neoclassical economics which Keynes discerned and tried to rectify with his 'in time' monetary theory.

Similarly, Arrow and Hahn (1971), in their desire to give a systematic exposition of general competitive analysis, have stumbled across Keynes's contract-time approach. In their chapter on 'The Keynesian Model', they discover that (pp. 356–7):

> The terms in which contracts are made matter. In particular, if money is the good in terms of which contracts are made, then the prices of goods in terms of money are of special significance. This is not the case if we consider an economy without a past and without a future. Keynes wrote that 'the importance of money essentially flows from it being a link between the present and the future' to which we add that it is important also because it is a link between the past and the present. If *a serious monetary theory* comes to be written, the fact that contracts are indeed made in terms of money will be of considerable importance. (Italics added)

Furthermore, Arrow and Hahn (p. 361) have concluded that in 'a world with a past as well as a future and in which contracts are made in terms of money, no [general] equilibrium may exist'.

For a decentralized market economy moving irreversibly through calendar time (where the future is uncertain), forward contracting for inputs to the production process is essential to efficient production plans (see the third section of this article). Moreover, in such an economy, when slavery is illegal the money-wage contract is the most ubiquitous forward contract of all; and since labour hiring precedes in time the delivery of newly produced goods, it is the money-wage relative to productivity that is the foundation upon which the price level of new goods rests. If Arrow and Hahn are correct, it therefore follows that the relevant analytical framework for a market economy is the monetary approach of Keynes rather than the traditional GE analysis.

Hence, it would appear that the fundamental soundness of the monetary analysis developed by Keynes is slowly being rediscovered as 'a serious monetary theory' once again – after a hiatus of almost forty years – and is being developed to make contact with the real world.

2 MONETARISTS VERSUS KEYNESIANS VERSUS KEYNES ON THE CROWDING-OUT EFFECT

A recent argument developed by monetarists (Spencer and Yohe, 1970) states that if the US government attempted to increase deficit expenditures to stimulate the economy during a recession, the effect would be to 'crowd out' private borrowers from credit markets, thereby further depressing private sector spending.

Since those who do not study history (of economic thought) tend to repeat the errors of the past, some American 'Keynesian' scholars blatantly dismissed the 'crowding-out' theory as lacking any understanding of the basic Keynesian principle that, before full employment, there can never be a shortage of savings 'to finance' any level of investment (or government) spending. Yet, it was a similar debate which caused Keynes to add the finance motive to his liquidity preference approach.

In *The General Theory*, Keynes (1936, p. 195) discusses the transactions demand for money (income deposits in the *Treatise*) as the motive for holding money in order 'to bridge the interval between the receipt of income and its disbursement'. Underlying this motive for spanning *institutional and contractually determined time intervals* is: (1) the behavioural pattern of households to avoid the embarrassment of insolvency between the time they expect to receive money as a result of contracting for the sale of goods and services (primarily labour) and the time they have to meet all their anticipated contractual commitments incurred while buying goods for money during the period; and (2) the need of entrepreneurs to redeem their promises to pay for inputs to the production process with money before the time when they will receive money receipts from the sale of goods produced by these inputs.

In the *Treatise*, the demand for income deposits by households and firms depended upon anticipated or expected spending that would come due during the contractual payments period. In the truncated monetary analysis of *The General Theory*, however, Keynes (1936, p. 170), while defining the transactions motive in terms of 'personal and business exchanges', tends to encourage viewing this demand for money as a means of settlement of obligations solely from the householder's position, while neglecting the business motive. Since, in *The General Theory*, planned household spending is primarily a function of *income*, many 'Keynesians' have been misled into incorrectly specifying the medium of exchange function of money as a simple function of income, for example,

$$L_t = f(Y) \tag{13.1}$$

or even

$$L_t = b(Y) \tag{13.2}$$

where L_t is the aggregate demand for transactions cash balances, Y is aggregate income, and b is a constant. In fact, Keynes (1936, pp. 199–200) used equation (13.1) as a 'safe first approximation' for the purpose of analysing a specific set of circumstances where it was hypothesized that M was exogenous and the planned spending propensities did not change. Nevertheless, when the demand for transactions balances is a demand to meet *planned* expenditures during the contractual income period, then the correct specification of L_t is:

$$L_t = \alpha C + \beta I \tag{13.3}$$

where C is planned consumption demand (at each Y level), I is planned investment spending, and α and β are constants.[3]

Equation (13.3) implies that all the parameters of the demand function for goods by households, investors, and governments are also parameters of the demand for money function. Thus, every time there is an exogenous shift in the aggregate demand for goods function, the demand for transaction balance function is displaced. (This interdependence should not be as shocking as it may first appear to some. After all, in 'Principles', textbook economists have always taught that the demand for goods depends on wants *plus the ability to pay*. In a monetary economy the ability to pay involves the possession of transactions balances.)

In 1937, Ohlin quickly spotted the error of Keynes's 'safe first approximation' as embodied in an equation such as (13.1). In reply to Ohlin's criticism, Keynes (1937, pp. 201–23) introduced a new and, to appearances, somewhat novel purpose for demanding money: namely, the finance motive. Keynes argued that entrepreneurs typically hold some cash balances between payments periods to assure themselves that, when they enter into forward contracts for the purchase of capital goods that will be produced during the period, they will be able to meet these obligations. Thus, as long as planned (contractual) investment expenditures are unchanged in each period, demand for transactions balances is a stable function of output flow.

'But,' Keynes (1973, p. 209) wrote, 'if decisions to invest are (e.g.) increasing, the extra finance involved will constitute an additional demand for money.' If, for example, profit expectations are increased exogenously, then at the given flow of output and rate of interest, entrepreneurs would desire to enter into more forward contracts for capital goods than before, and consequently the demand for money to use to pay for the hire purchase of these goods would increase[4] (Robinson, 1952, pp. 20–2). In other words, an increase in planned investment expenditures will normally result in an increase in the aggregate demand for money function, even before the expenditures are undertaken.

Once the finance motive is properly introduced, the interdependence of the real and monetary subsectors is readily demonstrated. For example, using the popular *IS–LM* framework as a pedagogical device, if equation (13.3) or (13.4) is utilized in developing the *LM* locus, then every upward shift of the *IS* curve due to an exogenous increase in aggregate demand implies a concomitant upward (but less than proportionate) shift in *LM* functions;[5] i.e. every increase in the aggregate demand for real goods induces an increase in the demand for money as contractual obligations per period increase at any level of Y.

Keynes (1973, p. 222) noted that his finance motive analysis highlighted the fact that *any* increase in planned spending will create 'congestion' (to use Keynes's term) in the money markets, while

> the public can save *ex ante* and *ex post* and ex anything else until they are blue in the face without alleviating the problem . . . the banks hold the key position in the transition from a lower to a higher scale of activity. If they refuse to relax [i.e. to provide endogenous additional finance] the growing congestion of the short-term loan market or the new issue market, as the case may be, will inhibit the improvement, no matter how thrifty the public purpose to be out of their future income. On the other hand, there will always be *exactly* enough ex-post saving to take up the ex-post investment and so release the finance which the latter had been previously employing. *The investment market can become congested through shortage of cash. It can never become congested through shortage of saving. This is the most fundamental of my conclusions within this field.* (Italics added)

Thus, exactly forty years ago Keynes recognized that the possibility of 'congestion' (or, in modern parlance, 'crowding out') was the 'most fundamental' of his conclusions in the monetary theory field in which he was a preeminent scholar. In terms of the *IS–LM* framework, this congestion is due to the fact that the parameters of the planned spending (*IS*) function are also parameters of the demand for money (*LM*) function; that is, the *IS* and *LM* functions are interdependent.

Unfortunately, confusion reigns in much of the recent monetary theory literature because these aggregate interdependencies have not been recognized by American Keynesians, and only, vaguely and incorrectly perceived by monetarists. Tobin (1974, p. 77), for example, has written that the 'main issue' separating monetarists from his brand of Keynesianism is 'the shape of the *LM* locus.' Friedman (1974, p. 142), on the other hand, has discovered that 'the main issue between us clearly is not and never has been whether the *LM* curve is vertical or has a positive slope'. Friedman, in an analysis similar in some respects to Keynes's fundamental conclusion regarding the finance motive, has at least recognized that under certain circumstances, when the *IS* curve shifts because of an increase in planned spending, the *LM* curve shifts concomitantly. Although Friedman has not perceived all the ramifications of the interrelationships of *IS* and *LM* curves, he at least appreciates the possibility of the principle of interdependence of the functions of the monetary and real sectors – a principle that is basic to Keynes's approach but that has so far escaped the perception of the leading proponents of the neoclassical branch of the Keynesian school.

Friedman, accepting the 'crowding-out' effect (without realizing its origin in Keynes's finance motive analysis), sketches his position with the following example. Assume a permanent, once-for-all shift in the *IS* function due to a deficit-financed increase in government spending from G_0 to G_1. The deficit, according to Friedman, must be financed by a concomitant increase in the money supply (to avoid 'congestion') not only in the first period when incomes increase from Y_0 to Y_1, but in each future period as long as the deficit continues, even though government expenditure remains unchanged at G_1. Thus, the *LM* curve continues to shift rightward in each future period so that its movement 'must swamp the effect of the once-for-all shift of the *IS* curve' (Friedman, 1974, p. 141).

Of course, Friedman has *not* recognized that when the *IS* curve shifts outward initially the finance motive will cause the *LM* curve to shift inward, and therefore an increase in the money supply in the initial period to finance the initial increase in government spending will merely offset the inward *LM* shift and *avoid* congestion. Whether the *LM* curve must continue to shift outward in each subsequent future period after the once-for-all shift of the *IS* function, however, depends on the flow-demand for securities out of savings in future periods. The flow demand for securities, as I have demonstrated in detail elsewhere (Davidson, 1978, ch. 13) depends on the magnitude of m, the marginal propensity to purchase securities out of each period's aggregate savings. Once the higher level of income Y_1 is established from the once-for-all shift in *IS*, the additional savings in each future period compared to savings that would be forthcoming if Y remained at Y_0 will just equal $G_1 - G_0$. If $m = 1$, then this additional savings sum will *all* be spent on securities, so that the additional new issue of government debt to finance the same $G_1 - G_0$ deficit in each future period, *ceteris paribus*, can just be absorbed by the private sector net flow demand for securities out of savings, and no additional money need be forthcoming to float the additional government debt. Thus if $m = 1$, the *LM* curve will not shift in future periods in response to the once-for-all shift in *IS*. In other words, both functions will shift about in the initial period only.

If, on the other hand, $m = 0$, then there will be no additional flow demand for securities by the private sector in each future period, and hence government bonds (at the current rate of interest) can be sold only to the banking system, so that Friedman's scenario of the money supply increasing *pari passu* with the $G_1 - G_0$ deficit in each future period is applicable.

Keynes (1973, p. 222) believed that $0<m<1$, and hence, *ceteris paribus*, some part of the new issue of government debt used to finance the $G_1 - G_0$ spending in each future period will be absorbed by the private sector and part will have to be financed by an increase in the money supply if tax revenues did not expand as income increased. Thus, whether the continuous shifting of the *LM* curve 'swamps' the once-for-all shift of *IS* depends on the magnitude of m. Money clearly matters, but so does the liquidity preference (and hence the asset-holding desires) of the private sector.

3 WHY MONEY MATTERS

3.1 Time, Liquidity, and Finance

At the outset of his *Treatise*, Keynes (1930a, p. 3) explicitly stated that money is 'that by delivery of which debt contracts and price contracts are *discharged*, and in the shape of which a store of General Purchasing Power is held'. Thus in 1930 Keynes started his analysis with the same 'hunted hare' that Arrow and Hahn finally glimpsed in concluding their analysis 41 years later; namely, that the existence of contracts in terms of money is essential to the phenomenon of money and that 'a serious monetary theory' cannot be developed unless this fact is explicitly accounted for.

Modelling of the real world requires an analysis of an economic system moving irreversibly through calendar time where the human institution of money and its related market institutions of money contracts for (a) immediate delivery and payments (spot contracts) and/or (b) future delivery and payment (forward contracts) play fundamental roles. This in turn requires a study of the relationship and organization of such time-related spot and forward markets similar to the one provided by Keynes in his *Treatise*, a framework which Keynes (1930b, pp. 140–6) proclaimed to be superior to the orthodox short-period theory of prices since it permitted a simultaneous analysis of the relationship of the (spot) price of stocks and the (forward) price of flows. Although Keynes's time-related market organization analysis has been virtually ignored – except perhaps in the writings of Kaldor (1939) and myself (1978) – in 1977 Clower (p. 209) rediscovered the principle that one of the objects of monetary theory is to explain 'how the organization of . . . markets tends always to take highly specialized form that permits us objectively to assert that certain objects (or documents representing the latter) play a distinctive role as "money"'.

Why must transactions on organized markets be time related? Time is a device that prevents everything from happening at once. Production takes time, and hence in a market-oriented economy most production transactions along the non-integrated chain of firms involve forward contracts. For example, the hiring of factor inputs (especially labour) and the purchase of materials for the production of goods will normally require forward contracting if the production process is to be planned efficiently. The financing of such forward-production cost commitments (i.e. taking a 'position' in working capital goods) requires entrepreneurs to have money available to discharge these liabilities at one or more future dates *before* the product is sold, delivered, and payment received, and the position is liquidated. Since orthodox neoclassical theory neglects the concept of contracting over calendar time in organized markets for future delivery *and* payment, this ubiquitous liquidity problem of entrepreneurs in capitalist economies is left unattended by mainstream economists, who consequently are deserving recipients of the businessman's traditional gibe: 'They have never had to meet a payroll!' Keynes, on the other hand, recognized that positions in working capital are necessary because final goods take time to produce.[6] Keynes's monetary theory of production explains why and how entrepreneurs attempt to meet their payroll (and other) contractual obligations.

The existence of money contracts for forward delivery *and* payment is fundamental to the concepts of liquidity and money (Davidson, 1977a). In such a setting, changes in money-wage rates – Keynes's wage unit – determine changes in the costs of production and the price level associated with the production of goods that profit-oriented entrepreneurs are willing to undertake. The view that inflation (i.e. a rising money price level of newly produced goods) is a monetary phenomenon makes logical sense only in an economy where time-oriented money contracts (especially labour hire) are basic to the organization of production activities.

Marshall (1950, p. vii) warned in the preface of the first edition of his *Principles* that the 'element of Time is the centre of the chief difficulty of almost every economic problem'. Most of the perplexing problems facing economic agents in the real world involve the temporal coordination of production, delivery and usage, and payments for both existing stocks and newly produced finished and intermediate goods. In order to aid in this coordination of production flows with stock-holding positions, economic man has organized, in a variety of ways, markets for dealing either with (a) immediate (spot) payment and delivery (and hence only pre-existing stocks can be sold) or (b) forward payment and delivery at a specific future date (so that transactions in goods and services still to be produced can also be handled).

Neoclassical theory tends to treat all transactions as if they are made in *spot* markets, for example, the emphasis on 'production to [spot] market' (and not to [forward] contract) in current textbooks on price theory. The Fisher quantity theory approach implicitly treats transactions as if they are made on the spot, as do Friedman and the monetarists with their emphasis on the relatively fast (instantaneous) speed adjustment in price. Even in GE models where future delivery is possible, payments (or at least the clearing of all payments) occurs at the initial instant, that is, on the spot (to assure Walras's law and the absence of false trades).[7] Any of these economic models implicitly assumes either that no production of goods is carried out, so that everything is inherited from the past (Patinkin's initial endowment) or all production is completed before goods are brought to market, or that aggregate future production is sold and paid for at market-clearing prices at the initial instant, so that the future (real) production flows are independent of money payment flows. Hence the basis is laid for the Fisher–Friedman 'quantity theory presumption' (Friedman, 1974, p. 27) that real income, at least in the long run, is not influenced by the supply of money, for the levels for the former are determined outside the market price system, which functions merely to allocate a given total of (current and future) goods or endowments. In the real world, however, as in Keynes's analytical system, spot prices and initial instant payment coexist with forward prices and future money payment obligations for goods still to be produced.[8] Forward prices for producible goods depend (if entrepreneurs are rational) on the short-run Marshallian flow supply costs of production and hence ultimately on money-wages (Davidson, 1978, pp. 149–50).

As early as 1939, Hicks (pp. 135–6) had explicitly presented his macro-analysis in terms of either a spot-trading or a forward-trading economy. Unfortunately Hicks, perhaps because of his GE orientation, tended to consider an economy either exclusively as spot market oriented or as forward market oriented. In later writings, Hicks's spot-market analysis was translated into flexprice markets (because the stock supply is, by definition, perfectly inelastic, and hence any change in the public's demand will be immediately and completely reflected in a change in the spot price)[9] while forward markets (because of the fixed money terms of the time-related contracts) became Hicks's fixprice markets in a calendar time setting. The popularity of Hicks's separate flexprice vs. fixprice analysis contributed significantly to the neglect of Keynes's monetary-market approach with its simultaneous spot-forward market analysis in the decades of the 1940s and 1950s.

Recently, however, Hicks has recognized the artificiality of permitting all prices to be fixed on the spot on the Monday of a Hicksian week while trying to develop a theory of 'production *in* time'. In 1976, Hicks (pp. 142–3) wrote of his *Value and Capital* spot-market GE analysis:

> It was quite an interesting exercise . . . but I have become abundantly conscious how artificial it was. Much too much had to happen on that 'Monday'! And even if that was overlooked (as it should not have been overlooked) I was really at a loss how to deal with the further problem of how to string my 'weeks' and my 'Mondays' together.

Following the principle of Robertson's 'hunted hare' analogy, Hicks has apparently rediscovered Keynes's view that if a community existed where *all* transactions require payment on the spot, nothing would possess liquidity over time; for such a spot-market system, as Keynes (1930a, p. 3) put it, would have 'scarcely emerged from a state of barter'.[10]

In the real world, however, it is the ubiquitous catenated forward contracts primarily (but not solely) for the purchase of inputs along the non-integrated chain of firms in the production process which form the string connecting Hicks's Mondays. Because production takes time, entrepreneurs require forward contracts whose duration exceeds the gestation period of production so that they can have some assurance of the monetary limits to the 'position' they will be undertaking when they initiate a production flow.[11] If a producer can enter into a forward contract for the sale of product at the maturation date at the same time that (or before) he makes a substantial commitment to hire inputs – a practice that is typically sought and often occurs at all stages of production except the retail stage – then the entrepreneur can be assured of the profitability of his 'position' in working capital goods and can therefore readily finance this position through the banking system. Accordingly, forward contracting can be considered as the way entrepreneurs in a 'free market' environment attempt to maintain wage and price controls – for such sales and cost controls are fundamental in obtaining sound financing. Bankers and businessmen abhor what GE economists love – namely, recontracting.

Since 1975, economists at the Brookings Institution have apparently discovered that any analysis of real world inflation requires an analysis of contracts as well as two different types of markets: '"auction" markets . . . with instantaneous market clearing and "customer" markets in which economic incentives induce long-term contractual arrangements' (Gordon, 1977; also see Okun, 1975, and Poole, 1976). Although there are obvious similarities between these auction and customer market concepts and the Keynes spot- and forward-market analysis, the former concepts have not been developed adequately. For the Brookings people, the difference appears to turn on the existence of an auction (and the implicit absence of contracts) in the one and the existence of contracts (and the absence of an auction) in the other. Contracts, however, are the essence of both 'auction' and 'customer' markets. It is the time duration of the contractual commitment in each type of market, and not whether the market is organized on an auction basis or not, that is the important feature in developing 'a serious monetary theory'. (It is possible to have well-organized auction markets for forward contracts – even though each contract involves long-time contractual arrangements.)

The existence of time-related markets and contracts for performance and money payments is the essence of a money economy, for it is basic to the concept of liquidity. Liquidity in a temporal setting, given the money-wage unit and the resulting price level, is the cornerstone of Keynes's revolution! Problems of liquidity and finance are the hallmarks of everyday business decision-making in a monetary economy.

Liquidity involves being able to have the means of settlement to meet all one's contractual obligations when they come due. Since money is the only thing that will discharge contract commitments (by definition), for any store of value besides money to be liquid, it must be easily resaleable for money in a spot market. Thus the degree of liquidity associated with any durable depends on the organization and orderliness of the spot market in which it is traded.[12] Those durables whose spot markets are very poorly organized, thin, or even notional are *illiquid assets*. Such assets (e.g. fixed capital and consumer durables) are held primarily for either the net money stream or utility stream they are expected to generate at specific dates in the future.[13]

Liquid assets are durables traded in well-organized and orderly markets. Hence, what are the liquid assets of any economy depends on the social practices and institutions that exist in that economy. In his *Principles*, Marshall (1950, pp. 325–7) indicated a number of factors that would affect the degree of organization of a market for any good. He omitted, however, the most essential factor for well-organized markets – namely, the institution of a *market maker*, or trade coordinator in Clower and Leijonhufvud's terminology (1975, p. 184). The function of a market-maker is to provide orderliness over time in the money price of the good traded, offsetting the random ebbs and flows of the market by utilizing sizeable inventories of both the good traded in the market and money (or other liquid assets) (Davidson, 1978, p. 87). Thus even spot prices need not respond with perfect flexibility to every change in the demand or supply of the good on the part of the public. Orderliness (i.e. sticky spot prices over time) is maintained by means of reservation demands by the market-makers. Orderliness in spot prices merely requires the existence of buffer stocks and the willingness of the holders of such stocks to utilize them to assure a continuity in market price over time (according to the rules of the games adopted by the market so organized).

If there is a market-maker who deals with the public as both the residual buyer and seller of a specific durable in economy A while no similar market-maker institution exists for the same item in economy B, then the same durable will be a liquid asset in A but not in B. In the most developed monetary economies, large private sector market-makers have evolved in many spot markets (e.g. security specialists and jobbers, bond houses, foreign exchange dealers, etc.) so that in such economies there is a large spectrum of financial assets besides money that are highly liquid. Often formal or even informal financing arrangements exist between these private market-makers and the banking system (and hence either directly or indirectly with the central bank). The public recognizes that such financial arrangements imply that, in any macroliquidity crisis, these private market makers will not experience undue financial pressure which would otherwise force them to liquidate their 'position' completely in a short period of time, causing the spot price to drop precipitously. Consequently, the continuity and orderliness of such spot markets appear assured – as long as the central banker ultimately acts as the lender of last resort and the community continues to use the 'money' of the system to denominate its contractual obligations.[14] If, however, these financial arrangements prove inadequate in a liquidity crisis, perhaps because the chain from the private market-maker to the central bank is weak and therefore the latter does not (or cannot) respond as lender of last resort swiftly enough, then some large private sector market-maker could collapse. This can in turn induce a chain reaction in other liquid spot markets as the financial structure of debt layering (as Minsky has eloquently described it) collapses like a house of cards.

In this era of central banks, it is their decisions and activities that ultimately provide the liquidity of any ongoing monetary economy which relies on the institution of forward contracting in money terms to organize its productive activities. And it is only in such an economic system that money matters and central banks matter!

Fully liquid assets are money (i.e. that which discharges contractual obligations) plus any asset that can be converted into money in a spot market where the market-maker 'guarantees' a fixed and unchanging net spot money price. Since ultimately only the central bank (in modern economies) can provide such guarantees, either the central bank or a market-maker institution with ready and direct access to the central bank can create the fully liquid assets of a modern economy.

The importance of the existence of a market-maker to provide liquidity for many durables has been ignored by Friedman in his attempt to differentiate his monetary analysis from that of Keynes and the Keynesians. The difference, according to Friedman (1974, p. 28), 'is in the transmission mechanism that is assumed to connect a change in the quantity of money with a change in total nominal income'; for Keynes only financial assets traded on well-organized spot markets are good substitutes for money, while Friedman insists that a far wider range of assets, including furniture, appliances, clothes, etc., are substituted for money by wealth owners in their portfolios as they attempt 'to restore or attain a desired balance sheet after an unexpected increase in the quantity of money'.

Tobin (1974, p. 89), on the other hand, believes that Friedman's claim that 'he is more catholic than nonmonetarists in the list of assets he includes in portfolios – in particular his inclusion of *durable goods for which there are not good organized markets*' (italics added) – does not do justice to Tobin's own conception of a portfolio that 'has always included consumer durables'.

In Keynes's original model, however, portfolio choice is associated with *liquidity preference*. Keynes (1936, p. 211) specifies that 'the act of saving implies . . . a desire for "wealth" as such, that is for a potentiality of consuming an unspecified article at an unspecified time'. Consequently, it would be foolish for savers to hold a specific physical durable that is not traded in a well-organized spot market, i.e. an illiquid asset, in their portfolio as a store of value. Instead Keynes (ibid., p. 166) insists that a saver must decide to store his wealth either

in the form of immediate liquid command (i.e. money or its equivalent) . . . [or] to part with immediate command for a specified or indefinite period, leaving it to future [spot] market conditions to determine on what terms he can, if necessary, convert deferred command over specific goods into immediate command over goods in general . . . In other words, what is the degree of *liquidity-preference*.

If wealth owners are saving for an unspecified expenditure at an unspecified future date, then portfolio choices can only be between fully liquid assets and liquid assets. Illiquid assets such as capital goods and consumer durables will never be a good substitute for money as an uncommitted store of value as long as well-organized, orderly spot markets for such goods do not exist. It is obvious that in the real world most fixed capital goods and consumer durables are not traded in well-organized spot markets and no market-maker has come forth to organize such markets. Accordingly, such reproducible goods cannot satisfy liquidity demands.

Keynes (ibid., ch. 17) insisted that the essential properties of money and other assets which possess the attribute of liquidity in large degree were zero or negligible elasticities of production (i.e. the asset could not be readily reproduced through the exertion of labour in response to an increase in demand), and a zero or negligible elasticity of substitution between liquid assets and goods that are readily reproducible through the exertion of labour.[15]

Rightly or wrongly, Keynes (ibid., p. 241) asserted that the 'attribute of liquidity is by no means independent of the presence of these two characteristics'. Fixed capital goods and consumer durables are normally not held as stores of value for liquidity purposes because they do not possess the characteristics which encourage the development of active, well-organized spot markets for their exchange (Davidson, 1978, ch. 4). Thus, in contrast to Friedman, Keynes insists that one of the basic 'peculiarities' of a monetary economy is that easily reproducible, labour-resource-using durables are illiquid and that such illiquid assets are never good substitutes for money. Consequently Say's Law is inapplicable and unemployment equilibrium is possible.

These peculiar elasticity properties do not mean that the quantity of money is unalterable. In a bank money economy, the money supply can be changed either exogenously (via open market operations) or endogenously, as the banks respond to an increased demand for money due to the finance motive – including the need to meet increased payrolls if the contractual money wage rate increases (Davidson, 1977b). Nevertheless, in an economy where liquidity is associated with these peculiar properties, an increased demand for money for precautionary or speculative purposes at the expense of planned transactions will, all other things being equal, reduce employment, while an exogenous increase in the money supply will not have a direct impact on spending on reproducible goods via portfolio adjustments. (This latter result is in direct conflict with Friedman's (1974, pp. 28–29) assumed transmission mechanism.)

Friedman, and to some extent Tobin, on the other hand, because of their GE approach implicitly assume that, at least in a GE long-run system, all markets are *well* organized (via the Walrasian auctioneer) and, therefore, all goods are ultimately gross substitutes. By ignoring the institutional questions of (a) market organization and market makers, (b) the non-universality of the gross substitution maxim, and (c) the essential properties of money, both Friedman and Tobin are to different degrees neglecting some of the most fundamental problems of real world economies. Consequently, the debate between Friedman's monetarism and Tobin's Keynesianism has shunted economic theory onto a wrong line and has therefore retarded the development of what Arrow and Hahn have labelled 'a serious monetary theory'.

3.2 General Equilibrium versus Keynesian Equilibrium

In the search for a microfoundation that is consistent with Keynesian macroeconomics, some theorists have attempted to 'alter' their basic GE models to permit a 'Keynesian' underemployment solution. What is happening in this search process is another example of Robertson's 'hunted hare' cycle since, consciously or otherwise, these GE theorists are rediscovering the elasticity properties Keynes labelled as essential to the concept of money.

Grandmont and Laroque (1976, p. 54), for example, have formulated a 'temporary Keynesian equilibrium' model which has (a) fiat money as the only store of value, and (b) only one producible commodity that is non-storable over time. Hence, without acknowledgement (or recognition?), Grandmont and Laroque have assumed a money that possesses zero elasticities of production and substitution (between money and the productible, perishable commodity). Unfortunately these authors have not focused on this money concept; rather, they claim (ibid., p. 53) to achieve a 'temporary Keynesian' underemployment equilibrium by making rigid money wages and/or monopolistic competition (fix prices) 'a central feature of the Keynesian model'.

Keynes would not deny the existence or the importance of monopoly power and money wage rigidities, but he did argue that these were not central features of underemployment equilibrium. A reduction in money wages (or prices) would not, *ceteris paribus*, have a direct tendency to increase employment (Keynes, 1936, pp. 260–2). 'Unemployment develops . . . because people want the moon; men cannot be employed when the object of desire (i.e. money) is something which cannot be produced and the demand for which can not be readily choked off' (ibid., p. 235). Thus for Keynes, if not for Grandmont and Laroque, it is the elasticity properties and not the existence of monopoly power which permits underemployment equilibrium[16] (ibid., 1936, pp. 229–35).

Professor Hahn (1977, p. 25) has recently noted that the view that Keynesian economics deals with important relevant problems and General Equilibrium theory deals with no relevant problems at all . . . has, alas, an element of truth'. Hahn, however, vainly tries to restore the usefulness of his GE research programme by simultaneously introducing the first of Keynes's 'essential properties' of money into a GE model while removing this property from its association with money. Hahn (ibid., p. 27) assumes an economy 'which can produce a single good by the aid of this good and labour. This good is perfectly durable if not consumed'. He (ibid., p. 31) claims that underemployment equilibrium can exist in his GE model as long as there are 'resting places for savings other than reproducible assets. In our model, this is money. But Land, as to his credit Keynes understood, would have the same consequences and so would Old Masters. It is, therefore, not money which is required to do away with a Say's-Law-like proposition that the supply of labour is the demand for goods produced by labour. Any non-reproducible asset will do.'[17]

Non-reproducibility alone, however, will not do in the real world! A second elasticity property is essential if Say's Law is to be inapplicable when income earners increase the demand for this non-reproducible good (which we may call stones) for liquidity purposes at the expense of the durable producible good (which we may call furniture). As the market price of stones rises, if furniture is a substitute (as both Friedman and Tobin explicitly suggest and the gross substitution maxim of Hahn's GE model requires), then the increased demand for stones spills over into a demand for furniture. The greater the elasticity of substitution between stones and furniture, the less the price of stones has to rise to resuscitate Say's Law in Hahn's model. Because Hahn has rediscovered only the first of Keynes's elasticity properties, his analysis is flawed.

Money, unlike the pure rent factors of Hahn's GE model, possesses a second elasticity property. 'The second *differentia* of money is that it has an elasticity of substitution equal, or nearly equal, to zero . . . Thus not only is it impossible to turn more labour on to producing money . . . money is a bottomless sink for purchasing power when the demand for it increases, since there is no value for it at which demand is diverted – so as to slop over into a demand for other things' (Keynes, 1936, p. 231).

In a world of uncertainty, where the institution of forward contracting in money terms for labour and other materials is an essential aspect of production decisions, a money that possesses these two elasticity properties enhances the expectations of sticky efficiency wages (ibid., p. 238; Davidson, 1978, chs. 6, 9). It is a combination of these properties and real world contracting institutions and economic organizations that can inhibit neoclassical 'natural market forces' from bringing about a full employment equilibrium (ibid., p. 235).

Explicit acceptance of the second elasticity property by Hahn, however,

would violate the fundamental gross substitutability tenet (the mos
important sufficient condition for demonstrating the uniqueness and sta
bility of the general equilibrium position). Thus, there is a fundamenta
logical incompatibility between the 'serious monetary theory' developed b
Keynes and the neoclassical GE approach of Hahn (and Friedman an
Tobin as well). As Keynes noted, such neoclassical theory has as muc
relevance to the real world as Euclidean propositions regarding paralle
lines has to a non-Euclidean world.[18]

4   CONCLUSION

Economic theory in general and monetary theory in particular are com
pleting another 'hunted hare' cycle. We have not advanced much furthe
than when Keynes was formulating his theory of a monetary economy ir
the late 1920s and early 1930s. Nevertheless, the role of and need fo
national and international central banks has increased as economies have
become more developed, more interdependent, and more monetized.

Events have not stood still in the last 50 years. The growth of labour
power under the protection of governmental full employment policies and
the growth of multinational corporations since the Second World War had
already created problems that by 1970 were threatening the basic monetary
institutions of free market economies and were creating the first major
crisis for capitalist economies since the Great Depression. In the last few
years, the sudden development of OPEC's economic power and the
resulting rapid changes in national and international monetary flows and
asset holdings further threaten the stability and, perhaps, even the viability
of many monetary institutions and organizations that have evolved slowly
over decades of a different environment. Mainstream neoclassical monetary theory has little advice to offer as to how these monetary institutions
should adapt to these tremendous stresses and strains except that, if we
maintain a steady increase in the money supply *in the long run*, though we
are all dead, the monetary waters will again be calm.

Keynes, on the other hand, never lost focus on the interrelations
between the money supply and the money-wage unit (or, in a larger
context, the cost unit including imports). Keynes's monetary analysis
(1936, p. 239) led him to the fundamental conclusion: that 'money-wages
should be more stable than real wages is a [necessary] condition of the
system possessing inherent stability' (ibid., p. 239). In both his *Treatise* and
his *General Theory*, Keynes emphasized the money-wage–money-supply
nexus. He noted that if we have control of both the earnings system
(incomes policy) and monetary system (monetary policy) and can control
the rate of investment, we can 'stabilise the purchasing power of money, its
labour power, or anything else – without running the risk of setting up

ocial and economic frictions or of causing waste' (1930a, p. 169). More-
ver, Keynes maintained that 'if there are strong social or political forces
ausing spontaneous changes in the money-rates of efficiency wages [or in a
nodern context, the money costs of energy] the control of the price level
nay pass beyond the power of the banking system' (1930b, p. 351).

Let us hope that, having come full circle in monetary theory, we can now
reak the 'hunted hare' syndrome and advance our theories so that we can
ninimize the deleterious effects of the inevitable future fluctuations and
isruptions of a monetary economy moving through time. Except in the
ong-run neoclassical models, human thought can never bring about the
ong-run calm waters of a state of economic bliss, but we can strive to
nodify and improve our economic environment in the short run by
ninimizing the economic waves generated by real world monetary econ-
mies when exposed to ever-changing pressures over time. The first
rerequisite to such an advance, however, is an understanding of how a
eal world monetary economy behaves in the short run as it moves through
ime. Keynes provided such a basic framework. Let us advance from
here.[19]

Notes

1. The term 'potted version' is used by Hicks (1967, p. vii) to describe his famous
   'Mr. Keynes and the "Classics"' article.
2. Weintraub (1957; 1960) was one of the first to call attention to this fact. More
   than a decade later. Leijonhufvud (1968) was more successful in focusing
   attention on the fact that macroeconomics deviated from the analysis of
   Keynes.
3. In an expanded model where planned government spending (G) is included,
   equation (13.2) would be written as:

$$L_t = \alpha C + \beta I + \sigma G \qquad (13.4)$$

4. To clarify the essence of the finance motive and indicate why it is not properly
   taken into account in the discussion of the transactions motive, Keynes wrote
   (1973, pp. 220–1):

   It follows that, if the liquidity-preference of the public (as distinct from the
   entrepreneurial investors) and of the banks are unchanged, an excess in the
   finance required by current ex-ante output (it is not necessary to write
   'investment,' since the same is true of *any* output which has to be planned
   ahead) over the finance released by current ex-post output will lead to a rise
   in the rate of interest; and a decrease will lead to a fall. I should not have
   previously overlooked this point, since it is the coping-stone of the liquidity
   theory of the rate of interest. I allowed, it is true, for the effect of an increase
   in actual activity on the demand for money. But I did not allow for the effect
   of an increase in *planned* activity, which is superimposed on the former . . .

> Just as an increase in actual activity must (as I have always explained) raise the rate of interest unless either the banks or the rest of the public become more willing to release cash, so (as I now add) an increase in planned activity must have a similar, super-imposed influence.

5. For proof see Davidson (1978, pp. 168–70, 185–8).
6. Similarly, positions in consumer durables, houses, plant, and equipment must be financed over some period of calendar time beginning with their initial purchase date, since such goods take time to consume or use.
7. Jaffe (1967, pp. 9–14) has demonstrated that Walras's own system was logically consistent only for an exchange economy where all goods are in essence traded on the spot.
8. Minsky (1975, ch. 4), for example, has provided a lucid illustration of these two coexisting price mechanisms in his discussion 'Capital Financing and the Pricing of Capital Goods'.
9. This is true only to the extent that public demand change is not offset by a change in reservation demand of the market makers of these spot markets. Even in spot auction markets the degree of price flexibility depends on this reservation demand of market makers, i.e. their reactions and interpretation of sudden changes in the public's market behaviour and the institutional rules governing how market makers are supposed to maintain 'orderliness' in spot prices over calendar time.
10. Or, as Hahn (1970, p. 3) stated in 1970, 'the Walrasian economy that we have been considering, although one where the auctioneer regulates the terms at which goods shall exchange, is essentially one of barter'.
11. Cost overruns, except when they are validated by forward cost-plus purchase contracts (e.g. in defence industries) can be a disaster to a firm.
12. In GE systems, since it is assumed that all goods can be traded in well-organized spot markets and all payments are made at the initial instant, there is never a liquidity problem. Everything appears to be equally liquid, although nothing is really liquid, for these are barter economies.
13. Friedman's transmission mechanism, however, as well as Tobin's portfolio balance approach, assumes that illiquid assets are held for the same reasons as money (see discussion below).
14. Only in the case of a 'flight from domestic money', i.e. when the economic agents of the domestic economy refuse to enter into forward contracts denominated in the domestic money of the economy, will the monetary system break down. In such cases, even money loses its attribute of liquidity and normally a foreign asset or currency will (at least temporarily) become the 'money' of the economy.
15. For a complete discussion of these two elasticity conditions, see Davidson (1978, chs. 6, 9). Keynes insisted that if demand is redirected from producible goods towards money, 'labour cannot be employed in producing more money and . . . there is no mitigation at any point through some other factor being capable, if it is sufficiently cheap, of doing money's duty equally well' (1936, p. 234). Of course, other liquid assets that possess a zero or negligible elasticity of production may be good substitutes for money (e.g. financial assets, foreign exchange) (see Davidson, 1977a).
16. For a more complete critique of the Grandmont–Laroque model, see Davidson (1977a).
17. At other places in his paper, Hahn indicates that underemployment equilibrium can also be attributed to fixed money wages and/or the absence of perfect

competition when wages or prices are changed. As already indicated above and developed in detail elsewhere (Davidson, 1977a) these latter aspects are not the central features of Keynes's world. Even in their absence, under-employment equilibrium is possible.

18. 'The classical theorists resemble Euclidean geometers in a non-Euclidean world who, discovering that in experience straight lines apparently parallel often meet, rebuke the lines for not keeping straight – as the only remedy for the unfortunate collisions which are occurring. Yet in truth, there is no remedy except to throw over the axiom of parallels and to work out a non-Euclidean geometry. Something similar is required today in economics' (Keynes, 1936, p. 16).

19. For those who find disconcerting the absence of any extended explicit discussion of inflation in this paper, let me indicate that my reason for not examining this aspect was twofold. First, I have just published a paper entitled 'Post Keynes Monetary Theory and Inflation' (Davidson, 1977b) and did not wish to repeat those arguments here; and, second, in Keynes's model the connection between money and the price level is indirect and occurs via money wage magnitudes.

Keynes did recognize two types of inflation: (i) a commodity inflation, i.e. rising spot prices; and (ii) an incomes inflation, i.e. rising production costs (forward prices). Keynes (1930a, p. 169) believed that the latter was the most threatening and even in the 1930s recognized the importance of what in modern parlance is called an incomes policy for dealing with an incomes inflation. Moreover, it follows from our analysis that a buffer stock policy is a method of fighting a commodity inflation if that is required.

References

Arrow, K. J. and Hahn, F. H. (1971), *General Competitive Analysis* (San Francisco: Holden-Day).

Clower, R. W. (1977), 'The Anatomy of Monetary Theory', *American Economic Review, Papers and Proceedings*, 67.

Clower, R. W. and A. Leijonhufvud, (1975), 'The Coordination of Economic Activities: A Keynesian Perspective', *American Economic Review, Papers and Proceedings*, 65.

Davidson, P. (1974), 'A Keynesian View of Friedman's Theoretical Framework for Monetary Analysis', in R. J. Gordon (ed.), *Milton Friedman's Monetary Framework: A Debate With His Critics* (Chicago: University of Chicago Press). (Chapter 8 in this volume).

Davidson, P. (1977a), 'Money and General Equilibrium', *Economie Appliquée*, 4 (Chapter 12 in this volume).

Davidson, P. (1977b), 'Post Keynes Monetary Theory and Inflation', in S. Weintraub, (ed.) *Modern Economic Thought* (Philadelphia: University of Pennsylvania Press).

Davidson, P. (1978), *Money and the Real World*, 2nd edn (London: Macmillan).

Fisher, I. (1911), *The Purchasing Power of Money* (New York: Macmillan).

Friedman, M. (1974), 'A Theoretical Framework for Monetary Analysis' and 'Comments on the Critics', in R. J. Gordon, (ed) *Milton Friedman's Monetary Framework* (Chicago: University of Chicago Press).

Friedman, M. (1977), 'Nobel Lecture: Inflation and Unemployment'. *Journal of Political Economics*, 85.

Grandmont, J. M. and G. Laroque (1976), 'On Temporary Keynesian Equilibria' *Review of Economic Studies*, 43.

Gordon, R. J. (1977), 'The Theory of Domestic Inflation', *American Economic Review, Papers* and Proceedings, 67.

Hahn, F. H. (1970), 'Some Adjustment Problems', Econometrica, 39.

Hahn, F. H. (1977), 'Keynesian Economics and General Equilibrium Theory Reflections on Some Current Debates', in G. C. Harcourt (ed.), *Microeconomic Foundations of Macroeconomics* (London: Macmillan).

Harrod, R. F. (1951), *The Life of John Maynard Keynes* (London: Macmillan).

Harrod, R. F. (1969), *Money* (London: Macmillan).

Hicks, J. R. (1937), 'Mr. Keynes and the Classics: A Suggested Interpretation' *Econometrica*, 1937, 5; reprinted in Hicks, 1967; all references are to reprint.

Hicks, J. R. (1939), *Value and Capital* (Oxford: Oxford University Press).

Hicks, J. R. (1967), *Critical Essays in Monetary Theory* (Oxford: Oxford University Press).

Hicks, J. R. (1976), 'Some Questions of Time in Economics', in A. M. Tang *et al.* (eds), *Evolution Welfare and Time in Economics* (Lexington: Lexington Books).

Jaffee, W. (1967), 'Walras' Theory of Tatonnement: A Critique of Recent Interpretations', *Journal of Political Economics*, 75.

Kaldor, N. (1939), 'Speculation and Economic Activity', *Review of Economic Studies*, 6.

Keynes, J. M. (1930a), *A Treatise on Money*, Vol I (London: Macmillan).

Keynes, J. M. (1930b), *A Treatise on Money*, Vol II (London: Macmillan).

Keynes, J. M. (1936), *The General Theory of Employment, Interest and Money* (New York: Harcourt).

Keynes, J. M. (1971), *A Tract on Monetary Reform*, reprinted as volume IV of *The Collected Works of John Maynard Keynes* (London: Macmillan, 1971). All references are to the reprint.

Keynes, J. M. (1973), *The Collected Works of John Maynard Keynes* (London: Macmillan). All references are to volume XIV unless otherwise specified.

Leijonhufvud, A. (1968), *On Keynesian Economics and the Economics of Keynes* (Oxford: Oxford University Press).

Leijonhufvud, A. (1974), 'Keynes' Employment Function: A Comment', *History of Political Economy*, 6.

Marshall, A. (1950), *Principles of Economics*, 8th edn (London: Macmillan).

Minsky, H. P. (1975), *John Maynard Keynes* (New York: Columbia University Press).

Modigliani, F. (1944), 'Liquidity Preference and the Theory of Interest and Money', *Econometrica*, 12.

Ohlin, B. (1937), 'Some Notes on the Stockholm Theory of Savings and Investment, pt. II',*Economic Journal*, 47.

Okun, A. (1975), 'Inflation: Its Mechanics and Welfare Costs', *Brookings Papers on Economic Activity*, 6.

Poole, W. (1976), 'Rational Expectations in the Macro Model', *Brookings Papers on Economic Activity*, 7.

Robinson, J. (1952), *The Role of Interest and Other Essays* (London: Macmillan).

Robertson, D. H. (1956), *Economic Commentaries* (London: Macmillan).

Spencer, R. W., and Yohe, W. P. (1970), 'The "Crowding Out" of Private Expenditures by Fiscal Policy Actions', *Federal Reserve Bank of St Louis Review*, October.

Tobin, J. (1974), 'Friedman's Theoretical Framework', in R. J. Gordon (ed), *Milton Friedman's Theoretical Framework: A Debate with His Critics* (Chicago: University of Chicago Press).

Weintraub, S. (1957), 'Micro Foundations of Aggregate Demand and Supply', *Economic Journal*, 67.

Weintraub, S. (1960), 'The Keynesian Theory of Inflation: "The Two Faces of Janus"', *International Economic Review*, 6.

14 Rejoinder to V. Kerry Smith*

In his comment, Kerry Smith admits that the financing of basically illiquid positions of 'goods in process' is an essential aspect of a production economy organized on a forward money contracting basis. Smith realizes the importance of money and contracts in the production processes of modern firms; however, he claims that this idea can be readily incorporated into a neoclassical production function concept.

Smith admits that 'the neoclassical production function originated as a *compact approximation* of the more complex underlying engineering activities'. Certainly he understands that the role of money in the production process is not one determined by strict engineering activities. The need for money is a manifestation of a monetary contract method of organizing production activities over calendar time; i.e. it is the man-made law of contracts, and not any law of physics, which determines money usage in the production process. Nevertheless, Smith claims there is no reason 'to reject *a priori* an extension' of the concept of a neoclassical production function to handle 'money as [if it were] a factor input' in the engineering sense, for Smith suggests that there is a 'potential for gaining insights into behaviorial patterns' by stretching the concept of a production function.

Despite the apparent reasonableness of Smith's desire to gain insights by expanding existing notions, I am afraid I must demur to his approach. Science advances only when essentially difficult ideas are clarified by using precise language, that is, flawless, simple, and unambiguous definitions. To appropriate the neoclassical concept of an *ex ante* production function by 'using duality theory to demonstrate the existence of a transformation set dualed to this profit function that includes money in a role analogous to a factor input' is to force the production function notion to cover aspects it was not defined to include. Such misuse of language can only confuse and mislead rather than clarify.

It is true, of course, that if one collects data on physical (value of?) stocks of inputs used by the firm and physical (value of?) output produced during a specified interval of time, as well as the cash requirements of the firm to pay for these physical inputs during the interval, one can find an empirical relationship in which output = f(real input quantities, money used.) What this function has to do with what we ordinarily mean by the blueprints of *technological* alternatives that neoclassical economists label a production function is not clear. Money is not merely an additional input in

* *Journal of Post Keynesian Economics*, vol. 2, no. 2, Winter 1979.

he production process; there is no elasticity of substitution between money and real capital or labour services along an isoquant. If anything, money is complementary to both labour and capital services; in other words, if entrepreneurs want, *ceteris paribus*, to increase the use of either capital or labour services during the interval covered by the prevailing contractual arrangements, they must demand additional money to meet these additional contractual obligations. Moreover, if the entrepreneur does not have sufficient funds to utilize a method of production that minimizes the cost of labour and capital services for a given flow of output during the interval, then he will have to adapt to an (inefficient?) method of production; that is, there can be liquidity constraints on an engineering production function that lead to non-cost-minimizing behaviour. For example, if the owner of the marginally more expensive (per unit of output) factor (e.g. capital) is willing to wait for some of the money payment for factor services until after the product is sold, while the owner of the less expensive factor (e.g. labour) demands payment at stated dates during the gestation period of production before the product is sold, entrepreneurs under a liquidity constraint will organize their production in a manner that allows them to 'meet their payrolls'. This cash flow problem occupies most of the time and effort of real world entrepreneurs, but never enters the typical neoclassical description of entrepreneurial production decisions. Moreover, any entrepreneurs who are unable to finance an illiquid position in goods in process during the production period face bankruptcy even if the neoclassical economist can show, using 'duality theory', that the production process chosen meets the first and second derivative conditions for maximizing (positive) profits given the engineering production function and the money prices of factor inputs.

In sum, Smith's desire to develop a concept of 'money as a factor input' can lead only to further confusion and less understanding of entrepreneurial behaviour in a production economy organized on a forward money contract basis. A rose by any other name may smell as sweet; but redefining garlic into the rose family can only foul the atmosphere of any economist's flower garden.

15 Is Monetary Collapse in the 1980s on the Cards?*

Is monetary collapse in the 1980s on the cards? At the risk of overgeneralization, the simple answer to this query is yes – unless economists provide a 'new deal' in monetary theory to guide 'practical men' in government and central banks with their policy decisions. We will get our policies right only when we get our theory of money right.

Adherence to monetarist policies for handling inflation, which now appear to dominate central banks and Western government thinking, will ultimately result in the breakdown of the capitalist system of financing productive activities by private sector entrepreneurs and/or state and local governments. In the last decade, monetarist brinksmanship policy by the Federal Reserve has brought the economy close to the precipice (for example, the Penn-Central, Lockheed, and New York City financial crisis). Only at the last moment, when decision-makers felt the hot breath of the dragon of financial collapse on their necks, did policy-makers 'temporarily' abandon strict monetarist principles to institute *ad hoc* practical medicines to avoid disaster. Fortunately, our economic system is strong enough to withstand many of these 'macho' monetarist episodes, but the cumulative effect is to make a permanent solution more difficult. It may already be too late to institute such reforms until the 'second great economic collapse' of the twentieth century is upon us.

Yet, history is warning us. At the end of the decade of the 1920s when the Quantity Theory and the benefits of unfettered market activity dominated economists' writings and provided rationalization for the acts of central bankers and politicians, one after another capitalist economy collapsed. It took the revolutionary ideas of Keynes about the workings of a developed monetary economy to provide the guidelines for saving capitalism. Keynes was primarily a Monetary Theorist and he believed money was so important that the words 'money', or 'currency', or 'monetary' appear in the titles of all of his major economic books. For Keynes (if not for Keynesians) money mattered, but not in the way it did for the quantity theorists of the 1920s and 1930s.

Currently, history is repeating itself as the neoclassical monetarist school threatens to dominate economists' writings. Monetarists, while paying lip

* *Nebraska Journal of Economics and Business*, vol. 18, Spring 1979.
  Paper presented at a joint session of the American Economic Association and the Public Interest Economics Foundation, Chicago, 30 August 1978.

service to unfettered market activity and the importance of money, are relying in their logical foundations of their analysis upon a world where money has no significant role to play. Such a model cannot provide guidelines for the problems of modern monetary economies.

Currently, practical men are not the 'slaves to some defunct economist' that Keynes declared.[1] Instead, because of the efficiency of communication conduits such as the financial pages of the *New York Times, Business Week*, and the like, and the respectability bestowed upon monetarist economists by these publications, politicians and central banks feel required diligently to pursue monetarist objectives for 'worldly wisdom teaches that it is better for reputation to fail conventionally than to succeed unconventionally'.[2]

The Carter administration, despite its claims of a desire to overthrow the tried and tired unrewarding policies of the past, once having taken office has shown a revealed preference for failing conventionally rather than attempting new and unconventional policies to improve our economic situation. Thus, despite campaign rhetoric promising to end stagflation, the current administration appears to be as paralysed as its predecessor. Each month there is the hope that next month's statistics will begin the dawn of a new era, while current bad news about inflation is dismissed as due primarily to unusual episodic events. Apparently, only when the economic game appears to be nearly lost are we willing to try out new ideas which can save us from the conventional follies of economists.

In no case is this more apparent than with money, which is the economic 'oil' which lubricates Adam Smith's Great Wheel of Commerce. Money is a human institution and not a gift from nature. To understand money and to control our monetary system we must, therefore, first understand this institution and its economic interrelation to the processes of production and pricing. I wish to provide some brief guidelines for comprehending these relationships so that we can perceive why money matters and then attempt to resolve the stagflation problem which threatens to bring the capitalist system down.

1 MONEY

Modern monetarists mistakenly believe that the use of illustrative examples of money can provide a definition of a concept; hence, modern monetary theory abounds with so-called 'definitions' of M_1, M_2, M_3, . . ., M_7, which are exemplifications rather than explanations. Imagine the confusion and chaos that would occur if astronomers defined 'planets' by using the name of specific heavenly bodies (how would you tell a planet from a moon?), or, even worse, if some chemists defined the term 'molecule' in terms of specific inorganic salts, while a second group included specific inorganic acids with the salts, and a third group included inorganic bases, and the like.

Scientific communication and progress can occur only when definitions are cast not in terms of specific illustrations but are formulated in terms of *essential* features and properties. Then, if a specific item possesses these essential properties and features, it is an example of the defined things no matter how strange this may appear to the layman, for example, a whale is a mammal, not a fish, or bamboo shoots are grass, not trees.

In this spirit of scientific definition, I shall insist that the concept of money in existence in a modern production, market-oriented economy involves two fundamental, concomitant features. These features, in turn, require two necessary properties. Money is that thing which by delivery permits economic agents to discharge obligations that are the result of spot and/or forward contracts. Thus the first definitional feature is that *money is the means of contractual settlement*. Money is also capable of acting as a vehicle to move generalized (non-specific) purchasing power over time, that is, the second feature involves *money as a one-way* (present to future) *time machine*.

In modern monetary economies, this second feature, which is known as liquidity, is possessed in various degree by some, but not all, durables. Since any durable besides money *cannot* (by definition) be used as a means of settlement of future contractual obligations, in order for a specific durable to be a vehicle for moving generalized purchasing power over time it must be readily resaleable at any time in a well-organized, orderly *spot* market. The degree of liquidity associated with any durable is a measure of its capability as a 'liquidity time machine' and that depends on the degree of organization of its spot market.

The means of contractual settlement or payment feature of money, on the other hand, is *not* possessed by any other durable except money. If some 'liquidity time machine' was suddenly also to possess this means of settlement feature (or to lose it), at that moment the durable would become (would no longer be) money. Thus, for example, when in the 1930s the US Supreme Court upheld the abrogation of the gold clause in business contracts, gold was no longer money in the United States – even though it may have retained a degree of liquidity to the extent it was saleable for money in spot markets.

It therefore follows that exemplifications of money in any economy (for example, M_1, M_2, and so forth) can only be identified in relationship to the existing *law of contracts* in the particular economic system under observation and the market organization and institutional arrangements which permit contracting in money terms over short (the initial instant or today) and longer periods of calendar time. Obviously, therefore, some monetarists have abused the concept of money in their extended 'definitions' which include corporate securities, bonds, and the like (for example, M_3,

M_4, and so forth), for they have improperly identified the time machine aspect as the essential feature of money and have basically ignored the means of contractual settlement feature – while the latter is the essence of anything which deserves the title of money.

Money plays an essential and peculiar role only when contractual obligations span a significant length of calendar time. If the economic system being studied only permits *spot* transactions, that is, contracts which require payments at the immediate instant, then even if its members utilize a convenient medium of account (the numéraire) and/or exchange, such a numéraire is *not* money in the full sense of the term. Spot transaction economies (which are equivalent to Hicks's flexprice economies) have, as Keynes insisted, 'scarcely emerged from the stage of barter'. In other words, a world in which economic activity never involves contracts for payment at specified future dates that are weeks, months, or even years in the future is an economy in which both the settlement concept of money and its related notion of liquidity are vacuous.

Money only matters in a world – our world – where there are multitudinous catenated forward contracts in money terms. In such an economy it is necessary that there be some continuity as to what will be the thing which by delivery settles the resulting obligations. The existence of market institutions which permit (and encourage) contracting for future payment creates the need for money and liquidity.[3] This is an essential aspect affecting the performance of all real-world, market-oriented, monetary economies where the activitity of production requires the passage of calendar time.

In a market-oriented economy most production transactions along the non-integrated chain of firms involve forward contracts.[4] For example, the hiring of factor inputs (especially labour) and the purchase of materials for the production of goods will normally require forward contracting if the production process is to be efficiently planned. The financing of such forward production cost commitments (that is, taking a 'position' in working capital goods) requires entrepreneurs to have money available to discharge these liabilities at one or more future dates *before* the product is sold, delivered, and payment received and the position is liquidated. Since orthodox neoclassical theory neglects the concept of contracting over calendar time in organized markets for future delivery and payment, this ubiquitous liquidity problem of entrepreneurs in capitalist economies is left unattended by mainstream economists who consequently are deserving recipients of the businessman's traditional gibe: 'They have never had to meet a payroll!'

The existence of money contracts for forward delivery *and* payment is fundamental to the concepts of liquidity and money. In such a setting, changes in money-wage rates – Keynes's wage unit – determine changes in the costs of production and the price level associated with the production of goods that profit-oriented entrepreneurs are willing to undertake. The view that inflation (that is, a rising money price level of newly produced goods) is a monetary phenomenon makes logical sense only in an economy where time-oriented money contracts (especially labour hire) are basic to the organization of production activities.

The attribute of liquidity requires that money possess certain 'essential properties', namely, a zero (or negligible) elasticity of production and a zero (or negligible) elasticity of substitution.[5] (Since I have developed this 'essential' elasticities property theme at great length elsewhere,[6] it will be assumed in what follows that the reader is familiar with that analysis.)

2   WHY MONEY MATTERS

Modelling of the real world requires an analysis of an economic system moving irreversibly through calendar time where the human institution of money and its related market institutions of money contracts for (a) immediate delivery and payments (spot contracts) and/or (b) future delivery and payment (forward contracts) play fundamental roles. This in turn requires a study of the relationship and organization of such time-related spot and forward markets which permits a simultaneous analysis of the relationship of the (spot) price of stocks and the (forward) price of flows.

Most of the perplexing problems facing economic agents in the real world involve the temporal coordination of production, of delivery and usage, and payments for both existing stocks and newly produced finished and intermediate goods. Because production takes time, it is the ubiquitous existence of catenated forward money contracts primarily (but not solely) for purchase of inputs along the non-integrated chain of firms which facilitates the production process. Entrepreneurs require forward contracts whose duration exceeds the gestation period of production so that they can have some assurance of the monetary limits to the 'position' they will be undertaking when they initiate a production flow. If a producer can simultaneously enter into a forward contract for the sale of product at the maturation date at the same time (or before) he makes a substantial commitment to hire inputs – a practice that is typically sought and often occurs at all stages of production except at the retail stage – then the entrepreneur can be assured of the profitability of his 'position' in working capital goods and can therefore readily finance this position via the banking system. Accordingly, forward contracting can be considered as the way entrepreneurs in a 'free market' environment attempt to maintain wage and price controls – for such price and cost controls are fundamental in obtaining sound financing. Bankers and businessmen abhor what neoclassical economists love – namely, recontracting.

The existence of time-related markets and contracts for performance and money payments is the essence of a money economy, for it is basic to the concept of liquidity. Liquidity in a temporal setting, given the money-wage unit and the resulting price level, is the cornerstone of Keynes's revolution! Problems of liquidity and finance are the hallmarks of everyday business decision-making in a monetary economy.

Liquidity involves being able to have the means of settlement to meet all your contractual obligations when they come due. Since money is the only thing which will discharge contract commitments (by definition), for any store of value besides money to be liquid it must be easily resaleable for money in a spot market. Thus the degree of liquidity associated with any durable depends on the organization and *orderliness* of the spot market in which it is traded. Those durables whose spot markets are very poorly organized, thin, or even notional *illiquid* assets. Such assets (for example, fixed capital and consumer durables) are held primarily for either the net money stream or utility stream they are expected to generate at specific dates in the future.

Liquid assets are durables traded in well-organized *and* orderly markets. Hence, what are the liquid assets of any economy depends on the social practices and institutions that exist in that economy. In his *Principles*, Marshall indicated a number of factors that would affect the degree of organization of a market for any good.[7] He omitted, however, the most essential factor for well-organized markets, namely, the institution of a *market-maker* or trade coordinator, in Clower and Leijonhufvud's terminology.[8] The function of a market-maker is to provide orderliness over time in the money price of the good traded, offsetting the random ebbs and flows of the market by utilizing sizeable inventories of both the good traded in the market and money (or other liquid assets).[9] Thus even spot prices need not respond with perfect flexibility to every change in the demand or supply of the good on the part of the public. Orderliness (that is, sticky spot prices over time) is maintained via reservation demands by the market-makers. Orderliness in spot prices merely requires the existence of buffer stocks and the willingness of the holders of such stocks to utilize them to assure a continuity in market price over time (according to the rules of the games adopted by the market so organized).

Often formal or even informal financing arrangements exist between private market-makers and the banking system (and hence either directly or indirectly with the central bank). The public recognize that such financial arrangements imply that, in any macroliquidity crisis, these private market-makers will not experience undue financial pressure which would otherwise force them to completely liquidate their 'position' in a short period of time, causing the spot price to drop precipitously. Consequently the continuity and orderliness of such spot markets appear assured – as long as the central bank ultimately acts as the lender of last resort and the community continues to use the 'money' of the system to denominate its contractual obligations. If, however, financial arrangements between market-makers and central banks prove inadequate in a liquidity crisis, perhaps because the chain from the private market-maker to the central bank is weak and therefore the latter does not (or cannot) respond as lender of last resort swiftly enough, then some large private sector 'market maker' could collapse. This can in turn induce a chain reaction in other liquid spot markets as the financial structure of debt layering (as Minsky has eloquently described it[10]) collapses like a house of cards.

In this era of central banks, it is their decisions and activities which ultimately provide the liquidity of any ongoing monetary economy which relies on the institution of forward contracting in money terms to organize its productive activities. And it is only in such an economic system that money matters and central banks matter!

For a decentralized market economy moving irreversibly through calendar time (where the future is uncertain), forward contracting for inputs to the production process is essential to efficient production plans. Moreover, in such an economy when slavery is illegal, the money-wage contract is the most ubiquitous forward contract of all; and since labour hiring precedes in time delivery of newly produced goods, it is the money wage relative to productivity which is the foundation upon which the price level of new goods rests. If Arrow and Hahn are correct (see note 4), it therefore follows that a 'serious monetary theory' must be based on a money-wage contract view of the economy. It is the stickiness of money-wages and prices (that is, the absence of rapid movements) guaranteed via the law of contracts which permits capitalist economies to engage in time-consuming production process and provides a basis for a sticky price level of producible goods. This view was the focal point of Keynes's revolutionary ideas on the workings of a monetary economy.

Events have not stood still since the writing of *The General Theory*. The growth of labour power under the protection of governmental full employment policies and the growth of multinational corporations since the Second World War had already created problems which by 1970 were threatening the basic monetary institutions of free market economies and were creating the first major crisis for capitalist economies since the Great Depression. In the last few years, the sudden development of OPEC's economic power and the resulting rapid changes in national and international monetary flows and assets holding further threatens the stability and, perhaps, even the viability of many monetary institutions and organizations which have evolved slowly over decades of a different environment. Mainstream neoclassical monetary theory has little advice to offer as to how these monetary institutions should adapt to these tremendous stresses and strains except that if we maintain a steady increase in the money supply *in the long run*, though we are all dead, the monetary waters will again be calm.

Keynes never lost focus on the interrelations between the money supply and the money-wage unit (or in a larger context, the cost unit including imports). Keynes's monetary analysis led him to the fundamental conclusion that 'money-wages should be more stable than real wages is a [necessary] condition of the system possessing inherent stability'.[11] In both his *Treatise* and his *General Theory* Keynes emphasized the money wage-money nexus. He noted that if we had control of both the Earnings System (incomes policy) and Monetary System (monetary policy) and can control the rate of investment, we can 'stabilise the purchasing power of money, its labour power, or anything else – without running the risk of setting up social and economic frictions or of causing waste'.[12] Moreover, Keynes maintained that 'if there are strong social or political forces causing spontaneous changes in the money-rates of efficiency wages [or in a modern context, the money costs of energy] the control of the price level may pass beyond the power of the banking system'.[13]

Thus, a monetary economy requires constraints on the movement of money-wages and the other factor prices which become the Marshallian flow-supply prices which are people's incomes. Contractually constrained input prices permit entrepreneurs to make production hiring contractual commitments with some assurance that the money costs of producing goods will not change violently from the initial date of the undertaking until the expected date of the final sale. Whatever historical accidents provided such stability in factor prices for capitalist societies during most of the last two centuries seem to have disappeared in recent decades. Unless we reinstitute deliberate policy to contain such flow-supply prices – a Permanent Incomes Policy – monetary collapse is inevitable, for strong social and political forces have removed control of the price level from both the international and domestic banking system.

Notes

1. J. M. Keynes, *The General Theory of Employment, Interest and Money* (New York: Harcourt, 1936), p. 383.
2. Ibid., p. 158.
3. 'It is, however, interesting to consider how far those characteristics of money as we know it . . . are bound up with money being the standard in which debts and wages are usually fixed . . . The convenience of holding assets in the same standard as that which future liabilities may fall due . . . is obvious,' (ibid., pp. 236–7).
4. As K. J. Arrow and F. H. Hahn have noted in *General Competitive Analysis* (San Francisco: Holden-Day, 1971), pp. 356–7:

    The terms in which contracts are made matter. In particular, if money is the good in terms of which contracts are made, then the prices of goods in terms of money are of special significance. This is not the case if we consider an economy without a past and without a future. Keynes wrote that 'the importance of money essentially flows from it being a link between the present and the future' to which we add that it is important also because it is a link between the past and the present. If *a serious monetary theory* comes to be written, the fact that contracts are indeed made in terms of money will be of considerable importance. (Italics added.)

Furthermore, Arrow and Hahn (p. 361) have concluded that in 'a world with a past as well as a future and in which contracts are made in terms of money, no [general] equilibrium may exist.'

5. 'The attribute of "liquidity" is by no means independent of these two characteristics. For it is unlikely that an asset, of which the supply can be easily increased or the desire for which can be easily diverted by a change in relative price, will possess the attribute of "liquidity" in the minds of owners of wealth' (Keynes, 1936, p. 241).
6. Paul Davidson, *Money and the Real World*, 2d edn (London: Macmillan, 1978).
7. A. Marshall, *Principles of Economics*, 8th edn (London: Macmillan, 1950), pp. 325–7.
8. R. W. Clower and A. Leijonhufvud, 'The Coordination Of Economic Activities: A Keynesian Perspective', *American Economic Review, Papers and Proceedings*, 65, (1975), p. 184.
9. Davidson, *Money and the Real World*, p. 87.
10. H. P. Minsky, *John Maynard Keynes* (New York: Columbia Universtiy Press, 1975).
11. Keynes, *The General Theory of Employment, Interest and Money*, p. 239.
12. J. M. Keynes, *A Treatise on Money* (London: Macmillan, 1930), p. 169.
13. Ibid., p. 351.

16 Keynes's Paradigm: A Theoretical Framework for Monetary Analysis*

The object of our analysis is, not to provide a machine, or method of blind manipulation, which will furnish an infallible answer, but to provide ourselves with an organized and orderly method of thinking out particular problems; and, after we have reached a provisional conclusion by isolating the complicating factors one by one, we then have to go back on ourselves and allow, as well as we can, for the probable interactions of factors amongst themselves. This is the nature of economic thinking. Any other way of applying our formal principles of thought . . . will lead us into error. (Keynes, 1936, p. 297)

Keynes started his revisions and extensions of his *Treatise on Money* in the belief that he was continuing his refinement of the theory of money. Instead, on his own admission, he finished by writing an entirely new and original theory of prices, employment, and output as a whole in which it was impossible to dichotomize the monetary and real relations of a modern production economy (Keynes, 1973, vol. XIII, pp. 408–9).

To me, the most extraordinary thing regarded historically, is the disappearance of the theory of demand and supply for output as a whole, i.e. the theory of employment, *after* it had been for a quarter of a century the most discussed thing in economics. One of the most important transitions for me, after my *Treatise on Money* had been published, was suddenly realizing this. (ibid., vol. XIV, p. 85)

It was in the enunciation of the principle of effective demand that Keynes showed that the monetary and real relations of a modern production economy were interdependent. Hence if we are to understand the analytical method that Keynes believed himself to be using, we must reject the 'old-time *ISLMic* religion' of Hicks, Modigliani, and Samuelson which has as its basic tenet that equilibrium in the real sector is an independent function of equilibrium in the monetary sector, i.e. that the parameters of the *IS* function are independent of the *LM* function's parameters. Implicit in all this is that Walrasian microtheory (as well as the axiomatic value

* *Growth, Property and Profits*, ed. E. J. Nell (Cambridge University Press, 1980), co-authored with J. A. Kregel.

theory derived from Walras by Arrow, Debreu and Hahn) is inherently incompatible with Keynes's theory of output as a whole.[1]

Keynes, the monetary theorist, did not begin his analysis by studying the behaviour of a world without money and then imagine why, in certain circumstances, 'money' should of necessity be invented. Instead he took the view that what should be described from the very beginning was the operation of a 'real world' monetary economy as he saw and lived in it. Keynes bypassed the impractical and irrelevant question of the behaviour of a barter system when money is imposed upon it (ibid., vol. XIII, pp. 408–11).

Modern general equilibrium analysis of monetary relations simply presupposes the existence of a world of institutions and behaviour identical to that found in the real world monetary economy, except that initially only pairwise trades are possible. The technical problem of equilibrium exchange or prereconciliation of all trading plans before any economic activity is undertaken is then considered as an investigation of monetary relations (e.g. Howitt, 1973; Ostroy and Starr, 1974). General equilibrium (GE) analysis becomes a search for complete consistency of plans before any economic actions are undertaken so that in a GE world prereconciled *ex ante* decisions always equal *ex post* realizations. This ultimately requires unchanging expectations and continuous fulfilment of plans (at least in an actuarial sense) in a timeless setting.[2]

Keynes's approach, on the other hand, asserts that the exact opposite situation is the nature of the economic problem. Decisions are made in the face of an uncertain future. Seriatim forward contracting through time is the most important institution yet devised for dealing with an uncertain future in a market economy. These contracts permit time-consuming economic activities to be undertaken even though all economic agents recognize that errors and inconsistencies are human frailties that no market mechanism can completely abolish (Keynes, 1973, vol. XIV, pp. 106–7).

How strange it must seem to the untutored reader of many 'advanced' economic textbooks to find, in one part of the text, the GE world (where markets assure consistency of *ex ante* plans and *ex post* results) presented as the microfoundation of Keynes's macrotheory while, in the other part of the text, the mechanism for explaining changes in the level of income is the difference between *ex ante* and *ex post*, i.e. inconsistency in plans as they are reflected in non-reversible market actions. Only those with advanced degrees from our most learned universities are clever enough to ignore this basic incompatibility between the micro and macrocomponents as they profess the 'neoclassical synthesis'.

In contradistinction to the GE approach, Keynes's method is one where from the very beginning 'money plays a part of its own and affects motives and decisions . . . so that the course of events cannot be predicted, either in the long period or in the short, without a knowledge of the behaviour of money between the first state and the last' (ibid., vol. XIII, pp. 408–9). Keynes insisted that economic decision-makers acted on the belief that their inexact expectations may be met, while recognizing that in all likelihood, they would not (ibid., vol. XIV, p. 107). Keynes took for granted that the economic system to be studied was a monetary–production economy in which the future is uncertain and in which there can be no market institutions that would permit the effective prereconciliation of all trading and production plans for all economic agents.[3]

Within the context of a production economy with an uncertain future, Keynes sought to shift the emphasis from actual to expected values of the economic variables (ibid., vol. XIII, p. 434). In essence Keynes was insisting that the economic paradigm should be 'composed of thoughts about thoughts' (Shackle, 1972, p. 71). Thus, Keynes made the general state of expectations an explicit independent variable of all the functional relationships in the system (Keynes, 1973, vol. XIII, pp. 441–2).

In order to develop his most fundamental contribution – the theory of effective demand – Keynes chose, in *The General Theory* (GT), to elaborate on a model where it was assumed that once the state of expectations is given, it would continue for a sufficient length of time for the effect on employment to have worked itself out (Keynes, 1936, p. 48). This static Keynes model permitted the specifications of simple, stable functional relationships that a dynamic or shifting expectational model would have rendered impossible.[4] The use of this simple static model was a pedagogical device to separate the effect of a given set of expectations in determining the equilibrium level of employment (which could be less than full employment) from the effect of disappointment and changes in expectations on shifting the level of employment; for it had already been understood that changing entrepreneurial errors of optimism and pessimism could result in a trade cycle. While recognizing the importance of expectations, Keynes thought that these parts of the economic nexus could be initially relegated to the background in order to give full scope to the role played by effective demand in producing an equilibrium level of employment which could be less than full employment.[5]

1 KEYNES'S TWO MODELS

In Chapter 5 of the GT, Keynes explicitly introduces the notion of two possible approaches to economic analysis. The first is a static analysis where the state of entrepreneurial expectations is unchanged so that expected propensities can be uniquely specified, and where actually realized results have (by assumption) no effect on long-term expectations. In this model even if small mistakes occur, such discrepancies may be eliminated by trial and error changes, while entrepreneurs are 'not confused or interrupted by any further change in expectations' (ibid., p. 49). The second approach is a dynamic model where expectational propensities shift over time, whether expectations are being fulfilled at any moment or not. In other words, this dynamic or shifting equilibrium approach is applicable whenever there is a change in the state of expectations due to either autonomous factors or induced by current realizations differing from past expectations.

For Keynes, the difference between a dynamic and a static model involved 'not the economy under observation which is moving in the one case and stationary in the other, but our expectations of the future environment which are shifting in the one case and stationary in the other' (Keynes, 1973, vol. XIV, p. 511).[6]

These two approaches to economic analysis are given differing weights in the GT, and especially when Keynes is discussing policy. It is not always crystal clear whether his prescriptions are based on the fully developed static model of the GT, where expectations are unchanged and so *as a logical exercise (and not as a projection over time)* the position of equilibrium can be determined; or whether the prescription is based on the less explicit, dynamic approach of the GT where expectations are changing while the economy is moving through time.

The usual interpretation is that Keynes held the state of expectations constant while discussing functional relationships, hoping that with 'the introduction of the concepts of user costs and of the marginal efficiency of capital' to give a role to expectations and bring static theory 'back to reality, whilst reducing to a minimum the necessary degree of adaptation' (Keynes, 1936, p. 146). On occasion however, Keynes did appear to introduce the effects of disappointment into the static discussion of the stable spending propensities (e.g. Keynes, 1936, p. 51), thereby tending to weaken the link between disappoinment and shifts in expectations.

After he completed the GT, Keynes recognized that his indiscriminate treatment of the relationship between disappointment and a given state of expectations in the GT could confuse the reader about the theory of effective demand. In his 1937 lectures, Keynes stated

> If I were writing the book again I should begin by setting forth my theory on the assumption that short period expectations were always fulfilled; and then have a subsequent chapter showing what differences it makes when short-period expectations are disappointed.
>
> For other economists, I find, lay the whole emphasis, and find the whole explanation in the *differences* between effective demand and income; and they are so convinced that this is the right course that they do not notice that in my treatment this is not so . . .[7] The main point is to distinguish the forces determining the position of equilibrium from the technique of trial and error by means of which the entrepreneur dis-

covers where the position is . . . *Ex ante* savings and *ex ante* investment *not* equal . . . *ex ante* decisions in their influence on effective demand relate solely to *entrepreneurs'* decisions . . . the disappointment of expectations influence the next *ex ante* decisions.

[but even if we] suppose the identity of *ex post* and *ex ante*, my theory remains . . . I should have distinguished more sharply between a theory based on *ex ante* effective demand, however arrived at, and a psychological chapter indicating *how* the business world reaches its *ex ante* decisions. (Keynes, 1973, vol. XIV, pp. 181–3)

Thus Keynes gives an insight into the intermingling of approaches that he used in the GT. On the one hand, there is the stark static model where, given expectations, the theory of effective demand is the prime determinant of the level of employment. In this model, where disappointment-induced shifts of expectations are removed, Keynes demonstrates that unemployment was not necessarily a short-run disequilibrium phenomena; that booms and slumps need not be the result of faulty entrepreneurial expectations, but that a monetary production system could settle, as a theoretical matter, in equilibrium at almost any level of employment.

To this stark model complicating factors of disappointment were added at some points in the GT, but not before the static model is completely laid out. Wholesale shifts in expectations were forcibly removed from the initial picture in order to permit the derivation of the stable functional relationships necessary for the elucidation of the theory of effective demand. When such large changes in expectations are discussed they are held separate form the static model of the GT, thus leading Friedman to catalogue these discussions of Keynes as 'many correct, interesting, and valuable ideas, although some wrong ones, and many shrewd observations on empirical matters . . . but all . . . strictly peripheral to the main contribution of *The General Theory*' (Friedman *et al.* 1974, pp. 148–9).

In his 1937 lecture notes, Keynes has suggested that he might have better convinced his audience if he had more clearly separated the principle of effective demand under a given set of expectations from the effect of disappointment on effective demand changes.

2 KEYNES AND HICKS ON EXPECTATIONS AND ECONOMIC ANALYSIS

Hicks's analysis of expectations in *Value and Capital* can be fruitfully used to clarify the distinctions between Keynes's static dynamic approaches. Hicks suggests that there are three influences which affect expectations. The first two are due to either 'noneconomic' or economic factors generated by forces other than those under discussion. These, Hicks suggests, cause autonomous changes in expectations, and although 'we must never forget that . . . expectations are liable to be influenced by autonomous causes . . . we must leave it at that' (Hicks, 1946, p. 205). Hicks's third influence occurs when today's realized values differ from previous expectations about today's realized values, thereby inducing a change in expectations about future values of the relevant variables. Hick's elasticity of expectations (E_e) measures the magnitude of this induced change in expectations. E_e is defined as the ratio of the proportionate change in the expected future values of X to the proportionate change in the current realized value of X *vis-à-vis* the previous expected value of the current X.[8]

Hence if there are no autonomous changes in expectations during the period of observation and if $E_e = 0$, then even though all variables are dated (Hicks's definition of dynamics) the analysis involves Keynes's static method.[9] If, on the other hand, either $E_e \neq 0$ and/or there are autonomous changes in expectations, then Keynes's dynamic analysis is applicable.

In sum, Keynes's static model where $E_e = 0$, permits stable aggregate demand and supply functions to be derived, and a point of effective demand to be developed which need not be full employment. Such a model need not have an unchanging equilibrium level of employment as long as existing expectations have correctly foreseen future changes (Keynes, 1936, p. 48 n. 1), but realizations cannot (by hypothesis) alter expectations. That this process was not one that Keynes expected to actually occur over time in the real world is emphasized by his calling the resulting equilibrium employment level a 'long-period' position (Keynes, 1936, p. 49) and his direct method of severing the extent to which anything can alter existing expectations about the future (ibid., p. 49).

Keynes's dynamic approach can provide models of shifting but stable equilibrium if $E_e \neq 0$ but it is not greater than unity, when, as Keynes assumed was the normal human condition, ex ante and ex post are unequal.[10] Nevertheless, in a dynamic economy there is no necessary constant relationship between realizations, E_e, and autonomous changes in expectations; nor need E_e, even be constant over time. Only in the unlikely event that $E_e = 0$, will realizations of errors not alter the state of expectations. 'The actual course of events is more complicated . . . for the state of expectations is liable to constant change' (ibid., p. 50), thereby shifting the independent behavioural propensities. Thus, Keynes's model of shifting equilibrium will describe an actual path of an economy over time chasing an ever-changing equilibrium – it need not ever catch it.

This latter approach of shifting equilibrium is, however, conceptually distinct from the GE approach and/or the adaptive expectations approach used by most American economists. In Keynes's full view of the system it is the conjectural and often figmental state of human expectations which are the prime movers of a free enterprise economic system. Thus, in the Keynes paradigm, supply and demand functions exist at a point in time but they need not exist over historical time. As Shackle argues, this is just as much a part of Keynes's message as the static exposition of effective demand, for 'stable curves and functions are *allergic* to the real human economic scheme of things' (Shackle, 1972, p. 517). It is in the shifting equilibrium analysis that the crucial role of historical time as well as the difficult methodological problems are most clearly seen.

3 METHODOLOGY AND THE TIME DIMENSION

Time is a device which prevents everything from happening at once. Keynes recognized that the essence of real world economics is that calendar time normally elapses between the point where decisions are made and the ultimate outcome of these decisions. This is the blunt message of chapter 5 of the GT.

Keynes believed that the time duration between the enacting of decisions based on *ex ante* expectations and the resulting *ex post* outcome was 'incapable of being made precise' so that there could be no specification of a 'definite relationship between aggregate effective demand [as expected by entrepreneurs] at one time and aggregate income [realizations] at some later time' (Keynes, 1973, vol. 14, p. 179–80). Thus, Keynes explicitly gave up on the *ex ante–ex post* approach to handling time.[11] 'I used to speak of the period between expectations and results as "funnels of process" but the fact that the funnels are all of different lengths and overlap one another meant that at any given time there was no aggregate realized result capable of being compared with some aggregate expectation at some earlier date' (ibid., vol. XIV, p. 185).

Instead of a Robertson period analysis or a Swedish *ex ante–ex post* approach, Keynes initially presented his static model which allowed, in a very arbitrary but exact way, the tracing through of the influence of a given state of expectations to the 'long-period level of employment' associated with it. Keynes chose to associate 'short run' with 'the shortest interval after which a firm is free to revise its decisions as to how much employment to offer.[12] It is, so to speak, the minimum effective unit of time' (Keynes, 1936, p. 47, n. 1). Simultaneously, he chose to blur the distinction between realized and expected sales proceeds by referring to a large overlap between them (ibid., p. 51), so that the static model could operate under the assumption that a state of expectation will 'continue for a sufficient length of time for the effect on employment to have worked itself out completely . . . the steady level of employment thus attained may be called the long-period employment corresponding to that state of expectation' (ibid., p. 48).

For example, in Figure 16.1, the aggregate supply curve (Z) is derived on the basis of expected production techniques and factor prices, and each

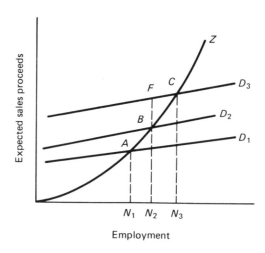

Figure 16.1

of the expected demand curves (D_1, D_2, D_3, etc.) represents a different state of expectations of possible sales in the minds of entrepreneurs.[13] Thus in Figure 16.1, there is a long-period level of employment associated with each possible expected point of effective demand, N_1 with point A, N_2 with B, etc.

Given a specific state of entrepreneurial expectations regarding the sales proceeds which can be expected to be spent by buyers for alternative levels of employment – as represented by D_2 in Figure 16.1 for example – entrepreneurs expected effective demand to be at point B. (Assume further, merely for expositional simplicity, that this point of effective demand is expected to prevail for a number of future production periods.) Acting on such expectations entrepreneurs hire N_2 workers in the current period. If D_2 is the realizable aggregate demand curve, the expectations will be fulfilled and N_2 will remain the equilibrium level of employment until there is a change in the state of expectations.

What if, however, the realizable demand function in the current period turned out to be D_3? Logically, the Keynes static model suggests that as long as entrepreneurs expect D_2 to prevail, i.e. as long as $E_e = 0$, employment will remain at N_2 even if realizations differ from expectations. 'The actual realized result . . . will only be relevant to employment insofar as they cause a modification of subsequent expectations' (ibid., p. 47), i.e. only if $E_e > 0$. That, however, would require dynamic, rather than static, analysis. Keynes's static model can apply to this situation only by stretching a verbal sleight of hand which Keynes used. If the actual aggregate demand curve is, say D_3, when they expected D_2, then entrepreneurs should be surprised by subsequent events when they find either an unexpected increase in spot market prices, and/or an unintended run-down of inventories, and/or an increased queue of buyers (as the realizable aggregate demand price associated with the actual hiring of N_2 workers is given by points F). The discrepancy between the expected and realizable aggregate demand functions (D_2 and D_3) should, it would seem, alter entrepreneurial expectations so long as $E_e \neq 0$. Keynes, however, blurred the difference between the state of entrepreneurial expectations underlying the initially expected aggregate demand curve (D_2 in Figure 16.1) and the expectations that would have brought forth the realizable demand curve (D_3) in the minds of entrepreneurs in order to maintain his static model assumptions by assuming

> in practice the process of revision of short-term expectation is a gradual and continuous one, carried on largely in the light of realised results; so that expected and realised results run into and overlap one another in their influence . . . Thus in practice there is a large overlap between the effects on employment of the realised sales-proceeds of recent output and those of the sales-proceeds expected from current input. (ibid., p. 51)

In other words, despite the surprises that the point of effective demand was C rather than B, Keynes can be interpreted as assuming within a static framework that entrepreneurs can switch from the expectations underlying D_2 to those underlying D_3 *without a change in the state of expectations occurring*.[14] Thus, market signals will push entrepreneurs to increase their hiring towards N_3, the 'long-period level of employment' (ibid., p. 48).

Of course, Keynes realized that 'the actual course of events is more complicated' since expectations 'are liable to sudden revision' before any state of expectation 'has fully worked itself out' (ibid., pp. 50–1), i.e the aggregate supply and/or demand curve could shift before point C (in Figure 16.1) is reached. Thus, Keynes envisioned his real world model as one of shifting equilibrium, a world in continuous movement without the necessity for the plans of the economic agents to ever be reconciled. It is unfortunate that only his pedagogical static model made any impact on the economics profession.

3.1 Equilibrium Versus Historical Models

In economic methodology, there are two types of models – timeless, general equilibrium models and historical–humanistic models. The former are used by GE theorists, the latter by Keynes, and some of his followers.[15]

An equilibrium model builder proceeds by specifying a sufficient number of equations to determine all the unknowns in the system and then concentrates on the simultaneous solution of the equations. All the equilibrium theorist can tell you is if the equilibrium position exists, i.e. if all plans can be prereconciled. 'A world where expectations are liable to be falsified cannot be described by the simple equations of the equilibrium path' (Robinson, 1963, p. 25). An equilibrium model is bound to a timeless system where all plans are prereconciled before any action takes place.

A historical model, on the other hand, specifies a particular set of values at a moment in calendar time. These particular values may or may not be in any sense in equilibrium.[16] The historical model can show (1) how entrepreneurial expectations lead to employment, output and pricing decisions, (e.g. Keynes's static model was supposed to explain 'the process of transition to a long period [employment] position due to a change in expectations' (Keynes, 1936, pp. 48–9); (2) whether entrepreneurial plans are consistent with buyer's realizable demands; and (3) for any given value of E_e, the possible effect of disappointment on future expectations. It should be obvious that a dynamic analysis of the real world, even more than the static analysis of the kind Keynes envisaged, can only be done in a historical model context. In the real world, the inevitable inconsistency of plans and unexpected changes in events must lead to shifts of economic relationships over time. This model of 'shifting equilibrium' with its unpredictable shifts in propensities 'is a far cry from smooth and quasi-stable curves or schedules, which Keynes paraded on the front of his stage to mask the horrid void of indeterminacy and nonrationality at its rear' (Shackle, 1972, p. 517).

3.2 Dynamics, Time, and Instability

If we are to utilize the dynamic Keynesian theory, where the state of expectations can and does change as the system moves irreversibly along the calendar time axis, it becomes essential to recognize that there is nothing in the logic of the dynamic theory which rules out violent instability. Nevertheless, Keynes noted that 'outstanding characteristic of the economic system in which we live, whilst it is subject to severe fluctuations . . . it is not violently unstable' (Keynes, 1936, p. 249). Hence there must be certain conditions in the economic environment which promote relative stability in a dynamic world so that inevitable disappointment and surprise does not lead to violent alterations in the state of expectations, so that the $E_e < 1$.

As long as the future is uncertain the state of expectations may be liable to rapid unpredictable changes and hence the economic system is potentially very unstable. Recognizing the mercurial possibility of the economic system, man has, over time, devised certain institutions and rules of the game, which, as long as they are operational, avoid such catastrophes by providing a foundation for a conventional belief in the stability of the system and hence in the quasi-stability of the state of expectations. It is the existence of spot *and* forward markets, money, and concurrent seriatim time–length money (forward) contracts[17] and their enforceability, as well is the expectations that these institutions will continue to operate with continuity or 'orderliness' for the foreseeable future, which limits the magnitude of E_e and keeps real world economic fluctuations in bounds (Hicks, 1946, pp. 264–7, 270–1, 297–98). If these institutions break down, as they did for example in Germany between 1921 and 1923, a modern monetary economy may exhibit violent instability. For most developed interdependent production economies, however, where production requires considerable calendar time and therefore contractual commitments for the hiring of resources must occur a long time before everyone can possibly know how valuable the outcome will be, such instability will mean the breakdown of production flows. This occurrence is so costly to society that most members of the economy will cling to the hope that even a crippled monetary system can be resuscitated. This hope maintains some stability in states of expectations, i.e. $E_e < 1$, but if the situation deteriorates so that almost everyone is completely uncertain as to the meaning of contractual commitments then a catastrophic breach in the continuity of the system is inevitable.

4 STABILITY OF ECONOMIC FUNCTIONS

The well defined, *stable* functions of Walrasian (or even Marshallian) microeconomics do not exist over calendar time, and are of little use in the real world for they can be defined only for a given state of expectations. What Keynes insisted on was not the stability of demand and supply functions – they could shift every time the unpredictable state of expectations changed – but their momentary existence. This means we cannot predict what will happen over a period of calendar time, only what can happen for any given state of expectations.

Keynes spent considerable time discussing the formation of expectations in his *Treatise* and in the GT (e.g. Keynes, 1936, ch. 12), but he remained adamant that there was no uniform relationship between a set of observable events and the subsequent state of expectations. In Keynes's paradigm, the '*indefinite* character of actual expectations' are the free autonomous variables which govern everything else, rather than being governed by everything else (Keynes, 1973, vol. XIV, pp. 106–7). In the real world expectations may only be tenuously related to past economic facts as politics, acts of God, thoughts, and life-styles are also determinants – thus Keynes's and the post-Keynesians' emphasis on 'animal spirits'.

Keynes's independent psychological propensities (Keynes, 1936, p. 245) – consumption, investment, and liquidity preference – would be stable *but not independent* in any system (such as the GE model) where time and uncertainty are absent. Keynes's assumption of a given state of expectations about an uncertain future, and the belief of economic agents that all

production, consumption, investment and liquidity decisions do not have
to be made simultaneously and for all time at the initial date (or at any
other point of time), permitted Keynes to deal with these propensities as
formally independent stable relations within his static framework. This
static Keynes model, although unrealistic because of its undue formalistic
approach, did form the core of the Keynesian revolution. It liberated
'men's thoughts from the concept of general equilibrium . . . [and] made
possible the construction of effective theories of a *varying* level of output
and employment' (Shackle, 1968, p. xxi).

Keynes's dynamic model is more applicable to a real world economic
system which lurches from one historical position to another without even
necessarily being in equilibrium. Unfortunately the dynamic model makes
predictions about the future a very tricky and unsafe business. Unlike the
GE system which is closed once tastes and endowments are given, Keynes's dynamic model is open with constantly changing unpredictable expectations driving the system onward through calendar time. Economists,
unlike astronomers (but like weathermen?), are stuck with an open system. They cannot use the mechanistic approach of general equilibrium.
They must instead provide a classificatory theory of economics using, when
relevant, the E_e concept which puts situations into one box or another
according to what can happen as a sequel under a given set of circumstances, not what will happen. This philosophy about the nature of economic models was summed up by Keynes in a letter to Harrod in which he
said

> Economics is a branch of logic; a way of thinking . . . *Progress* in
> economics consists almost entirely in a progressive improvement in the
> choice of models . . . but it is of the essence of a model that one does *not*
> fill in real values for the variable functions . . . The object of statistical
> study is not so much to fill in missing variables with a view to prediction
> as to test the relevance and validity of the model.

> Economics is a science of thinking in terms of models joined to the art
> of choosing models which are relevant to the contemporary world. It is
> compelled to be this, because, unlike the typical natural science, the
> material to which it is applied is, in too many respects, not homoge-
> neous, through time . . . Economics is essentially a moral science and
> not a natural one. That is to say, it employs introspection and judgments
> of value. (Keynes, 1973, vol. XIV, p. 296)

5   REAL WORLD STABILITY AND THE CURRENT INFLATION

Keynes's dynamic model threatens the logical possibility of violent instability. Yet, except for rare historical episodes, capitalism has been rela-

tively durable and homeostatic. Hence, it is important in these days of world-wide inflation and prophecies of economic cataclysm to delineate those characteristics of modern economic agents and institutions which have provided a homeostatic mechanism in an uncertain world.[18]

5.1 Contracts and Price Stability

Forward contracting is the most important economic institution yet devised for controlling the uncertain future course of markets. Since production takes time, entrepreneurs are always entering into forward contracts to assure the future costs of inputs, and in a non-integrated production chain, into sales contracts to assure prices and revenues in the future. In fact, one may look upon the private institution of contracts as the way free enterprise markets attempt to assure wage and price controls.[19]

Since the money-wage contract is the most ubiquitous forward contract in modern economies and since the duration of money-wage contracts normally exceed the gestation period for the production of most goods, it is the institution of forward labour contracting which provides a basis for the conventional belief in the stickiness or stability in prices over time. Such a convention is necessary if entrepreneurs are going to take long-term positions in productive facilities.

In a capitalist economy, some people will employ hired labour on forward contracts for future profits; while some desire to save, i.e. not to exercise all of their currently earned claims on new goods produced by labour. Savers must hold resaleable assets that can last through time with a minimum of carrying costs and therefore serve as a store of value, unless they know what specific thing they will want to possess at a specific future date, for then they can buy a forward contract for the production of the item wanted and its delivery at the desired future date. But Keynes stressed: 'an act of individual savings means . . . *not* . . . to consume any specified thing at any specified date' (Keynes, 1936, p. 210). Hence savings involves the possession of stores of value that are durable and liquid.

Durables possess liquidity or resaleability only if there is a well-organized spot market in which they can be readily resold at any future date for a claim on resources available at that date. (As long as labour-hire contracts are made in terms of money-wages, then money will be the primary claim on newly produced goods.) The current money value of any resaleable durable can increase or decrease *without limit* if expectations of future spot prices change. If, however, the durable has relatively high elasticities of production and substitution, a counterbalancing factor due to new production (or in the case of decrease in value – carrying costs and physical deterioration) comes into play, as over time the costs of production and new supplies limit the increase in future spot prices expected at future dates. Nevertheless, for those assets which have negligible elasticities of production and substitution and well-organized spot markets –

primarily financial assets – their conditions of supply (resource using reproducibility) do not, indeed cannot, act as a counterbalance to the effect of changing expectations of future spot prices on present (spot) market values.

Since all exchange values are relative and since the current values of all resaleable durables ultimately depend on their expected future spot prices, the only thing which will provide an anchor for the money price level over time is the belief in the stability or stickiness of money costs of production over time.[20] Hence as long as forward labour contracts are set in monetary terms for a period of calendar time which exceeds the gestation period of production, economic agents can expect stickiness in the price level of new goods and services. It is the money-wage contract and the resulting stickiness of money wages which permitted Keynes to produce a stable but potentially shifting equilibrium model. As Hicks emphasized, Keynes

> assumes a unity elasticity of expectations only for [spot] prices expected to rule in the near future; for prices expected in the further future [where new production can come to market], he [Keynes] assumes that they move with money wages . . . Consequently the instability of the system is . . . in abeyance so long as money wages are kept constant (for then more distant prices have a zero elasticity of expectations and this acts as a stabilizer). (Hicks, 1946, p. 256)

Of course, Keynes did not assume constant money-wage rates, merely 'sticky' ones so that E_e need not equal zero; E_e will be very inelastic as long as there are long-term forward contracts for money wages.

The stability of the level of money prices over time therefore depends on habit and/or convention which makes the money price of something relatively sticky over time so that people can 'expect' price stability. In the real world, in normal times, the efficiency money-wage, i.e. money-wages relative to productivity, is nearly enough constant so as to provide some basis for the convention of price stability to be incorporated into entrepreneurial expectations and therefore encourage them to undertake productive commitments.[21] The necessity of some conventional price stability is 'a fundamental assumption essential to *any* dynamic economies' (Townshend, 1937, p. 163).[22]

The staunchest defenders of the 'free enterprise system', however, advocate freely flexible money-wages to relieve capitalist economies of the problems of unemployment and inflation. Sticky or controlled money-wages (whether by private contract or social contract), in their view, inhibit a free enterprise economy from achieving a stable, full employment growth path over time – a state of bliss. Perfect flexibility of money-wages could be possible if the labour market were a 'bourse'. Hence, if there was a well-organized spot market for slaves then wages could be perfectly flexible nd continuous full employment of slaves could be attained. Rightly or wrongly, modern economies have made such slave markets illegal, and in capitalist countries almost all labour is hired on a forward contract basis with the duration of the contract equalling or exceeding the production period.

Recently, however, Friedman has publicly advocated reducing the duration of the labour contract to a time period less than the production period in order to fight inflation. Friedman's recommendation is to 'index' all labour contracts and most other contracts to a current price index.

Widespread indexing of labour contracts would create wage flexibility and simultaneously destroy the conventionality of price stickiness which is necessary for capitalist entrepreneurs to undertake production commitments. In his classic study of *The Economics of Inflation*, Bresciani-Turroni showed that although Germany had suffered from double digit inflation since almost the beginning of the First World War, the inflation really began to accelerate at the end of 1922 (Bresciani-Turroni, 1968, p. 442). The period from the end of 1922 to the end of 1923 was different in that it 'was characterized by an enormous rise in nominal wage-rates' as the system of indexing wages became general throughout Germany (ibid., pp. 308–10). The cost of living index which had been calculated monthly before 1922, was calculated twice a month in 1922, and weekly in 1923 as more wages were geared to the index. But even that was found to be insufficient as each increase in money-wages pushed up domestic prices. By mid-1923 a daily index was substituted by most industries as wages were paid daily. But that only accelerated price increases, so that by the end of 1923 a daily index of forecasted prices was being used (ibid., p. 310). The result was an accelerating inflation of over 400 per cent per month.[23]

This historical episode of widespread indexing can be viewed as simply a form of incomes policy. Unfortunately it is the worst form of an anti-inflationary incomes policy since it will keep wages and prices stable only if they are already stable and there is nothing which alters expectations of their remaining stable.[24] Anything which touches off expectations of inflation can, under the indexing scheme of Friedman's lead to unending inflation. In other words, under indexing, thinking can make it so!

This bootstrap theory of inflation under indexing can be readily analysed via a Marshallian analysis of the interaction of market period (spot) prices and short-run flow supply (forward) prices (Davidson, 1974, 1972). In Figure 16.2, *D* represents the initial Marshallian demand schedule (including Wicksteedian reservation demand) for a durable good, while the vertical line *S* represents the stock of the good inherited from the past. If this good is not reproducible (e.g. old masters) then the resulting spot price p_s would allocate the stock without remainder among demanders. If the good is reproducible, the stock can be augmented by a flow of output if buyers are willing to promise to pay the flow–supply price and wait the

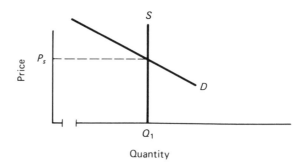

Figure 16.2

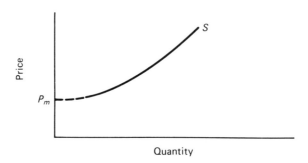

Figure 16.3

gestation period for delivery. The curve S (Figure 16.3) represents the industry's Marshallian flow–supply schedule, i.e. it shows the alternative production offerings at alternative flow–supply prices. If producers are short-run profit maximizers, then p_m is the lowest point on the average variable cost schedule and represents the minimum flow–supply price.

The total market situation for a good can be obtained by laterally summing the stock and flow–supply schedules to obtain $S + s$ in Figure 16.4. Superimposing the demand schedule D onto this figure indicates that the spot price, p_s, exceeds the forward or flow–supply price, p_f, as some buyers are willing to pay a premium for immediate delivery rather than wait the gestation period for a new unit to be produced.[25] This situation (where $p_s > p_f$) is known as *backwardation* and production of $Q_2 - Q_1$ units will be forthcoming at the delivery date.

Assume all money-wage contracts are geared to a price index which includes the spot price of many durables (e.g. housing, used cars, standardized commodities, tanker rates, etc.). Since the height of the S curve (Figure 16.3) depends on the money-wage rate or wage unit at any point in time, the higher the price index the higher the wage unit and the higher S.[26]

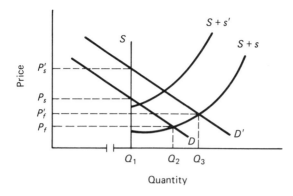

Figure 16.4

At some initial date there will be a given 'real' wage rate and hence a level of investment and aggregate output which is compatible with it; hence any attempt to change the rate of investment, the distribution of income, etc., will automatically upset the price index and induce shifts in the flow–supply curve as the indexing clauses in wage contracts become operative. Let us analyse an extreme situation where the initiating force for change is an autonomous change in the state of expectations so that (given current production costs) buyers expect prices of all goods to rise more rapidly in the future than they did when the demand curve, D, was derived. This expectation of inflation will raise the marginal efficiency of all durables thereby shifting D outward to D' in Figure 16.4 immediately increasing the spot price to p'_s (Keynes, 1936, p. 142) and encouraging some buyers to order more goods for future delivery.

Forward prices would rise, *as long as money-wage rates are unchanged*, from p_f to p'_f, only if the elasticity of supply was not perfectly elastic. Moreover, even if the forward price rose because of short-run flow supply elasticity was less than ∞, if money-wages were not indexed, the resulting increase in production flow would increase the existing stock over time (shifting S rightward) and returning the flow-supply price and the spot price to the initial p_f and p_s levels (assuming no further change in expectations). If, however, money-wages are indexed, the immediate rise in spot prices (and those forward prices of goods whose flow-supply elasticity is less than perfect) will shift up the flow-supply function and therefore the total supply function (in Figure 16.4) to $S + s'$, thereby raising forward prices even more. This increase in actual forward prices could induce an additional increase in Marshallian demand curves as (1) money-wage incomes increase and (2) the further increase in forward prices increases the marginal efficiency of durables even further as buyers recognize that indexing will assure that $E_e = 1$, indeed it will institutionalize this belief. Hence D' would shift out again (in Figure 16.4) and this will lead to money-wage increases shifting up the supply curve $S + s'$ once again. Thus, indexing, by establishing a unitary E_e, will cause an initial disturbance due to any cause to spill over into an unending *incomes inflation* (Davidson 1972, ch. 14), which can feed back into a further spot price inflation, etc.

This institutionalization of an $E_e = 1$ via indexing must create an unstable economy, for as Hicks has noted 'If all elasticities of expectation are unity, the stability of the system can only be maintained by the existence of rigid wage-rates; but if all elasticities of expectation are unity why should [money] wage rates be rigid?' (Hicks, 1946, p. 270). Hicks's response to this rhetorical question was money-wages could remain fairly rigid if wage earners 'have fairly *inelastic* price–expectations' (Hicks, 1946. p. 270) – the exact opposite of indexation. In fact, Hicks pointed out once workers' $E_e \rightarrow 1$, negotiators will have recourse to indexing and 'the rigidity of money wages ceases altogether' (ibid., p. 271). Stability requires, Hicks concludes, 'A tendency to rigidity of certain prices, particularly wage-rates, but there must also be a tendency to rigidity of certain price expectations as well' (ibid. p. 271). One must add, that these tendencies are to be found in the modern institutions of forward contracting in general and money-wage forward contracts for labour in particular.

Although in Figure 16.4, the destabilizing process was set off by an autonomous change in expectations creating an increase in demand, the process could have been initiated by a reduction in supply as well. Thus an act of God or man, such as either a drought, preventing replacements to the stock supply as a commodity is consumed, or an international cartel, deliberately withholding stock supplies from the market, will initially raise spot commodity prices and thereby, via indexing, start the process of a domestic incomes inflation which can only exacerbate the initial price increase problem.

Hence the unnerving conclusions that in a dynamic Keynesian model, where equilibrium may never have time to establish itself; or even if established may not long endure, it is only the stickiness and long duration of forward labour contracts which provide the conventional price stability required to avoid violently destabilizing processes. In the absence of the institution of seriatim forward contracting in money terms expectations of future price increases and/or spot market supply shortages could impinge on Marshallian supply and demand curves, shifting them up almost without limit as long as entrepreneurs can obtain working capital funds to finance their constantly escalating production commitments.[27]

In short, if conventional price stickiness is broken down by destroying the duration of private labour contracts fixed in money terms, then, since production takes time, a free enterprise system can become violently unstable. Furthermore, widespread indexing could destroy the liquidity of the existing monetary system, for no good produced in the system would have a sticky flow-supply schedule to limit its possible future price. In the absence of sticky flow-supply schedules the expected prices of all future goods are determined by the same expectations of the future prices of nonproducible durable goods.

6 CONCLUSION

In any perfectly indexed economy, any increase in the price index would start a process of continually shifting the flow supply curves of all goods upward, causing people to fly from currency (i.e. there is a dramatic fall in the liquidity of money) as people will prefer to hold liquid goods (whose future price is expected to be inflation proof). Thus without the 'expectations of a relative stickiness of wages in terms of money'[28] one does not have the corollary proposition that the 'excess of liquidity premium over carrying cost being greater for money than for any other asset' (Keynes, 1936, p. 238) and hence the way is open for the system to become a 'nonmonetary economy' where 'there is no asset for which liquidity premium is always in excess of the carrying costs' (ibid., p. 239). In such a world, time-consuming production processes will grind to a halt for no one will undertake the required long-term production commitments. Hence a dynamic capitalist economy with widespread indexing would be precariously perched on a knife edge. Anything which set off spot price changes or even expectations of spot price changes (a condition which is quite a normal state of affairs in the real world) will cause the system to oscillate violently with prices racing to infinity (or to zero if indexed in both directions) (ibid., pp. 269–70).

Under this conceptualization of the real world, the indexing of wage contracts is almost certain to bring about the destruction of any capitalist monetary system, especially if the index contains some spot price components whose basis is not anchored to the stickiness of production–flow prices. An upward movement (ephemeral or otherwise) in spot prices of producible goods will immediately set off a process of legalized and required upward wage and price recontracting which can continue as long as agents can finance their contractual commitments. Even if the money supply were not to increase endogenously as entrepreneurs required more working capital funds, expectations may encourage a flight from money sufficient to finance the ever increasing costs of production *and* inventory speculation for a long time.

Monetary stringency, if and when it comes, will occur when the debt structure of entrepreneurs becomes so precarious that they are unable to borrow additional sums to meet their forward contract production commitments. The inevitable chain of bankruptcies that will follow along the non-integrated production system will ultimately mean the end of the system, as all contracts become meaningless. Such a catastrophe, by wiping out all existing contracts simultaneously, provides a foundation for developing a new monetary unit of account which is not indexed and can be utilized in denominating new input price contractual commitments with a reasonable expectation of these prices being sticky. Thus the system will attempt to restore flexibility of real wages at the same time as it stabilizes money wages. Without this property, the economy could not adapt to inevitable changes with any degree of stability.

Hence, economic society in the unconscious recesses of its being, knew what it was all about when men developed long-term forward contracts for labour and abolished spot markets for slaves. In so doing, society provided institutions which assured that an uncertain future does not mean an unstable future for any dynamic monetary economy where expectations govern decisions that drive the system through its environment of shifting equilibria.

This view was summed up by Townshend, one of the first to recognize the implications of Keynes's dynamic model:

> There can be no such thing as long period dynamic economic theory failing the . . . discovery of a plausible long-term convention of price stability. It is perhaps now being generally realised that such long-term dynamic theories as there are conceal unplausible ones. It is not unnatural that those who forecast the future in algebra or geometry should be chastened by hard fact more slowly than those who have to forecast it in arithmetic. Nor is the conclusion that the search for laws to enable us to predict economic events far ahead, like eclipses, must be given up, so surprising – not to say nihilistic – as it may seem (to some economists) at first sight. (Townshend, 1937, p. 166)

Notes

1. Keynes believed that Walras was 'strictly in the classical tradition', a tradition which could not produce a general theory of employment, interest, and money (Keynes, 1936, p. 177).
2. In the most recent statements of GE not only does each economic agent have a complete set of punctiliously specified expectations for every conceivable state of the world for each future date, but all contracts for contingent commodities must be entered into at market clearing prices at the initial date *before* any production or exchange takes place and then no further contractual relations can be entered into for the rest of time. Moreover, all future contracts must be paid for at the initial date so that financial constraints do not bind expenditure plans. Thus GE is a *timeless* system where *all* decisions and payments are made at an instant of time.
3. As Hicks recognized there is a device whereby coordination of expectations can occur in a private enterprise system, namely, forward contracting. A

complete 'future economy' where all goods were always and only bought and sold forward should eliminate inconsistency in expectations, but the possibility of errors due 'to *unexpected* changes in wants or resources would *not* be removed' (Hicks, 1946, p. 136, italics added). Hence even in such an economy, markets cannot prereconcile all trading plans *and* eliminate unwanted occurrences.

4. Keynes, of course, was aware of how precarious it was to balance his static model on the parameter of long-term expectations. He noted that his analysis of spending propensities 'shall not in any way be precluded from regarding the propensity itself as subject to change' (Keynes, 1973, vol. XIII, p. 440). In an early draft of the GT, Keynes explicitly included in his propensity equations a variable, E, which represented the 'state of long term expectations' (ibid., pp. 441–2). Hence if there is either an autonomous change in expectations or if current realizations differ from previous expectations and thereby induce a change in expectations about the future (i.e. if *ex ante* does not equal *ex post* and this causes a shift in the state of expectations), then there will be shifts in the functional relations of the system and Keynes's static model is inapplicable.

5. 'Having, however, made clear the part played by *expectation* in the economic nexus and the reaction of realized results on future expectation, it will be safe for us in what follows often to disregard express reference to expectation. It is important to make the logical point clear and to define the terminology precisely so that it will apply without ambiguity in all cases. But when once this has been done, considerations of practical convenience may legitimately take charge' (Keynes, 1973, vol. XIII, p. 397).

6. This differs from Hicks's definitions where statics is 'where we do not trouble about dating', while dynamics is where 'every quantity must be dated' (Hicks, 1946, p. 115).

7. Keynes is referring primarily to D. H. Robertson's model where income is determined in a previous period while effective demand is determined in the current period and hence they may differ. But recently it has again become voguish to make differences between effective demand and income the basis of a Keynesian model (Tobin, 1975, p. 198). Nevertheless, Keynes insisted that 'the theory of effective demand is substantially the same if we assume that short-period expectations are always fulfilled . . . subsequent discussion has shown that this seems to differentiate my treatment much more than I realized at [the] time, from those of other contemporary economists who have been thinking more or less about the same problem' (Keynes, 1973, vol. XIV, p. 181).

Keynes believed that his approach would permit greater emphasis on why 'the economic system may find itself in stable equilibrium with N at a level below full employment, namely at the level given by the intersection of the aggregate demand function with the aggregate supply function' (Keynes, 1936, p. 30).

8. Elasticity concepts are taxonomic and permit a classificatory methodology to be applied to economics. Shackle has called this approach *Keynesian Kaleidics* and argued that economic 'theory ought explicitly to be a classificatory one, putting situations in this box or that according to what *can happen* as a sequel to it. Theories which tell us what *will* happen are claiming too much' (Shackle, 1972, pp. 72–3).

9. Even in Hicks's dynamic model, if $E_e = 0$, static conditions apply (Hicks, 1946, p. 250). Recently Hahn, recognizing the irrelevance of traditional GE methodology, redefined the concept of equilibrium so that 'an economy is in

equilibrium when it generates messages which do not cause agents to change theories which they hold or policies they pursue' (Hahn, 1973, p. 25). This equilibrium concept, Hahn claims, is 'not at all clear', it is an 'ill-specified hypothesis but it does permit application to 'rare instances' where realizations differ from expectations so long as these 'rare' occasions do not induce agents to change their plans (ibid., pp. 26–7). Contrary to Hahn's claim, however, this is the well-defined Keynes static approach where $E_e = 0$. Thus after millions of man hours of economic research and progress in GE theory, the latest development is to work with a model which might be labelled as a 'no learning by doing' system. For Keynes to start with such a pedigogical device 40 years ago in order to clarify the principle of effective demand to his 'fellow economists' (Keynes, 1936, p. v) is, at least, understandable. For modern savants to present this ancient tool as the culmination of decades of research is lamentable.

10. A system where $E_e > 1$ 'is definitely unstable' (Hicks, 1946, p. 255). Keynes recognized there was nothing in the logic of the analysis that required $E_e < 1$, nevertheless the real world was not violently unstable. Hence Keynes was continuously searching for conditions which are capable of causing the $E_e < 1$ (Keynes, 1936, p. 250).

11. As Keynes stressed in a letter to Harrod, *ex ante* is what entrepreneurs *plan* to do not what they *ought* to do to assure the equality of *ex ante* and *ex post* (Keynes, 1973, vol. XIV, pp. 322–7). In a dynamic (realistic) model of the real world, therefore, when entrepreneurs carry out plans which lead to a realized effective demand (actual rate of growth) which differs from that level of effective demand where plans are reconciled (warranted rate of growth), the result may be for economic agents to change their state of expectations (shifts in behavioural propensities) which may lead to a further divergence between actual and warranted paths.

12. Thus short-run decisions are not independent of contractual obligations.

13. The aggregate supply curve is derived essentially in the same conceptual manner as the Marshallian microsupply curve. Thus, for example, in the case of a profit–maximizing 'price–taker' firm, the microsupply curve is obtained from the points of intersection between a family of alternative 'expected' demand curves and the 'expected' marginal cost curve (Samuelson, 1973, p. 454).

14. This verbal legerdemain was necessary if the simpler Keynesian static model was to make any impact on Keynes's 'fellow economists'. Keynes tried to dress his models with stable relationships even though he believed that psychological propensities were not because he required a forceful clear-cut exposition if he was going to make an impression on his peers. But in blurring the distinction between static and dynamic models, Keynes created a schism between the growth model of Harrod and those of other English Keynesians such as Robinson and Kaldor (Davidson, 1972, Ch. 5).

In a similar analysis of Keynes's liquidity preference analysis, R. F. Kahn has demonstrated

> the unsuitability of thinking of a schedule of liquidity preference as though it could be represented by a well-defined [*stable*] curve or by a functional relationship expressed in mathematical terms or subject to econometric processes. Keynes himself often gave way to the temptation to picture the state of liquidity preference as a fairly stable relationship, despite his institutional horror of undue formalism, but his treatment can be justified by the need at the time for a forceful and clear-cut exposition if it was to carry any weight at all. (Kahn, 1954, p. 250)

5. The Keynesian Revolution involved a change in paradigm from equilibrium models to historical models.
6. The initial data contains values for tastes, endowments, and the state of expectations of the agents concerned.
7. In an economy where no contractual transactions are made for other than the current period, nothing will have much liquidity.
8. It follows from Hicks's analysis of expectations that this homeostatic mechanism requires the inelasticity of E_e and the absence of continuous large autonomous changes in expectations (Hicks, 1946, pp. 256–7). In what follows we show what institutions are needed to assure stable expectations.
9. Businessmen abhor what GE theorists love – namely, recontracting.
20. The purchase of non-resaleable durables is like marriage, 'indissoluble except for death and other grave causes' (Keynes, 1936, p. 160). Such durables are illiquid and if all durables (including money) were illiquid we would be in a non-monetary economy such as described by GE theory.
21. Keynes explained the historical relative stability of price level in terms of the balance between money wage ('wage-unit') increases and the increase in the efficiency of labour (Keynes, 1936, p. 308). Keynes predicted that 'the long run stability or instability in prices will depend on the strength of the upward trend of the wage unit (or more precisely of the cost unit) compared with the rate of increase in the efficiency of the productive system' (ibid., p. 309). In these days of rising raw material costs, the cost unit may be more relevant.
22. Hicks reminds us that if 'all prices were equally flexible and all price expectations equally flexible', any change will lead to a 'complete breakdown' of capitalism, and the only thing that prevents this instability is 'price-rigidities' and 'beyond price rigidity, . . . people's sense of normal [i.e. sticky] prices' (Hicks, 1946, pp. 297–8).
23. Real wages changed rapidly and drastically from month to month during this period, declining from a high in March 1923 (of 80 per cent of 1913 real wages) to a low (of approximately 45 per cent of 1913 real wages) in July and regaining the March level in August and October.
24. It also implies a fixed real wage or, given the rate of changes in labour productivity, it may incorporate a given rate of change in real wages. Hence indexing as an incomes policy is balanced on a Harrodian knife-edge.
25. If the good in question is not durable, then the stock supply schedule is coincidental with the ordinate axis and only a forward flow–supply market exists. If the good is not reproducible (i.e. its elasticity of production is zero), then only a spot market exists, or if forward markets are developed, the forward prices will, in a world of uncertainty, represent speculation as to future spot prices for goods where flow–supply consideration cannot affect the outcome.
26. If some basic raw material such as petroleum is also linked to the same index then we could adopt Keynes's 'cost unit' as underlying the position of the short-run flow supply curve, S, in Figure 16.3.
27. If inputs did not require payments until after sales were completed, the financial constraint would be on the buyers to meet their indexed forward contract commitments.
28. Keynes noted that in a flight from currency, e_w, the proportional change in money-wages compared to the proportional change in effective demand becomes 'large', wages are no longer sticky (Keynes, 1936, p. 306).

References

Bresciani-Turroni, C. (1968), *The Economics of Inflation* (London: Allen & Unwin).

Davidson, P. (1972) *Money and the Real World*. (London: Macmillan).

Davidson, P. (1974), 'Disequilibrium Market Adjustment: Marshall Revisited' *Economic Inquiry*, 12, pp. 146–58.

Friedman, M. *et al.* (1974), *Milton Friedman's Monetary Framework: A Debate with His Critics* (Chicago: University of Chicago Press).

Hahn, F. H. (1973), *On the Notion of Equilibrium in Economics* (Cambridge Cambridge University Press).

Hicks, J. R. (1946) *Value and Capital*, 2nd edn. (New York: Oxford University Press)

Howitt, P. W. (1973) 'Walras and Monetary Theory', *Western Economic Journal*, 11, pp. 487–99.

Kahn, R. F. (1954) 'Some Notes on Liquidity Preference', *The Manchester School*, pp. 229–57.

Keynes, J. M. (1936), *The General Theory of Employment, Interest and Money* (New York: Harcourt-Brace).

Keynes, J. M. (1973) *The Collected Works of John Maynard Keynes*, Vol. XIII (London: Macmillan).

Keynes, J. M. (1973) *The Collected Works of John Maynard Keynes*, Vol. XIV (London: Macmillan).

Ostroy, J. M., and Starr, R. M. (1974), 'Money and the Decentralization of Exchange', *Econometrica*, 42, pp. 1093–1113.

Robinson, J. (1963) *Essay in the Theory of Economic Growth* (London: Macmillan).

Samuelson, P. A. (1973) *Economics*, 9th edn (New York: McGraw-Hill).

Shackle, G. L. S. (1968) *Expectations, Investment and Income*. 2nd edn, (New York: Oxford University Press).

Shackle, G. L. S. (1972), *Epistemics and Economics* (Cambridge: Cambridge University Press).

Shackle, G. L. S. (1973) 'Keynes and Today's Establishment in Economic Theory', *Journal of Economic Literature*, 11, pp. 516–19.

Tobin, J. (1975) 'The Legacy of Keynes', *American Economic Review, Papers and Proceedings*, 65.

Townshend, H. (1937) 'Liquidity-Premium and the Theory of Value', *Economic Journal*, 47, pp. 157–69.

17 Post Keynesian Economics: Solving the Crisis in Economic Theory*

There appears to be a crisis in economic theory. The tide of events in the last decade has diminished the stature of economists of both neoclassical-Keynesian and monetarist persuasion in the eyes of the public, and the corpus of orthodox neoclassical theory is a shambles. Meanwhile, and even more importantly, there appears to be an economic crisis in the real world which is not unrelated to the crisis in economic theory. For this economic crisis – the second great economic crisis of the twentieth century – is being precipitated by policy advice derived from irrelevant schools of neoclassical economic thought.

The Keynesians of the so-called 'neoclassical synthesis', who reigned supreme in the American economics profession during the 1950s and early 1960s, must bear some responsibility for this state of affairs; for, despite its name, the neoclassical synthesis was not really a synthesis of neoclassical with Keynesian ideas (as it purported to be) but merely the reassertion of the neoclassical framework with the addition of some Keynesian 'macro' terminology. The flavour of some of Keynes's specific policy recommendations was retained, but the essential logic of Keynes's economic theory was discarded. Thus the neoclassical synthesis had the result that the fundamental Keynesian Revolution was aborted before it could establish roots in the economics profession.

The bearing of this on the present crisis is that the logic of the neoclassical synthesis is essentially pre-Keynesian. Since the pre-Keynesian systems were inadequate for analysing the real world economic problems of the 1930s, it is not surprising they are incapable of dealing with the more complex problems of the 1980s.

Keynes was pre-eminently a monetary theorist. The words 'money', 'monetary', or 'currency' appear in the titles of all his important economic books. Keynes was a firm believer in the importance of money and a passionate advocate of monetary and banking reform, both domestically and internationally. Keynes's writings provide a monetary framework for

* *The Public Interest* (1980), reprinted in I. Kristol and D. Bell (eds), *The Crisis in Economic Theory* (New York: Basic Books, 1980).

the analysis of twentieth-century production economies involving markets, contracts, money-wages, expectations, time, employment, and output. Although Keynes emphasized the problems of mass unemployment, he also provided a basic framework for dealing with the stagflation problems of modern economies. Economists who have worked to foster the further development of this logical approach are Post Keynesians.

In recent years, there has developed a 'Post Keynesian' literature and even a *Journal of Post Keynesian Economics*. As the brace at the bottom of Table 17.1 indicates, Post Keynesian economists[1] are primarily an amalgam of those from the Keynes and Neo-Keynesian schools, but are also joined by some right-leaning members of the socialist–radical group, such as Galbraith. Moreover, certain left-leaning members of the neoclassical Keynesian school have exhibited much sympathy for Post Keynesian analysis in recent years (e.g. John Hicks's writings of the late 1960s and 1970s). Thus Post Keynesians do not represent a monolithic or puristic approach to the study of either micro or macroeconomics. The analytical framework utilized by Post Keynesians does, however, share certain common propositions (which tend to be downgraded by the other schools, if they are noticed at all).

Post Keynesians also share the view that Keynes provided a revolutionary new *logical* way of analysing a *real world* economy; and, like Keynes, Post Keynesians believe that only models which are relevant to the contemporary world are worthy of economists' attention. Thus, in a chronological sense, the economists who share these features and views are the only Post Keynesians among the various schools of economics listed in the table. The other schools rely primarily on analytical foundations which were developed before Keynes and hence represent regress and not progress in economic science, despite a veneer of mathematical and econometric sophistication.

1 ECONOMIC MODELS AND THE REAL WORLD

Economics is a science of thinking in terms of models joined to the art of choosing models which are relevant to the contemporary world . . . Good economists are scarce because the gift for using 'vigilant observation' to choose good models, although it does not require a highly specialized intellectual technique, appears to be a very rare one.

J. M. Keynes, *Collected Works*, Volume IV

Models used in economics are of two basic types: (a) general equilibrium models, which are characteristic of all neoclassical economics; and (b) historical humanistic models, which were used by Alfred Marshall and by Keynes and are the models favoured by Post Keynesians.

Equilibrium is a concept that has not always been well understood, even by economists (see Hahn, 1973). Economists have often used the term with different meanings in different contexts. In the broadest, most generic, sense of it, a market is said to be in equilibrium when, given an initial set of conditions, the market price is such that neither buyers nor sellers wish to alter their market offers. General equilibrium theory, however, uses a restricted definition of equilibrium which asserts that a market is in equilibrium if, at the equilibrium price, the market *clears* – meaning that the quantity demanded equals the quantity supplied. It can be shown, however, that market clearing is a sufficient but not a necessary condition for market equilibrium in the generic sense (see Davidson, 1967). In other words, although it is true that any market which clears will be in a state of equilibrium (in the sense given above), there are conditions under which a market may be in a state of equilibrium – meaning that there are no market forces inducing buyers and sellers to change their offers at the going price – *even if the markets do not clear*. When Keynes and Post Keynesians use the term equilibrium (for example, when they speak of less-than-full employment equilibrium) they are using the concept in its generic sense. Neoclassical economists, on the other hand, use the term equilibrium to mean market clearing.

The notion of a general equilibrium is formed by taking this restricted definition of equilibrium, which originally applied only to a single-commodity market, and applying this concept to the whole economic system, which consists of a large number of interacting markets. Thus general equilibrium theory addresses the interaction among markets. This mode of analysis proposes to understand an economic system by positing, instead of a single market-equilibrium price, a set of relative prices at which, if they were simultaneously achieved, all markets would be in a state of equilibrium, both internally and with respect to one another.

Simply stated, a general equilibrium economic system is one in which there exists a set of relative prices for all goods and services (including labour and capital) which will bring about the simultaneous *clearing* of *all* markets. In such a system it is impossible (by definition) to have a situation of less than full employment (i.e. an uncleared labour market in which labour market exceeds labour demand).

In the 1950s, neoclassical economists (e.g. Patinkin), using this limited equilibrium concept, were able to 'prove' (by definition) that Keynes's theory was '*disequilibrium*' analysis, where unemployment occurred only because money-wages were 'too high' and were 'rigid', so they would not decline in a recession. Of course, neoclassical economists before Keynes were well aware that unemployment was 'caused' by wage rigidities, and if

Table 17.1 A Table of Political Economy

	Socialist-Radical	Neo-Keynesian	Keynes	Neoclassical synthesis Keynesian	Monetarist-Neoclassical
Politics	Extreme left	Left of centre	Centre	Right of centre	Extreme right
Money	Real forces emphasized – money merely a tool for existing power structure.	Real forces emphasized, money assumed to accommodate.	Money and real forces intimately related.	Money matters along with everything else.	Only money matters.
Wage rate and income distribution	Wage rate basis of value. Income distribution the most important economic question.	Money-wage is the linchpin of the price level. Income distribution very important.	Money-wage rate fundamental; income distribution question of less importance.	Wage rate one of many prices. Income distribution is the resultant of all the demand and supply equations in a general equilibrium system. Income distribution a matter of equity, not of 'scientific' inquiry.	
Capital Theory	Surplus generated by reserve army.	Surplus needed over wages.	Scarcity theory (quasi-rents).	Marginal productivity theory and well-behaved production functions.	
Employment Theory	Any level of employment possible. Assumes growth in employment over time. Full employment creates crisis for capitalism.	Growth with any level of employment possible, although growth at full employment emphasized.	Any level of employment possible; full employment desirable.	Full employment assumed; unemployment is a disequilibrium situation.	Full employment assumed in long run; no explicit short-run theory of employment.

Inflation	Primarily due to money wage changes, but can also be due to profit margin changes.	Due to money wage or profit margin changes.	Due to changes in money wages, productivity and/or profit margins.	In long run primarily a monetary phenomenon being related to money supply via portfolio decisions. In short run may be related to Phillips curve.	Primarily a monetary phenomenon in the sense of being related to the supply of money via portfolio decisions.
Well-known representatives:	Galbraith, Bowles, D. Gordon, All Marxists	Mrs Robinson, Kaldor, Sraffa, Pasinetti, Eichner, Kregel, Harcourt	Harrod, Shackle, Weintraub, Davidson, Minsky, Wells, Vickers	Solow, Samuelson, Tobin, Clower, Leijonhufvud, J. R. Hicks	Friedman, Brunner, Meltzer, Parkin, Laidler

Post Keynesians

This is entitled 'A Table of Political Economy' because it attempts to associate the various schools of modern economic thought with different positions on the political spectrum, from extreme right to extreme left. Obviously the divisions are not watertight, but the views of individuals within any one school tend to be very close, and where there is overlap among the schools, the overlap tends to be greatest between individuals in schools that are adjacent in the table.

Keynes was merely emphasizing these aspects he contributed nothing new to economic theory.

In a famous letter to George Bernard Shaw, Keynes claimed to be 'revolutionizing' the way the world thinks about economic problems. As a trained logician, Keynes knew that in order to transform the way the world thinks about economic problems, he had to displace the existing approach by a new set of axioms and logical analysis. He specifically denied that, in his logical framework, reducing money-wages would automatically assure full employment equilibrium (Keynes, 1936, pp. 260–2). Thus Keynes's analytical framework is logically incompatible with all general equilibrium systems for a number of reasons, not the least being that it is based on a wider definition of equilibrium than merely market clearing. Accordingly, Keynes's wider definition must provide a more *General* Theory.

The most crucial limitation of general equilibrium models, however, is their inability to deal with the passage of calendar time. All general equilibrium systems are essentially static or timeless, despite claims by some economists that they can be made to handle time. General equilibrium is timeless in the sense that the equilibrium position is thought to be uniquely determined by an initial set of conditions, preferences, and decisions, all taken at an arbitrary initial instant. Logically, there can be no activities which occur after the initial event which were unanticipated (at least in an actuarial sense). Thus there can be no activities which happen after the initial instant that have any effect of the predestined final outcome. Accordingly, the logic of general equilibrium analysis implies that such systems *cannot* provide practical answers for policy-makers facing hard decisions when unforeseen complications arise and involve activities which will have important ramifications in the uncertain, unpredictable future.

In effect the general equilibrium model depicts a world in which all contracts are signed (*and paid for*) in the Garden of Eden, without any erroneous (false) trades, and in which the 'initial instant' decision process completely determines the future history of mankind for every conceivable trick of Mother Nature. In the future course of events, economic actors merely read their agreed-upon lines, and the economic play is performed, though all know – or expect with actuarial certainty – that Hamlet and the others will die in a certain sequence in the last act.

There are certain purely imaginary intellectual problems for which general equilibrium models are well designed to provide precise answers (if anything really could). But this is much the same as saying that if one insists on analysing a problem which has no real world equivalent or solution, it may be appropriate to use a model which has no real world application. By the same token, if a model is designed specifically to deal with real world situations it may not be able to handle purely imaginary problems.

Post Keynesian models are designed specifically to deal with real world problems. Hence they may not be very useful in resolving imaginary problems that are often raised by general equilibrium theorists. Post Keynesians cannot specify *in advance* the optimal allocation of resources over time into the uncertain, unpredictable future; nor are they able to determine how many angels can dance on the head of a pin. On the other hand, models designed to provide answers to questions of the angel–pinhead variety, or imaginary problems involving specifying in advance the optimal-allocation path over time, will be unsuitable for resolving practical, real world economic problems. Moreover, even with regard to this question of optimal allocation, it has been shown by F. H. Hahn that by means of general equilibrium models one can only demonstrate that leaving allocation to market forces will *not* guarantee an optimal solution.[2] In fact, general equilibrium systems were not (and logically cannot be) designed to provide positive guides to resolving the macro–political–economic problems of inflation, unemployment, economic growth, or even the energy crisis. These horrendous economic problems are, however, the perfect grist for the Post Keynesian mill, because it is precisely this sort of problem that the historical and humanistic models employed by Post Keynesian economists are best suited to deal with.

2 THREE PROPOSITIONS

Post Keynesians recognize, of course, that all theories are abstractions and, hence, simplifications of reality. But the purpose of the theory is to make the real world intelligible, not to substitute an ideal world in place of it. The general equilibrium model, however, abstracts from precisely those features that make the real world real – namely, the irreversibility of time and the uncertainty of the future. The characteristics of the historical and humanistic models employed by Post Keynesians may be summarized in the following three propositions: (1) The economy is a historical process; (2) in a world where uncertainty is unavoidable, expectations have an unavoidable and significant effect on economic outcomes; and, (3) economic and political institutions play a significant role in shaping economic events.

1. *The economy is a process in historical time.* Time is a real world device which prevents everything from happening at once! The production of commodities takes time; and the consumption of capital goods and consumer durables takes time. These processes of production and consumption are essentially irreversible. Thus real time is an asymmetric variable, which means, among other things, that we know the past but cannot know the future. Yet economic decisions taken in the present require actions which cannot be completed until some future date. Hence, as Marshall stated in the preface to the first edition of his *Principles*: '[The] element of

time is the center of the chief difficulty of almost every economic problem.'
Keynes's revolution is in the Marshall tradition of emphasizing the presence of time at the centre of economic problems. The neoclassical synthesis, on the other hand, by attempting to reformulate the Keynesian
revolution in general equilibrium terms, emasculates it by removing from
the Keynesian terms their original reference to the historical process.

2. *In a world where uncertainty and surprises are unavoidable, expectations have an unavoidable and significant effect on economic outcomes.* In
an uncertain world, economic decisions are continually affected by the
decision-makers' expectations, and these expectations are shaped by the
'inherited stocks' possessed by economic actors – the accumulated results
of past guesses, both correct and incorrect. In other words, economic
decisions are rarely made on anything like a clean slate. As different
individuals or groups approach the same economic circumstances with
different 'slates', so their expectations and hence their decisions may also
differ. Post Keynesians, therefore, emphasize the role played by this
heterogeneity of expectations, as well as the importance of the fact that
future events *cannot be fully anticipated.* As J. R. Hicks recently noted,
'One must assume that people in one's models do not know what is going
to happen, and know that they do not know what is going to happen. As in
history!' (Hicks, 1977, p. vii). And Keynes himself clearly recognized that
money matters only when we wish to analyse the 'problems of the real
world in which our previous expectations are liable to disappointment and
expectations concerning the future affect what we do today' (Keynes, 1936,
pp. 293–4).

In a neoclassical world, on the other hand, all decisions involving present
and all future actions are taken at a single initial instant in time; errors are
(at least in the long run) *by assumption* impossible. Thus neoclassical
economics implicitly denies human fallibility, for to admit the possibility of
error is to admit that a general equilibrium solution via market prices
(which are suppose to coordinate people's plans and expectations without
altering the initial parameters) need not exist. In a neoclassical system, the
existence of competition *guarantees* that no one undertakes erroneous
(wasteful) activities, as resources must always be 'optimally' allocated.

Neoclassical theorists assume that the uncertainty of the future can be
adequately represented by means of probability statements about an
economic world which, without being absolutely determinate, is at least
statistically predictable. The monetarists Laidler and Parkin, for example,
have noted that in neoclassical theory:

[E]xpectations – even if erroneous – are usually treated as if held with
certainty, or it is assumed that any variance in expectations does not
influence behaviour. There exists a well-developed analysis, based on
probability theory, of individual behaviour in the face of risk elsewhere

in our subject and there surely are gains to be had from applying this analysis to aspects of the problems of inflation. This at least would be our view, but there are many economists, notably Davidson (1972) and Shackle (1955), who would presumably regard the application of such analysis as misconceived (though possibly better than assuming all expectations to be held with certainty). They would stress that *uncertainty* in the Knightian sense as opposed to risk lay at the root of the problem. Certainly an analysis of behaviour of this kind would provide an interesting alternative to the approach based on probability. There can be no guarantee *ex ante* as to which line of work will prove more fruitful, as a means of replacing the widespread assumption (often unstated) that people's actions are the same as if their expectations were held with certainty. (Laidler and Parkin, 1975, p. 795)

Replacing the concept of certainty by the concept of a known probability distribution merely replaces the assumption of perfect foreknowledge by the assumption that economic agents possess actuarial knowledge. In such a situation actuarial costs and benefits can be calculated, and the economic agent can act 'as if' he possessed absolute foreknowledge (or, in modern monetarist parlance, expectations are 'rational' and 'fully anticipate').[3] This semantic legerdemain permits neoclassical economists to develop sophisticated theories which replicate the solutions of pre-Keynesian perfect-certainty models while giving the specious appearance of dealing with time and decision-making by economic agents facing an uncertain (but fully anticipated!) future. Such literary deceptions are, in fact, required by the neoclassical economists to enable them to reach their invariable conclusion that government intervention to improve employment (by means of fiscal policy) or to fight inflation (by means of incomes policy) is always bound to be ineffective. In the 'rational expectations' models, for example, the conclusion that government intervention is futile is connected with the concept of a 'natural rate of unemployment' (which is the equivalent of full employment in a world of perfect certainty). As Laidler has argued,

> any rate of inflation is consistent with a state of zero excess demand in the economy provided it is *fully expected*. If to this we add the proposition that there is a unique level of unemployment in the economy associated with a situation of zero overall excess demand then we have it by implication that this *so-called "natural" employment rate is consistent with any fully anticipated rate of inflation*.
> (Laidler, 1976, p. 59, emphasis added)

Is there really a difference between 'fully anticipated' events and perfect certainty?

Modern neoclassical economists have developed models of expectation formation in an attempt to shore up their collapsing analytic structure.[4] These models are, as even their advocates have admitted, 'naive', 'arbitrary', or 'inconsistent' (ibid., p. 62f). 'The simplest lesson to be learned from consideration of the rational expectations hypothesis,' Laidler concedes, 'is that there is likely to be far more to the formation of expectations than the blind application of some mechanical formula to a body of data . . . [Moreover] we must face the implication that heterogeneity of expectations at any moment is more likely to be the rule than homogeneity' (ibid., p. 69).

Yet the fundamental monetarist concept of a 'natural rate of unemployment' *requires*, as the monetarists admit, a 'fully anticipated future' – which means a future which 'can only be perfectly anticipated in any actual economy if *all* people hold the same expectations since otherwise some expectations are bound to be wrong' (Laidler and Parkin, 1975, p. 743). Elaborate monetarist models which show that controlling the rate of growth of the money supply is an effective method of fighting inflation (in the long run!) are based, however, on a 'natural rate of unemployment' and hence on a fully anticipated future with everyone holding the same expectations.

Heterogeneity of expectations, which Laidler admits to be the more likely real world situation, however, precisely means that people have differing expectations about the future. This guarantees that most of those holding expectations today will find, as events unfold, that their expectations were in some degree incorrect.[5] Certainly mistakes, false trades, and, above all, changing economic parameters are unavoidable in the real world. Consequently, the monetarist proposal to fight inflation simply by controlling the money supply has no sound basis. It appears merely to be an article of faith!

In contrast to this neoclassical approach that handles uncertainty as if it were the same as predictable risk, Post Keynesians build upon the fact that the future is uncertain, and as Hicks observed, people know that they do not know the future when they undertake economic actions. By recognizing this obvious fact of life, the Post Keynesians aim, when discussing future events, to be approximately right; whereas the neoclassical economists, in aiming to be precise, end up being precisely wrong. The economic future, Post Keynesians note, is *created* by man, not simply discovered.

3. *Economic and political institutions are not negligible and, in fact, play an extremely important role in determining real world economic outcomes.* The logical world of general equilibrium theory contains no significant real world institutions – not even organized commodity or financial markets. That is to say, general equilibrium theorists treat institutions as theoretically negligible, for the same reason that they are committed to the view that the particular configuration of institutions *cannot* have any effect on

the final outcome (i.e. the general equilibrium position). In the Post Keynesian world, on the other hand, the real world in which the future is uncertain and events take place in time – in that world economic and political institutions are both influential and prominent in determining economic outcomes, and policy-makers neglect them at their peril.

The distribution of income and power is a basic concern of Post Keynesians, particularly in regard of the problems of inflation. With the growth of an industrial society and democracy, people have learned that they can and *should* attempt to control their own destinies. If one gains control of one's income, then one's fate is largely in one's own hands. In modern societies, there are three ways to affect and control one's own income: (1) possess a unique, marketable qualification and exercise the monopoly power it provides; (2) organize with others who have similar market capacities in order to exercise some joint monopoly control; and (3) organize and employ political activities to tilt government policy towards improving one's income.

Post Keynesians recognize that in a world whose future is not predetermined by the initial conditions, continuing inflation involves a redistribution of real income *from* the weaker groups to the more powerful. This induces powerful economic *and* political forces, as competing groups attempt to catch up with one another. Thus inflation is symptomatic of a struggle between organized groups, each trying to obtain a larger share of the available national or world income for themselves. Post Keynesians emphasize the importance of bearing in mind that every price is ultimately somebody's income. For example, OPEC's price increase is the way the oil cartel extorts real income from consumers who, if they have any market or political power, demand 'cost-of-living' adjustments to their pay so that they will not lose income to the Arabs. If the United States cannot or will not break the OPEC cartel, then we must give up some of our GNP to OPEC. The remaining income must be distributed some way. In an unfettered market system with large business, labour, and governmental units, where all are reluctant to accept a reduction in real income or profits, the struggle over the remainder of the pie will induce a continuing wage-price inflation. If one ignores this phenomenon, one cannot properly compare the effectiveness of incomes policies designed to restrain the income demands of competing groups with that of 'planned recessions' achieved by means of tight monetary or fiscal policy.

The goal of restrictive monetary and fiscal policy as anti-inflation devices is to so weaken the various domestic and foreign groups (the euphemism is 'squeezing out inflationary expectations') by creating business losses and unemployment that they will not have the strength to continue the struggle. Unfortunately, those that are most likely to be weakened are those with the least power to begin with, while any success with such a severe policy requires, as even its advocates would admit, several years of impoverishing the entire society (by means of recession or slow economic growth). Incomes policies, on the other hand, are designed to obtain a social agreement among the domestic competing groups to limit their demands for real income in a manner which is socially responsible for distributing the remaining GNP and hence limiting current inflation to the size of the OPEC tax on our resources.

In the general equilibrium world, the problem of how to deal with income redistributions over time due to *unanticipated* inflation cannot even arise, because, as we have seen, the system assumes the future is predictable and 'fully anticipated'. Thus the logic of neoclassical analysis does not even permit the analysis of the problem of distribution over time due to unanticipated inflation, despite pontifical neoclassical statements about the desirability of 'indexing' to avoid unanticipated inflation.

3   THE IMPORTANCE OF MONEY

Post Keynesians, following Keynes's lead, give particular attention to the human institution of money and other institutions with which it is organically connected. These include the banking and monetary systems; time-oriented markets for goods, factors of production, and financial assets; money contracts for spot and forward transactions; and especially, the money-wage contract as a necessary condition of liquidity over time in any market-oriented production economy organized on a forward money-contracting basis. (A production economy is one in which goods are produced as well as marketed. A pure exchange economy is an abstraction, used by many neoclassical economists, in which production is disregarded and only trade in pre-existing goods is studied. Liquidity involves the ability to discharge one's money–contractual obligations as they come due; this ability depends on either holding sufficient money balances to meet these obligations or holding readily marketable assets which can be quickly sold for money when needed.)

Keynes and the Post Keynesians base their logical analysis on the following inductive propositions: (1) modern monetary economies do not possess any automatic mechanism that assures a tendency towards full employment of resources over time; (2) underemployment equilibrium is a recurring phenomenon in money-using production economies; and therefore, (3) the existence of underemployment equilibrium must be associated with the characteristics of money and related institutions, and with how production is organized.

Money is first and foremost a human institution, organically connected to other economic institutions including the banking system; time-oriented markets for goods, factors of production, and financial assets; and money contracts for spot and forward transactions – especially the money-wage contract. The existence of these interrelated economic institutions produce the need for liquidity over time in any market-oriented, production economy organized on a basis of forward contracts in money terms.

In all modern market-oriented production economies, production is organized on a forward money-contracting basis. A forward contract is simply one that specifies a future date (or dates) for both delivery *and* payment. Since production takes time, the hiring of factor inputs and the purchase of materials to be used in any productive activity must precede the date when the finished product will be at hand. These hiring and material-purchase transactions will therefore require forward contracting if the production process is to be efficiently planned.

The financing of such forward production-cost commitments (the taking of a 'position' in working capital) requires entrepreneurs to have money available to discharge these contractual liabilities at one or more future dates before the product is sold and delivered, payment received, and the 'position' liquidated. This is the ubiquitous liquidity problem of entrepreneurs in capitalist economies, a problem which, however, is left unattended by mainstream neoclassical economists.

The logic of general equilibrium theory requires that *all* payments be made at the initial instant, and therefore neoclassical theory cannot logically deal with the question of meeting contractual payment obligations at any point of time after the initial instant. Consequently neoclassical economists, by remaining faithful to their theory, truly earn the businessman's traditional gibe: 'They have never had to meet a payroll!'

In a general equilibrium world, it is *assumed* that all goods are traded simultaneously in spot markets and all payments are also made simultaneously on the spot, while each person's expenditures are assumed to equal the value of his simultaneous sales. There is never a liquidity problem, for neoclassical models are actually barter systems where, in essence, goods pay for goods at equilibrium prices on the spot. In such a world there is no logical niche for the institution of money, a money price level, or future events that are not already 'fully anticipated' and dealt with on the spot. If the real world were similar to, and could therefore be represented by, a logical world of barter economies, then indeed money would *not* matter! Money only matters in an economic world where numerous interconnected sequences of forward contracts in money terms are used to organize productive activities. *But that is our world!*

In a decentralized market economy, then, moving irresistibly through historical time into the uncertain future, forward contracting for production inputs is essential to efficient production planning. And the most ubiquitous forward contract of all in such an economy, as long as slavery and peonage are illegal, is the money-wage contract. Since labour hiring and payment precede in time the delivery of newly produced goods, the price level of new goods depends in large measure on the relationship between the money-wage and the productivity of labour. As Arrow and Hahn (1971, p. 356f) have written:

> The terms in which contracts are made matter. In particular, if money is the good in terms of which contracts are made, then the prices of goods in terms of money are of special significance. This is not the case if we consider an economy without a past and without a future. Keynes wrote that "the importance of money essentially flows from it being a link between the present and the future" to which we add that it is important also because it is a link between the past and the present. If a *serious monetary theory* comes to be written, the fact that contracts are indeed made in terms of money will be of considerable importance. (Emphasis added)

If Arrow and Hahn are correct, a 'serious monetary theory' must give serious attention to the economic role of the *money-wage contract*. It is the 'stickiness' of money-wages and prices (i.e. the absence of rapid movements), as guaranteed by the law of contracts, that permits capitalist economies to engage in time-consuming production processes and provides a basis for a 'sticky' price level of producible goods. Accordingly, forward contracting can be considered as the way entrepreneurs in a 'free market' environment attempt to maintain wage and price controls! Indeed, such controls are fundamental to the financing of production processes.

The existence of fixed money contracts for forward delivery *and* payment is fundamental to the concepts of liquidity and money. In such a setting, changes in money-wage rates – Keynes's wage unit – determine changes in the costs of production and the price level associated with the production of goods that profit-oriented entrepreneurs are willing to undertake. The view that inflation (i.e. a rising money-price level of newly produced goods) is a monetary phenomenon makes logical sense only in an economy where time-oriented money contracts (especially labour hire) are basic to the organization of production activities. For clearly, as long as the time duration of fixed-money wage contracts exceeds the gestation period of production, entrepreneurs can limit their liabilities when undertaking any production process. If, however, the institution of long-duration fixed-money contracts begins to break down, the entrepreneur's liabilities may become prohibitively uncertain. Then a 'social contract' to limit wage and price movements over long periods of calendar time must be developed to buttress the private institution of lengthy forward contracts, if production processes which require lengthy periods of time are to be maintained.[6]

Post Keynesians contend, therefore, that the existence of some human institution which will guarantee income (i.e. production-cost) restraint over time is a necessary adjunct to developed capitalist economies. Devices that have been proposed for achieving this objective are frequently referred to as 'incomes policies'.

4 LIQUIDITY

Liquidity involves the ability to discharge one's contractual obligations when they come due. The capacity to remain liquid requires holding sufficient money balances to meet known upcoming obligations and, in an uncertain world, to meet unknown but potential obligations. (Instead of holding cash one can hold readily marketable [liquid] assets which can be quickly sold for cash when needed and which do not incur significant carrying costs while they are being held.)

According to Keynes (1936, ch. 17) money and all other liquid assets possess two 'essential properties', and it is these two properties which cause unemployment when people reduce their purchases of goods and increase their demand for liquid assets instead. Thus, in the real world, where the future is uncertain, any unexpected event which creates fears for the future may induce a rush towards liquidity which can thereby cause additional unemployment. The two essential properties of liquid assets are: (1) their elasticity of production must be zero (or negligible); and (2) their elasticity of substitution must be zero (or negligible).[7]

When a good is said to possess a positive elasticity of production, this simply means that any increase in the demand for this commodity will induce private suppliers to produce more of it by hiring additional workers. To say that money has an elasticity of production of zero is merely to state in the language of the economist the old adage that 'money does not grow on trees'. Hence money cannot be harvested (produced) by the use of labour. (Most laymen would be appalled to know that the weighty pronouncements and econometric projections given by neoclassical economists are based on a logical structure which assumes that money (or the 'numéraire' as it is called in general equilibrium models) can be any commodity and that it is often associated in such analysis with *peanuts* – which, if it does not grow on trees, does grow on bushes. If the logical foundations of neoclassical economists had any relevance to the real world, President Carter might have done better to name brother Billy rather than Mr Volcker to the chairmanship of the Federal Reserve Board.)

Money's zero elasticity of production does not mean that its supply is unalterable. Obviously the money supply can be expanded exogenously by means of deliberate actions of the central bank, or endogenously when the banking system responds to an increased demand for finance. But money's zero production elasticity does have the consequence that an increase in the demand for money does not induce a commensurate increase in the demand for workers to produce it.

If a good possesses a positive elasticity of substitution, this means that, if the *price* of this good *rises*, some of the demand for this commodity will be diverted to some other good (or goods) which is then said to be a substitute for the first. Thus if the price of coffee rises, some people will switch to tea; others may attend the cinema more often. The greater the relative diversion of demand away from coffee for any given percentage *increase in its price*, the greater the elasticity of substitution between coffee and other producible commodities. (One of the fundamental axioms of neoclassical theory is 'gross substitution', which assumes that ultimately anything is a substitute for anything else, so that if the price of anything rises, people will spend less on it and more on other producible things.)

The importance of these elasticity properties, and their implications for the Post Keynesian, as against the neoclassical, theory of employment, is easily illustrated. Suppose we start from a period of close-to-full employment and then hypothesize that some event causes people to become more worried and cautious about the uncertain future. Many people will wish to postpone or even permanently reduce their current purchases of goods and services, and use more of their current income to buy liquid assets (or just store it in the form of money). This reduction in the public's demand for goods will immediately reduce the sales of industry and cause lay-offs. The increased demand for liquid assets will cause *their* price to increase. But if liquid assets have a zero elasticity of production the laid-off workers cannot be re-employed to produce (or harvest) money or any other liquid asset. (In a neoclassical world where peanuts can be money (the *numéraire*), laid-off workers would be reallocated and re-employed – by the invisible hand of the rising price of liquid assets – in the peanut fields to harvest more numéraire in response to the increase in demand.)

Moreover, since the elasticity of substitution between liquid (non-producible via the use of labour) assets and producible goods is zero, the hypothetical increased demand for liquidity will *not* be diverted by the rising price of liquid assets back to things which are readily produced by labour (whose prices have not changed). Thus in a Post Keynesian world, the rush to liquidity not only causes workers to be laid-off in industry, but also they cannot be re-employed in producing more of the (liquid) objects that the public now desires.

In my recently published debate with Professor Friedman, he specifically indicates that, in contradistinction to the Post Keynesian analysis, his theoretical framework assumes easily reproducible commodities are good substitutes for money. Accordingly, any change in the demand for liquidity will, on Friedman's model, be diverted into a change in the demand for producible goods such as furniture, household appliances, clothes, and the like. Thus Friedman's logical framework requires the full employment of labour, *in the long run*, since he assumes that everything demanded by people as they spend their income leads, either directly or through a substitution effect, to an equivalent demand for workers. Hence, there can never be a shortage of effective demand.

Keynes thought differently, however, as he made clear in his *General Theory*: 'Unemployment develops, that is to say, because people want the moon; – men cannot be employed when the object of desire (i.e. money) is something which cannot be produced and the demand for which cannot be readily choked off' (1936, p. 235).

The acceptance of the 'essential properties' approach to liquidity, then, represents a fundamental logical difference between Post Keynesians (who reject the universality of the gross substitution axiom) and *all* neoclassical theorists. These essential properties entail that underemployment equilibrium *can* occur whenever there are what Hahn calls 'resting places for savings other than reproducible assets' (1977, p. 31). Neoclassical doctrine holds that equilibrium can occur only in a state of full employment; hence unemployment is regarded merely as a blemish due to some friction in an otherwise perfectly functioning market system. For this reason neoclassicists argue that unfettered markets will, in the long run, work out these blemishes and that government interference merely accentuates them.[8]

Post Keynesians, however, see unemployment as a fundamental problem of any money economy where liquidity considerations are important. Post Keynesians believe that unemployment tendencies are an inherent weakness in any money economy and that only public policy can prevent this weakness from manifesting itself and perhaps destroying an otherwise desirable system of organizing economic activities.

5 SOME CLOSING REMARKS

The purpose of this essay was to illustrate that there are fundamental logical differences between Post Keynesian theory and neoclassical general equilibrium analysis of either the Keynesian or monetarist persuasions.[9] If the neoclassical view is adopted as the starting point of any economic theory, observed real world unemployment and stagflation phenomena can only be 'explained' as *temporary* phenomena due to frictions, short-run price and wage rigidities, or (adaptive? rational?) expectational reactions. In the long run it is believed that a state of economic bliss will be attained by means of unfettered market processes. (This latter is, of course, not a conclusion of the analysis but merely a reiteration of the initial supposition of neoclassical systems.) The object of neoclassical modelling is an 'idealized state', i.e. the long-run equilibrium solution, and *all* neoclassical theorists begin with the assumption that full employment is the necessary long-run position of modern production economies.

Arrow and Hahn have shown that in 'a world with a past as well as a future and in which contracts are made in terms of money, no [general] equilibrium may exist' (1971, p. 361). In other words, even the *existence* of a full-employment equilibrium position cannot be logically demonstrated for a world of time and money contracts. Thus, economies such as ours – organized on a money-contracting basis over time – may settle down to equilibrium at any level of employment; that is, they may exhibit an unemployment equilibrium *in the long run*, as well as in the short run.

Keynes believed that from the outset economists should model the actual state of the real world, rather than idealized long-run solutions. He wrote in a famous passage: 'But this long run is a misleading guide to current affairs. *In the long run* we are all dead. Economists set themselves too easy, too useless a task if in tempestuous seasons they can only tell us that when the storm is long past the ocean is flat again' (Keynes, 1971, p. 65). For members of the Post Keynesian schools the notions discussed above – historical time, uncertainty, expectations, political and economic institutions (especially money and forward contracts) – represent fundamental characteristics of the world we inhabit – *the real world*. We have seen that the idealized state of the neoclassical model cannot exist, even as an ideal, in the temporal setting of the real world. Accordingly, Post Keynesian economists oppose neoclassical analysis as irrelevant to the macroeconomic problems of the twentieth century. They believe that their own approach, even if incomplete, is the only one that is able to look with unclouded vision at the problems which most earnestly require attention.

Notes

1. There is no hyphen between the words 'Post' and 'Keynesian'. In the past there has been a lack of uniformity in labelling schools of thought; hence perceptive readers will note that others have used the term Post-Keynesian (with the hyphen) to designate the school that I have labelled Neo-Keynesian. In order to provide a non-ambiguous terminology I have eliminated the hyphenated term from this text and request others to do the same.
2. Intelligent advocates of general equilibrium systems have come to realize that the one and only useful function of general equilibrium analysis is to demonstrate why optimal allocations can *never* be achieved in the real world. In this view, neoclassical systems are only:

   > very useful when for instance one comes to argue with someone who maintains that we need not worry about exhaustible resources because they will always have prices which ensure their 'proper' use. Of course there are many things wrong with this contention but a quick way of disposing of the claim is to note that an Arrow–Debreu equilibrium must be an assumption he is making for the economy and then to show why the economy cannot be in this state. The argument will here turn on the absence of futures markets and contingent futures markets and on the inadequate treatment of time and uncertainty by the construction. This negative role of Arrow–Debreu equilibrium I consider almost to be sufficient justification for it, since practical men and ill-trained theorists everywhere in the world do not understand what

they are claiming to be the case when they claim a beneficent and coherent role for the invisible hand. But for descriptive purposes of course this negative role is hardly a recommendation. (Hahn, 1973, pp. 14–15)

3. Moreover, in a general equilibrium world, *all* expectations must be realized by events; surprises and disappointments are logically incompatible with general equilibrium.

4. The monetarists have attempted to shore up their collapsing system by adding various expectational–formation hypotheses to their system. 'Expectations' permits any outcome in the short run, while expectations either 'adapt' or are 'rational', and therefore monetarists assume that economic actors either know *at the initial instant* what are the true parameters of the economic system or learn (adapt to) these unchanging parameters. Consequently 'in the long run', though we are all dead, the monetarist expectational analysis will be verified! (Elsewhere I have demonstrated that even with such expectational–formation models added to general equilibrium systems, one cannot rescue the neoclassical system (Davidson, 1978a, pp. 370–2).)

5. The rational expectations hypothesis, on the other hand, assumes that the public has complete knowledge of the parameters of the real economic system and hence cannot be 'fooled' by government intervention.

6. It would be foolish for entrepreneurs in a free enterprise, market-oriented system to enter into a production process whose gestation period greatly exceeded the duration of forward contracts with his workers (or even his material suppliers). To do so would be to undertake a potentially unbounded liability with no controls on the costs of production and hence no assurance that the entrepreneur had sufficient finance to meet his future payrolls and complete the production process.

7. For a complete discussion of these technical requirements see Keynes (1936, ch.17), Davidson (1978a, chs. 6–9; 1980). The latter item is followed by a discussion by Bronfenbrenner (1980) and a reply which discusses these matters and their relation to gold.

8. Logically consistent general equilibrium analysts would argue, for example, that unemployment can be cured by lowering the money-wage so that businessmen *substitute* workers for other productive inputs without lowering the level of GNP (income). Keynes and Post Keynesians, on the other hand, argue that reducing wages will not directly increase employment, for such wage cuts will *pari passu* reduce consumers' incomes and hence lower the demand for the output of industry. Instead, if government increases income, employment will rise both directly and indirectly via the multiplier.

9. Solow, on the other hand, believes that 'thus far so-called Post Keynesianism seems to be more a state of mind than a theory' (Solow, 1979, p. 344). Of course, Solow (as he readily admits) is far from an impartial judge of the merits of Post Keynesian analysis *vis-à-vis* neoclassical Keynesianism. Although Solow concedes that he now finds 'bits of unorthodoxy incomparably more credible than the things that impeccably orthodox equilibrium theory asks me to believe about the world' (ibid., p. 348), he still concludes: 'It is much too early to tear up the . . . [neoclassical synthesis] chapters in the textbooks' (ibid., p. 354). Perhaps it is 'too early' for professors who have made fame and fortune out of such models to be ready to abandon them, despite their common sense which suggests the incredible nature of neoclassical theory; for others who have an earnest desire to resolve the economic problems which are threatening the second great crisis of capitalism in the twentieth century, and who have no vested interest in neoclassical theory, time is running out.

References

Arrow, K. S. and F. H. Hahn (1971), *General Competitive Analysis* (San Francisco: Holden).

Bronfenbrenner, M. (1980), 'Davidson on Keynes and Money', *Journal of Post Keynesian Economics*, 2 (Spring).

Davidson, P. (1967), 'A Keynesian View of Patinkin's Theory of Employment' *Economic Journal*, 77.

Davidson, P. (1978a), *Money and the Real World*, 2nd edn (London: Macmillan)

Davidson, P. (1978b), 'Why Money Matters: Lessons from a Half Century of Monetary Theory', *Journal of Post Keynesian Economics*, 1 (Chapter 13 in this volume).

Davidson, P. (1980), 'The Dual Faceted Nature of the Keynesian Revolution: The Role of Money and Money Wages in Determining Unemployment and Production Flow Prices', *Journal of Post Keynesian Economics*, 2 (Spring).

Davidson, P. and E. Smolensky (1964), *Aggregate Supply and Demand Analysis* (New York: Harper & Row).

Eichner, A. S. (1976), *The Megacorp and Oligopoly* (Cambridge: Cambridge University Press).

Galbraith, J. K. (1978), 'On Post Keynesian Economics', *Journal of Post Keynesian Economics*, 1.

Hahn, F. H. (1973), *On the Notion of Equilibrium in Economics* (Cambridge: Cambridge University Press).

Hahn, F. H. (1977), 'Keynesian Economics and General Equilibrium Theory', in G. C. Harcourt (ed.) *Microeconomic Foundations of Macroeconomics* (London: Macmillan).

Harrod, R. F. (1969), *Money* (London: Macmillan).

Hicks, J. R. (1967), *Critical Essays in Monetary Theory* (Oxford: Oxford University Press).

Hicks, J. R. (1976), 'Some Questions of Time in Economics', in *Evolution, Welfare and Time*, ed. by A. M. Tang, F. M. Westfield, and J. J. Worley (Lexington: Heath).

Hicks, J. R. (1977), *Economic Perspectives* (Oxford: Oxford University Press).

Hicks, J. R. (1979), *Causality in Economics* (New York: Basic Books).

Kaldor, N. (1960a), *Essays on Value and Distribution* (Illinois: Free Press).

Kaldor, N. (1960b), *Essays on Economic Stability and Growth* (London: Duckworth).

Keynes, J. M. (1936), *The General Theory of Employment, Interest and Money* (New York: Harcourt).

Keynes, J. M. (1971), *A Tract on Monetary Reform*, reprinted as Vol. IV of *The Collected Writings of John Maynard Keynes* (London: Macmillan).

Keynes, J. M. (1973), *The General Theory and After: Part II; The Collected Writings of John Maynard Keynes*, Vol. XIV (London: Macmillan).

Kregel, J. A. (1971), *Rate of Profit, Distribution and Growth: Two Views* (Chicago: Aldine).

Kregel, J. A. (1973), *The Reconstruction of Political Economy* (New York: Halsted).

Laidler, D. (1976), 'Expectations and the Phillips Trade Off: A Commentary', *Scottish Journal of Political Economy*, 23.

Laidler, D. and M. Parkin (1975), 'Inflation – A Survey', *Economic Journal*, 85.

Marshall, A. (1980), *Principle of Economics*, 1st edn (London: Macmillan).

Minsky, M. P. (1975), *John Maynard Keynes* (New York: Columbia University Press).

Pasinetti, L. L. (1974), *Growth and Income Distribution* (New York: Cambridge University Press).

Robinson, J. (1956), *The Accumulation of Capital* (London: Macmillan).

Robinson, J. (1962), *Essays in the Theory of Economic Growth* (London: Macmillan).

Roncaglia, A. (1978), *Sraffa and the Theory of Prices* (New York: Wiley).

Sraffa, P. (1960), *Production of Commodities by Means of Commodities* (Cambridge: Cambridge University Press).

Solow, R. M. (1979), 'Alternative Approaches to Macroeconomic Theory: A Partial View', *Canadian Journal of Economics*, 12.

Weintraub, S. (1958), *An Approach to the Theory of Income Distribution* (Philadelphia: Chilton).

Weintraub, S. (1978), *Capitalism's Inflation and Unemployment Crisis* (Reading: Addison-Wesley).

18 A Critical Analysis of Monetarist–Rational Expectation–Supply-side (Incentive) Economics Approach to Accumulation During a Period of Inflationary Expectations*

David Laidler has written that 'Like beauty, "monetarism" tends to be in the eye of the beholder' (Laidler, 1981, p.1). Nevertheless, Laidler indicates that in his view the four key characteristics of monetarism are:

(1) a 'quantity theory' approach to the demand for money and a belief that 'fluctuations in the quantity of money are the *dominant* cause of fluctuations in money income' (ibid., italics added),
(2) a vertical long-run *Phillips* curve,
(3) a monetary approach to the balance of payments, and
(4) antipathy to any activist stabilization policy, and support for long-run policy rules for the target level of some monetary aggregate rather than the level of interest rates.

Since category (1) is as Laidler emphasizes 'the theoretical core of monetarism' (ibid.,) it is important to analyse whether the 'quantity theory' provides a viable theoretical nucleus, or whether it is only an empty shell. If the latter is closer to the truth (as I believe), then monetarism is more of an ideology than a theoretical construct and any attention economists pay to it makes them more like members of the priesthood than a community of scholars.

At various places over the years, I have analysed various theoretical deficiences in monetarist theory (Davidson, 1972; 1974; 1978; 1980a; 1980b). Here I wish to explore a flaw in a fundamental and well-known tenet of monetarism – namely, the belief that expectations of inflation

* *Kredit und Kapital*, vol. 14, 1981.

:reate a meaningful *ex ante* difference between the 'real' and 'money' rate
of interest. To Keynes (1936, p. 142), on the other hand, and to Post
Keynesians, the concept of the interest rate (as opposed to the marginal
efficiency of real goods) is always solely a monetary phenomenon in any
entrepreneurial economy which utilizes spot and forward money contracts
to organize exchange and production processes.

1 INFLATION EXPECTATIONS AND THE QUANTITY THEORY

Laidler notes that in Friedman's celebrated essay on the quantity of money
(1956), Friedman

> abstracted from any specific characteristics money might have because it
> is a financial asset; Friedman treated money instead 'as if' a service
> yielding consumer durables to which the permanent income hypothesis
> of consumption could be applied . . . Friedman explicitly recognized
> inflation as an own rate of return on money and postulated a well
> determined functional relationship between the expected inflation rate
> and the demand for money. (Laidler, 1981, p. 3)

This particular monetarist function relating expectations of future inflation and the market rate of interest is basic to the monetarist–rational
expectation-supply-side theories of conservative governments such as
Mrs Thatcher's and President Reagan's. In essence, this view holds that
current high market interest rates are a result of inflationary expectations
and not a cause of inflation (even though interest rates are a cost of doing
business in all entrepreneurial economies); *ergo* a lowering in the expected
rate of inflation will, *ceteris paribus*, reduce the high interest rates currently
plaguing Western capitalist countries. The argument asserts that potential
lenders (savers?) who are currently holding money balances will not make
any loans unless they are compensated for the real rate of interest (i.e. the
nominal rate of interest that would prevail in the absence of any inflation)
plus an inflation premium equal to the (rationally?) expected rate of
inflation.

Keynes specifically denied the validity of this monetarist argument
(Keynes, 1936, p. 142; 1973, p. 518). Harrod similarly held that 'the
occurence of a new-found belief firmly held, that a certain rate of inflation
will occur cannot affect the rate of interest' (Harrod, 1970, p. 62). Thus
there is a fundamental and irreconcilable conflict about the effect of
expectations of inflation on interest rates between Monetarists and Keynes
and his Post Keynesian disciples. This difference has important implications for the use of monetary policy as an anti-inflationary device.

2 MONETARISM, INFLATION HEDGES, AND THE RATE OF INTEREST

The theoretical validity of the Post Keynesian view can be developed vi
the following analysis:

Suppose we compare two economies, α and β, alike in all respects excep
in the α economy there is no inflationary expectation, while suddenly a
time t_0, in the β economy all lenders possess (homogeneous and rational?
expectations of say 15 per cent inflation in the foreseeable future. If th
nominal rate of interest (= the real rate) in the α economy is 5 per cent
then it is argued that lenders in β will not lend their money if the interes
rate is less than 20 per cent; 5 per cent of which is a real rate and 15 per cen
is the inflation premium.

The rationale for this alleged monetarist behaviour in the economy wa
originally developed by Fisher (1911) who argued that if $100 was worth
100 apples at the *current* (t_0) spot price, then a lender might be willing to
lend at 5 per cent if there was no inflationary expectation, so that at the end
of a year he received purchasing power equal to 105 apples. If, however
the lender expected a year from today $100 would only purchase 85 apples
(15 per cent expected inflation), then the lender would be willing to lend
only at a 20 per cent nominal rate so that one year from today the $120
maturity value of the bond would be expected to buy 105 apples (and hence
the *ex ante* real rate of interest would still be 5 per cent).

But, what alternative to lending their money holdings do lenders with
inflationary expectations in the β economy have at time t_0? If they hold
their money for the year, then it will be expected to lose purchasing power
at a 15 per cent rate; whereas if they lend it at 5 per cent they can expect to
lose purchasing power at only a 10 per cent rate (for they could buy 90
apples a year from today with the $105 maturity value of the bond). Would
not lending at 5 per cent still be just as preferable to holding cash,
therefore, when inflationary expectations suddenly occur?

The monetarist response to this query must be that in the β economy,
potential lenders at time t_0 would neither hold cash nor lend it at nominal
rates below 20 per cent. Instead, it would be claimed, these potential
lenders in β (as opposed to those in α) would be induced by their
new-found and widely held inflationary expectations to increase their
purchases of durables commodities (e.g. real estate, precious metals, etc.)
as hedges against inflation. In other words, potential lenders (savers?) in β
will increase their demand for the existing stocks of durables (*vis-à-vis* the
demand in α) whose spot (resale) price (net of carrying costs) is expected
to keep pace with the rate of inflation. This hypothesized induced additional demand (outward shift in the demand curve) for existing durables
will be the result of lenders desiring to use resaleable durables as a
'temporary abode of purchasing power' (to use Friedman's terminology)

instead of holding cash or purchasing negotiable bonds as long as the interest rate on bonds is less than 20 per cent. [If commodity durables are to be held for liquidity purposes, i.e. as temporary abodes of purchasing power, however, their carrying costs must be low and they must be readily resaleable in spot markets. Any durable which cannot be resold because there is no well-organized spot market for it will not be a hedge against inflation and hence will be shunned by savers in β.]

What will be the effect of this increased demand for existing durables when this hypothesized demand increase is due to widely held expectations of inflation originating at time t_0 in the β economy? The increase in demand for goods that are hedges against inflation (which will be concentrated on non-readily reproducible durables such as land, gold, Old Masters, etc.) implies that the spot (Marshallian market) price of these items at t_0 will instantaneously be higher than the equivalent spot prices in α. These higher spot prices in β are a reflection of the fully (and rationally) antici- pated inflation expected by the entire β community, including those who possessed legal title to these pre-existing durables in β at the moment before t_0. Thus, the original holders of the existing durables have a potential capital gain (as compared to the original holders in α); any lender in β who decides to buy a durable rather than a 5 per cent bond will discover that the spot 'prices of existing goods will be forthwith so adjusted that the advantages of holding money and of holding goods are again equalized, and it will be too late for holders of money to gain or to suffer a change in the rate of interest which will offset the prospective change during the period of the loan of the money lent' (Keynes, 1936, p. 142). In other words, the original holders of durables will receive a windfall increase in the capital value of their holding. If inflationary expectations fully anticipate' the future, the potential lenders in β will find that when the spot market of all durables opens on the morning of t_0, the opening offer prices already reflect the rational expectations of inflation of the economic agents in β.

In any monetarist model, as Laidler and Parkin explained in their famous Survey of Inflation article (1975): (a) expectations 'are usually treated as if held with certainty, or it is assumed that any variance in expectations does not influence behavior' (p. 795); while (b) monetarist concepts such as the natural rate of unemployment require the assumption of a 'fully anticipated' future rate of inflation – while the future 'can only be perfectly anticipated if all people hold the same expectations since other- wise some expectations are bound to be wrong' (p. 743). Thus, the monetarist theory of real versus nominal interest rates is mired in its own logical mudhole. If the expectations of inflation in β which create the difference between the money and real interest rates do 'fully anticipate' the future and are widely held (or at least any variance in expectations about future rates of inflation do not affect behaviour given the rational expected rate of price increase) as monetarist doctrine claims, then existing durables can never be a better hedge against inflation than bonds and/or money! The original holders of existing durables form the same expectations (at least on average) as do lenders and the rest of the public at the same moment in t_0. Consequently, the original holders of durables in the β economy will increase their reservation demand price (i.e. they will become as bearish on holding money as a store of value) at exactly the same instant in t_0 as the hypothetical original lenders do. Thus, the holding of money versus bonds versus other durables will again be equalized in the β economy as in the α economy without even a single transaction having to occur, as all spot (offer) prices adjust simultaneously. It will therefore be too late for competitive lenders of money in β to demand an inflation premium on loans when they suddenly form inflationary expectations. The holders of money at t_0 in the β economy will have no better alternative but to continue to lend the money out over time at the same rate as in α as long as the Monetary Authority in β increased the nominal supply *pari passu* with any increase demand in nominal transactions balances (for normal purchases) as the money prices of goods actually purchased rise over time.

In sum, a newly formed expectation of inflation in a monetarist world of rational expectational formation cannot affect the rate of interest. Of course, in the real world any sudden growth of uncertainty (nonpredictability) about what the future rate of inflation is can affect the nominal rate of interest. The interest rate in β can be higher than in α at t_0, if new expectations of inflation in β create a growth of uncertainty about the future and its many economic imponderables: uncertainty as to the rate of change in prices; uncertainty as to when governments, under monetarists' pressure, will restrict nominal money supply's growth and change government spending and tax policy; and, in an open economy, uncertainties as to when speculative flows by others among various currencies will affect exchange rates. In β where the uncertainties about the future are multiplied compared to α, then there can be a growth in the desire of the public to stay more liquid (than in α); for he who hesitates in the face of greater uncertainty is saved to make a binding (not recontractable) commitment another day. Thus the public in β may demand, *ceteris paribus*, a greater liquidity premium for giving up money because of greater uncertainty about the future, even if everyone in β is convinced that holding money over time results in a negative return on money (compared to a zero return on holding money in α) as the β price level is expected to rise.

To recapitulate, widely held, rational expectations of a positive rate of inflation, even if they fully and efficiently anticipate the future, cannot, in themselves, increase the rate of interest compared to an expectational state of zero per cent price level change. Of course, as Harrod noted, 'Uncertainty about whether they [prices] will rise and by how much can send up the rate of interest by making a larger number of people want to remain liquid in respect of a large proportion of their assets for the time being' (Harrod, 1970, p. 63).

3 INFLATIONARY EXPECTATIONS, REPRODUCIBLE ASSETS AND THE MARGINAL EFFICIENCY OF CAPITAL GOODS

Let us extend the comparison of α and β economies further to the analysis of the demand for readily reproducible durables such as investment goods. The creation of inflationary expectations at time t_0 in the β economy can have the *ceteris paribus* effect of stimulating the rate of investment in β compared to α.

The investment evaluating equation in each economy will be:

in the
$$\alpha \text{ economy: } SP \, t_0 = \frac{A_1}{(1 + r_\alpha)} + \frac{A_2}{(1 + r_\alpha)^2} + \dots + \frac{A_n}{(1 + r_\alpha)^n} \quad (1)$$

in the
$$\beta \text{ economy: } SP \, t_0 = \frac{\lambda_1 A_1}{(1 + r_\beta)} + \frac{\lambda_2 A_2}{(1 + r_\beta)^2} + \dots + \frac{\lambda_n A_n}{(1 + r_\beta)^2} \quad (2)$$

where SP is the supply price or cost of production of plant and equipment (assumed the same for any investment flow in α and β) at time t_0

A_1, A_2	expected difference between total revenue and total operating cost on new equipment in period 1, 2 . . . in the α economy
λ_1, λ_2	expected (change in) price level in β economy in period 1, 2 . . .
$\lambda_1 A_1, \lambda_2 A_2$	expected difference between money revenues and operating expenses on new equipment in period 1, 2 . . . in β economy
r_α	marginal efficiency of new capital goods in α economy at t_0
r_β	marginal efficiency of new capital goods in β economy at t_0

By the usual arguments, investment at t_0 will be carried out to the point where:

$i = r_\alpha$ in the α economy, and
$i = r_\beta$ in the β economy

where i is equal to the nominal rate of interest at time t_0. It follows from comparing equations (1) and (2) that to the extent expectations of inflation at t_0 increase the expected net money income stream in the future in β

(compared to α), given (by assumption) the same costs of producing capital goods at t_0 in both economies, and the same nominal interest rate, then investment and output will be stimulated in β as compared to α.

> If the rate of interest were to rise pari passu with the marginal efficiency of capital there would be no stimulating effect from the expectation of rising prices . . . Indeed Professor Fisher's theory could be best re-written in terms of a "real rate of interest" defined as being the [nominal] rate which would have to rule, consequently on a change in the state of expectations as to the future value of money, in order that this change should have no effect on current output. (Keynes, 1936, p. 143)

In other words, from a Post Keynesian view the monetarist argument that nominal rates rose sufficiently to provide the 'correct' inflation premium to keep the real rate of interest the same in α and β would be a theory of how much nominal rates would have to rise, *ceteris paribus*, so that there was no stimulus to the expansion of the capital stock due to inflationary expectations *vis-à-vis* a non-inflationary expectations situation. Thus, for those monetarists who advocate supply-side (or 'incentive') economic policies to encourage more rapid capital accumulation (and therefore eliminate stagnation tendencies), to be logically correct they should be encouraging expectations of even greater rates of inflation in the future while simultaneously recommending lower nominal interest rates today. We will be living in interesting times when we find monetarist economists abandoning their current ideology which requires constraining the growth in some (any) monetary aggregate, and ignoring the level of market interest rates, and following the logical results of their inflation expectation analysis as developed herein!

References

Davidson, P. (1972, 1978), *Money and the Real World* (1st edn 1972, 2nd edn 1978) (London: Macmillan).
Davidson, P. (1974), 'A Keynesian View of Friedman's Theoretical Framework for Monetary Analysis', in *Milton Friedman's Monetary Framework: A Debate with His Critics* edited by R. J. Gordon (Chicago: University of Chicago Press) (Chapter 8 in this volume).
Davidson, P. (1980a), 'The Dual Faceted Nature of the Keynesian Revolution: The Role of Money and Money Wages in Determining Unemployment and Production Flow Prices', *Journal of Post Keynesian Economics*, 2 (Spring).
Davidson, P. (1980b), 'Post Keynesian Economics: Solving the Crisis in Economic Theory', *The Public Interest*, special issue.
Fisher, I. (1911), *The Purchasing Power of Money* (New York: Macmillan).
Friedman, M. (1956), 'The Quantity Theory of Money: A Restatement', in *Studies*

in the *Quantity Theory of Money*, edited by M. Friedman (Chicago: University of Chicago Press).

Harrod, R. F. (1970), 'Discussion Paper', in *Monetary Theory and Policy in the 1970's*, edited by G. Clayton *et al.* (Oxford: Oxford University Press).

Keynes, J. M. (1936), *The General Theory of Employment, Interest and Money* (New York: Harcourt).

Keynes, J. M. (1973), *The Collected Writings of J. M. Keynes*, Volume XIII edited by D. Moggridge (London: Macmillan).

Laidler, D. (1981), 'Monetarism: An Interpretation and an Assessment', *Economic Journal*, 91.

Laidler, D. and M. Parkin (1975), 'Inflation – A Survey', *Economic Journal*, 85.

19 Monetarism and Reaganomics*

Despite the prolonged existence of idle plant and heavy unemployment among a literate, trained labour force, the United States seems unable to mobilize these resources to rebuild our decaying cities, to revitalize mass transit, to regenerate clear air and waterways, and so on. Why are we so impotent? Conventional wisdom suggests that any mobilization of idle resources for a war on such things as decay, pollution, poverty will require either additional government expenditures or private sector tax cuts. This means huge deficits financed by increasing the quantity of money which, monetarists claim, can only fuel the fires of inflation. Until we tame the dragon of inflation, we are told, these projects – no matter how desirable – must wait. Conventional wisdom says we must stoically accept tight money and stringent constraint on governmental spending for many years (the long run?) if inflation is to be stopped.

Five times since the Second World War, the United States has evoked the conventional restrictive monetary approach and restraints on government spending to fight inflation. Each time a recession followed the medicine; each slowdown was worse than the one preceding it. Moreover, even when the rate of price increase slowed in a recessionary pause, the expansion that followed brought an even higher underlying rate of inflation than the previous period of growth. In other words, tight money and recession were a temporary palliative, while the inflationary temperature jogged its long-term upward trend.

The philosopher Santayana once said, 'Those who do not study history are destined to repeat its errors.' Are our policy-makers in Washington so foolish that they have not learned the lessons of history and are therefore dooming us to repeat its errors? I think not. Policy-makers are trapped by pre-Keynesian economic theories which have little applicability to a modern entrepreneurial economy. Politicians know that tight money and fiscal policies cannot succeed; nevertheless, 'worldly wisdom teaches that it is better for reputation to fail conventionally than to succeed unconventionally'.[1] And, for politicians, reputation is everything.

These practical men cannot be blamed entirely for the possibility of economic collapse that awaits us. Conventional economic theory, as espoused by Nobel prize winners in economics, has not provided our politicians with any other course.

* *Reaganomics in the Stagflation Economy*, ed. S. Weintraub and M. Goodstein (University of Pennsylvania Press, 1983).

Adherence to monetarist policies for handling inflation, which now appear to dominate the thinking of the central banks and Western governments, will ultimately result in the breakdown of the capitalist system of financing productive activities by private sector entrepreneurs and/or state and local governments. In the last decade, the monetarist brinksmanship of the Federal Reserve has brought the economy close to the precipice (e.g. the Penn Central, Lockheed, and New York City financial crises). Only at the last moment, when decision-makers felt financial collapse was imminent, did they 'temporarily' abandon monetarist strictures to institute *ad hoc* practical medicines to avoid disaster. Fortunately, our economic system is strong enough to withstand many 'macho' monetarist episodes, but the cumulative effect is to make a permanent solution more difficult. It may already be too late to institute such reforms until the second great economic collapse of the twentieth century is upon us.

Yet history is warning us. At the end of the 1920s, when the quantity theory and the benefits of unfettered market activity dominated economists' writings and provided rationalization for the acts of central bankers and politicians, one after another of the capitalist economies collapsed. It took the revolutionary ideas of Keynes on the workings of a developed monetary economy to provide the guidelines for saving capitalism.

It is instructive to note that pre-Great Depression neoclassical analysis united a supply-side concept – Say's Law of Markets ('Supply creates its own demand') – with the quantity theory of money (which emphasizes limiting the money supply to prevent inflation) and the gold standard to establish full employment without inflation. Exactly one week before the stock market crash the world famous monetarist precursor of Milton Friedman, Irving Fisher of Yale, announced that the US economy was marching along a 'permanently high plateau' of economic prosperity. No doubt future historians will note Arthur Laffer, Robert Lucas, Arthur Burns, and Friedman in a similar lemming leadership role today![2]

It is difficult to identify a unique economic, or econometric model, that can symbolize monetarism. One prominent monetarist, David Laidler, has written, 'Like beauty, "monetarism" tends to be in the eye of the beholder.'[3] Having over the years analysed various theoretical deficiencies in monetarist theory,[4] I believe monetarists have adopted Milton Friedman's pragmatic debating philosophy, namely, 'It is very hard to hit a moving target.' Hence, every time a logical or practical deficiency of monetarism is publicly exposed, a new mutant rears its head.

Consequently, at best, one can only attempt to identify various 'unchanging' propositions as monetarist and then check these propositions against Federal Reserve statements and policies under the Reagan administration to see if the Fed is following a truly monetarist drift. We can thereafter evaluate whether the policies and goals are logically compatible (a) with monetarist theory and (b) with real world phenomena.

The four basic identifiable propositions of monetarism are:

1. Inflation is always a monetary phenomenon.
2. There is a conceptual *ex ante* difference between the real and nominal rates of interest.
3. Control of money supply growth at a rate compatible with the long-run growth of real output (exogenously determined by growth in labour force and technology) will impel a real world economy growing at its long-run real rate at market clearing prices without inflation.
4. A monetarist approach to the demand for money involves a belief that 'fluctuations in the quantity of money are *the dominant cause* of fluctuations in money income'.[5]

No one could seriously argue with the first principle enunciated above, for in the absence of a monetary system there could not be any phenomenon known as inflation. Nevertheless, it is my view that propositions 2, 3, and 4 are logically incorrect[6] and/or inappropriate to real world entrepreneurial economies as we know them. (By an entrepreneurial economy I mean an economic system that organizes production and exchange activities on the basis of *forward money contracts*.) Yet these propositions are fundamental to the monetarist tack which Paul Volcker and the Board of Governors have adopted ever since late 1979, when they smelled the victory of monetarism in the political wind. No wonder recent monetarist policy has been the disaster which now threatens the viability of basic financial institutions in our real world entrepreneurial system.

Volcker, in testimony before Congressional committees, public speeches, and so on, reiterates the 'technical aspects of monetary policy and our numerical targets for the various monetary aggregates', as if inflation can be harnessed *if and only* if the Federal Reserve would 'avoid excessive growth in money and credit'.[7] Apparently Volcker, under the watchful eye of Beryl Sprinkel and the Shadow Open Market Committee, like Margaret Thatcher in the United Kingdom, would be willing to tolerate unemployment rates of 12 per cent plus tidal waves of business bankruptcies as the necessary medicine that must be swallowed to achieve the long-run cure for our inflation malaise. After all, Volcker's job and pension are secure, and the Federal Reserve, as a non-profit organization, need not fear going bankrupt. Unfortunately, only when their jobs are in jeopardy do politicians abandon the puritanical medicine of monetarism – as President Richard Nixon and Prime Minister Edward Heath did in the early 1970s and as President Ronald Reagan and Prime Minister Thatcher are likely to do by 1983. By then, however, heavy damage and ugly scars will remain as a recurrent reminder of monetarist sawbones hacking away at capitalism's body.

In fact, those in Washington who are worrying about the employment of

Republican Congressmen and Senators after November 1982, such as Treasury Secretary Donald Regan and Council of Economic Advisors Chairperson Murray Weidenbaum, have already complained publicly that perhaps the Federal Reserve has already been too successful in its monetarist operation on the US economy. Weidenbaum, in an address to the walking wounded of the National Association of Savings Banks, was quoted by Leonard Silk in the *New York Times*, 16 September 1981, as declaring that an increase in the annual rate of growth of the money supply 'should not be viewed as alarming, even though individual month-to-month increases may appear at first blush to be excessive to the untrained observer'. Obviously, excessive growth of the money supply, like true beauty, is only to be revealed to the trained observer! What we need, apparently, is a Pavlovian training for market observers. But who gets to ring the bell?

There are only two basic (with many variants) competing anti-incomes inflation policies being advocated – one by neoclassical theory, one by Post Keynesian analysis. The traditional conservative analysis calls for restrictive monetary and fiscal policy – what Friedman calls 'bullet-biting' – which so impoverishes the economy that it cannot be held up for economic blackmail by powerful subgroups who are attempting to gain more of the national product for themselves. Thatcherism is symptomatic of this painful medicine offered to the unions in the United Kingdom. Monetarist Mach II, alias rational expectations theorists, however, have held out the hope that just the threat of such a painful medicine will be sufficient to achieve a painless remedy to incomes inflation in the United States. These 'supply-side' nostrum peddlers suggest that inflation can be stopped by merely announcing that the Reagan administration will have a tight monetary and fiscal policy and, like Margaret Thatcher, permit people to price themselves out of the market if they insist on raising wages and profit margins. If the unions and management believe Reagan, Regan, and Stockman, it is claimed, then 'rational expectations' will prevail as everyone recognizes that everyone else will stop asking for inflationary wage and profit margin increases, and inflation will stop dead in its tracks without the punishing depression of Thatcherism. (If you believe in this scenario, you probably believe in the Good Tooth Fairy.)

What is so odd about the current political–economic scene in Washington is the entertainment as gospel of the inane utterances of supply side gurus such as Laffer well after evidence has proved his previous locutions false. In the upside-down world of Reaganomics and the financial press, nothing succeeds like failure – everyone is too polite to remark that these supply-side impresarios are without clothes. (Apparently, blunt truths on official mandarins are hazardous to reporters. Readership is titillated by a serialization of fictional events which always rescue the economic damsel in distress – as in the fabled 'Perils of Pauline'. Limit the financial press to checking the official assertions against the unfolding facts, diagnosing the theories, and publications such as *Business Week* could scarcely survive even as a biennial issue, let alone a weekly!)

Recall that in the spring of 1981 the Laffer curve assured one and all that a reduction in marginal tax rates (even without any cut in government spending) would significantly reduce, even eliminate, the pending deficits of 1982, 1983, and 1984, while simultaneously stimulating enough gross national product activity to end stagflation – despite a lack of supporting evidence. Never mind the fact that upon coming into office in May 1979, Margaret Thatcher immediately slashed the higher marginal tax rates of the wealthy (by even more than was contemplated in the original Kemp- -Roth bill) and plunged the United Kingdom into the worst depression since the 1930s while her government deficits ballooned. Late 1981 saw Budget Director David Stockman confessing to the wild supply-sider deficit assertions as utterly lacking in original substantiation, as a $100 billion deficit mocked the promises of the Reagan people for 1982.

Summer is often dubbed the season of 'crazies' by reporters, and therefore it is possible to explain the Reagan budget and tax victories in Congress in July 1981. But the autumn (1981) cool shows the economy still ticking historically high inflation rates while activity tumbles as a result of the Federal Reserve's tight money policy and Reagan's budget attempts to 'get the government off our backs'. For the minor slowdown in the inflation rate since President Reagan took office, we must certainly remember to thank the Organization of Petroleum Exporting Countries (OPEC), as it pauses to catch its breath after its whirlwind increase in oil prices in 1979–80, rather than the Reaganomic budget which became effective only on 1 October 1981 and scarcely could have accomplished the inflation slowdown last spring (1981). Moreover, high nominal interest rates (and historically high real rates) still plague the economy despite monetary dogma which asserts that a *constant* real rate should have led to falling nominal rates as actual inflation declines and rational expectations conditioned by Reagan Congressional victories reduced the inflation premium in nominal rates even further.

But in 1981 autumn's early light it is evident that enormous deficits loom ahead despite the airy Laffer curve and that nominal interest rates will not decline until the Federal Reserve actively increases bank reserves sufficiently, no matter what the public's (rational?) expectations on future inflation. If I were a subscriber to a belief of 'rational' behaviour on the part of independent economic and political decision-making agents, I would think that recent events which indicated continuing and *increasing* deficits, and high nominal interest rates, would be sufficient for the market-place of ideas to bury the Laffer curve theorists and the real versus nominal monetarists in the Rube Goldberg cemetery for crackpot inventions.

Instead, supposedly serious economic publications such as *Business*

Week (e.g. 21 September 1981, pp. 114–20) continue to peddle and provide an aura of pseudo-credibility to the latest gibberings of the Laffers, namely, the need to reinstitute a gold standard to stabilize the purchasing power of money so as, according to Laffer, to 'dramatically change inflationary expectations'. Apparently, the greater the previous error in your prognosis, the more *Business Week* assigns current credibility, and therefore the greater fees the gurus can command from the lecture circuit. Apparently, 'failing conventionally' does, as Keynes suggested many years ago, pass the market test – especially if your failures are wrapped in a trickle-down format designed to redistribute more income to the most wealthy in the resulting impoverished community.

Monetarism Mach II, in its rational expectations armour, instantaneously market clearing twaddle, and bombastic mathematical pretensions demonstrates how economists are able to foist a horrendous superstructure based on wholly absurd assumptions on the gullible economics profession while pandering to the lecture market circuit (normally bankrolled by wealthy special-interest groups). Lucas monetarists and Laffer supply-siders join curiously in the rational expectation hypothesis that active monetarist (and fiscal) policy lacks ability to stabilize jobs and output. If the public swallows this pap with its 'rigorous' mathematical wrappings as high thought, then the Federal Reserve is relieved of all responsibility if it fails to stabilize employment or to stop inflation or the resulting skewness in income inequality. Ah, then the golden vision of a pure gold standard can be promised as the miracle cure in lieu of the Federal Reserve monetary authority, whose activities merely exacerbate our problems!

In the real world of entrepreneurial economies, however, as Friedman notes, returning to the gold standard is not a painless way of controlling inflation. *Business Week* (21 September 1981, p. 115) quotes Friedman as stating: 'In order to stabilize prices you will have to go through a recession. That has been the experience of most countries that have stopped inflation. If it is not politically possible to accept that cure without a gold standard, it will not be possible to do it with a gold standard.'

In sum, then, Monetarism Mach II, including its occasionally deviant but equally conservative rational expectations and supply-side wings, insists that if government announces an anti-inflationary policy – in some memory of Senator George Atken's spoof policy on Vietnam – and simultaneously rewards the wealthy first, then each of us will adopt a congenial 'rational expectations' to trust your neighborhood plumber, oil company, landlord, and so on not to raise his price if you do not raise yours. Friedman, in his Monetarism Mach I model, maintained a more familiar nineteenth-century 'liberal' approach – an approach more properly labelled 'economic Darwinism'. For the more traditional Friedman monetarists, once inflation has become widespread the cure for those whose inordinate wage and price demands are symptoms of the inflationary disease must come through economic deprivation, starvation, and even economic death via bankruptcy!

Friedman's statement, however, does imply that the ultimate cure for inflation rests on a political basis. Hence, enlightened twentieth-century social democratic nations should recognize that there are viable political alternatives to Friedman's nineteenth-century economic Darwinism, or the Laffer–Lucas twentieth-century version of Alice in Walrasland. One plausible alternative would involve a National Policy to Coordinate Income Claims (NPCIC) to assure each agent that there will be an equality of sacrifice when economic events are unfavourable and an equality in sharing of gains when our economy is prosperous. In other words, the economy must develop a policy to supplant the current Darwinian free market struggle for income shares which is the primary cause of our current inflation problems; the present arrangement is not endemic to entrepreneurial systems. Just as society encourages fair and efficient traffic flows by a judicial system which extracts penalties (related to the severity of the offense) for drivers who violate well-defined traffic laws, so we must develop institutions to provide a fair and efficient income shake to make sure that the aggregation of our individual income claims does not total more than 100 per cent of available real income. If the public was educated to the need for and objectives of a well-designed legal system for coordinating income claims, there could be overall compliance by a law-abiding people. Hence, the creation of an institution to carry out a fair NPCIC (such as a well-designed tax-based incomes policy) would immediately create an environment where success – without significant deprivation – could be assured.

No civilized nation leaves the decision about which side of the road to drive on to individual free choice, to see who is 'chicken' as cars approach each other and each driver tries to intimidate the other in determining who is 'king of the road'. Yet 'free marketeers' endure a similar process of intimidation and dominance for determining the distribution of income, under the guise of free market libertarianism. But just as war is too important to be left to the generals, income distribution is too important to be left to the god of unfettered markets to resolve. One would have hoped that the worship of Social Darwinistic determination of the distribution of income would have been long abandoned when we learned that cooperation under society's laws of contract – rather than plunder – was a better design for dominating transactions in a civilized society.

Adoption of a NPCIC does *not* mean that income must be distributed equally. There are social, economic, and psychological justifications for significant inequalities of income and wealth. The task is to manage human nature and the desire for income, not to transmute these desires. Enterprise and the production of desirable goods and services are the props of society, and most citizens would recognize that those who contribute most are deserving of a somewhat larger share and that each one's share is determined by some equitable and clear rules of the game, allowing for anyone who feels aggrieved by the current rules to have a day in court. If instead the rules of the game for the distribution of income are such that each *expects* the other to grab as much as he can without consideration of others, and therefore *expectations* are generated that there may not be enough to go around, then a mortal blow will be thrust at our entrepreneurial society because it would damage the psychological expectational equilibrium tolerating the societal acceptance of unequal economic rewards within the available output of a zero sum society.

Why then do most politicians and businessmen appear to support economically restrictive monetarist policies in their public oratory, rather than a permanent incomes policy? First, they are never told and they are never clear that the object of the restrictive policies is to involve business firms in losses and our people in unemployment. If they were told this and they still chose restrictive policies, they would have forfeited their right to complain when these results ensue; they would be voted out as either the impoverished electorate or the bankruptcy courts removed them from office. Instead, restrictive policies are always presented as if only *others* – painted as more greedy than your own group – will suffer! Second, and more important, with the development of industrial markets and the percolation of the democratic ethos through society, each group believes that it can, and has the right to, insulate itself against the market forces unleashed by restrictive policies and thereby to shift the burden to others. As Kenneth Galbraith has forcefully argued, with the growth of industrial society and democracy people have learned that they can, and should, attempt to control their own destinies.[8] If you can gain control of your income, then your fate is largely in your own hands. Galbraith indicates that there are three ways people can attempt to control their own income: (1) develop a unique marketable qualification, that is, establish a monopoly position; (2) organize with others who have similar market capacities in order to exercise some joint monopoly control; and finally, if market power still eludes such groups, (3) organize and employ political activities to tilt government policy toward augmenting your income. Thus, 'poor' farmers, poor people, senior citizens, rich and poor corporations, educational institutions, labour unions, and so on, each in turn march on Washington, and a lobbying industry grows and enriches itself.

These developments are permanent; we cannot return to the nineteenth century, when the ordinary person accepted his income as part of his kismet, beyond his control, believing that poverty on earth could be redressed by heavenly rewards. Today we must employ the democratic processes to work out a 'social contract' which permits the equitable sharing of an economic pie that is growing at its maximum potential.

In an economy when strong social and political forces have already gained control of the money costs of production, the power over the domestic price level has passed beyond the levers of the central bank, or the Office of Budget Management. The firm of Reagan, Regan, and Stockman can attempt to unleash recessionary forces to put 'labour' back in its place, that is, to induce future changes in money-wages relative to productivity so as to soften the future inflationary process. Even if such oppressive measures turn out successful, Reagan, Regan, and Stockman cannot control the pace or the route of the journey to the new era of 'non-inflationary expectations'. The path will be long and dreary, and our mainly enterprise economy, if it survives, will be the poorer for the experience. Luck alone cannot prevail for very long against the exactions of OPEC, internationally, and the uncoordinated domestic demands of unions, firms, and ordinary citizens for bigger shares of the gross national product.

Monetary policy and Reagan, Regan, and Stockman, with or without the always-subject-to-change vagaries of 'supply-side economics', are singularly ill-adapted for preventing domestic incomes inflation, for they cannot directly influence the major costs of production of reproducible goods. On this premise there is no viable set of options for any modern capitalist society which relies upon cooperation among the factors of production for its national production. As the private flow of long-duration money contracts breaks down and each group demands more rapid income increases, and we leapfrog over one another on our treadmill to higher money incomes, our society must either collapse or enter into a social contract to re-establish the 'rules of the capitalist game' – a game in which sticky money-wages and price contracts over a long future are at the core.

In keeping with the game analogy, it should be noted that President Jimmy Carter had likened the current incomes–inflation problem to a crowd at a sporting event – all standing on tiptoe to get a better view. The result is no better view, but instead aching leg muscles for all, with survival for the tallest. All would be better off if there was a permanent rule, equitably enforced, requiring everyone to sit down. Any temporary rule or any restrictive policy which reduced the tempo of the game *might* provide temporary relief as the crowd relaxed, but the throngs would be on their feet again at the next flurry of activity.

Why is a permanent incomes policy (or PIP) feared? For three reasons: (1) the uncertainty associated with anything new, (2) PIP may subsidize inefficiency (in others) by penalizing the productive and the skilled (i.e. me), and (3) by permanently freezing relative prices, resource misallocation creating greater economic losses than would otherwise occur.

The third fear is not well founded since (a) restrictive policies create worse economic losses and incite social conflicts and (b) incomes policies can be designed to permit relative price changes and/or resource reallocation as desired. The first and second fears contain substance; hence policy solutions must not only be developed upon correct economic analysis, but must also be designed in a form that is politically acceptable and encourages compliance. Economists can provide politicians with guidelines for being 'good', but it will also require the services of political scientists, social psychologists, and opinion research specialists to tell politicians how to be clever.

In sum, then, in twentieth-century entrepreneurial economies, central banks no longer have the power to control the price level (if they ever had). Unions, oligopolies, multinational corporations, international cartels, governments, and other groups who have positions of strong economic and political power share responsibility for our stagflation malaise.[9] Monetary policy cannot directly affect this distribution of power which, without any constrained legal rules in the capitalist game, is free to make excessive and incompatible claims on the gross income of modern economies. A democratically determined incomes policy, which coordinates claims to the maximum potential output of society, is the only *civilized* solution to this second great crisis of capitalism. It is in the vested interest of all groups to support such a policy, for as Benjamin Franklin noted, in an interconnected interdependent society 'We must all hang together or we will all hang separately.'

Notes

1. John M. Keynes, *The General Theory of Employment, Interest and Money* (New York: Harcourt, 1936), p. 58.
2. Since the latter two are associated with Rutgers University (Friedman as an undergraduate mathematics major was introduced to economics by Arthur Burns, who was his instructor at Rutgers), Post Keynesians at Rutgers today bear an extra burden in trying to set economic theory and policy right!
3. David Laidler, 'Monetarism: An Interpretation and an Assessment', *Economic Journal*, 91 (1981), p. 1.
4. Cf. Paul Davidson, *Money and the Real World* (London: Macmillan, 1972; 2d edn, 1978); 'A Keynesian View of Friedman's Theoretical Framework for Monetary Analysis', in R. J. Gordon (ed), *Milton Friedman's Monetary Framework: A Debate with His Critics* (Chicago: University of Chicago Press, 1974); 'The Dual-Faceted Nature of the Keynesian Revolution: The Role of Money and Money Wages in Determining Unemployment and Production Flow Prices', *Journal of Post Keynesian Economics*, 2 (Spring 1980), pp. 291–307; 'Post Keynesian Economics: Solving the Crisis in Economic Theory', (1980), pp. 151–73, *The Public Interest*, special issue; Paul Davidson and Sidney Weintraub, 'Money as Cause and Effect', *Economic Journal*, 83 (December 1973), pp. 1117–32.
5. Laidler, 'Monetarism'. Italics added.
6. In an appendix omitted in final publication, I demonstrated that proposition 2 is logically flawed. Propositions 3 and 4 have been demonstrated to be faulty in Davidson, *Money and the Real World*; Davidson and Weintraub, 'Money as

Cause and Effect'; and Davidson, 'The Dual-Faceted Nature'.

7. Paul A. Volcker, 'Prepared Statement Before US Committee on Banking, Finance and Urban Affairs', House of Representatives, 21 July 1981, p. 13.

8. John K. Galbraith, 'On Post Keynesian Economics', *Journal of Post Keynesian Economics*, 1 (Fall 1978), pp. 8–11.

9. Monetary policy cannot and should not exogenously 'control' some arbitrary and vague aggregate known as 'the' money supply. An endogenous money supply is a necessary institutional arrangement to ease financing of economic growth. Monetary policy can and should affect the spot prices of bonds (the rate of interest) and other liquid assets (e.g. foreign exchange, commercial paper) in such a way as to avoid any potential shortages of liquidity which threaten the growth of real output and employment. See the works cited in note 6.

20 Why Deficits Hardly Matter*

The conventional economic wisdom being dispensed this election year by Democrats and Republicans alike is that the current size of the Federal deficit is ruining our nation's economic health. In the past deficits might have been useful, we are told, but in 1984 our rising debt is 'bad governmental policy' because:

1. We are approaching full production capacity (even with 7.5 per cent unemployment?).
2. It is being financed by excessive monetary expansion and is therefore inflationary.
3. It is absorbing half of net savings and hence is reducing productive capital formation.
4. The resulting high interest rates are necessary to shield the economy from inflation.
5. Foreigners who buy US Treasury bonds are laying claim to future American wealth.

Thus the conventional wisdom maintains that eliminating the deficit is a top national priority. Blind acceptance of this nineteenth-century sophistry has caused many liberal economists and politicians docilely to concur that entitlement programmes designed to alleviate poverty must be trimmed, and that the US is too poor a country to afford the public works needed to rebuild its decaying cities, bridges, highways, and waterways. Moreover, it is often argued that any additional taxes levied have to be earmarked for deficit reduction so that they will not be diverted to providing useful public goods and services for our citizens.

In truth, a shortage of leadership and will inherited from the Carter administration, not a shortage of resources, has prevented the US from completing the New Deal, Fair Deal and Great Society reforms of the last 50 years. The seeming 'success' of Reaganomics in limiting inflation and restoring economic growth has deflected the media from critically analysing the benefits and costs of the conservative counter-revolution engineered by Ronald Reagan and Federal Reserve Board Chairman Paul Volcker, contributing to the image of the man in the White House as a Teflon President.

* First published in *The New Leader* (20 August 1984).

Stripped of its rhetoric and jingoism, Reaganomics has always had as its basic objective a reversal of the trend over the past half-century towards an expanding government service sector and a more progressive tax and expenditure structure. In the 1980 campaign Reagan was fond of asking, 'Why should the government do a better job of spending your income than you?' Simply by raising the question he was suggesting that individuals had no social responsibility to contribute to the investment in education and community institutions, to aid those in ill health or poverty, beyond what they deemed to be in their own interests.

The popularity of Reaganomics is readily explainable, for it appeals to those unpleasant yet ubiquitous human traits, selfishness and greed. We prefer to imagine the possibility of getting rich, rather than face the reality that, without the help of the community, most of us will remain relatively poor.

Domestically, the New Deal, Fair Deal and Great Society programmes – and, internationally, the Marshall Plan, Aid to Developing Nations, etc. – appealed to our sense of cooperation. In so doing, these undertakings enriched everyone spiritually as well as economically. The historical record indicates that when people join together out of a feeling of kinship and compassion, growth and prosperity for all inevitably follow. Reaganomics, by contrast, has caused a greater disparity between the rich and the poor, and has reduced community services at a pace that, if allowed to continue for the next four years, may result in their regressing to levels where the middle class will virtually disappear.

The ability of Reaganomics to tame inflation is not very difficult to understand either once one abandons conventional wisdom's clichés. Despite the rapid growth of the money supply during the past few years, inflation has not heated up, as Milton Friedman and his fellow monetary economists had warned. This is due to the Reagan–Volcker nineteenth-century-type 'incomes policies', which create slack markets and high unemployment to limit the power of labour and others to force wage and price increases onto buyers. These ancient tactics, based on a philosophy that New York's Governor Mario Cuomo in his keynote address to the Democratic Convention aptly called 'Social Darwinism', have involved the deliberate reduction of aggregate demand to create the worst world-wide recession in a half-century, plus direct union bashing (remember the air traffic controllers).

But no one should pursue low inflation at the price of high unemployment. What is required is the kind of incomes policy Sidney Weintraub advocated in the pages of this magazine during the five years prior to his death in June 1983 – specifically, a tax-based incomes policy, or TIP, that would control production costs and hold down inflation while preventing unemployment. With such a civilized incomes policy, there would be no need for high interest rates to protect us from inflation. The rates could then drop dramatically, reducing the cost of servicing the national debt and consequently helping somewhat to bring down the deficit.

As for the current recovery, it is being sparked by traditional Keynesian manoeuvres to stimulate the components of aggregate demand. The first year of the Reagan tax cut (starting in July 1981) was largely offset by higher Social Security and other levies, but the second and third stages of the tax cut raised real incomes (except for those with very low earnings), stimulating consumer spending and retail sales. Lower business taxes since 1981 increased the after-tax profitability on these additional sales, encouraging more investment. Additional purchases of goods by the government, especially for the military, began to come on stream in significant volume by 1982.

Although still quite high compared with past history, the lower interest rates of the last two years are the result of the Federal Reserve, in its 'lender of last resort' function, deliberately abandoning its monetarist experiment and rapidly expanding the money supply to avoid an impending debt crisis. The decline in interest rates since August 1982 has added to the value of the expected discounted cash flow from new investments, thereby reviving investment expenditures. The present surge in investment spending from its depressed levels of 1979–81 is directly attributable to the August 1982 reversal of monetary policy, just as the Reagan tax cuts were finally improving the after-tax income of employed middle- and upper-income families.

The belief that today's huge government deficits are absorbing too much savings and therefore squeezing out productive investment that otherwise would be occurring might have some validity if the United States, and the rest of the industrialized world, were already at full employment and businessmen were clamouring for more capital goods. Further, only at that point could government deficits be throttled with the hope that private spending would immediately pick up the ensuing slack. Increasing taxes before that state of bliss is achieved would merely slide us back into recession. The extent of the backward slide would be directly related to the amount of tax increase earmarked for deficit reduction.

In these uncertain times, the desire for liquidity is quite high, and net investment is still constrained by the existence of some unused capacity as well as by concern about the profitability of added capital outlays. The problem is not that there has been no increase in investment and consumption since 1982; it is that the stimulating Keynesian policies have not stepped up capital formation and consumer expenditures sufficiently to generate full employment in the US and simultaneously act as the engine for creating full employment abroad. New taxes now would adversely affect any drive towards world-wide full employment.

In sum, the unprecedented deficit is not a symptom of illness in the economy. Quite the contrary, it is the medicine that promoted the robust recovery of 1982–4 and lifted profits from the terrible depths induced by the 1979–82 Volcker monetarist experiment.

Preachers of the conventional wisdom about the danger of deficits forget George Santayana's warning that those who do not study history are doomed to repeat its mistakes. A half-century ago, the conventional wisdom had it that the unprecedented New Deal deficits would bankrupt this country. In the election year of 1936, the government, bending to the warnings, moved vigorously to improve the situation – mainly by (shades of Ronald Reagan) reducing 'unnecessary' government spending. The result was a drastic nine-month plunge in GNP in 1937, matching the rates of decline experienced during the Hoover era.

In this election year of 1984, many prestigious economists are providing similar counsel and suggesting programmes for an immediate reduction in the deficit to head off economic disaster. If followed, however, these prescriptions could make the 1982–5 period a replay of the 1933–7 years.

We would do well to remember that after 1937 (admittedly under the threat of war) the admonitions of conventional wisdom were ignored. By 1945 the annual deficit was approximately 25 per cent of GNP and government spending was roughly 40 per cent of GNP. Even though much of the deficit-financed expenditures were for wholly unconsumable war materials, the fact is that between the mid-1930s and the mid-1940s the US economy was transformed from its depressed condition to a modern cornucopia. The long-term growth in living standards (from the 1940s to the 1960s) was born in the huge deficits of the New Deal and the Second World War. Why must it take calamities like a great depression or a world war to force us to dispense with the conventional wisdom and recognize some obvious economic fundamentals?

Part of the problem may be that because we have not adopted a civilized incomes policy, such as TIP, the high interest rates used to shield us from inflation in tandem with the rapid growth of the deficit have had undesirable side-effects on domestic and international income distribution. The great interest cost on government borrowing has fattened the purses of wealthy residents and foreigners who hold Treasury debt obligations at the expense of middle- and low-income taxpayers. This redistributive effect is not surprising, though, given the Reagan philosophy of 'survival of the wealthiest'.

In any case, despite the huge deficits from 1981 on, the heavens have not fallen. Nor will they fall if we overthrow the conventional wisdom that Federal deficits are inherently bad and moves towards a balanced governmental budget are necessarily good.

President Reagan, who pays homage to that notion and goes so far as to support a balanced budget amendment (which would not take effect until after 1988), has ignored the conventional view in his economic policies aimed at rewarding the rich and starving the public sector, except for the military. As a result, he is the first incumbent since 1964 to face an electorate where the majority appears satisfied with the recent progress of the economy. Indeed, the public's complacency regarding the large government deficit suggests that the average citizen is instinctively more sensible than many politicians running for office, let alone the conventional wisdom of their economic advisers.

21 Financial Markets and Williamson's Theory of Governance: Efficiency Versus Concentration Versus Power*

The orthodox theory of the firm and of markets assumes structural rationality, that is, the organization is capable of the efficient translation of purpose into action. In orthodox analysis the purpose is assumed to be self-evident; for the firm it is to produce goods for the market in order to maximize profits, and for the market it is to bring buyers and sellers together to maximize utility in consumption. The firm and the market are conceived of as 'black boxes' and little analysis is done as to what is happening in those real world black boxes – or even whether the black boxes exist in the real world.

Oliver Williamson has been in the forefront of analysing the black boxes of the real world – and noting that there are many shades of black (that is, organizational variety) – and hence he has partly broken with mainstream theory. His organizational analysis, however, remains firmly within the bounds of expanded orthodox microtheory; where by expanded orthodoxy is meant the dropping of the assumptions of (1) a costless dispersal of information via a Walrasian auctioneer and/or (2) recontracting without penalty, and/or (3) perfect foreknowledge for at least rational expectations based on ergodic processes.

For Williamson, following Adolf Berle and Gardiner Means, managers use their discretion in their own interests, which may be different from the purposes of black-box firms maximizing profits in a world where there are transaction costs. The existence of transaction costs in (1) interpreting market signals, (2) developing markets in the absence of the costless auctioneer, and (3) probing the dark uncertain future, affects real output flows.

Williamson's unifying principle for the study of firms and markets is the economizing of transactions costs (Williamson, 1983, p. 2). This is in contrast to that of J. Kenneth Galbraith where organizational control is not a means to a purpose. Although both Williamson and Galbraith follow the

* *Quarterly Review of Economics and Business*, 24 (Winter). This chapter with Greg Davidson.

lead of Berle and Means, for Galbraith the organization is simply a state of being; in a complex world, decisions involving a complex technology in a complex market cannot be taken by individuals, only by groups. Hence for Galbraith (1967) *social analysis* – rather than behaviourism and marginalism is called for (1984). Management or the technostructure is a class of society like the proletariat, or the leisure class. Like all social classes, the goals of management are associated with prestige in a certain social–historical context; there is, however, no presumption that the organization will effectively pursue the goals that its employees value. The organization does not have goals of its own, only the managers who seek to keep the organization as a going concern and, within that framework, seek their own advantage. The organization per se aspires to nothing, it maximizes nothing.

Williamson, although deviating from strict orthodox theory, does not go nearly so far as Galbraith in this rupture. Williamson instead follows the consensus as expressed by R. W. Solow (1971) that 'it is useful to think of a "typical" firm as maximizing something . . . it may not matter very much exactly what firms are trying to maximize'. Thus the first question one needs to address in assessing whether organization analysis is free of orthodox shackles is whether organizations are a means to a purpose that can be expressed as maximizing or minimizing some truly objective, observable function no matter how varied in its attributes, or whether organizations are a state of being – such as species are in evolutionary biology. This evolutionary biological state does not mean that organizations do not perform functions in their pursuit of everyday living – but it does imply that to understand the organization – as one would understand an organism in a biological study – requires a descriptive analysis of the organic system and its environment. This leads to fundamentally different interpretations of existing human institutions, such as the law of contracts and the existence of financial markets other than those developed by Williamson.

1 WHY CONTRACTS?

Williamson (1983, p. 2) endorses the view of James Buchanan that 'economics comes closer to being a "science of contracts" than a "science of choice" . . . [on which account] the maximizer must be replaced by the arbitrator, the outsider who tries to work out compromises among conflicting claims' (Buchanan, 1975, p. 229). Williamson substitutes an 'institutional design specialist' for the arbitrator for he asserts that 'the object is less to resolve conflict . . . than to recognize potential conflict in advance and devise governance structures which forestall or attenuate it' (ibid., p. 3).

In emphasizing the possibility of future rather than present conflict,

Williamson has put his finger on the issue while never adequately explaining why conflict can occur *after* the signing of a contract that, after all, is 'a meeting of the minds'.

For orthodox economists such as Buchanan, there should be no conflict after a contract is signed. The analysis of the contract curve of the Edgeworth Box logically does not permit such conflict if the future is either perfectly foreseen or if 'rational expectations' are held by both parties. Each party accepts the final contractual agreement as maximizing its expected utility. No future conflicts are to be expected.

Williamson asserts that his 'transactions–cost' economics requires studying contracting not solely or even mainly in *ex ante* terms. This implies that human beings, in their conduct of everyday business in modern, real world economies recognize that all conflicts are not necessarily resolved with the 'meeting-of-the-minds' signing of binding contracts. Thus, as Williamson recognizes, the neoclassical economic person, as a high-powered maximizer given to simple self-interest seeking, cannot be the foundation of an analysis of real world organizations.

Having almost cut himself off from the mainstream economics, Williamson is unwilling to go the final step since he insists that (1) *rationality* and (2) *motivation* still are necessary systematic concepts for explaining organizational behaviour. (A third attribute that Williamson recognizes, but does not systematically integrate into his analysis, is dignity.)

Rather than neoclassical maximizing rationality, Williamson relies on 'bounded rationality'; when he accepts H. A. Simon's theory that economic actors are to be '*intendedly* rational, but only *limitedly* so' (1972, p. xxiv). Williamson embraces bounded rationality for it implies that parties to any transaction will seek out and attempt to implement opportunities to realize efficiencies even though cognitive competence is limited (Williamson, 1983, p. 5).

Interestingly Williamson recognizes an even weaker form of rationality, 'organic rationality', which *he* associates solely with the 'modern evolutionary approach' of the 'Austrian school' and the institutions of money, markets, property rights, and so on. These societal institutions are not planned, they are associated with situations of ignorance. Williamson (1979, p. 6) asserts that the research agenda of 'organic rationality' is different from, but still complementary to, his 'bounded rationality', transactions–cost approach.

Williamson does not cite a similar strand of thought, the Keynes/Post Keynesian view of rationality – or what might be better called 'sensibility', that is, where individuals in organizations recognize that they are facing an *uncertain* and not statistically predictable future, that is, a future where ignorance of the outcome of current actions prevails. In such a non-ergodic world individuals, operating within existing evolutionary organizations, try to form sensible expectations regarding the future.

Time is a device that prevents everything from happening at once. Production and consumption processes take time, and hence, the decision to organize production must occur at an earlier time than the outcome. If the economic world has, or can have, important non-ergodic circumstances associated with it, then the outcome of an economic process can never be forecasted with statistical accuracy at the onset of the process. It is only in a non-ergodic environment, where people recognize that the future may be non-predictable in any stochastic sense, that the sensibility of human beings prevails. Sensible expectations rely on diverse organizations that have evolved to permit human beings to cope with the unknowable. Only in such a world are the attributes of dignity and human motivation necessarily geared *not to rationality* but to sensibility.

For Keynes and the Post Keynesians, non-ergodic circumstances are a necessary condition for the human institutions/organizations of money, contracts, and financial markets. Only in such a world does money affect the real sector in both the short run and the long run. That is, money is not neutral. Thus, it is 'animal spirits – of a spontaneous urge to action rather than inaction' . . . [and not the *rational* calculation (bounded or otherwise) of the] 'outcome of a weighted average of quantitative benefits multiplied by quantitative probabilities' (Keynes, 1936, p. 161) that makes the financial and industrial world go round.

Although lower life-forms enter into organizational structures for the efficient operation of production and consumption activities (for example, herds of elephants, schools of fish, colonies of ants, groups of beavers, and so on), none of these lower animals' activities is driven by 'animal spirits' *interacting* with contracts, money, and marketing institutions to achieve the production and consumption objectives of the species in question. Only homo sapiens, amongst all life-forms, recognizes the passage of calendar time and the fundamental uncertainty of a non-ergodic world. Thus human economic activity has evolved institutions of contracts, money, and so on, in order to be able to 'assure' legal future outcomes in a non-ergodic environment.

In the real world, money is anything that discharges a contractual liability under the civil law of contracts. All contracts are calendar-time-oriented – either spot or forward time-oriented. A spot contract specifies delivery and payment at the instant of signing. A forward contract, although signed today, indicates a specific future date for delivery *and* payment.

Only in a non-ergodic world, where the future is non-predictable, can future conflicts arise after a forward contractual 'meeting of the minds'. When the uncertain future becomes the actual present, some parties to some contractual transactions will discover that they are *unable* or *unwilling* to deliver on their contractual obligations.

Each party to a forward contract recognizes that the other party, *despite possessing good faith at the time of signing of the contract*, may be unable or unwilling to execute the contractual terms at the specified future date. Enforcement via the law of contracts permits each party to have *sensible* expectations that if the other party does not fulfil its obligations, the injured party will be entitled to just compensation. In the real non-ergodic world – unlike the neoclassical ergodic system – recontracting without penalty whenever a buyer or seller has made an error is simply *not* permitted. *Forward contracts for purchase and sale of goods and services are human institutions devised to enforce money, wage, and price controls on future outcomes over the life of the contracts.* Business firms and households abhor what neoclassical economists love – namely, a flexible price system and recontracting without penalty. Contracts, therefore, attenuate potential conflicts by assuring both parties that even if uncertain future events should adversely affect one party's ability to meet its commitments, the other party will have a remedy in law. The law of contracts does not guarantee that conflicts will not occur in an uncertain future, it merely guarantees that the innocent party will not unduly suffer from the conflict *when and if it arises.*

2 MOTIVATION

Williamson distinguishes various forms of self-interest – the strongest being *opportunism* – which includes stealing, cheating, lying, and even deceit. Moreover, Williamson blurs the line between those opportunism attributes that are primarily violations of *criminal* rather than contract law and the use of 'incomplete or distorted disclosure of information' (1983, p. 7). Incomplete information, it is claimed, 'vastly complicates problems of organization by compounding the sources of uncertainty'.

2.1 Governance and Creative Opportunities

Yet in a wider context of law as the governor of acceptable civilized human behaviour, Williamson has raised an important point. He notes the existence of human attributes of what he labels 'self and social regard', but he does not systematically incorporate them into his transactions–cost economics. It is not surprising, therefore, that he sees motivation primarily as a problem of opportunism and the pursuit of self-interest. 'Plainly if it were not for opportunism,' Williamson asserts (ibid.) 'all behaviour could be rule governed.'

Williamson (ibid., p. 5), in his discussion of bounded rationality, equates limited rationality with limited competence. He thus loses sight of the special human abilities of cooperative creativity and constructiveness. Though he seeks governance functions to 'recognize potential conflict in advance and devise governance structures which forestall or attenuate it' (ibid., p. 13), he does not appear to recognize the powerful social forces that can create the structures that induce human beings to behave in a civilized manner under the 'rules of the game' that we call social norms. The governance structures of civilized humanity are designed to protect members and existing organizations not only from each other but also from the dark forces of time and uncertainty.

In his discussion of human dignity, Williamson makes the crucial point that orthodox utilitarian calculations will systematically undervalue human dignity, thereby inflicting a loss on to society as 'the political and social competencies of the parties are degraded' (ibid., p. 11). Williamson obviously values social cohesion, but he does not properly value the forces of human dignity and social cohesion as a means to continued existence – and hence to the prevention or attenuation of conflict.

2.2 Shared Values and Motivation

The existence of a shared language of definitions and rules of the game are essential for all governance structures to be effective. This sort of linguistic certainty is not readily available in many short-run interactive environments. Williamson recognizes that the development of long-term relationships between parties is necessary for them to develop mutually and adopt a common language of meanings. Thus, involved parties develop a societal hub amongst themselves in which bonds of social regard are formed. These bonds act as a motivational force that counters the socially destructive forces of opportunism. An individual's interdependence with and trust of other individuals may lead to the betrayal of one party dealing with an unethical opportunistic other; but where two or more parties enter into an organizational agreement, there is the chance for additional benefits for both parties. Cooperative species often thrive better in a Darwinian environment than does each individual organism alone.

Although Williamson does not specifically identify this social bond in determining contractual organization, he does emphasize the need to build structures to channel potentially destructive incentives in a way that supports *mutual* confidence and cooperation. Through these structures, opportunistic motivations are kept in check but, more important, opportunism itself is attacked. Williamson echoes the broader thought of Machiavelli, who wrote of the need for good institutions to channel properly the interests of individuals so that individual *and* social wants could be satisfied in concert with one another.

3 UNCERTAINTY, MOTIVATION, AND DIGNITY

Williamson suggests that 'incomplete or distorted disclosure of information' vastly complicates the problem of uncertainty (ibid., p. 7). But what information, in Williamson's system is distorted or incomplete – the past or the future? Surely it cannot be the past for the past is history that is always complete and, in the Williamson approach, is available to all (at a transactions cost of searching out the facts). (Opportunistic agents can distort the past, that is, withhold past facts from the other party, only if the other party is not willing to pay the price to search for the true 'facts.')

But bygones are always bygones. Ultimately it *must* be future information that is incomplete or distorted. Who is distorting this future? If it is (an opportunistic?) Mother Nature who provides incomplete information, then Williamson is implicitly assuming that the future already exists along the time axis and is therefore (1) known to all omnipotent parties and (2) can be forecasted with actuarial certainty via rational expectations by others who process sufficient existing data (the ergodic hypothesis).

If, on the other hand, the concept of uncertainty involves important non-ergodic circumstances, then there currently does *not* exist information (complete, incomplete, distorted, or otherwise) that will aid human beings to discover the future. Instead human beings will have to invent or create the future for themselves by their actions within evolving and existing organizations.

Acting on expectations about an uncertain future helps shape the future. Uncertainty in this latter context means non-predictability, and the law of contracts permits agents and organizations to continue to exist and function in a homeostatic manner, even in a potentially threatening environment. Without contractual 'rules of the game', no time-consuming game could be played by either the ultimate winners or losers in the game of economic life. It is because Williamson has not truly cut the Gordian knot that ties him to assuming some form of 'rationality' in the operation of the real world's organizations that he misinterprets the concept of statistically predictable risk for non-ergodic uncertainty; and, hence, he finds that the concept of *dignity* cannot be integrated into his transaction–cost economics – any more than dignity can be integrated into neoclassical economics (ibid., p. 10).

In a non-ergodic world, *dignity* involves maintaining a modicum of decency in the face of unforeseen and unforeseeable events that may make any party to a transaction embarrassingly unable or unwilling to meet its contractual commitments. Enforcement of the law of contracts, as developed in modern democratic societies, provides an opportunity to regain or retain social dignity for any party who finds himself involved in a situation of contractual default. Contract law, by allowing each party to have 'one's day in court', permits each to 'prove' publicly the propriety of one's behaviour when a contractual conflict arises. In a world where organization behaviour is not a means to a maximizing purpose but is, instead, simply a state of being, the dignity involved in the law of contracts governing interacting transactors permits each party to believe that it can maintain its dignified being by defending (when necessary) its actions in a court of law.[1] Dignity therefore does, as Williamson correctly notes, 'have important social consequences' (ibid.).

4 CONTRACTS, ASSET SPECIFICITY, AND UNCERTAINTY

Some valuable lessons involving asset specificity in Williamson's transactions–costs economics have been incorporated in the literature of negotiations. D. A. Lax and J. K. Sebenius (1984) emphasize the importance of the alternatives facing the parties in determining their power in interactive bargains. Investment in firm–specific human capital makes both labour and management dependent on each other. Asset specificity makes less palatable those alternatives, which would involve both parties in capital-asset-valuation losses. Opportunism is thereby discouraged and cooperation encouraged, as the existence of firm–specific assets makes both parties aware that their opposite is similarly constrained.

In bargaining, a credible constraint is a strength, not a weakness (Schelling, 1960, pp. 21–52). Once known credible constraints resulting from, say, asset-specificity are placed on both parties, they are more likely to trust each other. The mere threat of one-party domination creates a strong incentive to avoid entering into a vulnerable relationship unless each party is very sure that its opposites are going to face a similar range of alternatives once they begin to lower their defences. Bargaining situations where one or both parties cannot be credibly constrained are unstable, because there are no assets uniquely specified to them that can be lost if either side withdraws from cooperative activity. Asset-specificity can therefore play a useful role in creating an environment for contractual agreements in a non-ergodic world.

4.1 Franchising and Asset-Specificity

In the domain of public utilities involving asset-specificity, Williamson endorses a form of renewal franchise bidding as an alternative to regulation, with the proviso that government retains the power to force a new franchise auction whenever unforeseen circumstances evolve. If, Williamson argues, 'nontrivial', specific, real assets possess liquidity in the sense that they are readily resaleable in well-organized, second-hand spot markets, then these assets are no longer firm- (or user-) specific; and therefore refranchising with new auctions is a viable alternative to regulation, since no serious asset-valuation problems occur with a change of operator. Williamson recognizes however that real assets – especially long-lived specific real assets such as buildings, plants, and so on, are not liquid – even if some shorter-lived assets (for example, fleet vehicles) could be. Consequently, displacing the old utility supplier with the new winning bidder for the franchise creates serious asset valuation problems and potential devastating wealth effects. To rescue the possibility of efficient renewable franchising as an alternative to government regulation, Williamson requires the government to own the illiquid (non-resaleable) base plant (1983, p. 34). In other words, only if *all* assets are resaleable or liquid can private ownership of capital and renewable auction markets for franchising result in an efficient solution.

It is very unlikely that advocates of franchising auctions such as Milton Friedman will endorse Williamson's approach, that involves government ownership of all the specific physical *illiquid* assets necessary to provide the public utility service. For this dodges the question of who is to make the investment–resource decision as to what base plant. Is it the private franchisee who, not owning the facilities, will have a vested interest in requiring the government to provide the most capital-intensive plant possible? Or is it that the government bureaucrat in whom the Friedmanites have no confidence, has any business acumen?

Williamson's suggested solution of franchising and government ownership of non-liquid assets as an alternative to regulation raises more problems than it resolves. But it does expose a major fault in the facile 'franchising' solutions of the Chicago School. Without clearly realizing it, Williamson has located one of the Achilles' heels of neoclassical economics and its efficiency approach – namely, the implicit assumption that all assets are *not* agent-specific. Neoclassical theory always presumes that all assets are liquid and readily resaleable for use by others. In a neoclassical world, capital is liquidity-fungible if not malleable.

In this, Williamson's efficient franchising analysis is close to W. J. Baumol's 'contestable market' hypothesis (1982) for in both cases entry and exit is assumed to be costless in terms of asset-specific investment, although Williamson at least recognizes a role for government when illiquid user-specific assets exist. In the contestable market case, it is assumed that either assets are not user- or market-specific or else there is an active second-hand market for all real assets, that is, all real assets are liquid. Liquidity, in the real world, is, however, restricted to a very small group of the universe of existing assets. Only assets resaleable in well-organized, continuous spot markets can possess liquidity, and, as a stylized fact about the real world, only non-specific financial assets possess any significant degree of liquidity. (Davidson, 1972)

5 MONEY, CONTRACTS, FINANCIAL MARKETS, AND NON-SPECIFIC ASSETS

Spot financial markets by their very nature provide liquidity, by providing a market for the resaleability among 'faceless' buyers and sellers of non-specific assets. Only in a money contract economy is liquidity – and therefore financial markets – important.

As Williamson (1983, pp. 5–6) explicitly recognizes, money does not play an important role in his transaction–cost analysis. Unable to throw over the vestiges of a 'rationality' concept to analyse the 'being' of *sensible* organizations in a non-ergodic world, he is unable to integrate money into his system. Yet Williamson's governance analysis cries out for a non-neutral money approach. In our world, contracts are almost always made in nominal terms – and indeed are enforceable in a court of law only in nominal terms. And as K. J. Arrow and F. H. Hahn have warned:

> The terms in which contracts are made matter. In particular, if money is the goods in terms of which contracts are made, then the price of goods in terms of money are of special significance. This is not the case if we consider an economy without a past or future . . . *if a serious monetary theory* comes to be written, the fact that contracts are made in terms of money will be of considerable importance. (1971, pp. 356–7, italics added)

Moreover, Arrow and Hahn demonstrate (ibid., p. 361) that if contracts are made in terms of money (so that money affects real decisions) in an economy moving along in calendar time with a past and future, then *all existence theorems are jeopardized*. The existence of money contracts – a characteristic of the world in which Keynes lived and in which we still do – implies that there need never exist, in the long run or the short run, any rational expectations or general equilibrium, market-clearing price vector. In such a world, 'money matters', it is not neutral. Money and its related financial markets affect real variables including real asset choices. As Keynes (1930) reminded us in the first page of his *Treatise on Money*, money comes into existence with the presence of money contracts. Money and contracts are intimately and inevitably tied. And it is only in a world of non-ergodic uncertainty that money is not neutral (Keynes, 1936, pp. 408–9 and 411; Davidson, 1972, 1980a, 1980b, 1982).

To achieve a non-neutrality of money analytical system, Keynes had to reject three basic axioms of orthodox neoclassical theory: (1) the axiom of gross substitution, that is, that everything is ultimately a substitute for everything else; (2) the axiom of reals, that is, that the objectives of agents that determine their actions and plans do not depend on any nominal magnitudes; agents care only about relative prices and real things; and (3) the axiom of an ergodic economic world.

The characteristics of the real world that Keynes believed could be modelled only by overthrowing these aforementioned neoclassical axioms are (1) money matters in the long and short run, that is, money is not neutral, it affects real decision-making.[2] (2) The economic system is moving through calendar time from an irrevocable past to an uncertain future. Important monetary time-series realizations will be generated by non-ergodic circumstances; hence decision-making agents know that the future need not be predictable in any probability sense (Davidson, 1982–3). (3) Forward contracts in terms of money are human institutions developed to organize efficiently time-consuming production and exchange processes (ibid., 1980a, p. 299). The money-wage contract is the most ubiquitous of these efficiency-oriented contracts. Modern production economists are, therefore, on a money-wage-based contract system. (4) Unemployment, rather than full employment, is a common *laissez-faire* situation in a market-oriented, monetary-production economy. (5) In such a world, the concept of liquidity is fundamental to the operation of real economic processes.

6 LIQUIDITY AND FINANCIAL MARKETS

In an economy organized over calendar time on a money-contract basis, 'liquidity involves being able to discharge one's money contractual obligations as they come due; this ability depends on either holding sufficient money balances to meet these obligations or holding readily marketable assets which can be quickly sold for money when needed' (ibid., 1980b, p. 164). Money as defined by Keynes and Post Keynesians, is *the* medium of contractual settlement. For all assets except money, resaleability on well-organized, continuous spot markets is the requirement for any degree of liquidity.

Liquidity is the necessary preventive medicine that provides protection against the indignity of insolvency or the *fatal* economic disease of bankruptcy. Liquidity is the key that unlocks the gate to a world of alternatives to which illiquid agents do not have access. Consequently the possession of liquidity assures continued existence to organizations and human beings facing a non-ergodic and potentially hostile environment. Assured continued existence assures access to alternatives and gives agents negotiating power even if these alternatives are never chosen. Well-organized, spot financial markets, by continuously dealing with faceless buyers and sellers, create non-specific assets that provide liquidity with a minimum of transactions costs.

In order for a well-organized market to exist, certain attributes must be present, namely, (1) the good must be an article of general demand, (2) it must be capable of standardization, (3) it must be durable and valuable in proportion to bulk, and finally (4) there must exist a financial institution that 'makes' the market by acting as residual *buyer or seller* when necessary (ibid., 1972, p. 87). Markets for financial assets easily meet all of these criteria; markets for *real* capital assets rarely do. Hence, there is, in a non-ergodic world, a fundamental unbridgeable difference between liquid financial assets and illiquid real assets. The former are economically non-specific assets, the latter are agent-specific assets.

Although two types of financial markets coexist – the new issues market and the organized spot market for 'second-hand' seasoned securities – most economists emphasize the latter when they speak of financial markets. It is only in the latter market where faceless buyers and sellers meet to exchange very standardized goods in the presence of a 'market-maker'. (For most new issues, the identities of the buyers and sellers are usually known to each other.) Thus the real world of resaleable liquid assets via organized exchanges is incompatible with the underlying dimensions of *asset specificity* that Williamson indicates is essential to his organizational analysis (1983, pp. 11–12).[3]

Only in a non-ergodic world can the precautionary demand for liquidity be comprehended as a shield against forces that may threaten the very existence of individuals and organizations. These forces are a threat to the very dignity that is at the heart of the Galbraithian analysis of organizations, but that is not systematically incorporated in the Williamson approach.

In the absence of well-organized, spot financial markets, only the possession of money could provide the assurance of continued existence to business and household organizations and 'liquidity preference due [solely] to the precautionary motive would be greatly increased' (Keynes, 1936, p. 170). The existence and evolution of organized, spot financial asset markets, however, permits the managers of organizations to vary widely the amount of money they hold as an assurance of the continued being of the organization and to include resaleable financial assets among the guarantors of continued existence.

The greater the wealth stored in financial assets, including money, the greater the power of an organization to assure its continual survival, no matter how hostile the future environment may become. Flexibility due to access to many potential alternatives is power. Thus the second-hand market for seasoned securities is not organized primarily to promote an efficient allocation of 'saved' resources among various investment projects; instead, it has evolved as a market organization that encourages business and household managers to attempt to build up financial power that can be used to protect the very economic being of the possessing organization.

Since the potential hostility of future events towards each organization striving to maintain its being in a non-ergodic world is unbounded (since it is unknown and unknowable), there can never be a satiation of individuals' desires to accumulate 'more' liquid assets. Moreover, since liquidity provides power via permitting access to more alternatives, the more power one individual or organization amasses, the more the threat to others. Every marginal increase in the power of an individual or organization will reduce the relative strength of all existing liquid-asset holdings of others.

A bull market may run out of steam not because organizational managers' appetite for liquidity has been satiated, it can end either because
buyers have lost confidence in the ability of the liquid assets to continue to
grow or even maintain nominal values, and/or participants have to 'cash-in'
their liquidity in order to protect their being from a sudden threatening
change in the economic environment.

In a non-ergodic world where the possession of liquidity is essential for
the preservation of the organization's being, it is the current nominal price
vis-à-vis the expected future nominal value of financial assets (that is, the
money rate of interest on money) that 'rules the roost' (ibid., ch. 17). In
such a world with organized financial markets, each manager will maintain
a 'position' in resaleable liquid assets only as long as its nominal value is
expected to rise or at least be maintained. When the manager no longer
expects the nominal value to be maintained, he will pass off this liquid asset
to the next (unsuspecting) person who has not yet realized that the future
nominal value will decline. Thus,

> Of the maxims of orthodox finance none, surely, is more anti-social than
> the fetish of liquidity, the doctrine that it is a positive virtue on the part
> of investment institutions to concentrate their resources upon the hold-
> ing of 'liquid' securities. It forgets that there is no such thing as liquidity
> of investment for the community as a whole. The social object of skilled
> investment should be to defeat the dark forces of time and ignorance
> which envelop our future. The actual, private object of the most skilled
> investment today is 'to beat the gun,' as the Americans so well express it,
> to outwit the crowd, and to pass the bad, or depreciating, half-crown to
> the other fellow. (ibid., p. 155)

7 CONCLUSION

Williamson deserves kudos from the economics profession for his heroic
attempt to break away from the 'black-box' approach of orthodox
neoclassical theory to organizational analysis. In some areas, for example,
negotiation theory, franchising versus regulation, contestable markets, and
so on, Williamson has provided fruitful insights into organizational behaviour. In the area of financial markets, however, Williamson's use of the
concept of bounded rationality and its association with 'uncertainty' and
contracts is not a sufficient break with orthodox economic theory to
provide useful insights into this most important of all sectors in a capitalist
economy.

As Berle and Means discovered a half-century ago, in such a
finance–capitalist world, the evolution of financial markets has severed the

demand for real assets (involving control and management of future production flows) from the liquidity-portfolio, balance decision (involving legal ownership of corporate entities). Those households and firms 'investing' in corporate securities (or governmental bonds) are merely looking for a liquid resting place for the economic power to maintain and strengthen their organizational being; they are not primarily interested in the actual investment decisions of the corporate entities they own or the governments who are indebted to them. They willingly hold such liquid assets as long as they believe they can 'beat the gun' and push onto others the securities that are about to go sour before the others realize the extent of the threat to the organization that initially floated the securities.

The faceless stock and bond market investor is virtually uninterested in 'controlling' the corporate organization he owns or to which he is a creditor. He requires only that the management attempt to maintain the *being* of the organization – and failing that, signals of the potential collapse of the organization should be more readily available to the current faceless security-holder than the market at large. Managers of these organizational bodies that float securities to the faceless public have a similar interest. The managers also wish to maintain the being of the corporate or governmental organization without any significant interference regarding control of the organization by the bond- and/or stockholders. Managers can then manipulate the organization to obtain for themselves the prestige and dignity that is associated with the social class of managers in a given socio-historical structure.

Notes

1. If all contracts had to be enforced in the courts, justice would be bogged down in administrative detail. *Trust* is the social cohesive cement that permits contract law to operate and provide social dignity.
2. Despite Milton Friedman's use of the motto 'money matters', he remains faithful to the axiom of reals (see what follows) and does not permit money to affect the long-run, real outcome of his system. In his own description of his logical framework, Friedman (1974, p. 27) states:

   That changes in the quantity of money as such *in the long run* have a negligible effect on real income so that nonmonetary forces are "all that matter" for changes in real income over decades and money "does not matter". . . I regard the description of our position as 'money is all that matters for changes in *nominal income* and for *short-run* changes in real income' as an exaggeration but one that gives the right flavor to our conclusions.

3. The use of the banking system to finance illiquid positions in working capital arising from forward production contractual commitments is closer to Williamson's underlying dimensions. This aspect is not discussed here. The interested

reader is referred to (Davidson, 1972, 1980a) for a discussion of liquidity and working-capital commitments.

References

Arrow, K. J. and F. H. Hahn (1971), *General Competitive Analysis* (San Francisco: Holden-Day).

Baumol, W. J. (1982), 'Contestable Markets: An Uprising in the Theory of Industrial Structure', *American Economic Review*, 72 (March), pp. 1–15.

Berle, A. A. and G. C. Means (1932), *The Modern Corporation and Private Property* (New York: Commerce Clearing House).

Buchanan, J. M. (1975), 'A Contractarian Paradigm for Applying Economic Theory', *American Economic Review*, 65 (May), pp. 225–30.

Davidson, Paul (1972), *Money and the Real World* (London: Macmillan).

Davidson, Paul (1980a), 'The Dual-faceted Nature of the Keynesian Revolution', *Journal of Post Keynesian Economics* 2 (Spring), pp. 291–307.

Davidson, Paul (1980b), 'Post Keynesian Economics: Solving the Crisis in Economic Theory', *The Public Interest*, Special issue, pp. 151–73 (Chapter 17 in this volume).

Davidson, Paul (1982), *International Money and the Real World* (London: Macmillan).

Davidson, Paul (1982–3), 'Rational Expectations: A Fallacious Foundation for Analyzing Crucial Decision Making', *Journal of Post Keynesian Economics*, 5, pp. 182–98.

Friedman, Milton (1974), 'A Theoretical Framework for Monetary Analysis', in R. J. Gordon (ed.), *Milton Friedman's Monetary Framework: A Debate with His Critics* (Chicago: University of Chicago Press).

Galbraith, J. K. (1967), *The New Industrial State* (Boston: Houghton Mifflin).

Galbraith, J. K. (1984), 'Galbraith and the Theory of the Firm', *Journal of Post Keynesian Economics*, 7 pp. 43–60.

Keynes, J. M. (1930), *Treatise on Money* (London: Macmillan, 1930).

Keynes, J. M. (1936), *The General Theory of Money, Interest and Employment* (New York: Harcourt).

Keynes, J. M. (1973), *The Collected Writings of John Maynard Keynes*, Vol. 13 (London: Macmillan).

Lax, D. A. and J. K. Sebenius (1984), 'The Power of Alternatives or the Limits to Negotiation', *Harvard Negotiation Journal*, 1.

Schelling, T. E. (1960), *The Strategy of Conflict* (London: Oxford University Press).

Simon, H. A. (1972), 'Theories of Bounded Rationality', in C. McGuire and Radnisk (eds), *Decision and Organization* (Amsterdam: North-Holland).

Solow, R. W. (1971), 'Some Implications of Alternative Criteria for the Firm', in R. Morris and A. Wood (eds), *The Corporate Economy, Growth, Competition, and Innovative Potential* (Cambridge, Mass.: Harvard University Press).

Williamson, O. E. (1979), 'Transaction-Cost Economics: The Governance of Contractual Relations', *Journal of Law and Economics*, 22 (October), pp. 233–61.

Williamson, O. E. (1983), 'The Economics of Governance: Framework and Implications', Yale University Discussion Paper, 153 (July).

22 Can We Afford to Balance the Budget?*

Public opinion polls taken in recent months have indicated that a large majority of citizens favours reducing the huge Federal deficit. There has been no public ground swell, though, for either raising taxes or cutting government services that affect middle-income living standards. Nor has a cry gone up against letting inflation whittle down income transfers to the poor.

Numerous observers therefore doubt that Americans are really willing to pay the price of deficit reduction. In Congress, the apparent selfishness of individuals and vested interests has reinforced the feeling that tax increases per se remain unpopular, and that a significant segment of the voting population is opposed to any lessening of government largess.

How, then, does one explain the polls supporting a balanced budget, which prompted Congress's rush last month to vote for the bill sponsored by Senators Phil Gramm (R-Tex.), Warren B. Rudman (R-N.H.) and Ernest F. Hollings (D-S.C.) forcing deficit cutbacks over the next five years that will achieve this? Well, it appears the public's response to the pollsters has merely reflected what television and the print media have continually publicized as the 'conventional wisdom' that deficits are bad.

In the Eisenhower administration, Secretary of the Treasury George M. Humphrey verbalized the conventional wisdom by noting that he 'had never heard of a person who could spend himself rich'. If the government did not end its profligate ways, he cautioned, the US would 'have a depression that would curl your hair'. Although current purveyors of the judgement have not been able to coin such delicious epigrams, they have effectively bombarded the public with an equivalent message.

The deficit has doubled since Ronald Reagan took office in 1980. Today the Federal government 'owes' $2 trillion. This rate of indebtedness cannot go on, many have exclaimed. Both the former chairman of the President's Council of Economic Advisors, Martin Feldstein, and the former director of the Office of Management and Budget, David Stockman – the Chicken Littles of the first Reagan Administration – repeatedly warned of the impending doom due to such spending. And the more readily observable facts have contradicted the dire pronouncements of the professionals, the more prestigious and acclaimed have they become – in the *New York Times*, on Wall Street and at Harvard.

Given these circumstances, it is not surprising the public has been

* First published in *The New Leader*, 13 January 1986.

brainwashed to fear deficits will cause the economic sky to fall. Still, they
were responsible for nudging the economy out of the Great Recession of
1979–82, and the subsequent steady improvement has primarily been a
function as well of not attempting to rein in Reagan's deficits. Past
experience further suggests this was predictable. As I have pointed out
previously ('Why Deficits Hardly Matter', *NL*, 20 August 1984), in 1937
explicit legislative actions aimed at balancing the budget induced a dramatic nine-month plunge in GNP, matching the rates of economic decline
under Hoover. By contrast, those years where Franklin D. Roosevelt did
not worry about the deficit were the basis of economic growth and prosperity.

President Reagan, ignoring his own balanced budget-amendment rhetoric during the 1984 election year, was triumphantly returned to office.
Walter Mondale, whose domestic platform rested on the same thinking
that underlies Gramm–Rudman, was buried in a landslide of good economic news as Reagan continued to pursue the largest Keynesian deficit
spending programme the country ever experienced. Indeed, his unswer-
ving Keynesian actions seemed to virtually ensure him a place in history as
the saviour of American capitalism and the most popular President since
FDR.

The US economy – its present 7 per cent unemployment notwithstanding
– has also shown remarkable vitality compared with the rest of the free
world over the last three years. At the onset of the international depression
of 1980–2, the other major nations started reducing their deficits as a
percentage of GNP. They have enjoyed little growth – except for the sales
of their export industries to the US, which have risen *pari passu* with the
Reagan recovery.

Clearly our Federal deficit will become a serious economic problem (not
only to ourselves, but to our friends abroad) only when, as Gramm–Rudman requires, we start doing something to lower it. No wonder President
Reagan signed this bill in the privacy of the Oval Office, without any public
display or photo opportunity. Its adoption signals the end of the euphoric
phase of expansionary Reaganomics, and paves the way toward reducing
Reagan's image in the history books as the promoter of unprecedented
prosperity. From a cynical standpoint, it could be argued that Gramm–
Rudman is one of the best things that has happened to the Democrats
politically since passage of the Smoot–Hawley Tariff in the Hoover administration.

Ultimately, the real issue raised by the new legislation is not whose taxes
will have to be increased, or whose goodies Uncle Sam will have to curtail
or eliminate. The real question is, can we as a society afford the reduction
in jobs and GNP – the recession – that the activation of Gramm–
Rudman will produce? For the road to a balanced budget will return us to

the era of more than 10 per cent unemployment, substantially reduced profits, and large-scale bankruptcies brought on by the reduction in aggregate demand that must be a consequence of some combination of less government spending and tax hikes to meet the terms of Gramm–Rudman.

You might wonder whether Congressmen who preached the urgency of mandating an end to the deficit realized that, all other things being equal, this amounted to legislating a recession and significant increases in unemployment. Of course they did! But the politicians, faced with the public opinion polls, wanted something to satisfy their constituents. Backing Gramm–Rudman permitted incumbents to demonstrate that they are against the sin of excessiveness without explicitly lowering the voters' living standards.

Where consciences troubled, there were two possible rationales for agreeing to support a measure that could plunge the nation into a severe recession: the first assumes that reducing Federal borrowing will cause interest rates to drop, and thereby stimulate sufficient investment in new plant and equipment to offset the decline in government demand for the products of industry. Unfortunately, the well-meaning legislators who reason in this fashion fail to recognize a critical fact: although much idle plant and equipment was put to work again in 1982–3 as Reagan's Keynesian recovery got under way, plant utilization has *fallen* since mid-1984 despite the GNP's continued growth because of deficit spending. Hence, even if interest rates were to come down as a result of Gramm–Rudman, there is no reason to expect businesses will embark on a spontaneous investment boom. No one is going to build more capacity, regardless of the interest rates, when too much already exists.

The second rationale is, in its substance, more pernicious to our social structure. It is an extension of what *New York Times* columnist Tom Wicker calls the 'shrewd political theory', which seeks to reverse the trend of the last half century towards a more equitable redistribution of income. As economic conditions worsen during the coming recession, it holds pressure will build to resolve the situation in a manner similar to the solution of 1980–2 – namely, a regressive redistributive tax cut under some supply-side slogan.

Whatever the rationale, it does not change the true cost of Gramm–Rudman. And that cost, in my view, will be the impoverishment of America and the stripping of the cohesive social fabric woven via cooperative redistributive legislation that has made us an enduring, civilized economic society.

23 A Post Keynesian View of Theories and Causes for High Real Interest Rates*

1 INTRODUCTION

The doctrine of monetarism had tended to dominate economic discussions regarding inflation and economic policy – even when the facts, since 1980, have shown there is very little correlation between growth in the domestic money supply and consumer price increases. Considerable time and energies are still being expended, and in my view wasted, trying unsuccessfully to provide a cogent policy analysis of real world problems in the face of the popularity of unhelpful monetarist concepts. The concept of the 'real rate of interest' is an excellent case in point. Accordingly, if we are to have a useful discussion regarding why 'real' interest rates internationally have risen so dramatically since 1979, we must first clarify the theoretical meaning of *the real rate of interest*. For until we get our 'theory' right, it is impossible to get a good diagnosis of real world 'facts', the problems implicit in these 'facts', and possible policy actions.

The facts for the years since 1973 are presented in Tables 23.1 and 23.2. The upper portion of Table 23.1 provides end-of-period nominal yields on major corporate bond yields; while the lower portion estimates *ex post* real yields which are computed by dividing the nominal yields by the change in the consumer price level in the various nations during the previous year. Table 23.2 provides similar information on the average yield on central government bonds in nominal and real terms. Table 23.2 also presents similar yield estimates for London Interbank Offer Rates (LIBOR) on one-year US dollar deposits.

Both tables, with minor variations, tell a similar story for the period since the breakdown of the Bretton Woods Agreement. In the United States there was an eight-year upward trend movement in nominal interest rates, peaking in 1981. Nominal interest rates declined in 1982–3, then showed a renewed upward advance in 1984. In 1985, nominal interest rates declined continuously, returning to 1979–80 levels. Real interest rates in the United States, on the other hand, were only slightly positive over the period 1973–8, with negative rates in years of rapidly increasing inflation

* *Thames Papers in Political Economy*, Spring 1986.

Table 23.1 Corporate Bond Yields in Major Financial Markets, in Nominal and Real Terms, 1973–84, End of Period (percentage)

	1973–8	1979	1980	1981	1982	1983	1984	Feb. 1985	Jul. 1985
Nominal yields									
United States	8.4	10.8	13.0	15.5	11.8	12.6	12.3	13.0	11.7
Japan	9.1	8.3	8.6	7.7	7.6	7.1	6.2	7.0	6.6
Federal Republic of Germany	8.2	8.2	9.5	10.5	8.2	8.3	7.2	7.2	7.1
France	11.1	12.9	15.2	17.3	15.9	14.1	12.1	12.2	12.1
United Kingdom	14.9	15.0	14.2	16.7	12.3	11.6	11.6	12.0	11.2
*Real yields**									
United States	0.7	-0.4	-0.5	4.6	5.4	9.1	8.0	9.5	8.3
Japan	-2.0	4.6	0.6	2.7	4.8	5.2	3.9	5.6	4.3
Federal Republic of Germany	3.0	3.9	3.9	4.0	2.8	4.8	4.8	4.9	5.0
France	0.8	2.0	1.3	3.5	3.7	4.1	4.8	5.8	6.5
United Kingdom	0.1	1.3	-3.2	4.2	3.5	6.7	6.6	6.6	5.0

*Nominal yields deflated by the rate of change in consumer prices during the immediately preceding year.
Source: Morgan Guarantee Trust Company, *World Financial Markets* (New York), various issues.

rates. In 1979 and 1980 real rates were more strongly negative, but from 1981 to early 1985, in the face of rapidly declining inflation rates, real interest rates in the United States climbed to very high positive levels. Since then real rates have declined somewhat despite continuing huge Federal government deficits, a declining exchange rate, and well-publicized financial difficulties for some state depository institutions.

Nominal interest rate movements in other major capital markets throughout the 1970s are similar to those in the United States. The LIBOR rate (both nominal and real) in Table 23.2 tracked movements in the US rate fairly closely, at least till mid-1985, when the nominal (and hence real) rate decline significantly more rapidly.

Real interest rates in other countries, on the other hand, have shown more divergent movements since 1972 with only the Federal Republic of Germany having relatively stable positive real rates throughout. Beginning in 1981, however, real rates have increased in all developed nations but the magnitudes of change among the various nations differ with real rates peaking in 1983 in Japan, in 1984 in West Germany, and in early 1985 in the UK.

In sum then, the facts are that different nations' nominal and real interest rates exhibit somewhat different patterns over time, e.g. since 1978, Japan and Germany's rates showing a smaller upward secular trend than others, while the nominal rates of France and the UK follow the US pattern somewhat more closely. Only since 1981 do real rates, although at different levels in each country, tend to trace a similar pattern of higher values.

The facts are therefore clear. Nevertheless, the question remains: in the years since 1980 why have *ex post* international real interest rates on average increased so dramatically and remained so high, especially when inflation appears to be much more contained than it has been since the international oil price shocks of the 1970s?

Ex post real interest rates are always merely the result of a statistical calculation, namely, the division of the observed nominal rate by an appropriate price index. Since, however, we are discussing the monetarist concept of the real interest rate and since Friedman considers money 'as if' it is a consumer durable (see Laidler's remarks cited below), the consumer price index of each nation was used in calculating *ex post* or hindsight 'real' interest rates in Tables 23.1 and 23.2. Thus, the *ex post* real interest rates in Tables 23.1 and 23.2 are, at best, a measure of the after-the-fact real income claims earned by debt-holders during the particular period.

Most monetarist theorists, however, are not primarily interested in the real rate of interest as a measure of income claims actually earned. Monetarist doctrine assumes that the real rate is a variable which affects behaviour, affecting the demand for money *vis-à-vis* real durables to be held for the future. Thus, they are assuming that it is not hindsight but

Table 23.2 Average Yield on Central Government Bonds in Major Financial Markets, and LIBOR Rate, in Nominal and Real Terms, 1973–85, End of Period (percentage)

	1973	1974	1975	1976	1977	1978	1979	1980	1981	1982	1983	1984	Feb. 1985	Aug. 1985
Nominal yields														
United States	7.1	8.1	8.2	7.9	7.8	8.5	9.3	11.4	13.7	12.9	11.3	12.5	11.7	10.7
Japan	7.3	9.3	9.2	8.7	6.5	6.1	7.7	9.2	8.7	8.1	7.4	6.8	6.8	6.6*
Federal Republic of Germany	9.3	10.5	8.5	7.8	5.7	5.8	7.4	8.5	10.4	9.0	7.9	7.8	7.4	6.4
France	8.3	10.5	9.5	9.2	9.6	9.0	9.5	13.0	15.7	15.6	13.6	12.4	11.4	10.7
United Kingdom	10.7	14.8	14.4	14.4	11.1	12.5	13.0	13.8	14.7	12.9	10.8	10.7	11.1	10.4
LIBOR on US $ deposits						9.3	11.7	13.5	16.1	13.6	10.1	11.8	10.9	8.7
*Real yields**														
United States	1.0	-0.2	-0.9	1.9	1.3	0.8	-1.9	-2.1	1.8	6.7	8.1	8.2	8.2	7.3
Japan	-4.0	-15.1	-2.7	-0.6	-1.5	2.1	3.1	1.2	3.8	5.4	5.6	4.5	5.4	4.6**
Federal Republic of Germany	2.4	3.4	2.5	3.5	2.0	3.0	3.3	3.1	4.1	3.7	4.6	5.4	5.1	4.3
France	1.0	-3.2	-2.3	-0.4	-0.2	0.0	-1.3	-0.5	1.3	3.8	4.0	5.1	5.0	5.1
United Kingdom	1.6	-1.2	-9.8	-2.1	-4.8	4.2	-0.4	-4.2	2.8	4.3	6.2	5.7	5.7	4.2
LIBOR on US $ deposits							0.4	-0.1	2.4	7.5	6.9	7.5	5.3	5.3

*As in Table 23.1
**As of end of first quarter 1985 (latest data available from IMF).
Source: International Monetary Fund, *International Financial Statistics*, vols. 32 (1979), 38 (1985).

foresight which affects behaviour. This implies there is a forward looking or *ex ante* real interest rate which affects agents' decisions. (An *ex ante* real interest rate requires an *ex ante* or expected consumer price index for its calculation since only nominal interest rates are established in financial markets in the real world.) Is the real rate of interest a viable *ex ante* concept in a monetary economy?

Section 2 briefly traces the development of the concepts of the real versus nominal interest rate from Fisher to Friedman and notes that Keynes specifically disagreed with the view that one could identify an *ex ante* real rate differently from a nominal interest rate in an entrepreneurial monetary, production economy. Section 3 develops Keynes's argument by showing that if one assumes that, on average, agents have a sudden change in expectations about future consumer prices (even if these changed expectations are rational and/or financial markets are efficient), then there can be no *ceteris paribus* effect of this average change in inflationary expectations on the nominal rate of interest. Accordingly, there can be no 'inflation premium' in observed nominal interest rates. Keynes's analysis therefore debunks the relevance of the monetarist *ex ante* real interest concept.

Section 4 provides a brief review of the fundamental axioms underlying neoclassical monetary theory and contrasts this with the role of money in an entrepreneurial, monetary-production system. In the latter the nominal interest rate is a measure of liquidity preference and it 'rules the roost' (Keynes, 1936, ch. 17). By an entrepreneurial monetary–production economy, we mean one where the institutions of spot and forward money contracts are used to organize production and exchange efficiently. Consequently, money is not neutral and financial markets are not efficient (in the neoclassical sense) in either the short run or the long run – and only nominal returns are relevant for liquidity decisions of lenders.

This non-neutrality of money requirement for an entrepreneurial monetary economy conflicts with a basic axiom underlying most mainstream macro and international monetary models. For many, a non-neutrality assertion is so repugnant to their beliefs that it may induce a negative tropistic reaction against the monetary–production analysis presented here. I, therefore, request the goodwill of all fair-minded readers to make an exerted effort against such a thoughtless 'knee-jerk' reflex to the idea of non-neutral money as a characteristic of real world economies and to at least consider the argument presented, rather than to unthinkingly close their minds.

Section 5 will, in the light of the monetary–production analysis developed, discuss some of the possible 'causes' of the observed rise in *ex post* real rates of interest (in Tables 23.1 and 23.2) suffered in the last few years by the entrepreneurial economies of the real world.

Finally, section 6 provides a short epilogue to the paper.

2   THE FISHER–FRIEDMAN REAL INTEREST RATE CONCEPT

Irving Fisher initially introduced the distinction between the nominal and real rate of interest into the literature. Fisher initially defines '*the rate of interest as the per cent premium* paid on money at one date in terms of money to be in hand one year later' (1930, p. 13). Thus the interest rate is defined strictly in nominal terms of money now vs. money in the future (Cf. Keynes, 1936, p. 222). Then by introducing a Robinson Crusoe economy analogy, *where by construction no money exists and therefore money must be neutral*, Fisher (1930, p. 22) switched definitions of the rate of interest from a nominal to a real concept. In a Robinson Crusoe non-monetary economy, the rate of interest is 'described as the percentage premium on present goods over future goods of the same kind' (ibid., p. 36). Of course, if one assumes a non-monetary economy, it is not surprising that the discounting idea must be defined solely in real, rather than in nominal, terms.

Nevertheless, as even Fisher conceded, in the real world which we inhabit the rate of interest on world financial markets is always observed in nominal terms. Hence Fisher, attempting to carry over his analogy of a real interest rate from the Robinson Crusoe system to a real world monetary, production economy, faced the dilemma that there is no readily observable real interest rate determined in major real world financial markets. Accordingly, he was forced to argue that it was at the theoretical level one had to distinguish *ex ante* 'between interest expressed in terms of money and interest expressed in terms of other goods' (ibid., p. 42). In the absence of inflation, Fisher conceded that these two interest rate concepts reduce to the same thing (ibid., p. 43). Only if a change in the purchasing power of money 'is foreseen', Fisher insisted, will inflation affect the money rate of interest and cause it to differ from the real rate by an inflation premium. This Fisherian argument *assumes* that there is something which is the *ex ante* real interest rate which is either exogenous or solely determined by real factors while the nominal rate is just a veil, i.e. money is neutral.

Of course, Fisher warned that 'in actual practice, it is the rate in terms of money with which businessmen deal and hereafter the rate of interest, unless otherwise specified, will in this book be taken to be this *money* rate' (ibid.,). Moreover, Fisher conceded that in an inflationary period in the real world, the money rate of interest in the market might take inflation account 'but only slightly, and, in general, indirectly' (ibid.). Thus from a pragmatic standpoint, Fisher conceded that only the nominal rate of interest is observable in financial markets and that rate will only slightly, if at all, reflect any inflation premium.

In sum, although Fisher drew a theoretical distinction between the money rate of interest (as a premium of future money against spot money) and the real rate (future real goods versus current real goods), the latter

had a clear cut *ex ante* meaning while the former was irrelevant for decisio
makers *in a Robinson Crusoe economy* which could not have a nomina
rate (because it had no money!). Fisher clearly recognized that in the rea
world business decisions were made on the basis of the money rate o
interest, and that expectations of future inflation would only 'slightly' affec
monetary interest rates. Accordingly, the real versus money rate of interes
was a theoretical distinction which would, at most, only 'slightly' affect rea
decisions in a monetary world. Consequently, one might question whether
even for Fisher, the *ex ante* real interest rate was really an importan
concept for real world economic decision-making analysis.

Many years later, however, Milton Friedman (1956) revived and empha
sized the Fisherian distinction between the real and monetary interest rate
as an important variable affecting real decisions in an economy where
'money matters'. Friedman thereby put his distinctive monetarism empha
sis and interpretation on this Fisherian categorization. In order to avoid
any suggestion that I, a non-monetarist, have misrepresented Friedman's
views to make my case stronger, I quote from Laidler – an ardent mon
etarist – who succinctly described Friedman's argument as follows:

> First, it abstracted from any specific characteristics that money migh
> have because it is a financial asset; Friedman treated money instead 'as
> if' a (real) service yielding consumer durable to which the (real) perma
> nent income hypothesis of consumption could be applied . . . In thi
> respect Friedman's approach stands in sharp contrast to the analysis o
> William Baumol (1952) and Tobin (1956) (1958) as it does in its claim to
> be a theory of the total demand for money in the macro-economy rather
> than some component of that demand. Second, *Friedman explicitly*
> *recognized inflation as an own rate of return on money and postulated a*
> *well determined functional relationship between the expected inflation rate*
> *and the demand for money, a relationship whose existence Maynard*
> *Keynes (and some of his disciples) explicitly denied.* (Laidler, 1981, p. 3
> italics added)

This peculiar Friedman–monetarist function relating expectations of
future inflation and the market demand for money is fundamental to a
conceptualization of an *ex ante* real rate of interest as an important factor
affecting agents' portfolio–real savings behaviour. If this monetarist *ex ante*
function really exists, and if it is as important as monetarists claim, then the
high nominal market rates of interest observed over the last few years can
be interpreted as due to the public's average expectation of high future
rates of inflation. For monetarists, recent high nominal rates cannot be
either a cause of inflation (even though interest rates are a cost of doing
business in all entrepreneurial monetary, production economies) or a
reflection of the excess demand for liquidity in a period of increased
non-ergodic)[1] uncertainty. Thus, accepting the monetarists' argument, the

observed increasing *ex post* real interest rates since 1979 suggest that average world-wide expectations of inflation have been increasing substantially since Ronald Reagan took office, even as he and Paul Volker pursued a 'successful' anti-inflation policy.

Accordingly monetarists should argue that once the public realized that the back of inflationary price increases has been 'permanently' broken, then the own rate of return on money will be significantly reduced and nominal and *ex post* real rates will come back down towards the more reasonable long-term levels of the 1960s and early 1970s (where some inflation was occurring). Instead, as Tables 23.1 and 23.2 indicate, all that we have observed, despite several years of reduced inflation, is a peaking of nominal and real rates. Thus, if monetarists are correct, there is no need for central banks to provide more liquidity to reduce nominal rates; all we need now is a policy oriented towards lowering expectations regarding rates of future inflation which will, *ceteris paribus*, encourage a dramatic reduction in the high nominal interest rates that have been plaguing capitalist economies in the 1980s.

2.1 Why Should an Inflation Premium Exist?

The Fisher-Friedman argument of high nominal interest rates due to an inflation premium over the real rate of interest ultimately assumes that potential optimizing lenders (savers?) who are currently holding money balances will not make money loans (i.e. give up liquidity), unless they are compensated for the 'own' cost of holding money in a period of expected inflation. Monetarists argue that this lender-required inflation premium over the exogenously (technologically?) determined long-run real rate of interest can be demanded, because lenders can hold real physical durable goods (even consumer durables, see Friedman, 1974, p. 28–9), *as a substitute for money as a temporary abode of purchasing power*, i.e. all durables are good inflation hedges for temporarily storing purchasing power.

As Laidler correctly points out, Keynes (1936, p. 142; 1973, p. 518) specifically denied the validity of this monetarist 'real durables as an inflation hedge' argument in a world where the market on average correctly foresees inflationary trends. Harrod similarly argued that 'the occurrence of a new-found belief firmly held, that a certain rate of inflation will occur, cannot affect the market rate of interest. But the growth of *uncertainty* about what rate of inflation, if any, is in prospect, can send up the rate of interest.' (Harrod, 1971, p. 62).

There is therefore a fundamental and irreconcilable difference regarding the effects of inflation, *ceteris paribus*, on nominal market interest rates between monetarists and Keynes and his followers. This difference has important implications for the role of monetary policy as an anti-inflationary device.

3 MONETARISM, INFLATION HEDGES AND THE RATE OF INTEREST

The theoretical validity of the Keynes–Post Keynesian view of the inapplicability of a Friedman *ex ante* real rate of interest concept to a monetary, production economy concept can be developed via the following analysis:

Suppose we compare two closed economies, A and B, alike in all respects except that in the A economy there are no inflationary expectations, while suddenly at time t_0 in the B economy, lenders possess homogenous (or on average) expectations of, say, a 15 per cent inflation in the foreseeable future. If the nominal rate of interest (=the real rate) in the A economy is 5 per cent, then monetarists would argue that lenders in B will not lend their money if the nominal interest rate is less than 20 per cent; 5 per cent of which is the real rate and 15 per cent is the inflation premium.[2]
per cent of which is the real rate and 15 per cent is the inflation premium.[2]

But what alternative to lending their money holdings do lenders with inflationary expectations in the B economy have at time t_0? If they hold their money for the year, then it will be expected to lose purchasing power at a 15 per cent rate; whereas if they lend it out at interest at 5 per cent they can expect to lose purchasing power at only a 10 per cent rate. Would not lending at 5 per cent still be just as preferable as holding cash, therefore, when inflationary expectations suddenly occur?

The monetarist response to this query must be that in the B economy, potential lenders at time t_0 would neither hold cash nor lend it at nominal interest rates below 20 per cent. Instead, it would be claimed, these potential lenders in B (as opposed to those in A) would be induced by their newly found and widely held inflationary expectations to increase their purchases of durable commodities (e.g. real estate, precious metals, etc) as hedges against inflation. In other words, potential lenders (savers?) in B will increase their demand (*vis-à-vis* demand in A) for the existing stocks of durables whose spot (resale) price (net of carrying costs) is expected to keep pace with the rate of inflation. This hypothesized-induced additional demand (outward shift in the demand curve) for existing durables will be the result of lenders desiring to use resaleable durables as a 'temporary abode of purchasing power' (to use Friedman's terminology) instead of holding cash or purchasing negotiable bonds as long as the interest rate on bonds is less than 20 per cent. For *real* durables to be substitutes for money and bonds as a liquid store of value (i.e. temporary abodes of purchasing power), however, their carrying costs must be low and they must be readily resaleable in well-organized spot markets. Any durable which cannot be resold because there is no well-organized spot market for it will not be a hedge against inflation and hence will be shunned by savers in B.

In a monetary economy, liquidity means the ability to meet your monetary contractual obligations as they come due. Hence to possess liquidity requires immediate access to the medium of contractual settlement (which is the definition of money, see Keynes, 1930, p. 3; Davidson, 1977; 1982). Consequently, all assets other than money must be readily convertible into money by being resaleable in well-organized, continuous spot markets *if they are to be liquid*.

What will be the effect of this hypothesized increase in demand for existing liquid durables due to a change in expectations of inflation originating at time t_0 in the B economy? The increase in demand for goods that are to be used as hedges against inflation (which will be concentrated on not readily reproducible durables such as land, gold, Old Masters, etc.) implies that the spot (Marshallian market) price of these items at t_0 will *instantaneously* be higher than the equivalent spot price in A. These higher spot prices in B are a reflection of the 'fully anticipated' inflation expected (on average) by the B community *including those who possess legal title to these pre-existing durables in B at the moment before t_0*. Thus the original holders of the existing durables have a potential capital gain (compared to the original holders of similar durables in A); any lender in B who decides to buy a durable rather than a 5 per cent bond will discover that the spot 'prices of existing goods will be forthwith so adjusted that the advantages of holding money and of holding goods are again equalized, and it will be too late for holders of money to gain or to suffer a change in the rate of interest which will offset the prospective change during the period of the loan in the value of the money lent' (Keynes, 1936, p. 142). In other words, the original holders of durables will receive a windfall increase in the capital value of their holdings.

If inflationary expectations on average affect spot markets of all assets, the potential lenders in B will find that when the spot markets open on the morning of t_0, the opening offer prices already reflect the markets' average (rational?) expectation of inflation. In other words, at the opening of spot markets the change in the average of expectations will already be capitalized into the spot price of all durables. (In Monetarism Mach II, based on rational expectations, expectations are on average correct so that, in B, the market has already correctly discounted the inflation to come.)[3]

Thus the monetarist theory of a real versus nominal interest rate is mired in its own logical mudhole. If expectations of inflation in B which create the difference between the real and nominal interest rates do 'fully anticipate' the future so that, in Fisher's term, inflation is 'foreseen' (and any variance in expectations around the average does not affect average behaviour in spot markets) as monetarist doctrine claims, then the existing stock of real durables can never be a better *ex ante* inflation hedge than before the change in expectations occurred. The original holders of real resaleable durables form the same expectations (at least on average) as do lenders and the rest of the public at the same moment t_0. Consequently, the original holders of real durables will increase their reservation demand price (i.e. they will become as bearish on holding money as a store of value as all other agents) at the exactly same moment as the lenders do. Thus the holding of money versus bonds versus real resaleable durables will again be equalized in the *B* economy as in the *A* economy without even a single transaction having to occur as all spot prices adjust instantaneously.

It will therefore be too late for lenders of money in *B* to demand any inflation premium on loans when they suddenly have a change in inflationary expectations. The holders of money in *B* at time t_0 will have no better alternative but to continue to lend money at the same rate as in *A* as long as the Monetary Authority in *B* increases the nominal money supply *pari passu* with any increases in demand for nominal transactions balances (for normal purchases) as the money prices of goods actually purchased rise over time.

In sum, then, a newly formed expectation of changes in inflation cannot affect, *ceteris paribus*, the nominal rate of interest. Of course, in the real world any sudden growth of uncertainty (non-predictability) about the future rate of inflation can affect the nominal rate of interest by inducing a greater demand for liquidity. The interest rate in *B* can be higher than *A* at t_0, if new expectations of inflation in *B* create a growth in uncertainty about the future and many of its economic imponderables; uncertainty as to the rate of change in prices; uncertainty as to when governments, under monetarist pressure, will restrict nominal money supply growth and alter fiscal policy, etc. In *B* where uncertainties are multiplied compared to *A*, then there can be a growth in the desire to remain more liquid and avoid making monetary contractual binding commitments in the *B* economy. Thus the public may demand, *ceteris paribus*, a greater liquidity premium for giving up money now for the delivery of more of the same money in the future – even if everyone in *B* is convinced that holding money over time results in a loss of purchasing power compared to holding money in the *A* economy.

To recapitulate, widely held changes in the average expectations of a positive rate of inflation, even if agents fully and rationally anticipate future events, cannot in themselves cause an increase in the nominal interest rate compared to an expectational state of no change. Of course, as Harrod noted, 'Uncertainty about whether they (prices) will rise and by how much can send up the rate of interest by making a large number of people want to remain liquid in respect to a large proportion of their assets for the time being' (Harrod, 1971, p. 63).

4 CALENDAR TIME AND ECONOMIC STRUCTURAL STABILITY

Underlying monetarist and neoclassical synthesis Keynesian monetary theory is the conception of observed economic events being generated by an ergodic stochastic process. Samuelson, for example, notes that neoclassical monetary theory requires

> an interesting assumption . . . I shall call it the ergodic hypothesis . . . Technically speaking we theorists hope not to introduce *hysteresis* phenomena into our model, as the Bible does when it says, 'We pass this way only once' and in so doing, takes the subject out of the realm of science into the realm of genuine history (Samuelson, 1969, pp. 184–5)

In other words, a fundamental assumption of neoclassical monetary theory is that the future economic structure is already determined in the current period, at least in a stochastic sense. Under this view, human beings can only discover the future, they cannot create it.

As Samuelson suggests, technically this implies that all future economic events are the result of an already operating *ergodic* process. In an ergodic world, the probability function which governed the occurrence of past events is the same probability distribution which determines today's outcomes and it is also identical with the probability function out of which future events will be drawn (see Davidson, 1982–3). The past, current, and future economic universe is therefore presumed to be in a state of statistical control and therefore future economic outcomes can be predicted in a statistically reliable manner from past and current information.[4]

If this 'scientific' foundation of neoclassical theory is relevant and the economic system is ergodic, then there can be no unique role for money, i.e. money is neutral. But the very existence and obvious importance of money in the real world is in conflict with this orthodox economic theory. Hahn (1983, p. 1) has recognized the problem and has warned: 'The most serious challenge that the existence of money poses is this: the best developed model of the economy [an Arrow–Debreu general equilibrium model] cannot find room for it.'

Since neoclassical general equilibrium theory has no room for money in its logical structure, semantic confusions and obfuscations pervades professional discussions of the role of money in the real world. The Fisher–Friedman *real* rate of interest concept is, if it is logically consistent with what Hahn calls 'the best developed [general equilibrium] model of the economy' – which most neoclassical monetarists claim is their logical analytical base – applicable only to economies which have no room or role for money!

If money really matters, then the fact that neoclassical theory has no role for money should be an embarrassment to all honest neoclassical theorists. They should, therefore, be willing to examine objectively another model in which money does play a role in both the long and short run, i.e. a model where money is not neutral. For that is the logical system initiated by Keynes in his 'revolution' and it has continued to be developed by some of his Post Keynesian followers (Davidson, 1984).

It should have been obvious to Hahn, but apparently is not, that his acceptance of one of the fundamental axioms of neoclassical economic theory is the reason why there is no room for money in orthodox theory. This axiom, which Hahn argues 'most economists would accept' (Hahn, 1983, p. 34) can be stated as

> the objectives of agents that determine their actions and plans do not depend on any nominal magnitudes. Agents care only about 'real' things, such as goods (properly dated and distinguished by states of nature), leisure and effort. We know this as the axiom of the absence of money illusion, which it seems impossible to abandon in any sensible analysis. (ibid.).

What seems 'sensible' to Hahn, however, is absurd if one wishes to portray the role of money in the real world. For this axiom (which Hahn labels 'the absence of money illusion' but is better termed 'the axiom of reals') suggests that *money is neutral*, i.e. that it has no *real* effects. No wonder there is 'no room' for money in an economic theory which is built on a postulate that money does not matter.[5]

Keynes, of course, argued that money was not neutral (Keynes, 1973, p. 411) and that in the theory which he was articulating 'money plays a part of its own and affects motives and decisions' (ibid., pp. 408–9) in both the long run and the short run! In other words, in a Keynes–Post Keynesian theory, there is a unique role for money – money is not neutral and hence it matters.

Elsewhere I have developed the Post Keynesian analysis which argues that (a) in an economy moving through calendar time and (b) in a world of uncertainty where the future is not merely the result of an ergodic random draw from a given and unchanging probability distribution, while (c) production takes time, the most efficient way to organize production is via forward monetary contracts (Davidson, 1972, 1982, 1982–3). This creates a need for liquidity – a concept which only has meaning and relevance in a world which does not rely on the axiom of reals (Davidson, 1984). Liquidity, the ability to meet your contractual monetary obligations as they come due, is the name of the game when we want to discuss a role for money in the real world.

Of course, Frank Hahn should have realized all this since Arrow and Hahn meticulously demonstrated that:

> the terms in which contracts are made matter. In particular, if money is the goods in terms of which contracts are made, then the price of goods in terms of money are of special significance (nominal magnitudes matter!). This is not the case if we consider an economy without a past or a future . . . *If a serious monetary theory* comes to be written, the fact

that contracts are made in terms of money will be of considerable importance (Arrow and Hahn, 1971, pp. 356–7; italics added).

Moreover, Arrow and Hahn (p. 361) demonstrate that if contracts are made in terms of money (so that money affects real decisions) in an economy moving along in calendar time with a past and a future, then *all existence theorems are jeopardized*. The existence of money contracts – a characteristic of the world in which Keynes lived and which we still do – implies that there need never exist, in the long run or the short, any general equilibrium market clearing price vector.

4.1 The Need for Money Contracts

Time is a device which prevents everything from happening at once. Production processes take time and hence the decision to organize production in a certain manner must occur earlier in time than the outcome. If the economic world has, or can have, important non-ergodic circumstances associated with it, then future outcomes of any economic process can never be forecasted with statistical precision at the onset of the process. In any non-ergodic environment, people recognize that the future may be unpredictable in any stochastic sense, and hence the sensibility of human beings prevails.

Sensible expectations rely on existing human institutions which have evolved to permit fallible humans to cope with the unknowable. In such a world, the attribute of dignity associated with *all human motivation is necessarily geared not to rationality, but to sensibility*. In such a world, the institution of fixed money contracts which limit nominal liabilities is an essential adjunct of organizing production processes (Davidson and Davidson, 1984).

Only if entrepreneurs' monetary liability is contractually limited, *and if* entrepreneurs obtain reasonable assurances from their bankers that they can obtain the necessary monetary financing of their nominal working capital production contractual commitments, will their animal spirits be bolstered and their dignity protected sufficiently to undertake the burdensome organization of large-scale production. In the absence of money contracts limiting nominal liabilities and controlling expected cash flows, it is unlikely that entrepreneurs, facing a statistically unpredictable and unknowable future, would undertake large-scale, long-lived, complex production processes.

For Keynes and the Post Keynesians, non-ergodic circumstances are necessary conditions for the human institutions/organizations of money, contracts, and financial spot markets. Only in such a world does money affect the real sector in both the short and long run, i.e. *money is never neutral*. Thus, it is 'animal spirits – of a spontaneous urge to action rather than inaction and not the outcome [rational calculation, bounded or otherwise] of a weighted average of quantitative benefits multiplies by quantitative probabilities' (Keynes, 1936, p. 161) that makes the financial and industrial world go round!

Lower life forms enter into organizational structures for the efficient operation of production and consumption processes (e.g. herds of elephants, schools of fish, colonies of ants, etc.). None of these lower life animal activities utilizes 'animal spirits' interacting via contracts and money to achieve the production and consumption objectives of the species in question. Only *homo sapiens*, who can recognize the passage of time and the fundamental uncertainty of a non-ergodic world, uses monetary contracts as an essential adjunct to complex interdependent production and consumption processes. Thus, human economic activity has evolved institutions of contracts and money in order to 'assure' legal future outcomes in a non-ergodic environment.

In the real world, money is anything that legally discharges a contractual liability under the civil law of contracts. All contracts are calendar time – whether spot or forward – oriented. A spot contract designates delivery and payment at the moment of signing; while a forward contract, designates a specific future calendar date for delivery and payment. Each party to a forward contract recognizes that the other party, *despite possessing good faith at the time of signing of the contract*, may be unable and/or unwilling to execute the contractual terms at the specified date. Legal enforcement permits each party to have *sensible* expectations that if the other party does not fulfil its contractual obligations, the injured party will be entitled to just monetary compensation (Davidson and Davidson, 1984).

In the real non-ergodic world – unlike the ergodic neoclassical system – recontracting *without penalty* whenever a buyer or seller has made an error is simply not permitted as a normal way of running an economic system. *Forward nominal contracts for sale of goods and services are human institutions devised to enforce money-wage and price controls over the life of the contracts.* Business firms and households abhor what neoclassical economists love – namely, a flexible price system and recontracting without penalty.

Money contracts, therefore, attenuate potential conflicts by assuring both parties that even if uncertain future events adversely affect one party's ability to meet its commitments, the other party will have a remedy in law. The existence of contracts in terms of money, and the means to discharge contractual obligations, i.e. money, affect the real production decisions in a monetary production economy.

That thing (money) which discharges contracts in an entrepreneurial monetary–production economy has certain essential properties – namely money's elasticity of production and substitution (with producible goods) are zero or negligible (Cf. Keynes, 1936, ch. 17; Davidson, 1972, ch. 7–9).

These properties mean that money does not grow on trees, i.e. is not producible by the use of labour in the private sector, nor are easily producible durable goods substitutes for money as a temporary abode of purchasing power.

Since money is not producible by the use of labour in the private sector, it is not simply a general equilibrium *numéraire*, like peanuts. Money is unlike producible commodities; it plays a special and unique role in a monetary–production economy. Since money is not a normal, readily producible good, nor are any readily reproducible goods substitutes for money, therefore the rules under which financial institutions provide for changes in the money supply and the nominal terms at which it can be borrowed, affect the real outcomes of the economy in both the short run and the long run.

5 WHY HAVE *EX POST* REAL INTEREST RATES BEEN SO HIGH IN THE PERIOD 1980–5?

If we are to model a world in which money and money contracts are essential to the organization of production and exchange activities, then the concepts of liquidity and nominal cash outflow problems become an essential aspect of decision-making economic agents. In an entrepreneurial economy where cash flows and liquidity are important, 'the firm is dealing throughout in terms of sums of money. It has no object in the world except to end up with more money than it started with. *That is the essential characteristic of an entrepreneur economy*' (Keynes, 1979, xxix, p. 89; italics added).

For Keynes and Post Keynesians, investment in fixed and working capital goods depends on the expected future net cash flows that will be generated by these activities in an entrepreneurial economy *vis-à-vis* the expected nominal return on liquid (easily resaleable in a spot market) assets (Keynes, 1936, ch. 17). Consequently, the rate of interest, *which is strictly a monetary phenomenon* in a monetary production economy, rules the roost. In such a world money is not neutral, i.e. money is a real phenomenon which affects real outcomes and the rate of interest is strictly a monetary phenomenon (see Kregel, 1983).

It therefore follows that the real rate of interest can only be an *ex post* calculated phenomenon; its magnitude depends on two independent (in the sense that knowing the magnitude of one does not uniquely explain the value of the other) variables – (i) the nominal rate of interest charged on loans and (ii) the current rate of inflation.

To explain the recent *ex post* high real rates shown in Tables 23.1 and 23.2, therefore, we must investigate the reasons for (a) high nominal rates, and (b) the decline in the actual rate of inflation in recent years.

5.1   US Monetary Policy – Changes in Fed Targets and US Banking Law

The United States is, for all intents and purposes, the central banker for the world. The US economy, despite its many stumbles over the last fifteen years, is gargantuan compared to others. In 1980, for example, the World Bank (1983) estimates that the GNP of the United States exceeded 25 per cent of the free world's GNP. The importance of being so important is that monetary and financial developments in the United States must spill over to the major financial markets in the rest of the free world. Thus if Paul Volker catches the flu, world financial markets are threatened with pneumonia.

As Table 23.2 suggests, from 1973 to 1979, the trend in nominal interest rates in the US was moderately up as the Federal Reserve practised orthodox (marginally) restrictive monetary policies, in expansionary phases of the business cycle during the 1970s, in an attempt to reduce inflationary pressures. With the second oil price shock of 1979 and the success of Carter policies of 'talking' down the dollar in the hopes of stimulating exports, inflation in the United States began to accelerate dramatically to double-digit levels by the end of 1979.

The then newly appointed Chairman of the Fed, Mr Volker, believed that drastic monetary action was necessary to stem the inflationary flood. Dramatic new non-accommodating policies which broke with post-Second World War tradition were announced in the autumn of 1979. These Fed policy changes were widely interpreted as indicating that the Fed would no longer attempt to limit movements in nominal interest rates; rather the target would be to limit the growth of the money stock. This generated tremendous uncertainties in financial markets as to future interest rates. Almost all market participants believed that the dramatic change in US monetary policy would cause nominal rates to rise rapidly but no one could make any statistical predictions based on existing time series realizations as to how high nominal rates would go.

Technically speaking, financial market participants believed they were entering an uncertain (non-ergodic) environment where past times series evidence provided little statistical reliability in forecasting the quantitative changes in future nominal interest rates. In such a world of recognized unpredictability, *sensible agents* realize that it is important to remain as liquid as possible so as to take advantages of unforeseeable commitments that could become financial disasters if unforeseen misfortunes occur. Indeed in the years immediately following the Fed's announced change in policy targets, uncertainty increased and the result was greater desires for liquidity; and nominal interest rates rose to new highs not seen for many years.

Thus sensible agents formed expectations that were not 'rational' in the Muth–Lucas sense. These *sensible expectations*, however, are essential for survival in a non-ergodic world. Those who strived for greater liquidity as soon as the Fed announced a change in policy in 1979 were more able to survive the unpredictable liquidity problems of the early 1980s. In a world of uncertainty, liquidity is freedom and any sensible agent, in a monetary-production economy, who hesitates and avoids becoming illiquid is saved to make a decision another day.

Almost simultaneously with Mr Volker's revolutionary policy changes, the Congress passed the Monetary Control Act of 1980 which, while attempting to reduce the cash outflow problems of some banks due to disintermediation, severely impacted on the nominal costs of the liabilities of the existing banking system in the United States. Prior to this legislation and since the Great Depression, interest payments on demand deposits were prohibited by law and normal competitive banking activities for funds were circumscribed by close legal regulation which limited the customary behaviour of bankers. Thus up until 1980, a major portion of bank liabilities (demand deposits) were carried interest free. Accordingly, bankers could afford on the average to make commercial loans at overall lower nominal rates for any given cost of borrowed funds. Simultaneously, at least till 1979, it was Fed policy to stabilize the cost of borrowed funds at any one time, and only permit a slow upward drift of the cost of borrowing reserves during periods of rapid economic growth. With the imposition of the Monetary Control Act of 1980, the prohibition against interest rate payments for cheque accounts was lifted and even though some limits remained these interest ceilings are being phased out and will disappear by 1986.

For US bankers, therefore, the change in legislation meant that the average cost of funds, *ceteris paribus*, rose dramatically with the passage of the Monetary Control Act of 1980. Hence even if the Fed had not embarked on a dramatic change in policy in late 1979, the nominal costs of bank loans would have, *ceteris paribus*, increased in 1980 as an institutional increase in bankers' cost of carrying demand deposit liabilities was legislated. At approximately the same time, the cost of borrowing funds either directly from the Fed or indirectly via liability management through money markets rose dramatically because of the announced changes in Fed policy and the sensible increased liquidity preferences they created. Consequently, the cost of liability management for US bankers rose significantly, requiring them to obtain higher nominal interest rates on all bank loans. No wonder interest rates rose to unprecedented heights in 1980–1 in the US.

The impact on the rest of the world's major financial markets of these 1979–80 changes in the Fed policy is clear. The initially higher nominal interest rates in the US created interest rate differentials which encouraged a flow of short-term funds to the United States. Foreign central banks were forced to raise domestic nominal interest rates to help reduce the capital outflow. Nominal interest rates rose rapidly and substantially in all major capital markets, reducing private sector world aggregate demand and contributing to world-wide recession. Moreover, to the extent that some nations (e.g. the UK and Austria) specifically attempted to maintain high exchange rates on an anti-inflationary device, the Fed's high nominal interest rate policy required them to raise their nominal interest rates even more to protect the exchange rate.

The world-wide drop in aggregate demand was a major attack on inflation. The effect of the world-wide recession of 1981–2, and the political union bashing activities of newly elected leaders such as Reagan and Thatcher, significantly reduced labour's power to push up money wages. Simultaneously, US legislative energy policies of the mid-1970s which had mandated increases in the mileage per gallon performance of the changing stock of cars on US roads caused aggregate petrol consumption to peak in 1979 even though mileage *per capita* continued to rise. This decline in petrol demand which started in 1980 in the US – the biggest market for oil in the world – plus energy conservation policies world-wide induced a downward trend in the demand for fossil fuels which was reinforced by the recession of 1981–2. Also by the end of the 1970s the compensation for the nationalization of the vast Saudi Arabian oil fields (as well as other OPEC producing properties) had been accomplished. Having received compensation settlements based on the projection of high cartel prices of underground reserves, the major multinational companies, since the second oil price shock in 1979, have had incentives to develop and bring on stream alternative oil reserves outside the Persian Gulf, thereby weakening the power of the Saudis to act as the cartel's balancing wheel. This has put additional downward pressure on world-wide energy prices and slowed inflationary trends throughout the developed consuming nations of the world.

Thus, the continuous growth in nominal wage rates and energy prices that major nations of the world had suffered for most of the 1970s were dealt severe and concurrent body-blows. The result was to slow increases drastically in (if not actually lower) nominal unit labour and energy costs of domestic production in the US and in most of the industrialized nations of the world. Hence inflation in the nominal production cost of domestically produced goods declined dramatically. This decline in inflation of domestically produced goods was reinforced by the lower cost of imports for the US where the inflow of funds raised the international value of the dollar. For other developed nations, on the other hand, this slowing of the rise in domestic unit labour costs was at least partially offset by the inflation in imported goods in those nations whose exchange rate declined *vis-à-vis* its trading partners and/or in terms of the dollar (the standard for pricing standardized commodities such as food, energy and metals in international trade).

While non-US nominal interest rates had to follow the Volker lead to stem capital outflows, the fall in exchange rates *vis-à-vis* the dollar between 1981 and 1984 meant a *ceteris paribus* slower rate of decline in the inflation rates for Japan and Western Europe due to the relatively higher prices of dollar-dominated imported goods such as food and energy. The resulting high real interest rates (but not as high as those in the US) for Japan, Germany, France and the UK in the 1980s as shown in Tables 23.1 and 23.2 are the *ex post* result of several concurrent forces.

6 EPILOGUE

Real *ex post* US interest rates increased from 1980 through early 1985 as a result of (i) high *nominal* interest rates precipitated by the type of monetary policies pursued during this period and (ii) lower inflation rates. Non-US *ex post* real interest rates have also been increasing. This can be explained by (a) the need to follow the increases in nominal rates dictated by US monetary authorities, and (b) the differential (and less decline) in inflationary forces unleashed by a floating exchange rate system in which the dominant industrial and agricultural power is forcing nominal interest rates up world-wide regardless of the rate of inflation in the various nations.

Since the economic world is non-ergodic, it is not possible to forecast the future with any degree of statistical reliability. As Shackle has noted, proper economic theory does not possess the power to predict actual future outcomes. Economic theory is fundamentally taxonomic or classificatory. It is useful in

> putting situations in this box or that according to what *can* happen . . . Theories which tell us what *will* happen are claiming too much: too much independence from their turbulent surroundings; too much capacity to remain upright in the gale of politics; diplomacy and technical chance and change. Kaledic theories give insight; preparedness for what cannot, in its nature, be known for sure . . . but which need not spring a total surprise. Classification is no second-rate technique. It is the method of medicine . . . of the law . . . of the organization of libraries . . . of stellar astronomy . . . of botanical and zoological organization. . . . Even the procedure for finding solutions of differential equations is a question of groping in a catalogue of possibilities. The efficiency of formal codes is the efficiency of classification. (Shackle, 1972, pp. 72–3)

And Shackle might have added, the greatest contributions to the development of economic theory have come via refinements in classification, e.g. Ricardo's division of income into wages, rents, and profits, or Marshall's introduction of elasticity classes into economics.

In this humble view of the power of economic theory then, one cannot predict what will happen to nominal and *ex post* real interest rates in 1986. And such a prediction was not a goal of this analysis. This chapter will have succeeded in its purposes if it has encouraged others to, in the future, consider analytical models where money is not neutral in either the short run or the long run. In such a world, the role of policy is to develop institutions which can reinforce voluntarily entered into contractual arrangements which make price and nominal interest rate movements sticky over times at levels which encourage the full employment of resources. In a non-ergodic world with non-neutral money, dedicated and vigilant policy decision-makers, ready to respond to unknown future events in a manner to encourage full employment and social harmony, are essential to the efficient operation of highly developed interdependent entrepreneurial economies.

Notes

1. The terms non-ergodic/ergodic can be defined as follows. Stochastic processes generate time series data (realizations) which can be used to form statistical averages. *Space averages* are statistical averages formed over a universe of realizations observed at a fixed point of time (i.e. estimates from cross sectional data). *Time averages*, on the other hand, refer to averages calculated from a single realization over an indefinite period of calendar time. If the process is *ergodic*, then, for infinite realizations, the space average and the time average will coincide, while for finite realizations the space and time averages will tend to converge (with the probability of unity).

   Hence, if an economic process is *non-ergodic*, then the calculation of either a time and/or space average based on past data cannot be expected to provide a statistically reliable estimate of either (1) the current space average or (2) any time or space averages that will be observed over future calendar time. Nor can any currently estimated space average provide reliable estimates of future time or space averages. *In other words, in a non-ergodic environment, past observations do not produce knowledge about current and/or future events, while current observations of events provide no statistically reliable unbiased estimates about future time and/or space averages.*

   One type of non-ergodic economic process is one which moves in historical time so that its distribution function is not independent of historical time, i.e. history matters. Such an historical process is labelled nonstationary by statisticians. Nonstationarity is a sufficient but not a necessary condition for non-ergodicity.

   Some stationary stochastic processes, e.g. limit cycles, are also non-ergodic. An example of an economic limit cycle would be many accelerator–multiplier trade cycle models with ceilings and floors (see Davidson, 1982–3, pp. 186–7).

2. The rationale for this alleged behaviour was originally developed by Fisher (1911) who, in essence, argued that if $100 was worth 100 apples at the *current* (t_0) spot price, then a lender might be willing to lend at 5 per cent if there were no inflationary expectations so that at the end of the year when the loan was

paid off she/he expected to receive purchasing power sufficient to buy 105 apples. If, however, the lender expected a year from today that $100 would only purchase 85 apples (15 per cent expected inflation), then the lender would be willing to lend only at a 20 per cent nominal interest rate so that one year from today the $120 maturity value of the bond would be expected to buy 105 apples (and hence the *ex ante* real rate of interest would still be 5 per cent).

3. If, from hindsight, today's expectations are not proved correct, today's spot price will merely reflect the discounted value of the expected (incorrect) inflation.
4. Stationarity is a necessary, but not sufficient condition for predictability (see Davidson, 1982–3, p. 186, n. 1).
5. Despite Friedman's use of the motto 'money matters', he remains faithful to the axiom of reals and does not permit money to affect the long-run outcome of his system. In his own description of his logical framework, Friedman states

> that changes in the quantity of money as such *in the long run* have a negligible effect on real income so that nonmonetary forces are 'all that matter' for changes in real income over decades and money 'does not matter' . . . I regard the description of our position as 'money is all that matters for changes in *nominal income* and for *short-run* changes in real income' as an exaggeration but one that gives the right flavor to our conclusions. (Friedman, 1974, p. 27)

References

Arrow, K. W. and Hahn, F. H. (1971), *General Competitive Analysis* (San Francisco: Holden-Day).

Davidson, P. (1972), *Money and the Real World* (London: Macmillan).

Davidson, P. (1977), 'Money and General Equilibrium' *Economie Appliquée*, 30; reprinted as Appendix to chapter 3 of Davidson (1982).

Davidson, P. (1982), *International Money and the Real World* (London: Macmillan).

Davidson, P. (1982–3), 'Rational Expectations: A Fallacious Foundation for Analyzing Crucial Decision Making', *Journal of Post Keynesian Economics*, 5, (Winter).

Davidson, P. (1984), 'Reviving Keynes's Revolution', *Journal of Post Keynesian Economics*, 6, (Summer).

Davidson, P. and Davidson, G. S. (1984), 'Financial Markets and Williamson's Theory of Governance: Efficiency vs. Concentration vs. Power', *Quarterly Review of Economics and Business*, 24 (Winter) (Chapter 21 of this volume).

Fisher, I. (1911), *The Purchasing Power of Money* (New York: Macmillan).

Fisher, I. (1930), *The Theory of Interest*, (original edition), reprinted in 1961 in New York by Augustus M. Kelley.

Friedman, M. (1956), 'The Quantity Theory of Money: A Restatement', in *Studies in the Quantity Theory of Money*, by M. Friedman, (ed.) (Chicago: University of Chicago Press).

Friedman, M. (1974), 'A Theoretical Framework for Monetary Analysis', in *Milton Friedman's Monetary Framework: A Debate with His Critics*, by R. J. Gordon, (ed.) (Chicago: University of Chicago Press).

Hahn, F. H. (1983), *Money and Inflation*, (Cambridge, Mass: MIT Press).

Harrod, R. F. (1971), '*Discussion Paper*', in *Monetary Theory and Policy in the 1970s* by G. Clayton *et al.*, (eds) (Oxford: Oxford University Press).

Keynes, J. M. (1930), *A Treatise on Money* (London: Macmillan).

Keynes, J. M. (1936), *The General Theory of Employment Interest and Money*, (New York: Harcourt).

Keynes, J. M. (1973), *The Collected Writings of John Maynard Keynes*, Vol. XIII, by D. Moggridge (ed.) (London: Macmillan).

Keynes, J. M. (1979), *The Collected Writings of John Maynard Keynes*, Vol. XXIX, by D. Moggridge (ed.) (London: Macmillan).

Kregel, J. A. (1983), 'The Multiplier and Liquidity Preference: Two Sides of the Theory of Effective Demand', (mimeo).

Laidler, D. (1981), 'Monetarism: An Interpretation and An Assessment', *Economic Journal*, 91.

Samuelson, P. A. (1969), 'Classical and Neo-Classical Monetary Theory', in *Monetary Theory* by R. W. Clower, (ed.) (Harmondsworth: Penguin). Originally published under the title 'What Classical and Neoclassical Monetary Theory Really was', *Canadian Journal of Economics*, 1, (1968).

Shackle, G. L. S. (1972), *Epistemics and Economics: A Critique of Economic Doctrines* (London: Cambridge University Press).

World Bank (International Bank of Reconstruction and Development) (1983), *1983 World Bank Atlas* (Washington: The World Bank).

24 Finance, Funding, Saving, and Investment*

One of the most difficult aspects of monetary theory is to distinguish between the necessary (short-term) financing of an investment project while it is being constructed and the (long-term) funding of an investment project after it is completed. In a monetary economy, real investments flows are not usually undertaken until short-term bank financing arrangements have been made. Once undertaken, the real savings comes into existence *pari passu* with the real investment flow. Once built, the investment goods exist whether the long-term funding process is successful or not.

Since a clear distinction is rarely made between the short-term bank financing and the long-term security market funding concepts, confusion regarding the roles of saving, investment, and the banking system in a monetary production economy is rife in the literature.

In an earlier book (Davidson, 1982), I attempted, apparently unsuccessfully, to draw the distinction between short-term construction fund finance and long-term investment fund finance. I am grateful that Professor Asimakopulos's (1986) latest analytical intercharge with Professor Kregel gives me the opportunity to clarify my view of the role of the banking system whose function it is to create additional short-term finance whenever entrepreneurs wish to increase the flow of real investment. This bank-created (non-resource using) finance must be distinguished from the role of long-term financial markets which require the public to give up an amount of liquidity equal to real savings (i.e. unexercised income claims on resources) in the process of funding the investment.

1 FINANCE VERSUS FUNDING REVISITED

A stylized narrative of the finance–investment–funding–savings process of a monetary, production economy where entrepreneurs use forward money contracts to efficiently organize long-duration production processes can provide our basic analytical framework.

In a monetary economy, entrepreneurs tend to buy plant and equipment from firms specializing in the production of specific goods needed as capital inputs in the production process of the investing firm. Even firms that are

* *Journal of Post Keynesian Economics*, Fall 1986, vol. 9 # 1.

capital goods producers normally do not produce their own plant and equipment – rather, they purchase these tools from others.

Since production takes time, and capital goods are typically those that have very long gestation periods, most capital goods are ordered on forward contract. The forward contract assures the seller of the commitment of a buyer willing to pay for, and take delivery of, the output of a long duration, expensive production process. This output typically has been customized (e.g. plant built and affixed to buyer's property) to fit the buyer's requirements. Moreover, with the signed contract in hand, the capital goods producer can readily borrow short-term finance from his banker to meet his production costs while fabricating the goods.

The buyer, on the other hand, needs the cost control assurance that an *explicit* forward money contract provides, for, when delivery occurs, the purchase price (cash-outflow obligation) has been limited in advance. With the possession of the sales commitment, the buyer need only worry whether he possesses the liquidity (or can obtain it from the financial market) to meet this contractually fixed nominal cash-outflow obligation at the time of delivery.

Thus both producers and buyers of capital goods benefit from *explicit* forward money contracting.

1.1. The Finance and Funding of Contractual Commitments

When managers have expectations that the present value of the future net cash flows (discounted by a long-term interest rate) of an investment project exceeds the supply price (production cost) offer quoted by the manufacturer of the capital goods involved, the project is deemed worthwhile.

If the buyer does not have sufficient liquidity to pay for the project, the firm will require *external* funding on the specified delivery and payment date. The firm will typically engage an underwriter (investment banker), who will contractually commit his institution to provide for the flotation of a new issue, at a specified long-term interest rate.[1] (For simplicity we will assume external debt rather than equity funding is used.[2]) The sales receipts of the new issue are expected to generate an 'investment fund' for the buyer to make payment to the seller at the delivery date.[3] The long-term interest rate quoted by the underwriter will be used by the prospective investor to discount the project's expected cash flows.

Armed with the underwriter's guarantee to provide liquidity via an 'investment fund' (cf. Davidson, 1978, p. 37), the investing entrepreneur can safely enter into a forward purchase order thereby providing the capital goods producer with a sales contract. In the process, the capital goods buyer has contractually matched his forthcoming capital cash-outflows and inflows.

The capital goods producer's supply price offer is based on (1) his estimate of the production costs of labour and raw materials (typically purchased on forward contract so that the seller's production–cost cash-outflows are controlled by contract) plus (2) the short-term interest cost charged by his banker for financing payroll and material suppliers' bills from the moment when production is started to the date when final payment from the buyer is contracted to be received.

Normally, the capital goods producer has an established customer–client relationship with his commercial banker. Consequently, the signed purchase order contract is usually more than sufficient collateral for the commercial banker to be willing to commit the bank to finance the producer's production costs via a short-term (working capital) loan for the duration of the production period (cf. ibid., pp. 36–7). Hence the producer has, via this process, not only matched his production cash-outflows on payrolls and materials with his bank loan cash-inflow, but he has also matched his loan repayment cash-outflow with his forward sales receipts cash-inflow. Having assured himself of the ability to meet all his cash-outflows with matching cash-inflows, the producer can now settle down to the job of producing new investment goods by hiring (assumed) otherwise unemployed resources.

Consequently, at the signing of the order contract, both parties can confidently expect that there will be no financial (i.e. liquidity) difficulties in carrying out all their commitments.

As long as the producer's commercial banker provides (creates) short-term bank money, the real (additional) investment flow will be undertaken – without anyone's precommitment of planned (additional) savings – as long as the idle resources necessary to produce the goods are available. Of course, when the investment flow is actually produced, then the rights to the real savings flows (i.e. unused claims on resource production) must have occurred somewhere in the economy. It will be up to the investment banker to accumulate these liquidity claims on resources equal to these real savings by successfully floating the new issue.

1.2 The Role of the Banks to Create Finance

Commercial banks create money every time they increase the aggregate volume of bank loans outstanding in the economy. If the investment project under consideration is an addition to the current investment flow, and if there exist unemployed resources available to produce these additional capital goods, then as soon as the producing firm hires the unemployed resources (paid out of increases in bank credit) aggregate real investment increases. All that is needed to initiate this additional real investment flow therefore is *the working capital finance provided by an increase in total bank loans*. At this stage, no plans or desires explicitly to increase savings by the public are required to finance any hypothesized *additional* investment project, as long as the banker can create new finance via acceptable bank accounting practices. The bank liabilities created are sufficient to mobilize (hire) the idle resources necessary to bring this additional investment project on stream.

The mere fact that previously idle resources are now producing *real investment goods* which cannot be used by households for consumption purposes means that, out of the increased income flow, a greater *real savings* flow must be *pari passu* occurring. Hence, Kregel is correct in his claim that – assuming idle resources are available – only a liquidity constraint resulting from the banks refusing to create additional loans to permit the financing of additional profitable investment projects can abort this planned hypothesized increase in real investment.

1.3   Funding the Payment for Completed Investment Projects

When the investment project is completed and delivery is made, the capital goods produced have been *accounted* for as part of the real income flow of the community for the relevant accounting period. This real investment flow, by its physical nature, is unavailable for purchase and use by consumers. Thus, there must be a real savings flow in the same period equal to that portion of the real income flow that is unavailable for consumption. This real savings is widely dispersed among households and other agents who have earned income this period but have not exercised all the claims on the products of industry that their income provided for them. In a monetary economy, these unexercised claims initially take the form of the possession of fully liquid money.

When the real investment has been produced and the associated real spending flows have already been completed, the investment underwriter can float the new issue, whose nominal value equals the purchase price of the investment. If the underwriter is successful in floating the issue at the interest rate quoted in the underwriting agreement as the cost of funding, the underwriter makes a profit. At that long-run rate of interest, members of the public will have given up their current (liquid) claims on resources equal to the extra liquidity created by the banking system and used by the capital goods producer to meet his production cost commitments. Even if the underwriter is unsuccessful at floating the entire new issue at the expected interest rate, he will still provide the funds to the buyer (as he is legally required to do) while taking a loss on this flotation.[4]

The investment buyer will then have sufficient *funding* to meet his contractual purchase order payment. The seller, upon receipt of payment from the buyer, will be able to repay his bank loan. The repaid bank loan will then be able to be utilized as 'a revolving fund of short-term finance' to permit other capital producers to finance their new production operations

if they get orders which maintain the current (higher) investment production flows.[5]

2 WHAT DOES ASIMAKOPULOS MEAN?

Asimakopulos posits a situation in which a new investment project has
already taken place (raising real investment) but, for some unexplained
reason, the 'increase in desired [planned?] saving does not occur simultaneously with the [investment] expenditure . . . [desired savings] takes
place only when the full multiplier effects of an increase in investment have
worked themselves out' (1986, p. 83). Like Kregel, I suspect that at this
point Asimakopulos's exposition has been trapped by the usual textbook
terminology which confuses investment and income flows for levels[6] – and
hence his criticism involves a semantic misunderstanding.

Assume that an entrepreneur is willing to undertake an additional
investment of ΔI, where ΔI equals the supply price of this additional
investment project. When the additional investment contract is signed and
the bank provides additional working capital finance, then the increase in
the money supply (ΔM) initially equals the supply price of the additional
investment (cf. Davidson, 1978, pp. 270–1); that is,

$$\Delta M = \Delta I \tag{24.1}$$

If there are unemployed resources, the additional bank finance advanced
will allow the capital goods producer to marshall these resources into
productive employment and there will be an increase in real income flows.

At this point, what does Asimakopulos mean when he says that the
'multiplier effects' have not yet worked themselves out? I understand him
as assuming that the consumption goods producers do not realize that the
additional employment would increase the market demand for consumption goods and hence they do not build up their working capital in order to
have additional consumption goods available when the newly employed
workers came to market with their paychecks.[7] Hence, the induced increases in real consumption goods that make up the multiplier effects have
not yet 'worked themselves out'. Nevertheless, there will still be a relationship between actual real investment and real income flows such that

$$Y = kI \tag{24.2}$$

This equation is, however, based on an accounting identity stating that
all income flows are either investment goods or consumption goods and
hence income flow must be some multiple of investment flow at each point
of time. If k is to reflect Asimakopulos's 'worked out' multiplier effects,

then he must assume that the expansion was foreseen by the consumption goods producers. If the expansion was not foreseen, then the additional money incomes of newly employed workers cannot buy additional real consumption goods. Additional worker spending merely bids up the market price of consumer goods (whose flow rate is, by hypothesis, unchanged) leading to windfall profits for consumption goods producers (and no real income gains for workers as a group, at least until consumption goods production expands). These windfall profits will, by definition, be equal to additional 'planned' savings – as it is impossible to plan to spend (unexpected) windfalls!

Kregel, on the other hand, interprets Asimakopulos as assuming a Robertsonian period so short that the newly employed workers (1) have not yet been paid, or (2) having been paid these workers have not had a chance to spend their incomes. In either of these cases, as Kregel has noted, some 'forced saving' concept by workers is implied. For long-duration capital goods production processes where payrolls are going to have to be met for many weeks before the project is completed, I find it difficult to accept the existence of such arbitrary payment barriers as cases (24.1) or (24.2) to explain 'forced savings' by workers. Instead I would argue that, if the expansion was foreseen, the multiplier holds instantaneously at all points of time – as it is merely an expression between two equilibrium production flow rates. Asimakopulos must be assuming either that the expansion was not foreseen and hence additional consumption goods have not come on stream, or else that the underwriter attempts to sell the new issue before the real investment has been undertaken (see note 5).

3 LIQUIDITY CONSTRAINTS EVEN WHEN SAVINGS EQUALS INVESTMENT

Assume all financing of increased real investment flows is accomplished via the banking system creating credit – without any prior availability of planned household savings. At delivery and payment date for the new investment project, there will always exist enough additional liquidity (and additional savings) to fund the capital goods buyers' additional forward purchase commitments. All that is required is that the investment underwriter mobilize these liquid additional savings funds at the initial interest rate via the new issue market.

Assume also that, in Asimakopulos's terminology, the multiplier effects have worked their way out, so that actual investment (I) equals (desired?) household savings (S^h). Since all investment is to be externally financed, then whether the volume of new issues (ni) can be floated at the initial interest rate or not depends on whether

$$ni \gtreqless mS^h \tag{24.3}$$

where m is equal to the marginal propensity to purchase securities out of household savings.

If, as is often assumed, the marginal propensity to buy securities out of savings at the existing long-term interest rate is equal to unity ($m = 1$) (see Brechling, 1957; Davidson, 1978, pp. 324ff.), then, at the current long-term interest rate,

$$I = ni = mS^h \tag{24.4}$$

and all the new issues will be successfully floated to the public at the offer price.

If, however, the marginal propensity to purchase securities out of savings is less than unity, so that

$$I = ni > mS^h \tag{24.5}$$

at the initial rate of interest, then the volume of new issues exceeds the public's demand for additional securities at the original offer price. In this case, a shortage of liquidity can constrain real output expansion even though *the additional planned savings flow is equal to the additional investment flow*. If $m < 1$, then the underwriters will be unsuccessful in funding all the investment projects in the new issue market at the long-term rate of interest which they anticipated when they made the underwriting commitment to the investment buyers.

When $m < 1$, at the initial interest rate, some households desire to hold some of their savings in the form of fully liquid money. Hence, all the new issues cannot be sold at the original offer price even though desired household savings equals investment. A higher long-term interest will have to be offered sufficient to induce savers to give up the additional liquidity they wished to hold at the initial interest rate (*or* some long-term securities will have to be absorbed by the central bank to ease the liquidity constraint).

With a higher interest rate, even though desired household savings as a function of income is unchanged, the form in which savings will be held will be altered. Savers are induced by higher interest rates to give up fully liquid money to hold less liquid new issues.

Consequently, when savers' liquidity preference is sensitive to long-term interest rates, then the fact that savers have a marginal propensity to buy securities (at the initial interest rate) of less than unity will, *ceteris paribus*, increase the costs of long-term funding, lowering the profitability of prospective investments and thereby slowing down future additional in-

vestment flows and depressing the economy – even though the 'multiplie
effects' have 'worked their way out'.

The solution to any scenario in which liquidity constraints limit invest
ment no matter how much the public 'desires' to save out of income *e*
ante, *ex post*, or *ex anything else* is for the monetary authority to provide
via the banking system, all the liquidity the public desires. Ultimately, in
monetary economy, where 'money matters', that is, money is never neu
tral, it is liquidity constraints and *never* an income (or savings) constrain
that limits expansion before full employment.

Notes

1. If the buyer has a contractual commitment from his investment banker (or
   underwriter) to provide the funds to purchase the capital goods, then the buyer
   can proceed with the contract signing without fear of illiquidity in a statistically
   unpredictable future (cf. Davidson, 1978, ch. 11). Of course, a good underwriter will also limit future surprises by contacting professional pension fund
   managers, insurance company portfolio managers, and so on in order to get
   these disbursers of public funds to commit themselves to buy the new issues
   when they come to market. It is these formal and informal forward liquidity
   commitments which permit decision-makers to assure themselves of future
   financial outcomes in a nonergodic (uncertain) environment.
2. For a discussion of the conceptual differences between debt and equity funding,
   see Hicks (1967, p. 47) and Davidson (1978, pp. 410–13).
3. Normally the investment underwriter provides contractual guarantees that he
   will be liable for any funds not received if the sale of the new issue to the public
   falls short of expectations.
4. The way the investment banker adjusts to this problem, and his ability to finance
   unsuccessful new issue flotations by further borrowings from the banking
   system, is discussed in Davidson (1978, ch. 11). The upshot is, however, that the
   financial system ultimately can restrict accumulation because of a shortage of
   liquidity, even when idle resources and entrepreneurial 'animal spirits' exist.
5. For completeness, it should be noted that if the underwriter should try to
   borrow the liquidity generated by the real savings *before* it exists, for example,
   at the moment of the signing of the forward order contract for new capital
   goods, then tightness in the money market will constrain output. An early
   example of this situation was given by Keynes in the 18 April 1939, edition of
   The Times when he wrote: 'If an attempt is made to borrow them [the savings
   which result from the increased production of non-consumption (war) goods]
   before they exist, as the Treasury have done once or twice lately, a stringency in
   the money market must result, since, pending the expenditure, the liquid
   resources acquired by the Treasury must be at the expense of the normal liquid
   resources of the banks and public.'
6. A problem that, I recognize, I have often encountered in my own writings over
   the years.
7. If the income flow has risen more than the additional investment flow (the
   multiplier effects), then some of the increased real output is the result of
   increased production of consumption goods by producers anticipating the ad-

ditional induced consumption expenditures of newly hired workers. Since the production of consumption goods takes time, this must also be financed via working capital loans from the banking system. Consequently, the total increase in the supply of money provided by bankers for working capital loans to both investment and consumption goods producers equals the increase in aggregate working capital (equals the increase in real income flows) (cf. Davidson, 1978, pp. 270–2; Moore, 1986). Once aggregate income flows are no longer increasing, then there is no requirement for additional bank money. The existing money supply becomes a revolving fund of finance available each production period to finance the same total flow of work-in-process goods.

References

Asimakopulos, A. (1986), 'Finance, Liquidity, Saving, and Investment', *Journal of Post Keynesian Economics*, 9 (1), pp. 79–90.
Brechling, F. P. R. (1957), 'A Note on Bond Holding and the Liquidity Preference Theory of the Interest Rate', *Review of Economic Studies*, 24.
Davidson, P. (1978), *Money and the Real World* (London: Macmillan).
Davidson, P. (1982), *International Money and the Real World* (London: Macmillan).
Hicks, J. R. (1967), *Critical Essays in Monetary Theory* (Oxford: Clarendon Press).
Kregel, J. A. (1984–5) 'Constraints on the Expansion of Output and Employment: Real or Monetary?' *Journal of Post Keynesian Economics*, 7 (2), pp. 139–52.
Moore, B. J. (1986), *Horizontalists and Verticalists*, unpublished manuscript.

25 Endogenous Money, the Production Process, and Inflation Analysis*

Recently, Hahn, a distinguished neoclassical theorist, wrote. 'The mo:
serious challenge that the existence of money poses to the theorist is thi:
the best developed model of the economy cannot find room for it' (Hahr
1981, p. 1).

Because orthodox economic theory dominates the discussion in th
professional literature, and because orthodoxy has 'no room' for money i:
its search for existence proofs, semantic confusion and obfuscations pe:
vade the professional discussions on whether 'money matters' and th
related question as to whether the money supply is exogenous or endogen
ous. Yet, Keynes and some Post Keynesians have striven to develop a:
analytical structure where not only does money play a unique role, bu
where a money economy operates differently from a non-monetary system

In section 1, a brief outline of the role of money in a monetary
production economy is outlined. Section 2 indicates that the terms exogen
ous and endogenous in relation to the money supply have often been use
in different and sometimes conceptually incompatible manners. Then :
taxonomic scheme for distinguishing exogenous versus endogenous mone:
is developed which is consistent with the Post Keynesian monetary theor:
where money plays an important role in both the long run and the shor
run. Section 3 describes the two possible processes for changing the suppl:
of money. Finally, section 4 analyses the financing of real bills and inflatio:
bills.

1 MONEY'S ROLE

It should have been obvious to Hahn, but apparently is not, that his
acceptance of one of the fundamental axioms of neoclassical economic
theory is the reason that there is no room for money in orthodox theory.
This axiom, which Hahn argues 'most economists would accept' (Hahn,
1981, p. 34) can be stated as

* *Economie Appliquée*, XLI, 1988. Papers presented at An International Conference of the
Faculty of the Social Sciences, University of Ottawa, 3–6 October 1984 – organized jointly
by the University of Ottawa and the Institut de Sciences Mathématiques et Economiques
Appliquées of Paris.

the objectives of agents that determine their actions and plants do not depend on any nominal magnitudes. Agents care only about 'real' things, such as goods (properly dated and distinguished by states of nature), leisure and effort. We know this as the axiom of the absence of money illusion, which it seems impossible to abandon in any sensible analysis.

What seems 'sensible' to Hahn, however, is absurd if one wishes to portray the role of money in the real world. For this axiom (which Hahn labels 'the absence of money illusion' but is better termed 'the axiom of reals') suggests that *money is neutral*, i.e. that it has no *real* effects. No wonder there is 'no room' for money in an economic theory which is built on a postulate that money does not matter.

Keynes, of course, argued that money was not neutral (Keynes, 1973, XIII, p. 411) and that in the theory which he was articulating 'money plays a part of its own and affects motives and decisions' (ibid. pp. 408–9) in both the long run and the short run! In other words, in a Keynes–Post Keynesian theory, there is a unique role for money – money matters!

Elsewhere I have developed the Post Keynesian analysis which argues that (a) in an economy moving through calendar time and (b) in a world of uncertainty where the future is not merely a result of an ergodic random draw from a given and unchanging probability distribution, while (c) production takes time, the most efficient way to organize production is via forward monetary contracts (Davidson, 1982–3). This creates a need for liquidity – a concept which only has meaning and relevance in a world which does not rely on the axiom of reals (Davidson, 1984). Liquidity, the ability to meet your contractual monetary obligations as they come due, is the name of the game when we want to discuss a role for money in the real world.

Of course, Frank Hahn should have realized all this since Arrow and Hahn meticulously demonstrated that

> the terms in which contracts are made matter. In particular, if money is the goods in terms of which contracts are made, then the price of goods in terms of money are of special significance [nominal magnitudes matter!]. This is not the case if we consider an economy without a past or a future . . . *If a serious monetary theory* comes to be written, the fact that contracts are made in terms of money will be of considerable importance. (Arrow and Hahn, 1971, pp. 356–7; italics added)

Moreover, Arrow and Hahn demonstrate (ibid., p. 361) that if contracts are made in terms of money (so that money affects real decisions) in an economy moving along in calendar time with a past and a future, then *all existence theorems are jeopardized*. The existence of money contracts – a characteristic of the world in which Keynes lived and which we still do – implies that there need never exist, in the long run or the short, any general equilibrium market clearing price vector.

1.1 The Need for Money Contracts

Time is a device which prevents everything from happening at once. Production processes take time and hence the decision to organize production in a certain manner must occur earlier in time than the outcome. If the economic world has, or can have, important non-ergodic circumstances associated with it, then future outcomes of any economic process can never be forecasted with statistical precision at the onset of the process. In a non-ergodic environment, people recognize that the future may be unpredictable in any stochastic sense, and hence the sensibility of human beings prevails.

Sensible expectations rely on existing human institutions which have evolved to permit fallible humans to cope with the unknowable. In such a world, the attribute of dignity associated with all human motivation is necessarily geared not to rationality but to sensibility. In such a world, the institution of fixed money contracts which limits nominal liabilities is an essential adjunct of organizing production processes.

Only if entrepreneurs' monetary liability is contractually limited, *and* if entrepreneurs obtain reasonable assurances from their bankers that they can obtain the necessary financing of their working capital production contractual commitments will their animal spirits be bolstered and their dignity protected sufficiently to undertake the burdensome organization of large-scale production. In the absence of money contracts, it is unlikely that entrepreneurs, facing a statistically unpredictable and unknowable future, would undertake large-scale, long-lived, complex production processes.

Lower life forms enter into organizational structures for the efficient operation of production and consumption processes (e.g. herds of elephants, schools of fish, colonies of ants, etc.). None, however, utilizes contracts and money to achieve its production and consumption objectives. Only *homo sapiens*, who can recognize the passages of time and the fundamental uncertainty of a non-ergodic world, uses monetary contracts as an essential adjunct to complex interdependent production and consumption processes. Thus, human economic activity has evolved institutions of contracts and money in order to 'assure' legal future outcomes in a non-ergodic environment.

In the real world, money is anything that legally discharges a contractual liability under the civil law of contracts. All contracts are calendar time – either spot or forward – oriented. A spot contract designated delivery and payment at the moment of signing; while a forward contract designates a specific future calendar date for delivery and payment. Each party to a forward contract recognizes that the other party, *despite possessing good faith at the time of signing of the contract*, may be unable and/or unwilling to execute the contractual terms at the specified date. Legal enforcement permits each party to have *sensible* expectations that if the other party does not fulfil its contractual obligations, the injured party will be entitled to just monetary compensation.

In the real non-ergodic world – unlike the ergodic neoclassical system – recontracting without penalty whenever a buyer or seller has made an error is simply not permitted. *Forward nominal contracts for sale of goods and services are human institutions devised to enforce money wage and price controls over the life of the contracts.* Business firms and households abhor what neoclassical economists love – namely, a flexible price system and recontracting without penalty.

Money contracts, therefore, attenuate potential conflicts by assuring both parties that even if uncertain future events adversely affect one party's ability to meet its commitments, the other party will have a remedy in law. The existence of contracts, and the means to discharge contractual obligations, i.e. money, affect the real production decisions in a monetary production economy. Moreover, financial institutions which play an essential role in governing the money supply affect the short-run and long-run real outcomes of the economy.

2 EXOGENOUS VERSUS ENDOGENOUS MONEY: THE CONCEPTUAL FOUNDATIONS

A recurring theme in the long evolution of monetary theory is the dispute whether changes in (bank) money supplies play a causal part in influencing economic activity or whether variations are an effect of economic activity, overcoming the obstacles of barter in an interdependent production economy. The view of money as causal represents a Currency School legacy, descending from Lord Overstone and the charter revision of the Bank of England in the 1840s. Money, viewed as an effect, constituted the core of the 'real bills' Banking Principle doctrine espoused at the time of William Tooke. Precursors abound as Marget's (1938) careful documentation reveals.

In recent times, this Currency cause versus Banking School effect controversy has evolved into a dispute between the monetarists who argue that the quantity of money supplied is (should be) exogenous and therefore is a *cause* of inflation and the Post Keynesians who, following Keynes (1973, XIV, pp. 222–3), believe that changes in the quantity of money supply should be endogenous or an effect, i.e. responsive to changes in the demand for liquidity, and hence observed changes in the stock of money are often an endogenous *effect*. Thus cause versus effect has, in the recent literature, become intertwined with the terms exogenous versus endogenous.

If the money supply is exogenous, as monetarists believe, then to the extent that changes in quantity of money are associated with changes in the price level it can only play (by definition) a causal role. If the money supply is often endogenous or an effect, on the other hand, then anti-inflation policies aimed at restricting the growth of the money supply will be effective only if they restrict changes in aggregate demand. Thus the theoretical issue of whether money supplies are exogenous or endogenous has important implications for the cause versus effect role of monetary policy in a modern market-oriented production economy.

Unfortunately, the conceptual basis of the terms exogenous versus endogenous has not been clearly defined. The participants in the debate have often used and confused two different concepts, (a) the magnitude of the interest elasticity of the money supply function and (b) the independence (stability) of the money supply function.

2.1   The Quantity of Money Supplied (Elasticity) Concept

Under the elasticity of supply approach, if, and only if, the *quantity of money* supplied by the banking system is perfectly inelastic with respect to interest rates, then money is exogenous. If the quantity of money supplied in the system is less than perfectly inelastic, then money is endogenous. If, and only if, the quantity of money *supplied* is assumed to be always and only determined by policy rules, actions, or other non-economic forces, then the money supply function must be perfectly interest inelastic. Hence, the only postulated cause of changes in the observed quantity of money is specific policy actions by the Monetary Authority or other non-economic forces. Thus (by hypothesis), change in the measured money supply may be the cause of some economic event, it cannot be the result (effect)!

An *exogenous quantity of money supplied* concept must and will be associated with a perfectly interest *inelastic* money supply function in the interest rate versus quantity of money quadrant as, for example, S_x in Figure 25.1a. Providing one can properly define what is meant by money, the quantity of (bank) money supplied will be solely and exogenously determined as a policy variable by the Monetary Authority. Any change (shift) in the demand function for money from say D^1 to D^2 in Figure 25.1a will play against the perfectly inelastic or vertical supply function of money (S_x) to induce *pari passu* changes in the rate of interest from i_a to i_b. Thus, in this case, a perfectly inelastic money supply is also associated with an independent supply of money function (i.e. independent of factors affecting the demand for money function).

Contrary to the obvious facts, monetarists have assumed this extreme case governs the real world. Hence monetarists have argued for a 'rule' to

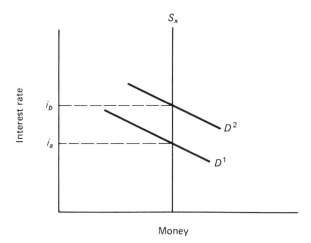

Figure 25.1a

govern an independent time rate of growth of the *quantity of money supplied*. This rule would shift the perfectly inelastic money supply function solely due to the passage of time and independently of any short-run changes in the demand function for money. B. J. Moore has termed those who believe in a monetarist rule verticalists.

If an exogenous money supply is defined strictly and solely with a perfectly inelastic money supply function, then any money supply function which either is less than perfectly inelastic must be associated with an endogenous money supply. Consequently, a perfectly elastic (horizontal) supply function such as S_n^1 in Figure 25.1b is only one form of money supply endogeneity; endogeneity can also be associated with an upward sloping, less than perfectly inelastic function (S_n^2 in Figure 25.1b) or even conceivably a downward sloping money supply function (S_n^3 in Figure 25.1b).

Moore has associated those who believe that the quantity of money supplied by the banking system will alter in response to the demand for money changes as horizontalists. These horizontalists, of whom Kaldor (1982) is the prime example, conceive of an endogenous money supply in terms of a perfectly elastic (horizontal) money supply function, S_n^1 in Figure 25.1b. Thus, for the horizontalists, when the demand for money function exogenously shifts from D_1 to D_2, the quantity of money supplied increases from M_a^1 to M_b^1 in Figure 25.1b, even if the money supply function has not shifted. But as the above discussion indicates, strict horizontalists represent only an extreme (or corner position) of those who profess the endogeneity of the quantity of money supplied elasticity approach. For example, if S_n^2 in Figure 25.1b is the money supply function then with an exogenous shift in money demand from D_1 to D_2, the quantity

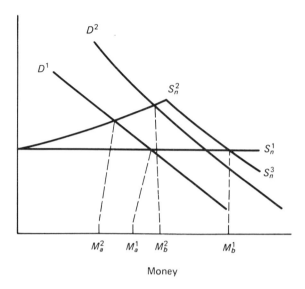

Figure 25.1b

of money supplied endogenously increases from M_a^2 to M_b^2 in Figure 25.1b.

In sum, exogenity versus endogenity hinges on the magnitude of the elasticity of supply of money. An exogenous money system is only associated with the extreme case of a perfectly inelastic supply function. All endogenous money supply advocates have a less than perfectly inelastic supply function in mind when they argue that observed or measured change in the quantity of money is normally an effect (of a change in the demand for money), rather than a cause.

2.2 The Independent (Stability) Money Supply Function Concept

The other possible view involves whether the *supply function of money* is strictly and always independent of the shift factors which exogenously change the demand function for money or not. This independence (or stability) of the supply function of money is not constrained by the actual elasticity of money supply function at any point of time.

In this stability of supply approach, the emphasis is on the independence versus the interdependence of the supply function of money *vis-à-vis* the demand function of money. As long as the money supply function is assumed to always be independent of the factors affecting the demand function for money, any independent shift in the supply function must be interpreted as an exogenous change in the money supply which can be a cause but not an effect. On the other hand, as long as the money supply *function* is stable and does not change, observed changes in the quantity of money supplied can not be the *initiating* cause of any economic event.

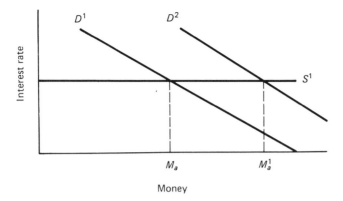

Figure 25.2a

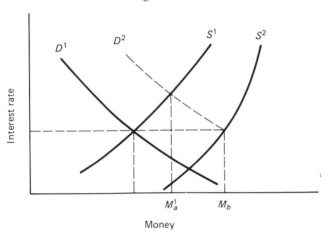

Figure 25.2b

2.3 These Two Views Do Not Always Provide a Common Ground for Exogenous Versus Endogenous Money Concepts

These elasticity and stability concepts do not necessarily provide a common ground for distinguishing between exogenous and endogenous money as cause or effect. Hence both must be used to provide clear definitions.

If, for example, every time there is an exogenous change in the demand for money such as D_1 to D_2 in Figure 25.2b, if the supply function is interdependent, then the quantity of money supplied is always endogenous in that it responds to changes in demand for money. (This would be true under the interdependence criteria even if S_1 and S_2 were vertical – as in the elasticity view). If, however, the money supply function S_1 in Figure 25.2b (or S^1 in Figure 25.2a) remains unchanged while the demand curve shifts from D_1 to D_2, the money supply function is independent (exogenous under the stability view) but the *quantity of money supplied* increases from M_a to M_a^1 and is endogenous under the elasticity approach – just as the horizontalists claim.

Thus, in this latter view, even if the money supply function is unchanged as long as it is not perfectly inelastic with respect to the price (interest rate) variable, an observed or actual (measured) change in the quantity of money supplied to the system is an effect rather than a cause.

These two – elasticity versus independence – conceptions therefore do not necessarily provide a common ground and are not therefore strictly alternatives for classifying all possible money supply cases as either exogenous or endogenous. A perfectly inelastic *and* always independent money supply function is uniquely associated with an exogenous money supply. In such a regime, any observed change in the quantity of money such as from M_a to M_b in Figure 25.3b must be due to an exogenous (independent!) policy variable shifting the entire supply function from S_1 to S_2 as the demand function shifted from D_1 to D_2. This independent *and* perfectly inelastic supply of money function conception implicitly underlies monetarists's arguments that the money supply is exogenous, for in this case the change in the measured money supply can only be a cause not an effect!

If, however, the money supply function is perfectly inelastic (exogenous under the elasticity interpretation) at any point of time, e.g. S_1 in Figure 25.3a, *and* if this vertical supply function shifts concomitantly to S_2 every time the demand for money function exogenously shifts from D_1 to D_2, then the money supply function is interdependent and the measured change in the quantity of money supplied from M_a to M_b in Figure 25.3a is an effect due to a change in the demand for money rather than a cause. Hence, the observed change in the money stock is an *endogenous* quantity of money supply response despite the inelasticity of the money supply function.

Similarly, if the money supply is not perfectly elastic, (e.g. horizontal) it is endogenous (under the elasticity interpretation), but if the supply function is unchanged (at say S_n^2 in Figure 25.1b) when the demand for money function shifts from D_1 to D_2 in Figure 25.1b, then money supply function is independent, while any observed changes in the quantity of money supplied (from M_a^2 to M_b^2) is always an effect, not a cause. Of course, a less than perfectly inelastic money supply function may also shift when the demand for money function changes, and hence the money supply would be endogenous under either view in this case.

Every elementary principles textbook in economics stresses the importance of distinguishing between a change in the quantity of a commodity supplied (or demanded), i.e. a movement along a supply (or demand) curve, and a change in supply (or demand), i.e. a shift in a supply (or demand) curve. Most economic principles instructors warn of horrendous

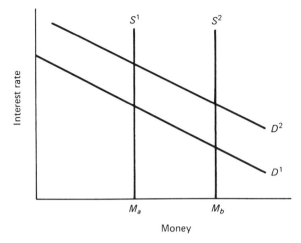

Figure 25.3a

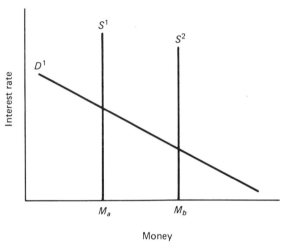

Figure 25.3b

errors (and failing grades) in any economic analysis of changes in prices
and quantities by any freshman who cannot distinguish between movements along a curve (changes in quantities supplied or demanded) and a
shift in a curve (changes in supply or demand). Yet just such a confusion
has hindered the professional discussion regarding the 'quantity of money'
and its role in the economy as either cause and/or effect and whether
money is exogenous or not.

No wonder that even after a century of discussion, there continues to be
considerable debate over this cause versus effect – and exogenous versus
endogenous – and independent versus interdependent money supply issue.

Since the words and concepts have not been clearly, crisply and uniquely defined, the various combatants in the continuing controversy often use the same terms to convey somewhat different meanings. Until we get our concepts semantically in order, little progress in the dialogue and discussion over the cause versus effect role of money can be expected.

For conceptual simplicity and completeness, therefore, differences in conceptualization of the 'money supply' can be distinguished by:

(1) the elasticity of the money supply function, i.e. perfectly interest inelastic versus any interest elasticity; and/or
(2) independence versus interdependence of the money supply and money demand functions.

An *exogenous* money supply then can always be identified as a *causal* factor if it is defined as when either the money supply function is perfectly inelastic *and* when the money supply function shifts independently of the demand for money function. An *endogenous money supply can be identified as an effect therefore if it is defined as associated either with a less than perfectly interest inelastic money supply function or* an interdependent shift of the supply function.

3   THE SUPPLY OF MONEY PROCESS REVISITED

For many years, Post Keynesians have been warning that orthodox macroeconomic theorists have not properly depicted the money supply process (e.g. Davidson and Weintraub, 1973; Davidson, 1978). Keynes's (1936, ch. 17) 'essential properties' of money (and all liquid assets) involving a zero (or negligible) elasticity of production of the money commodity immediately determines the market supply behaviour of producers of the money commodity in the private sector. If one is to specify properly how observed changes in the supply of money come about, one must relate them to the relevant banking institutions and operations which bring forth money. In the real world, Keynes reminded us at the very beginning of his *Treatise on Money* (1930, p. 3), money 'comes into existence along with debts, which are contracts for deferred payment and . . . offers of contracts for sale or purchase', that is, the supply of money, and debt and production-offer contracts are intimately and inevitably related. For Keynes, money does not enter the system like manna from heaven, nor is it dropped from the sky via a Friedmanian helicopter (i.e. the money supply function is not always independent of demand factors), nor is it produced from the application of labour to the harvesting of money trees. For Keynes and Post Keynesians, the supply of money in a modern economy can increase only via two distinct money supply processes – both of which are related to contracts; one is associated with endogenous money, the other with exogenous money.

3.1 The Income Finance Process

In the first money supply process, which may be called the income generating-finance process, an increased desire to buy more reproducible goods per period – the finance motive (Keynes, 1973, XIV, pp. 215–23; Davidson, 1965, 1978) – induces individuals, firms, governments, and foreigners to enter into additional debt contracts with the banking system. If these contracts are accepted by the banking system without any simultaneous intervention or action by the central bank, then the money supply elasticity cannot be perfectly inelastic. The additional debts of banks are issued and used to accept and pay for additional offer contracts of producers and workers. In the finance process, therefore, changes in the quantity of money supplied are always endogenous under the elasticity interpretation. If, however, these private debt financing contracts can, on a system wide basis, only be accepted by private bankers if there is an accommodation by the central bank via its lender of last resort function then the institutionally based money supply function will be interdependent if the central bankers do their jobs, by permitting an endogenous (less than perfectly interest inelastic) money supply response. If the central bankers are to be lenders of last resort to prevent a banking system collapse, all they can control is the bankers' cost of obtaining reserves and hence the interest rate.

In the income-generating finance process, an exogenous increase in aggregate demand for goods provokes the demanders for money to initiate the process which increases the quantity of money supplied, as long as banks are willing and able to make additional bank-debt contracts available under the rules of the game (and, of course, it is in the self-interest of bankers to do so). This increase in the measured money supply is used to finance additional orders for producible goods. Depending on the various cost elasticities of the various industries stimulated, increases in real income and prices will expand along with the increase in the endogenous quantity of money supplied.

3.2 The Portfolio Change Process

In the second money supply process, which may be labelled the portfolio-change process, the central bank *initiates* the change in the money supply by buying existing liquid assets from the portfolios of the banking system and/or the general public. These sold assets are initially replaced in the banks' portfolios by bank reserves or in the portfolio of the general public of bank-debt contracts as an alternative store of value at a rate of exchange which the sellers find very favourable. In the portfolio money supply process, the initiating cause of a change in the money supply is an explicit *ceteris paribus*, policy decision on the part of the Monetary Authority to shift the supply function of money at any given rate of interest. Thus the portfolio money supply process always involves an exogenous change in the money supply function.

In the portfolio-change process, changes in the money supply are immediately used by the public as a substitute for securities as a vehicle for transferring purchasing power to the indefinite uncertain future. This independent increase in the money supply function due to open market operations *initiated* by the central bank, will increase the demand for real produced goods only via the usual Keynesian effect of lowering the cost of financing the purchasing of durables.

4 FINANCE: REAL VERSUS INFLATION BILLS

The income generating finance process demonstrates that the financial system holds the key to facilitating the transition from a lower to a higher level of economic activity. As long duration, mass production processes must be planned ahead if they are to be efficiently organized in any non-slave or non-cooperative economies, then entrepreneurs will require the institution of long duration forward contracts to ensure the cooperation of owners of factors inputs in delivering *on time* factor services and materials according to the production schedule. Since these contractual commitments require monetary payments (cash outflows) to factor owners before the product is sold and sales revenues (cash inflows) are received, entrepreneurs must be assured that they can obtain sufficient finance to meet these production cash outflow commitments. Any inability to obtain sufficient financial commitments today prevents entrepreneurs from initiating production activities, no matter how profitable these production processes are expected to be at a later date when the product is finally sold.

In an entrepreneurial system of organizing production, economic growth requires a banking system that will provide an 'elastic currency' so that the expanding needs of trade can be readily financed. In the absence of a financial system which can provide such an endogenous money supply system, an entrepreneurial, market-oriented, monetary, production economy will find that its best made plans for expansion will be stymied.

Unfortunately, the same banking system which provides a mechanism for the endogenous expansion of the money supply to meet the needs of trade (the real bills doctrine) cannot normally distinguish between entrepreneurial increased requirements to finance larger payrolls due to (a) increased employment (at a given money wage) associated with a larger production flow and (b) higher money pay per unit of labour (or other factor) effort (after adjusting for changes in labour productivity), i.e.

higher efficiency wages or unit money costs of production. Consequently, any banking system designed to provide a financial environment which eases the transition from a lower to a higher level of employment and output is also capable of supporting inflationary forces due to economic, social, and political demands from various groups for higher money incomes in order to obtain, *ceteris paribus*, a greater share of any aggregate output flow. In other words, any financial structure which is appropriately designed to provide an endogenous money supply under the real bills doctrine is simultaneously capable of creating a permissive environment for wage or profit inflation. Any healthy banking system apparatus which meets the needs of trade can be subverted to create an elastic currency of 'inflation bills' rather than 'real bills'. Any deliberate policy aimed at restricting the banking system's ability to issue 'inflation bills' will therefore concurrently limit its ability to supply sufficient real bills to maintain economic expansion.

As modern banking institutions evolved from asset management activities to liability management processes to organize their loan activities, they essentially evolved a money supply function which would realistically never be perfectly inelastic under the fractional rules of the game.

In a textbook world of the process of money creation, of course, it is the exogenous introduction of new reserve assets into the banking system's balance sheet which is the initiating cause of an increase in the money supply, *at any interest rate*. Under these textbook conditions, the money supply function can be conceived of as being perfectly interest inelastic and independent of the money demand function. Only an exogenous change in the aggregate reserve asset position of the banking system can induce a change in the money supply. Unfortunately, this artificial construct has been misinterpreted by many economists as a proper description of current real world banking systems.

Under a liability management banking system, however, with a Monetary Authority charged with the responsibility of preventing any systematic liquidity crisis from creating a banking collapse, however, an endogenous money supply is assured. The only question is the interest rate costs to the banking system of inducing additional reserve assets into their balance sheets during any expansion. As long as there are additional borrowers who are willing to pay the going interest rate or more (at which bankers can make a profit), bankers will have an incentive to expand their loans.

In a liability management context, bankers can, even on a system-wide basis, increase the lending power of their existing reserve asset base by paying the public to give up very liquid assets and accepting less liquid bank liabilities in return. Since the reserve requirements on the very liquid demand deposits is greater than on less liquid time and savings deposits even if no additional bank reserves are created, liability management by the banks (i.e. paying the public to switch from more to less liquidity bank liabilities or vice versa) means that the same reserve base can endogen-ously expand or contract to meet the changes in net demand for loans by borrowers.

The central bank can moderate the interest elasticity of supply resulting from liability management by providing the banks with an alternative source of bank reserves compared to paying the public to alter the liquidity of its portfolio. Thus in a modern banking – liability management – system, the central bank can never prevent some money endogenity. The Monet-ary Authority can only increase the elasticity of the money supply function in response to a change in the public's demand for money, or produce an exogenous shift in the money supply function via the portfolio balance process. Consequently, the central bank's power to 'lean against the wind' in inflation is much more limited than monetarists claim.

ABSTRACT

This chapter demonstrates that a good deal of confusion is involved in the definition of endogenous money. For some people endogeneity is defined relative to the elasticity of the money supply function, namely, any money supply function which is not perfectly inelastic is considered endogenous. Alternatively, endogenous can be defined as a shift in the money supply function independent of its elasticity. Using the latter definition of endo-geneity, the chapter distinguishes between changes in the supply of money (endogenous shifts of the supply function) which is due to real bills or increase in production flow effect, from that due to inflation bills, i.e. an increase in the costs of production effect.

References

Arrow, K. and H. Hahn, (1971), *General Competitive Analysis* (San Francisco: Holden-Day).
Davidson, P. (1965), 'Keynes's Finance Motive', *Oxford Economic Papers*, 17 (Chapter 1 in this volume).
Davidson, P. (1978), *Money and the Real World*, 2nd edn (London: Macmillan).
Davidson, P. and S. Weintraub (1973), 'Money As Cause and Effect', *Economic Journal*, 83 (Chapter 9 in this volume).
Hahn, F. H. (1981), *Money and Inflation* (London: Basil Blackwell).
Kaldor, N. (1982), *The Scourge of Monetarism* (Oxford: Oxford University Press).
Keynes, J. M. (1930), *A Treatise on Money* (London: Macmillan).
Keynes, J. M. (1936), *The General Theory of Employment, Interest and Money*, (New York: Harcourt).
Keynes, J. M. (1973), *The Collected Writings of John Maynard Keynes*, vol. XIII and XIV (London: Macmillan).
Marget, A. (1938), *The Theory of Prices* (New York: Prentice-Hall).

26 Keynes and Money*

The basis of Keynes's revolution in economic theory has been placed in the multiplier (Johnson, 1961, p. 144; Patinkin, 1982, p. xxi), or in the fixity of money-wages and prices (Modigliani, 1944), or in the reversal of the Marshallian price and quantity adjustment velocities (Leijonhufvud, 1968;[1] Friedman, 1974, p. 18), or in the failure of markets to coordinate nominal effective demand and actual effective demand (Clower, 1965; Clower and Leijonhufvud, 1975).

None of these commentators has suggested that Keynes's monetary analysis was the innovative element in the *General Theory*. In fact, assessments by most monetarists have suggested that Keynes minimized the importance of the monetary mechanism. Thus, monetarists have chosen as their motto 'money matters' to distinguish their version of macrotheory from that of Keynes.

Such conclusions are not plausible when one considers the history of Keynes's intellectual development and his writings. Keynes was pre-eminently a monetary theorist, as well as a practitioner of 'high finance'. At Cambridge, he lectured in courses on monetary theory, while in 'the City' he was an active and successful player of the financial markets. Throughout his life Keynes was a firm believer in the importance of money and a passionate advocate of monetary reform, both domestically and internationally. The titles of all his major academic books in economics include the words money, monetary, currency, or finance – certainly an indication that the role of money in the economy was always a primary focus of his analytical attention.

In his *Tract on Monetary Reform* (1923, p. 30), Keynes insisted that the quantity theory of money is 'fundamental . . . [and] not open to question. Nevertheless, it is often misstated and misrepresented' – a statement that is just as true today as it was more than a half century ago. Keynes's 1923 version of the quantity theory differs from Fisher's, or Friedman's, or even Lucas's, in that Keynes argued that the demand functions for goods and money were not entirely independent of the supply of money. Keynes's criticism of the monetarist interpretation of the quantity theory was that it relied on assumptions as to what variables are to be taken as mathematically independent, so as to provide a unique and unidirectional cause and effect relationship running from money to prices (or money incomes.)[2]

'In actual experience', Keynes argued, changes in the quantity of money could affect either velocity or real income or both; moreover, *in certain*

* *Keynes Money and Monetarism*, ed. R. Hill (London: Macmillan, 1989).

circumstances changes in spending propensities induced changes in the money supply, i.e. the money supply could be endogenous. Starting from this more 'general' approach to the quantity theory, Keynes went on to develop a monetary framework for the operation of an entrepreneurial economy in his *Treatise on Money* and *General Theory*. Harrod (1969, p. 151) has characterized Keynes's monetary analysis as 'a study in depth of a magisterial quality not matched in the present century'.

1   THE IMPORTANCE OF MONEY

In trying to assess the importance of money, it is enlightening to compare the views of Keynes and Friedman on the relationship of money to the economic system. In a 1933 article entitled 'A Monetary Theory of Production', Keynes insisted that what should be modelled from the very beginning is the operation of a real world monetary production system, and not a barter system upon which money has been imposed. In Keynes's words (1933, pp. 408–10):

> In my opinion the main reason why the problem of crisis is unsolved, or at any rate why this theory is unsatisfactory, is to be found in the lack of what might be called a *monetary theory of production*. An economy which uses money as a neutral link between transactions in real things and real assets and does not allow it to enter into motives or decisions might be called – for want of a better name – *a real exchange economy*. The theory I desiderate would deal . . . with an economy in which money plays a part of its own and affects motives and decisions and is, in short, one of the operative factors in the situation, so that the course of events cannot be predicted either in the long period or in the short, without a knowledge of the behaviour of money between the first state and the last. And it is this which we ought to mean when we speak of a *monetary economy*.

Keynes then specified his research agenda by noting: 'Booms and depressions are peculiar to an economy in which . . . *money is not neutral* . . . I believe that the next task is to work out in some detail a monetary theory of production . . . that is the task on which I am now occupying myself in some confidence that I am not wasting my time' (Keynes, 1933, p. 410; italics added). For Keynes, money really matters in the determination of production and employment flows, in both the short and long run. Money is never neutral.

Milton Friedman (1974, p. 27), on the other hand, summarized his views on the quantity theory and the role of money as follows:

> We have accepted the quantity theory presumption . . . that changes in the quantity of money as such *in the long run* have a negligible effect on real income so that nonmonetary forces are "all that matter" for changes in real income over decades and money "does not matter" . . . we have emphasized that changes in M [money] are a major factor, though even then not the only factor, accounting for short run changes in both nominal income and the real level of activity (y). I regard the description of our position as "money is all that matters for changes in *nominal* income and for *short-run* changes in real income" as an exaggeration but one that gives the right flavor of our conclusions.

Friedman thereby 'misstated' and 'misrepresented' the quantity theory (in Keynes's sense) by presuming growth in the money supply cannot affect long-run real output and employment. In the long run money, according to Friedman, is neutral and changes in the quantity of money cause changes in nominal income (by affecting the price level), but not vice versa. Moreover, in Friedman's Nobel Prize lecture (1977, p. 470), he noted that the attainment of long-run results 'may take a long chronological time . . . time to be measured by quinquennia or decades, not years'. If the monetarist theory can only provide anti-inflation policy guidelines for such a long run, then we are all truly dead!

In the short run (in which we live), Friedman (1974, p. 50) admits that his quantity theory explanation of the determination of nominal income 'does not specify anything about the division of nominal income between prices and output'. Thus, unlike Keynes's theory of prices (1936, ch. 21), Friedman's monetarism is devoid by any short-run theory of inflation. Keynes's analysis, on the other hand, explicitly provided for a short-run and long-run theory of inflation:

> The general price level depends partly on the rate of remuneration of the factors of production which enter into marginal cost and partly on the scale of output as a whole [i.e., on productivity] (Keynes, 1936, p. 294) . . . And the long-run stability or instability of prices will depend on the strength of the upward trend of the wage-unit (or, more precisely, of the cost unit) compared with the rate of increase in the efficiency of the productive system. (p. 309)

In his earlier *Treatise* (1930, I, pp. 168–70, 273–4) Keynes had already noted the importance of controlling the 'earnings system' to prevent inflation and how 'singularly ill-adapted' is monetary policy for exercising such constraints. Keynes's analysis has always implied the need for a workable incomes policy to prevent inflation.[3]

To avoid the implication of short-run policy impotency in Friedman's brand of monetarism, others have introduced rational expectations (RATEX) into their monetarist analysis. This form of monetarism (what Tobin has labelled 'Monetarism Mach II') permits Friedman's long-run analysis to be 'capitalized' into short-run outcomes. Monetarism Mach II assumes the neutrality of money, in the market period, in the short run, and Friedman's long run. Monetarism Mach II, therefore, is a logical expansion of the Fisher–Friedman tradition to every instant of time. It is an even further retrogression from Keynes's revolutionary monetary theory.

2   THE LOGICAL BASIS OF KEYNES'S REVOLUTION

It is clear from Keynes's own writing that he believed that his analysis of the role of non-neutral money in determining the flow of production and employment was *the* novel and innovative aspect of his *General Theory*. He compared those economists whose theoretical system was based on a neutral money assumption to Euclidean geometers in a non-Euclidean world who

> discovering that in experience straight lines apparently parallel often meet, rebuke the lines for not keeping straight – as the only remedy for the unfortunate collisions which are taking place. Yet, in truth, there is no remedy except to throw over the axiom of parallels and to work out a non-Euclidean geometry. Something similar is required today in economics. (Keynes 1936, p. 16)

To throw over an axiom is to reject what the faithful believe are 'universal truths'. Keynes's revolution in economic theory was therefore truly a revolt since it expelled orthodox tenets and substituted a more general foundation for a non-Say's Law model more closely related to what Keynes called 'the facts of experience' (ibid., p. 3). Unfortunately, since Keynes, mainstream macrotheorists, seduced by a technical methodology which promised precision and unique results at the expense of applicability and accuracy, have reintroduced more sophisticated forms of the very axioms Keynes rejected a half century ago.

Consequently, the Keynesian Revolution was almost immediately shunted onto a wrong track as more obtuse versions of the axioms underlying a Say's Law world became the keystone of the Hicks–Samuelson–Modigliani version of Keynesian theory. Joan Robinson labelled this approach 'Bastard Keynesianism' because of its illegitimate mixing of Keynes's effective demand analysis with the microfoundations of a real exchange economy. By using the Walrasian system as the microfoundations of their macroanalysis, these Neoclassical Synthesis Keynesians, as well as Monetarists Mach I and II, had rehabilitated pre-Keynesian analysis by reintro-ducing the 'universal truths' that Keynes struggled to overthrow.

In contradistinction to these monetarist and Bastard Keynesian systems, the facts of experience which Keynes modelled are: (1) Money matters in the long and short run, i.e. money is never neutral – it affects real decision-making. (2) The economic system is moving through calendar time from an irrevocable past to an uncertain future. (3) 'The character-istics of money as we know it' (ibid., p. 236) are bound up with the existence of money contracts, or as Keynes put it on the first page of his *Treatise On Money* (1930), money 'comes into existence along with . . . contracts'. (Hence in a monetary system recontracting without income penalty is not permitted.) (4) Forward contracts in money terms are the human institution developed to organize time-consuming production and exchange processes efficiently. The money-wage contract is the most ubiquitous of these efficiency-oriented contracts. Modern production econ-omies are therefore organized via a money-wage contract system. (5) Unemployment, rather than full employment, is a normal equilibrium outcome of a money-using, market-oriented economy.

In order to explain why money is not neutral,[4] Keynes had to, in effect, reject two assertions that are basic to orthodox theory; namely, (1) the presumed ubiquitousness of the axiom of gross substitution, and (2) the supposition that the economic system is ergodic.

The axiom of gross substitution is the backbone of neoclassical econ-omics: it is the assumption that any good is a substitute for any other good. If the demand for good x goes up, its price will rise inducing demand to spill over to the now relatively cheaper substitute good y. For an economist to deny the omnipresence this 'universal truth' is revolutionary heresy – punishable by banishment from mainstream professional journals.[5]

2.1 The Essential Properties of Money

Yet in chapter 17 of his *General Theory*, Keynes states that an *essential* property of money (and all other liquid assets) is that its elasticity of production and its elasticity of substitution are zero or (negligible) relative to reproducible goods. A zero elasticity or production means that entrepre-neurs cannot produce the money commodity by hiring labour. A zero elasticity of substitution means that producible assets are not gross substi-tutes for the asset, money. Hence, gross substitution is not a universally applicable axiom.

All liquid assets, including money, possess an obvious – but rather peculiar property – they do not grow on trees. This may seem so self-evident that one may wonder why the issue is raised. Keynes's assumption that money has a negligible production elasticity is merely technical jargon to say that money cannot be grown on trees. Friedman, on the other hand insists (1974, p. 153) that neither of these zero elasticity properties is essential for money 'and neither has in fact characterized actual moneys' He claims that over most of history, 'money has consisted of a commodity that was capable of being produced by the exertion of labour, often at roughly constant costs' (ibid.). In other words, in Friedman's theoretical world money can grow on trees, and in his reading of history money has, in essence, 'grown on trees'.

This apparently astounding assertion by Friedman is, however, not surprising. Friedman, like all mainstream theorists, accepts the Walrasian system as the microfoundation of macroeconomic theory. These Walrasian equations not only permit, but *require*, money to be a producible commodity, e.g. corn or bananas, or peanuts, etc. – a numèraire – so that the market value of all other goods can be expressed in terms of this producible numèraire. (Peanuts – which grow on the roots of bushes if not on trees – are typically used as the example of the numèraire commodity in many neoclassical textbooks.)

If money can have a large elasticity of production, as Friedman claims, i.e. if money was an easily producible commodity, then there can never be any unemployment. If the money commodity grew on trees, then unemployed persons, who want to work but who are not hired by any firm, can always become self-employed entrepreneurs who can harvest money trees in order to earn income. As long as the marginal yield of working in the money-tree orchard exceeds the marginal disutility of harvesting, workers can always be employed. Involuntary unemployment is logically impossible as supply (production) of the monetary commodity creates its own demand.

It therefore follows from Friedman's acceptance of the Walrasian system's conception of money as a readily producible commodity that anyone who is unemployed does not want to work for a living. Accordingly, the unemployed can be pictured as parasites living off government handouts. It is then easy to justify policies which, in the real world, cause long-term unemployment – and then treat the unemployed callously.

If only money could grow on trees, as it does in Friedman's logical world, recessions would be impossible not only from the supply side (as explained above) but also from the aggregate demand side. When people become more worried about the possibility of future 'rainy days' and therefore cut their spending on goods, such as cars, in order to build up liquidity, employment will decline in the car industry. If, however, money is a producible crop, such as peanuts, the resulting increased demand for liquidity will increase the demand for peanuts and hence employment in the peanut industry. Increased unemployment in Detroit's car factories would be offset by increased employment in Georgia's peanut farms. If money really was peanuts, President Carter might have fared better had he appointed his brother Billy rather than Paul Volker to be chairman of the Federal Reserve.

A zero elasticity of substitution of money (and all other liquid assets) implies that (illiquid) producible goods are *not* gross substitutes for liquid assets as stores of liquid values in savers' portfolios. Whenever savers use some of their current earnings to buy additional non-producible assets for storing their increments of wealth in liquid forms, this increase in demand will increase the price of non-producibles.

The resulting price rise for non-producibles relative to the price of producibles will, if the axiom of gross substitution is applicable for *all* assets, induce savers to substitute newly producible durables for non-producibles in their wealth holdings. Accordingly, even if the demand for savings out of income is initially directed to the purchase of non-producibles, this demand will always spill over into a demand for producibles and therefore generate employment opportunities – assuming universal gross substitutability permits the propensity to save to create jobs just as much as the propensity to consume. The gross substitution axiom thereby restores Say's Law and denies the logical possibility of involuntary unemployment.

In his *Debate with His Critics*, Friedman correctly attacks Tobin and other 'Bastard' Keynesians since they rely on Walrasian microfoundations and hence on the gross substitutability of all durables as objects of savings. Friedman (ibid., p. 28) attacks these Keynesians who, while relying on Walrasian microfoundations, limit the 'range of assets considered' as possible gross substitutes for money (and marketable financial assets) in their analysis of portfolio balance. For Friedman the total spectrum of assets including 'houses, automobiles, let alone furniture, household appliances, clothes [underwear?] and so on' (ibid., p. 29) is eligible for portfolio savings. (After all, in his permanent income hypothesis, Friedman (1957, p. 11) deliberately defines savings to include the purchase of producible durable goods such as Lamborgini cars, yachts, etc.)

Thus, Friedman, like 'Ricardo offers us the supreme intellectual achievement, unattainable by weaker spirits, of adopting a hypothetical world remote from reality, as though it was the world of experience and then living in it consistently' (Keynes, 1936, p. 182). In such a world Friedman can 'prove' that savings does not create unemployment. For the Samuelsons, Tobins, and Modiglianis of the world, their common sense, if not their microfoundations, tells them better.

In an entrepreneurial economy it is the presence of a money that does *not* grow on trees in combination with the public's desire to hold such money (for liquidity purposes) which refutes Say's Law. Whatever income is earned via the production of goods does not assure sufficient effective demand to sell all the goods produced, as long as people can 'spend' some portion of their current income on money (or other liquid assets) rather than spending it on producible goods (cf. Keynes, 1979, p. 86). Whenever the public reduces its total spending on goods in order to try to enhance its liquidity position sales will decline, causing entrepreneurs to lay off workers.

In the real world, an increase in the public's demand for liquidity, at the expense of the public's spending on goods, cannot be translated into new job opportunities in the private sector. Business firms cannot meet the increased demand for liquidity by hiring workers to harvest more liquidity from trees, or to print more money! In the absence of the applicability of the axiom of gross substitution to liquidity demand, income effects (e.g. the Keynesian multiplier where butter and guns are complementary) can predominate and swamp any hypothetical neoclassical substitution effects (butter versus guns), as the Reagan administration has demonstrated over the last seven years. Consequently, relative price changes via a flexible pricing mechanism will not be the cure-all 'snake-oil' medicine usually recommended by many neoclassical doctors for all the unfortunate economic maladies that are occurring in the real world.

Keynes associated these essential zero elasticity properties with people's need to hold liquid assets rather than producible goods as a store of value (Keynes, 1936, p. 241, n. 1). His theory of liquidity preference was based on his *Treatise* recognition that humans developed the institution of forward money contracts to organize time-consuming production and trading activities effectively. These fixed money contracts can only be explained as necessary in a world where the future is uncertain in the sense of it being statistically unpredictable.

To postulate a statistically unpredictable future meant overthrowing the axiom of ergodicity – an axiom which was implicitly fundamental to the economic theory of Keynes's day, and has since been promoted to the *sina qua non* of economics as a science.

2.2 Outcomes Are Predictable in a Neutral Money World

Samuelson (1969, p. 184) has argued that the basis of economics as a hard science is 'the "ergodic hypothesis"', where he uses ergodic 'by analogy with the use of the term in statistical mechanics'. Samuelson states that by invoking the concept of ergodicity, 'technically speaking we theorists hoped' to remove economics from 'the realm of genuine history' and move it into the 'realm of science'. The presumption that the economic system operated under the ergodic hypothesis permitted economists to assert that there exists a 'unique long run equilibrium independent of the initial conditions' (ibid.).

The word 'ergodic' does not often come up in ordinary discourse except among mathematicians and some physical scientists. In using this ergodic terminology, Samuelson is, as he readily admits, drawing an analogy with nineteenth-century statistical mechanics where the long-run 'equilibrium' outcome is inevitable. For example, the ergodic presumption permits physicists to predict that an unhindered pendulum will always come to the same (long-run equilibrium) point of rest at the bottom of its path no matter where in the swing we start it off from. In economics, the 'ergodic' analogy of the swinging pendulum is that an unhindered economy will always come to the same long-run position of rest (at full employment[6]), no matter where in the business cycle swing the system starts from. Only random shocks disturb the pendulum or the economy from its equilibrium position.

The axiom of ergodicity permits economists to act 'as if' they were dealing with a 'hard' science like nineteenth-century physics where data are homogeneous with respect to time. In a 'hard science' world, the probability distribution which governed economic outcome in the past will also govern future events; the future is merely a statistical reflection of the past. By studying the past as generated by an ergodic situation, present and future events can be forecasted in terms of statistical probabilities (cf. Davidson, 1982–3). The future may be risky in an ergodic system, but it is not uncertain any more than the probability of rolling a seven at the gaming table is uncertain.

Keynes (1937b, p. 308) specifically noted that 'the economic environment is not homogeneous over a period of time'. He further stated (ibid., p. 316), 'we cannot be sure that such [time homogeneity] conditions will persist in the future, even if we find them in the past'. These statements are logically incompatible with the assumption that the economic system is ergodic.

In the *General Theory* Keynes (1936, pp. 161–2) denied the applicability of ergodicity when he argued

> our decisions to do something positive, the full consequences of which will be drawn out over many days to come, can only be taken as a result of animal spirits – of a spontaneous urge to action rather than inaction, and not as the outcome of a weighted average of quantitative benefits multiplied by quantitative probabilities . . . if the animal spirits are dimmed and the spontaneous optimism falters, leaving us to depend on nothing but a mathematical expectation, enterprise will fade and die; – though fears of loss may have a basis no more reasonable than hopes of profit had before.

In 1937, Keynes reiterated the importance of non-ergodic circumstances when he wrote (1937a, p. 114):

> Actually . . . we have . . . only the vaguest idea of any but the most direct consequences of our acts . . . By uncertain knowledge . . . I do not mean to distinguish what is known for certain from what is only probable . . . About these matters there is no scientific basis on which to form any calculable probability whatever.

And in explaining his *General Theory* in 1937, Keynes (1973, pp. 113
accused the older 'classical' economic system of asserting that 'the calculus
of probability . . . was supposed to be capable of reducing uncertainty to
the same calculable status as that of certainty itself'.[7]

All these statements by Keynes describe a non-ergodic environment
*where the future is uncertain in the sense that history and current events do
not provide a statistical guide to knowledge about future outcomes!* In a
non-ergodic environment people 'do not know what is going to happen and
know that they do not know just what is going to happen. As in history'
(Hicks, 1977, p. vii).

In the real world, some economic processes may be ergodic, at least for
short subperiods of calendar time, while others are not. The problem
facing every economic decision-maker is to guess whether (a) the phenomena involved are currently being governed by probability distribution
functions which are sufficiently time invariant as to be presumed ergodic –
at least for the relevant future – so that the past patterns are expected to be
reliable guides to future events, or (b) non-ergodic circumstances are
involved – so that the future is uncertain.

Keynes (1936, p. 147–8) argued that 'future changes in the type and
quantity stock of capital assets and in the tastes of the consumer, the
strength of effective demand from time to time during the life of the
investment under consideration, and the changes in the wage-unit in terms
of money' are some important factors which are 'very uncertain' – and for
which we cannot calculate statistical probabilities based on past observations. For Keynes, then, sensible rather than rational expectations regarding these factors would have to be formed!

Thus, as long as decision-makers believe they operate in a non-ergodic
environment, they 'know' that those who hesitate are saved to make a
decision another day. For as Keynes (1936, p. 210) noted: 'An act of
individual savings means – so to speak – a decision not to have dinner
today. But it does *not* necessitate a decision to have dinner or to buy a pair
of boots a week hence or a year hence or to consume any specified thing at
any specified date.'

The desire to postpone commitments varies with a person's assessment
of the current situation and their perception of the uncertain future. People
do, of course, recognize that some commitments have to be made even if
the future cannot be reliably predictable on the basis of past statistical
evidence alone. The use of fixed money contracts permits the parties, in a
non-ergodic environment, legally to assure a future outcome in terms of
performance and payment.

2.3 Contracts and Real Bills

In undertaking specific contractual commitments, *only* the possession of
sufficient liquidity to meet these obligations and to be able to take advan-

age of unforeseen opportunities can lull people's distrust of their 'own calculations and conventions concerning the future' (Keynes, 1937, p. 116). Thus, the human propensity to use some portion of currently earned wealth claims to purchase (and maintain) liquidity instead of committing income completely to the purchase of producible goods and services reflects a *sensible* behaviour by decision-makers, – a behaviour which negates Say's Law.[8]

Although lower life-forms enter into organizational and societal structures (e.g. beaver and ant colonies, schools of fish, herds of elephants, etc.) for the efficient operation of production and consumption processes, none of these lower animals' activities is driven by 'animal spirits' *interacting* with forward contracts, money, and markets to achieve the objectives of the species in question.

Only humans have evolved the institutions of *explicit* enforceable forward money contracts to assure legal future outcomes of performance and payment, where the future is uninsurable and conflicts can arise *after* a 'meeting of the minds' (i.e. a contract curve solution) between the contracting parties. When the uncertain future becomes the actual present, sometimes parties to contractual agreements will discover that they are *unwilling and/or unable* to deliver their *explicit* contractual obligations.

Each party to a forward contract recognizes at the time of signing that the other party, *despite possessing good faith at the time of signing*, may not execute the contractual terms at the specified date. Legal enforcement of contracts permits each party to have *sensible* expectations that if the other party does not fulfil its obligation, the injured party is entitled to just compensation and hence will not suffer a pecuniary loss. Thus as long as the legal system of contract law remains in force, entry into forward hiring and material purchase contracts permits entrepreneurs to control (and therefore predict) their legal future cash outflows, while assuring the availability of inputs for production in an otherwise uncertain future. If the entrepreneur already possesses the liquidity to finance these contractually controlled production costs (or he can borrow the liquidity from his banker), then the entrepreneur-producer not only 'knows' that he can efficiently organize the long duration production process, but also that he has the financial wherewithal to carry out the production process to its successful completion.

The ability of the banking system to create 'real bills' to finance *increases* in production flows is, therefore, an essential expansionary element in the operation of a (non-neutral) money production economy.[9] If entrepreneurs cannot obtain additional bank money commitments when, in the aggregate, they wish to increase their position in working capital by expanding their production flows (and the liquidity preference of the public is unchanged), then entrepreneurs will not be able to meet their additional payroll obligations before the additional output is completed and sold. Accordingly, in the absence of the creation of additional bank money commitments, entrepreneurs will not be willing to sign additional hiring contracts – and long-run employment growth will be stymied, even when expected future effective demand is sufficient to warrant expansion. In this situation money is not neutral – a shortage of money can hold up the expansion of real output!

If, on the other hand, an entrepreneur can obtain sufficient liquidity from the banking system to finance expansion in working capital, then his only (and not insignificant) worry is whether he can sell the product profitably at its future gestation date, thereby liquidating his position in working capital and assuring his ability to begin a new production cycle.[10]

In the absence of money production–hire contracts over time in a non-ergodic environment, entrepreneurs would be foolish to start up a long duration production process for they would not possess any knowledge of the ultimate future costs of production! (How could a profit-maximizing manager calculate the marginal costs associated with varying production flows, in a non-ergodic world, without fixed nominal contracts?) The institution of forward money contracts where delivery and payment is specified at a future date is an institutional arrangement which permits agents to deal with, and control the outcomes of, an otherwise uncertain future. Long-lived forward contracts are the way a free market economy, in an uncertain world, builds in institutional price and wage controls over time. In an uncertain world, such explicit money contractual anchors for future events are necessary conditions for encouraging entrepreneurs to carry out economic activities in a market economy.

3   MONEY, BANKS, AND THE PRICE LEVEL

As firms expand production in anticipation of greater future sales, additional production commitments will require an increase in borrowing from the banking system. Given the liquidity preference of the public, only if the total volume of loans is permitted to rise as entrepreneurs desire to expand production can our economy grow. If impediments are placed in the way of the banks responding to entrepreneurial needs, the economy will stagnate and die.

The money supply increases envisioned under this process are 'real bills' because it is assumed that commercial bank loans are used to finance entrepreneurial positions in working capital. Increases in bank deposits (money) is, therefore, associated with the financing of the growth in the production costs associated with the needs of managers to expand *real* output.

Under the real bills doctrine the additional bank money created via expanded commercial bank loan activity would be chasing additional goods; therefore, increases in the money supply would never cause inflation. Monetarists avoid this relationship between commercial bank loans and working capital needs by *assuming* that (a) in the initial instant there can be no significant increase in production so that the increase in the money supply must immediately be 'chasing too few goods', while (b) in the long run we will always produce the full employment output no matter what the money supply! Thus, by assertion and assumption, rather than demonstration, monetarists deny the need for a banking system to provide discretionarily for varying needs of trade as changing conditions warrant.

In contrast, Keynes was a firm believer in the real bills doctrine. He wrote (1930. ii, p. 220) that bank 'credit is the pavement along which production travels, and the bankers if they knew their duty, would provide the transport facilities to just the extent that is required in order that the productive powers of the community can be employed at their full capacity'.

Keynes argued that in a money-using entrepreneurial society there is no natural tendency (invisible hand) to guide the system towards the full utilization of all its potential resources. Instead the economy will only perform up to the level of effective demand expected to be forthcoming from buyers. This aggregate demand can be classified into two parts, D_1 which will be related to, and hence (in principle) financed from, current aggregate income, and D_2 which will not be related to current income, and therefore will be financed by borrowing (cf. Keynes, 1936, p. 29). To the extent that the D_1 expenditure is less than full employment income, then D_2 spending financed by borrowing is necessary to fill the full employment spending gap.

If private borrowers do not or cannot fill this gap, then the government must. The size of the government deficit necessary to promote sufficient effective demand to achieve full employment, and the resulting expansion of the bank credit money supply, should be of secondary importance. It is of no value for a civilized community to have a government that maintains a balanced budget while its citizens are impoverished because of a lack of income earning opportunities due to an insufficiency of private borrowing and spending. It is of great value to a civilized society to have a government that goes as deeply into debt as necessary to provide for the full employment and prosperity of its citizens.

Similarly, it is of no value for a civilized society to restrict the growth of the money supply to some constant rate, as monetarists recommend to fight inflation and stabilize the economy, when there are unemployed resources. If the government tries to expand spending in order to increase demand to generate jobs for all who want to work in a period of unemployment, while the money supply is constrained under a monetarist rule, then the banks will be unable to accommodate the additional entrepreneurial financial needs to carry the position in working capital necessary to support a full employment production flow. A monetarist policy, in a period of less than full employment, merely perpetuates unemployment and recession.[11]

3.1 Inflation Bills

Unfortunately, the same banking system which provides a mechanism for the endogenous expansion of the money supply to meet the needs to trade (the real bills doctrine), does not normally distinguish between entrepreneurial increased requirements to finance larger payrolls due to (a) increased employment (at a given money-wage) associated with any enlarged production flow and (b) higher money pay per unit of labour effort (after adjusting for changes in labour productivity), i.e. higher efficiency wages or unit labour costs of production. Consequently, a banking system designed to provide a financial environment which eases the transition to greater employment and output flows, is also capable of passively supporting inflationary forces due to economic, social, and political demands from various groups for higher money incomes in order to obtain, *ceteris paribus*, a greater share of any aggregate output flow. In other words, any financial structure which is appropriately designed to provide an endogenous money supply under the real bills doctrine is simultaneously capable of creating a permissive environment for wage or profit margin inflation. Any healthy banking apparatus which meets the needs of trade can be subverted to create an elastic currency of 'inflation bills' rather than 'real bills', and any deliberate policy aimed at restricting the banking system's ability to issue 'inflation bills' will therefore concurrently limit its ability to supply sufficient real bills to maintain full employment.

Keynes did not deny that the banking system might accommodate inflationary income demands of production inputs. He never lost focus of the interrelations between the money supply and the money-wage unit (or, in a larger context, the cost unit including imports). Keynes's monetary analysis (1936, p. 239) led him to the fundamental conclusion: that 'money-wages should be more stable than real wages is a [necessary] condition of the system possessing inherent stability' (Keynes, 1936, p. 239).

In both his *Treatise* and his *General Theory*, Keynes emphasized the money-wage–money-supply nexus. He noted that if we have control of both the earnings system (via an incomes policy) and the monetary system (monetary policy) and can control the rate of investment, we can 'stabilise the purchasing power of money, its labour power, or anything else – without running the risk of setting up social and economic frictions or of causing waste' (1930, I, p. 169). But Keynes maintained that 'if there are strong social or political forces causing spontaneous changes in the money-rates of efficiency wages the control of the price level may pass beyond the power of the banking system' (ibid., II, p. 351).

4 WHO HAS PRODUCED A SERIOUS MONETARY THEORY: KEYNES OR THE MONETARISTS?

Arrow and Hahn (1971, pp. 356–7) have written:

> the terms in which contracts are made matter. In particular, if money is
> the good in terms of what contracts are made, then the prices of goods in
> terms of money are of special significance. This is not the case if we
> consider an economy without a past or a future . . . *If a serious monetary
> theory* comes to be written, the fact that contracts are made in terms of
> money will be of considerable importance. (Italics added)

By stressing the need for contracts made in terms of non-neutral money, in
a world where there is a future which differs from the past, Keynes and the
Post Keynesians have already met the Arrow and Hahn criterion for a
'serious monetary theory'. In contrast, the analysis underlying Monetarism
Mach I and II as well as Bastard Keynesianism assumes (i) an ergodic
system, a timeless economy where the past and the future are statistically
the same, *and* (ii) Walrasian microfoundations where money is merely a
neutral *numéraire* and recontracting without income penalties is fundamental to the adjustment process. Ultimately, in such a system goods are
contracted for not in terms of money but in terms of other goods as the
economy achieves a long-run general equilibrium position. As Arrow and
Hahn demonstrated (ibid., p. 361), however, all general equilibrium
existence proofs are jeopardized in a world with fixed money contracts
over time; no general equilibrium need exist in a 'serious monetary
theory'.

Since Keynes's concept of a monetary economy facing an uncertain
future provides the analytical basis for the use of fixed money contracts, it
analytically provides for the possibility of the existence of long-period
unemployment equilibrium – and the possibility of the non-existence of a
general equilibrium. Persistent inflation is due to a struggle over the
distribution of incomes within a nation and between countries. To attempt
to stem inflationary pressures by restricting bank money advances in such a
system perpetuates global unemployment and depression.

The key to resolving the world's economic problems is not to constrain
the money supply and thereby perpetuate unemployment, scarcity, and
economic misery. Rather, as Keynes recognized decades ago, the key is to
expand output and employment so as to make 'goods so abundant . . . this
may be the most sensible way of gradually getting rid of many of the
objectionable features of capitalism' (Keynes, 1936, p. 231).

In the quarter century since the Second World War, when most governments pursued Keynes's policies – even when their economists did not
really comprehend his monetary analysis, the free world experienced the

most dramatic growth in real income in the history of mankind. On the other hand, the free world's recent flirtation with monetarism in recent years has revived, in the name of free enterprise, some of the most undesirable features of capitalism, e.g. massive unemployment, slow rates of economic growth, protectionism and competitive exchange devaluations to stimulate national employment, and the growth of unpayable international debt commitments.

The results of the adoption of Keynes's policies by capitalist economies during the years 1940 and 1965 have demonstrated that Keynes's monetary analysis can deliver the goods. Just think of the advances that our economies could make if only mainstream economists could jettison the archaic neutrality of money analysis and help to develop Keynes's real world monetary system and apply it to our current economic problems.

Notes

1. Leijonhufvud (1968, p. 52) asserted that 'The "revolutionary elements" in *The General Theory* cannot perhaps be stated in simpler terms' than the reversal of output and price velocities. However, Leijonhufvud (1974) recanted after reading a draft of my paper (Davidson, 1974) arguing that the reversal of the price and output adjustment velocities could not be found in Keynes. Leijonhufvud (1974) now insists, 'It is *not* correct to attribute to Keynes a general reversion of the Marshallian ranking of relative price and quantity adjustment velocities.'

2. In a perceptive passage which precedes his most often-quoted words, Keynes noted that the quantity theory 'has often been expounded on the further assumption that a *mere* change in the quantity of money cannot affect k [velocity] . . . that is to say, in mathematical parlance that n [the quantity of money] is an *independent variable* . . . Now "in the long run" this is probably true'.

   Then Keynes continued: 'But this *long run* is a misleading guide to current affairs. *In the long run* we are all dead. Economists set themselves too easy, too useless a task if in tempestuous seasons they can only tell us that when the storm is long past the ocean is flat again.'

3. For a closed economy model, Weintraub (1959) developed an ingenious algebraic simplification of Keynes's inflation theory, starting from the truism that nominal GNP (PY) was equal to some multiple (k) of the aggregate wage bill (wN), i.e. $PY = kwN$, where Y was real GNP and N was aggregate employment. He showed that the price level (P) was equal to the ratio of the money-wage rate (w) divided by the average productivity of labour (A) multiplied by a profit margin mark-up (k), i.e. $P = k\,(c/A)$. Thus if one could control the ratio of w/A and profit margins directly via an incomes policy, one could prevent inflation. (For an open economy, Weintraub (1976) recognized that an additional variable representing the terms of trade had to be included in his mark-up equation).

4. The assumption of non-neutral money by Keynes requires the rejection of what I have labelled the axiom of reals (Davidson, 1984, pp. 569–70). This axiom

asserts that 'The objectives of agents that determine their actions and plans do not depend on nominal magnitudes. Agents care only about real things, goods . . . leisure and effort' (Hahn, 1983, p. 34). (See also note 10.)

5. Given the 'publish or perish' criterion for achieving academic tenure, if Keynes was a young, non-tenured faculty member today trying to explain the existence of unemployment he would clearly perish. His general theory would be found to violate the basic principles of mainstream economics by the editors of major economic journals and hence 'unworthy' of professional discussion.

6. As we have shown, full employment is the inevitable long-run equilibrium outcome of assuming the universality of gross substitution in a producible money commodity world.

7. Hence both RATEX and the Arrow–Debreu models, where probabilistic risk is substituted for uncertainty, are, from Keynes's perspective, throwbacks to the older nineteenth-century analyses.

8. Sensible behaviour is not 'rational' in the Walrasian sense of optimizing the intertemporal consumption of producible real goods. Liquid assets such as money are non-producible (by the use of labour in the private sector) goods (see Keynes, 1936, ch. 17; Davidson, 1978, ch. 6–9). When held for precautionary and/or speculative purposes, liquid assets provide utility by protecting the owner, in a monetary production economy, from adverse, statistically unpredictable events. The utility value of possessing liquid assets, in an uncertain world, is not the present value of a utility index for the consumption of some specific future consumption goods at a specific future date. Rather it is the value of preserving flexibility for future actions! Utility flows associated with liquidity holdings which protect and insure holders from unpredictable outcomes are omitted from the preference functions of inhabitants of an ergodic neoclassical world, where rational expectations would make such long-run liquidity demands superfluous.

9. In a revision of his famous Keynesian Counter-Revolution article, Clower recognized the fact that the creation of 'real bills' must precede increases in economic activity (and therefore money cannot be neutral). He argued that

> implicit in this entire line of argument that at some 'initial' stage in the evolution of market trading arrangements, the marketing [monetary?] authority advances a nominal quantity of book [bank?] credit to one or more of the transactors to set the trading process in motion (without such initial advances, no sales order could ever be executed since no purchase order would ever be validated). (Clower, 1969, p. 289)

Of course, every repayment of the credit advanced by the authority must *immediately* be lent out again if activity is to be maintained, otherwise the sales order receipts that are used to pay back the advance are unavailable to validate an equivalent purchase order. But then every increase in activity (not only the increase from an initial zero level activity) must also be *preceded* by additional bank money creation, if the public's liquidity preference is unchanged.

10. Keynes, like Marx, believed that firms operated in an $M - C - M'$ production cycle where C represents goods, and M is a quantity of money (and $M'>M$). The firm 'has no object in the world except to end up with more money than it started with. This is the essential characteristic of an enterprise economy' (Keynes, 1979, p. 89).

11. In so doing, it may weaken the market power of firms and workers and thereby limit their ability to demand inflated incomes. Moreover, such an anti-

inflationary policy implies that the slack in the market must be perpetually maintained, for otherwise, improving job prospects and profit opportunities will set off a renewed demand for inflated incomes. The long-run cost of such a monetarist anti-inflationary policy, which Balogh has called the 'incomes policy of Karl Marx', is barbaric considering that there are other methods for directly limiting income demands without foisting a loss of real income on society. Monetarists avoid talking about this long-run loss in real income *by assuming* that in the long run money is neutral, and therefore it does not affect the long-run growth in real income of society.

References

Arrow, K. J. and F. H. Hahn (1971), *General Competitive Analysis* (San Francisco. Holden-Day).

Clower, R. W. (1965), 'The Keynesian Counter-Revolution: A Theoretical Reappraisal', in *The Theory of Interest Rates* by F. H. Hahn and F. Brechling (eds) (London: Macmillan); reprinted in *Monetary Theory* by R. W. Clower (ed.) (London, Penguin, 1969). All references are to the reprint.

Clower, R. W. and A. Leijonhufvud (1975), 'The Coordination of Economic Activities: A Keynesian Perspective', *American Economic Review Papers and Proceedings*, 65.

Davidson, P. (1974), 'Disequilibrium Market Adjustment: Marshall Revisited', *Economic Inquiry*, 12.

Davidson, P. (1978), *Money and the Real World*, 2nd edn (London: Macmillan).

Davidson, P. (1982–3), 'Rational Expectations: A Fallacious Foundation for Studying Crucial Decision-making Processes', *Journal of Post Keynesian Economics*, 5 (Winter).

Davidson, P. (1984), 'Reviving Keynes's Revolution', *Journal of Post Keynesian Economics*, 6.

Friedman, M. (1957), *The Theory of Permanent Income* (Princeton; Princeton University Press).

Friedman, M. (1974), 'A Theoretical Framework for Monetary Analysis' and 'Comments on the Critics', in *Milton Friedman's Monetary Framework: A Debate With His Critics* by R. J. Gordon (ed.) (Chicago: University of Chicago Press).

Friedman, M. (1977), 'Nobel Lecture: Inflation and Unemployment', *Journal of Political Economy*, 85.

Hahn, F. H. (1981), *Money and Inflation* (London: Basil Blackwell).

Harrod, R. F. (1969), *Money* (London: Macmillan).

Hicks, J. R. (1977), *Economic Perspectives* (Oxford: Oxford University Press).

Johnson, H. G. (1961), 'The General Theory After Twenty Five Years', *American Economic Review Papers and Proceedings*, 71.

Keynes, J. M. (1923), *A Tract on Monetary Reform*; reprinted in *The Collected Writings of John Maynard Keynes*, Vol. IV, edited by D. Moggridge (London: Macmillan, 1973). All references are to the reprint.

Keynes, J. M. (1930), *A Treatise on Money* (London: Macmillan).

Keynes, J. M. (1933), 'A Monetary Theory of Production' (1933) in *The Collected Writings of John Maynard Keynes*, Vol. XIII, edited by D. Moggridge (London: Macmillan, 1973). All references are to the reprint.

Keynes, J. M. (1936), *The General Theory of Employment, Interest, and Money* (New York: Harcourt).

Keynes, J. M. (1937a), 'The General Theory of Unemployment', *Quarterly Journal of Economics*; reprinted in *The Collected Writings of John Maynard Keynes*, Vol. XIV, edited by D. Moggridge (London: Macmillan, 1973). All references are to the reprint.

Keynes, J. M. (1937b), 'Professor Tinbergen's Method', *Economic Journal*; reprinted in *The Collected Writings of John Maynard Keynes*, Vol. XIV, edited by D. Moggridge (London: Macmillan, 1973). All references are to the reprint.

Keynes, J. M. (1979), in *The Collected Writings of John Maynard Keynes*, Vol. XXIX, edited by D. Moggridge (London: Macmillan).

Leijonhufvud, A. (1968), *Keynesian Economics and the Economics of Keynes* (London: Macmillan).

Leijonhufvud, A. (1974), 'Keynes' Employment Function: Comment', *History of Political Economy*, 14.

Modigliani, F. (1944), 'Liquidity Preference and the Theory of Interest and Money', *Econometrica*, 12.

Patinkin, D. (1982), *Anticipations of the General Theory* (Chicago: University of Chicago Press).

Samuelson, P. A. (1969), 'Classical and Neoclassical Theory', in *Monetary Theory* by R. W. Clower (ed.) (London: Penguin).

Weintraub, S. (1959), *A General Theory of the Price Level, Output, Income Distribution, and Economic Growth* (Philadelphia: Chilton).

Weintraub, S. (1976), 'The Price Level in an Open Economy', *Kyklos*, 30.

27 Macroeconomic Policy and the Twin Deficits

Many people think that the pressing economic problems facing the United States can be cured by eliminating its twin deficits – the budget deficit and the trade deficit – via a more stringent fiscal policy. In my view, however, these twin deficits are not the problem. They are, instead, the levers that were used to extricate the industrialized world from the great economic depression of 1979–82. Hence, any deliberate attempt by the US government to initiate a 'saving' process via a tight fiscal policy will reverse the progress made in the 1980s – as the entire free world will, *ceteris paribus*, suffer from another great recession.

I should point out that when, in the *New York Times*, Leonard Silk quoted both Robert Eisner and myself for making similar statements after last October's Bloody Monday, Professor Larry Summers of Harvard attacked both Eisner and myself as 'hard-core Keynesians'. (I prefer the title of Post Keynesians.) Summers disparagingly compared such 'hard-core' (Post) Keynesian views to those whom he labelled the 'eclectic Keynesians' at Harvard and MIT, who wanted to eliminate these deficits by stringent fiscal policies which could reduce US real *per capita* income significantly in the next five years. Luckily, most politicians in Washington, while paying lipservice towards deficit reduction, have not read the lips of Harvard's eclectic Keynesians such as Martin Feldstein and Larry Summers. Instead, for perhaps the wrong reasons,[1] they have acted in a more responsible manner and have not significantly further reduced the budget deficit which has been a primary force for global economic growth since 1982.

Hard-core Post Keynesians recognize the Midas touch of all modern industrial economies – especially in a global context. The problem of industrial economies is rarely, except in times of war and/or Keynesian full employment prosperity, a real supply-side constraint – that is, a shortage of workers, or a Malthusian scarcity of raw materials. Rather the Midas problem is that every accumulation of wealth via net investment creates additional productive capacity, and hence acts as a damper on further accumulation unless *aggregate demand* can be nurtured to grow vigorously. The need to stimulate effective demand growth is too important to be left to the vagaries of the free market.[2]

Consequently, the first priority of any advanced civilized society with the Midas touch must be to develop policies which encourage higher consumption standards rather than induce greater domestic savings out of any given aggregate income flow. (This will increase the magnitude of the multiplier for autonomous spending as well as help deliver the fruits of economic growth to society.) If the *laissez-faire* market determined consumption plus investment expenditures cannot generate enough effective demand to reach full employment, then it is the responsibility of civilized government to increase aggregate demand via fiscal policy, even though this may increase budget deficits (even at full employment).

In an open system, however, nations may have an uncivilized mercantilistic mechanism for generating demand, income and employment growth – namely, export-led growth. This approach is heavily favoured nowadays by industrialized countries such as Germany, Japan, Korea, Taiwan, etc. Export-led growth provides output growth and employment for the individual country – but only by exporting one's unemployment to other nations. Moreover, in a regime of flexible exchange rates, a mercantilist policy of export-led growth can simultaneously be an anti-inflationary policy for the export surplus nation and, via exchange rate appreciation, can also export inflation (see Davidson, 1989). This export surplus induced state of bliss lasts only as long as the other nations are willing – and able – to finance both their persistent trade deficits and the resulting increasing international debt service obligations.

In the context of the 1980s, this mercantilist mechanism was used by the United States' trading partners when that great 'hard-core' Keynesian in the White House, Ronald Reagan, acted as the engine of growth pulling the industrialized free world, rather than just the US, from the second greatest depression of the twentieth century. When Japan, Germany, and others resorted to mercantilism rather than adopting similar domestic Keynesian expansionary policies, the result was to dilute the growth impact on the US economy of Reagan's Keynesianism.[3] The resulting trade deficit means that the US will continue to be the world's engine for growth only as long as the US acquiesces in absorbing our prosperous trading partners' persistent tendency to oversave. This willingness of America to accommodate foreigners' savings is the solution, not the problem – as long as our trading partners refuse to live up to their means!

Conventional wisdom, on the other hand, states that our current economic woes are the result of the US living beyond its means, i.e. spending more than its exports earnings. Conventionality, therefore, requires a substantial reduction in the US budget deficit be made immediately! Immediately after the election, a group headed by Presidents Ford and Carter provided such conventional advice to President-elect Bush by urging him to raise taxes! These two former Presidents who were followers of the conventional wisdom (see note 6) during their terms of office, presided over the precipitous decline of the US economy. Their economic policies (remember WIN – whip inflation now – buttons, and MEOW – the moral equivalent of war) did nothing to ease the economic problems of their day. Why should we believe that they are wise enough now to be better able to solve today's economic problems?[4]

The 'hard-core' Post Keynesian truth is that without the big-spending, tax reduction policies of Ronald Reagan, the economies of Europe, Asia and America would have been hopelessly mired in the depression and financial crisis that began in 1979. The forced reversal (because of the Mexican default) of Chairman Volker's high interest policy in 1982 would not, by itself, have provided an engine of growth for the free world; it merely provided the liquidity lubricant that allowed Reagan's Keynesian-ism to have a successful launch to promote the industrial world's economic growth.

Our twin deficit 'problem' is, in large measure, due to the fact that the prosperity party initiated by Ronald Reagan is not being sufficiently promulgated by his conservative counterparts in Germany, Japan, Korea Taiwan,[5] etc. who are not even coming close to living up to their means. These nations steadfastly refuse to spend much of their export earnings on the products of foreign industries. Instead they tend to hoard, Silas Marner fashion, international reserves. For example, in the twelve months ending September 1988 Japan's foreign reserves rose by 26 per cent to $90.3 billion.

The Governor of the Bank of Japan and the Japanese Finance Minister were reported by the *New York Times* (15 November 1988) as ready to buy US dollars to support the dollar. They apparently prefer to buy and hold US dollars rather than encourage their citizens to buy and consume US beef, leather goods, pharmaceuticals, grain, and other imports! If these Japanese bureaucrats would develop policies to encourage the purchases of US production rather than US dollars, the US trade and US budget deficits could be substantially reduced, the Japanese living conditions could be substantially improved, and there would be an overall increase in global real income – without (read my lips) any new US taxes.

The problem facing both the developed and developing world is a lack of sufficient global effective demand – not a shortage of global savings. The problem is the persistent underconsumption (oversavings) of modern mercantilist nations such as Japan, Germany, and the NICs. If they would only consume more, the world's international debtors would earn more. This would allow these debtors to invest more and to further improve the standard of living of their citizens. We need more global belt loosening, not tightening, if the free world is to continue to prosper in the 1990s.

But if the new Bush administration succumbs to the pressure of the conventional wisdom, then we will not continue to spend ourselves and the industrial world rich, but rather we will save ourselves and the free world poor![6]

If the marginal propensities of Japan, Germany and the NICs to con-sume and to import had not been so low, then more of the Keynesian multiplier effect of the Reagan budget deficits would have been fedback to the United States. Instead, the effect was to permit the multiplier to leak out into foreign GNP growth. Japan and Germany, in an era of flexible exchange rates, found that they could benefit in at least three ways from the resulting export-led growth. Initially, they achieved lower unemployment rates. Secondly, higher real wages – lower inflation – were achieved (due to their currency appreciation) *vis-à-vis* the real wage that would have resulted from internally generated demand growth. Finally, as the dollar fell, these mercantilistic nations also gained via a real wealth effect which permitted the 'bargain' transference of ownership of national treasures such as Old Masters, valuable real estate, and domestic enterprises from the trade deficit nations such as the US and Latin America. These real wage and real wealth effects could not have occurred under a fixed exchange rate system. Hence the incentive to pursue mercantilist export-led growth policies was much less under the Bretton Woods system.

Thus, to act as the engine of growth in a flexible exchange rate world, as the US has done since 1982, is to permit much of the resulting improvement in real income to leak out to other nations who are willing to take advantage of the 'engine' beneficence. The income gains remaining for the engine are therefore minimal relative to the exertion required – and, moreover, the effort leads to a trail of foreign and domestic debts and a loss of real wealth as real estate and enterprises become 'bargains' to nations whose currencies have appreciated.

According to conventional wisdom, however, this trail of foreign debts leaves the benefactor 'engine' between a rock and a hard place, for financial prudence (in the guise of financial market opinion) will not 'permit' debtors to continue forever to contribute to the well-being of the global community. Just as in an earlier era, the media continually suggests that the financial market knows the future and 'the market' is telling us we cannot continue to spend ourselves and our trading partners rich. If, however, the 'wisdom'[7] of the market is followed, the result will be that by 'tightening our belt' the entire world, including the US, will be worse off! Hard-core Post Keynesians recognize, as Keynes did, that financial markets have no godly gift for foretelling the future; instead, market 'valuation is established as the outcome of the mass psychology of a large number of ignorant individuals' (Keynes, 1936, p. 154). Earlier this month, ex-Fed Chairman Paul Volker, in testimony before the National Economic Commission stated, 'We are hostage to the psychology of the market.' But to permit such mass psychological ignorance to dictate our economic policies can only be the height of foolishness.

The solution to the spending 'binge' which has generated whatever prosperity the world has experienced after the dreadful decade of the 1970s is not for the US to cut the federal spending unilaterally and raise taxes merely to reduce the budget deficit. For the United States to initiate such a stringent fiscal policy significant reduction in its budget deficit is a mug's game – a negative sum game where if the engine acts in a 'fiscally

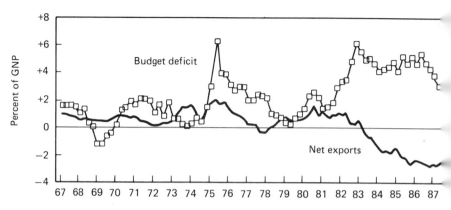

Figure 27.1   Budget-Deficit and Net Exports as a Percentage of Nominal GNP, 1967:1–1987:3

Source: Peter L. Berstein, Inc

responsible' manner, the entire globe will suffer a loss of real income! Those nations currently pursuing persistent mercantilist export-led growth must reverse these actions and by spending more save their own prosperity, as well as that of the free world. Moreover, the accumulated reserves from their persistent trade surpluses provide these nations with the wherewithal to pursue global belt-loosening policies which will lighten the debt burden of their trading partners.[8]

1   WHAT IS THE RELATIONSHIP BETWEEN THE BUDGET AND TRADE DEFICITS?

The fallacy that the primary cure for the US foreign debt problem must involve an immediate and significant reduction of the budget deficit seems so ingrained in the media,[9] is it worthwhile to digress slightly to explore the relationship between government deficits and trade deficits?

If one charts budget deficits and net exports as a percentage of GNP from 1967 to 1987 (see Figure 27.1), there is no clear relationship. It is true that since 1982 high US budget deficits have been associated with historically high trade deficits. But this experience appears to be a unique episode. In the past, rising budget deficits have been associated with rising export surpluses, e.g. 1974–7; or rising budget deficits with relatively stable trade surpluses (as a percentage of GNP), e.g. 1967–9; 1971–3; 1979–81. Also the US government surplus of 1969–70 was associated with a basically stable (or slightly declining) trade surplus.

A simple, stable regression analysis to relate the twin deficits statistically does not provide any further clarification. Tables 27.1 and 27.2 show some naive regressions where the trade balance (or balance on goods and services, or current account balance) as a percentage of GNP is the dependent variable, while independent variables include the Federal Government Debt as a per cent of GNP, total government debt as a percentage of GNP, and the unemployment rate. Perusal of these tables indicates that there is no simple and significant statistical relationship. These results suggest that there is not any robust basis for making any kind of reliable prediction that cutting the budget deficit will reduce our trade deficit.

Cutting the budget deficit is hardly a necessary condition for reducing the trade deficit. In fact, if the trade surplus nations were to accept their global responsibility to resolve the international debt crisis, then positive action on their part to reduce their trade surplus, in the context of expanding global aggregate demand, would simultaneously reduce the US budget and trade deficits without the need to change government spending and taxing policies.

Cutting spending and/or raising taxes, on the other hand, can lower the trade deficit, *if, and only if*, the consequence is to reduce employment and real income in the US and therefore reduce US demand for imports via an income effect. Such policies, however, will be the equivalent of throwing the US international engine of world growth into reverse, pushing the rest of the free world, *ceteris paribus*, into recession or even depression.

2   ARE WE OVERCONSUMING AND LIVING BEYOND OUR MEANS?

As a result of the rapid US economic recovery between 1982 and 1988 compared to the slower growth of Europe and the rest of the Western Hemisphere, US purchases of imports have soared relative to exports, causing significant annual deficits in the balance of payments between the United States and its trading partners.

Conservatives see this trade deficit as indicating that Americans are consuming beyond their means; and they add, with a tone of moral righteousness, that Americans are not saving enough – they are using foreign savings to finance a sinful splurge of wanton consumption! The statistics do not support this 'sinful' interpretation. As Table 27.3 indicates both real consumption and real government spending and real GNP increased 21 per cent over the period 1982 to 1987. Hence consumption and government absorbed the same proportion of the GNP in 1987 as in 1982 when the US had a small net goods and services export surplus. Real gross domestic investment had grown by more than 53 per cent since 1982, and increased from 14 to 18 per cent of GNP.[10]

There is no more overconsumption currently than there was in 1982

Table 27.1 1960–87

Dependent variable	Intercept	FGD/GNP	TGD/GNP	Unemployment rate	R2	D–W
1 MTB/GNP	.509 (1.96)	.574 (5.86)			0.55	0.99
2 MTB/GNP	+8.48 (.29)		.545 (3.50)		0.32	0.72
3 MTB/GNP	-.797 (-.88)	.775 (4.66)		.273 (1.50)	0.59	1.09
4 MTR/GNP	.712 (.69)		.434 (1.88)	-.122 (.59)	0.33	0.70
5 BGS/GNP	.971 (3.72)	.487 (4.80)			0.47	0.93
6 BGS/GNP	.630 (2.33)		.469 (3.27)		0.29	0.79
7 BGS/GNP	-1.185 (1.41)	.818 (5.33)		.451 (2.68)	0.59	1.20
8 BGS/GNP	.160 (0.15)		.545 (2.51)	.913 (0.47)	0.30	0.83
9 BCA/GNP	.580 (2.13)	.478 (4.49)			0.43	0.88
10 BCA/GNP	.253 (.91)		.465 (3.16)		0.28	0.78
11 BCA/GNP	-1.709 (-1.96)	.829 (5.18)		.480 (2.73)	0.50	1.16
12 BCA/GNP	-0.397 (-0.37)	.570 (2.97)		.126 (.64)	0.29	0.83

Where MTB = merchandise trade balance   FGD = federal government deficit
         BGS = balance of goods and services   TGD = total government deficit
         BCA = balance on current account   GNP = gross national product

Table 27.2 – period 1974–87

Dependent variable	Intercept	FGD/GNP	TGD/GNP	Unemployment rate	R2	D–W
MTB/GNP	.332 (.46)	.386 (1.87)			0.23	0.62
MTB/GNP	-1.033 (-1.75)		.252 (1.07)		0.09	0.42
MTB/GNP	-5.285 (-3.12)	.896 (3.93)		.894 (3.03)	0.59	0.64
MTB/GNP	-5.262 (-2.13)		.685 (2.09)	.697 (1.76)	0.29	0.46
BGS/GNP	.808 (1.02)	.463 (2.04)			0.26	0.77
BGS/GNP	.029 (.04)		.332 (1.28)		0.12	0.57
BGS/GNP	-5.613 (3.72)	1.124 (5.53)		1.158 (4.50)	0.74	1.00
BGS/GNP	-5.99 (-2.40)		.948 (2.91)	.992 (2.52)	0.44	0.68
BCA/GNP	-.481 (.57)	4.69 (1.94)			0.24	0.75
BCA/GNP	-.295 (-.43)		.342 (1.29)		0.12	0.56
BCA/GNP	-6.52 (-4.22)	1.188 (5.72)		1.262 (4.80)	0.75	1.09
BCA/GNP	-7.063 (-2.84)		1.034 (3.13)	1.115 (2.79)	0.48	0.71

Where MTB = merchandise trade balance
     BGS = balance on current account
     BCA = balance on current account

BGD = federal government deficit
TGD = total government deficit
GNP = gross national product

Table 27.3

	% change 1982–7	Share of GNP 1982	1987
Real consumption	21	65	65
Real gross domestic investment	53	14	18
Real government expenditures	21	20	20
Real net exports	–615	1	–3
Real GNP	21	100	100

when consumers took 65 per cent of the GNP pie and we ran an exports of goods and services surplus! The high global savings rate of 1982 appeared in the high US unemployment rate of 9.5 per cent.

3 A DIGRESSION ON THE IMPORTANCE OF PERSONAL SAVINGS RATIOS

Why all the fuss about the reported low US personal savings ratios? If personal savings rates were higher, with no change in the propensity to import among major trading partners in Europe and Asia, then the inflow of foreign savings into the US would be less – as in 1982 – but only because the US economy was in recession with higher unemployment. Most commentators calling for a significant raise in taxes and/or government spending cuts to cure the US trade deficit do not publicly admit that what they want is to cure the patient by giving him a good case of recession. Yet, in the 14 November issue of the *New York Times*, one professor of international trade was caught with his guard down and quoted as saying that the only way to lower the US trade deficit significantly was to reduce economic activity in the United States. But a reduction in economic activity is more likely to result in less capital accumulation and lower economic growth *vis-à-vis* what has occurred under Reagan!

Query: Why do we 'want' higher personal savings?

In real terms, higher personal savings ratios should be advocated only when the following conditions exist: (a) there is an excess of consumer demand that cannot be met from any available source, while simultaneously (b) there is a global excess demand for investment goods to produce capacity to meet this unfulfilled consumption demand. Only if both these excess demand conditions exist can it make sense, from the standpoint of global economic well-being, to suggest that we need to *free* (i.e. unemploy) resources *now* from the consumer goods sector to be put to work *immediately* in the investment goods producing sector.

Neither the US nor the free world economy is currently in such an excess demand environment where, *ceteris paribus*, a higher US personal savings ratio is in the economic interests of the free world. Hence, I conclude that the case for encouraging additional personal savings is far from proven.

4 IS HOW WE MEASURE THE PERSONAL SAVINGS RATIO IMPORTANT? A FURTHER DIGRESSION

For intellectual delight and to display academic prowess, economists often engage in discussions regarding whether certain variables have been correctly measured. Currently, it is in vogue to ask if it is possible that the 'low' personal savings ratio observed is due to the government agency incorrectly measuring savings? (For example, see L. Summers and C. Carroll, 1987.)

What difference does the reported level of personal savings make if the objective (under the excess demand conditions specified above) is to free *additional* resources for *additional productive investment*? If there is a supply-side shortage of resources to build up our capital stock, then how a governmental agency measures personal savings is irrelevant. With excess demands, more savings will, *ceteris paribus*, lead to more growth.

It is, therefore, unfortunate that some talented economists have been side-tracked into worrying whether we should include the purchase of consumer durables as 'personal savings', as Friedman does in his *Theory of Permanent Income* (1957). If the purchase of newly produced consumer durables occurs, then labelling such expenditures as 'personal savings' will not free any additional resources to be engaged in producing *productive* capital. The purchases of durables, e.g. Porsche cars, does not increase capital accumulation in real terms for further growth in output – even though Professor Friedman insists on labelling such expenditures savings!

5 IS THE AGEING OF AMERICA THE CAUSE OF UNDERSAVINGS? ANOTHER DIGRESSION

Summers and Carroll, reflecting an idea made popular by Professor Martin Feldstein's attack on the Social Security system for undercutting personal savings habits, state: 'Our judgment is that the improving relative economic fortunes of the elderly probably is the single most important cause of reduced savings' (1987, p. 631). Yet a study based on 9494 economic units, by investigators at the Poverty Institute of the University of Wisconsin, indicated that 'the elderly spend less than the nonelderly at the same level of income and the very oldest of the elderly have the lowest average propensity to consume' (Danziger *et al.*, 1982–3, p. 224). The empirical results suggest that 'the sharp rise in the percentage of the population aged 65 and over by early in the next century could lead to increased, not

Table 27.4

Variable	Total percentage	
	Change 1962–9	Change 1954–61
Real GNP	39.8	21.3
Real gross investment	55.5	21.8
Real govt spending	42.3	7.5
Real consumption	37.5	27.0
Real savings (GNP–C)	43.5	9.6

decreased, personal savings' (ibid.). The authors conclude that 'the expectation created by the LCH [life-cycle hypothesis] about the relationship between savings and age which underlies much theorizing, many measures of economic well being and important policy judgments does not appear to accord with the facts. It seems rather late for this discovery' (ibid., p. 226).

6   DO THE HISTORICAL FACTS SUPPORT THE VIEW THAT INCREASED CAPITAL ACCUMULATION REQUIRES LOWER GOVERNMENT DEFICITS AND LESS CONSUMPTION?

Santayana once said that those who do not study history are bound to repeat its errors. Keynes pointed out many years ago that reducing consumption expenditures does not automatically increase the actual volume of savings; nor does increasing government spending automatically retard capital accumulation. Inspection of the data on the prosperity of the Kennedy–Johnson era *vis-à-vis* the Eisenhower prosperity should send a clear message to those who want to learn the economics of the real world rather than repeat the conventional wisdom.

Table 27.4 indicates that the Kennedy–Johnson years of high growth in government spending were the years of high growth in GNP,[11] consumption *and domestic savings*, especially when compared to the more conventional approach to budget balance (and even running surpluses) adopted by the Eisenhower administration. The net increase in government debt in the Eisenhower period 1954 to 1961 was $5.5 billion while between 1962 and 1969 it was $19.3 billion.

The CPI rose 16.3 per cent over the 1962–9 period with over 7 percentage points of that rise occurring in the last two years of the period. When the Kennedy–Johnson voluntary guidelines policy broke down in 1967, the government had no 'incomes policy' to prevent inflation from occurring before full employment. As the dreadful data of the decade of the 1970s clearly demonstrated, accelerating inflation was compatible with higher and higher NAIRUs each year – except for the Nixon wage–price control period of 1971–3 – and until the Great Volker–Carter Depression of

1979–82. Under the Kennedy 'guideline-income policy' the unemployment rate could fall from 6.7 per cent to 3.8 per cent in a few years, while the annual per cent change in the CPI was between 1.0 and 1.7 in each year! Never was historical record so clear and supportive of the 'hard-core' Keynesian view that policy decisions and not natural economic forces determine the economic results.

7   ARE THERE CIVILIZED POLICY OPTIONS WHICH CAN RESOLVE OUR CURRENT TWIN DEFICIT PROBLEMS?

In an interdependent world any attempt by the US to reduce its trade deficit unilaterally by the conventional policy of deflating the economy is likely to lead merely to world-wide recession. But the US can take the lead unilaterally in creating the environment where the surplus nations have the incentive to institute policies which change the trade balances within a context of global expansion – not contraction! (For a detailed discussion of such a policy see G. Davidson and P. Davidson, 1988, pp. 179ff.)

The orthodox daydream that the US can cut its spending and increase taxes without causing a recession while simultaneously reducing our trade deficit requires:

(a) that the unemployed resources resulting from these government policy changes are immediately put to work in the capital goods producing sector, as the Fed lowers interest rates *parri passu* with a reduction in the budget deficit,

and

(b) although no loss of GNP (aggregate income) is assumed, Americans, for some unexplained reason, will lower their aggregate demand for imports solely because of these changes in governmental fiscal policy.

This conventional daydream is more than likely to be a real world nightmare for the following reasons.

(1) Reducing US imports means loss of export markets for our trading partners – Germany, Japan, the NICs, and especially Latin America. Reducing our markets to these countries and especially to Latin American debtors, who are already sinking under their crushing international debt service obligations, will merely precipitate a financial crisis. Moreover, our own export markets in Latin America would all but disappear, and hence our trade balance would not improve as significantly as expected (even if Japan, Germany, etc. did not retaliate via protectionism to keep their unemployment rates from rising).

(2) US industries would not respond to lower interest rates by increasing their capital accumulation in the face of declining consumer markets at

home and export markets in Latin America and elsewhere. Under the orthodox daydream, however, domestic markets must slacken as a result of fiscal policy changes. And US export markets are bound to shrink somewhat as our trading partners lose export sales in the United States.

Only if some version of Say's Law is presumed, in the short run, could the conventional scenario for changing fiscal policy achieve a reduction in the trade deficit without recession. But if Say's Law held in the 1980s there would have been no great recession in 1979–81 and the entire Reagan supply-side 'voodoo economics' would never have been adopted and the twin deficits would never had occurred. But, in the real world, without the 'voodoo economics' of Reagan's Keynesian demand expansion due to tax cuts and spending increases providing the whole world with a free lunch, we would have had the continuation of the second great depression of the twentieth century.

8   WHAT TARGETS?

Those who ask, 'What should the major fiscal monetary, budget targets be for the next four years?' are asking a beat-your-wife question. Merely to mouth such an inquiry implies that one could solve our economic problems via a neoclassical 'eclectic Keynesian' pipedream based on the conventional, but fallacious, wisdom.

As my coauthor and I wrote on pp. 131–2 of *Economics for a Civilized Society*,

> The size of the government deficit necessary to promote sufficient demand to achieve full employment and the resulting expansion of the bank credit money supply, should be of secondary importance. It is of no value for a civilized community to have a government that maintains a balanced budget while its citizens are impoverished because of a lack of [employment and business] opportunities due to an insufficiency of private borrowing and spending. It is of great value to a civilized society to have a government that goes as deeply into debt as necessary to provide for the full employment and prosperity of its citizens.

APPENDIX: WHAT ABOUT LOWERING THE EXCHANGE RATE TO CURE THE TRADE DEFICIT? WHY THE POLICY OF DELIBERATE REDUCTION IN THE VALUE OF THE DOLLAR IS WRONG[12]

Those who, in September 1985, recommended a 'soft landing' devaluation of the US dollar – the so called Baker initiative – did not realize that any reasonable decline in the dollar's value would neither eliminate our payments imbalance nor substantially alter our merchandise trade imbalance, which has been in deficit for fifteen years. This soft landing approach is based on the false premise that there is a *given and unchanging* world aggregate demand so that a reduction in the value of the dollar will, via the gross substitution axiom, encourage foreigners to buy sufficiently more US goods and for US residents to buy fewer imports to eliminate the multi-billion dollar deficit.

In 1985, when the Baker initiative was begun, oil imports accounted for $55 billion of our trade deficit. Since oil prices are fixed in terms of dollars, a dollar devaluation cannot *per se* reduce the cost of these imports. The fall in the dollar price of crude oil between 1985 and 1988 has contributed to holding down our trade deficit – but that gain is independent of the fall of the dollar.[13] To the extent that oil prices are expected to rise, it will exacerbate our future trade deficit position.

Secondly, in 1985, $22 billion of our trade deficit was with non-OPEC nations (e.g. Korea, Taiwan, Canada) whose exchange rate has been kept in line with the dollar and/or would not be allowed to rise as rapidly as the yen or Deutsche Mark. Hence a 'lower dollar' in terms of the yen and the Deutsche Mark does not increase the dollar price of imports from these other nations as much, and consequently it will not significantly increase the competitiveness of US industries *vis-à-vis* those in countries such as Korea or Canada.[14]

The major gain for the US from the dollar devaluation might have been expected to occur in increased agricultural exports such as grain, where international markets are relatively free from cartels. Since the US grain embargo of 1979–80 disrupted international grain markets, however, many former importers of US grains (e.g. India, China, Saudi Arabia) decided not to be left to the mercy of political whims, and have subsidized farmers to produce grain. (By 1985, Saudi Arabia was a grain exporter!) It was therefore very unlikely that these countries would increase the dollar value of their grain imports significantly even if the dollar is devalued in terms of their own currency. Nevertheless, as Table 27.5 below indicates, the US net exports of food products appear to have risen from $2.1 billion in 1985 to over $7 billion in 1988. (In 1982, however, our net food exports exceeded $14 billion.)

In sum, it seemed that somewhere between $70 and $90 billion of the US import product surplus in 1985 could not be significantly reduced by any soft landing reduction in the value of the dollar.

What of the remaining trade imbalances in 1985 – involving industrial products such as Japanese TV sets, Japanese and German cars, etc.? The evidence since the Baker initiative in September 1985 further supports the position that I took before the Joint Economic Committee in September 1985. I argued that the trade deficit in these 'competitive' foreign products

Table 27.5 US Merchandise Export Surplus (billions of dollars)

Year	Food	Industrial supplies	Capital goods	Cars	Consumer goods	Other	Total	Exchange rate	
								DM	Yen
1982	+14.2	−50.3	+37.3	−19.7	−25.4	+14.2	−27.5		
1985	+2.1	−54.4	+8.8	−43.9	−55.7	+17.9	−126.5		
1986	−2.1	−44.0	+4.0	−56.5	−65.2	+25.5	−138.3	3.14	2.50
1987	−.5	−44.3	+1.7	−60.6	−71.0	+22.5	−152.1		
1988	+6.9	−33.6	+7.4	−57.4	−73.0	+28.2	−120.5	1.80	1.30
(7 months annualized)									
% change since 1985								−43%	−48%

would be only minimally affected by a dollar decline of 35 per cent. Table 27.5 shows that despite a 48 per cent decline of the dollar against the yen and a 43 per cent decline against the Deutsche Mark, the net export position of the US in terms of cars and consumer goods has actually continued to rise since the institution of the Baker initiative.

Manufacturers in Japan and Germany experienced huge windfall profits and increased their market shares dramatically between 1982 and 1985 when the dollar was rising. With dollar devaluation, these manufacturers could afford to reduce yen and mark prices significantly to maintain a competitive dollar price and US market share at least into 1987.

Even if there is a significant reduction in Japanese or German imports as the dollar continues to fall, the lost German and Japanese shares of the US market are more likely to be scooped up by factories in Korea and other NICs, rather than being recouped by US industries. Often these factories will be making 'Japanese' brand items.

The magnitude of a fall in the dollar that would be necessary to eliminate the US payments deficit is probably so large as to threaten the stability of the economies of the free world. Any 'reasonable' further diminution in the dollar's value will be responsible for a savage reduction in the real income of America's industrial workers, and, in the longer run, spill over into a reduction in the real income of our Japanese and German trading partners. Increasing global real income and living standards requires a more innovative approach.

Yet, right after the Bush election, Professor Martin Feldstein suggested than an additional 20 per cent decline in the dollar would resolve the US trade deficit. It is difficult to understand where Professor Feldstein expects this correction in the export versus import accounts to occur.

Table 27.5 shows the changes in the US export surplus by major categories between 1982 and 1988. In 1985, the dollar peaked. Since then the dollar has declined by approximately 45 per cent. Yet our total net export surplus (import deficit) improved by only 4.7 per cent between 1985 and 1988. Although some categories such as food, industrial supplies and 'other' improved, deterioration occurred in our net exports of capital goods, cars, and consumer goods.

Thus, unless Professor Feldstein and others expect either substantial export gains to be made in major product classes that have not shown up at all as yet in the figures, a *ceteris paribus* change in the exchange rate of the magnitude expected by Feldstein is unlikely to 'cure' the trade deficit. Tables 27.6 and 27.7 provide more detailed product category statistics for US exports markets in Japan and West Germany. I cannot find convincing evidence as to where sufficient further growth in US exports markets will come from if the dollar declines by another 20 per cent.

If, alternatively, Feldstein is really arguing that a 20 per cent further fall will provide benefits primarily from the reduction of US imports (rather

Table 27.6 Leading Items in US Total Exports (F.a.s. value) to Japan (Thousands of dollars)

Schedule E commodity	1983	1984	1985	1986	1987
Total all commodities	21,600,318	23,173,163	22,190,791	26,619,426	27,808,368
792 Aircraft, spacecraft, & associ	1,346,532	1,079,618	1,486,592	1,830,960	1,906,346
247 Wood, nspf, in the rough, rough s	699,879	642,722	684,138	790,912	1,128,578
044 Corn or maize, unmilled	1,764,357	1,999,257	1,305,307	877,983	1,036,028
759 Parts of office machs & adp ma	470,882	586,538	691,703	731,880	934,625
011 Meat, fresh, chilled or frozen	553,799	547,388	528,049	746,741	882,167
752 Auto data proc (adp) machs & a	478,770	595,081	694,714	746,478	877,365
222 Oilseeds, etc, for soft fixed oi	1,227,681	1,190,842	953,446	855,137	802,178
875 Measuring, checking etc instru	507,493	566,257	592,464	633,140	782,334
517 Organic chemicals & related pr	562,814	603,037	609,163	643,066	778,690
034 Fish, fresh, chilled, or froze	368,605	365,780	517,556	635,278	728,105
541 Medicinal and pharmaceutical p	524,173	554,142	582,234	635,644	683,533
776 Electronic components and part	335,875	504,420	408,498	428,638	649,110
251 Pulp and waste paper	328,491	371,485	316,002	414,993	572,600
524 Uran, thor; etc; radio & non-r	440,377	605,573	583,396	653,863	547,784
334 Petroleum products	533,087	562,297	613,006	443,113	540,367
122 Tobacco manufactures	81,193	96,063	95,860	128,537	495,196
322 Bituminous coal and peat moss	1,002,088	865,524	769,197	554,730	484,581
248 Wood, shaped or simply worked	204,059	199,872	203,207	312,686	446,055
764 Telecommunications equip nspf	210,849	224,485	267,768	329,940	435,675
057 Fruits & nuts, nspf, prepared.	285,057	297,176	308,228	377,294	432,434

Code	Commodity				
588	Syn resins; rubber and plastic	345,219	324,596	338,437	423,958
714	Internal combustion engines, n	265,312	299,186	377,008	418,170
263	Cotton and cotton waste	504,873	372,834	243,765	417,732
288	Non-ferrous waste and scrap, ns	250,249	312,065	318,643	405,965
641	Paper and paperboard, not cut.	272,855	272,295	336,963	383,123
211	Hides, skins, exc furskins, undr	239,527	298,347	331,455	369,885
684	Aluminum and alumm alloys, wr	374,841	258,662	188,487	358,575
041	Wheat, incl spelt or meslin, w	589,324	468,970	424,330	352,280
896	Artworks, collectors pieces &.	49,916	79,496	184,845	347,204
990	Under $251 entries, estimated.	41,694	179,531	205,493	315,677
121	Tobacco, unmanufactured; tobacco	338,480	302,387	227,115	301,688
525	Inorganic chemicals & products	195,129	221,832	232,771	289,170
774	Electro-medical & radiological	138,852	162,895	210,825	278,098
882	Photographic supplies	220,879	219,383	268,297	272,738
728	Specialized industrial machine	295,876	375,754	277,976	247,942
036	Shellfish, fresh, frozen, salt	68,101	82,691	141,349	237,089
081	Animal feeding stuff, excl unml	158,595	161,265	232,731	228,057
778	Electrical machinery & apparat	131,795	175,143	209,679	221,064
784	Bodies and chassis, motor vehi	94,949	184,025	200,568	210,749
898	Musical instruments etc & reco	84,048	95,649	141,264	206,002
	Total of items shown	16,586,573	17,057,537	17,863,014	21,429,415
	Total other	5,013,745	5,133,254	8,756,412	6,378,953

Note: Compiled from official statistics of the US Department of Commerce.
NOTE: TRADE DOES NOT INCLUDE SPECIAL CATEGORY EXPORTS.
Top 40 commodities sorted by total exports, F.a.s. value in 1987.

Table 27.7 Leading Items in US Total Exports (F.a.s. value) to West Germany (Thousands of dollars)

Schedule E commodity	1983	1984	1985	1986	1987
Total all commodities	8,473,966	8,830,353	8,925,044	10,373,594	11,559,247
759 Parts of office machs & adp ma	580,924	666,169	709,617	810,892	1,024,180
792 Aircraft, spacecraft, & associ	450,286	526,566	802,792	1,024,382	962,887
752 Auto data proc (adp) machs & a	520,322	670,329	678,064	825,896	913,443
875 Measuring, checking etc instru	369,006	410,572	436,701	479,966	523,711
776 Electronic components and part	232,794	310,154	286,656	285,944	326,708
714 Internal combustion engines, n	180,186	139,149	178,404	255,984	318,742
541 Medicinal and pharmaceutical p	162,194	203,544	216,897	301,373	317,787
222 Oilseeds, etc, for soft fixed oi	444,886	237,402	200,900	246,204	305,297
081 Animal feeding stuff, excl unml	533,496	272,550	166,015	207,436	282,916
990 Under $251 entries, estimated	36,874	120,574	157,172	173,025	266,311
251 Pulp and waste paper.	218,912	218,536	193,702	218,454	254,921
784 Bodies and chassis, motor vehi	189,414	200,444	243,384	227,794	244,513
774 Electro-medical & radiological	119,605	138,228	155,848	184,836	229,409
588 Syn resins; rubber and plastic	110,333	130,742	157,075	205,728	205,673
517 Organic chemicals & related pr	111,935	152,211	176,388	157,764	202,013
728 Specialized industrial machine	131,908	163,409	219,941	234,241	201,779
524 Uran, thor, etc; radio & non-r	302,411	315,978	256,658	256,778	189,115
772 Elect eq, current carry, resis	104,942	129,758	131,020	140,848	180,559
778 Electrical machinery & apparat	155,671	185,041	153,887	159,821	175,942
764 Telecommunications equip nspf.	189,120	204,021	164,722	150,997	170,742

Code	Commodity					
121	Tobacco, unmanufactured; tobacco	150,745	177,955	216,924	209,733	170,023
057	Fruits & nuts, nspf, prepared.	65,381	89,032	216,924	108,897	120,974
898	Musical instruments etc & reco	54,324	61,997	68,841	86,533	133,182
896	Artworks, collectors pieces &.	59,516	55,247	44,870	123,097	132,303
781	Passenger motor veh (exc publi	38,008	50,220	40,315	82,028	131,905
713	Internal combust piston engine	72,540	95,084	94,087	103,694	109,098
263	Cotton and cotton waste	68,800	81,649	56,690	53,826	106,475
741	Heating and cooling equip (exc	71,416	109,360	96,256	98,313	91,672
872	Medical instruments & applianc	53,807	60,301	63,196	75,717	90,314
881	Photographic apparatus & equip	45,806	35,559	38,841	85,835	87,552
749	Non-electric parts napf for ma	68,411	73,637	85,694	82,371	86,014
598	Miscellaneous chemical product	57,908	63,747	65,573	81,729	81,158
699	Manufctrs & semi-mfrs, base mo	54,837	62,448	75,112	76,977	80,767
288	Nonferrous waste and scrap, ns	28,334	58,403	73,913	48,817	77,586
394	Baby carriages, toys etc & spo	67,479	46,806	35,837	61,126	75,851
736	Metal-working machine tools, p	55,770	53,394	61,333	73,235	75,518
525	Inorganic chemicals & products	68,071	108,415	85,945	77,192	74,268
891	Articles of rubber or plastics	48,607	59,331	54,209	57,415	69,384
745	Non-elect machy & mechan appar	58,656	62,510	52,966	57,393	68,507
641	Paper and paperboard, not cut.	67,696	60,658	28,835	49,500	66,376
	Total of items shown.	6,401,332	6,861,128	7,134,178	8,244,869	9,271,811
	Total other.	2,072,633	1,969,225	1,790,866	2,128,724	2,287,435

Note: Compiled from official statistics of the US Department of Commerce.
NOTE: TRADE DOES NOT INCLUDE SPECIAL CATEGORY EXPORTS.
Top 40 commodities sorted by total exports, F.a.s. value in 1987.

than the expansion of exports), then the question is, why not use protective tariffs to achieve the same results? For tariffs at least have the benefit that the US will reduce its trade deficit *without having to provide the Germans and Japanese with a further gratuitous real wealth effect, which makes our real estate and our enterprises such bargains to foreigners.*

Notes

1. Milton Friedman is quoted as saying that the large federal deficit is a blessing – since it acts as a constraint on a 'liberal' Congress to expand government spending (even if the spending is to improve the welfare of its citizens). Thus we are too much in debt to repair our highways, harbours, and city infrastructures, while in our midst we have over 6.5 million workers who cannot find a job in these same cities.
2. Neoclassical economists including eclectic Keynesians merely *assume* that, in a free market economy, in the long run, real economic growth will track along a full employment growth path. Keynes and hard-core Post Keynesians believe that the historical record demonstrates that entrepreneurial economies do not automatically achieve full employment economic growth, even in the long run!
3. Between 1982 and September 1985, Germany, Japan, and other surplus nations experiencing export-led growth induced by US trade deficits were also experiencing inflation, as the costs of their imports rose as the dollar appreciated due to speculative capital flows swamping net trade payments. Accordingly, in those years, conservative governments in West Germany and Japan would not stimulate domestic demand for fear of further exacerbating inflationary pressures. After 1985, as the dollar declined, these nations continued to enjoy export-led growth but now were doubly blessed by the absence of inflation as they continued to expand. Consequently, there was no pressure to change orthodox policies limiting domestic demand growth.
4. It is a mark of the low analytical discrimination of the media when the economic ideas of such 'proven' Presidents are given such prominence. Would sports columnists in the media recommend that the new manager of 6 pennant winners in a row take advice from two former managers who directed baseball teams towards the bottom ranks in their leagues?
5. And, until recently, the UK.
6. 'Worldly wisdom teaches us that it is better for reputation to fail conventionally than to succeed unconventionally' (Keynes, 1936, p. 158). Ronald Reagan had the personality where he could act unconventionally (remember voodoo economics) and succeed in promoting economic growth, if not balanced budgets. George Bush is too much of a pragmatist, according to the media, to scoff at conventions, and hence, I fear, he will fail conventionally – despite the campaign pledge of no new taxes.
7. How wise can 'the market' be when it eagerly snaps up things which are advertised as 'junk' bonds?
8. For a full discussion of these matters, and the part that the US can play in encouraging Japan and Germany to initiate such policies, see Davidson and Davidson, 1988, ch. 8.
9. Everyone in the media conveniently seems to forget that Harvard's eclectic Keynesian, Martin Feldstein, when he was President Reagan's Economic

Advisor in the early 1980s was playing the Chicken Little role of running around the country indicating that the budget deficits of the time were threatening an immediate collapse of the sky. The fact that half a decade later, the sky has not fallen, does nothing to diminish the aura in which Feldstein's policy prognostications and pronouncements is held in the media.

10. Preliminary figures for the third quarter of 1988 indicate that the share of GNP going to consumption and investment, and government remained relatively unchanged from 1987 at 65 per cent and 18 per cent respectively, while the government share fell slightly to 19 per cent and the net export share rose to –2 per cent. Unemployment declined from 5.8 per cent in the fourth quarter of 1987 to 5.4 per cent in September 1988 as the demand for exports created a significant number of new jobs. For the first and second quarters of 1988, the results were approximately the same, with the government share closer to 20 per cent and the net export share less than –2 per cent but not as low as –3 per cent.

11. Real GNP growth between 1962 and 1969 was 4.5 per cent per annum; capacity utilization was equal to or greater than 87 per cent. Real GNP *per capita* grew by 28 per cent while the population grew by over 9 per cent during the 1962–9 period.

12. The analysis of the following section is not based solely on hindsight. The arguments presented were provided in written testimony to the Joint Economic Committee on 18 September 1985 – one week before the Baker initiative – by Paul Davidson.

13. If, however, the dollar had not depreciated, then it could be argued that the current global oil glut would have been larger, and hence the dollar price of oil might have fallen further and made a greater contribution to reducing our trade deficit.

14. Moreover, to the extent that US manufacturers use the rising price of Japanese and German imports (e.g. cars and electronics) as an excuse for raising their profit margins and prices, US industries will lose competitiveness against industries from such countries as Korea and Taiwan.

References

Danziger, S., J. van der Gaag, E. Smolensky and M. Taussig (1982–3), 'The Life Cycle Hypothesis and the Consumption Behavior of the Elderly', *Journal of Post Keynesian Economics*, 5.

Davidson, G. and P. Davidson (1988), *Economics for a Civilized Society* (London: Macmillan).

Davidson, P. (1989), 'Monetary Theory and Policy in a Global Context with a Large International Debt', in S. Frowen (ed.), *Monetary Theory and Monetary Policy: New Tracks for the 1990s*, (London: Macmillan).

Friedman, M. (1957), *Theory of Permanent Income* (Princeton, NJ: Princeton University Press).

Keynes, J. M. (1936), *The General Theory of Employment, Interest and Money* (New York: Harcourt).

Summers, L. and C. Carroll (1987), 'Why Is the US Savings Ratio So Low?', *Brookings Papers on Economic Activity*, no. 2, p. 608.

Part II
Macroeconomic Employment

28 Rolph on the Aggregate Effects of a General Excise Tax*

In a stimulating and provocative analysis of the fiscal aspects of taxation, Rolph has stressed the deflationary property of a general and uniform excise tax.[1] In sum, he argues that under competitive pricing conditions, sellers cannot arbitrarily raise prices when an excise tax is levied. Instead, each firm has an incentive to reduce output as the tax lowers the 'net' prices of products. Thus there is a corresponding reduction in the demand for hired resources. Given government expenditures, the distribution of income and assets, and assuming full employment of a given quantity of resources, Rolph concludes that factor owners are forced to take a lower price for their services 'and hence the money income of owners are proportionately reduced'.[2] Thus, according to Rolph, a system of general and uniform excise taxes in an economy with flexible factor prices, (1) leaves the level and composition of output unchanged, (2) does not raise product prices, but (3) does proportionately reduce the money income of all resource owners.

Developing his analysis via a hypothetical arithmetic example, Rolph demonstrates the deflationary characteristics of a general excise tax, which 'by reducing money incomes of private groups . . . *ceteris paribus*, reduces private demand'.[3] If prior to the tax levy the government budget was balanced, Rolph argues that the surplus created by the tax receipts *lowers prices*.[4] He concludes, however, that 'in real terms, there is no change in the private take from the economy . . . which follows from the assumption that government expenditures remain unchanged and *the supply of resources remain constant*'.[5]

This is truly an interesting and, if valid, surprising result even for a world of pure competition. It implies constant employment of all resources independent of factor returns, i.e. that all factor supply functions are, in real terms, perfectly inelastic. This last implication, it should be emphasized, is but an assumption of Rolph's, *not a condition of pure competition*. Once upward sloping factor supply schedules are permitted, then it can be demonstrated that any deflationary effect of a general excise tax will have an employment and output incidence as well as a price effect.[6]

* *Southern Economic Journal*, July 1960.
The author is indebted to Sidney Weintraub and C. Harry Kahn for many helpful comments on an earlier draft of this paper.

Before outlining this output–employment effect, however, it might be well to probe further for what seem to be additional, and, I think, unrealistic aspects of the Rolphian system. For one thing, he argues that the imposition of a general excise tax will fail to affect the composition of output or the nature of the product mix. Thus, following this simplification of his analysis, we may assume the production of a composite commodity. Due to the fall in factor prices after the imposition of the tax, the price of this commodity will not rise; nevertheless, if the government budget was initially balanced and if the tax proceeds are not spent, then, according to Rolph, the equilibrium price after the tax levy will fall as demand proceeds (taken through a reduction in factor incomes) are reduced.

Let us outline the basic scheme of Rolph's argument. The following symbols can facilitate the presentation. We shall want to examine phenomena before and after the tax; hence, subscript b refers to the post-tax equilibrium situation, while subscript a refers to the pre-tax position.

P product price
Q output quantity
Z total sales proceeds $= PQ$
Z^* total receipts accruing to firms $= W + C$
W total money wage bill
C gross capitalist income including depreciation
D total money expenditures
y fraction of sales proceeds turned over to government as excise tax revenue where $(0 < y < 1)$
x fractional fall in market prices after the imposition of the tax (where $0 \leqq x 1 <$)

The following six conditions are imposed, according to Rolph:

$$Q_a = Q_b \tag{28.1}$$

$$P_b = (1 - x)P_a \tag{28.2}$$

$$Z_a{}^* = Z_a \tag{28.3}$$

$$Z_b{}^* = (1 - y)Z_b. \tag{28.4}$$

$$Z_a = D_a \tag{28.5}$$

$$Z_b = D_b \tag{28.6}$$

Since $Z_a = P_aQ_a$, while $Z_b = P_bQ_b = P_bQ_a = (1 - x)P_aQ_a$, it follows that

$$Z_b = (1 - x)Z_a \tag{28.7}$$

and

$$D_b = (1 - x)D_a. \tag{28.8}$$

Furthermore, from (28.4) and (28.7)

$$Z_b{}^* = (1 - x)(1 - y)Z_a \tag{28.9}$$

or

$$W_b + C_b = (1 - x)(1 - y)[W_a + C_a]. \tag{28.10}$$

Assuming no fixed income recipients, Rolph argues that the money incomes of all resource owners are proportionately reduced, i.e.

$$W_b = (1 - x)(1 - y)W_a \tag{28.11}$$

$$C_b = (1 - x)(1 - y)C_a. \tag{28.12}$$

Furthermore, Rolph indicates that the total reduction in private money income is equal to the tax yield[7] $(= yZ_b)$, therefore

$$W_a - W_b + C_a - C_b = yZ_b. \tag{28.13}$$

Rearranging terms, we obtain:

$$W_a + C_a - (W_b + C_b) = Z_a - Z_b{}^* = yZ_b$$

or

$$Z_b{}^* = Z_a - yZ_b,. \tag{28.14}$$

Substituting equation (28.4) into (28.14) we obtain:

$$(1 - y)Z_b = Z_b - yZ_b = Z_a - yZ_b. \tag{28.15}$$

Consequently,

$$Z_b = Z_a \tag{28.16}$$

which, according to equation (7) implies that $x = 0$, and therefore $P_a = P_b$.

In words, when prices do not fall money incomes are reduced in proportion to the tax rate; and it follows from equations (16), (5), and (6) that $D_b = D_a$. This implies that despite the fall in money incomes (with constant product prices), factor owners maintain the same level of money expenditures, or that they maintain their real consumption[8] intact at the expense of their real savings. Curiously, this suggests a constant real aggregate demand entirely independent of the level of real income of factor owners,[9] which, in turn, implies a perfectly inelastic aggregate demand curve for labour. It is these implicit assumptions which appear rather strange and restrictive, and which give Rolph his surprising results.

It also follows from equations (28.2), (28.11) and (28.12) that no matter what money price (above zero) factor owners are willing to accept, the market price of the product must always fall at a proportionately slower rate than factor incomes (at the same level of employment). Consequently, *resource owners can not collectively receive enough income to clear the market*. Ultimately, assuming a constant aggregate output quantity and an initially balanced government budget, the after-tax equilibrium position of the Rolphian system could only be realized when all factor prices (and hence product prices) fall to zero – that is, when all goods are free.[10] This implication is the inevitable result of Rolph's assumption of perfectly inelastic supply curves of factors and a constant quantity of output.

In view of the restrictive nature of his system, the entire analysis calls for reconsideration. Upon renouncing Rolph's assumption of constant and invariant demand and supply quantities, it can be demonstrated that even with flexible factor prices, a general excise tax *must* involve a change in the level of employment as well as factor incomes. On this tactic it will be disclosed that part of the loss in real income (i.e. the burden of the tax) comes from the unemployed. On the following pages, two models are presented. The first one, although highly unrealistic, traces the consequences of a general excise tax (in a flexible price system) when the money price of the factors falls by a percentage equal to the tax rate (as Rolph claims). The second model introduces the more realistic assumption of a downward rigidity in the money wage rate.

1   MODEL I

To facilitate the analysis, the following assumptions (which parallel Rolph's scheme) are made: (1) a purely competitive system, (2) profit maximization, (3) given production functions, (4) a homogeneous labour force is the only hired variable factor of production, (5) a flexible money-wage rate, (6) fully integrated industries, (7) a balanced government budget prior to the tax levy, and (8) the level of autonomous investment is constant.

Furthermore, to avoid the possibility that the stock of money in the private sector decreases as the government 'impounds' the tax surplus after the tax is instituted, we may assume a perfectly elastic money supply. (Such a supposition is reasonable for it implies that the monetary authority will pursue an easy money policy as aggregate effective demand declines.) Alternatively, and perhaps more realistically, we could assume that the government uses the surplus to reduce the publicly held portion of the national debt and that these funds are then made available to finance new investment. It is evident, therefore, that at the post-tax equilibrium output level, resource owners can collectively receive enough funds to clear the market. (This was not possible in Rolph's scheme.)

Our analysis will employ a relationship between entrepreneurs' expectation of total sales proceeds (Z) and the level of employment (N) such expectations will bring forth, i.e. $Z = f(N)$. This relationship, the aggregate supply function, has been fully developed from its Keynesian origin[11] by Weintraub. Given the level of factor prices, Weintraub derives an aggregate supply function relating employment to money proceeds 'in the sense that each expected-proceeds level generates a particular amount of employment'. Each proceeds quantity is obtained from the individual industry supply curves by multiplying the supply price by the associated output and summating over all industries. This sum is then related to the volume of employment required for the particular output quantities. Thus, a Z-function can be described from industry supply curves, if the latter are determinate and 'if the distribution of proceeds for each expected aggregate volume of proceeds is determinate'.[12]

The price level is implicit at every point on the aggregate supply function. Under our assumptions

$$P = MC = w/M \tag{28.17}$$

where P is the product price, MC is marginal costs, w is the money wage rate, and M is the marginal product of labour. Assuming diminishing returns, M declines with increasing employment levels. Hence, given the money-wage rate, prices rise as employment increases.

We will also employ a Keynesian aggregate demand function which, given factor prices, relates employment levels to money expenditure propensities, i.e. $D = g(N)$.[13] The equilibrium level of employment is given by the intersection of the aggregate demand and aggregate supply functions.

Assuming a money-wage rate of w_a in the pre-tax period, then, in Figure 28.1, OW_a represents the relationship between the money-wage bill and the level of employment. OW_a is a straight line with a slope equal to w_a. Given the factor prices, the aggregate demand and aggregate supply curves are determinate. Thus, in the pre-tax period, let Z_a represent the aggregate supply curve and D_a the aggregate demand curve (in Figure 28.1). Consequently, N_a is the equilibrium employment level and Z_1 is the level of money proceeds (GNP) in period 1.

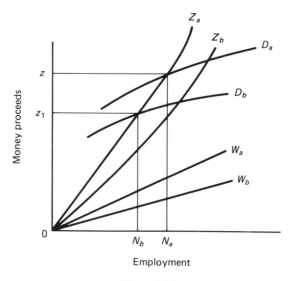

Figure 28.1

Following Rolph, we will *assume* that after the general excise tax is instituted, the money price of factors declines by the same percentage as the tax rate. Hence, in Figure 28.1, OW_b represents the new wage bill line which is $y.100$ per cent lower than OW_a at each N-level (i.e. the new money wage rate, $w_b = (1 - y)w_a$). Similarly, Z_b represents the 'net' sales proceeds expected to go to industry at each N-level in period 2, while Z_a remains the aggregate supply (or gross proceeds) curve. The ordinate difference between Z_a and Z_b at any employment level measures the tax yield. At any N-level, there is a discrepancy between the market price and the 'net' price of the product.[14]

$$P^* = (1 - y)P \tag{28.18}$$

where P is the market price, P^* is the 'net' price, and y is the tax rate.

At any given N-level, private aggregate money income is lower in the post-tax period than in the pre-tax period, while the market price for that output level is the same. Consequently, the real income of the private sector, at any given N-level, is lower in period 2 than in period 1. If real consumption is a function of real income, then real aggregate demand at each employment level will decline. Since market prices are the same, at any given N-level, in both periods, this implies that total money expenditures along the entire aggregate demand schedule declines, i.e. D_a shifts downward to D_b. The post-tax equilibrium position will be found at the intersection of the aggregate demand curve (D_b) with the aggregate (market) supply curve (Z_a). Thus, in period 2, the employment level is N_b,

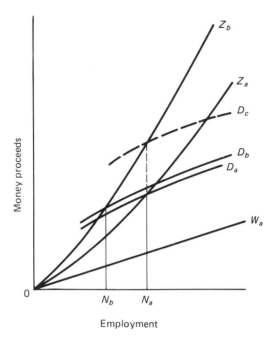

Figure 28.2

total money expenditures (GNP) are Z_2, while market prices are lower than in the pre-tax equilibrium situation.

Hence, with flexible money-wage rates, a general and uniform excise tax will reduce the level of employment, total expenditures, and market prices.[15]

2 MODEL II

In this model, we maintain all the assumptions of the previous one, except the going money-wage rate is assumed to be inflexible downwards.[16] In Figure 28.2, the OW_a, Z_a and D_a curves are identical to their counterparts of the previous model. The rigid wage rate assumption, however, prevents the tax from affecting factor prices. Instead, after the tax is levied, the aggregate supply (gross proceeds) curve is shifted upward to Z_b, while, in period 2, Z_a represents the 'net' proceeds going to industry at each N-level.[17]

Thus, aggregate private money income at any given N-level is unchanged, while market prices are higher in the post-tax period; hence real income in the private sector is lower. It is unlikely, therefore, that the pre-tax real consumption level (at a given employment level) will be maintained in the post-tax period. Accordingly, the post-tax aggregate demand function could not shift upwards enough to maintain the pre-tax equilibrium levels of output and employment (e.g. to D_c). In other words, the tax reduces real effective demand. Let us tentatively assume that factor owners increase their aggregate money expenditures at each N-level by an amount sufficient to dislodge the D-curve upward to D_b. Despite this movement, it nevertheless follows that employment declines from N_a to N_b.

Hence, assuming a downward rigidity in the money-wage rate, a uniform and general excise tax will, *ceteris paribus*, reduce the level of employment. Indeterminateness, however, extends to the fate of the market price level in the post-tax period, for the equilibrium prices in period 2 may be more than, equal to, or less than the market prices of period 1.

In period 1, when the tax rate is zero ($y = 0$), it follows from equations (28.17) and (28.18) that

$$P_1 = P_1{}^* = w_a/M_a \tag{28.19}$$

where P_1 is the aggregate market supply price of output, $P_1{}^*$ is the aggregate 'net' supply price, w_a is the money-wage rate, and M_a is the marginal physical product of N_a workers. Since entrepreneurs' decisions are based on the 'net' prices, in period 2 when $0 < y < 1$, it follows from equations (17) and (18) that

$$P_2 = \frac{P_2{}^*}{(1 - y)} = \frac{w_a}{M_b(1 - y)} \tag{28.20}$$

where P_2 is the aggregate market supply price in period 2, $P_2{}^*$ is the aggregate 'net' supply price, and M_b is the marginal physical product of N_b workers. Assuming diminishing returns, since $N_a > N_b$, therefore $M_a < M_b$. Comparing equations (19) and (20) we note that P_1 is greater than (equal to, less than) P_2, if $\Delta M/M$ is greater than (equal to, less than) y.

Accordingly, if the percentage increase in the marginal physical product of labour (as employment declines) is greater than the tax rate, then the post-tax price level is lower than the pre-tax price level. (Since the money-wage rate is constant, changes in the real wage rate are inversely related to changes in market prices.) In this case, the real wage rate is higher in the post-tax period, and the workers who become unemployed will bear a real burden *in excess of the tax yield*, while the still employed workers will enjoy a higher real income level. If, on the other hand, the percentage increase in the marginal physical product is less than the tax rate, then post-tax prices are higher than pre-tax prices, and the real wage rate is lower. Consequently, the unemployed bear only a portion of the tax burden, since the employed factors' real income will also decline.

3 CONCLUSIONS

Our initial analysis of Rolph's system has disclosed that, on the simplification of a constant level of employment, if a general excise tax is deflationary, then factor incomes must fall proportionately faster than product prices.[18] The seeming contradiction and contrariness of Rolph's model becomes apparent when it is shown that his argument implies that resource owners will not earn enough money incomes to clear the market, which indicates a further cumulative deflation till all prices reach zero! He avoids this result only by building in an expenditure lag. Nevertheless, we are entitled to employ an equilibrium analysis devoid of lags; they hardly constitute the essence of tax analysis.

Once the level of employment is allowed to vary, we have demonstrated that in a competitive economy with flexible factor prices (Model I), a general and uniform excise tax will reduce the level of employment as well as lower product prices. Assuming a downward rigidity in the money-wage rate (Model II), we have shown that an excise tax will decrease the level of employment. The effect on market prices, on the other hand, is not uniquely determinate. Market prices will decrease (increase) if the percentage change in the marginal product of labour is greater (less) than the tax rate.

If prior to the tax levy there was no idle capacity, then for any given tax rate, it is likely that the increase in marginal product will be substantial, and consequently it is possible that $\Delta M/M > y$. In this case, market prices fall in the post-tax period, and the unemployed lose more in real income than the tax yield. On the other hand, if idle capacity existed before the imposition of the tax, then the increase in the marginal product is likely to be small and therefore it is possible that $\Delta M/M < y$; in which case, the post-tax market prices are higher.

Notes

1. E. Rolph, *Theory of Fiscal Economics* (Berkeley: University of California Press, 1954), ch. 56.
2. Ibid., p. 129. Rolph notes, however, that fixed income recipients are left in the same money and real position by a general excise tax, implying no change in product prices.
3. Ibid., pp. 131–2.
4. Ibid., p. 131. This implies that rentiers improve their real income position, contrary to Rolph's other statements on pp. 129, 132.
5. Ibid., p. 131. Italics mine. Yet if prices decline while government money expenditures are constant, then the government 'take' must increase.
6. Cf. J. M. Keynes, *The General Theory of Employment, Interest, and Money* (New York: Harcourt, 1936), ch. 20.

7. For example, see Rolph's arithmetic example, *Theory of Fiscal Economics*, p. 130.

8. If resource owners do not maintain their real consumption levels, then, *ceteris paribus*, the level of employment must fall.

9. The assumption of a constant product mix despite the fall in real income of the factor owners implies that every individual exhibits a unitary income elasticity for each good produced. It then follows that the composition of the consumers' market basket is independent of the level of income. Once the possibility of different income elasticities is introduced, then the composition of effective demand will differ in the post-tax period as compared to the pre-tax situation. Thus, a general excise tax is likely to have an allocative as well as a deflationary effect.

10. Rolph avoids this by either assuming income is constant or lagging outlay behind income. We are entitled, however, to use an equilibrium solution which is devoid of lags – they hardly constitute the essence of tax analysis.

11. Keynes, *The General Theory*, pp. 25, 29.

12. S. Weintraub, *An Approach to the Theory of Income Distribution* (Philadelphia: Chilton, 1958), pp. 25–6.

13. See Keynes, *The General Theory*, pp. 25, 28–9, See Weintraub, *An Approach to the Theory of Income Distribution*, pp. 30–8, for a graphical derivation of the aggregate demand function.

14. Cf. Rolph, *Theory of Fiscal Economics*, p. 129.

15. A complete discussion of a flexible price system should include the analysis of the determination of the money-wage rate necessary to clear the labour market when the labour supply curve (in real terms) is upward sloping. Such an analysis can be derived from Weintraub's system (see, *An Approach to the Theory of Income Distribution*, ch. 6) but for reasons of expediency and simplicity I have not included such an analysis in this chapter. Suffice to say that the conclusions given are consistent with clearing the market in a flexible wage system although the lower post-tax money-wage rate (w_b) need not be less than the pre-tax money wage rate (w_a) in the same proportion as the tax rate.

16. This may be due to legislation on minimum wages, or union power, or ethical notions of a 'just' wage.

17. This upward shift of the aggregate supply curve is the macrocounterpart of the usual microanalysis of the effect of a particular excise tax on the supply schedule of a commodity.

18. Rolph's system is but a variant of the classical tradition of full employment and is hardly applicable in an economy where employment itself is a variable.

29 Wells on Excise Tax Incidence in an Imperfectly Competitive Economy*

In his stimulating article, Wells has attempted to substitute 'an aggregate equilibrium model of the Keynesian type' for the usual general equilibrium models, since the latter 'appear inadequate to deal with tax incidence in a "world of monopolies"'.[1] Although I agree with Wells that general equilibrium models cannot handle his problem. I cannot concur in his rationale. It is not because he deals with a world of monopolies but rather because he is interested in aggregate conclusions that the general equilibrium method proves inadequate. General equilibrium assumes a constant level of real income for the economy;[2] however, it is the determination of the level of real income and its distribution which are the essential elements of aggregate analysis. Elsewhere, I have presented a Keynesian-type analysis of the aggregate effects of a general and uniform excise tax in a purely competitive economy.[3]

Moreover, there are certain aspects of Wells's model which appear to be inconsistent with established aggregate economic theory. For example, Wells, although characterizing his model as Keynesian, adopts some assumptions that should appear rather strange to 'Keynesians', e.g. he assumes

(1) 'that trade unions always succeed in establishing their wage demands which are . . . *to maintain a fixed real wage rate in the event of rising prices and employment*'.[4] Keynes, on the other hand, has written, that 'given organisation, equipment, and technique, real wages and the volume of output (and hence employment) are uniquely correlated so that, in general, *an increase in employment can only occur to the accompaniment of a decline in the rate of real wages*'.[5]

(2) 'neither the size of the labor force nor its productivity changes'.[6] The first part of this assumption implies that the supply function of labour is perfectly inelastic and hence completely unaffected by changes in the real wage rate,[7] while the second part is obscure in its meaning. Does Wells assume a constant marginal product of labour, or a constant average product of labour, or a given production function?

* *Public Finance*, 1961.

In his analysis of the effect of government demanding 'an additional x per cent of output deciding to finance its additional demand entirely by levying an excise tax of x per cent' on the output of the community, Wells reaches at least one conclusion which should immediately be suspect. He deduces that the post-tax equilibrium level of employment will be lower than the pre-tax equilibrium level.[8] This implies that the balanced budget multiplier is negative (which is contrary to a large literature on this topic).[9]

Wells's surprising conclusion is due to an oversight in his analysis of the 'employment determining function', $E = g(P)$ (where E is the level of employment and P is the price level). This function is really a disguised aggregate demand function for, according to Wells, it is uniquely determined only when the consumption and investment functions of the community are given.[10] Although Wells recognizes that his 'price determining function', $P = f(E)$, (an incognito aggregate supply function) shifts with the imposition of the tax,[11] he fails to note that this movement of the aggregate supply function must involve a dislodgement of the employment determining (aggregate demand) function, since the community's consumption function is unique only if the distribution of income is unaltered at each employment level. (A change in the price level and the presence of fixed income recipients assures a redistribution of income at each employment level.) Wells indicates that points on the employment determining function 'obey Say's Law', but he apparently is not aware of the interdependence between aggregate supply and aggregate demand which Say's Law implies.[12] Every change in the distribution of income implies a shift in the $E = g(P)$ function.

Finally, Wells's conclusion that 'the greater the monopoly power of a given group relative to the rest of the economy, the less will the real income of this group suffer as a result of an excise tax'[13] is tautological since he defines monopoly powers as 'the bargaining strength, or capacity, of an individual or group to maintain the same (or increased) real prices for its services or products as the general price level rises (or falls)'.[14]

In view of the shortcomings of Wells's model, the problem bears reconsideration; hence, in the next section. I will suggest a model which is applicable to a 'world of monopolies'.

1   THE MODEL

To facilitate the analysis the following assumptions are made: (1) imperfectly competitive economy, (2) profit maximization, (3) given production functions, (4) a homogeneous labour force is the only hired factor of production, (5) the presence of involuntary unemployment prior to the excise tax levy, (6) a constant money wage rate, (7) fully integrated industries, (8) the level of investment is constant,[15] (9) a balanced government budget prior to the tax levy, (10) the government increases its demand for the products of the community and decides to finance this increment in demand entirely by the levying of an excise tax of x per cent on the output of the community.

Our analysis will employ a relationship between entrepreneurs' expectations of total sales proceeds (Z) and the level of employment (E) such expectations bring forth, i.e. $Z = z(E)$. This relationship, the aggregate supply function, has been fully developed from its Keynesian origin[16] by Weintraub. Given the level of factor prices, Weintraub derives an aggregate supply function relating employment to money proceeds, 'in the sense that each expected-proceeds level generates a particular amount of employment'. Each proceeds quantity is obtained from individual supply curves by multiplying the supply price by the associated output and summating over all industries. This sum is then related to the volume of employment required for the particular output quantities. Thus, a Z-function can be described from industry supply curves, if the latter are determinate and 'if the distribution of proceeds for each expected aggregate volume of proceeds is determinate'.[17]

The price level is implicit at every point on the aggregate supply function. Under our assumptions:

$$P = MR\ (1 - 1/E_d) = MC(1 - 1/E_d) = (w/M)\ (1 - 1/E_d) \qquad (29.1)$$

where P is the product price, MR is the marginal revenue, MC is marginal costs, w is the money-wage rate, M is the marginal productivity of labour, E_d is the price elasticity of demand for the product, and $1/E_d$ is the Lerner measure of the degree of monopoly. Assuming diminishing returns, M declines with increasing employment levels. Hence, given the money-wage rate and the degree of monopoly, it follows from equation (29.1) that prices and employment move in the same direction.

We will also employ a Keynesian aggregate demand function which, given factor prices and the degree of monopoly, relates employment levels to money expenditure propensities, i.e. $D = d(E)$.[18] The equilibrium level of employment is given by the intersection of the aggregate demand and aggregate supply functions.

Assuming a money wage rate of w_a in the pre-tax period, then, in Figure 29.1, OW_a represents the relationship between the money-wage bill and the level of employment. OW_a is a straight line with a slope equal to w_a. Given the factor prices, the aggregate demand and supply functions are determinate. Thus, in the pre-tax period, let Z_a represent the aggregate supply curve and D_a the aggregate demand function (in Figure 29.1). Consequently, E_1 is the equilibrium level of employment and Z_1 is the level of money proceeds (GNP) in period 1.

After the tax is levied, the aggregate supply (gross proceeds) curve is

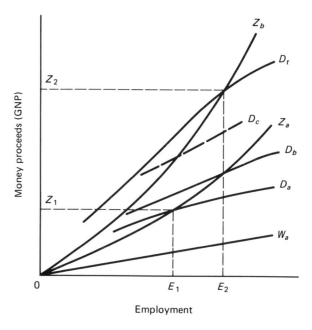

Figure 29.1

shifted upwards to Z_b, while in the post-tax period, Z_a represents the net proceeds going to industry at each employment level.[19] The ordinate difference between Z_b and Z_a at each employment level measures the tax yield. Thus, aggregate private money income at any given employment level is unchanged; while market prices are higher in the post-tax period. Hence, the real income of the private sector is lower at each employment level. It is unlikely, therefore, that private pre-tax real consumption at each employment level will be maintained. Accordingly, the post-tax private aggregate demand function could not shift upwards enough to maintain the pre-tax equilibrium level of employment (e.g. to D_c). In other words, the tax reduces real private effective demand at each level of employment. Let us assume that the private sector increases its aggregate money expenditures at each employment level by an amount sufficient to dislodge the pre-tax aggregate demand curve to D_b.[20] To this D_b function we must add the additional government expenditures at each employment level to obtain the total post-tax aggregate demand curve (D_t). Assuming the government spends the entire tax receipts at each E-level, then the ordinate difference between Z_a and Z_b is added to the D_b function to obtain in the D_t curve. The post-tax equilibrium situation is obtained where the D_t and D_b curves intersect.[21]

Hence, it follows that:

(a) the price level increases by a greater percentage than the tax rate. This rise in prices is due to the sum of two influences, (i) the tax rate (shifting the Z-curve upwards), and (ii) diminishing returns (due to a movement along the Z-curve);
(b) employment increases from E_1 to E_2;
(c) the real wage rate falls, but the fate of the real wage bill is uncertain, since the increase in employment may more than offset the decline in the wage rate;
(d) the real income of fixed income recipients declines by more than the tax rate (due to diminishing returns);
(e) profit recipients improve their relative and absolute income positions.[22] If there is no change in the number of profit recipients, this can be translated into a per capita gain.

Thus we may conclude that a general and uniform excise tax is borne mainly by fixed income groups and previously employed workers, while the newly employed and the profit recipients will gain in real income.

Our analysis of the effect on profit recipients would be less conclusive if we allow the degree of monopoly to vary with the level of employment. In this case, ultimately whether this group gains or not depends mainly on the changes in the degree of monopoly power as employment varies. Theoretical views on this relationship differ: (a) some argue that monopoly power varies directly with employment as buyers become less discriminate with prosperity, (b) others feel that it varies inversely as the decline in aggregate demand leads to price-fixing agreements, (c) still others believe it does not vary at all.[23] If view (a) is correct, profit recipients stand to gain even more as employment expands, while if (b) is applicable, then their gain may be small or even negative. Finally if view (c) is acceptable, then monopoly has little to offer as an explanatory determinant of differences in excise tax incidence as employment varies. Which view is realistic awaits further empirical studies.

Furthermore, as Weintraub notes:

> that monopoly can support output in certain productivity and demand configurations while a purely competitive – or a $P = MC$ type – adaptation cannot, eliminates any easy means of comparing the income result under the one pricing mode with that under the other. Although the income division for the same *employment* volume can be compared, as the output composition will differ, then not too much meaning can be assigned to the comparative results in this typical index number riddle.[24]

Finally, if we replace assumption (6) with the supposition that the money-wage rate is inflexible downwards but will increase as employment rises, then the ultimate post-tax aggregate supply function will be Z_c (Figure

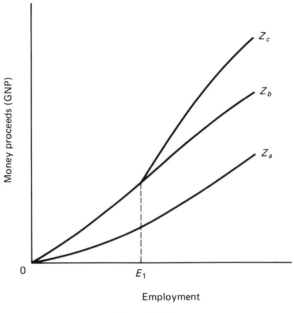

Figure 29.2

29.2). The steeper slope of Z_c over Z_b, after the E_1-level, is derived from cross-cutting through a family of aggregate supply functions where each member of the family assumes a given money wage rate[25] (in a manner similar to the one presented by Wells on pp. 213–14). The new aggregate demand curve could be elicited and the equilibrium solution determined. The direction of tax incidence should be similar to the conclusions listed above, but differences in the magnitudes of the burdens and gains would involve a comparison of the price and employment results in the two cases.

2 WELLS'S GENERALIZATIONS

Wells has generalized that the more competitive the economy, the smaller the rise in the general price level and the more even the burden of the tax. We have argued, on the other hand, only changes in the degree of monopoly (not the level) are important in tax incidence. Furthermore, we have indicated that it is difficult (if not impossible) to compare competitive and monopolistic results.

Wells believes that the key to the analysis of the incidence of an excise tax 'lies . . . with the changed distribution of income it brings about'.[26] Our analysis has emphasized, however, that changes in the level of employment are as important as changes in the distribution of income.

Notes

1. P. Wells, 'Excise Tax Incidence in an Imperfectly Competitive Economy', *Public Finance*, XIV, 1959, p. 203.
2. S. Weintraub, *An Approach to the Theory of Income Distribution* (Philadelphia: Chilton, 1958), p. 10.
3. P. Davidson, 'Rolph on the Aggregate Effects of Excise Taxation', *The Southern Economic Journal*, XXVII, July 1960, pp. 37–42, and Chapter 28.
4. Wells, 'Excise Tax Incidence', p. 205; italics mine.
5. J. M. Keynes, *The General Theory of Employment, Interest and Money* (New York: Harcourt, 1936), p. 17.
6. Wells, 'Excise Tax Incidence', p. 204.
7. Compare my criticism of Rolph's system, Chapter 28, pp. 433–41 and Weintraub's analysis of the labour supply function, *An Approach Theory of Income Distribution*, pp. 117–30.
8. Wells, 'Excise Tax Incidence', p. 209.
9. For example, W. A. Salant, 'Taxes, Income Determination, and the Balanced Budget Theorem', *Review of Economics and Statistics*, May 1957, especially p. 158, '*in any event*, the balanced budget multiplier will be greater than zero'. Italics mine.
10. Wells, 'Excise Tax Incidence', p. 205.
11. Ibid., p. 211. Note the similarity to the shift of the aggregate supply function with the imposition of the tax in my competitive model, Chapter 28, pp. 436–40.
12. Weintraub, *An Approach to the Theory of Income Distribution*, p. 8. Almost as an after-thought, on page 216, Wells notes that under a full employment fiscal policy, government spending can shift the $E = g(P)$ function.
13. Wells, 'Excise Tax Incidence', p. 216.
14. Ibid., p. 213 n.
15. Wells assumes a constant level of investment. This assumption is inconsistent with his suppositions of a constant money supply, constant marginal efficiency of capital schedule, and rising prices and interest rates. See Wells, 'Excise Tax Incidence', pp. 207 and 207 n. We do not make any such monetary assumption in our model.
16. Keynes, *The General Theory* pp. 25, 29.
17. W. Weintraub, *An Approach to the Theory of Income Distribution*, pp. 25–6, also see pp. 68–68 n. 10.
18. Keynes, *The General Theory* pp. 25, 28–9. See Weintraub, ibid., pp. 30–8 for a graphic derivation of the aggregate demand function.
19. This upward shift of the aggregate supply function is the macrocounterpart of the usual microanalysis of the effect of a particular excise tax on the supply schedule of a commodity.
20. See F. Gehrels, 'Inflationary Effects of a Balanced Budget Under Full Employment', *American Economic Review*, XXXIX, 1949, p. 1227.
21. This is true if we assume that the government pays the excise tax on its purchases from business enterprises. Otherwise the gross proceeds curve (Z_b) would have to be reduced somewhat to allow for government purchases at less than market prices.
22. Weintraub, *An Approach to the Theory of Income Distribution*, p. 92.
23. Ibid., p. 68.
24. Ibid.
25. For the technique, see Weintraub, ibid., pp. 77–8.
26. Wells, 'Excise Tax Incidence', p. 216.

30 Income and Employment Multipliers, and the Price Level*

Although Keynes suggested that 'the general price-level depends partly on the rate of remuneration of the factors of production which enter into marginal cost and partly on the scale of output as a whole, i.e. (taking equipment and technique as given) on the volume of employment' (Keynes, 1936, p. 294), the typical Keynesian multiplier analysis has ignored the problem of changing price and wage levels as output expands or contracts.

The pedagogical simplicity of existing 'real' multiplier formulations has obstructed attempts to analyse concurrent price movements. Multiplier analysis has usually been applied to the following cases: (1) the involuntary unemployment case, where prices are assumed constant and output is variable,[1] and (2) the full employment case, where output is assumed constant and prices are variable. Hence in (1) changes in money income can be directly related to changes in real income, while in (2) changes in money income are directly related to changes in the price level.

Although the usual multiplier models have given valuable insight into income generation and contraction processes, they have not been helpful for policy purposes, for they are unable to deal with simultaneously occurring economic events, e.g. price movements before full employment, changes in employment levels, money-income determination, and distributive effects of expansionary and contractionary forces (Robertson, 1959, pp. 177–8). For example, the typical Keynesian multiplier model is incapable of explaining the continuous rise in the Consumer Price Index since the bottom of the 1958 recession despite the persistent presence of high rates of unemployment and excess capacity.

The purpose of this paper is to develop simple multiplier formulations which (a) are compatible with the conceptual framework of *The General Theory*[2] and the modern theory of the firm, and (b) are useful for policy purposes in that they permit the analysis of the effects of changes in aggregate demand on price and wage levels, employment and output levels, and money-income determination and its distribution.

Our analysis will emphasize (1) the heterogeneity of economic interests

* *American Economic Review*, September 1962.
The author is indebted to S. Weintraub, E. O. Edwards, L. R. Klein, A. Lerner, and E. Smolensky for helpful comments on earlier drafts of this paper, to I. B. Kravis for making available some unpublished empirical estimates, and to C. L. Leven for checking the mathematical analysis.

among members of the same economic group (e.g. employed versus unemployed workers, rentier versus entrepreneur capitalists) on such economic policy issues as inflation and/or changes in the level of employment (Robinson, 1956, pp. 278–9; Weintraub, 1958, pp. 58–9); (2) the asymmetry of price-level changes and the employment multiplier in an expansion as compared to a contraction; and (3) the effect of changes in the distribution of income on expansions and contractions.

In the appendix some crude statistical estimates of the magnitude of the multipliers developed in this paper are presented.

1 THE FIRST MODEL: MONEY-WAGE RATE CONSTANT

The analysis will be based on the concept of an aggregate supply function as developed from its Keynesian origin (Keynes, 1936, pp. 25, 29) by Weintraub. Given the level of factor prices, an aggregate supply function relating employment (N) to expected money proceeds (Z) can be derived 'in the sense that each expected-proceeds level generates a particular amount of employment'. Each proceeds quantity (i.e. expected total revenue) is obtained from individual industry supply curves by multiplying the supply prices by the associated output and summating over all industries. These sums are related to the volume of employment required for the particular output quantities via production functions (Weintraub, 1958, pp. 25–7).

The following symbols will be used in this presentation:

A	average physical product of labour
b	marginal (= average) propensity to consume of wage-earners
C_r^i	rentiers' real consumption
C_r^r	real consumption out of the gross profit residual
C_r^w	wage-earners' real consumption
D	aggregate demand in money terms
D_r	aggregate demand in real terms
f	marginal (= average) propensity to consume of rentiers
F	fixed money income payments
I	money expenditures on investment
I_r	real investment
k	the reciprocal of the wage share
K	the stock of capital
M	marginal physical product of labour
MC	marginal cost
N	employment
P	price level of composite commodity
Q	output quantity of composite commodity

r marginal (= average) propensity to consume out of the gross profit residual

w money-wage rate

Z aggregate supply in money terms (GNP)

Z_r aggregate supply in real terms ($= Q$)

α, β production function constants

The following assumptions will facilitate the analysis: (1) we are concerned with a purely competitive closed economy with profit-maximizing entrepreneurs; (2) the money-wage rate is constant; (3) a homogeneous labour force is the only hired variable factor of production; (4) involuntary unemployment exists; (5) a composite commodity is produced by fully integrated firms using an identical technology; (6) the aggregate production function is of the Cobb–Douglas type; (7) there are no government expenditures or receipts; (8) there are three income recipient groups (wage earners, rentiers, and profit recipients) and the real consumption of each group is a simple proportional function of the real income of that group (Kaldor, 1955–6, p. 95); and (9) the level of money investment expenditures is exogenously determined. This last assumption would be apropos if businessmen were to budget a given amount of money for investment and did not alter their decisions. If the period of analysis is relatively short, this supposition may approximate reality.

These assumptions impose the following conditions on the system: The aggregate production function takes the form:

$$Q = \beta N^{\alpha} K^{1-\alpha} \tag{30.1}$$

Consequently, at any level of factor hire, the ratio of average product to marginal product of labour (and the reciprocal of the wage share) is a constant (Davidson, 1959, p. 194; 1960, p. 110),

$$A/M = 1/\alpha = k \tag{30.2}$$

The price level of the composite commodity is a function of the money-wage rate and the marginal productivity of labour:

$$P = MC = w/M \tag{30.3}$$

Accordingly, the price level varies directly with the level of employment and consequently is different at each point on the aggregate supply function which relates employment to expected GNP. As Weintraub has shown (1958, p. 51), the shape and position of the aggregate supply curve will depend on the ratio of average to marginal product and the money-wage rate, i.e.

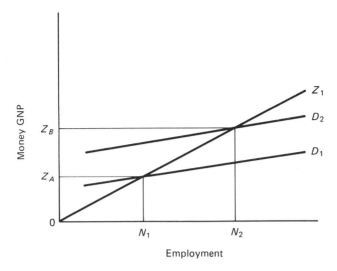

Figure 30.1

$$Z = (A/M)wN = kwN \tag{30.4}$$

Thus, in Figure 30.1, Z is a linear function of N.

Money aggregate demand is equal to the sum of the money consumption expenditures of the three income groups plus money investment expenditures. Hence, an aggregate demand function in money terms can be derived given the consumption behaviour of the three income groups and the investment decisions of businessmen.

Given the aggregate demand and supply functions of D_1 and Z_1 in Figure 30.1, then N_1 is the equilibrium level of employment and Z_A is the equilibrium level of GNP (with an implicit price level of P_1). If there is a parametric shift in the aggregate demand function to D_2 because of an autonomous rise in investment expenditures, then the new equilibrium values, *ceteris paribus*, are N_2 and Z_B, while the new price level (P_2) is higher than the old price level (P_1) because of diminishing returns.

1.1 The Multiplier

Let us now analyse this system in greater detail. Underlying the monetary aggregate supply and demand functions will be real phenomena. The real aggregate supply curve (Z_r) relating physical output with employment is, of course, the familiar total product curve (Figure 30.2). Since the production function is of the Cobb–Douglas type, the total product curve rises at a continuously decreasing rate.

The real aggregate demand function can be decomposed into separate

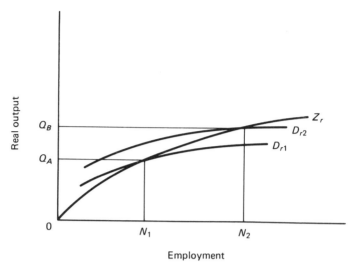

Figure 30.2

real consumption functions for each income group and real investment expenditures,

$$D_r = C_r^w + C_r^r + C_r^f + I_r \qquad (30.5)$$

For simplicity we have assumed that the consumption of each income group is a simple proportionate function of the real income of each group. Thus, the consumption functions would be:

wage earners: $C_r^w = b\dfrac{wN}{P}$ $\qquad\qquad$ (30.6)

rentiers: $C_r^f = f\dfrac{F}{P}$ $\qquad\qquad$ (30.7)

profit recipients: $C_r^r = r\left(\dfrac{Z - F - wN}{P}\right) \ = \dfrac{r[(k-1)wN - F]}{P}.$ (30.8)

These functions have several interesting implications. Equation (7) is particularly noteworthy in that it suggests that as employment and prices rise, the real consumption of rentiers declines (although their money consumption spending remains constant). Hence rentiers are 'forced' to save without accumulating either any real or monetary assets.[3] Implicit in equation (8) is the assumption that a constant proportion of the real gross profit residual is distributed and that the proportion of the distributed profits spent on consumption is constant; or, if changes in the proportion of the profit residual distributed were to occur they would be offset by changes in the proportion of the distributions that are consumed (Kaldor, 1955–6, p. 95; Robinson, 1956, pp. 258–9).

Equations (30.6) and (30.8) suggest the important proposition that it is the consumption behaviour of wage earners and profit recipients which tends to give the real aggregate demand function its positive slope. On the other hand, since real investment declines as employment rises (assumption (30.9)), rentiers' and investment spending tends to reduce the upward slope of the real aggregate demand function (Figure 30.2).

In equilibrium, aggregate supply equals aggregate demand,[4] i.e. $Z_r = D_r$. Since $Z_r = Z/P$, therefore, using equations (30.4) through (30.8), the equilibrium condition can be written as:

$$\frac{kwN}{P} = \frac{bwN}{P} + \frac{r[(k-1)wN - F]}{P} + \frac{fF}{P} + \frac{I}{P} \tag{30.9}$$

Multiplying through by P and expanding terms, we obtain

$$kwN = bwN + r(k-1)wN + (f-r)F + I \tag{30.10}$$

Solving for N:

$$N = \frac{1}{w[k - b - r(k-1)]} [(f-r)F + I] \tag{30.11}$$

Consequently, for a given change in I, we obtain the resultant change in N, or the employment multiplier as:

$$\frac{\Delta N}{\Delta I} = \frac{1}{w[k - b - r(k-1)]} \tag{30.12}$$

The employment multiplier relates the additional employment created by an increment in money expenditures, assuming w is constant.[5]

Similarly, substituting Z/kw for N in equation (11), we may solve for Z:

$$Z = \left[\frac{k}{k - b - r(k-1)} \right] [(f-r)F + I] \tag{30.13}$$

Consequently, the money income (GNP) multiplier is:

$$\frac{\Delta Z}{\Delta I} = \frac{k}{k - b - r(k-1)} \tag{30.14}$$

The money-income multiplier relates the change in money GNP due to an exogenous increase in money expenditures.

Inequality (10a) in note 4 implies that the term $[k - b - r(k - 1)]$ which appears in the denominator of both multipliers, is positive, hence both of the multipliers are positive. These multipliers offer a useful contrast to conventional 'real income' multipliers which have become commonplace in the literature.[6] Our multipliers indicate that for a given change in I, the change in GNP depends on (1) the marginal propensities of wage earners and profit recipients and (2) the distribution of income as expressed through k. The change in employment for a given change in I, however, depends on the money-wage rate, as well as the marginal propensities (b and r) and the distribution factor (k).

As might be expected, the magnitude of the multipliers varies directly with the marginal propensities to consume, i.e. the greater the additional real consumption out of a given increment in the real income for wage earners and/or profit recipients, the greater the multiplier effects. Moreover, the magnitude of the multipliers varies inversely with changes in the magnitude of k, the income distribution factor. For example, should k increase, the shift in relative income away from the usually higher marginal-spending wage earners and towards the usually higher marginal-saving profit recipients would reduce aggregate spending repercussions.

Fixed income recipients do not appear to affect the magnitude of the multipliers. This result is not as surprising as it might at first seem since, as we have already noted, the assumption of a simple proportionate real consumption function for rentiers implies constant money expenditures by rentiers at any level of employment and prices. To the extent that rentiers consist primarily of pensioners, widows and orphans who are already spending almost all of their income to subsist, they are unable significantly to increase their money expenditures out of their current money income when employment and prices rise. Furthermore, for small changes in prices, the moral tradition against living off one's capital may be sufficiently strong to prevent these rentiers from using previous savings for consumption. Hence the money expenditures of 'income poor' rentiers may be constant as their real consumption declines with rising prices. These rentiers will have a vested interest in preventing any increase in output associated with rising prices (Keynes, 1936, p. 328).

On the other hand, wealthy individuals who receive rentier income actually receive most of their income in forms conceptually similar to wages and/or profit distributions.[7] Hence the consumption pattern of these 'income rich' quasi-rentiers may be subsumed under functions (30.6) and/or (30.8).

1.2 The Price Variable

The price of the composite commodity is given by equation (30.3); its differential is:

$$PdM + MdP = dw \qquad (30.15)$$

If w is assumed constant, then

$$\frac{dP}{P} = -\frac{dM}{M} \qquad (30.16)$$

or, in words, proportionate changes in the price level are inversely related to proportionate change in the marginal product of labour. Since the production function is $Q = \beta N^{\alpha} K^{1-\alpha}$, the proportionate change (neglecting signs) in M is equal to $(\alpha - 1)$ times the proportionate change in N.[8] Since $\Delta N/N$ can be obtained from equations (30.11) and (30.12), the proportionate change in price can be computed via

$$\frac{\Delta P}{P} = -\frac{\Delta M}{M} = -(\alpha - 1)\frac{\Delta N}{N} \qquad (30.17)$$

Thus, for example, if $\alpha = \frac{1}{2}$, a 2 per cent increase in employment will lead to a 1 per cent increase in price.

An important implication of equation (30.17) is that increasing employment levels are a mixed blessing to employees as a group. Since prices rise while the money-wage rate is constant, the real wage rate declines. Workers who were employed before the increase in aggregate demand find their real income declining (Keynes, 1936, pp. 10, 17; Robinson, 1956, p. 265). Increased employment, therefore, implies a real cost to the previously employed wage earners as well as to rentiers. The newly employed, who were formerly members of a 'null-income' group (Weintraub, 1958, pp. 58–60), on the other hand, experience a substantial increase in real income. Hence, the higher the initial level of employment, the fewer the wage earners who have a vested interest in a further increase in employment and output, and the more who will bear some real cost in any further expansion. Accordingly, given a fixed money-wage rate, there is a heterogeneity of interests between employed and unemployed workers.

If dividend distributions tend to lag behind rising profit levels as the economy approaches full employment, most of the incremental profits will remain the property of the firm. Given diminishing returns and fixed money contracts, therefore, it is only (1) the fictitious legal individual – the corporation, and (2) those entrepreneurs (mainly of unincorporated enter-

prises) whose incomes are geared directly to profit levels who will tend to
reap unmistakeable benefits from an unfettered economic expansion.

2   THE SECOND MODEL: MONEY-WAGE RATE VARIABLE

The analysis thus far has assumed a constant money-wage rate. Let us now
relax this assumption and take the money-wage rate as a function of the
level of employment, i.e. $w = \varphi(N)$. This money-wage function should not
be interpreted as the supply function of labour. Following Keynes, our
model assumes the labour supply to be a function of the real-wage rate.
Nevertheless, Weintraub has demonstrated that a function relating labour
offerings to money-wage rates can be derived from the demand function
for labour and its implicit real wage phenomena. Whenever aggregate
demand changes, *ceteris paribus*, the money demand and supply functions
of labour derived by Weintraub are displaced. Our function $w = \varphi(N)$, is
the locus of equilibrium points traced out by the simultaneous shifts of
these two Weintraub curves (1958, pp. 109–29).

2.1   The Multiplier

In this model equation (30.10) can be written as

$$kN\phi(N) = bN\phi(N) + r(k - 1)N\phi(N) + (f - r)F + I \qquad (30.10')$$

Solving for ΔN as before, we obtain the employment multiplier as

$$\frac{\Delta N}{\Delta I} = \frac{1}{[\phi(N) + N\phi'(N)][k - b - r(k - 1)]} \qquad (30.12')$$

A priori reasoning suggests that the money-wage rate function should
have a positive minimum value and should be an increasing function of the
level of employment. Hence, for illustrative purposes, we assume that
$\varphi(N) = m + nN^2$. Accordingly equation (30.12') becomes

$$\frac{\Delta N}{\Delta I} = \frac{1}{[m + 3nN^2][k - b - r(k - 1)]} \qquad (30.12'')$$

Thus the additional employment created by a given increment in money
expenditures depends on the distribution of income (k), the marginal
propensities to consume out of wages and profits, and the initial level of
employment. The relationship between changes in the magnitude of the
employment multiplier and changes in k, b, and r are the same as in the

irst model. When the money-wage rate is a function of employment, however, the higher the initial N-level, the smaller the increment in employment from the multiplier repercussions, as more of the increase in money spending spills over into bidding up money wages and less into increasing real output (Keynes, 1936, pp. 284–6).

Substituting $Z/k\ \phi(N)$ for N in equation (30.10') and solving for ΔZ, we obtain the same money-income multiplier as we did in the first model, i.e.

$$\frac{\Delta Z}{\Delta I} = \frac{k}{k - b - r(k - 1)} \tag{30.14'}$$

Hence, the money-income multiplier is the same whether the money-wage rate is constant or not. What is important in determining the magnitude of the money-income multiplier is the marginal propensities of the two income groups who share in the increments of income and the relative distribution (as expressed through k) of the income increment between wage-earners and profit recipients.

2.2 The Price Variable

Dividing equation (30.15) by $MP = w$ and rearranging terms, we obtain

$$\frac{dP}{P} = \frac{dw}{w} - \frac{dM}{M} \tag{30.16'}$$

i.e. the proportionate change in the price level varies directly with the proportionate change in the money-wage rate and inversely with the proportionate change in the marginal product of labour. Since the relative price increase for any given change in employment will be greater than the relative money-wage increase, therefore any autonomous increase in spending must decrease the real-wage rate while increasing the level of employment (Keynes, 1936, pp. 10, 17).

Moreover, if some immobility or other imperfection exists in the labour market, higher starting wages may accompany increasing employment levels, while the money-wage paid to previously employed workers need not change very much (a phenomenon that is often observable in white collar occupations). Thus the average money-wage rate may be an increasing function of employment, while the previously employed workers do not share as fully in wage increases as the newly employed. In this case, the real cost of expansion borne by the previously employed workers, as well as by rentiers, will be greater than in the constant money-wage case, and the lack of zeal for increasing employment displayed by these groups is understandable.[9]

When the employment rate hovers around the 5 to 7 per cent level (as it has since the recession of 1958) most of the voters will be either rentiers, or already employed workers. Consequently, the overwhelming majority of the electorate are more interested in preventing inflation than in reaching full employment. It is only the remaining unemployed (many of whom are probably disenfranchised because of race, age, residential or educational requirements), the owners of small unincorporated enterprises, executives in family or closely held corporations, and the impersonal large publicly held corporations who will benefit from further increases in output and employment. It is not surprising, therefore, that the United States tolerated a 7 per cent unemployment rate throughout most of 1961, while politicians and financial writers claimed that 1961 was a year of unprecedented prosperity. The political fears of inflation overshadow the desire to mop up the remnants of unemployment once a relatively high level of employment has been obtained.

2.3 Ratchet Effect of the Money-Wage Rate

Finally if we assume that changes in the money-wage rate produce a ratchet effect, then once a given money-wage rate is established in the marketplace it is inflexible downwards. In such a situation, the employment multiplier presented in equation (12′) is applicable to an increment in money expenditures, while the employment multiplier of equation (12) is the relevant one for decrements in money expenditures. Accordingly, the employment multiplier may be asymmetric, its magnitude being larger in a contraction than in an expansion.

Given a ratchet effect for the money-wage rate, equation (16′) implies that the price variable may be relatively more stable during a contraction than during an expansion. Thus it is not surprising that the 1957–8 and 1960–1 recessions chiefly affected the level of employment, while the expansions beginning in 1958 and 1961 (at less than full employment) tended to affect both employment and prices.

3 CONCLUSIONS

Given the simplifying assumptions, the magnitudes of both the employment and money-GNP multipliers vary directly with the marginal propensities to consume of wage earners and profit recipients, and inversely with the distribution factor (k). The money-wage rate is inversely related to the employment multiplier but does not affect the magnitude of the money-income multiplier. If the money-wage rate is an increasing function of the level of employment, then the higher the initial employment level, the weaker the multiplier repercussion will be on further increases in employment. If the money-wage rate is inflexible downwards, then the employment multiplier may be larger in a contraction than in an expansion.

The apparent complacency about recent unemployment levels in the United States is basically due to the heterogeneity of economic interests among the members of the community. As our analysis has shown, with expansions in economic activity the real income of fixed income groups and already employed workers declines, while the real income of the unemployed workers and the entrepreneurs of unincorporated and small corporate enterprises increases. As a consequence, once the level of employment is relatively high, most members of the community fear inflation more than they desire further expansion.

APPENDIX: AN ESTIMATE OF THE INCOME AND EMPLOYMENT MULTIPLIERS

A.1   The Value of the Parameters

1. *The income distribution factor (k)*. Weintraub (1959) has presented statistical evidence that the value of k is approximately 2 for the United States economy.
2. *The marginal propensity to consume out of wages (b) and out of the gross profit residual (r)*. Although a number of statistical studies on the consumption–savings behaviour of various economic groups have been published, none of the marginal (or average) propensity estimates has precise applicability to our theoretical concepts. Nevertheless, by using a study by Klein (1960) and unpublished estimates of consumption propensities by occupational groups done by I. B. Kravis, in conjunction with the national income data of the Department of Commerce, crude estimates of b and r can be made.

Estimate of b. The consumption behaviour of 'all employees' can be used as an approximation for the marginal propensity to consume out of wages. Klein's and Kravis's figures tend to suggest that b would be in the .75 to .85 range, or approximately .80.

Estimate of r. The marginal consumption out of the gross profit residual is more difficult to estimate. The aforementioned studies suggest that entrepreneurs' marginal propensity to consume out of their disposable income is between ½ and ⅔. These estimates, however, are only for entrepreneurs of unincorporated enterprises, self-employed professionals, and farmers, whose total income receipts were only approximately one-third of the total gross profit residual in 1960 (see Table A.1). From the other two-thirds of the gross profit residual, a little more than 10 per cent was paid out as dividends and was consequently available for consumption by profit recipients. If we assume that the marginal propensity to consume

Table A.1   Gross Profit Residual, 1960 (billions of dollars)

Business and professional income	$36.2	
Farm income	12.0	
Rental income	11.7	
		$59.9
Capital consumption allowances	$43.1	
Indirect business taxes	45.6	
Corporate profits before taxes	45.1	
		133.8
Gross profit residual		$193.7
Dividends – $14.1		

Source: *Federal Reserve Bulletin*, September 1961, pp. 1102–3.

out of profit distributions is approximately the same as the marginal propensity to consume out of wages (i.e. 4/5), then the marginal propensity to consume out of the total gross profit residual can be computed as a weighted average:

$$r = (e)(g) + (d)(h)(1 - g)$$

where e is the marginal propensity to consume out of entrepreneurial income, g is the fraction of the gross profit residual going to entrepreneurs, d is the marginal propensity to consume out of profit distribution, h is the fraction of the corporate gross profit residual that is distributed, and $(1 - g)$ is the fraction of the gross profit residual accruing to corporations. Hence,

$$r = (.50 \text{ to } .67)(.33) + (.80)(.10)(.67) = .220 \text{ to } .275$$

$$r \approx .25$$

Thus the marginal propensity to consume out of the gross profit residual (r) would approximate .25.

3. *The money-wage rate (w)*. The money-wage rate may be estimated by dividing total employee compensation in 1960 by total employment in that year ($293.7 billion ÷ 66.7 million), i.e. $w = \$4.40$, or approximately $4400 per annum per employee.

4. *The parameters of the function for the money-wage rate (m, n)*. Our posited money-wage function in the second model, $w = m + nN^2$ suggests an a priori relationship, where (1) there is a minimum money-wage rate

:vel (m), and (2) as employment increases and the pools of unemployment ry up, the money-wage rate tends to rise at an increasing rate. Crude stimates for m and n can be made as follows:

Given a legal minimum wage rate of $1.00 per hour in 1960 and a 0-hour work week, the value of m would be $2.08 (i.e. $2080 per annum). f, in 1960, the level of employment was 66.7 million, while the going ioney-wage rate was $4.40 and the minimum was $2.08, then n would be 000521.

.2 The Magnitude of the Multipliers

Jsing the above values for the parameters, the money-income multiplier an be estimated from equation (30.14) to be 2.11. If w is constant, then he employment multiplier in equation (30.12) is .239; if w is an increasing unction of N, then the employment multiplier [equation (30.12″)] is .116. Thus, for example, an increment of $1 billion in exogenous spending would ncrease GNP by $2.11 billion, while employment would rise by 239 000, if he money-wage rate were constant, or by 116 000 if the money-wage rate vere an increasing function of employment.[10]

With these multiplier values, the output, income, and price effects and onsequently the anti-recessionary policy implications of President Ken-iedy's decision, in July 1961, to increase military expenditures by $3.5 iillion (without increasing taxes) can be estimated. If wages increase with :mployment (as in our second model) then the additional defence expendi-ures will induce a 1 per cent increase in prices and a $7.39 billion increase n money GNP. The reduction in unemployment would be only 406 000, as nuch of the increase in total spending will raise the average money-wage ate by almost .7 per cent. Consequently, unemployment (which was 5.1 nillion in July of 1961) would still be significantly large. On the other hand, f the money-wage rate could be constrained (by moral suasion or legislat-ve action) then, for the same initial increase in expenditures, the employ-nent effect would be more than twice as large; 837 000 new jobs would be :reated, while the concurrent price rise would be relatively small (approxi-nately .6 per cent).

Notes

1. The typical involuntary unemployment multiplier system, although designated a Keynesian model, is incompatible with Keynes's *General Theory* since he there indicated that any changes in effective demand at less than full employ-ment will affect prices as well as output and employment (Keynes, 1936, pp. 284–6).
2. The extent to which the Keynesian framework has been obscured is most

obvious in the modern theory of international adjustments. Machlup, for example, in his comprehensive study of foreign trade multipliers assumes infinitely elastic supply curves because he is 'not equipped' to deal with changing price and distributional effects. He defends his stable price assumption on the grounds that it rules out a great many complications and 'there is little that a general theory can do about this mass of "possibilities"'' (Machlup 1950, pp. 204, n. 205). Nevertheless, it is just these wage, price and distributional complications which are relevant for trade policies and which have attracted the attention of economists since Ricardo. (Elsewhere, I have suggested how these complications could be handled in a macroanalysis of an economy engaging in international trade (Davidson, 1960, pp. 114–19).)

3. Weintraub has previously noted this phenomenon in analysing his system and has some cogent comments on the often observable 'forced' savings of rentiers (1958, pp. 42–3, 124). Also see Keynes's comments on 'unproductive consumption' (1930, pp. 124–5).

4. A stable equilibrium exists if the excess of aggregate demand over aggregate supply decreases with increasing employment levels, i.e.

$$\frac{d(D_r - Z_r)}{dN} < 0 \tag{30.9a}$$

This implies that the slope of the aggregate demand function is less than the slope of the aggregate supply function.

$$\frac{dD_r}{dN} < \frac{dZ_r}{dN}$$

or

$$b + r(k - 1) < k \tag{30.10a}$$

Rearranging terms

$$b - r < k(1 - r) \tag{30.10b}$$

Since normally $k > 1 > b > r$, a stable equilibrium is assured.

5. Our employment multiplier differs from Kahn's concept which stressed the relationship between the increment in total employment and a given increase in employment in the investment industries (1931). Although Kahn's ratio is designated as the employment multiplier in *The General Theory*, Keynes noted that Kahn's intention was to lay down 'general principles by which to estimate the actual quantitative relationship between an increment of net investment and the increment of aggregate employment which will be associated with it' (Keynes, 1936, pp. 113–14). Since equation (12) deals directly with this latter relationship, I've designated it as the employment multiplier.

6. The employment and money-income multipliers may be reduced to a more familiar algebraic form by dividing their numerators and denominators by k, i.e.

$$\frac{\Delta N}{\Delta I} = \frac{1/k}{w/k[k - b - r(k - 1)]} = \frac{1}{kw\{1 - [b(1/k) + r(1 - 1/k)]\}}$$

and $$\frac{\Delta Z}{\Delta I} = \frac{1}{1 - [b(1/k) + r(1 - 1/k)]}$$

where $[b(1/k) + r(1 - 1/k)]$ is simply a weighted average of the marginal propensities to consume of the different economic classes which share in the increments of income.

7. For example, in 1948, the top 5 per cent of the personal income recipients received 26 per cent of all the interest payments in the United States. Nevertheless, 44 per cent of their total income was derived from employee compensation, while 52 per cent was derived from income which is conceptually similar to profit income (34 per cent entrepreneurial income, 15 per cent dividends, and 3 per cent rental income). Fixed income payments (interest) was only 4 per cent of the total income received by this group (Kuznets, 1953, pp. 570–1, 676; Smolensky, 1961.)

8. From equation (2) we know that $M = \alpha \frac{Q}{N}$ or $MN = \alpha Q$. Hence

$$NdM + MdN = \alpha dQ$$

Dividing both sides of this equation by NM, it can be shown that

$$\frac{dM}{M} = (\alpha - 1)\frac{dN}{N}$$

9. A. Lerner was helpful in developing this portion of the discussion.

10. After this paper was submitted, Suits published a study which corroborates our estimate. Using a 32-equation econometric model of the United States, Suits calculated that an exogenous increase in plant and equipment expenditures of $1 billion would increase total employment by 115 000 (as compared to our estimate of 116 000). See D. B. Suits, 'Forecasting and Analysis with an Econometric Model', *American Economic Review*, March 1962, pp. 52, 128.

References

Davidson, P. (1959), 'A Clarification of the Ricardian Rent Share', *Canadian Journal of Economics*, 25, (May) pp. 190–5.

Davidson, P. (1960), *Theories of Aggregate Income Distribution* (New Brunswick).

Kahn, R. F. (1931), 'The Relation of Home Investment to Unemployment', *Economic Journal*, 41 (June), pp. 174–98.

Kaldor, N. (1955–6), 'Alternative Theories of Distribution', *Revue of Economic Studies*, 23, pp. 83–100.

Keynes, J. M. (1930), *Treatise on Money*, Vol. II (London).

Keynes, J. M. (1936), *The General Theory of Employment Interest and Money* (New York).

Klein, L. R. (1960), 'Entrepreneurial Savings', in I. Friend and R. Jones (eds), *Consumption and Savings*, Vol. II (Philadelphia), pp. 297–335.

Kuznets, S. (1953), *Shares of Upper Income Groups in Income and Savings* (New York).

Machlup, F. (1950), *International Trade and the National Income Multiplier* (Philadelphia).

Robertson, D. H. (1959), *Money*, 4th edn (Chicago).
Robinson, J. (1956), *The Accumulation of Capital* (London).
Smolensky, E. (1961), 'Industrialization and Income Inequality: Recent United States Experience', *Journal of Regional Science Association Proceedings*, 7.
Weintraub, S. (1958), *An Approach to the Theory of Income Distribution* (Philadelphia).
Weintraub, S. (1959), *A General Theory of the Price Level, Output, Income Distribution, and Economic Growth* (Philadelphia).

31 More on the Aggregate Supply Function*

Veendorp and Werkema[1] have raised some questions about the necessary productivity requirements underlying the slope of the aggregate supply function as developed from its Keynesian origins[2] by Weintraub and Wells.[3]

The aggregate supply function is a relationship between entrepreneurs' expectations of total sales proceeds (Z) and the level of employment (N) such expectations bring forth, i.e. $Z = f(N)$. Given the level of factor prices, Weintraub derives an aggregate supply function relating employment to money proceeds 'in the sense that each expected proceeds level generates a particular amount of employment'. Each proceeds quantity is obtained from the individual industry supply curves by multiplying the supply price by the associated output and summating over all industries. This sum is then related to the volume of employment required for the particular output quantities via production functions. Thus, a Z-function can be described from industry supply curves, if the latter are determinate and 'if the distribution of proceeds for each expected aggregate volume of proceeds is determinate'.[4]

Wells, on the other hand, has assumed a single commodity output and an aggregate supply function in order to develop the inverse of Keynes's aggregate supply function, the employment function, $N = N(Z)$. Nevertheless, conceptually Wells's and Weintraub's systems are equal.

Veendorp and Werkema's criticisms are not new, and though their comments are mathematically true, they do not always describe economic possibilities. Veendorp and Werkema accept Wells's assumption of production occurring under conditions of diminishing returns, but object to his supposition that the third derivative of the production function with respect to employment equals zero, i.e. that the marginal productivity curve of labour is a (downward sloping) straight line. This latter supposition of Wells implies that the aggregate supply function must be convex to the employment axis.[5] (Veendorp and Werkema note that Weintraub had suggested that the convexity of the Z-function merely required diminishing returns.)[6] Veendorp and Werkema argue that diminishing returns in no way restrict the shape of the marginal product curve to a straight line, and that convex or concave marginal productivity curves are possible. Finally,

* *Economic Journal* (June 1962).
   The author is grateful to Professor S. Weintraub for helpful comments on an earlier draft of his paper.

they demonstrate that if, and only if, a convex marginal productivity curve does not meet a certain mathematical condition, then 'the aggregate supply function will be either a straight line or concave to the N-axis, characteristics contrary to the conclusions of Wells and Weintraub'.[7]

In replying to Veendorp and Werkema's cricitism, Wells states that 'in the absence of any definite knowledge concerning the third derivative of the aggregate production function, I am willing to make the unfastidious assumption that it is zero'.[8]

In this exchange of commentaries, both Wells and Veendorp and Werkema have failed to appreciate that it is not the slope of the marginal productivity curve, but the change in the ratio of the average product to the marginal product of labour which determines the slope of the aggregate supply function. In pure competition dZ/dN varies inversely with the elasticity of productivity, which, in the one variable factor case, is equal to the ratio of the marginal to the average product.[9]

Using this productivity ratio, I have suggested elsewhere that diminishing returns were not sufficient to ensure a convex aggregate supply curve. *If the production function is of the Cobb–Douglas type*, then the marginal product function is a downward sloping convex curve, the M/A-ratio is a constant, the aggregate supply function is *linear* and the relative wage share does not change as employment varies.[10]

Horlacher and Smolensky, in commenting on my remarks, demonstrated that with a certain type of production function which had a marginal product curve whose slope was 'very small', the elasticity of productivity would increase with increasing employment levels.[11] Implicit in the Horlacher–Smolensky function is confirmation of Veendorp and Werkema's belief that the aggregate supply function may be concave to the N-axis. Nevertheless, the Horlacher–Smolensky type function is economically unrealistic. As I remarked in an earlier discussion, their function

> can be more formally characterized by stating that, if the M/A-ratio is to increase within some range of inputs, then the total product curve must, in this range, asymptotically approach (from above) either an upward sloping straight line emanating from the origin or a line parallel to such a ray. In other words, Horlacher and Smolensky posit a situation where as the proportion of variable to fixed factor increases, diminishing returns rapidly becomes a relatively unimportant and practically negligible phenomenon.[12]

Thus, the concave aggregate supply function suggests an unrealistic world which approaches constant returns as the ratio of variable to fixed factor increases. Certainly, the economic realities rather than the mathematical conditions should govern the admissibility of such functions.[13]

Accordingly, Veendorp and Werkema are mathematically correct but economically wrong when they conclude 'diminishing returns phenomena alone, therefore, are not a sufficient condition for any particular shape of the Keynesian aggregate supply curve'.[14] If we assume an aggregate production function (as Wells does) that is economically plausible, then an aggregate supply curve concave to the *N*-axis is impossible.

1 CONCAVITY IN THE WEINTRAUBIAN SYSTEM

In two highly restrictive situations concavity of the *Z*-function is possible, although not probable, in the Weintraubian system.

1.1 The Weighted Average Elasticity of Productivity

In a multifirm, multiproduct economy, Weintraub's aggregate supply function depends on a *weighted* elasticity of productivity, where the *M/A*-ratio of each firm is weighted by the importance of its total sales proceeds in the total GNP.[15] Consequently, implicit in any smooth convex or linear *Z*-function is the notion that the 'average' elasticity of productivity does not rise as employment rises, and that, therefore, as *N* increases, the composition of output does not *radically* shift from industries with low *M/A*-ratios to industries with high *M/A*-ratios. Otherwise, it would be possible, because of the changing importance of different industries, for the 'average' elasticity of productivity to increase with increasing employment levels, even though the elasticity of productivity of each firm was declining. Hence, it would be possible to have a concave aggregate supply curve.[16]

There is no reason to believe, however, that this possibility will occur. Since most expansions tend to affect almost all industries in the economy, the probability of radical changes in weights in an economy producing a great many different products is likely to be quite small.

1.2 The Degree of Monopoly

Weintraub has shown that 'not only productivity phenomena . . . but also the elasticity of demand – the degree of monopoly power – influences the income division',[17] and hence the shape of the aggregate supply curve.

In a mixed competitive–monopoly economy Weintraub indicates that if the degree of monopoly is invariant to employment changes, then conclusions about the shape of the *Z*-function follow competitive theory, i.e. productivity phenomena determine the result. On the other hand, if changes in monopoly power are related to changes in the level of employment, then the slope of the aggregate supply function will be affected.[18] If, for example, restrictive business policies are more important in a recession, then the average degree of monopoly may decline with rising N-levels and may more than offset any declines in the average M/A-ratio, so that a Z-function concave to the N-axis would be possible. On the other hand, if buyers become less price conscious in prosperity, then the average degree of monopoly would tend to rise with employment levels and augment any possible convexity in the Z-function.

Although recognizing that monopoly conditions could alter the slope of the Z-function, in the absence of strong empirical evidence favouring one hypothesis over the other, a tentative assumption of no change in the degree of monopoly appears to be acceptable. Accordingly, there would be little justification for assuming a concave aggregate supply function.

2   PROFESSOR MARTY AND THE AGGREGATE SUPPLY FUNCTION

In the same issue of the *Economic Journal* in which Veendorp and Werkema's commentary appeared, A. L. Marty developed a geometric exposition of the Keynesian aggregate supply function.[19] Although employing different units, Marty's function is essentially equivalent to those derived by Weintraub and Wells; hence, no further commentary on Marty's derivation is necessary.

Nevertheless, one might question why Marty attempted to apply his aggregate supply analysis to a perverse case raised by Patinkin where real output falls from a previously achieved level of full employment and 'the time path of wages and prices is such that they fall proportionately so that the real wage-rate remains at the full employment level'.[20] Patinkin's hypothetical situation violates the assumptions underlying Marty's derivation and hence Marty's function is not applicable.

Marty has assumed: (1) the constancy of the money-wage rate; (2) the ubiquity of perfect competition and profit maximization (and hence production occurring under conditions of diminishing returns); and (3) the equality of the real wage rate and the marginal product of labour at each level of employment.[21] Because of these assumptions, the real wage rate cannot be constant when employment and output decline. Only if entrepreneurs were not profit maximizers could the real wage rate remain unchanged in the face of declining employment levels. But, of course, if entrepreneurs are not profit maximizers, then it is not surprising that Patinkin finds that they do not adhere to profit maximizing supply schedules. If managers do not attempt to maximize profits, however, then some other guiding principle of entrepreneurial behaviour must be posited before a unique supply schedule can be derived.

Notes

1. E. C. H. Veendorp and H. G. Werkema, 'Mr Wells' Aggregate Supply Function: A Comment', *Economic Journal*, 71, 1961, pp. 634–6.
2. J. M. Keynes, *The General Theory of Employment, Interest, and Money* (New York: Harcourt, 1936), pp. 25, 29.
3. S. Weintraub, *An Approach to the Theory of Income Distribution* (Philadelphia: Chilton, 1958), chapter 2. Also P. Wells, 'Keynes' Aggregate Supply Function: A Suggested Interpretation', *Economic Journal*, 70, 1960. Weintraub's development is more complete in that it is derived from microsupply curves. Moreover, it predates Wells's analysis by more than two years. It is surprising, therefore, that in his 1960 article, Wells fails to cite Weintraub's *Income Distribution* book or an earlier article on the same topic, 'The Micro-Foundations of Aggregate Demand and Supply', *Economic Journal*, 67, 1957. Instead, he refers only to Weintraub's less complete account of aggregate supply in 'A Macroeconomic Approach to the Theory of Wage Determination', *American Economic Review*, 46, 1956.
4. Weintraub, *An Approach to the Theory of Income Distribution*, pp. 25–6.
5. Veendorp and Werkema, 'Mr Wells' Aggregate Supply Function', p. 635.
6. Weintraub, *An Approach to the Theory of Distribution*, pp. 46, 56. A convex aggregate supply function implies a decreasing relative wage share with increasing employment levels.
7. Veendorp and Werkema, 'Mr Wells' Aggregate Supply Function', p. 636. The condition they suggest is

$$X''' < \frac{2(X'')^2}{X'} - \frac{X'X''}{X'}$$

where X is output.
8. P. Wells, 'A Further Comment', *Economic Journal*, 71, 1961, p. 637.
9. Weintraub (*An Approach to the Theory of Income Distribution*, p. 53) demonstrates that

$$\frac{wN}{Z} = \bar{E}_q$$

where w is the money-wage rate (assumed constant), N is the level of employment, Z is the total sales proceeds (GNP), $\bar{E}_q \left[= \sum_{i=1}^{n} \frac{Z_i}{Z} \left(\frac{M_i}{A_i} \right) \right]$ is the weighted average elasticity of productivity, Z_i is the sales proceeds of the ith firm, M_i is the marginal-, and A_i is the average productivity of labour employed in the ith firm. Thus:

$$Z = (1/\bar{E}_q)wN$$

and

$$\frac{dZ}{dN} = w \left[1/\bar{E}_q + N \frac{d(1/\bar{E}_q)}{dN} \right]$$

10. P. Davidson, 'A Clarification of the Ricardian Rent Share', *Canadian Journal of Economics and Political Science*, 25, 1959, p. 193, n. 12, and P. Davidson, *Theories of Aggregate Income Distribution* (New Brunswick: Rutgers University Press, 1960), pp. 97–8, 108–111.
11. D. E. Horlacher and E. Smolensky, 'Increasing Employment, Diminishing Returns, and Relative Shares', *Canadian Journal of Economics and Political Science*, 26, 1960, pp. 144–5.
12. P. Davidson, 'Increasing Employment, Diminishing Returns, Relative Shares and Ricardo', *Canadian Journal of Economics and Political Science*, 26, 1960, pp. 147–8. Using the function suggested by Horlacher and Smolensky, $X = \log_e, (N + 1) + N$, if N is increased tenfold (starting from the point where the M/A-ratio begins to increase), then the marginal product of labour declines by 16.5 per cent; whereas, if N is increased a thousandfold, then the total decline in the marginal product is 18.7 per cent.
13. Although a concave marginal product curve assures a decreasing M/A-ratio, and hence a convex aggregate supply function, it may also be considered to be somewhat unrealistic for in some range of inputs, as the third derivative becomes much less than zero, labour's absolute as well as its relative income share will decline as employment rises.
14. Veendorp and Werkema, 'Mr Wells' Aggregate Supply Function', p. 636.
15. See note 5.
16. Davidson, *Theories of Aggregate Income Distribution*, p. 142, n. 23.
17. S. Weintraub, *An Approach to the Theory of Income Distribution*, pp. 66–7. Since in the monopoly situation

$$\frac{wN}{Z} = \sum_{i=1}^{n} \frac{M_i}{A_i} (1 - 1/E_d) \frac{Z_i}{Z}$$

where E_d is the absolute value of the elasticity of demand facing the firm and $1/E_d$ is the Lerner measure of the degree of monopoly, therefore

$$Z = \frac{1}{\bar{E}_q\left(1 - \frac{1}{\bar{E}_d}\right)} wN$$

where the bar over a letter indicates a weighted average.
18. S. Weintraub, *An Approach to the Theory of Income Distribution*, pp. 67–8, and P. Davidson, *Theories of Aggregate Income Distribution*, p. 103.
19. A. L. Marty, 'A Geometrical Exposition of the Keynesian Supply Function', *Economic Journal*, 71, 1961.
20. Ibid., p. 564.
21. A. L. Marty, 'A Geometrical Exposition of the Keynesian Supply Function', *Economic Journal*, 71, 1961, p. 560.

32 The Aggregate Supply Function*

John Maynard Keynes wrote *The General Theory* (1936) in order to show that Say's Law, where (aggregate) supply created its own (aggregate) demand, was not applicable to a monetary, production economy. In a Say's Law world, the aggregate demand function would be coincident with the aggregate supply function so that 'effective demand, instead of having a unique equilibrium value, in an infinite range of values all equally admissible; and the amount of employment is indeterminate except in so far as the marginal disutility of labour sets an upper limit' (Keynes, 1936, p. 26). In other words, Say's Law assumes there is no barrier to the economy obtaining, in the long run, a full employment output level.

Keynes claimed that Say's Law 'is not the true law relating the aggregate demand and supply functions' (ibid.) and hence the 'true' relationship between the aggregate demand and the aggregate supply functions 'remains to be written and without which all discussions concerning the volume of aggregate employment are futile' (ibid.).

For Keynes, unlike the 'neoclassical synthesis Keynesians', both aggregate supply and aggregate demand functions played equally important roles in determining the equilibrium level of employment. As Keynes (1973) pointed out in a letter to D. H. Robertson, however, his aggregate supply function was 'simply the age-old supply function'. Keynes's revolutionary analysis stemmed from his belief that in a monetary economy, the aggregate demand function differed from, and was *not* coincident with, the aggregate supply function.

Keynes argued that the aggregate supply function could be readily derived from ordinary Marshallian microsupply functions (1936, pp. 44–5) and that, therefore, the properties of the aggregate supply function 'involved few considerations which are not already familiar' (ibid., p. 89). Keynes believed that 'it was the part played by the aggregate demand function which has been overlooked' (ibid.). Hence, though Keynes briefly described the aggregate supply function (ibid., pp. 25, 44–5) and its inverse, the employment function (ibid., pp. 89, 280–1), the bulk of *The General Theory* was devoted to developing the characteristics of aggregate demand while the aggregate supply function was given short shrift and treated perfunctorily.

Consequently, the 'Keynesian Revolution' analytical structure (which

---

* *The New Palgrave* (London: Macmillan, 1987).

473

Samuelson dubbed 'neoclassical synthesis Keynesianism') which was developed by Hicks (1937) in England and American economists such as Klein (1947) and Modigliani (1944) only emphasized the novelty of the aggregate demand-side of Keynes's economic system. In losing sight of Keynes's well-known 'age-old' aggregate supply function, the Keynesian Revolution went off at half-cock and lost its foundations in Marshallian microeconomics.

In the 1954–7 period, in the *Economic Journal*, there was a flurry of activity attempting to rediscover the basis of Keynes's aggregate supply function. This discussion culminated in Weintraub's classic article (1957) which Clower, in personal correspondence (dated 1 November 1957), characterized as 'a beautifully clear statement of what Keynes "should have meant" if we suppose that he was a rational being'.

Unfortunately, the leaders of the Keynesian Revolution at the time did not adopt the Weintraub approach. Instead, they continued to use their 'neoclassical synthesis Keynesian' structure which did not possess a strong enough aggregate supply foundation to permit it to provide a cogent analysis to deal with the stagflation of the 1970s. Accordingly, this popular brand of 'bastard Keynesianism' (to use Joan Robinson's descriptive phrase) – a hybrid of Walrasian microfoundations and Keynes's macro-analysis – lost its appeal as it failed to be able to account for supply-side problems such as money-wage inflation and the monopoly power of oil-producing countries who foisted oil (raw material) price shocks on Western nations during the 1970s. Consequently, 'bastard Keynesianism' was replaced in many academic circles and popular texts by monetarist and pre-Keynesian 'Supply-Side' philosophies. (Despite its name, the so-called Supply-Side school of economics did not incorporate Keynes's aggregate supply function into its system.)

'Keynesianism' failed because the most prestigious 'bastard Keynesians' had developed a variant of Keynes's analytical structure which had lost sight of his aggregate supply function. Had the derivation of Keynes's aggregate supply function concept been properly incorporated into the popular brand of Keynesianism that prevailed in the 1960s and 1970s, Keynesian analysis would still have dominated academic and popular economic discussions.

The following description of the derivation of the aggregate supply function has its origins in Keynes's *General Theory* (1936) as elucidated by Weintraub (1957) and further developed by Davidson (1962) and Davidson and Smolensky (1964).

The aggregate supply function relates the aggregate number of workers (N) that profit-maximizing entrepreneurs would want to hire for each possible level of expected sales proceeds (Z) – given the money-wage rate, technology, the degree of competition (or monopoly), and the degree of integration of firms (cf. Keynes, 1936, p. 245). For any given degree of firm integration in the aggregate, GNP is directly related to total sales' proceeds. If firms are fully integrated, aggregate sales' proceeds equals GNP.

Following Keynes's argument (ibid. p. 41) that money values and quantities of employment are the two 'fundamental units of quantity' to be used when dealing with aggregates, the aggregate supply proceeds is normally specified either in money terms (Z) or in Keynes's wage unit terms (Z) which is money sales' proceeds divided by the money-wage rate. Hence the aggregate supply function is specified as:

$$Z = f_1(N) \qquad\qquad 32.1$$

or

$$Z_w = f_2(N) \qquad\qquad 32.2$$

For purposes of simplicity and ease of comparability with the ordinary Marshallian microsupply function, only the form of equation (32.1) will be developed in the following discussion. Equational form (32.2) of the aggregate supply function can then be derived merely by dividing all money sums expressed in equation (32.1) by the existing money rate.

The Marshallian supply curve for a single firm (s_f) indicates the profit-maximizing output possibilities for alternative market demand conditions. The supply schedule of profit-maximizing, alternative price–quantity combinations depend on the degree of competition (or monopoly) of the firm (k) and its marginal costs (MC).

The degree of monopoly of the firm depends on the market demand condition it faces. In the most simple case as aggregate demand changes, the demand curve facing the firm shifts without altering the degree of monopoly of the firm, e.g. in the perfectly competitive case, shifts in the firm's demand curve do not alter the competitive market conditions. In more complex cases, the degree of monopoly may vary as aggregate demand changes and the firm's demand curve shifts, i.e. $k = f(N)$.

Thus the firm's supply schedule can be specified in terms of its degree of monopoly power as given by a mark-up – whose magnitude depends on the price elasticity of demand facing the firm and its marginal costs:

$$s_f = f_3(k_f, MC_f) \qquad\qquad 32.3$$

where k_f is the firm's mark-up over its marginal costs (MC_f).

The profit-maximizing firm's mark-up is equal to Lerner's (1935) measure of the degree of monopoly power which is $(1 - 1/E_{df})$ where E_{df} is the price elasticity of demand facing the firm for any given level of effective demand. Thus, for a perfectly competitive firm, $k = 0$ for all potential production flows and only marginal costs affect the position and shape of its marginal cost curve. For conditions of less than perfect competition, $k > 0$, and hence both marginal costs and monopoly power at each potential output level affect the firm's market offerings as reflected in its supply curve offerings.

The firm's marginal cost (MC_f), assuming labour is the only variable input in the production process, equals the money-wage (w) divided by marginal labour productivity (MP) where the latter is a function of employment (and the laws of returns involved in the technology of the firm). For any given 'law of returns' facing the firm, there will be a different marginal production cost structure. For example, with diminishing returns, the marginal production costs increase with increasing output; for constant returns, marginal production costs are constant, while for increasing returns marginal costs decline with increases in output and employment. (Of course, the latter two cases are incompatible with perfect competition; they require some degree of monopoly and hence some positive mark-up, ($k > 0$) over marginal costs, so that market price covers average unit costs.) If marginal user costs (MUC) are not negligible, then $MC_f = (w/MP + MUC)$.

The Marshallian industry flow-supply schedule(s) is simply obtained by the usual lateral summation of the individual firm's supply curves; it is, therefore, related to the average industry mark-up or 'average' degree of monopoly *and* the industry's marginal costs schedule, i.e.

$$s = f_4(k, MC) \qquad\qquad 32.4$$

where the symbols without subscripts are the industry's equivalent to the aforementioned firm's variables. Thus given (a) the production technology, (b) the money-wage, and (c) the degree of monopoly based on specified market conditions for any given potential output and employment level, a unique industry supply function can be derived.

Although output across firms in the same industry may be homogeneous and therefore can be aggregated to obtain the industry supply schedule (equation (32.4)); this homogeneity of output assumption cannot be accepted as the basis for summing across industries to obtain the aggregate supply function (Keynes, 1936, ch. 4). Accordingly, the Marshallian industry supply function, s, which relates prices (p) and quantities (q) must be transformed into Keynes's industry supply function which relates total industry sales proceeds into money terms (z) with total industry employment hiring (n), i.e.

$$z = f_5(n) \qquad\qquad 32.5$$

Since given returns, the money-wage and the degree of monopoly, every point on the Marshallian industry supply function, s, is associated with a unique profit-maximizing price–quantity combination whose multiple equals total expected sales proceeds (i.e. $pxq = z$) and since every industry output level (q) can be associated with a unique industry hiring level, i.e. $q = f(n)$ then every point of equation (4) of the s-curve in p versus q space can be transformed to a point on a z-curve in pq versus n space to obtain equation (5).

Hence for each industry in which traditional Marshallian supply function can be formulated in terms of equation (4), a Keynes industry supply function (equation (32.5)) can also be uniquely specified. All of Keynes's industry supply functions can then be aggregated together to obtain the aggregate supply function in terms of aggregate money proceeds (Z) and the aggregate quantity of employment units (N) as specified in equation (1), provided one reasonably assumes that corresponding to any given point of aggregate supply there is a unique distribution and employment between the different industries in the economy (ibid., p. 282).

References

Davidson, P. (1962), 'More on the Aggregate Supply Function', *Economic Journal*, (June) (Chapter 31 in this volume).

Davidson, P. and E. Smolensky (1964), *Aggregate Supply and Demand Analysis*, (New York: Harper & Row).

Hicks, J. R. (1937), 'Mr Keynes and the Classics', *Econometrica* (January).

Keynes, J. M. (1936), *The General Theory of Employment, Interest and Money*, (New York: Harcourt).

Keynes, J. M. (1973), *The Collected Writings of John Maynard Keynes*, XIII, edited by D. Moggridge (London: Macmillan).

Klein, L. R. (1947), *The Keynesian Revolution* (New York: Macmillan).

Lerner, A. P. (1934–5), 'The Concept of Monopoly and the Measurement of Monopoly Power', *The Review of Economic Studies*.

Modigliani, F. (1944), 'Liquidity Preference and the Theory of Interest and Money', *Econometrica* (January).

Weintraub, S. (1957), 'The Micro-Foundations of Aggregate Demand and Supply', *Economic Journal* (September).

33 Modigliani on the Interaction of Monetary and Real Phenomena*

In an important article,[1] Modigliani has renewed his analysis of the relationship between the real and monetary parts of the Keynesian system. One of Modigliani's major points in his latest article is that his famous 1944 model[2] embodied an error, for, in his opinion, it incorrectly specified the forms of the real aggregate consumption and investment demand functions.[3] While we find much to agree with in this new model, we do not agree with him as to the fundamental source of error in the 1944 model. Consequently, we are in disagreement with some important aspects of the latest formulation and, as a result, with some of his more important conclusions.

The basic flaw in Modigliani's 1944 model is not the fact that the aggregate real spending functions were not homogeneous of degree zero with respect to prices.[4] A quite different source of error was involved, and this error has been partly perpetuated in the 1963 model. While Modigliani's 1944 system contains a direct relationship between the price level and the money-wage rate,[5] this relationship is omitted entirely from the monetary equilibrium subset of equations. It is this relationship, however, which provides an essential link between the monetary and real sectors.

In 1944, Modigliani claimed that the four equations which defined 'the system of monetary equilibrium' were completely independent of the other equations in the system and formed a determinate subset.[6] Consequently, Modigliani concluded that 'Since the money income is determined exclusively by the *monetary* part of the system, the price level depends only on the amount of output' and therefore a change in the money-wage rate could affect the price level only if it resulted in a change in the level of output.[7]

This surprising result is not only in conflict with Keynes's analysis of the effects of money-wage changes,[8] but it is also incompatible with Modigliani's own conclusion in a later section of that same 1944 paper. Towards the end of his 1944 article, Modigliani argued that a reduction in the money-wage rate will 'depress the interest rate, the money income, and money wages without affecting the real variables of the system, employment, output, real wage rate'.[9] But how then can a change in the money-wage

* *Review of Economics and Statistics*, November (1964) with E. Smolensky.

rate affect the rate of interest? *If* the money-wage rate change does not affect real output, then, by Modigliani's earlier assertion, it cannot affect the price level. If both the price level and the level of real output are unaffected, there should be no change in the transactions demand for cash balances and consequently no change in the rate of interest! Of course, a change in the money-wage rate does affect prices and output and, therefore, the rate of interest. Accordingly, Modigliani's belief that the monetary equilibrium subset is independent of the money-wage rate must be in error.

In his latest formulation, Modigliani explicitly introduces the price level variable into his demand for money equation in order to demonstrate that, given nominal money balances, changes in the money-wage rate will shift the entire money market function relating the rate of interest and the level of output.[10] This implies that contrary to the 1944 model, *at any given level of output*, a decrease in the money-wage rate involves a reduction in prices and money incomes and therefore a decrease in the demand for transactions balances.

Modigliani can now demonstrate that the money-wage rate has an impact on the demand for money equation, but, in his system, a change in the money-wage rate still does not have any impact on the real spending functions. Modigliani now asserts that 'money wage reductions act *only* through shifts in the *MM* curve'.[11] Although Modigliani labels this conclusion 'a "Keynesian" result', it is in conflict with Keynes's expressed belief that changes in the money-wage rate will affect the real aggregate consumption function (via redistributional effects) and the marginal efficiency of capital schedule (via expectational effects), as well as the demand for money function.[12] In other words, Keynes believed that changes in the money-wage rate would affect both the *MM* and *yy* functions of Modigliani's 1963 model.

Modigliani's conclusions differ from those of Keynes because of some restrictive assumptions. Modigliani's demonstration that changes in the money-wage rate do not affect real spending functions follows directly from his assumptions that (1) the real aggregate consumption function is homogeneous of degree zero with respect to prices, and (2) the elasticity of expectations with respect to prices is unity. Neither of these assumptions is required or desirable.[13]

Although, as Modigliani correctly asserts, rational economic behaviour requires each individual's real consumption function to be homogeneous of degree zero with respect to prices (i.e. there is no money illusion), there is good reason to believe that the homogeneity postulate is *not* a characteristic of the real *aggregate* consumption function. Modigliani suggests two conditions under which the homogeneity postulate will not hold for the real aggregate consumption function: when (1) the Pigou effect and/or (2) redistributional effects are significant. Modigliani spends several pages (correctly) demonstrating the insignificance of the wealth effect and thereby justifying its omission, for all practical purposes, from the model. Modigliani does not even discuss income redistribution aspects, even though he suggests that redistributional effects are far more important than the Pigou effect.[14]

A homogeneity assumption for aggregate real consumption completely ignores income redistributional effects due to price level changes – effects which will have a significant impact on the real demand for consumption goods, since, in the real world, a substantial proportion of personal income results from pre-existing contracts for fixed money payments. Thus, if the money-wage rate and price level increase *at any given level of employment*, there will be a redistribution of real income from fixed money income recipients towards gross profits.[15] If the marginal propensity to consume out of gross profits is less than the marginal propensity to consume of rentiers, then real consumption demand at any given level of output will decline.[16] Accordingly, the real aggregate consumption function is *not* homogeneous of degree zero with respect to prices, even if each household's real consumption function is homogeneous of degree zero. Keynes was well aware of these distributional aspects[17] and they play an important role in both the Keynesian and classical models.[18]

Modigliani's omission of these important distributional aspects results in some strange policy implications. For example, if Modigliani's description of demand-pull inflation is taken at face value, it is difficult to understand why (in a closed economy) the monetary authority need take deliberate action to curb inflation. Modigliani states that:

> if the initial money supply were such that the *MM* curve passes above the full employment point . . . [and] if wages are only rigid downwards . . . [then] the rate of interest being initially too low, there is excess demand in the commodity market which bids up prices and wages; the rise in wages eventually reduces the effective money supply *M/W*, shifting down the *MM* curve, until it intersects the *yy* curve at the full employment point.[19]

This implies that demand-pull inflation has no effect on real investment or real consumption output; i.e. that there is a unique distribution of the full employment output between consumption goods and investment goods. Accordingly, if, following Keynes, we ignore the effect of interest rate changes on consumption behaviour, then, once full employment is reached, all attempts to restrict consumption (i.e. to 'force savings') in order to reallocate resources to bring forth additional real investment goods will be frustrated. Moreover, since the ensuing inflation merely raises money wages and prices in the Modigliani model, real spending decisions and the level of output are unchanged. Thus, no one's real income is not reduced by the inflationary process. Why then should Modigliani imply that demand-pull inflation be viewed as undesirable? Furthermore, Modigliani's analysis suggests that there is no need for a conscious monetary policy to reduce nominal money balances, since the ensuing increases in money-wages and prices will have the same result.

Modigliani's discussion of inflation suffers from the omission of two significant factors. These are (1) individuals whose money incomes do not keep pace with the rise in prices will suffer,[20] and (2) since the supply curve of labour is an increasing function of real wages (equation (6) in Modigliani's 1963 model), full employment is a schedule of different labour offerings at different real wage rates, and does not connote a fixed number of workers (as Modigliani implies).[21] Full employment is not an absolutely rigid ceiling on output; rather, it is more like an elastic constraining factor.

If we start from an initial full employment level and, if we postulate an increase in real aggregate demand (say, the demand for investment goods increases), then the economy can expand output by moving from the initial full employment level to a higher full employment level, *if* the real wage rises so as to induce more workers to enter the labour force. This can occur, in the short run, only if the money-wage rate rises more rapidly than the price of consumption goods which, in turn, implies that the marginal product of labour in the wage-goods (all consumption goods) industries (and therefore the real wage rate) increases. A rise in the marginal product of labour in the consumption goods industries implies that aggregate real consumption must decline, when real investment (and total real output) is increasing. Since the real income and, therefore, the real consumption, of workers and profit recipients will increase during this expansionary process, the money-wage rate and consumer prices must rise sufficiently so that real consumption of rentiers is reduced by more than the increase in real consumption of workers and profit recipients. Under these circumstances, real aggregate consumption will fall and allow the economy to move from one full employment level to a higher full employment level.[22] It is the reduction in the real income of rentier groups (particularly pensioners) and those wage and salary earners whose after tax money income does not keep pace with the rise in consumer prices who suffer during inflation[23] and who consequently fear inflation. It is these individuals (and at full employment they constitute the vast majority of the electorate) who demand that a deliberate monetary policy be taken to prevent inflation rather than to allow the adjustment to occur through rising wages and prices.[24]

Since prices will rise as output expands (due to diminishing returns and/or money-wage rate increases) even before full employment,[25] there will always be significant redistributional effects due to price level changes at any level of employment. Consequently, the real aggregate consumption function can no longer be assumed to be homogeneous of degree zero with respect to prices. Moreover, since changes in the price level will have significant ramifications for real consumption and output (and real investment demand)[26] as well as on the demand for money function, it is not correct to dichotomize the system into independent monetary and real subsets. The money-wage rate and its price level implications provide a link for demonstrating the inherent interdependence of the monetary and real mechanisms.

Notes

1. F. Modigliani, 'The Monetary Mechanism and Its Interaction with Real Phenomena', *Review of Economics and Statistics*, XXXXV (February 1963), pp. 79–101.
2. F. Modigliani, 'Liquidity Preference and the Theory of Interest and Money', *Econometrica*, 12, (January 1944), pp. 45–88; reprinted in *Readings in Monetary Theory* (New York: Blakiston, 1951), pp. 186–239. All references are to the reprint.
3. F. Modigliani, 'The Monetary Mechanism and Its Interaction with Real Phenomena', p. 82.
4. In fact, we shall argue that the real aggregate consumption function is incorrectly specified in the 1963 model.
5. F. Modigliani, 'Liquidity Preference and the Theory of Interest and Money', p. 188, equation 7.
6. Ibid., p. 190.
7. Ibid., p. 210.
8. J. M. Keynes, *The General Theory of Employment, Interest and Money*, (New York: Harcourt, 1936), chap. 19.
9. F. Modigliani, 'Liquidity Preference and the Theory of Interest and Money', p. 220.
10. F. Modigliani, 'The Monetary Mechanism and Its Interaction with Real Phenomena', pp. 89–90.
11. Ibid., p. 90. Italics added.
12. Keynes, *The General Theory*, pp. 262–5.
13. F. Modigliani, 'The Monetary Mechanism and Its Interaction with Real Phenomena', footnote 26.
14. F. Modigliani, Ibid., p. 88.
15. S. Weintraub, *An Approach to the Theory of Income Distribution* (Philadelphia, 1958), pp. 42–3 and 92–5.
16. P. Davidson, 'Income and Employment Multipliers, and the Price Level', *American Economic Review*, 52 (September 1962), pp. 743, 745, and 748–9.
17. J. M. Keynes, *The General Theory*, pp. 79, 262, and 290; and J. M. Keynes, *A Treatise on Money*, Vol. 2 (New York: Harcourt, 1930), pp. 124–7.
18. Modigliani was aware of these redistributional aspects in his 1944 paper (page 202), but he ignores them (by assertion) in his 1963 model (page 84).
19. F. Modigliani, 'The Monetary Mechanism and Its Interaction with Real Phenomena', p. 90.
20. Davidson, 'Income and Employment Multipliers', pp. 748–9.
21. F. Modigliani, 'The Monetary Mechanism and Its Interaction with Real Phenomena', p. 91.

22. See Keynes's analysis of 'unproductive consumption' in Keynes, *Treatise on Money*, pp. 124–7. The classical position that increases in real investment can occur only at the expense of real consumption (that is, when people 'save' more at any level of employment) is correct only when moving from one full employment level to another.

23. Although the total real wage bill rises, this does not imply that the real income of each worker rises. See Davidson, 'Income and Employment Multipliers', pp. 748–9, and Keynes, *The General Theory*, pp. 13–14 and 81.

24. Davidson, 'Income and Employment Multipliers', pp. 748–9.

25. P. Davidson and E. Smolensky, *Aggregate Supply and Demand Analysis* (New York: Harper & Row, 1964), chaps. 11 and 12.

26. Elsewhere, we have presented a system which takes into account both redistributional and expectational effects of changing money-wage rates and prices on the real aggregate consumption *and* investment demand functions. In such a system, the real aggregate spending functions are not normally homogeneous of degree zero with respect to prices, and, consequently, the real and monetary sectors are interdependent. Ibid., chap. 13.

34 Disequilibrium Market Adjustment: Marshall Revisited*

It is often argued that certain fundamental differences between Keynes and the neoclassics derive from different implicit assumptions about relative speeds of adjustment of prices and quantities in response to changes in demand. Indeed, Leijonhufvud has asserted that 'The "revolutionary" elements in *The General Theory* can perhaps not be stated in simpler terms' (1968, p. 52). Moreover, certain issues currently in dispute among monetarists and between monetarists and Keynesians appear to turn on much the same issue. For example, Friedman and Patinkin have quarrelled over whether Fisher and the quantity theorists 'simply took over Marshall's assumption [that] prices adjust more rapidly than quantities' (Friedman, 1972, pp. 933–4; also Patinkin, 1972, pp. 892–7). Friedman insists that Fisher and all other quantity theorists must adopt Marshall's assumption, which Friedman describes as follows:

> prices adjust more rapidly than quantities, indeed, so rapidly that the price adjustment can be regarded as instantaneous. An increase in demand (a shift to the right of the long-run demand curve) will produce a new market equilibrium involving a higher price but the same quantity. The higher price will, in the short run, encourage existing producers to produce more with their existing plants . . . it takes time for output to adjust but no time for prices to do so. (Friedman, 1972, p. 934)

Keynes and the Keynesians, according to Friedman, 'deviated from Marshall . . . in reversing the roles assigned to price and quantity' (ibid., pp. 934–5). Patinkin, on the other hand, suggests that Fisher and the Chicago school of the 1930s concentrated on short-run simultaneous variations in prices and output in their 'formal theoretical framework' (Patinkin, 1972, pp. 888–90).

Brunner and Meltzer, however, seem to support Friedman's view of relative speeds of adjustment when in a recent paper they state:

> The response of output and prices to money and other variables summarizes the interaction on the markets for money, output, and credit

* Previously published in *Economic Enquiry*, 12 (June 1974) pp. 146–58.
I am grateful to Paul Wells.

. . . We assume, throughout, that . . . asset markets are cleared by suitable adjustment of asset prices *within the time units relevant for our analysis*. Output prices do not adjust rapidly enough to maintain equilibrium on the output market. (Brunner and Meltzer, 1972, pp. 953–4; italics added)

Thus, it appears that some prominent monetarists base their models and policy prescriptions on hypothesized differential speeds of reaction of prices and output to changes in demand, despite Patinkin's claim that this did not differentiate the earlier quantity theorists from Keynes.

In this connection, it is interesting to note that Leijonhufvud (1974), who argued initially that the faster speed of adjustment of output was the revolutionary aspect of Keynes, now believes that:

It is *not* correct to attribute to Keynes a general reversion of the Marshallian ranking of relative price and quantity adjustment velocities . . . [Although] most recent writings on Keynes's theory, including my own, insist on examining it from a Walrasian prospective . . . Keynes was, of course, a price-theoretical Marshallian and . . . ignoring this fact will simply not do.

Like Patinkin, therefore, Leijonhufvud now regards the relative speed of adjustment issue as a red herring.

Even if the adjustment speed issue is irrelevant, the question remains: how may we best approach the study of real world price and output adjustment processes? In my opinion, these problems are most conveniently dealt with by utilizing the traditional Marshallian concepts of market- and short-run period analysis or, to use an alternative and more descriptive terminology, in terms of *spot* and *forward market* analysis.

A *spot market* involves transactions in pre-existing durables for immediate delivery and payment. A *forward market* involves current contractual agreements for delivery and payment at future dates. Implicit in all discussions of the flow of output in the real world is the notion that, as long as production takes time and involves contractual obligations, all production decisions involve forward contracts. In an ongoing market economy, therefore, magnitude and direction are given to aggregate output and employment by entrepreneurs entering into forward contracts to purchase labour services *and* to supply producible goods in the future.

Now, for any durable goods, there is a possibility of two separate, but related markets existing side by side – a spot market and a forward market. If a spot market exists, the spot price will be whatever is necessary to allocate the existing stock of goods among willing holders. (The spot price is equivalent to Marshall's market-period price, or the price determined by the Walrasian auctioneer in a pure exchange economy.) A spot market, by its very nature, deals solely with the determination of the price of existing stock of a commodity, hence for truly non-durable goods (e.g. services) no spot market can exist. A forward market, on the other hand, permits the quantity of goods to be augmented by short-period flow supply considerations. The forward price for a future date corresponding to the normal length of a production process can never exceed the short-period flow-supply price associated with that gestation period. If it did, it would be possible to make a profit by placing an order with a producer of the good to buy the commodity at the future date at its short-period flow-supply price and simultaneously selling a forward contract to deliver at the higher forward price at the future date. Hence, the short-period flow-supply price must always set an upper limit to the forward price, and as long as production is going on, the short-period flow-supply price will equal the forward-price.[1]

Any market in which buyers enter into contracts to make payments in the future while suppliers agree to make delivery at future specified dates is inherently a forward market. In practice, virtually all transactions for the flow of output of industry in a non-integrated chain occur via such contractual agreements; that is, all stages before the retail state (and often at retail, e.g. cars) the buyer orders goods for production and delivery at a later date.[2] The existence of a well-organized, freely competitive forward market would permit, of course, the entrepreneur to operate as if he were a price taker in the traditional neoclassical sense. He could observe the forward price and compare it with his short-period flow-supply price schedule to determine his short-period production decision. If the forward price 'shows a profit on his costs of production, then he [the entrepreneur] can go full steam ahead, selling his product forward and running no risk. If, on the other hand, this price does not cover his costs (even after allowing for what he loses by temporarily laying up his plant), then it cannot pay him to produce at all' (Keynes, 1930, pp. 142–3).[3]

In the real world, of course, newly produced goods are normally sold via forward contracts; but forward markets for most of the products of industry are neither freely competitive nor well-organized, nor are forward prices always public information. Consequently, although the outputs of producers are typically sold via forward contracts, the price may be agreed upon by negotiation, or via sealed bids, or simply set by sellers and announced as available to all buyers with or without quantity restrictions. In these cases, entrepreneurs have to make flow-supply offers before knowing anything certain about buyer responses.[4]

The costs underlying the short-period flow-supply schedule are partly a function of the length of the period between the beginning of production and the delivery of output (Alchian, 1959). Thus, if the forward price is associated with a future date when the flow-supply can be delivered, it must be equal to the price at which the market demand price equals the flow-supply price. There are only two major cases when the forward price may not equal the flow-supply price: (1) when the future date is so close to the present date that technology prevents any flow-supply from coming forth (in the extreme, the good has a zero elasticity of production), or (2) when there is such redundancy of existing stocks that there is no incentive for entrepreneurs to commit themselves to produce any new goods during the period (i.e. the demand price is less than the shutdown point for the industry). The first situation can be eliminated by treating it under the spot market analysis, the second can be treated in the analysis of contango market situations where no production occurs. Hence, for the purpose of this argument, if we limit ourselves to discussing changes in demand in which production is occurring we can treat the forward price as synonymous with the short-period flow-supply price.

In order for *well-organized* spot and forward markets to exist for a commodity, it must have certain characteristics, namely; (1) the good must be an article of general demand; (2) the commodity must be capable of standardization; (3) there must be a high degree of substitutability between old and new items; (4) the existing stock must be relatively large compared to short-period production flows; (5) the good must be durable; and (6) it must be valuable in proportion to bulk (cf. Kaldor, 1939, p. 20). Furthermore, continuity of markets in an uncertain world requires (7) the existence of a financial institution that 'makes' the market by acting, when necessary, as a *residual buyer or seller*.

Obviously different goods may have these features in different degrees. As long as production takes time, item (5) is a necessary condition for the existence of a spot market, while the other factors are important in determining how well organized or perfect the existing spot and/or forward markets will be. The degree of organization of spot and forward markets for each good will depend on the extent to which these characteristics are possessed by the good in question. Thus some raw material or working capital goods, because they are durable and readily standardized, have well-organized spot and forward markets. Second-hand fixed capital and most consumer durables, by their very nature, become destandardized as they age and so, although conceptually spot markets for all durables must exist, spot markets for such second-hand goods are likely to be poorly organized or even notional.[5] Nevertheless, for expositional purposes at this stage, it will be useful to discuss spot markets for durables as if all such markets were well-organized.

In his *Treatise on Money*, Keynes recognized that spot and forward markets (Marshallian market-period and short-period markets) existed *simultaneously*. Moreover, Keynes noted that an excess of the spot price over forward price (backwardation) is necessary for production to occur. In the *Treatise*, changes in demand would lead to immediate changes in prices in spot markets *and* to simultaneous changes in supply quantities and flow-supply prices in forward markets. Given the gestation period of production, the magnitudes of the changes in forward market prices and quantities depend on the short-run elasticity of supply (e.g. Keynes, 1930, pp. 140 ff.). In the simplification of Keynes's system that became *The General Theory* only flow-supply prices and quantities of capital goods and aggregate output were emphasized (Keynes, 1936, pp. 23–4, 135–9, 292–306) as Keynes attempted to focus attention on the production and pricing of new goods and services. Hence, in *The General Theory*, Keynes ignored spot markets for consumption goods and highlighted forward markets in which the flow of output and price adjust simultaneously. Moreover, if short-period flow-supply was very elastic, most of the adjustment to an increase in demand would occur via production flows and little via flow-price changes. Since few economists have paid serious attention to Keynes's *Treatise*, it is no wonder that many have been misled into believing that the Keynesian Revolution involved the reversing of '*The Marshallian ranking of price- and quantity-adjustment speeds*' (Leijonhufvud, 1968, p. 52; also see Friedman, 1972, p. 934). Although nothing could be further from the truth, any attempt at a complete exegesis of Keynes's theory of markets at this stage would require a lengthier exposition than can be given here. Instead the following paragraphs suggest how a change in demand affecting spot and forward markets could be explained by any student – as Keynes was – of Marshall.

For expositional clarity, I adopt the Bushaw–Clower geometric apparatus of adding stocks and flows in a Marshallian demand and supply quadrant (Bushaw and Clower, 1957, pp. 20–2; Clower, 1954). In Figure 34.1a, D represents the initial Marshallian demand schedule (including Wicksteedian reservation demand) for a durable good, while the vertical line S represents the stock of the good inherited from the past. If this good is not reproducible (e.g. Old Masters) then the resulting spot price p_s would allocate the stock without remainder among demanders. If the good is reproducible, the stock can be augmented by a flow of output if buyers are willing to promise to pay the flow-supply price and wait the gestation period for delivery. The curve s (Figure 34.1b) represents the industry's Marshallian flow-supply schedule, i.e. it shows alternative production offerings at alternative flow-supply prices. If producers are short-run profit maximizers, then p_m is the lowest point on the average variable cost schedule and represents the minimum flow-supply price.

The total market situation for a good can be obtained by laterally summing the stock- and flow-supply schedules to obtain $S + s$ in Figure 34.2. Superimposing the demand schedule D onto this figure indicates that the spot price, p_s, exceeds the forward or flow-supply price, p_f, as some buyers are willing to pay a premium for immediate delivery rather than wait the gestation period for a new unit to be produced.[6] This situation

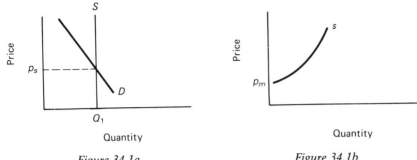

Figure 34.1a

Figure 34.1b

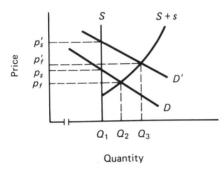

Quantity

Figure 34.2

(where $p_s > p_f$) is known as *backwardation* and production of $Q_2 - Q_1$ units will be forthcoming at the delivery date.

To trace the impact of an increase in demand let us hypothesize a shift in demand[7] to D'. It is obvious that in the spot market there will (by definition) be no increase in quantity; rather the spot (or asset) price for the durable will rise promptly to p'_s. In the (production) forward market the increase in demand will involve an *immediate* increase in the rate of acceptance of contracts for forward delivery causing an immediate increase in hiring and production flow, a change in the flow-supply (or forward) price to p'_f, and a building up of work-in-progress goods until by the delivery date final output has risen from $(Q_2 - Q_1)$ to $(Q_3 - Q_1)$. How much increase in the flow of output and how much increase in the forward price is induced by the hypothesized increase in demand will depend on the elasticity of the Marshallian flow-supply schedule.

Thus, it is obvious that in all spot markets there will be an instantaneous price adjustment to any change in demand, while the magnitude of price and quantity adjustments for the forward markets, which are relevant to the production of goods and hiring of workers, will depend, as always, on the homely and intelligible concept of the elasticity of the short-run supply schedule. If supply elasticities are large, and if the components of the flow-supply price (i.e. money wage rates relative to productivity, and profit mark-ups) are sticky, adjustments to changes in demand that are made operational via changes in the rate of acceptance of forward contracts will impinge primarily on output and not on prices – a result which is similar to Friedman's caricature of Keynes's model (e.g. Friedman, 1970, pp. 209–10). If, on the other hand, the flow-supply schedule is inelastic and/or the components of the flow-supply price are very sensitive to changes in demand,[8] then price rather than final output-flow will show the greatest adjustment. In either case, it is not relative speeds of adjustment of price vs. quantity that are at issue.

It is important to note that there normally is a significant difference between speed of adjustment and elasticity of short-run supply. According to Allen (Allen, 1956, p. 21):

$$\frac{dP}{dt} = -\lambda_1(S-D) = \dot{p}$$

where λ_1 is *the speed of response of price*, S is supply, D is demand, P is price, and t is time. It follows that

$$\frac{dQ}{dt} = -\lambda_2(S-D) = \dot{q}$$

where λ_2 is *speed of response with respect to output* and Q is output. Hence for any initial difference between demand and supply, λ_1 and λ_2 are measures of speed of response, but unless the short run supply elasticity is either zero or infinite, the relative speed of response is not equal to, or the same as, the elasticity of supply, i.e.

$$\frac{\lambda_2}{\lambda_1} \neq \frac{d \log Q}{d \log P}$$

In sum, a change in demand will induce an instantaneous adjustment in the spot market for pre-existing goods, while forward contract prices *and* the rate of flow of newly produced goods will adjust simultaneously and immediately even though the actual payment of forward prices associated with a change in final output will not be observed until later – the exact time depending on the gestation period for final output. In this model, as in the real world, orders for durable goods (e.g. machine tools, construction, etc.) are a leading indicator of the flow of output that will be forthcoming and changes in wholesale prices are an indicator of future changes in retail prices.

1 SHELF-INVENTORIES: AN EXTENSION OF SPOT AND FORWARD MARKET ANALYSIS

In the previous analysis, entrepreneurs were associated with production mainly 'to contract'. Hence changes in orders induced changes in production flows and in stocks of works-in-progress goods. Stocks of finished goods or shelf-inventories were ignored. As a stylized fact, this is probably a better representation of the real world than the traditional view that entrepreneurs produce only 'to market' i.e. that production is converted to shelf-inventory before any sales commitments are made. (The latter view may be epitomized by Marshall's 'fish market' example; where no orders are taken by sellers until market day. In modern industrial economies, 'fish markets' are far from representative.)

Although almost all labour markets and most commodity production transactions are, in practice, conducted primarily on a forward contract basis, there are some markets where producers may be required to make labour and raw material contractual commitments for short-period production flows before *all* planned output has been contracted for by the buyers.[9] At first blush, such situations may suggest that the traditional 'produce to market' analysis is relevant for the output market but not the input hire market, and thereby encourage the resurrection of the question whether price or quantity adjusts more rapidly to a change in demand.

However, if it is assumed that the producers are interested in maintaining an orderly product market when demand changes then, as in our previous analysis, it can be shown that both price and output of new production adjust *simultaneously* after a change in demand, while the spot price adjusts *immediately*.

Let us analyse the demand and supply of beer as a commodity representative of sectors where technology requires bunch processing and a given gestation period, while marketing institutions, at least at the retail stage, do not require a forward purchase contract as most sales are made from shelf-inventory. Let d_e^1 (Figure 34.3a) represent entrepreneurial expectations of the demand by consumers during period *1*, while s^1 represents the Marshallian flow-supply schedule. Since sales of beer will occur throughout the period, while the newly produced beer will not be available until some time after the beginning of the period, entrepreneurs will normally carry a quantity of shelf-inventory. Thus in Figure 34.3b, S^1 represents the on-hand inventory at the beginning of the period. The demand for inventory by producers at the beginning of the period will be a function of expected sales, and can be represented by D_I^1. Hence Q_o is the beginning of the period inventory volume, whose present value (or spot price) of P_a is given by the intersection of S^1 and D_I^1. As Kaldor has noted, in orthodox equilibrium theory

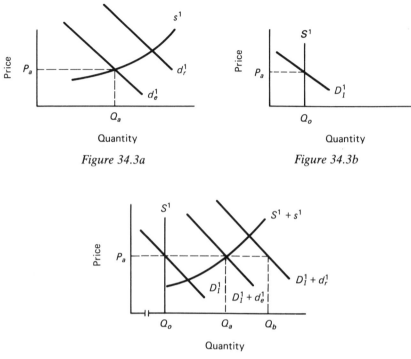

Figure 34.3a

Figure 34.3b

Figure 34.3c

this 'stock' demand is ignored . . . production and consumption, or 'flow'-demand and 'flow'-supply are necessarily equal in each market [as in Figure 34.3a] and in the rarefied world of Walrasian perfection where markets are continually in equilibrium, the question of how markets respond to 'disequilibria' [change] does not arise because all such 'disequilibria' are ruled out – all equilibrating adjustments are assumed to be instantaneous, either because change is timeless or because all changes have been perfectly foreseen. (Kaldor, 1972, p. 1247)

Since the accepted equilibrium theory does not explain reaction to unexpected changes in demand (and it is these changes that are involved in the speed of reaction controversy), different macrotheorists have merely postulated different speeds of reaction in order to buttress their intuitive arguments. Nevertheless, it is possible to analyse market responses to any postulated changes in demand by explicitly taking account of 'stock' or 'inside demand' (and supply) as well as flow-demand and flow-supply behaviour via our spot-forward market analysis. This requires that we laterally add the expected flow-demand (d_e^1) and flow-supply (s^1) functions of Figure 34.3a to the shelf-inventory stock-supply and demand of Figure

34.3b to get the total demand $(D_I^1 + d_e^1)$ and total supply $(S^1 + s^1)$ functions of Figure 34.3c. This figure can be used to determine the equilibrium situation and then, by hypothesizing a change in demand, market responses can be analysed.

Figure 34.3c is constructed on the assumption that the shelf-inventory, on hand at the beginning of the period, was considered by entrepreneurs to be optimal relative to their expectations of sales during the period and therefore they desire to set production (flow-supply) equal to expected consumption (flow-demand) over the period. Thus, according to Figure 34.3c, entrepreneurs will produce a target volume of $Q_a - Q_o$ during the period, while offering to sell beer at a price of P_a. If producers correctly anticipated consumption, then $Q_a - Q_o$ will be sold during the period (even though each unit of output may have to pass through the shelf-inventory bin), and, assuming unchanged expectations about future period sales, entrepreneurs will begin period 2 with a desired level of inventory[10] equal to Q_o.

Suppose, however, the realized flow-demand during period 1 (d_r^1) was greater than expected consumption (d_e^1) as in Figure 34.3a, say – because of an unanticipated increase in demand. Hence, in Figure 34.3c, the realized total demand for beer $(D_I^1 + d_r^1)$ will be greater than expected $(D_I^1 + d_e^1)$. If beer producers schedule a target production volume of $Q_a - Q_o$ at the beginning of period 1, and then offer beer to consumers at a price of P_a (from shelf-inventory), and if sales of beer occur stochastically over the period, then it will take some time for producers to gather sufficient information to realize that their target production volume involves an underestimation of flow-demand. Although $Q_a - Q_o$ will be produced, more than this, say $Q_b - Q_o$, will be consumed during the period, while $Q_b - Q_a$ will be subtracted from normal shelf-inventory as neither price nor production flow is adjusted in this period,[11] although the (notional) spot price (or present value) of the less-than-planned-for shelf-inventory increases as soon as entrepreneurs recognize that demand has increased.

In this situation, the stock supply schedule at the beginning of period 2 will be located to the left of S^1. Consequently, as entrepreneurs begin period 2 with lower shelf-inventories, the total supply curve for period 2 (i.e. $S^2 + s^2$) will be displaced leftward even if the Marshallian flow-supply schedule (of Figure 34.3a) is (by assumption) unchanged. If entrepreneurs perceive the higher sales as a permanent increase in demand (i.e. a shift to the right of the long-run demand curve in Friedman's terminology (see 1972, p. 934)), then expected total demand $(D_I^2 + d_e^2)$ would shift rightwards. If, on the other hand, entrepreneurs perceived higher sales as 'accidental' and expect consumption demand in period 2 to be identical with the demand expected in period 1, the total demand curve would be the same as in period 1. In either case, since total supply had been displaced to the left, the new point of expected effective demand would be further along the flow-supply schedule and hence, at the beginning of period 2, producers would *simultaneously* increase their production flow and their offer price – the magnitude of output and price change between period 1 and 2 would be dependent on the elasticity of the short period supply schedule.

Hence, even in the case where producers are required by technology, marketing institutions, etc., to target production volumes and sell from shelf-inventory rather than enter into forward contracts for output before production begins, rational behaviour requires that the offer price and production flow change simultaneously as entrepreneurs adjust to changes in demand.[12]

2 IMPLICATION FOR MONETARIST MODELS

If monetarists wish to discuss the effects of changes in the money supply on GNP and the price level associated with any given flow of aggregate production, then they must explicitly discuss how their models handle the forward (flow-supply) markets for producible goods. They have to indicate clearly how hypothesized changes in demand impinge on major components of flow-supply prices (money-wages and profit margins) and on relevant elasticities associated with the flow-supply schedules of producers.[13]

Thus, for example, if Brunner and Meltzer (1972) had explicitly used a spot–forward market framework, they would have noted that their model is incomplete and/or defective. As the previously cited Brunner–Meltzer quotation indicates, these authors use an arbitrary time unit that is sufficiently long to permit spot (or asset) prices to adjust to changes in demand, while assuming little or no adjustment in the output (or forward) markets. This implies that either (1) the time unit is less than the gestation period for output so that production flows are, by assumption, irrelevant, or (2) buyers can accept contract offers in spot markets, but for some unexplained reason cannot place contractual orders in forward markets for producible goods.

Accordingly, many monetarists are building models that achieve their strange results by utilizing an analytical framework that contains a defective time frame for forward market analysis. It is the failure to deal explicitly with complete spot and forward (flow-supply) markets that has led many modern theorists into a dead-end controversy about relative speeds of adjustment of price and output variables.

Notes

1. By definition, the price that buyers are offering to pay for forward delivery can never exceed the flow-supply price since the latter is the money price required to call forth the exertion necessary to produce any given amount of the commodity for any given delivery date.
2. This does not deny that some recently produced durable goods may be sold out of 'shelf inventory'. Nevertheless, if the supplier of the shelf-inventory goods operates as an on-going concern, the cost of ordering replacement for the inventory sold will be the short-period flow-supply price, and this will determine the offer price of the supplier of shelf-inventory goods. Hence, Marshallian short-run flow-supply prices and quantities will be associated with the flow of GNP at all stages of production in the non-integrated chain. (The problem of shelf-inventories is dealt with in more detail in the second half of this paper.)
3. Even if the entrepreneur did not accept a forward contract, he could use the current forward price as the best estimate of the spot price that would prevail on the delivery date.
4. The ability to bunch process orders with the existence of negotiated contracts and non-publicized prices will further encourage the use of short-run marginal cost in determining some offer prices. Thus phenomena such as secret price discrimination has always been considered important by economists interested in 'industrial organization' but usually has been ignored by economic theorists who abstract from the institutional setting of markets.
5. The spot market for financial assets, on the other hand, should be well organized.
6. If the good in question is not durable, then the stock supply schedule is coincidental with the ordinate axis and only a forward flow-supply market exists. If the good is not reproducible (i.e. its elasticity of production is zero), then only a spot market exists, or if forward markets are developed, the forward prices will, in a world of uncertainty, represent speculation as to future spot prices for goods where flow-supply considerations cannot affect the outcome.
7. This shift is equivalent to the one hypothesized by Friedman in his analysis of the Marshallian assumption regarding relative speeds of adjustment (1972, p. 934).
8. Since (a) the money-wage contract is the most ubiquitous forward contract in modern economies, and (b) the time-duration of forward money-wage contracts normally exceeds the gestation period for the production of most goods, there is a built in (i.e. contractual) stickiness to the wage cost component of flow-supply schedules. Moreover, as long as wage cost is an important component of short-run flow-supply prices, then flow-supply schedules will also be 'sticky'. Hence, the sensitivity of flow-supply prices to changes in demand will depend primarily on the elasticity of short-run supply schedules.
9. This situation is likely to rise in those industries where (a) technology does not permit rapid change in production flows, and/or (b) bunch processing involves large cost savings over producing only for forward contract, and/or (c) market rules, regulatory institutions, or other demand factors do not permit separate forward contractual arrangements with each buyer. Steel bars, airlines, chemicals and hotels are some industries which may exhibit these characteristics.
10. For simplicity we are assuming that entrepreneurs expect consumption demand in period 2, to be the same as in period 1, so that they will want to start the second period with the same Q_0 inventory as they had at the beginning of the preceding period. (Other assumptions about the growth – or decline – of

expectations of future period sales could be handled by this analysis, but for expositional simplicity, only this simplest case will be discussed.)
11. Following Keynes, the length of the period is defined as 'the shortest interval after which the firm is free to revise its decision as to how much employment to offer. It is, so to speak, the minimum effective unit of economic time' (1936, p. 47n).
12. It should be obvious to the reader, that the analysis would lead to a similar conclusion if there was a *decrease* in demand.
13. The relative speed of adjustment controversy does not involve short-run prices of output being more responsive than long-run money wages. Friedman ((1972), p. 207ff) and Leijonhufvud (1968, p. 52) have stated the difference as solely involving relative speeds of adjustment in *the same period and time frame*.

References

Alchian, A. (1959), 'Cost and Output', in M. Abromavitz *et al.*, *The Allocation of Resources*, (California).
Allen, R. G. D. (1956), *Mathematical Economics* (London).
Brunner, E. K. and A. H. Meltzer (1972), 'Money, Debt, and Economic Activity', *Journal of Political Economics*, 80 (September–October), pp. 951–77.
Bushaw, D. and R. W. Clower (1957), *An Introduction to Mathematical Economics*, (Homewood).
Clower, R. W. (1954), 'An Investigation into the Dynamics of Investment', *American Economics Review*, 44 (March), pp. 64–81.
Friedman, M. (1970), 'A Theoretical Framework for Monetary Analysis', *Journal of Political Economy*, 78 (March–April) pp. 193–238.
Friedman, M. (1972), 'Comments on the Critics', *Journal of Political Economy*, 80 (September–October), pp. 906–50.
Kaldor, N. (1939), 'Speculation and Economic Growth', *Revue of Economic Studies*; reprinted in *Essays on Economic Stability and Growth* (London, 1960). All references are to the reprint.
Kaldor, N. (1972), 'The Irrelevance of Equilibrium Economics', *Economic Journal*, 82 (December), pp. 1237–55.
Keynes, J. M. (1930), *Treatise on Money*, Vol. II (London).
Keynes, J. M. (1936), *The General Theory of Employment, Interest and Money* (London).
Leijonhufvud, A. (1968), *Keynesian Economics and the Economics of Keynes* (London).
Leijonhufvud, A. (1974), 'Keynes' Employment Function: Comment', *History of Political Economics*.
Patinkin, D. (1972), 'Friedman on the Quantity Theory and Keynesian Economics', *Journal of Political Economics*, 80 (September–October), pp. 883–905.

35 Disequilibrium Market Adjustment: Marshall Revisited. A Rejoinder*

Sampson contends that the results of Figure 2 in my paper (Davidson, 1974, p. 151) where the spot price (p_s) exceeds the forward price (p_f) 'only holds under a special form of market segmentation', i.e. that my analysis and diagram is not a general case. If Sampson's argument is that $p_s > p_f$ only under certain conditions, there is no argument between use. I have already stated (pp. 151–2) that 'this situation (where $p_s > p_f$) is known as *backwardation*' and I have indicated that other situations, known as 'contango market situations where no production occurs' were not analysed in this paper (p. 149).[1]

Sampson, however, implies that his argument with my analytical approach is not simply a question of backwardation versus contango markets, but rather what is involved is the dating of demand and supply curves and assumptions regarding the patience of *all* buyers. Sampson considers two cases which he believes highlight the limitations of my analysis. In the first case, Sampson assumes 'all buyers as so impatient that they would never buy contracts for future delivery at *any* forward price' (italics added). In the second case, '*all* buyers being patient . . . [regard] delivery now and contracts for future delivery as *perfect* substitutes' (italics added).

I see no logical inconsistency between these cases and my Marshall-Keynes analytic approach. Sampson has properly applied my temporal analysis of spot and forward markets to two extreme and obviously unrealistic situations in which the concept of time has been emasculated. Nevertheless, logically my model can handle Sampson's cases.

In Case I, Sampson assumes that *all* buyers have an infinite time preference for current over future goods, i.e. the marginal rate of substitution between present and future goods is zero. In the second case, Sampson assumes a zero marginal time preference for present goods by *all* buyers since present and future goods are perfect substitutes. Finally, Sampson concedes that my Figure 2 'is valid only if the following is true: any buyer who would rather pay p_s than forgo the commodity forever is so

* *Economic Inquiry*, (April 1977)

impatient that he would prefer delivery now at p_s, to delivery later at any price below p_s and any buyer not prepared to pay p_s is willing to wait'.

Except for Sampson's phrase 'than forgo the commodity forever' in the above statement, I believe Sampson's statement and analysis of his two cases (as opposed to his claims and contentions) is not only consistent with my model, but he has demonstrated the generality and analytical power of this approach[2] for handling stocks and flows in a temporal context. By presenting cases with explicit assumptions that suggest (as in Case I) that only the present is important and the future is irrelevant, or (as in Case 2), if there is no difference between the present and the future, Sampson has provided a demonstration of how the Marshall–Keynes analysis (which I presented) is *the general case* which can be reduced to the traditional 'timeless' analysis of neoclassical economics only by making heroic and unrealistic assumptions which remove calendar time from the buyers' decision making calculations.

In my article (p. 149) I specifically indicated that for well-organized spot *and* forward markets 'to exist for a commodity . . . they must be a high degree of substitutability between old and new items'. My Marshallian demand curve relating these spot and forward markets was drawn on this explicit substitutability assumption and its implicit corollary that buyers have a positive and not zero or infinite marginal time preference (at least in backwardation). If Sampson desires to utilize other assumptions about buyers' behaviour then obviously the Marshallian demand curve will have to be drawn to reflect these different assumptions.

In Sampson's first case, since buyers are so impatient that they have a zero elasticity of substitution between present and future goods, the future is irrelevant and forward markets are, by assumption, trivialized. If all buyers live only for the present, we are in a Walrasian exchange economy where no one ever demands goods for future delivery and hence there is no demand for production. The Mashallian demand curve, if it is to reflect Sampson's assumption in this case, must be perfectly inelastic at any price below the spot price. With this modification of the demand curve my diagram would be relevant to Sampson's unrealistic assumption that all buyers have the philosophy of eat, drink and be merry today for tomorrow you die.[3]

In Sampson's second case, the time of delivery of goods is irrelevant since *all* buyers are so patient that they value a bushel of wheat today as much as one a year from today, or even a century from today. Hence no buyers will pay a premium for immediate over future delivery. Of course, if all buyers view any quantity of goods in the future as 'perfect substitutes' for the same quantity of goods today then existing stocks (and the spot market) become trivial things relative to the potential flow of the commodity over an infinite period of time. In essence then the stock supply curve (SQ_1 of Sampson's diagram) is assumed to be (almost) coincident with the ordinate axis when the proper scale for production flows over the infinite future time period is considered along the Q axis.

Of course, if time of delivery is irrelevant, then the calendar time analysis of Marshall and Keynes which I presented collapses to an analysis based on the timeless flow-supply and demand curves for a neo-classical world where stocks are ignored and a single price exists for each commodity (or as Sampson states 'the spot and forward markets would both clear at a common price p_f.') Since in footnote 6 of my paper I have already indicated how the case where the stock supply schedule becomes coincident with the ordinate axis can be handled via my diagrammatic analysis, there is no conflict between my paper and Sampson's second case. (Although given its highly unrealistic assumption, can this case be worth more than a footnote?)

The only note of discord that remains in Sampson's comment is his qualifying phrase indicating that the backwardation diagram requires for its 'validity' buyers who rather 'pay p_s than forgo the commodity forever'. Contrary to Sampson's statement, a premium of spot over future price does not require the spot buyers to buy now or 'forgo the commodity forever'; backwardation merely requires that spot buyers prefer immediate to future delivery and they are willing to reveal their preference by paying a premium.[4]

Notes

1. In contango situations the spot price will be below the forward price. For a fuller discussion of the conditions underlying backwardation and contango markets, see (Keynes, 1930, pp. 141–5).
2. The conceptual analysis was developed by Keynes in his *Treatise on Money* (Davidson, pp. 142–7) while the diagram I utilized was adapted from the ingenious geometric analysis of stocks and flows developed by Bushaw and Clower (1957, pp. 13–22).
3. If such behaviour is widespread, the resulting economic system would have strange macroeconomic characteristics, e.g. the marginal propensity to consume would equal unity and Say's Law would prevail.
4. Space does not permit me in this rejoinder to elaborate further on the dating of Marshallian demand curves, especially during contango situations (which were not analysed in my paper (Davidson, 1974)). The reader who is interested can find a detailed analysis in chapter 4 of my *Money and the Real World* (esp. pp. 77, 82–103).

References

Bushaw, D. W. and R. W. Clower, (1957), *Introduction to Mathematical Economics* (Irwin: Homewood).

Davidson, P. (1974), 'Disequilibrium Market Adjustment: Marshall Revisited', *Economic Inquiry*, 12, (June), pp. 146–58 (Chapter 34 in this volume).
Davidson, P. (1972), *Money and the Real World* (London: Macmillan).
Keynes, J. M. (1930) *A Treatise on Money*, Vol. II (London: Macmillan).
Sampson, A. A. (1977) 'Disequilibrium Market Adjustment: A Comment', *Economic Inquiry*.

36 A Keynesian View of Patinkin's Theory of Employment*

Professor Patinkin has recently elaborated his views on the integration of value and monetary theory in a clearer, more comprehensive and even more reflective fashion than before (1965). Undoubtedly this new volume with its masterly command of monetary doctrine will evoke even wider praise and attention – in classrooms and from professional economists – than did the first edition of Patinkin's book (1956).

The obvious future influence of this new volume makes a critical examination of certain key elements in it important, especially since some of these fundamental notions have gone unexamined in the intervening years since 1956. Before the dialogue becomes immersed in a critical discussion of the many fine analytical points raised by Patinkin, it is essential to start with a statement of the fundamental differences between the analytical system developed by Keynes – and elaborated by others – for a macroeconomic integration of value and distribution theory into employment, output and price-level analysis, and Patinkin's application of value theory in monetary theory and the analyses of a production economy. Accordingly, this paper is not designed as a critical overall review of Patinkin's latest work. Rather it is an attempt to illuminate the basic theoretical concepts that separate modern neoclassical economists (for this is where Patinkin's work must be classified) and at least one branch of post-Keynesian writers, i.e. those who (following Keynes's lead) have restored the aggregate supply function for commodities to a position of equivalence with aggregate demand in the analysis of the equilibrium level of employment and output.

Differences between Patinkin's model and the Keynesian aggregate supply–demand approach are probably overemphasised in the following pages in the interests of providing a clear and sharp contrast. Patinkin's analysis has many admirable aspects, and the areas of agreement between the two approaches are significantly greater than the areas of difference, although it is the latter aspects which, of course, lead to diverse conclusions about important theoretical and policy matters. Consequently, the ultimate purpose of this paper is not merely to get the 'right' model; rather it is

* *Economic Journal*, 77 (1967). The author is grateful to M. Fleming, I. F. Pearce, E. Smolensky, and S. Weintraub for helpful comments on earlier drafts of this paper.

hoped that by focusing on the difference in the models, professional discussions on the 'right' full employment policy mix may be reoriented Before examining these areas of disagreement it seems desirable to remind the reader of some of the more important elements of agreement.

1 AREAS OF AGREEMENT

First and foremost, one must shout a strong amen to Patinkin's statement that the traditional 45° 'Keynesian' cross does not take account 'of the supply side of the commodity market' (Patinkin, 1965, p. 339, also see p. 325). This popular diagrammatic representation of a simple Keynesian model[1] has inverted Say's Law and has led many economists into a position of arguing that (at less than full employment) demand creates its own supply. It should also be clear, however, that *The General Theory* did not ignore commodity supply aspects, and that Keynes believed that 'the true law relating the aggregate demand and supply functions . . . is a vitally important chapter of economic theory . . . without which all discussions concerning the volume of aggregate employment are futile' (Keynes, 1936, p. 26).[2]

Secondly, the 'Savings equal Investment' equilibrium condition can be (and Patinkin suggests should deliberately be) avoided in an analysis of a market-oriented economy (Patinkin, 1965, p. 271), since this condition is merely an indirect way of stating that, in equilibrium, the revenue expected by the sellers of commodities (aggregate supply) equals the intended expenditures of the buyers of commodities (aggregate demand) (cf. Weintraub, 1958, pp. 44, no. 24).[3] When savings is less than (more than) investment, then expected sales revenue is less than (more than) intended purchases and the system is not at rest.

Thirdly, it is true that the real balance effect was commonly ignored in the pre-Patinkin literature. Patinkin, however, has consistently maintained that the real balance effect is irrelevant for policy purposes (e.g. Patinkin, 1956, pp. 233, 235; 1965, pp. 21, 57, 335); rather 'the significance of the real balance effect for economic theory . . . is [in] being concerned with the stability of an equilibrium position – with the possibility of its being reached by the automatic workings of a market economy' (Patinkin, 1965, p. 57).

Since Patinkin, it is unlikely that economists will ignore the real balance effect in an analytical discussion. It is unfortunate, however, that some writers in their zeal to enshrine automaticity in the economy have underestimated the impracticality of relying on an effect whose magnitude is significant only for rather disastrous price-level movements. From the outset Patinkin has indicated the absurdity of relying primarily on a real balance effect in a full-employment policy. Since he has also suggested that the real balance effect is not sufficient to assure the stability of full-employment equilibrium under all market conditions (ibid., p. 236), it would appear that Patinkin may be overemphasizing this aspect in relation to other factors, e.g. the existence of fixed money contracts and their redistributive effects (when money-wages and prices alter) on the spending behaviour of firms and households. Unfortunately, Patinkin merely assumes away these latter elements (ibid., pp. 207, 216–17, 220–1, 285, 336). Concerned with the operation of a 'pure' economy, these contractual rigidities are suppressed as apparently bothersome matters which prevent the operation of the *tâtonnement* mechanism for achieving equilibrium (ibid., p. 534).

Fourthly, it is essential to understand the distinction, as set out by Patinkin, between a demand curve and a market equilibrium curve (ibid., pp. 48, 50, 265). Confusion and wrong theoretical inferences abound if the latter is mistaken for the former. According to Patinkin, a demand curve attempts to explain variations in the dependent variable (usually demand quantities) when the exogenous independent variables – which are not subject to explanation – vary. In other words, the demand curve explains what the effect of an unexplained change in the independent variable will be on the dependent variable with other things held constant. A market equilibrium curve, on the other hand, is the locus of intersection points of demand curves and their corresponding supply curves. The latter is derived from a family of functions as a cross-cut; the former refers to an individual function where the parameters are specified and held constant.

In the circumstances, it is surprising that some confusion over these matters still persists in some parts of Patinkin's argument. For example, it will be argued below that Patinkin has mistaken the market equilibrium curve in the labour market for the demand curve for labour. Not unexpectedly, since Patinkin starts with an incorrect representation of the demand curve for labour, he elicits some rather curious conclusions about the equilibrium level of employment and its relationship to the aggregate supply function.

Finally, the invalidity of a dichotomy between the real and monetary sectors in a monetised, production economy is one of the basic tenets of both Patinkin's analysis and *The General Theory* (Keynes, 1936, p. 293). Disagreement can still persist, however, on the principal substantive grounds for this interdependence.[4]

2 PATINKIN VERSUS THE KEYNESIANS

The fundamental disagreement between Keynesians and Patinkin resides in his belief that Keynesian economics 'is the economics of unemployment *dis*equilibrium' (Patinkin, 1965, pp. 337–8). Keynes and most of the post-'Keynesian' writers have argued that underemployment was not only possible but normal.[5]

It is my contention that this divergence between Patinkin and the Keynesians is partly due to a semantic confusion resulting from the fact that Patinkin defines the concept of market equilibrium as identical with that of market clearing (ibid., p. 11) and partly (and probably more importantly) as a result of Patinkin's mistakenly identifying the market equilibrium curve in the labour market for the demand curve for labour (ibid., equation (2), p. 203). As a result, Patinkin spends most of his time analysing the economy under the classical assumption of a constant (full-employment) level of income, where Walras's Law *and* the budget re-straint are relevant (ibid., pp. 258, 261). Once the level of income is a variable, however, Walras's Law is no longer applicable, at least in the way that Patinkin wishes to apply it. Neither Walras nor Patinkin allow changes in the level of output (i.e. effective demand) to affect the *tâtonnement* process (i.e. to affect the shape or position of the excess demand function). In fact, Patinkin admonishes Walras for arguing that a production econ-omy differs from an exchange economy where in the latter the supply volume is fixed. Patinkin insists that Walras failed to realise that all input quantities are fixed (perfectly inelastic?) in a production economy, and therefore, there is no logical difference between the excess-demand func-tions in the two types of economies (ibid., pp. 534–5). Accordingly, Patinkin introduces Walras's Law under the assumption of *a fixed level of output* (i.e. a vertical aggregate supply curve), even in a production econ-omy. It is as if, in the Marshallian short run, output has no flexibility, and consequently, the difference between temporary market equilibrium and short-run equilibrium has been obliterated. This use of Walras's Law on the aggregate level in a production economy, however, involves Patinkin in a fallacy of composition, for he implicitly aggregates individual excess demand functions *under a budget restraint* into an aggregate demand function *where* income and therefore effective demand is a variable.[6] The short-comings of this analysis will be elaborated below.

2.1 Equilibrium, Clearing and Disequilibrium

In a commodity market the concept of 'clearing', as Marshall (among others) long ago taught, implies that at a given market price the quantity demanded by buyers exactly equals the quantity that sellers are willing to supply. On the other hand, equilibrium (merely) implies that the motiva-tion of buyers (for utility maximization) and sellers (for income maximiza-tion) are, at the given market-price–quantity situation, being just balanced out so that neither the sellers nor the buyers will act to alter the price or quantity offered or purchased. Accordingly, clearing is a sufficient but not a necessary condition for equilibrium.

In the usual case (Figure 36.1a) clearing and equilibrium are obtained simultaneously at a price of p_1. Without at this time inquiring into the setting which causes the buying and selling behaviour to be as represented by Figures 36.1b and 36.1c, it can be shown that in these latter cases *equilibrium will be achieved* at a price of p_1, while q_1 will be bought, but *the market will not clear*. In the equilibrium situation suggested Figure 36.1b, q_1 will be purchased, but a maximum of q_2 will be offered at a price of p_1, so that $q_2 - q_1$ will remain unsold. Nevertheless, if the demand and supply schedules actually depict the behaviour of buyers and sellers to alternative *market prices* nothing tends to change in the system (cf. Patinkin, 1965, p. 643). If the commodity in question is durable it may be held over in inventory for a future period. If, on the other hand, it is perishable, then we normally say that the quantity $q_2 - q_1$ has been lost to the economy (and in the case of labour we would call it involuntary unemployment – and a permanent loss of services that might have been rendered has occurred).

In Figure 36.1c, on the other hand, at the equilibrium price of p_1, the quantity q_1 will be offered and purchased, although q_2 could be sold if it were forthcoming at a price of p_1. Thus the market will be in equilibrium at a price of p_1 with q_1 being sold, and consequently some form of non-price rationing (e.g. lengthening of the order books) will develop in equilibrium.

Despite the common textbook practice, which evidences an apparent preference for demand and supply schedules being drawn as in Figure 36.1a, the horizontal segments of the supply curve in Figure 36.1b and of the demand curve in Figure 36.1c are representative of some real world markets. (Compare Figures 36.1b and 36.1c with Patinkin's money demand curve in Fig. IX–7b (ibid., p. 226) and his representation of other's view of labour supply in Fig. XIV–1 (ibid., p. 342).) Thus it is essential that we recognize that *clearing is not a necessary condition for equilibrium*.

Patinkin, however, defines equilibrium as synonymous with clearing (ibid., p. 11). In analysing the labour market, therefore, Patinkin asserts that the real 'wage rate will not be an equilibrium one unless it equates the amounts demanded and supplied of labour' (ibid., p. 203), i.e. unless the labour market is cleared. Obviously, if the labour market is not cleared, that is, if there is involuntary unemployment, then by Patinkin's limited definition of equilibrium,[7] Keynesian economics must be *dis*equilibrium economics. Disequilibrium becomes merely a definitional matter – in a context where institutional elements are bypassed.

Once the distinction between clearing and equilibrium is recognized, it is possible to demonstrate the existence of unemployment equilibrium, if it can be shown that the demand and/or supply curves for labour are not represented by Figure 36.1a (Patinkin's Fig. IX–1; ibid., p. 204) but rather by Figure 36.1b (Patinkin's Fig. XIV–1; ibid., p. 342).

The crux of the Keynesian–Patinkin disagreement, therefore, involves the question of what is the correct formulation of the aggregate demand

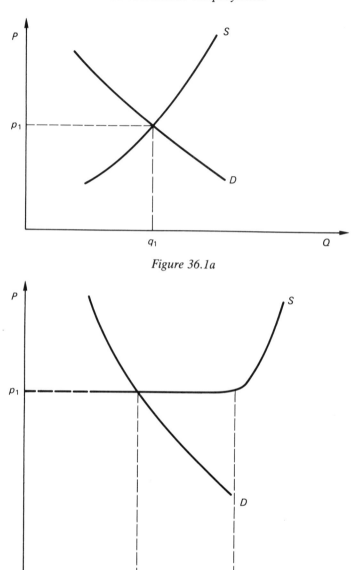

Figure 36.1a

Figure 36.1b

and supply curves for labour. It is at this stage that Keynes and Keynesians are at loggerheads with Patinkin. The former group have argued that the demand for labour is derived directly from the effective demand for goods. Patinkin, on the other hand, has interpreted an equation relating the level of employment to the real wage rate (i.e. to the marginal product of

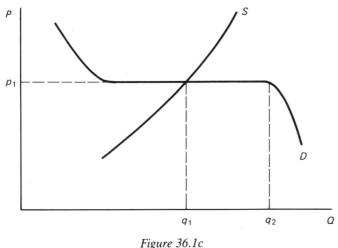

Figure 36.1c

labour) as the aggregate demand for labour function (ibid., p. 203). This divergence of views involves a much more substantial matter than the confusion between the concepts of clearing and equilibrium.

2.2   The Demand for Labour Function

Since the 1930s innumerable writers have argued that the marginal product curve *cannot* be the demand curve for labour as long as the level of output is a variable. (For example, Davidson, 1960, ch. 3, 4; Davidson and Smolensky, ch. 11; Hicks, 1939, p. 95 n. 2; Keynes, 1936, ch. 2, 20; Mishan, 1964; Weintraub, 1956; 1958, ch. 6) What is rather disappointing is that Professor Patinkin, who has displayed a mastery of so much of the Keynesian literature, and who has spent so much energy in making the profession aware of the difference between demand curves and market equilibrium curves, has not realised that the curve relating the real wage-rate and the level of employment (the inverse of the marginal product curve) may be a market equilibrium curve; *it is not*, as he describes it, *an aggregate demand curve for labour* (ibid., p. 203).

Patinkin explicitly assumes that in a production economy the demand for productive factors by business firms is based *solely* on relative prices, the rate of interest and the initial level of real assets (ibid., p. 77), which in turn, implies (a) that excess demand functions of households are independent of the quantity of factors demanded by business firms (ibid., pp. 76–77) (and *consequently the aggregate demand for commodities must be unrelated to total factor incomes!*), and (b) the aggregate demand for labour schedule is independent of the level of output, i.e. independent of the level of effective demand (ibid., p. 319). Moreover, Patinkin asserts that the

absence of output (i.e. effective demand) as a determinant in the demand
for labour function is the result of deriving the labour supply function from
the usual principle of profit-maximization (ibid., p. 319). Inevitably, Patinkin decides that there is no difference in the market-excess demand
functions of an exchange economy where output is fixed (and the above-
mentioned assumptions may be applicable) and the market-excess demand
functions in a production economy where effective demand *and* labour
supply quantities are variable (ibid., pp. 76–7) (and where, therefore,
Keynesians argue these assumptions are inapplicable). In essence *Patinkin
has revived the classical position that the Marshallian-type demand schedules* (i.e. Patinkin's excess demand curves) *can be assumed to remain
unchanged as aggregate income and effective demand varies.* This, of
course, implies that factor prices and factor incomes can vary without
altering the demand for commodities; in Patinkin's terminology, factor
incomes can change without altering excess-demand curves. Consequently,
there can be a change in total factor income without any change in initial
endowments (i.e. in real income).

In a production economy, however, the level of employment and output
can vary, and therefore the level of real income cannot be part of the
'givens' of the system. Accordingly, an analysis which aggregates excess-
demand curves based on the assumption of fixed initial endowments is
inapplicable in any economy where output and employment, as well as
prices, are variable (cf. Hicks, 1939, p. 95 n. 2; Weintraub, 1958, ch. 1;
Davidson and Smolensky, 1964a).

Without reviewing the entire analytical argument further, it is interesting
to quote Mishan, the most recent of many writers who have argued that
even though in perfect competition price equals marginal cost,

> and, therefore, that – since a common wage prevails – marginal physical
> product equals the real wage, this condition holds not only in some
> full-employment equilibrium but for any amount of labor that happens
> to be employed. The most we could say of the marginal product curve in
> this connection is that it traces a locus of all possible equilibrium
> positions in which this condition obtains . . . a decline in the real wage
> being properly regarded as the *result* of an expansion of aggregate
> demand; the wage decline is not the 'cause' of the expansion. (Mishan,
> 1964, p. 610)

Thus, to paraphrase Patinkin's description of market equilibrium curves
(Patinkin, 1965, pp. 266–7), the real wage-rate and the level of employment are dependent variables in the analysis (hence the equilibrium values
cannot be dependent on each other, but only on the independent variables). Accordingly, Patinkin's demand for labour curve is not a demand
curve at all; rather it is best to interpret this market equilibrium curve as a

real wage determining function, i.e. *given* the level of employment, it indicates what the equilibrium real wage will be.

Patinkin's model is therefore devoid of a useful, complete analysis of the labour market. Since he has not presented any demand function for labour, all his conclusions about equilibrium in the level of employment must be suspect. But then, the reader might ask, if the marginal product curve is not the demand curve, what is the *correct* specification of the demand function for labour? As Mishan suggests, the demand curve for labour in either a classical or Keynesian framework is 'primarily derivable from the effective demand for goods' (20, p. 610). Elsewhere I have adopted what I believe is the simplest geometric apparatus for analysing the demand and supply curves of labour when the demand is derived from the effective demand for commodities as output varies, and the supply of labour is based on real wage-rate (i.e. there is no money illusion) (Davidson and Smolensky, 1964a, ch. 11; also see Weintraub, 1958, ch. 6). Mishan provides a different geometrical apparatus to display the same market phenomena (1964). While this is not the place to compare these alternative geometric systems, the point remains that Patinkin's model does not have an explicit complete demand for labour function. Consequently, his claim that Keynesian economics is the economics of unemployment disequilibrium is illusory.

2.3   The Aggregate Supply Function

Patinkin's mislabelling of the market equilibrium curve as the demand curve for labour leads him to an inadequate specification of the aggregate supply function for commodities. According to Patinkin, the aggregate supply function 'indicates the amount of commodities the firms of the economy would like to supply in order to maximize the profits at the given real wage with which they are confronted in the market' (Patinkin, 1965, p. 210).[8] Since Patinkin has not identified the demand for labour function, he incorrectly indicates that there is only one equilibrium real wage rate, the rate which clears the labour market – the full-employment rate. Consequently, he concludes that the aggregate commodity supply function must appear as a vertical line, Y_0, on the 45° diagram (ibid., p. 211).

If Patinkin had recognized that his equation (3) on p. 203 was not the market demand curve for labour (rather it is the real wage rate determining equation), then his own definition of the aggregate supply function would have forced him to introduce a non-vertical aggregate supply curve on the 45° diagram. Moreover, he might have noticed that a vertical aggregate commodity supply function is inconsistent with his assumption of profit-maximizing firms in a perfectly competitive economy. This latter assumption implies, of course, that increasing levels of employment can occur only under conditions of diminishing returns, and consequently for each level of

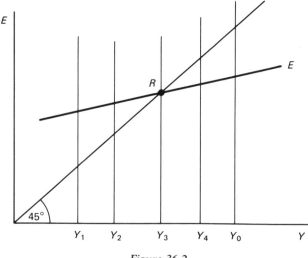

Figure 36.2

employment and output there will be a different real wage rate. In other words, at each given level of output on the 45° diagram there is a unique real wage, and consequently a unique vertical 'Patinkin-type' aggregate supply curve (Figure 36.2). Only one of this family of vertical supply curves, Y_0, represents supply at full employment, i.e. when the labour market has cleared. The equilibrium level of employment, however, would occur when the aggregate demand function (E in Figure 36.2), a vertical aggregate supply line, and the 45° line have all intersected at a single point (R in Figure 36.2).

If Patinkin had introduced aggregate supply conditions correctly into his model he would have noted some patent inconsistencies in his system. For example, in a perfectly competitive world the relationship between commodity prices and the money wage rate varies at each level of output because of diminishing returns. Consequently, the assumption of constant prices as output varies (which underlies Patinkin's aggregate demand curve, E (Patinkin, 1965, p. 206)) could be applicable only if the money wage rate declined as the level of employment expanded – a situation which is not usual in the 'classical system' and which is obviously not what Patinkin intended to imply.

Similarly, Patinkin's statement of the classical position 'as seen with Keynesian eyes' appears odd and unrecognizable (ibid., p. 357). In his Keynesian version of Say's Law, Patinkin interprets it as meaning that the 45° line becomes the aggregate demand for commodities function. What is surprising is that he then argues that aggregate demand will intersect with aggregate supply only at the full-employment level of output! This is not only inconsistent with his own statement (ibid., p. 356), but it is also in

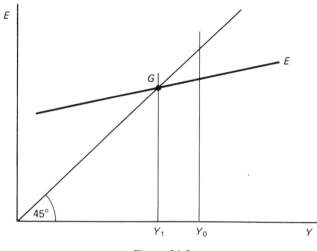

Figure 36.3

conflict with Keynes's interpretation of the statement that 'Supply creates its own Demand' (1936, pp. 25–6). Keynes argued that under Say's Law aggregate demand accommodates itself to the commodity output supplied by firms, i.e. *that the aggregate demand and supply curves are coincident with the 45° line throughout their entire length*. On this, Keynes wrote, 'effective demand, instead of having a unique equilibrium value, is an infinite range of values all equally admissible; and the amount of employment is indeterminate except in so far as the marginal disutility of labour sets an upper limit' (ibid., p. 26). According to Keynes, therefore, at any level besides full employment the economy is in *neutral* equilibrium and there is no obstacle to full employment. This is obviously quite a different view of Says's Law than the one Patinkin interprets 'through Keynesian eyes'.

Another inconsistency suggests itself when Patinkin indicates that his aggregate supply function

assumes the more familiar form of an upward-sloping curve if it is drawn within the [price and quantity] coordinate system of Figure III–Ia (p. 42). For the higher the price level, the lower the real wage rate, the greater the input of labour, and *the greater, therefore, the aggregate amount of commodities supplied*. Similarly it is clear from the discussion on p. 41 that the aggregate demand function for commodities (9) can be represented in Figure III–Ia (*as of a given level of Y and r*) by the negatively sloping curve which now appears there. (Patinkin, 1965, p. 211; italics mine)

Thus Patinkin suggests a diagram similar to our Figure 36.1a above.

The placing on the same price–quantity coordinate system of a supply curve which allows for changing levels of aggregate output with a demand curve explicitly based on a constant output level is strongly incongruous to one reared on Keynesian economics. Similarly, the representation of an aggregate demand curve which depicts desired expenditure at alternative levels of output, with a vertical aggregate supply curve which assumes a given (full-employment) level of output, in the same 45° diagram (ibid., p. 212) entails some contradiction.

Since Patinkin has not properly introduced aggregate supply phenomena into his model, it is inevitable that he tends to emphasize excess demand *at full employment* as the primary cause of price changes, and to ignore those 'homely but intelligible' supply concepts of marginal costs and the elasticity of short-period supply in the determination of the money-price level (cf. Keynes, 1936, pp. 292 ff.). What is so vexatious about Patinkin's painstaking efforts to integrate value theory with monetary theory is his almost complete neglect of the supply aspects of value theory. For example, he states that in a purely competitive economy an actual decline in output will occur *without changing the full-employment money wage–price structure* (Patinkin, 1965, p. 325). The classical economists, however, recognized that diminishing returns (i.e. a less than infinitely elastic supply condition) must affect the price level when output levels change – a proposition which Patinkin implicitly denies (although this same phenomenon was the basis for his labelling the inverse of the marginal product curve as the demand curve for labour).

Once prices are allowed to vary with output and employment levels and the aggregate commodity supply function is properly introduced into the system, Patinkin's neatly built model starts to become defective at several points. Patinkin's assumption that redistributive income effects are normally unimportant is acceptable only as long as money wages and prices are assumed constant, since then the presence of fixed money contracts – which are essential for the operation of a production-specialization economy – do not result in either income or wealth redistribution. Once prices and money wages are permitted to vary, however, then those people who received their income as a result of money contracts – and in the real world a large proportion of personal income is the result of such contracts – will see their income eroded by price rises;[9] and there will be redistribution of real income from households to business firms and governments (cf. Davidson and Smolensky, 1964a, ch. 11, 12). Since aggregate spending by these latter two sectors is not as closely related to income levels as is the spending of households, the aggregate demand function will not be homogeneous in relation to money price changes, even in the absence of the money illusion. Consequently, the interdependence of the real and monetary sector can be established via redistribution effects and without appeal to the real balance effect. (This argument and its consequence for labour market analysis has been developed elsewhere (Davidson and Smolensky, 1964b).) In fact, Patinkin ultimately notes that 'the real-balance effect is itself a distribution effect' (1965, p. 288). Since the real balance effect is admittedly relatively unimportant for policy, while it is obvious that fixed money contracts and changing money wages and prices are commonplace in the very nature of a modern production economy, one may ask why, at this late stage, has Patinkin spent so much time exploring the intricacy of the former, and ignoring, by assumption, the redistributive aspects of the latter?

2.4 Voluntary Versus Involuntary Unemployment – On Versus Off Schedules

Patinkin indicates that all individuals are acting voluntarily when they are all on their supply and/or demand schedules simultaneously. In his view involuntary unemployment implies that workers and firms are off their respective supply and demand for labour schedules (ibid., pp. 313–15). Patinkin, at this point, finally admits that his demand for labour function is imperfect in that it does not show the 'connection between the firms' output of commodities and the input of labour . . . Indeed, to all outward appearances, this function depends only on the real wage rate, and *not on the volume of output*' (ibid., p. 319; italics mine). In this statement apparently Patinkin admits that his demand-for-labour curve is not derived from the effective demand for commodities. Nevertheless, Patinkin argues that as effective demand declines, firms will 'offer a real wage rate below that indicated by the demand curve . . . or alternatively, at the real wage rate (w/P_0) they now demand a smaller input' (ibid., p. 320). But given technology, the stock of capital and profit-maximizing firms in a perfectly competitive system, the marginal productivity curve is anchored; therefore Patinkin's demand curve *cannot* shift, and Patinkin is forced by the logic of his position to suggest that firms will *move off* their labour demand schedule.

If the reader becomes a bit incredulous at this stage, Patinkin rebukes him for having 'the ingrained mental habit' of seeing only the points on the demand or supply curve (ibid., p. 323).[10] Nevertheless, this off-schedule type of analysis does lead to at least one implication which should give pause and arouse more than a mild suspicion. According to Patinkin, when effective demand is deficient firms move off their demand-for-labour curve. Market forces are thereby generated which ultimately shift the aggregate-demand-for-commodities curve back to the full-employment intersection (ibid., pp. 320 ff.). Thus, given Patinkin's demand-for-labour curve, it is market forces resulting from movements away from the demand curve for labour which ultimately increase aggregate demand. In its most bizarre form, this leads to the conclusion that, in Patinkin's model, the demand-for-commodities is derived from his demand-for-labour function, and the demand for labour is *not* derived from the demand for commodities.

If Patinkin had recognized that his function was *not* a demand-for-labour curve but rather a real wage determining equation he would have avoided the difficulty of defining involuntary unemployment as people 'being off their schedule'. Instead he is forced to twist and turn to avoid the inevitable inconsistencies of his system. He argues, for example, that at point G in Figure 36.3 above), although perfectly competitive firms are selling what they are actually producing, it is not an equilibrium situation, for given the relationship between money wages and prices of w/P_0, the firms *desire* to produce Y_0. But this *must* imply that firms are not profit maximizing at income level Y_1. Instead, given any money-wage rate, the marginal cost must be less than the market price at Y_1, so that profit-maximization should lead to an expansion to Y_0. According to Patinkin, however, the market will not purchase the entire Y_0 output at the given relationship between money wages and prices; therefore firms are pressured by the thread of potential unsold, unwanted inventories to remain at the Y_1 level *while the price level relative to money wages remains at the full employment level.*[11] Firms, however, can maintain the full-employment money-wage and price-level structure in the face of a lower output (and therefore lower marginal costs) only *if either* they do not maximize profits *or* they do not remain in a perfectly competitive market. If either of these latter aspects is true it is not surprising, of course, that firms are conceived as being off their competitive profit-maximizing schedules, or that, as Patinkin puts it, 'the demand curve . . . does *not* describe the actual behaviour of firms' (ibid., p. 321). If this curve doesn't describe the actual behaviour of firms to alternative situations, however, why should it be labelled the demand curve for labour?

What is vexing about this Patinkin apparatus for simultaneous departure from Patinkin-type demand and supply curves for labour is not, as he suggests, that 'a force majeure' has 'coerced' firms and workers off their respective schedules (ibid., p. 322); rather it is that Patinkin continues to call this 'function' an aggregate-demand-for-labour curve. The confusion is compounded when Patinkin reveals that this analysis results in 'a basic analytical problem here whose full solution is still not clear to me' (ibid., p. 323). Patinkin will be unable to remove this obscurity from his analytical system until he realizes that he has yet to derive a demand curve for labour.[12] Until such time as he derives a demand curve to place against his supply curve for labour, Patinkin's theory of employment will remain inchoate and incomplete, and his statement that the 'essence of dynamic analysis is involuntariness' will remain an unproven assertion.

Elsewhere I have summarized what I believe to be a reasonably consistent analysis of the labour market (Davidson and Smolensky, 1964a, ch. 11). This is not the place to repeat that analysis nor to argue for its advantages or reveal its limitations. The burden of the present argument is that the fundamental difference between Patinkin and Keynesian economics is centred on the analysis of the labour market, and that from a Keynesian point of view it appears that Patinkin has reinstated the classical restriction of attempting to derive a demand curve for labour under the implicit assumption of a given level of aggregate effective demand. In saying this, it should be absolutely clear that nothing has been said here which implies that Patinkin's analysis of the money and bond markets is necessarily faulty.[13]

The basic differences between Patinkin and Keynesians, however, hinge on the analysis of the labour market. Perhaps the best way that the arguments developed above can be brought into sharp focus is by concluding with a short discussion of Walras's Law, which is the necessary connecting link between the various markets in the Patinkin system.

2.5 Walras's Law Once More

The crux of Patinkin's entire analysis rests on the applicability of Walras's Law, which for him is inextricably connected with the budget restraint. Although Patinkin indicates that one could conceive of an economy where the budget restraint does not imply Walras's Law (Patinkin, 1965, pp. 36, 613), this does not imply that the reverse is true, i.e. that one can have Walras's Law in the absence of the budget restraint. In fact, in any number of places in his book Patinkin argues that the budget restraint is necessary for Walras's Law (ibid., pp. 37, 38, 41, 42, 45, 51–3, 70, 201, 211). Yet the budget restraint is often irrelevant in macroeconomics. *For an economy the budget restraint is full employment.* Thus below the full-employment level the economy is not subject to Walras's Law in the sense that Patinkin would have it. Consequently, it does not follow that if there is an excess demand for money there must always be an excess supply of commodities of equal aggregate value (cf. ibid., p. 35). That this is clearly so can be demonstrated by considering an example where the economy starts from a less than full employment position. Assume that there is an increase in investment plans because of improved profit expectations. Accordingly, there will be an increase in the demand for money to finance the additional proposed investment projects (and, *ceteris paribus*, there will be an excess demand for money), even before there is any increase in output (i.e. the supply of commodities is not in excess) (Davidson, 1965, pp. 54–6; Keynes, 1937b; Robertson, 1948, pp. 10–12; Robinson, 1952, pp. 80–7). Only if the level of output is constant will money and commodities always be the substitutes suggested by Walras's Law. Once income is a variable, the transaction and finance motives for holding money and finance imply that as the demand for goods rises, the demand for money will also rise in a sympathetic relationship.

It *is only when the level of output is predetermined* that Walras's Law must lead to the result that flexible prices alone, via the *tâtonnement* process, act as the equilibrating mechanism. If Patinkin, in his integration of value theory into monetary theory, had followed Keynes's lead and allowed both prices and output to vary concomitantly he would have discovered (as we have always taught in courses in price theory) that *normally both prices and quantities alter when demand changes*. Patinkin develops most of his concepts in an exchange economy where supply is explicitly fixed. When he extends his argument to a production economy Patinkin, recognizing that supply may be a variable, states 'the essential point is that – according to the marginal productivity theory – once the technical conditions of production are specified, the decisions of a firm with respect to these inputs and outputs are based entirely on relative prices' (Patinkin, 1965, p. 76). *This statement is true only if the level of output has been predetermined*. It is indeed surprising that almost thirty years after *The General Theory* an economic model based on the classical assumption of a constant (full-employment) level of output is served up as a refutation of Keynesian underemployment equilibrium analysis.

Patinkin is on weak ground when he argues that 'markets excess-demand equations of a production economy have exactly the same basic property . . . as do those of our simple exchange economy' (ibid., p. 77). In aggregating the former equations, one must explicitly analyse intended expenditures by households as the total factor incomes and their distribution alter; in the aggregation of an exchange economy's excess demand functions the total factor incomes are constant and only their distribution matters (cf. Keynes, 1936, p. 281; Weintraub, 1958, pp. 30–2). Patinkin slurs this point by remarking that 'no pretence of showing how this process of aggregation [of individual excess demand functions] is actually carried out' (Patinkin, 1965, p. 200). Had Patinkin executed this aggregation exercise with the same extraordinary skill he displays in other portions of his book, he might have become aware that his analytic system was based on the classical obsession with a given income level.

3 POLICY IMPLICATIONS OF PATINKIN VERSUS THE KEYNESIANS

Although the purpose of this paper has been to clarify the conceptual differences between the Patinkin neoclassical model and the Keynesian model, an equally important aspect is to isolate the different policy implications of each model.

Patinkin explicitly recognizes that 'the necessity of a major price decline' makes reliance on the real balance effect 'unacceptable as a primary ingredient of a modern full employment policy' (ibid., p. 335). Accordingly, he argues that monetary policy alone can be an efficacious alternative policy for full employment provided the automatic (flexible wage and price) market processes do not subject 'the economy to an intolerably long period of dynamic adjustment' (ibid., p. 339). Moreover, money-wage rigidities will, according to Patinkin, tend to aggravate the depth and duration of involuntary unemployment (ibid., p. 342). Thus, for Patinkin an efficiently operated monetary policy with freely flexible money wages and prices i.e. inflationary and deflationary price movements) are desirable *and* essential elements for a stable full-employment policy.

Keynesians, and particularly those who use an aggregate supply and demand approach, reach a considerably different policy conclusion. This does not mean that Keynesians do not think that 'money matters', for in a monetized production economy it would be foolish to deny the importance of money. After all, it was the neoclassicists and not Keynes who thought money was a veil! Keynes's entire life was devoted to showing that 'money matters' – that monetary management was essential. He was essentially a monetary economist, and considered it so important that the words money, monetary, or currency appear prominently in the titles of most of his major works. His legacy to the world includes the IMF and the World Bank. To Keynes money did matter – despite some curious deviations of some Keynesians!

From the policy standpoint, however, it is clear that the *essential* difference between Patinkin and the Keynesians does not lie merely in differing views of the efficacy of monetary policy, for, as Patinkin showed, this is simply a question that can be decided 'by empirical consideration of the actual magnitudes of the relevant economic parameters' (ibid., p. 340).

The basic conceptual difference in the two models involves an analysis of the labour market, and it is therefore not surprising that the fundamental policy difference is found there as well. The intrinsic difference is involved in the Keynesian argument that flexible money-wages exert a destabilizing influence in a market-oriented production economy. It is essential to the Keynesian model that there be some factor, such as wages, whose value in terms of money is at least sticky (if not fixed) if we are to have 'any stability of values in a monetary system' (Keynes, 1936, p. 304). As Keynes observed:

> The chief result of . . . [a flexible money-wage] policy would be to cause a great instability of prices, so violent perhaps as to make business calculations futile in an economic society functioning after the manner of that in which we live. To suppose that a flexible wage policy is a right and proper adjunct of a system which on the whole is one of *laissez-faire*, is the opposite of the truth. (ibid., p. 269)

Keynes recommended that a short-run stable money-wage level was the proper policy for a closed system; while a constant money-wage level and fluctuating exchange rates was the desirable policy for an open system. In the long run Keynes suggested that money-wages should rise with productivity increments (ibid., p. 271).

The importance of a wage or incomes policy in both open and closed economies has been recently re-emphasized by some Keynesians (Davidson and Smolensky, 1964a, chs. 11, 12; Davidson and Smolensky (mimeo); 12, ch. 2; Weintraub, 1958, ch. 6). Indeed, for Keynesians short-run stability in the money wage-rate is a desirable policy objective for both efficiency and equity reasons, since: (1) any given monetary measure is likely to be more efficacious in a market economy where wage and price movements are minimized, since changes in money-wages will have an impact on liquidity preferences which may offset the effects of changes in the money supply (Keynes, 1936, p. 263; Davidson and Smolensky, 1964, ch. 13), and (2) as long as many people have their personal incomes 'contractually fixed in terms of money, in particular the rentier class and persons with fixed salaries on the permanent establishment of a firm, an institution, or the State . . . social justice and social expediency are best served if the remunerations of *all* factors are somewhat inflexible in terms of money' (Keynes, 1936, p. 268).[14]

Clearly Keynes's original ideas on the desirability of stability in wages and prices with changes in demand underlie both the Council of Economic Advisors 'wage-guidelines' in the United States and the Labour Government's incomes policy in the United Kingdom. Indeed, it is the indisputable fact that most economic policy decision-makers in Western market-oriented economies have already chosen between the Keynesian and modern neoclassical models. Keynes has already won the ideological battle in the world of practical men. Should not our models and our textbooks deal with these facts of life?

Notes

1. The fact that 100 pages of the September 1965 issue of the *American Economic Review* was devoted to a discussion of the relative predictive value of a simple Keynesian model (essentially based on the 45° diagram) *vis-à-vis* a velocity model is clear evidence of the ubiquitous identification of this traditional 45° cross as representative of Keynesian economics.
2. Considering the short shrift the aggregate supply function is given in most popular 'Keynesian' writings, one may be surprised at the large number of economists who have discussed it (e.g. Davidson, 1960; 1962; Davidson and Smolensky, 1964a; DeJong, 1954; Edwards, 1959; Gruber, 1962; Hawtrey, 1954; Keynes, 1936; Marty, 1961; Patinkin, 1956; 1965; Robertson, 1948; 1956; Robertson and Johnson, 1955; Saito, 1962; Weintraub, 1958; Wells, 1960; Vibe-Pedersen, 1964).

3. Just as Patinkin deliberately avoids stating the savings–investment equilibrium condition in his book, so has an entire 'Keynesian' work been written where the equilibrium emphasis is always on the equality of aggregate supply and aggregate demand, and the savings equal investment condition is avoided (and apparently never missed by the many reviewers and instructors using the text (Davidson and Smolensky, 1964)).

4. Elsewhere I have suggested factors other than the real balance effect which will lead to this interdependence (Davidson, 1965; Davidson and Smolensky, 1964a, ch. 13).

5. The history of the labour market in the United States since the Korean War suggests the ubiquitous nature of unemployment. Can this be disequilibrium? And, if so, how long can it persist?

6. It is just this aggregation problem which Keynes was addressing himself to in *The General Theory* (Keynes, 1936, p. 281).

7. In his Note K, however, Patinkin admonishes Keynes for not using equilibrium in 'the usual sense of the term that nothing tends to change in the system' (1965, p. 643).

8. At this stage it must be pointed out that firms are *not* confronted with real wage rates in the labour market. What is relevant to the firm's hiring decision is the relationship between the money wage rate (assumed equal in each industry) and the price of the firm's product, i.e. the real cost in terms of the own-product of the firm. *This is not the same as real wage rate*, which relates the money wage to the price of wage goods, i.e. to the price of consumption goods (cf. Robinson, 19, p. 356). The difference between the real cost in terms of own-product and the real wage is most obvious in the hiring decision of a firm where its workers do not buy any of its products, e.g. in an investment-goods industry.

9. In a modern economy much of personal income is a result of fixed money contracts. Besides the traditional pensioners and coupon-clipping rentiers, government employees, university teachers, individuals engaged in non-commercial research, employees in philanthropic and religious organizations, as well as some salaried workers of business enterprises, receive their incomes are a result of fixed contractual commitments. As note 14 below indicates, significantly more than 30 per cent of personal income in the United States in any one year may be the result of contracts.

10. My conception of a schedule is that it is a logical representation of the behaviour of buyers or sellers (given their motivational principles and certain parameters, such as tastes, technology, etc.) when they are confronted by alternative situations. If these schedules do represent the observable behaviour of individuals as they are confronted with alternative situations, then we are involved in a logical inconsistency when we say that they can be off their schedules. Either people behave in the way their schedules say they should or they are operating on a different schedule from the one shown (perhaps because they are not motivated by the same factors as we assume they are, or something has changed in the environment which is assumed to be constant under the usual *ceteris paribus* derivation of the schedule). (See, for example, my discussion of the concept of the aggregate supply function as a schedule (Davidson, 1962, pp. 456–7).)

11. At this point Patinkin is arguing that market clearing can occur in a disequilibrium situation, – that equilibrium is not a necessary condition for clearing (1965, p. 320) – while previously Patinkin defined equilibrium as synonymous with clearing (ibid., p. 11).

12. Others have shown concern over Patinkin's 'off schedule' analysis of the labour market (e.g. Cross and Williamson, 1962; Gogerty and Winston, 1964). They have attempted to rescue Patinkin's conclusion that underemployment is a disequilibrium phenomenon by substituting different explanations for the adjustment process when aggregate demand declines from the full-employment level. Cross and Williamson assume that unwanted inventories and money-wage and price inflexibility cause firms to move up Patinkin's labour demand curve, so that unemployment disequilibrium is the initial result. Ultimately, in this model, wages and prices fall, bringing the real balance effect into play, and commodity demand curves shift rightward and employment 're-expands until the process comes to a halt when the [aggregate] demand curve once more intersects the 45° line at B [full employment]' (Cross and Williamson, 1962, p. 80).

Gogerty and Winston, on the other hand, rightly reject the notion of unwanted inventories and inflexible prices as incompatible with the assumption of pure competition. Instead, they introduce a *temporary* departure from pure competition in the commodity market when aggregate demand declines, so that firms are no longer on Patinkin's competitive labour demand curve; rather, they are, temporarily, on a monopoly labour demand curve, which, it is asserted, is to the left of Patinkin's curve. (The complications of introducing monopoly – even temporarily – are not pursued by Gogerty and Winston, and it would divert us from our main purpose to pursue this aspect in detail here. Suffice it to say that: (1) they ignore the fact that distributive effects of even a temporary monopoly structure will feed back on aggregate demand, and (2) the leftward position of Gogerty and Winston's monopoly labour demand curve is not conclusively demonstrated in the presence of this feedback.) Nevertheless, if prices and money-wages are flexible, then, according to Gogerty and Winston, equilibrium will be restored when 'the demand curve for labour will have returned to its original position – to Patinkin's labour demand curve' (Gogerty and Winston, 1964, p. 125). Thus, both Cross and Williamson and Gogerty and Winston provide alternative adjusting mechanisms to arrive at the same conclusion as Patinkin, i.e. underemployment is a disequilibrium phenomenon. Patinkin properly rejects both suggestions as unsatisfactory (1965, p. 670). Nevertheless, these alternative models suffer from the same limitation as Patinkin's original system, i.e. they imply that the equilibrium demand curve for commodities is derived from the labour demand curve, and not vice versa. None of these writers has realized that the marginal productivity curve is *not* the competitive aggregate demand-for-labour schedule, and that therefore their models do not have any explicit demand curve for labour when output and effective demand are variable.

13. In a future paper I hope to compare the Keynesian view of these markets with Patinkin's analysis. At this stage one can only point out a surprising assumption underlying Patinkin's capital–market analysis. Patinkin assumes an imperfection which prevents the supply of bonds from becoming infinite. This imperfection is an assumption that all debtors operate on the belief that they must repay all their debts by the end of their economic horizon, and therefore they can pay for all their planned borrowing accordingly. Given that some of the major borrowers in the modern economy are business firms and governments which may never retire their outstanding debt, it is surprising that this wholly unrealistic assumption is so readily accepted, whereas the somewhat more realistic imperfections that may exist in the system because of (a) the presence of fixed money contracts, and (b) the inability of labour to bargain for its own

real wage, are dismissed out of hand by Patinkin. Patinkin manages to spend many pages discussing the bond market, and yet he has no fixed money contracts in the system. Walras's Law, as Patinkin is well aware, logically requires the ability to recontract (1965, p. 534). Nevertheless, he sweeps aside the fact that bonds themselves are long-term fixed money commitments which do not permit the original debtors to recontract during the life of the bond. Patinkin avoids this problem by neutralizing the influence of the firm's initial outstanding bonds (ibid., p. 217 n. 13).

14. A cursory examination of the 1962 data on personal income is most revealing. It shows that out of a total personal income of $442.1 billion the compensation to fixed contract groups was as follows:

	$ billion
Employees of government	55.5
Employees of educational institutions	2.8
Employees of non-profit organisations	3.6
Rentier income (interest and rental income)	42.0
Transfer payments	34.8
	138.7

Thus, excluding salaries paid out to the employees of the profit-making business sector of the economy, we have already accounted for over 30 per cent of personal income. Accordingly, it would not be surprising that if figures on the compensation of this latter group could be obtained as much as 40 or even 50 per cent of personal income could be attributable to contractual commitments.

References

Cross, J. G. and J. Williamson, (1962), 'Patinkin on Unemployment Disequilibrium', *Journal of Political Economy*, 70 (February), pp. 76–81.

Davidson, P. (1960), *Theories of Aggregate Income Distribution* (New Brunswick).

Davidson, P. (1962), 'More on the Aggregate Supply Function', *Economic Journal*, (June), pp. 452–7.

Davidson, P. (1965), 'Keynes's Finance Motive', *Oxford Economic Papers*, 17 (March), pp. 47–65.

Davidson, P. and E. Smolensky (1964a) *Aggregate Supply and Demand Analysis* (New York).

Davidson, P. and E. Smolensky (1964b) 'Modigliani on the Interaction of Real and Monetary Phenomena', *Review of Economics and Statistics*, 46 (November), pp. 429–31.

Davidson, P. and E. Smolensky, 'The Popular Appeal of Five Percent Unemployment' (mimeo).

DeJong, F. J. (1954) 'Supply Functions in Keynesian Economics', *Economic Journal*, (March), pp. 3–24. Also see his comments in the December 1954, September 1955 and September 1956 issues of the *Economic Journal*.

Edwards, E. O. (1959), 'Classical and Keynesian Employment Theories: A Reconciliation', *Quarterly Journal of Economics*, 73 (August), pp. 407–28.

Gogerty, D. C. and G. C. Winston, (1964), 'Patinkin, Perfect Competition and

Unemployment Disequilibria', *Review of Economic Studies*, 31 (April), pp. 121–5.

Gruber, U. (1962), 'Keynes' Aggregate Supply Function and the Theory of Income Distribution', *Jahrbucher fur Nationalokonomie und Statistik*, 18 (May), pp. 189–219.

Harrod, R. F. (1965), *Reforming the World's Money* (London).

Hawtrey, R. G. (1954), 'Comment', *Economic Journal* (December), pp. 834–9. Also see his note in the September 1956 issue of the *Economic Journal*.

Hicks, J. R. (1957), 'A Rehabilitation of "Classical" Economics?' *Economic Journal* (June), pp. 278–89.

Hicks, J. R. (1939), *Value and Capital*, 2nd edn (London).

Keynes, J. M. (1936), *The General Theory of Employment, Interest and Money* (New York).

Keynes, J. M. (1937a), 'Alternative Theories of the Rate of Interest', *Economic Journal* (June), pp. 241–52.

Keynes, J. M. (1937b), 'The Ex-Ante Theory of the Rate of Interest', *Economic Journal* (December), pp. 663–9.

Marty, A. L. (1961), 'A Geometrical Exposition of the Keynesian Supply Function', *Economic Journal* (September), pp. 560–5.

Mishan, E. (1964), 'The Demand for Labor in a Classical and Keynesian Framework', *Journal of Political Economy*, 72 (December), pp. 610–16.

Patinkin, D. (1956), *Money, Interest and Prices*, 1st edn (Evanston).

Patinkin, D. (1965), *Money, Interest and Prices*, 2nd edn (New York).

Robertson, D. H. (1948), *Essays on Monetary Theory* (London, 1948).

Robertson, D. H. (1956), 'Two Comments', *Economic Journal* (September), pp. 485–7.

Robertson, D. H. and H. G. Johnson, (1955) 'Keynes and Supply Functions', *Economic Journal* (September), pp. 474–8.

Robinson, J. (1952), *The Rate of Interest and Other Essays* (London).

Robinson, J. (1956), *The Accumulation of Capital* (London).

Saito, K. (1962), 'Aggregate Supply Function and Income Distribution', *Keizai Kenkyu*, 13 (October), pp. 314–21.

Vibe-Pederson, J. (1964), *National Income and Aggregate Income Distribution* (Copenhagen).

Weintraub, S. (1958) *An Approach to the Theory of Income Distribution* (Philadelphia).

Weintraub, S. (1956), 'A Macroeconomic Approach to the Theory of Wage Determination', *American Economic Review*, 46 (December), pp. 835–56.

Weintraub, S. (1957), 'The Micro-Foundation of Aggregate Demand and Supply', *Economic Journal* (September), pp. 455–70.

Weintraub, S. (1963), *Some Aspects of Wage Theory and Policy* (Philadelphia).

Wells, P. (1960), 'Keynes' Aggregate Supply Function: A Suggested Interpretation', *Economic Journal* (September), pp. 536–42.

37 A Keynesian View of Patinkin's Theory of Employment: A Rejoinder*

The gist of Gramm's comment is that perfectly elastic segments of demand and supply curves are 'unrealistic' and therefore 'the existence of an aggregate labour supply curve with a perfectly elastic section . . . must be considered a special case', and 'may be irrelevant for the labour market'. Gramm's proof of the irrelevance of this type of aggregate labour supply curve is merely to cite a textbook on price theory (Stigler, 1966). Appeals to such authority are not likely to advance this important discussion very far.

In this brief reply I cannot properly present the entire analysis which suggests the generality and the relevance of macro demand and supply curves with elastic segments. In my article I gave several citations as to where the relevant analysis of the aggregate labour market could be studied in detail (Davidson and Smolensky, 1964a; 1964b). As have others, Gramm seems to have failed to understand why this view is the relevant *general* case for a labour market in a *monetary* (as opposed to a barter) economy. In a forthcoming article I have tried to spell out in even greater detail, and hopefully greater clarity, the Keynesian view that a perfectly elastic labour-supply segment is an essential property of money and therefore of any monetary economy (Davidson). Accordingly, such a labour-supply analysis is the only general basis for a *General Theory of Employment* in a modern, market-oriented, monetary economy. I can only hope that after Gramm has studied this analysis he will understand the relevance of this general case.[1]

Note

1. The generality of the analysis is developed in chapter 17 of Keynes's *General Theory* (1936). For a similar view, see Lerner (1952).

* *Economic Journal* (March 1969).

References

Davidson, P. (1969) 'A Keynesian View of the Relationship Between Accumulation, Money, and the Money Wage Rate', *Economic Journal*.

Davidson, P. and E. Smolensky (1964a) *Aggregate Supply and Demand Analysis* (New York).

Davidson, P. and E. Smolensky (1964b) 'Modigliani on the Interaction of Real and Monetary Phenomena', *Review of Economics and Statistics* 46 (November) pp. 429–31.

Keynes, J. M. (1936) *The General Theory of Employment, Interest and Money* (London).

Lerner, A. P. (1952) 'The Essential Properties of Interest and Money', *Quarterly Journal of Economics* (May) pp. 172–93.

Stigler, G. (1966) *The Theory of Price*, 3rd edn (New York).

38 Patinkin's Interpretation of 'Keynes and the Keynesian Cross'*

Professor Patinkin (1988) has provided yet another interesting but, in my view, incorrect attempt to redeem the 45° cross as the 'proper' interpretation of Keynes's *General Theory*. Patinkin rejects the Fusfeld (1985) description of a report by Arthur E. Burns of the latter's discussion with Keynes regarding the graphical representation of Keynes's aggregate supply and demand analysis.

Professor Patinkin's refutation is fundamentally based on two analytical points: First, Patinkin claims that Fusfeld's Figure 1 is inconsistent with the 'basic properties' of Keynes's 'description of the aggregate demand function in Chapter 3 of this book (pp. 29, 31)'. According to Patinkin, these basic properties are (a) the marginal propensity to consume is less than one, and (b) this marginal propensity 'decreases with income, which is directly related to the level of employment'. Patinkin states that 'neither of these basic properties is depicted by the convex aggregate demand curve $D=f(N)$ presented in Figure 1 of Fusfeld's note'.[1]

Visual inspection of Fusfeld's aggregate demand curve indicates that it does not appear to have a slope of less than unity throughout; moreover, since it is convex the slope is increasing as employment rises. Apparently, Patinkin would require Fusfeld's aggregate demand function *in Figure 1* to have a slope (a) that is less than unity and (b) is continuously decreasing as employment rises.

Patinkin is not mathematically correct. A less than unity marginal propensity to consume merely requires $(\Delta D/\Delta Y) < 1$, where D is aggregate demand (in this case consumption) and Y is income. The slope of Fusfeld's aggregate demand function, however, is $(\Delta D/\Delta N)$ where D is in monetary terms and N is aggregate employment.[2] Since $(\Delta D/\Delta N)=(\Delta D/\Delta Y)\cdot(\Delta Y/\Delta N)$, it follows that a marginal propensity to consume of less than one, by itself, places no mathematical restriction on either the magnitude of the slope or the shape of Fusfeld's aggregate demand function. If $(\Delta Y/\Delta N)$, i.e. the change in money income with a change in employment, is sufficiently large, then Fusfeld's aggregate demand function in money proceeds versus employment units can be convex and have a slope greater than unity. Moreover, if

* *History of Political Economy*, 21, 1989.

($\Delta Y/\Delta N$) increases sufficiently as employment expands,[3] then the slope of Fusfeld's aggregate demand function will be convex, *even if the marginal propensity to consume is declining with money (and real) income.*

In sum, since employment rather than real income is on the X-axis, Fusfeld's convex D-function is consistent with both the properties that Patinkin claims are basic to Keynes's description of the aggregate demand curve.

To demonstrate a unique and stable underemployment equilibrium in the money proceeds versus employment quadrant of Fusfeld's Figure 1, all that is required is that (a) the slope of the D-function be less than the slope of the Z- (aggregate supply) function at any level of employment, and (b) the D-function be at a higher level of money proceeds than the Z-function at very low levels of employment. Fusfeld's Figure 1 meets these requirements and hence would have been completely acceptable to Keynes in a discussion with Arthur E. Burns.

Secondly, according to Patinkin, in *How to Pay for the War* (1940), 'Keynes essentially made use of the $C + I + G = Y$ analytical framework for which the 45° diagram is the geometric counterpart.' Hence, Patinkin implies that Keynes implicitly accepted the 45°-cross diagram which was to be derived later by Samuelson and Klein.

What Keynes had accepted and utilized in his *General Theory* and hence in his *How to Pay for the War* was the double-entry bookkeeping system for the National Accounts, not the 45° diagram.[4] Accepting double-entry bookkeeping logic that total output equals total expenditures does not require accepting the Samuelson–Klein 45° diagrammatic analysis. Accounting identities are compatible with many diagrammatic approaches.[5]

Patinkin has here confused a bookkeeping identity, or truism, for a diagrammatic approach which can be faulty, in that the latter provides an analysis of aggregate demand but is devoid of any meaningful aggregate supply analysis. Patinkin apparently suffered from a similar puzzlement in his 1956 classic, *Money, Interest, and Prices*, where he was forced to introduce a third function, a *vertical* aggregate supply function, in his 45° diagrams (e.g. p. 356) in order to provide supply characteristics to his model.[6]

Keynes's *How to Pay for the War* analysis assumed (for obvious reasons) that aggregate demand would exceed full employment supply causing inflation. In this specific situation a reduction in some component of aggregate demand is required to prevent rising prices. Such a National Accounts analysis of a full employment situation may be the arithmetic equivalent of the 45° 'inflationary gap' analysis – but it would also be the arithmetic equivalent of Fusfeld's analysis where the aggregate demand function intersected the aggregate supply function in its vertical (full employment) segment. What the 45° system could not analyse, however, and what Fusfeld's diagram is capable of analysing is the magnitude of inflation that might be expected[7] under various hypothetical full employment wartime situations.

In this context, it is important to point out that Patinkin has misinterpreted Keynes's (1936, p. 32) statement that 'the Theory of Prices falls into its proper place as a matter which is subsidiary to our general theory'. Patinkin (1988) relies on these words to insist that the 'central message of the *General Theory* had to do with output and employment, not with prices'.[8]

It is clear that Keynes's novel and revolutionary insight involved the determination of employment and output, not the determination of the price level. But as Allan Meltzer (1981) correctly pointed out in his interpretation of the *General Theory*, Keynes's method was to analyse one piece of the macropuzzle at a time. This Marshallian approach allowed Keynes to deal initially with the determination of employment question, ignoring changes in money-wages and prices in the early chapters. As Keynes noted in chapter 19, 'It would have been an advantage if the effects of changes in money-wages [and prices] could have been discussed in an earlier chapter . . . It was not possible, however, to discuss this matter fully until our own theory [of employment] had been developed . . . it could not be set forth clearly until the reader was acquainted with my own method' (Keynes, 1936, p. 257).

Only after fully developing his anti-Say's Law analysis of employment and output determination, and the effects of changes in money-wages (chapter 19), could Keynes spend an entire chapter (21) of *The General Theory* on 'The Theory of Prices'. Keynes's price analysis was based on a Marshallian microfoundation where in a single industry

price depends on the rates of remuneration of the factors of production which enter into marginal cost, and partly on the scale of output. There is no reason to modify this conclusion when we pass to industry as a whole. The general price level depends partly on the rates of remuneration of the factors of production which enter into marginal cost and partly on the scale of output as a whole, i.e. (taking equipment and technique as given) on the volume of output. It is true that, when we passed to output as a whole, the costs of production in any industry partly depend on the output of other industries. But the more significant change, of which we have to take account, is the effect of changes in *demand* both on costs and on volume. It is on the side of demand that we have to introduce quite new ideas when we are dealing with demand as a whole and no longer with demand for a single product taken in isolation, with demand as a whole assumed unchanged. (Keynes, 1936, pp. 294–5)

In his *General Theory*, Keynes was attempting to develop a new theory of employment determination when demand 'as a whole' was changing; he was not trying to develop a *new* theory of prices. Instead Keynes merely carried over Marshall's theory of short-run (flow) supply prices to an 'aggregate' supply function.[9] Hence Keynes's theory of prices is 'subsidiary' to his *General Theory* in the sense that, unlike his employment theory, it is not new and revolutionary. Nevertheless, only in his analysis of aggregate demand and supply functions in terms of money proceeds versus employment units[10] could Keynes provide a theory of the general price level which was integrated with, and compatible with, his theory of employment. For, as even Patinkin admits, it is not possible to analyse both price and employment effects with the 45° Keynesian cross diagram.

Notes

1. A marginal propensity to consume out of income of less than unity (when measured *in wage units*) (Keynes, 1936, p. 96) is a basic property. On the other hand, Keynes (ibid., p. 120) merely suggested: 'It is probable that there will be, as a rule, a tendency for it [the marginal propensity to consume] to diminish as employment increases.' There is nothing in Keynes's *General Theory* that requires the marginal propensity to decline with increases in real income. Patinkin's second 'basic' property is not fundamental to *The General Theory*. Nevertheless, as we demonstrate below, there is nothing in the Fusfeld diagram which is inconsistent with this second property specified by Patinkin.
2. Since the vertical ordinate in Fusfeld's Figure 1 is in money proceeds terms (not wage units or real output) both D and Y must be converted to money terms before their implication for the Fusfeld diagram can be derived.
3. Since Fusfeld's diagram is in terms of money proceeds versus employment, (Y/N) can be increasing if diminishing returns is occurring as employment expands, when total money proceeds is rising faster than employment.
4. Keynes had already utilized Colin Clark's and Simon Kuznets's National Accounts in *The General Theory* (1936, p. 102) itself. These national accounting systems had led Keynes to define income differently in *The General Theory* from how it was defined in his earlier *Treatise on Money*. In *The General Theory*, the use of accounting concepts permitted Keynes to define income 'to conform as closely as possible to common usage. It is necessary, therefore, that I should remind the reader that in my *Treatise on Money* I defined income in a special sense' (Keynes, 1936, p. 60).
5. In microeconomics, for example, the accounting identity that for each buyer there is a seller does not require one to necessarily use a 45° geometric counterpart for demand and supply diagrams.
6. Patinkin (1988) asserts that in his 1982 book he has 'shown . . . that Keynes himself was confused about the properties of this [aggregate supply] curve . . . indeed in the only place where he specified its mathematical form (*GT, p. 55, fn. 2*), he did so incorrectly'. This is not the time or place to reply to Patinkin's (incorrect, I believe) assertion that the aggregate supply function is not correctly specified in *The General Theory* or that Keynes was confused about its properties. I can only note that I believe that Patinkin has always had trouble coming to grips with Keynes's concept of aggregate supply. In fact, in the past, Patinkin has admitted that his 'criticism of the *General Theory* on the grounds

that it did not provide for an analysis of supply was not well taken' (Patinkin, 1976, p. 91, n. 12). I believe that Patinkin's inability to see that there is a difference between the National Accounts income identity $Y = C + G + I$ and the use of the 45° diagram *vis-à-vis* Fusfeld's aggregate demand–supply diagram indicates that he has still been unable to clearly comprehend Keynes's concept of the aggregate supply function. (In *The New Palgrave* I (Davidson, 1988) have provided the mathematical derivation of the aggregate supply function that can be obtained from Keynes's *General Theory*.)

7. Based on how high in the vertical segment of the Z-function the point of intersection with the D-function occurs *vis-à-vis* the money proceeds level where the Z-function first becomes vertical.

8. The fact that two complete chapters (43 pages) or approximately 10 per cent of the book are devoted to a discussion of changes in money-wages and the price level makes it difficult to accept the claim that the determination of the price level was not an integral part of Keynes's *General Theory*.

9. In a letter (20 February 1935) to D. H. Robertson, Keynes wrote that his aggregate supply function 'is simply the age-old supply function' and that his 'employment function [which in his *General Theory* (p. 280) Keynes describes as the "inverse function" of the aggregate supply function] can be derived from the ordinary supply function'. Finally, to reinforce these Marshallian origins, Keynes noted, in this letter, that he did not 'spend much time' on aggregate supply 'except for some embroideries at a later stage, since it is only a re-concoction of our old friend the supply function' (Keynes, 1973, Vol. XIII, p. 513).

   Patinkin recognized this relationship between the Marshallian microsupply curve and the aggregate supply function when he admitted that 'it is true' that 'Keynes explicitly equates the supply price [of the aggregate supply function] with marginal costs' (Patinkin, 1982, p. 126).

10. 'In dealing with the theory of employment I propose, therefore, to make use of only two fundamental units of quantity, namely, quantities of money value and quantities of employment' (Keynes, 1936, p. 41).

References

Davidson, Paul (1988), 'The Aggregate Supply Function', *The New Palgrave*.

Fusfeld, Daniel R. (1985), 'Keynes and the Keynesian Cross: A Note', *History of Political Economy*, 17 (Fall), pp. 385–9.

Keynes, John Maynard (1936), *The General Theory of Employment Interest and Money* (New York: Harcourt).

Keynes, John Maynard (1940), *How to Pay for the War*. As reprinted in Keynes, *Collected Writings*, Vol. IX.

Keynes, John Maynard (1973), *The Collected Writings of John Maynard Keynes*, Vol. XIII (London: Macmillan).

Meltzer, Allan H. (1981), 'Keynes's General Theory: A Different Perspective', *Journal of Economic Literature*, 19 (1).

Patinkin, Don (1956), *Money, Interest, and Prices* (New York: Harper & Row). References are to 2nd edition (1965).

Patinkin, Don (1976), 'Keynes's Monetary Thought', *History of Political Economy*, 8 (Spring), pp. 1–150.

Patinkin, Don (1988), 'Keynes and the Keynesian Cross: A Further Note', *History of Political Economy* 21 (Winter) (1989)

39 The Dual-faceted Nature of the Keynesian Revolution: Money and Money-wages in Unemployment and Production Flow Prices*

The Keynesian Revolution has often been sited in the multiplier, the consumption function, animal spirits and investment, liquidity preference, dynamic disequilibrium, involuntary unemployment equilibrium, and perhaps several elements in combination. Most assessments, especially those by monetarists, have accused Keynes of *underplaying* the operation of the monetary mechanism – at least in *The General Theory*, though not in his *Treatise on Money* and in earlier work.

In contrast to these partly conflicting and partly complementary expressions, though it may take time to revise the conventional judgements, we should view Keynes's novel and incisive reflections on money as the clue to his theoretical system. Implications abound for economic theory in sustaining this interpretation: to wit, that Keynes's revolutionary take-off originated in the denial of the gross substitution axiom in a modern, monetized-production economy. Of course, gross substitution is a latter-day concept, so that Keynes's disclaimer covered the thought, not the name.

1 DISEQUILIBRIUM ECONOMICS

Often it is asserted that Keynes's theory of employment was *not* revolutionary in the sense of representing a change in paradigm. Instead, the allegation is that Keynes's analysis comprises merely a specific example of a general equilibrium (GE) system which produces an underemployment solution only because Keynes stressed either: (1) errors of foresight of entrepreneurs; and/or (2) badly behaved aggregate supply and demand relationships due to wage and price 'rigidities'.

* *Journal of Post Keynesian Economics*, 2(3) (1980).

With regard to errors of foresight by entrepreneurs, the argument is that unemployment is merely a short-run 'disequilibrium' solution where the 'speed' of quantity adjustments exceeds that of price adjustment, and free market price flexibility would lead to a long-run full employment. Friedman (Friedman *et al.*, 1974, p. 16 n.), for example, cites with approval Leijonhufvud's claim that 'in the Keynesian macrosystem the Marshallian ranking of price and quantity adjustment speeds is reversed . . . The "revolutionary" elements in *The General Theory* perhaps cannot be stated in simpler terms' (Leijonhufvud, 1968, p. 52).[1] Similarly, Patinkin (1965, pp. 337–8) has averred that if market prices were flexible and could adjust by means of a *tâtonnement* process, then Keynes's theory must be 'disequilibrium economics', where, by Patinkin's definition of equilibrium, Walras's Law (i.e. the simultaneous clearing of all markets) does not apply.

2   ILL-BEHAVED FUNCTIONS

If macro demand and/or supply curves are *not* well behaved, then either:

(a) these curves do not intersect in the first quadrant, and thus 'normal' market resolution is precluded (e.g. an interest-inelastic investment function faces a similarly interest-inelastic savings function); or
(b) horizontal segments of supply and/or demand functions (due to monopolies or economic 'irrationalities') prevent the price system from working (e.g. sticky money-wages or the liquidity trap); or
(c) some systemic impediments in income flows over time constrain demand to less than full employment. Essentially, this argument is that income receipts are necessary to finance expenditures. As the former precedes the latter in time, demand curves are constrained by actual income receipts so that 'effective excess demand may be insufficient to induce price adjustment despite the obvious sufficiency of notional excess demand [to achieve full employment]' (Clower, 1965, p. 123).[2]

Of course, if Keynes's unemployment analysis depended either on erroneous expectations and ensuing 'disequilibrium' or on badly behaved supply–demand functions, then Keynes was mistaken in his 1935 letter to George Bernard Shaw, in which he saw himself 'to be writing a book on economic theory which revolutionizes . . . the way the world thinks about economic problems' (1943, p. 492). Long before Keynes wrote his *General Theory*, economists (e.g. Pigou) had often concluded that business cycles were attributable to entrepreneurial errors of optimism and pessimism; even more universal was the recognition that unemployment persisted because workers refused to lower their money-wages. Thus, unemployment, based on errors or rigidities, was a pre-Keynesian concept. Indeed, if Keynes's model merely emphasized these aspects, he contributed nothing new to economic theory.

For completeness, it should be noted that although Clower's 'constrained' demand curves concept may not appear to be a pre-Keynesian concept, it is in fact similar to Keynes's analyses of the classical doctrine of 'Supply creates its own Demand' (Keynes, 1936, pp. 25–6). For Keynes this doctrine meant that the aggregate demand function, $f(N)$, and the aggregate supply function, $\phi(N)$, were 'equal for *all* values of N, i.e. for all levels of output and employment; and that when there is an increase in $Z(= \phi(N))$ corresponding to an increase in N, $D(= f(N))$ necessarily increases by the same amount as Z' (ibid.). In other words, if $f(N) = \phi(N)$, then, when firms hire less than the full employment level of workers, income will be constrained and aggregate demand will equal supply at less than full employment. Thus, any level of income can be equilibrium one if $f(N)$ and $\phi(N)$ are equal for all levels of N; i.e. there 'is an infinite range of [equilibrium] values all equally admissible' (ibid., p. 26). Hence, if firms initially produce the full employment level of output and if $f(N) = \phi(N)$, then there will be no shortage of effective demand; i.e. there is 'no obstacle to full employment' (ibid.).

Thus Clower's construction, though it may seem to some GE theorists to obtain 'Keynesian' results, does not get to the essence of the underemployment problem of monetary economies. In a monetary, production, market-oriented economy, even if entrepreneurs hire the full employment level of workers, there can be an insufficiency of aggregate effective demand when all goods currently produced cannot be profitably sold *at any price-money wage level*. It is the prospect of possible insufficient effective demand at full employment that clearly differentiates Keynes's analysis of a monetary economy from either a general equilibrium system or Clower's model.

3 GROSS SUBSTITUTION

As judged from the title of his 1936 book, his letter to Shaw, and elsewhere, Keynes surely thought he had altered the substance of economic theory. As a trained logician he well knew that if he was to transform the way the world *thinks* about economic problems, he had to dispel one of the fundamental axioms of orthodox theory. As Keynes explicitly stated:

> If the classical theory is only applicable to the case of full employment, it is fallacious to apply it to the problems of involuntary unemployment – if there is such a thing (and who will deny it?). The classical theorists resemble Euclidean geometers in a non-Euclidean world who, discover-

ing that in experience straight lines apparently parallel often meet, rebuke the lines for not keeping straight – as the *only* remedy for the unfortunate collisions which are occurring. *Yet, in truth, there is no remedy except to throw over the axiom of parallels and to work out a non-Euclidean geometry. Something similar is required today in economics.* (Keynes, 1936, p. 16; italics added)

Which axiom did Keynes select for the rebuke and 'throw-over'? Unfortunately, in his day Keynes did not have meticulous neoclassical workers such as Hicks, Patinkin, Arrow, Debreu, Hahn, and others to spell out in exacting detail the fundamental axioms of the now standard general equilibrium analysis. Hence, in retrospect an extended, revised interpretation of his fine intuition can be made. Keynes detected the mischief as located in wage theory: he stated his obvious need to 'throw-over the second postulate of the classical doctrine' (ibid., pp. 16–17); that is, 'the utility of the wage when a given volume of labour is employed is equal to the marginal disutility of that amount of labour' (ibid., p. 5). Thanks to neoclassical writers such as Arrow and Hahn as well as the others, however, it can now be demonstrated that Keynes's jettisoning of this 'second postulate' of the classical theory of employment, which defined equilibrium in terms of the clearing of the labour market, entailed repudiation of the axiom of gross substitution (GS) as a fundamental precept of a monetary, production economy. Gross substitution can be defined as the predominance of substitution effects in the economy, with substitution influences overwhelming negative income consequences.

Arrow and Hahn have noted that gross substitution is *the* predominant sufficient condition theorists rely upon to prove the *existence, uniqueness,* and *stability* of a GE solution (Arrow and Hahn, 1971, pp. 15, 127, 215, 305). In the absence of gross substitution, some excess-demand functions may *not* exhibit downward-sloping shapes; hence, there may be no price vector that clears all markets simultaneously (Walras's Law). Furthermore, even if such a market-clearing price vector exists, starting from any given disequilibrium position, a sequential price adjustment mechanism – without the GS axiom – need not converge to a general equilibrium at all (ibid., p. 305)!

Thus, in so far as neoclassical analysis is identified with the problem of reconciling all conditional intentions of economic agents within the productive capacity of the economy,[3] the axiom of gross substitution is a fundamental building block of the system. To reject the GS axiom, therefore, is to overthrow all general equilibrium systems and to render them inapplicable to the problems which Keynes staked for his study.

4 ESSENTIAL PROPERTIES OF MONEY

Keynes, in his chapter 'Essential Properties of Interest and Money' (1936, ch. 17), declares that the *essential* properties of money (*and* any other assets that have the attribute of liquidity) are that (1) its elasticity of production and (2) its elasticity of substitution, are zero (or negligible). Because of this second essential property of money, however, Keynes must reject the neoclassical axiom of gross substitution, just as non-Euclidean geometry throws out the axiom of parallel lines. Here, rightly or wrongly, Keynes has imported a new and revolutionary way of thinking about real world economic problems that involve money and liquidity.[4]

Economists who utilize gross substitution in the logical foundations of their models (i.e. all general equilibrium theorists) are forced by the logic of their system to respond as a Euclidean geometer in the real world: on observing the persistent unemployment and inflation in prices of producible goods – the equivalent of parallel lines crashing into each other – they 'rebuke' the dual disorder in events and deplore government interference with normal market forces for the unseemly outcome. Logically, the only policy guideline that can be derived from GE systems – *if Keynes's view of the essential properties of money is relevant* – is that if only the world complied with GE logic the perverse 'accident' could not occur. But from Keynes's standpoint, models based on gross substitution are irrelevant for monetary policy, for in any model that uses the GS axiom, money does *not* matter! Consequently, if the attribute of liquidity requires the elasticity properties postulated by Keynes, then general equilibrium models must be abandoned despite their air of precise and elegant structure. Economists will have to dwell in a world where gross substitution does not permeate every economic decision and where unemployment equilibrium *and* inflation are plausible potential outcomes of well-behaved (i.e. consistent with the axioms) aggregate demand and supply parameters.

5 THE DEFINITION AND ESSENTIAL PROPERTIES OF MONEY

Any analytical method requires the tools of an unambiguous set of definitions, for controversy too often is generated by mere semantic obfuscation. Fruitful policy development impels a tidy language so both the problem and steps to its resolution can be well defined. Unfortunately, in many on-going policy debates, the concepts of money and inflation are ambiguous. [The remainder of this section was first published as part of the article, 'Money and General Equilibrium' *Economie Appliquée*, 1977, pp. 4–77. We need not repeat it here.]

6 FORWARD TRANSACTIONS

In a market-oriented economy most production transactions along the non-integrated chain of firms involve forward contracts. For example, the hiring of factor inputs (especially labour) and the purchase of unfinished materials will normally entail forward contracting if the production process is to be efficiently planned. The financing of such forward production-cost commitments (i.e. taking a 'position' in working capital goods) compels entrepreneurs to have money at hand to discharge these liabilities at one or more dates *before* the product is sold, delivered, and payment collected, and the position liquidated. Since orthodox neoclassical theory neglects the fact of contracting over calendar time in organized markets for future delivery *and* payment, the ubiquitous liquidity provision of entrepreneurs in capitalist economies is left unattended by mainstream economists in their non-monetized theory of the firm. Consequently, they are irresistible targets of the businessman's gibe: 'They never met a payroll!'

7 MONEY-WAGES AND THE PRICE LEVEL

For a decentralized market economy moving irreversibly through and towards *uncertain* calendar time, forward contracting for inputs for the production sequence is essential to the execution of efficient production plans. Moreover, with slavery and peonage illegal, *the money wage contract* is the most ubiquitous forward contract of all. Since labour hiring, and wage payments, precede the delivery of newly produced goods, it is the (average) money-wage, relative to productivity, that is the foundation upon which the price level of new goods rests. (Following Keynes, Weintraub (e.g. 1978) has been most persistent in this recognition and challenge to the Hicks–Samuelson 'Keynesian' stream.)

As Arrow and Hahn have noted:

The terms in which contracts are made matter. In particular, if money is the good in terms of which contracts are made, then the prices of goods in terms of money are of special significance. This is not the case if we consider an economy without a past and without a future. Keynes wrote that 'the importance of money essentially flows from it being a link between the present and future' to which we add that it is important also because it is a link between the past and the present. If *a serious monetary theory* comes to be written, the fact that contracts are indeed made in terms of money will be of considerable importance. (1971, pp. 356–7; italics added)

Furthermore, as Arrow and Hahn recognized, in 'a world with a past as well as a future and in which contracts are made in terms of money, no [general] equilibrium may exist' (ibid., p. 361), i.e. the presence of time-related money contracts is a sufficient condition for the possibility of nonexistence of general equilibrium.

Granted this Arrow–Hahn vision of the necessity of recognizing the importance of money-denominated contracts stretching over a period of calendar time, it follows that a 'serious monetary theory' must be based on a system of *sticky* money wages and prices, i.e. the absence of rapid and explosive movements over time, generated by a system where economic agents are willing to enter into forward contracts that limit wage and price movements over the life of such contracts. Only a contractually fixed wage and product price system permits capitalist economies to engage in time-consuming production processes; for such a system provides the sticky (meaning normal) price level of producible goods that are the basis of decisions involving future economic consequences. This was the focal point of Keynes's view on the workings of a monetary capitalist economy.

Capitalist entrepreneurs are, in theory and practice, agents who (as managers of business firms) are willing to commit themselves contractually today to the purchase of working and/or fixed capital goods in order to provide an expected flow of produced goods at specific dates in the future. Since production takes time, for the production process to be organized efficiently, contractual commitments must be entered into at the start of the production process, so that delivery of components can be made as the goods-in-process (working) capital is fabricated from basic raw materials to finished product by the use of instruments of production and labour.[5] Over the non-integrated chain of firms linking raw materials to finished consumer goods, these overlapping forward money contracts are essential to providing an orderly market, when producers have sufficient demand and money–cost information to make 'rational' decisions about time-consuming production processes that, once begun, are difficult and very costly if not impossible to interrupt (see Davidson, 1978, chs. 3 and 4).

Moreover, in a capitalist production economy organized on a money forward-contracting basis, hiring depends on entrepreneurs' being willing *and* able to finance a 'position' in working capital goods. Keynes's theory of underemployment equilibrium is therefore *simultaneously* a theory of money and liquidity and a theory of the determination of the money prices of production flows. The Keynesian Revolution was a *dual* revolution, for it not only explained why, in the real world, unemployment equilibrium could be a natural outcome of market forces, but also why, in a production monetary economy, forward money contracts (which are essential to production management decisions) require sticky money-wages and production flow prices over time. Flexible money-wages and production flow prices, rather than assuring full employment equilibrium in real world economies that organize production on a forward-contracting basis, would, whenever exogenous disturbances occurred, lead to the breakdown of capitalist production, since entrepreneurs would be unwilling and/or unable to take on the resulting potentially unlimited monetary 'positions' in working capital goods required because of price flexibility over the time interval necessary for production to occur. The existence of fixed money-wage and price contracts for forward delivery and payment is therefore a *necessary* institutional arrangement for limiting liabilities in capitalist production processes.[6]

The existence of money contracts for forward delivery *and* payment is fundamental to the liquidity and money concepts. In such a setting, changes in money-wage rates – Keynes's wage unit – determine changes in the costs of production and the price level associated with the production of goods that profit-oriented entrepreneurs are willing to undertake. The view that inflation, meaning a rising money price level of newly produced goods, is a monetary phenomenon makes logical sense only in an economy where time-oriented money contracts (especially labour hire) are basic to the organization of production activities.

8 THE ESSENTIAL ELASTICITY PROPERTIES OF MONEY

The attribute of liquidity entails that money (and all other liquid assets) possess certain 'essential properties', namely, a zero (or negligible) elasticity of production and a zero (or negligible) elasticity of substitution between such liquid assets and goods that have a high elasticity of production, i.e. that are readily producible through the exertion of labour.[7] Since the rationale for these salient properties for liquidity is developed at length elsewhere (Davidson, 1978), their implications will be summarized here.

1. To denote that the elasticity of production is zero is merely to recognize, in the language of economists, the old adage that 'money doesn't grow on trees', and hence cannot be harvested (i.e. produced) by the use of labour. Because the elasticity of production is zero, if households, for example, decide to buy less automobiles (or space vehicles) and buy more time vehicles (for liquidity) out of current income, while no one else concurrently spends more on the producible goods of our industries, then employment will decline in the automobile (space machine) industry, while the unemployed resources cannot be deflected into the production of time machines. (As Keynes noted (1936, p. 210), a decision to save is *not* a decision to order future goods.) Moreover, since the unemployed car workers will buy less goods, additional or secondary unemployment (through a multiplier process) will occur in other industries that ordinarily sell goods to car workers.

2. Since the elasticity of substitution is also zero (or negligible), as the

hypothesized demand for money (or similar financial assets) increases, households will not substitute *other producible items* for these desired time machines. The demand for liquidity is 'a bottomless sink', and when the demand for liquidity increases at the expense of the demand for goods, there is no price at which this demand will be diverted back to the products of industry.[8]

These salient elasticity properties, it should be noted, do *not* mean that the money supply is unalterable. The money supply can be expanded exogenously (i.e. by the deliberations of the central bank) or endogenously when the banking system responds to an increased demand for money; in the latter instance, when part of the public wishes to enlarge its 'positions' in capital goods and other durables (the 'real bills' doctrine).

9   HAHN ON THE ESSENTIAL PROPERTIES

Recently, Hahn has noted that 'to many economists Keynesian economics deals with important relevant problems and General Equilibrium Theory deals with no relevant problems at all. This view . . . has, alas, an element of truth' (1977, p. 25). Hahn, however, tries (vainly) to salvage the relevance of his GE research programme by simultaneously incorporating the first of Keynes's 'essential properties' of money into a general equilibrium model, while severing the property from its tie to money.

Hahn assumes an economy 'which can produce a single good by the aid of this good and labour. This good is perfectly durable if not consumed' (ibid., p. 27). He elicits underemployment equilibrium from his general equilibrium model as long as there are 'resting places for savings other than reproducible assets. In our model, this is money. But Land, as to his credit Keynes understood, would have the same consequence, and so would Old Masters. It is, therefore, not money which is required to abolish a Say's Law-like proposition that the supply of labour is the demand for goods produced by labour. Any nonreproducible asset will do' (ibid., p. 31).

Non-reproducibility alone, however, will *not* be sufficient in the real world! A second elasticity property is essential if Say's Law is to be suspended when income earners divert demand to absorb the non-reproducible good (say, Marshall's stones) for liquidity purposes in supplanting the durable producible good (say, furniture). As stones rise in price, if furniture is a substitute (as both Friedman and Tobin explicitly suppose in their portfolio balance approach to wealth holding, and the gross substitution maxim of Hahn's GE model requires), then the increased demand for stones spills over into a furniture demand. The greater the *elasticity of substitution* between stones and furniture, the smaller the necessary price rise of stones to resuscitate Say's Law in Hahn's model. Because Hahn has injected only the first of Keynes's elasticity properties, his analysis of unemployment equilibrium is flawed.

Money, unlike the non-reproducible assets of Hahn's general equilibrium model, possesses a second elasticity property. 'The second differential of money is that it has an elasticity of substitution equal, or nearly equal, to zero . . . Thus not only is it impossible to turn more labour on to producing money . . . but money is a bottomless sink for purchasing power when the demand for it increases, since there is no value for it at which demand is diverted – as to slop over into a demand for other things' (Keynes, 1936, p. 231).

In a world of uncertainty where the institution of forward contracting, in money terms, for labour and other materials is an essential concomitant of production decisions, a money that carries these two elasticity properties enhances the expectations of sticky efficiency wages (Keynes, 1936, p. 238; Davidson, 1978, chs. 6, 9). In combination, these properties, and real world contracting institutions and economic organization, can inhibit neoclassical 'natural market forces' from assuring a full employment equilibrium (Keynes, 1936, p. 235).

Explicit acceptance of the second elasticity property by Hahn, however, would *violate* the gross substitution axiom. Consequently, there is an elemental logical incompatibility between the 'serious monetary theory' advanced by Keynes and the neoclassical general equilibrium analysis of Hahn (and Friedman and Tobin).

10   THE KEYNESIAN REVOLUTION

The 'revolutionary' aspect in Keynes thus originates in his association of money, *and liquidity*, with essential properties that dislodge the axiom of gross substitution as a building block for analysing an organized forward money contract, production economy. Since the money-wage contract is the most ubiquitous of all forward contracts, the money-wage relative to productivity is the anchor to which the general level of reproducible goods prices is tied.

Since gross substitution is an essential axiom of general equilibrium theory, it follows that Hicks 'shunted the car of economic science to a wrong line' when he wrote

I believe I have had the fortune to come upon a method of analysis which is applicable to a wide variety of economic problems . . . The method of General Equilibrium . . . was specially designed to exhibit the economic system as a whole . . . [with this method] we shall thus be able to see just why it is that Mr Keynes reaches different results from earlier economists on crucial matters of social policy. (1939, pp. 1–4)

After a 'mere' thirty-two years of rigorous and profound general equilibrium theorizing, Arrow and Hahn have finally conceded that a serious monetary theory had to be identified with money contracts (1971, pp. 356–7) and that, in a contract economy, a general equilibrium model may tumble (ibid., p. 361)! This same view, however, was expressed by Keynes on the first page of the text of his *Treatise* (1930, vol. 1, p. 3), where he specifies the coexistence of contracts with the institution of money, and in chapter 17 of his *General Theory* (1936), where he explicitly associates liquidity with properties that violate the gross substitution 'axiom'.

11   PRICE-LEVEL POLICY IMPLICATIONS

Events have not stood still in the last fifty years. The ascent of labour power under full employment policies, and the bulge of multinational corporations since the Second World War, have spawned problems that, by 1970, were menacing the basic monetary institutions of free market economies and posing the first major crisis for capitalist economies since the Great Depression. Aggravated by the economic power of OPEC (Organization of Petroleum Exporting Countries), the concomitant rapid disruptions in national and international monetary flows, as well as asset redistribution, jeopardize the viability of monetary institutions that developed slowly for a more leisurely environment. Bretton Woods exchange rate agreements have dissolved; dirty floats have evolved – to nobody's satisfaction. Mainstream neoclassical monetary theorizing does not meet the Arrow–Hahn criteria for a serious monetary theory; moreover, it has little advice to proffer on how the monetary framework can survive and adapt to the strains, except to advocate a steady hand at the money supply tiller for the long run – despite Keynes's disparagement of such 'theory'. Though we die and the system writhes, the monetary waters will at last be calm, claim the neoclassicists.

Going beyond the implications for underemployment 'equilibrium' in the 'essential' properties of money, Keynes never missed a chance to stress the interrelations between the money supply and the money-wage unit (or, in a larger context, the cost unit including imports) for determining the price level. His monetary analysis led him to this penetrating conclusion, overlooked too often: that 'money-wages should be more stable than real wages is a [necessary] condition of the system possessing inherent stability' (Keynes, 1936, p. 239).

In both the *Treatise* and *General Theory*, Keynes emphasized the money-wage/money supply nexus. He noted that if we have control of both the earnings system (incomes policy) and the monetary system (monetary policy), and if we can control the pace of investment, we can 'stabilize the purchasing power of money, its labour power, or anything else – without running the risk of setting up social and economic frictions or of causing waste' (Keynes, 1930, vol. 1, p. 169). Moreover, 'if there are strong social or political forces causing spontaneous changes in the money-rates of efficiency wages [or in a modern context, energy costs], the control of the price level may pass beyond the power of the banking system' (ibid., vol. 2, p. 351).

Having come full circle in economic theory to the point where eminent general equilibrium theorists in the 1970s reach conclusions basic to Keynes's writings of the 1930s, economists may be inspired to nudge our theories ahead by ejecting the gross substitution axiom from macroeconomics. Once the money wage contract is sighted as the fulcrum upon which the price level of producibles turns in both the short and the long run, much of the opaqueness regarding the confluence of incomes and monetary policies will evaporate.

Notes

1. My 1974 article demonstrated that relative speeds of adjustment were not critical to the Keynesian Revolution. Leijonhufvud, aware of my paper before publication, conceded that 'it is *not* correct to attribute Keynes a general reversal of the Marshallian ranking of relative price and quantity adjustments . . . most of the recent writing on Keynes' theory including my own, insist on analyzing it in a Walrasian perspective . . . But Keynes was, of course, a price theoretical Marshallian, and . . . ignoring this fact simply will not do' (Davidson, 1974, pp. 164–5).
2. Thus, for Clower (at least) unemployment occurred because there was no market mechanism, in a monetary economy, to *coordinate* full employment hiring decisions with the full employment *purchasing* decisions that would then be forthcoming. Apparently, in a Clower context, if entrepreneurs hire the full employment level of workers, then notional and actual household income receipts would be equal, and actual purchases would equal desired (notional) demand at full employment. Sufficiency of *current* effective demand for the product of workers, and full employment, could be maintained.
   Interestingly, although Clower declares that he cannot find any passage in Keynes to indicate that the latter utilized the 'dual decision hypothesis' of income-constrained demand curves, either Keynes had this 'hypothesis at the back of his mind, or most of the General Theory is nonsense' (Clower, 1965, p. 120).
3. And if GE is not involved with the reconciling of all conditional intentions, then what is the function of the market system in GE analysis?
4. 'It is, however, interesting to consider how far those characteristics of money as we know it . . . are bound up with money being the standard in which debts and wages are usually fixed . . . The convenience of holding assets in the same standard as that in which future liabilities may fall due . . . is obvious' (Keynes, 1936, pp. 236–67).
5. As *The Economist* (10–16 March 1979, p. 12, Survey) noted, the Japanese car industry became an important world force when Toyota

   implemented its radical production control system, known as the 'just in time' method. This process was quickly copied by the rest of Japan's motor industry. It likens each manufacturing stage to a customer . . . The customer collects his goods in the precise quantity and at the exact time he needs them. The component producer, which may be part of the same company, thus has an orderly market and so can adjust its production (using the same approach) accordingly.

6. Only in an economic system that organizes all production and distribution on a purely communal basis (e.g. a monastery or a kibbutz) so that (a) no factor inputs require payment *before* the completion of the production gestation period and (b) the initial division of the product is determined by some traditional non-market formula, will full employment of resources in the production process be assured. Of course, in such economies money is not necessary for either production or distribution.

7. 'The attribute of "liquidity" is by no means independent of these two characteristics. For it is unlikely that an asset, of which the supply can be easily increased or the desire for which can be easily diverted by a change in relative price will possess the attribute of "liquidity" in the minds of owners of wealth' (Keynes, 1936, p. 241).

8. In my published dispute with Professor Friedman he remarks that his theoretical framework specifically assumes that *easily reproducible commodities are good substitutes for money* (Friedman *et al.*, 1974, pp. 27–9, 107–10).

References

Arrow, K. S. and F. H. Hahn (1971), *General Competitive Analysis* (San Francisco: Holden Day).

Clower, R. W. (1965), 'The Keynesian Revolution: A Theoretical Appraisal', in R. H. Hahn and F. P. R. Brechling (eds), *Theory of Interest Rates* (London: Macmillan).

Davidson, P. (1974), 'Disequilibrium Market Adjustment: Marshall Revisited', *Economic Inquiry*, 12. (Chapter 34 in this volume).

Davidson, P. (1978), *Money and the Real World*, 2nd edn (London: Macmillan).

Friedman, M. (1974), *et al.*, *Milton Friedman's Monetary Framework: A Debate with His Critics*, ed. by R. A. Gordon (Chicago: University of Chicago Press).

Hahn, F. H. (1977), 'Keynesian Economics and General Equilibrium Theory: Reflections on Some Current Debates', in G. C. Harcourt (ed.), *Microeconomic Foundations of Macroeconomics* (London: Macmillan).

Hicks, J. R. (1939), *Value and Capital* (Oxford: Oxford University Press).

Keynes, J. M. (1930), *A Treatise on Money*, Vols. 1 and 2 (London: Macmillan).

Keynes, J. M. (1936), *The General Theory of Employment, Interest and Money* (New York: Harcourt).

Keynes, J. M. (1943), *The Collected Works of John Maynard Keynes*, Vols. XIII and XIV (London: Macmillan).

Leijonhufvud, A. (1968), *On Keynesian Economics and the Economics of Keynes* (Oxford: Oxford University Press).

Leijonhufvud, A. (1974), 'Keynes's Employment Function: A Comment', *History of Political Economy*, p. 5.

Patinkin, D. (1965), *Money Interest and Prices*, 2nd edn (New York: Harper & Row).

Weintraub, S. (1978), *Capitalism's Inflation and Unemployment Crisis* (Reading, Mass.: Addison-Wesley).

40 On Bronfenbrenner and Mainstream Views of the 'Essential Properties' of Money: A Reply*

> In economics you cannot convict your opponent of error – you can only *convince* him of it. And, even if you are right, you cannot convince him, if there is a defect in your powers of persuasion and exposition or if his head is already so filled with contrary notions that he cannot catch the clues to your thought which you are trying to throw at him. (Keynes, 1973, p. 470)

Professor Bronfenbrenner graciously accepted my invitation to provide a critique of the 'essential properties' views of money. His published comments[1] parallel several other reactions received in correspondence from other mainstream economists; they also overlap Friedman's criticism in our earlier published debate (Friedman *et al.*, 1974).

Bronfenbrenner's main criticism is that the elasticities of production and substitution of money 'are generally *not* zero, and cannot . . . be made zero by any redefinition . . . [for] there is at least potential commodity money [and] there are both near-moneys and money substitutes . . . A "monetary" reformulation of international economic theory is now based precisely on substitution between domestic and foreign moneys, and likewise between assets denominated in domestic and foreign moneys.'

In awareness of this 'monetary reformulation of international economic theory', I have been a small contributor to the literature (see Miles and Davidson, 1978). The fact that foreign money and other liquid assets (i.e. durables not readily reproducible by the exertion of labour but easily resaleable in organized *and* orderly spot markets) are good substitutes for domestic money is *not* inconsistent with Keynes's elasticity properties view of money. In fact, substitutability between money and liquid assets (*but not illiquid real durables*) is the essence of Keynes's liquidity preference theory. I therefore find it hard to see why Bronfenbrenner believes that the substitution of foreign moneys (or other liquid assets) for domestic liquid time machines (as long as there are orderly spot markets for exchange conversion) negates the zero substitution elasticity property. The question

* *Journal of Post Keynesian Economics*, 2 (Spring 1980).

of substitutability entails using liquid assets that have a negligible elasticity of production as temporary abodes of purchasing power (time machines) *vis-á-vis* reproducible durables. I have argued, however, that when the demand for liquidity rises, 'households will not substitute *other producible items* for these desired time machines'. Moreover, as Hahn (1977, p. 31) has conceded, as long as savings find 'resting places' in non-reproducible assets, Say's Law is broken and neoclassicism's claim that flexible prices assure labour market clearing is rejected!

Thus the real cutting edge of Keynes's Revolution lies in the 'essential properties' approach to liquidity. Can substitutes for money as a means of contractual payment, and a liquidity time machine, really be easily reproducible, i.e. possess a linear and homogenous production function?

Bronfenbrenner suggests that gold (which is producible by labour) can be money and that some union leaders even want wages paid in gold; moreover, since 1977 the gold clause in contracts has been 'restored to enforceability'. Implicit in this suggestion is that the essential properties do not pertain to gold; of course, gold was money before the Supreme Court abrogated the gold clause. Gold, however, is not easily reproducible and hence does not violate the negligible elasticity of production property.

1   GOLD VERSUS PEANUT MONEY

Friedman has also used gold as a counterexample to the elasticity properties approach; he goes even further in arguing that actual money can be a 'commodity capable of being produced by the exertion of labour, often at roughly constant costs' (Friedman, *et al.*, 1974, p. 153).

Against such 'commodity money' claims, I would insist that any developed monetary economy that organizes production on a forward money contract basis (as opposed, for example, to a system of production organized on the basis of tradition and custom, such as feudalism) will, if a 'commodity' money is adopted, utilize as money something which is *not* easily reproducible *within its boundaries* either because (a) the commodity is subject to rapidly diminishing returns in production, or (b) there are institutional arrangements to control its supply.

Why is it that in developed contractual production economies, if a commodity money is used, the society typically utilizes rare metals such as gold or silver as money?[2] Why not peanuts? After all, every student of general equilibrium knows that peanuts will do the job as *numéraire* as well as anything else. Certainly there must be some finance minister somewhere who received a Ph.D. from Chicago, or MIT, or Duke, or some other prestigious university where general equilibrium is the economist's touchstone. Why does such a minister not have the courage of his professors' convictions and use peanuts as the money of his economy?

If only peanuts (which are easily reproducible) were money, then the logical foundations of neoclassical economics would apply to a peanut money economy, for full employment would always be predestined, in the long run, as the unemployed could always be put to work in the peanut fields. Of course, if peanuts were money, or even a good substitute for it, then President Carter might have done better to name brother Billy rather than Paul Volcker as chairman of the Fed.

2 IS LONG-RUN FULL EMPLOYMENT EQUILIBRIUM INEVITABLE?

Friedman has characterized my 'essential properties' approach as follows: 'He [Davidson] appears to *start* from the proposition that there does not exist a long-run equilibrium position characterized by full employment, and then try to *deduce* the empirical characteristics of money (and other elements of the economy) from that proposition' (Friedman, *et al.*, 1974, p. 154). If the word 'necessarily' is inserted before the word 'exist', and 'real world' before 'long-run', then I believe the amended statement is a fair representation of my position. Surely, it should be more desirable to start from such a view rather than to begin, as general equilibrium theorists must, with the supposition that there exists a full employment solution that is the necessary long-run equilibrium position for real world economies (organizing production on a money contract basis) and then try to deduce the characteristics of a system which assure that unfettered market activity will achieve this outcome. Unfortunately, if the neoclassical proposition is adopted as the starting point, then observed real world unemployment and stagflation phenomena can only be explained as due to frictions, or price rigidities, or short-run phenomena caused by slowly changing (adaptive? rational?) expectational reactions; over the long run a state of economic bliss will be attained. (The latter, of course, is not a conclusion of the analysis but merely a reiteration of the initial supposition of neoclassical economics.)

Keynes would not deny the existence or importance of frictions, monopoly, union power, and wage rigidities, or even slowly changing expectations. Nevertheless, Keynes did argue that these were complications and aggravating factors; they were not the central feature of the logic of underemployment equilibrium. Even if the complications are assumed away, Keynes specifically argued that, if the economy is at less than full employment (with, say, a price level of p_e in Bronfenbrenner's diagram), then a cut in money-wages (and therefore a shift down of the S curve in his diagram) would *not*, *ceteris paribus*, in either the short run *or* the long run, have a *direct* tendency to enlarge employment (as from Y_e to Y_f in Bronfenbrenner's diagram) (Keynes, 1936, pp. 260–2).

In other words, Bronfenbrenner's no. 4829 re-examination of Keynes was specifically refuted by Keynes; every drop of the S curve induces an *additional* decline in Bronfenbrenner's D curve!

Like Samuelson's neoclassical synthesis, and the more recent rational expectation hypothesis of monetarists, the Bronfenbrenner view is so cluttered by neoclassical vestiges as to inhibit recognition of the primacy of Keynes's essential properties of money and liquid assets. These properties together with the ubiquitous liquidity needs are the logical foundations of Keynes's revolutionary monetary and employment theory.

Post Keynesians are indebted to Professor Bronfenbrenner for his candour and willingness to express his views and open a dialogue that can have a profound influence on the development of the economics discipline.

Notes

1. His critique was actually based on an earlier draft of my 'Dual-faceted Nature' article. I believe, however, that an identical analytical structure involving the elasticity properties of money is central to the earlier draft.
2. Why did the residents of Yap use stone money rather than money made from leaves?

References

Friedman, M. *et al.* (1974), *Milton Friedman's Monetary Framework: A Debate with His Critics* (Chicago: University of Chicago Press).

Hahn, F. H. (1977), 'Keynesian Economics and General Equilibrium Theory: Reflections on Some Current Debates', in G. C. Harcourt (ed.), *Microeconomic Foundations of Macroeconomics* (London: Macmillan).

Keynes, J. M. (1936), *The General Theory of Employment, Interest and Money* (New York: Harcourt).

Keynes, J. M. (1973), *Collected Works of John Maynard Keynes*, Vol. XIII (London: Macmillan).

Miles, M. A. and P. Davidson (1978), 'Monetary Policy, Regulation and International Adjustments', *Economies et societés*.

41 The Dubious Labour Market Analysis in Meltzer's Restatement of Keynes's *Theory**

Allan Meltzer has given the economics profession an interesting and alternative monetarist perspective to Keynes's *General Theory* (Meltzer, 1981).[1] Although Professor Meltzer generously acknowledges our useful exchange on an earlier draft of his fascinating paper, there still remain many unresolved analytical disagreements regarding Keynes's theory. Some of these differences may be questions of interpretation, hence open to differing views, but there is at least one vital relationship in Meltzer's model that deserves an airing for Meltzer's version is (a) inconsistent with Keynes's model and (b) logically inconsistent within Meltzer's own restatement of Keynes's theory. The disagreement turns on the specification of the demand for labour function.

1 THE LABOUR MARKET AND THE WAGE VARIABLE

Meltzer marshals convincing evidence that the 'main conclusions of *The General Theory* do not depend on rigid money wages' (ibid., p. 52). Moreover, Meltzer quotes Keynes's 1939 statement that *The General Theory* model is applicable even 'if we treat *real* wages as substantially constant in the short period' (Keynes, 1939, pp. 42–3; italics added). Meltzer also argued that constant real wages at any equilibrium level of employment less than full employment is not contradictory with *The General Theory* model (Meltzer, 1981, p. 51, n. 28).

Meltzer's eight equation model which represents 'a condensed restatement of Keynes' theory' (ibid., p. 52), however, is *not* consistent with the stable *real wage* argument which Meltzer affirmed just one page earlier. In his equational model, the demand for labour function equation (6) is written in the traditional neoclassical (non-Keynesian) form which makes real wages the independent variable determining the level of employment demanded, i.e.:

$$N^d = f\left(\frac{W}{P}\right)$$

* *Journal of Economic Literature*, 21, 1983, pp. 52–6.

where W is the money-wage and P is the price level. If, however, Meltzer accepts Keynes's claim that a *constant* real wage is compatible with under-employment equilibrium, then equation (6) must imply that the demand for labour is infinitely elastic (in real wage and employment space), independent of the level of autonomous real spending by government and investing firms. Thus, contrary to Keynes's framework, changes in the aggregate demand function do not change the demand for labour function in Meltzer's restatement.[2] Since, in Meltzer's model, equation (7), which represents the supply of labour, is written as

$$N^s = g(W) \quad \text{or} \quad g(W, P)$$

and is therefore strictly a function of nominal wages, *or* nominal wages and nominal prices as *separate* independent variables, while the demand for labour can be infinitely elastic with respect to the real wage, Meltzer cannot demonstrate that this model will determine a stable and unique labour market equilibrium regardless of the level of employment. Something is obviously amiss in this 'restatement of Keynes's theory' for Keynes believed his *General Theory* included the possible existence of a *stable and unique underemployment equilibrium* (Keynes, 1936, pp. 26, 30).

What Meltzer and most other neoclassical interpreters (e.g. Don Patinkin, Paul Samuelson, Robert Solow) of Keynes do not comprehend is that while Keynes accepted the first postulate of orthodox theory, i.e. at the *equilibrium* level of employment, the wage is equal to (or a function of) the marginal product of labour (ibid., p. 5), Keynes did *not* accept Meltzer's interpretation (1981, p. 53) that the demand for labour function is derived from a standard (aggregate) production function. In other words, Keynes would accept the view that the marginal productivity of labour function was, in Patinkin's (1965, pp. 391–2, 396) terminology, a market equilibrium curve which specifies the real wage outcome for any given market equilibrium level of employment and degree of monopoly (or degree of competition as Keynes states on p. 245 of his *General Theory*) but Keynes rejected the notion of a marginal product curve as the demand for labour function.[3] (For a fuller discussion of why the marginal product of labour curve is *not* the demand for labour function in a monetary economy see Davidson, 1967, and Thomas Tuchscherer, 1979).

The difficulty with Meltzer's equational system emerges if we focus on Keynes's early chapters of *The General Theory*. As Meltzer notes, 'Keynes discusses a more restricted solution in which the price level is constant, throughout most of the first seventeen chapters [of The General Theory]' (1981, p. 54). If, however, P is fixed and independent of the level of employment in these chapters, *and* if the money wage is fixed as well, and if the *real* wage is (or can be) stable for any given short period level of equilibrium employment, what is the role of Meltzer's demand for labour function, equation (6), where $N^d = f\left(\dfrac{W}{P}\right)$ in the first 17 chapters of Keynes's *General Theory*?

If real wages can be unchanged over a relevant range of employment levels, then in Meltzer's system there are no decreasing returns to labour in that range and labour's marginal product curve (MP_L) must be perfectly elastic in the $\left(\dfrac{W}{P}\right)$ versus N quadrant. Simultaneously, Meltzer's labour supply equation must also be assumed to be perfectly elastic in $\left(\dfrac{W}{P}\right)$ versus N space over the relevant range of employment in these early chapters of *The General Theory* whenever, as Meltzer suggests, W and P are assumed constants. Consequently, given Meltzer's interpretation of these early chapters, the MP_L and Meltzer's N^s functions are *either* (a) coincident over a relevant range of employment values and therefore any underemployment equilibrium is *not* unique, *or* (b) parallel to each other in real wage and employment space and hence no underemployment equilibrium exists. In either case (a) or (b) of Meltzer's system, the results are *not* compatible with Keynes's claim that his analysis could demonstrate the existence *and* uniqueness of a stable equilibrium at less than full employment.[4] Meltzer argues that 'Keynes relied on wage inflexibility to explain why output fluctuates' (Meltzer, 1981, p. 49) – at least until chapter 19.[5] But earlier, Meltzer declares that money-wage rigidity is not 'the central tenet on which the *General Theory* stands or falls' (ibid., p. 52). Hence, any restatement of Keynes's general demand for labour function should comprehend *both* the fixed and variable wage (money and real) cases. Meltzer's equational restatement should – almost a half century after Keynes – be able to encompass fixed as well as variable wages and prices. Can Meltzer's labour demand function, where real wages is the independent variable, and his labour supply function, where money-wages *or* money-wages and the price level are *separate* independent variables, assure a unique, stable labour market equilibrium when wages (*real* and money) are fixed *and independent of the level of effective demand*? The confused and confusing aspect of Meltzer's treatment comes from relying on real wages as the independent variable in his labour demand function and an inchoate mix for his labour supply function.

Keynes devotes chapter 20 in *The General Theory* to the employment function. 'The object of the employment function being to relate the effective demand measured in terms of the [nominal] wage unit . . . with the amount of employment' (Keynes, 1936, p. 280). Using this employment function concept, a demand for labour function in money wage and employment space (or given the degree of monopoly and productivity relations in real wage and employment space) can be derived from a locus of effective demand points (Davidson and Smolensky, 1964, ch. 11; Weintraub, 1958, ch. 6, 7). This is not the place to restate in complete detail this Post Keynesian analysis of labour markets which provides *a general theory of employment* in a monetary economy. Interested readers, however, should be aware that there exists a restatement of Keynes's theory which can provide an underemployment equilibrium whether wages (money, real) are fixed or not and is fully compatible with the entire corpus of *The General Theory*.

Some simple diagrams at this stage can illustrate compatibility of this Post Keynesian approach with the keystone of Keynes's model – *The Principle of Effective Demand* (chapter 3) and encourage the reader to explore the basic analysis elsewhere (Weintraub, 1958; Davidson and Smolensky, 1964).

In chapter 3, Keynes summarizes his effective demand analysis when he states:

> the volume of employment is not determined by the marginal disutility of labour measured in terms of real wages, except in so far as the supply of labour available at a given real wage sets a *maximum* level of employment. The propensity to consume and the rate of new investment determine between them the volume of employment. (1936, p. 30)

Thus, given technique, the stock of capital, the degree of monopoly or competition, etc. (ibid., p. 245) an aggregate supply function relating proceeds, either in money wage units (Z_w in Figure 41.1a) or in nominal units (Z in Figure 41.1b), can be expressed as a function of employment (ibid., pp. 25–6). Against this Z function an aggregate demand function (D_w in wage units in Figure 41.1a or D in nominal units in Figure 41.1b) can be derived given the propensity to consume and the rate of investment (ibid., pp. 25, 29, 30). The intersection of the aggregate supply and demand curves (pt E_w in Figure 41.1a and E in Figure 41.1b) is defined by Keynes (p. 25) as the *effective demand* which determines the equilibrium level of employment N_1 in the appropriate Figures 41.1a and 41.1b.

Figure 41.2 draws the market equilibrium curve (MP_L) relating real wages and employment as either perfectly elastic over the relevant range if the MP_L is constant (Figure 41.2a) or declining throughout (Figure 41.2b), if there are diminishing returns to labour. In these figures, N^s is Keynes's labour supply relationship which follows from Keynes's 'proposition that labour is always in a position to determine what real wage shall correspond to *full* employment, i.e. the *maximum* quantity of employment which is compatible with a given real wage' (Keynes, 1936, p. 12). The corresponding N_1 employment level associated with effective demand of E_w in Figure 41.1 is determined at point A on Figure 41.2a or 41.2b (as the case may be) and hence the market equilibrium real wage will be w_r^1, while the full or

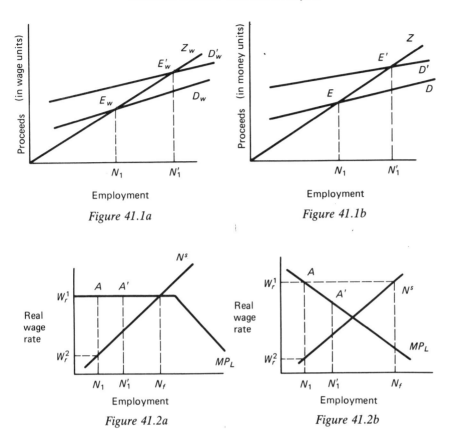

Figure 41.1a

Figure 41.1b

Figure 41.2a

Figure 41.2b

maximum employment level associated with a real wage of w_r^1 is given by N_f in Figure 41.2a (or 41.2b).

Keynes would describe this situation as follows (ibid., p. 30): 'If the propensity to consume and the rate of new investment result in a deficient effective demand, the actual level of employment will fall short of the supply of labour potentially available at the existing real wage $[N_1 < N_f]$, and the equilibrium real wage will be *greater* than the marginal disutility of the equilibrium level of employment $[w_r^1 > w_r^2]$.' If we then hypothesize an arbitrary (exogenous) change in aggregate demand from D_w to D_w' in Figure 41.1a (or D to D' in Figure 41.1b) then *ceteris paribus* the new equilibrium level of employment is N_1', the economy will be at A' rather than A on the market equilibrium (MP_L) curve and real wages either are constant (Figure 41.2a) or falling (Figure 41.2b) depending on whether there are decreasing returns to labour or not. Thus, a sufficient exogenous increase in aggregate demand can always move the point A' along the market equilibrium curve (MP_L) to the point where it intersects the N^s curve to obtain a full employment equilibrium; while if there is no change in D_w (or Z_w) then, *ceteris paribus*, the economy can languish at N_1 indefinitely whether money wages and/or prices are variable or not. This is the essence of Keynes's analysis.

It is obvious from this analysis, that if the economy is stuck at a less than full employment equilibrium such as N_1, then a reduction in money-wages in a flexible wage economy will, *ceteris paribus*, increase the level of employment *only if* it induces an increase in the consumption and/or investment components of aggregate demand in wage units (D_w) in Figure 41.1a. (By construction, money-wage changes cannot, *ceteris paribus*, affect the aggregate supply function [Z_w] in wage units.) Thus, Keynes's obvious conclusion: what is required is an increase in the aggregate demand function (D_w) in Figure 41.1a to expand an economy stuck at an underemployment equilibrium. As a practical matter Keynes could then explain why falling money-wages were not likely to produce any significant increase in the aggregate demand function in terms of wage units (Keynes, 1936, chapter 19) while there were other more efficacious methods (e.g. fiscal policy) to stimulate expansion. Moreover, in this model, it is clear that the real wage is, (given productivity and competitive conditions), determined by the equilibrium level of employment and not vice versa.

2   CONCLUSION

Meltzer's use of the orthodox, perfunctory, labour demand function (which may have some relevance in a non-monetary economy) is not a valid restatement of Keynes's general theory of employment. The road-block for mainstream neoclassical economic analysis of real world problems of employment and inflation has been the feckless use of the first derivative of aggregate production functions to denote the demand curve for labour for entrepreneurial economies which use the institutions of money and money contracts to organize productive activities in trying to cope with a world of uncertainty. Keynes's supply-side blade must be compatible with the Keynesian aggregate demand blade, if Keynes's theory – which invoked Marshall's scissors imagery – is to cut a correct pattern to explain real world employment–inflation problems. The marginal product–labour demand approach (which underlies the aggregate supply-side of goods in all *neoclassical* models) is simply incompatible with Keynes's analysis of the aggregate demand for goods in a monetary, entrepreneurial economy. The Post Keynesian theory of labour demand developed in S. Weintraub, 1958, and in Davidson and Smolensky, 1964, is, at least, consistent with the theory of effective demand in Keynes's *General Theory*.

Notes

1. In many respects Meltzer's views are, in my opinion, superior to Milton Friedman's monetarist perspective on Keynes's theory as he presented it (Friedman, 1974, pp. 15–40, 132–4, 148–57, 168–77).
2. This has always created difficulties for neoclassical interpretations of Keynes's model. Patinkin (1965), for example, insists that Meltzer's labour demand curve, $N_D = f\left(\dfrac{W}{P}\right)$ 'does not describe the actual behaviour of firms' (p. 321) and urged that we 'free ourselves of the mental habit . . . of seeing only the points *on* the demand and supply curves' (ibid., p. 323). Instead, Patinkin invoked a 'force majeure' to coerce firms off this so-called labour demand curve (ibid.). The correct diagramatics, however, do not require an overpowering or divine force to compel a correct analysis.
3. As demonstrated below Keynes (1936, p. 17) insisted that employment is determined by effective demand – i.e. the intersection of the aggregate supply and demand functions for goods. He did not deny that once the employment level is so determined, then 'the real wage earned by a unit of labour has a unique (inverse) correlation with the volume of employment. Thus, *if* employment increases, then, in the short period, the reward per unit of labour must . . . decline . . . This is simply the obverse of . . . working subject to decreasing returns.' Thus Keynes argued that if the equilibrium employment level increased in the face of diminishing returns, then real wages decline according to the market equilibrium curve $\dfrac{W}{P} = \phi(N)$ – which is the inverse of Meltzer's equation (6).
4. On page 26 of *The General Theory*, Keynes specifically rejects 'Say's law, that the aggregate demand price of output as a whole is equal to its aggregate supply price for *all* volumes of output' (italics added), i.e. that output and employment equilibrium is *not* unique. Instead he argues that if Say's law is not true then the uniqueness of underemployment equilibrium theory 'remains to be written', while on p. 30 Keynes summarizes how 'the economic system may find itself in *stable* equilibrium with N at a [unique] level below full employment' (italics added).
5. Early in his paper, Meltzer suggests he agrees with Roy Weintraub's view that 'Keynes's use of fixed wages prior to chapter 19 is an expositional device' (Meltzer, 1981, p. 49, n. 25).

References

Davidson, P. (1967), 'A Keynesian View of Patinkin's Theory of Employment', *Economic Journal*, 77 (September), pp. 559–78.
Davidson, P. and E. Smolensky (1964), *Aggregate Supply and Demand Analysis* (New York: Harper & Row).
Friedman, M. *et al.*, (1974), *Milton Friedman's Monetary Framework: A Debate With His Critics*, edited by Robert J. Gordon (Chicago: University of Chicago Press).

Keynes, J. M. (1936), *The General Theory of Employment, Interest and Money* (New York: Harcourt).

Keynes, J. M. (1939), 'Relative Movements of Real Wages and Output', *Economic Journal*, 49 (March), pp. 34–51.

Meltzer, A. H. (1981), 'Keynes's *General Theory*: A Different Perspective', *Journal of Economic Literature*, 19(1), pp. 34–64.

Patinkin, D. (1965), *Money, Interest, and Prices*, 2nd edn (New York: Harper & Row).

Tuchscherer, T. (1979), 'Keynes's Model and the Keynesians: A Synthesis', *J. Post Keynesian Econ.*, (Summer), *1*(4), pp. 96–109.

Weintraub, S. (1958), *An Approach to the Theory of Income Distribution* (Philadelphia: Chilton).

42 The Marginal Product Curve Is Not the Demand Curve for Labour and Lucas's Labour Supply Function Is Not the Supply Curve for Labour in the Real World*

In attempting to explain their views about recent levels of unemployment in the United Kingdom, Messrs Maynard and Rose (1983) mistakenly argue that the marginal product of labour curve (hereafter MP_L) is the macro demand curve for labour in a Keynesian macroanalytical system. They claim that Brothwell (1982) has not comprehended that their analysis is based on a downward shifting labour demand (net marginal product) curve juxtaposed upon a constant labour supply (real wage) function. It is the shift of this labour demand function (and not the slope of the MP_L curve) which they claim demonstrates an unambiguous decline in the demand price for labour.

In an article (Davidson, 1983), I demonstrated why Meltzer's (1981) restatement of Keynes's *General Theory* foundered on the mistaken notion that the MP_L is the macro demand curve for labour. Professor Brothwell in the previous article correctly suggests that Maynard and Rose, in the context of the open economy, make a similar error.

Since neoclassical theorists continue to perpetuate this fallacious interpretation of the MP_L I think it would be useful to reiterate why the MP_L is *not* the macro labour demand curve in any macrosystem based on Keynes's analytical structure. It is important not only to demonstrate that the Maynard–Rose analysis is faulty, and hence leads to wrong policy conclusions, but even more importantly, to demonstrate (i) why other modern macro-neoclassical theorists such as Patinkin (1965, 1976, 1977) and Barro and Grossman (1976) are incorrect in their off-marginal product curve analysis of unemployment (as a disequilibrium) phenomena, and finally (ii) to show why the Lucas-type (1983) labour supply analysis, which

* *Journal of Post Keynesian Economics*, 6(1) (1983).

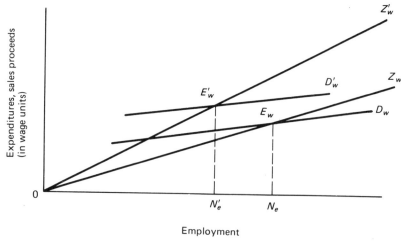

Figure 42.1

has been incorporated in most recent neoclassical models, is logically incompatible with a Keynes's real world monetary analysis. Until we get our theory of employment demand and supply logically correct, economists are unlikely to provide useful guidelines for employment policy.

In Keynes's *General Theory* (1936, pp. 25–6), given technique, the stock of capital, the degree of competition, etc., there is an aggregate supply function relating sales proceeds in money-wage units[1] which entrepreneurs expect to receive for any employment-hiring offered by entrepreneurs (Z_w in Figure 42.1). This Z_w function is derived from the profit-maximizing-hiring functions of firms (see Davidson and Smolensky, 1964, ch. 9; Weintraub, 1958, ch. 2). Against this Z_w function, an aggregate demand function relating planned expenditures in wage units to employment (D_w in Figure 42.1) can be derived given the propensity to consume and the rate of investment. (In an expanded model, D_w would consist of the propensity to consume domestically produced goods, the rate of investment and government expenditures on domestic output, and the rate of export sales – all in wage units.) The intersection of the aggregate supply and demand curves (E_w) is defined by Keynes (1936, p. 25) as the *effective demand which determines the equilibrium level of employment N_e.*

In Keynes's analysis the net marginal product of labour (MP_L) is, in Patinkin's (1965, pp. 391–2) terminology, a market equilibrium curve which specifies the real wage outcome associated with any given equilibrium level of employment *as determined by the point of effective demand.* In other words, once the equilibrium level of output is determined, given the conditions of physical productivity, the degree of competition, etc., MP_L shows the resulting real wage, i.e.

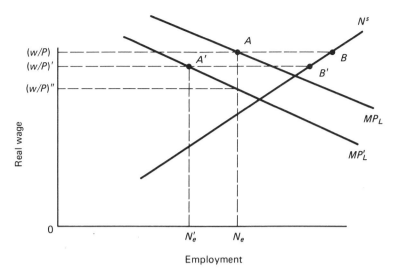

Figure 42.2

$$(w/P) = MP_L = f_1(m, g, j) \qquad\qquad (42.1)$$

where w is the money-wage, P is the price level, m is the Lerner measure of the degree of monopoly, $g[= f_2(N)]$ is the physical productivity returns to labour, and j is the price of imported inputs.

Since Maynard and Rose admit that their argument does not depend on 'the shape of the marginal product curve of labor' we can take the marginal product curve as sloping downward (MP_L in Figure 42.2) because of diminishing returns.[2] The real wage labour supply function, N^s in Figure 42.2, is, for simplicity, assumed to be upward sloping (although vertical or even a backward bending N^s curve could be utilized). For expositional purposes, it is also assumed that the position of the N^s is unchanged during the period of observation.[3]

On this MP_L market equilibrium curve, point A is the level of real wages which is associated with the equilibrium level of employment of N_e as determined by the point of effective demand, E_w in Figure 42.1. The amount of involuntary unemployment is given by the distance A–B in Figure 42.2. Point B is the (full employment) quantity of labour that is being offered at the market equilibrium real wage of (w/P).

Accepting the Maynard–Rose argument that the price increase of an imported input (e.g. oil) in the production process shifts the MP_L downward to MP'_L (Figure 42.2), it is still necessary in this system to analyse the impact of the oil price increase on the point of effective demand, i.e. on changes in Z_w and D_w before one can specify the impact on the demand for labour. Maynard and Rose are simply incorrect when they claim that this downward shift of the MP_L function can be immediately interpreted as a decline in 'the demand price' for labour in a Keynesian system. This hypothesized shift in the market equilibrium curve merely indicates that the real wage will be lower at *any given equilibrium level of employment*.

The higher cost associated with the importation of oil, assuming no change in $f_2(N)$ or monopoly power of domestic firms, must shift the aggregate supply function up to Z'_w in Figure 42.1, as more revenue (in terms of wage units) is needed for profit-maximizing firms to recoup their increased total variable input costs *for any given level of employment*.

How much the D_w function will shift depends on (a) the marginal propensity to consume domestically produced goods by foreign oil producers *vis-à-vis* the marginal propensity to consume of domestic residents (given the redistribution of income associated with the change in the terms of trade *at any given level of employment*) and (b) changes in government and investment spending on domestically produced goods. The latter depends in part on whether monetary policy is used to squeeze domestic spending as the price level increases due to rising oil prices and any wage–price spiral it induces.

Brothwell suggests that the upward shift of the aggregate demand function to D'_w should be proportionately less than the shift in aggregate supply to Z'_w in Figure 42.1, so that there is a fall in effective demand to E'_w. The level of employment declines from N_e to N'_e (Figure 42.1), while the A point in Figure 42.2 moves to the A' on the lower MP'_L curve. Real wages declines to $(w/P)'$ and involuntary unemployment is equal to the distance $A'-B'$ in Figure 42.2.

The level of employment could have remained at N_e if the aggregate demand function (in wage units) had shifted up proportionately (as a result of demand management policy?) with the aggregate supply function; real wages would have declined to $(w/P)''$, this decline being entirely due to the change in the international terms of trade.[4]

1   PATINKIN AND BARRO–GROSSMAN'S UNEMPLOYMENT LABOUR DEMAND ANALYSIS

The claim that the MP_L curve *is* the macro demand curve for labour has always created logical analytical problems for conscientious neoclassical theorists trying to explain the real world phenomenon of involuntary unemployment.

Patinkin, for example, was forced by the logic of his analysis to declare that 'Keynesian economics is the economics of unemployment *disequilibrium*' (1965, pp. 337–8). Despite labelling the MP_L curve as the demand for labour curve, Patinkin admits that this demand curve 'does *not* describe the actual behavior of firms' (ibid., p. 321) except perhaps at full employment.

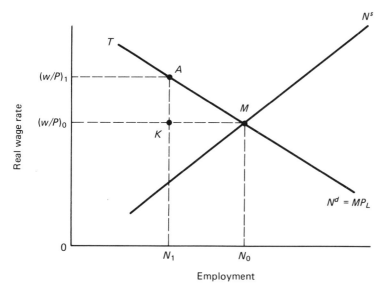

Figure 42.3a

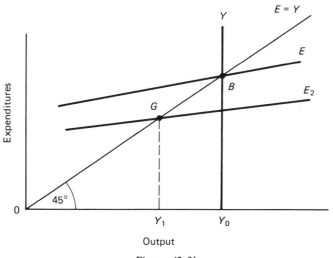

Figure 42.3b

Figure 42.3a and Figure 42.3b reproduce the relevant portions of Patinkin's Figure XIII–1 and XIII–2 (1965, pp. 316–17) respectively. Figure 42.3a is also equivalent to Barro and Grossman's figure 2–1 (1976, p. 44). Patinkin, arguing that the MP_L curve in Figure 42.3a is the demand curve for labour, indicates that point M represents full employment. Based on this, Patinkin builds an aggregate supply function[5] for commodities as the vertical line

$$Y = S[(w/P)_0, K_0] \qquad\qquad 42.2$$

in Figure 42.3b, where $(w/P)_0$ in Figure 42.3a represents the real wage associated with the full employment level of output, Y_0 (Figure 42.3b) when firms maximize profits and employ N_0 workers (Figure 42.3a). According to Patinkin (1965, pp. 211, 316), equilibrium exists only at the intersection of the MP_L and N^s curves (point M) which is the equivalent of point B in Figure 42.3b where the full employment aggregate demand function (E), the vertical aggregate supply function (Y), and the 45° line simultaneously intersect.

If the aggregate demand function was to decline exogenously to E_2 in Figure 42.3b, then, according to Patinkin, although the 'level of production is unchanged at Y_0' (1965, pp. 316–18), lower interest rates and a real balance effect (assuming flexible prices) would drive E_2 back to E, i.e. to a full employment equilibrium. If, however, interest rates or prices do not fall when E_2 prevails:

> It cannot be then realistically assumed that firms will continue producing at an unchanged level, for this would require them to accumulate inventories at ever increasing levels . . . they must eventually take some step to bring current output – and consequently current input – into line with current sales. And this is the beginning of involuntary unemployment . . .
>
> For though it is obvious that there must be some connection between the firms' output of commodities and their input of labor, *this connection is not explicit in our demand function for labor* . . . this function depends only on the real wage rate, and not on the volume of output. Furthermore, it must be emphasized that this absence of an express dependence on the volume of output is not a property peculiar to our function, but one that holds for *any labor demand function derived in the standard way from the principle of profit maximization.* (Patinkin, 1965, pp. 318–19; italics added)

(Patinkin is simply in error in the last sentence, for Weintraub, 1958, and Davidson and Smolensky, 1964, have shown how to derive an aggregate labour demand function for profit-maximizing entrepreneurs from a locus of effective demand points.)

In Patinkin's model, when the aggregate demand curve E_2 prevails while the assumed interest rate and/or real balance mechanisms are not sufficient to immediately return the economy to full employment, then N_1 workers are hired at the *unchanged* real wage rate of $(w/P)_0$ and firms' actual demand for labour is described at point K (rather than A or M) in Figure 42.3a (ibid., p. 321); since K is off the MP_L curve the latter cannot describe the actual behaviour of firms!

Patinkin defends this off-demand-curve analysis despite its apparent semantic inconsistency because it permits 'precise expression to many intuitive, common-sense ideas which have all too frequently been unjustifiably rejected as violating the precepts of rigorous economic analysis' (ibid., p. 323). In other words, an expedient analysis is preferable to a logically rigorous and consistent one! In all honesty, however, Patinkin admits that the insufficiency of aggregate demand case does raise 'a basic analytical problem whose full solution is still not clear to me' (ibid., p. 323, n. 9), when he argues that at less than full employment 'the corresponding "demand" conditions in the labor market are described by the kinked curve TAN_1' (ibid., p. 322) in Figure 42.3a. Constancy of real wages at employment levels below N_0 in Figure 42.3a is obtained by Patinkin by admitting that the MP_L curve does not represent labour demand by firms. Instead, Patinkin argues, firms are on a vertical segment (below the corresponding point of the MP_L curve) of a kinked demand curve. The existence of this kink, however, is, as Patinkin recognizes, inconsistent with the definition of behaviour by purely competitive profit-maximizing firms. In Patinkin's neoclassical world, unemployment is *always* associated with a real wage which is *less* than the marginal product of labour.

To salvage this neoclassical muddle, others have suggested that at less than full employment in the Patinkin system there is either (i) a *temporary* departure from pure competition (competition apparently becomes less intense when sellers find there are not enough buyers to go around); or (ii) the accumulation of inventories (while output remains at Y_0) causes prices to fall relative to money-wages (and money production costs) thereby increasing real wages and causing firms to march up the MP_L (labour demand) function[6] until they reach point A in Figure 42.3a. Patinkin, to his credit, rejects both these *ad hoc* explanations and insists that his off-curve involuntary unemployment analysis remains intact. 'This intactness reflects, not my satisfaction with the discussion, but rather my inability to revise it' (Patinkin, 1965, p. 670).

Barro and Grossman (hereafter B–G) have also attempted to model Keynesian underemployment phenomena, by utilizing some semantic legerdemain which distinguishes between notional and actual (effective) demand curves.[7] In the B–G analysis, *actual (or effective) demand for labor responds only to changes in output and not to the real wage, while notional demand responds only to the real wage and not to output* (1976, p. 43).

In B–G's non-market-clearing models, 'voluntary exchange implies that employment and output are demand determined' (ibid., p. 41). Hence if output is determined at the Y_1 level by the aggregate demand curve E_2 in Figure 42.3b, then in the B–G system, the MP_L curve merely represents 'notional labor demand' – a demand which is relevant *only* for market-clearing models (BG, ibid., pp. 42–3). In a world of involuntary unemployment, notional demand curves are defective; 'the essential problem is that the notional demand functions fail to take account of the fact that the failure of one market to clear creates a constraint which will influence behavior in other markets' (ibid., p. 41).

In the demand-determined involuntary unemployment model of B–G, the 'effective' or actual demand for labour at any real wage rate below points on the MP_L curve 'is depicted as vertical and distinct from [the notional demand curve]' (ibid., p. 44). In essence, therefore, B–G have refined Patinkin's kinked demand for labour curve (TAN_1 in Figure 42.3a), where firms are represented as being on a vertical segment of a kinked *actual* demand curve, such as at point K in Figure 42.3a, whenever there is involuntary unemployment.

In both the Patinkin and the B–G analysis of less than full employment, *the actual real wage is less than the MP_L*. This bizarre result is not only incompatible with the concept of profit maximizing firms operating in a world of pure competition, but even more importantly it is logically irreconcilable with Keynes's fundamental analysis and conclusions. Keynes explicitly accepted the first classical assumption that *in a purely competitive economy the real wage is equal to the marginal product of labour at any level of employment* (1936, pp. 5, 17). In this case, increased employment levels required lower real wages *only* because of diminishing returns. If, over a range of output there is no diminishing returns then, in Keynes's system, the *real wage would be constant and still equal to* the MP_L function as described in equation (1). In every conceivable case, the profit-maximizing assumption requires the acceptance of the pre-Keynesian first fundamental postulate. '*The wage is equal to the marginal product of labour*' (ibid., p. 5). Nevertheless, as our analysis has shown, this MP_L is not the demand curve for labour.

2   WHAT ABOUT THE LABOUR SUPPLY FUNCTION?

A complete analysis of the shape of the N^s function must wait for another article. Nevertheless, since the Lucas-type supply function of labour underlies much of what passes for modern mainstream macroeconomics, it may be useful to indicate that the S_L function in the Keynes model is quite different from a Lucas labour supply analysis.

Lucas believes that there is no way to explain real world unemployment patterns except via an analysis of intertemporal substitutability of labour by optimizing households (Lucas, 1983, p. 4). Keynes's real wage–labour supply analysis, however, does not require and, as shown below, is *logically incompatible* with Lucas's specification (Lucas and Rapping, (hereafter L–R), 1969, pp. 24–5) of this intertemporal relation.

Unemployment does not require workers to be off their long-run supply curve as in the Lucas analysis (ibid., p. 26). Rather, in a Keynesian world, the quantity of labour supplied for any given market real wage is given by the N^s function. The *involuntarily unemployed* ($A-B$ in Figure 42.2) know that they are suffering a permanent loss in real income; they are not engaging in a Lucas optimizing decision to take more leisure today in the expectation that by so doing they will obtain more consumption goods tomorrow when they expect to be rehired at a higher ('normal') real wage than today's market real wage (see ibid., p. 32).

Workers can be involuntarily unemployed because the marginal propensity to spend (from income earned in the production process) on producible goods is less than one, and the income thus saved can be stored in non-reproducible assets such as money, bonds, collectibles, etc. (Davidson, 1980). Hahn has shown that if there are 'resting places for savings other than reproducible assets', then this is all that is 'required to do away with a Say's law-like proposition that the supply of labor is the demand for goods produced by labor' (Hahn, 1977, p. 31); i.e. there can be a long-run deficiency in effective demand. In this case, there will be no behavioural actions that can be taken by workers to bring 'their real wage into conformity with the marginal disutility of the amount of employment offered by employers at that wage . . . there is no . . . tendency towards equality between the real wage and the marginal disutility of labour' (Keynes, 1936, p. 11).

Thus, whenever there is an insufficient effective demand (in money-wage units), actual behaviour in the goods, assets, and labour markets cannot be logically consistent with households' maximizing utility solely in terms of the four commodities specified by Lucas, namely: (1) today's consumption, (2) today's labour supply, (3) tomorrow's consumption, and (4) tomorrow's labour supply (L–R, 1969, p. 24). In order for households to be able to achieve utility maximization solely in terms of these four arguments of the Lucas's utility function, Lucas must assume that households have an intertemporal marginal propensity to spend on producible goods of one.

Given the usual neoclassical assumption that substitution effects dominate (negligible) income or asset effects (ibid., pp. 25, 49) in the Lucas equilibrium system, it is the expected changes in tomorrow's real wage relative to today's that motivates households to allocate all their time intertemporally either in (i) planned leisure or (ii) planned work to earn income. For households to achieve intertemporal utility maximization they must plan to spend, either today or tomorrow, *all* the income they expect to earn over time on producible goods – since producible commodities and leisure time are the only important gross substitutes in the household's utility function assumed by Lucas.

The Lucas claim (1983, p. 4) that this intertemporal substitutability of labour is the *only* way to explain unemployment patterns is true only for a

Say's Law world. In the Lucas–Say's Law world, in the long run (i.e. over two periods called today and tomorrow) and on the statistical average, optimizing households have a marginal propensity to spend of one as the intertemporal long-run labour supply function assumed by Lucas is also the intertemporal demand for goods produced by labour.[8] Of course, a world where Say's Law is assumed to prevail is a world where Keynesian prescriptions are irrelevant – as even Keynes would admit (1936, pp. 25–6). Lucas and other modern mainstream macroeconomists, by assuming Say's Law prevails, have solved the real world's unemployment problems, by assumption, not by analysis!

Notes

1. Keynes (1936, p. 43) insisted that 'unnecessary perplexity can be avoided if we limit ourselves strictly to . . . two units, money and labor' in developing the analysis. Since Brothwell has already explained the Maynard–Rose case in nominal units terms, we will use the alternative of measuring the system in terms of (money) wage units.
2. Of course, constant returns to labour implies a horizontal MP_L curve over the relevant range (see Davidson, 1983, p. 55).
3. As Darity and Horn (1983) have demonstrated, if real wealth as well as real wages affects labour supply, then the S_L curve will shift any time there is a change in effective demand which alters the price level and workers hold their wealth in assets whose nominal prices do not change *pari passu*.
4. As Brothwell suggests, if the oil price increase creates a balance of payments problem at the original N_e level, this may force the government to reduce effective demand in terms of wage units in order to improve the external balance.
5. Under criticism from Post Keynesians, Patinkin recently admitted that his *Money, Interest, and Prices* criticism of Keynes's analysis of the relationship of employment, the real wage, and the aggregate supply of goods 'was not well taken' (Patinkin, 1976, p. 91, n. 12). Patinkin then provided a new formulation for the aggregate supply function (1976, p. 88) which unfortunately was still faulty. Admitting these flaws in his 1976 analysis, Patinkin (1977) provided still another interpretation of Keynes's aggregate supply, real wage, and employment analysis which, in my view, is still incorrect! But that is another story.
6. Mechanism (ii), however, where money prices fall *relative* to money-wages at any given employment level, is clearly incompatible with profit maximizing behaviour by competitive firms.
7. Elsewhere (Davidson 1977; 1982) I have demonstrated that the notional versus actual demand function construction first introduced by Clower (1965), in an attempt to achieve Keynesian results from a neoclassical analysis, does not get to the essence of the underemployment analysis for monetary, entrepreneurial economies. It is *not* income or output constrained demand curves which distinguish real world monetary economies and Keynes's model from the BG or Patinkin (or Meltzer) neoclassical equilibrium system. Clower has specifically admitted that 'the essential character of the dual decision process would come out more clearly . . . (in) a model with income and *without money*' (1965,

p. 305; italics added). Thus, the notional versus actual demand framework which can provide a rationalization for less than full employment does not require money for its operation. Yet, Keynes insisted that it was the *existence* of money and/or other liquid assets (in his *General Theory of Employment, Interest and Money*) which created the possibility of underemployment equilibrium and assured that the MP_L is not the correct specification of the labour demand function in any entrepreneurial economy which utilized forward money contracts as the institution for organizing production and other economic activities (1936, ch. 17, especially pp. 236–42).

8. This requirement appears in L–R under the seemingly innocuous assumptions that 'future goods and leisure are substitutes for current leisure, that leisure is not inferior, and that the asset effect is small' (L–R, 1969, p. 25). Thus by assuming no significant income effects and all the 'commodities' in the consumer utility function are either gross substitutes producible by labour (or labour itself), Lucas has reintroduced Say's Law. (For a discussion on the inapplicability of the Gross Substitution Theorem in Keynesian analysis, see Davidson, 1980).

References

Barro, R. J. and H. I. Grossman (1976), *Money, Employment, and Inflation* (Cambridge: Cambridge University Press).

Brothwell, J. F. (1982), 'Monetarism, Wages, and Employment Policy in the United Kingdom', *Journal of Post Keynesian Economics*, 4 (3), pp. 376–87.

Clower, R. W. (1965), 'The Keynesian Revolution: A Theoretical Appraisal', in F. H. Hahn and F. P. R. Brechling (eds), *The Theory of Interest Rates* (London: Macmillan).

Darity, W. A. and B. L. Horn (1983), 'Involuntary Unemployment Reconsidered', *Southern Economic Journal*, 49, pp. 717–33.

Davidson, P. (1967), 'A Keynesian View of Patinkin's Theory of Employment', *Economic Journal*, 77, pp. 559–78 (Chapter 36 in this volume).

Davidson, P. (1977), 'Money and General Equilibrium', *Economie Appliquée*, 30, pp. 541–64 (Chapter 12 in this volume).

Davidson, P. (1980), 'The Dual-Faceted Nature of the Keynesian Revolution: Money and Money Wages in Unemployment and Production Flow Prices', *Journal of Post Keynesian Economics*, 2(3), pp. 291–307 (Chapter 39 in this volume).

Davidson, P. (1982), *International Money and the Real World* (London: Macmillan).

Davidson, P. (1983), 'The Dubious Labor Market Analysis in Meltzer's Restatement', *Journal of Economic Literature*, 21, pp. 52–6.

Davidson, P. and E. Smolensky (1964), *Aggregate Supply and Demand Analysis* (New York: Harper & Row).

Hahn, F. H. (1977), 'Keynesian Economics and General Equilibrium Theory: Reflections on Some Current Debate', in G. C. Harcourt (ed.), *The Microfoundation of Macroeconomics* (London: Macmillan).

Keynes, J. M. (1936), *The General Theory of Employment, Interest and Money* (New York: Harcourt).

Lucas, R. E. (1983), *Studies in Business Cycle Theory* (Cambridge, MA.: MIT Press).

Lucas, R. E. and L. A. Rapping (1969), 'Real Wages, Employment, and Inflation', *Journal of Political Economy*, 77, pp. 721–54; reprinted in Lucas (1983). All page references are to reprint.

Maynard, G. and H. B. Rose (1983), *Journal of Post Keynesian Economics*, vol. VI no. 1.

Meltzer, A. (1981), 'Keynes's General Theory: A Different Perspective', *Journal of Economic Literature*, 19, pp. 34–64.

Patinkin, D. (1965), *Money Interest and Prices*, 2nd edn (New York: Harper & Row).

Patinkin, D. (1976), 'Keynes's Monetary Theory', *History of Political Economy*, 8.

Patinkin, D. (1977), 'Keynes's Aggregate Supply Function: A Correction', *History of Political Economy*, 9.

Weintraub, S. (1958), *An Approach to the Theory of Income Distribution* (Philadelphia: Chilton).

43 Reviving Keynes's Revolution*

Addressing *The General Theory* chiefly to his 'fellow economists' (1936, p. v), Keynes insisted that

> the postulates of the classical theory are applicable to a special case only and not to the general case . . . Moreover, the characteristics of the special case assumed by the classical theory happen not to be those of the economic society in which we actually live, with the result that its teaching is misleading and disastrous if we attempt to apply it to the facts of experience. (ibid., p. 3)

Keynes (ibid., p. 26) believed that he could *logically* demonstrate why 'Say's Law . . . is not the true law relating the aggregate demand and supply functions' when we model an economy possessing real world characteristics; and until we get our theory to mirror and apply accurately to the 'facts of experience', there is little hope of getting our policies right. That message is just as relevant today.

Keynes compared those economists whose theoretical logic was grounded in Say's Law to Euclidean geometers living in a non-Euclidean world,

> who discovering that in experience straight lines apparently parallel often meet, rebuke the lines for not keeping straight – as the only remedy for the unfortunate collisions which are taking place. Yet, in truth, there is no remedy except to throw over the axiom of parallels and to work out a non-Euclidean geometry. Something similar is required today in economics. (ibid., p. 16)

To throw over an axiom is to reject what the faithful believe are 'universal truths'. The Keynesian Revolution in economic theory was therefore truly a revolt since it aimed at rejecting basic mainstream tenets and substituting postulates which provide a logical foundation for a non-Say's Law model more closely related to the real world in which we happen to live. Unfortunately, since Keynes, mainstream macrotheorists, seduced by a technical methodology which promised precision and unique results at the expense of applicability and accuracy, have reintroduced more sophis-

* *Journal of Post Keynesian Economics*, 6 (4) (1984).

ticated forms of the very axioms Keynes rejected almost a half century ago. Consequently, the Keynesian Revolution was almost immediately shunted onto a wrong track as more obtuse versions of the axioms underlying a Say's Law world became the keystone of modern mainstream theory. Monetarists and the new classical economists, as well as neoclassical synthesis Keynesians, have reconstructed macrotheory by reintroducing the 'universal truths' that Keynes struggled to overthrow.

The major neoclassical axioms rejected by Keynes in his revolutionary logical analysis were (1) *the axiom of gross substitution*, (2) *the axiom of reals*, and (3) *the axiom of an ergodic economic world*. The characteristics of the real world which Keynes believed could be modeled only by overthrowing these axioms are: (1) Money matters in the long and short run; i.e. money is not neutral – it affects real decision-making.[1] (2) The economic system is moving through calendar time from an irrevocable past to an uncertain future. Important monetary time series realizations will be generated by non-ergodic circumstances; hence decision-making agents know that the future need not be predictable in any probability sense (see Davidson, 1982–3). (3) Forward contracts in money terms are a human institution developed to organize time consuming production and exchange processes efficiently (Davidson, 1980, p. 299). The money-wage contract is the most ubiquitous of these efficiency-oriented contracts. Modern production economies are therefore on a money-wage contract-based system. (4) Unemployment, rather than full employment, is a common *laissez-faire* situation in a market-oriented, monetary production economy.

Only the monetarists and the new classical theorists (like Ricardo)

> offer us the supreme intellectual achievement, unattainable by weaker spirits, of adopting a hypothetical world remote from experience as though it was the world of experience and then living in it consistently. With most of . . . [the Keynesians?] common sense cannot help breaking in – with injury to their logical consistency. (Keynes, 1936, pp. 192–3)

1 SPENDING, CONSTRAINED DEMAND, SAY'S LAW AND GROSS SUBSTITUTION

Keynes's *General Theory* is developed via an aggregate supply–aggregate demand function analysis which can be used to illustrate the difference between Say's Law and Keynes's analytical structure (ibid., pp. 25–6).

The aggregate supply function (Z) relates entrepreneurs' expected sales proceeds with the level of employment (N) entrepreneurs will hire for any volume of expected sales receipts. In Figure 43.1a this aggregate supply

(Z) function is drawn as upward sloping, indicating that the higher entrepreneurs' sales expectations, the more workers they will hire. The aggregate demand function relates buyers' desired expenditure flows for any given level of employment. In Figure 43.1b, the aggregate demand (D) function is drawn as upward sloping, indicating that the greater the level of employment hire, the more buyers will spend on goods and services.

The aggregate supply and demand functions can be brought together in a single quadrant to provide the equilibrium employment solution. In Figure 43.2a the aggregate supply (Z) and aggregate demand (D) functions are drawn as they would be developed in a Say's Law world where supply creates its own demand. In a Say's Law world (as explained below and as shown in Figure 43.2a), the aggregate supply and demand functions are coincident throughout their entire length. Thus if at any point of time the actual employment level is N_1^a, actual demand is constrained to point G. Any coordinated expansion in hiring by entrepreneurs to provide additional output (say to point H in Figure 43.2a) will increase actual demand concomitantly to point H and full employment (N_f^a) could be established. In a Say's Law world there is no obstacle to full employment.

In Figure 43.2b, on the other hand, the aggregate demand and supply functions are distinguishable functions which intersect at a single point, the point of *effective demand* (E); and in a manner consistent with Keynes's theory (ibid., p. 25) the equilibrium level of employment is N_1^b. At the full employment level (N_f^b in Figure 43.2b) there is a deficiency in effective demand equal to the vertical distance JK, and hence all the full employment output cannot be profitably sold.

As defined by Keynes, Say's Law required that the aggregate supply curve be coincident with the aggregate demand curve over its entire length so that supply could create its own demand. Accordingly, *effective demand* 'instead of having a unique equilibrium value, is an infinite range of values, all equally admissible' (ibid., p. 26). If, therefore, Say's Law prevails, then the economy is in neutral equilibrium where actual demand is *constrained* only by actual income (supply). In other words, Say's Law requires that aggregate demand is a *constrained demand function* (in the terminology of Clower, 1965, or Barro and Grossman, 1976), and a 'short-side of the market rationing' rule limits employment opportunities. This short-side rule is specifically adopted by Malinvaud (1977, pp. 12–35) to 'explain' Keynesian unemployment. It has also been used by most of the 'Keynesians' who have manned the Council of Economic Advisers under Democratic administrations to explain what their logical unconstrained model cannot.[2]

In the Clower–Leijonhufvud neoclassical synthesis version of the Keynesian system, which has been labelled the dual-decision hypothesis with a coordination failure, purchasing decisions are always equal to, and constrained by, *actual* income (Clower, 1965). The economy is in neutral

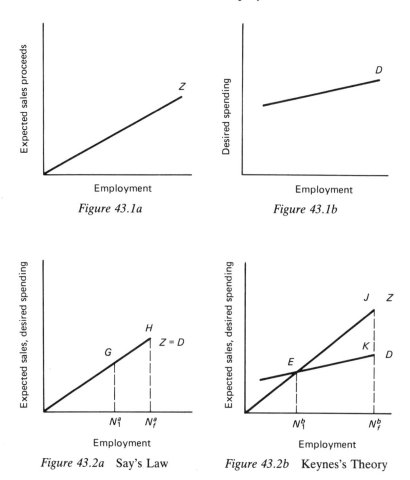

Figure 43.1a

Figure 43.1b

Figure 43.2a   Say's Law

Figure 43.2b   Keynes's Theory

equilibrium at any level of actual income. There is no obstacle to full employment except that entrepreneurs do not receive a market signal that they would be able to sell the full employment output profitably if only they would coordinate and march together to the full employment hiring level. Unemployment is solely due to a 'coordination failure' of the market system to signal to entrepreneurs that, if they would only hire the full employment level of workers, actual income would equal *notional* (full employment) *income* and the spending decisions by income earners would be equal to, and constrained by, the full employment budget line and all markets would clear.[3] Hence, in contrast to Keynes (1936, pp. 30–1), these 'Keynesians' argue that if only entrepreneurs would hire all workers there would never be an insufficiency of aggregate demand.

Those who believe a short-side rule or constrained demand function limits employment opportunities should, if they follow their logic and not their common sense, support President Reagan's proposal for solving the unemployment problem. In the spring of 1983 Reagan suggested that unemployment could be ended if each business firm in the nation immediately hired one more worker. Since there are more firms than unemployed workers, the solution is obviously statistically accurate – but unless the employment by each of these additional workers created a demand for the additional output at a profitable price (additional supply creating *pari passu* additional demand), it would not be profitable for entrepreneurs to hire additional workers.

Neoclassical Keynesians should applaud Reagan's clarion call for firms to coordinate increased hiring. If each firm does hire an additional worker so that full employment is (at least momentarily) achieved, then actual income flows earned would be equal to notional income and therefore aggregate demand would not be constrained short of full employment. There is no coordination failure – and no short-side rule limits job opportunities.

In a Keynes world, on the other hand, involuntary unemployment is due to an insufficiency or lack of effective demand (at full employment) as shown by the vertical distance JK in Figure 43.2b. The sales of the additional output produced by private sector entrepreneurs hiring workers above the N_1^b level in Figure 43.2b cannot be profitable.

Keynes would never have endorsed Reagan's Say's Law solution to the unemployment problem. In a closed economy context, Keynes held that neither of the two private sector components of the aggregate demand function (D_1 and D_2 or aggregate consumption and investment spending) are constrained by actual income, although D_1 may be related to income earned! To put it bluntly and in its most irritating – thought provoking – form, the underlying axioms of Keynes's revolutionary theory of effective demand require that *the demand for goods produced by labour need never be constrained by income; spending is constrained only by liquidity and/or timidity considerations*. Thus the budget constraint, in a Keynes model, need never limit individual spending – or aggregate spending at less than full employment.

In the real world, planned spending need never be equal to, or constrained by, actual income as long as (a) agents who earn income by selling their labour (or goods produced by labour in the private sector) are not required to spend all their earned income on goods produced by labour, and/or (b) agents who plan to spend on currently producible goods are not required to earn income (previously or concurrently) with their exercise of this demand (where by 'demand' we mean 'want' *plus the ability to pay*).

Hahn (1977, p. 31) has put point (a) as meaning that Say's Law is done away with and involuntary unemployment can occur whenever there are 'resting places for savings in other than reproducible assets' so that all income earned by engaging in the production of goods is not, in the short or long run, spent on assets producible by labour. For savings to find such ultimate resting places, the axiom of gross substitution must be thrown over (see Davidson, 1980, pp. 303–5).

This axiom is the backbone of mainstream economics; it is the assumption that any good is a substitute for any other good. If the demand for good x goes up, its price will rise inducing demand to spill over to the now relatively cheaper substitute good y. For an economist to deny this 'universal truth' is revolutionary heresy – and, as in the days of the Inquisition, the modern day College of Cardinals of mainstream economics destroys all non-believers – if not by burning them at the stake, then by banishment from the mainstream professional journals. Yet in Keynes's analysis (1936, ch. 17) 'The Essential Properties of Interest and Money' requires that the elasticity of substitution between all liquid assets including money (which are not reproducible by labour in the private sector) and producible (in the private sector) assets is zero or negligible. These properties which Keynes (ibid., p. 241, n. 1) believed are *essential* to the concepts of money and liquidity necessitate that a basic axiom of Keynes's logical framework is that non-producible assets that can be used to store savings are not gross substitutes for producible assets in savers' portfolios.

Instead, if the gross substitution axiom is true,[4] then even if savers attempt to use non-reproducible assets for storing their increments of wealth, this increase in demand will increase the price of non-producibles. This relative price rise in non-producibles will, under the gross substitution axiom, induce savers to substitute reproducible durables for non-producibles in their wealth holdings and therefore non-producibles will not be ultimate resting places for savings (cf. Davidson, 1972; 1977; 1980). The gross substitution axiom therefore restores Say's Law and denies the logical possibility of involuntary unemployment.

In *Debate With His Critics*, Friedman could correctly attack Tobin and other neoclassical Keynesians for logical inconsistencies involving 'differences in the range of assets considered' as possible gross substitutes in savings portfolios. For Friedman, the total spectrum of assets including 'houses, automobiles, let alone furniture, household appliances, clothes and so on' (1974, p. 29) is eligible for savings. (After all in his *permanent income hypothesis*, Friedman deliberately defines savings to include the purchase of producible durable goods.) Thus, Friedman, in his logical world, remote from reality, can 'prove' that savings does not create unemployment; for the Samuelsons, Tobins, and Solows of the world their common sense if not their logic tells them better.

To overthrow the axiom of gross substitution in an intertemporal context is truly heretical. It changes the entire perspective as to what is meant by 'rational' or 'optimal' savings, as to why people save or what they save. Recently, Sir John Hicks noted that all Keynes needed to say was that income was divided between current consumption and a vague provision for the uncertain future. The mathematical assumption that 'planned expenditures at specified different dates in the future have independent utilities [and are gross substitutes] . . . this assumption I find quite unacceptable . . . the normal condition is that there is strong complementarity between them [consumption plans in successive periods]' (Hicks, 1979, pp. 76–7, n. 7). Indeed Danziger *et al.* (1982–3) have shown that the facts regarding consumption spending by the elderly are incompatible with the notion of intertemporal gross substitution of consumption plans which underlie both life-cycle models and overlapping generation models currently so popular in mainstream macroeconomic theory.

In the absence of the axiom of gross substitution, income effects (e.g. the Keynesian multiplier) predominate and can swamp any hypothetical neoclassical substitution effects. Consequently, relative price changes via a flexible pricing mechanism will not be the cure-all 'snake-oil' medicine usually recommended by many neoclassical doctors for the unfortunate economic maladies that are occurring in the real world.

2 INVESTMENT SPENDING, LIQUIDITY, AND THE AXIOM OF REALS

Point (b) above is that agents who planned to spend in the current period are not required to earn income currently or previously to their exercise of demand in the market. This implies that spending for D_2, the demand for fixed and working capital goods (or even consumer durables) reproducible by labour in the private sector, is constrained by neither actual income nor endowments. For Keynes, given animal spirits and not timidity on the part of entrepreneurs, D_2 is constrained solely by the *monetary*, and not the real, *expected return on liquid assets* (Keynes, 1936, ch. 17). The rate of interest, which is strictly a monetary phenomenon in Keynes, rules the roost.

Keynes (ibid., p. 142) believed that the 'real rate of interest' concept of Irving Fisher was a logical confusion. In a monetary economy moving through calendar time towards an uncertain (statistically unpredictable) future, there is no such thing as a forward-looking real rate of interest. Moreover, money has an impact on the real sector in both the short and long run. Thus, money is a real phenomenon, while the rate of interest is a monetary phenomenon (cf. Kregel, 1983).

This is just the reverse of what classical theory and modern mainstream theory teaches us. In orthodox macrotheory, the rate of interest is a real (technologically determined) factor while money (at least in the long run for both Friedman and Tobin) does not affect the real output flow. This reversal of the importance or the significance of money and interest rates for real and monetary phenomena between orthodox and Keynes's theory is the result of Keynes's rejection of a second neoclassical universal truth – the axiom of reals.

For the D_2 component of aggregate demand not to be constrained by actual income, agents must have the ability to finance investment by borrowing from a banking system which can create money. Such money creation is therefore inevitably tied to the creation of money (debt) contracts. This financing mechanism involves the heresy of overthrowing what Frank Hahn calls the 'axiom of reals' (cf. Minsky, 1984). Hahn describes this axiom as one where:

> The objectives of agents that determine their actions and plans do not depend on any nominal magnitudes. Agents care only about 'real' things such as goods . . . leisure and effort. We know this as the axiom of the absence of money illusion, which it seems impossible to abandon in any sensible sense. (Hahn, 1983, p. 44)

The axiom of reals implies that money is a veil so that all economic decisions are made on the basis of real phenomena and relative prices alone. Money does not matter!

To reject the axiom of reals does not require assuming that agents suffer from a money illusion. It only means that 'money is not neutral' (Keynes, 1973, p. 411); money matters in both the short run and the long run, or as Keynes put it:

> The theory which I desiderate would deal . . . with an economy in which money plays a part of its own and affects motives and decisions, and is, in short, one of the operative factors in the situation, so that the course of events cannot be predicted in either the long period or in the short, without a knowledge of the behaviour of money between the first state and the last. And it is this which we ought to mean when we speak of a *monetary economy*. (Keynes, 1973, pp. 408–9)

Can anything be more revolutionary? In this passage from an article entitled 'The *Monetary* Theory of Production' (and I emphasize the word *Monetary*) Keynes specifically rejects the axiom of reals! The only objective for a firm is to end the production process (which takes time) by liquidating its working capital in order to end up with more money than it started with (Keynes 1979, p. 82).

Let me illustrate: suppose during the next great depression a firm has a production process gestation period of one year. At the beginning of the year it hires workers, buys materials, and so on, on forward money contracts for the entire production process and thereby has, except for acts of God, controlled its costs of production. Suppose that during the year, the CPI falls by 10 per cent but the price at which the firm expected to sell its product at the end of the gestation period falls by only 5 per cent. In relative real terms the firm is better off; but in the real world the firm is really worse off. Now change the numbers to say 50 per cent and 45 per cent respectively. The firm still has a 5 per cent improvement in real terms, but in all likelihood if this continues the firm will soon have to file for bankruptcy. (Of course, a good neoclassical economist would respond that the firm will not go bankrupt if it can recontract without penalty – but such recontracts without penalties are not a characteristic of the world we live in.)

If on the other hand we had assumed the CPI goes up by 10 per cent (or 50 per cent) while the firm's product price went up by 5 per cent (or 45 per cent), although the firm's real position has deteriorated its real world position is better. As long as money contracts are used to plan the production process efficiently, production decisions will be affected by nominal values and money is a real phenomenon![5]

Once we admit that money is a real phenomenon, that money matters, then the traditional axiom of reals must be rejected. Hahn should realize this, since Arrow and Hahn have demonstrated that:

> The terms in which contracts are made matter. In particular, if money is the goods in terms of which contracts are made, then the prices of goods in terms of money are of special significance. This is not the case if we consider an economy without a past or future. . . . *If a serious monetary theory* comes to be written, the fact that contracts are made in terms of money will be of considerable importance. (1971, pp. 356–7; italics added)

Moreover, Arrow and Hahn demonstrate (ibid., p. 361) that, if contracts are made in terms of money (so that money affects real decisions) in an economy moving along in calendar time with a past and future, then *all existence theorems are jeopardized*. The existence of money contracts – a characteristic of the world in which Keynes lived and which we still do – implies that there need never exist, in the long run or the short run, any rational expectations equilibrium or general equilibrium market clearing price vector.

3 THE PERVASIVE ERGODIC AXIOM – PRECISION VERSUS ACCURACY

Most neoclassical and new classical economists suffer from the pervasive form of envy which we may call the 'economist's disease'; that is, these economists want to be considered as first-class scientists dealing with a 'hard science' rather than be seen as 'second-class' citizens of the scientific community who deal with the non-precise 'social' and 'political' sciences. These economists, mistaking precision (rather than accuracy) as the hallmark of 'true' science, prefer to be precise rather than accurate.

Precision conveys the meaning of 'sharpness to minute detail'. Accuracy, on the other hand, means 'care to obtain conformity with fact or truth'. For example, if you phone the plumber to come and fix an emergency breakdown in your plumbing system, and he responds by indicating he will be there in exactly 12 minutes, he is being precise, but not exercising care to obtain conformity with fact or truth. If he says he will be there before the day is over, he is being accurate, if not necessarily precise.

Most economists, unfortunately, prefer to be precisely wrong rather than roughly right or accurate. The axiom of ergodicity permits economists to act 'as if' they were dealing with a 'hard' science where data are homogeneous with respect to time. In an ergodic world, observations of a time series realization (i.e. historical data) are useful information regarding the probability distribution of the stochastic process which generated that realization. The same observations also provide information about the probability distribution over a universe of realizations which exist at any point of time such as today, and the data are also useful information regarding the future probability distribution of events. Hence by scientifically studying the past as generated by an ergodic situation, present and future events can be forecasted in terms of statistical probabilities (cf. Davidson, 1982–3).

Keynes (1936, ch. 12) rejected this view that past information from economic time series realizations provides reliable, useful data which permit stochastic predictions of the economic future. In a world with important non-ergodic circumstances – our economic world – liquidity matters, money is never neutral, and neither Say's Law nor Walras's Law is relevant (cf. Davidson, 1982–3). In such a world, Keynes's revolutionary logical analysis is relevant.

4 CONCLUSIONS

Mainstream economic theory has not followed Keynes's revolutionary logical analysis to develop what Arrow and Hahn have called a 'serious monetary theory' in which contracts are made in terms of money in an economy moving from an irrevocable past to an uncertain, non-ergodic future (cf. ibid., 1982–3). At the very beginning of his *Treatise on Money*, Keynes (1930, p. 3) reminded the reader that, in a modern economy, money exists only because there are contracts and therefore money is intimately related to the existence of money contracts.

In his writings Keynes explicitly assumed things which are incompatible with (a) the gross substitution axiom, (b) the axiom of reals, and (c) ergodicity. Unfortunately, many of the popularizers and professional interpreters of Keynes's analysis either did not read what he wrote, or did not comprehend his revolutionary logic requiring the overthrow of these fundamental neoclassical axioms. Nevertheless, Keynes's policy prescriptions made a great deal of common sense. Hence Keynes won the policy battles of the first three decades after the publication of *The General Theory*, even though 'Keynesians' had erected a 'neoclassical synthesis' microfoundation to Keynes's macroeconomics which could not logically support Keynes's general case.

From a logical standpoint the neoclassical synthesis Keynesians had created a Keynesian Cheshire Cat – a grin without a body. Thus, Friedman and the rational expectations – new classical – theorists were able to destroy the rickety neoclassical Keynesian scaffolding and replace it with a technologically advanced, logically consistent, but irrelevant and inaccurate theory.

In this one hundred and first year after Keynes's birth, it is surprising how few in the economics profession are willing or able to defend the logical basis of Keynes's analysis. It is almost as if many believed that, as Clower (1965, p. 120) indicated, 'the *General Theory* is theoretical nonsense' unless Keynes believed in the constrained demand function, dual decision hypothesis. Yet, we have shown above that this constrained demand function analysis implies Say's Law. Hence, if Clower is correct in his claim that Keynes had the dual-decision hypothesis at the back of his mind, then Keynes was a theoretical charlatan in claiming his analysis eliminated Say's Law. Of course, it is Clower and the other neoclassical Keynesians who maintain axioms rejected by Keynes who are in error in trying to apply Keynes's label to their logical system.

At the Royal Economic Society's Centennial Celebration of Keynes's birth in July 1983, the detractors of Keynes on the programme far exceeded those who were attempting to honour Keynes's accomplishments and build on the legacy he left. Some, such as Professors Samuelson and Solow, proudly labelled themselves as 'reconstructed Keynesians' to differentiate their theory from the 'unreconstructed' Keynesians of Cambridge in England. As Samuelson put it – a reconstructed Keynesian was one who found the Keynesian structure imperfect and had therefore to reconstruct it.

This 'reconstructed Keynesian' appellation is, however, a misnomer when applied to the neoclassical synthesis Keynesian approach of Samuelson and Solow. These mainstream American 'Keynesian' models never began with the same logical foundations and axioms as Keynes's model. Hence these Keynesians cannot, and will not, reconstruct Keynes until they throw over the neoclassical axioms rejected by Keynes.

The 'unreconstructed' Keynesians – or Post Keynesians as I would call them – recognize that there may be many flaws in the Keynes superstructure and that the times have brought forth new and different pressing problems. Post Keynesians may not have worked out all the answers but at least they recognize that Keynes started with a logically different theoretical system – a system which accurately reflects the characteristics of the real economic world – those of Wall Street and the corporate boardroom, rather than those of Robinson Crusoe or the medieval fair.

Post Keynesians recognize that their logical model is neither fully developed nor as neat and precise as the neoclassical one – after all, the number of person-hours put into developing the orthodox model exceeds those invested in the Post Keynesian analysis several millionfold. Nevertheless, Post Keynesians believe it is better to develop a model which emphasizes the special characteristics of the economic world in which we live than to continually refine and polish a beautifully precise, but irrelevant, model. Moreover, when one is dealing with human activity and institutions, one may be, in the nature of things, outside the realm of the formally precise. For Keynes as for Post Keynesians the guiding motto is 'it is better to be roughly right than precisely wrong!'

After the revolution comes evolution. Post Keynesians are trying to build on the logical foundations of Keynes's real world analysis to resolve modern day economic problems. They invite all who possess open minds to undertake the further evolution of Keynes's logical heresy and to explore a Keynesian (non-Euclidean) world where the axioms of ergodicity, of gross substitution, and of reals are not universal truths applicable to all economic decision-making processes.

Unlike Samuelson's 'reconstructed Keynesians', Post Keynesians do not believe that a regression to pre-Keynesian (Euclidean) axioms represents progress no matter how much technological garb these postulates are wrapped in. Only in the world of 1984 and doublespeak can a regressive analytical structure be considered an advance!

Notes

1. Despite Friedman's use of the motto 'money matters', he remains faithful to the axiom of real (see below) and does not permit money to affect the long-run real outcome of his system. In his own description of his logical framework, Friedman states:

   that changes in the quantity of money as such *in the long run* have a negligible effect on real income so that non-monetary forces are 'all that matter' for changes in real income over decades and money 'does not matter'. . . I regard the description of our position as 'money is all that matters for changes in *nominal income* and for *short-run* changes in real income' as an exaggeration but one that gives the right flavour to our conclusions. (Friedman, 1974, p. 27)

2. These liberal Democratic Economic Advisers, however, have the difficulty that their logic is based on Say's Law, but their common sense tells them that unemployment is a problem which the system cannot solve without direct government interference. Thus they turned to *ad hoc* modifications of their neoclassical model – a short-side rule or a constrained demand function – to abrogate Say's Law and achieve a non-Walrasian equilibrium, at least in the short run.

3. Since in this neoclassical world, engaging in a production process is assumed distasteful it would seem axiomatic that no agents would contribute to production unless they planned to spend all their income on producible goods. Consequently, full employment hiring decisions should always bring forth sufficient demand to buy all the products of industry.

   This belief also underlies the rational expectations hypothesis via Lucas's aggregate supply analysis. Lucas believes there is no way of explaining real world unemployment patterns except via an analysis of intertemporal substitutability of labour by optimizing households (Lucas, 1983, p. 4). In order for households to achieve utility maximization solely in terms of the four arguments of Lucas's utility function – (1) today's consumption, (2) today's labour supply, (3) tomorrow's consumption, (4) tomorrow's labour supply – Lucas must assume that the intertemporal marginal propensity to spend on producible goods is unity. Say's Law therefore prevails by assumption. Unemployed workers are optimizing by preferring leisure today with rational expectations that they will get more real income per unit of effort tomorrow when they go back to work. Hence today's unemployed are not suffering any loss in permanent real welfare; i.e. the colliding lines that we observe are not really colliding – it is all apparently an optical illusion.

   If, on the other hand, you believe, as Keynes did and Post Keynesians do, that today's unemployed know they are suffering a permanent loss in real well-being then you must throw off the classical axioms of gross substitution *and* the axiom of reals and enter the world of Keynes's non-Euclidean economics! In such a world, the desire to possess liquidity – liquid assets not producible by labour – is also an argument in any labour (factor owner) supply function.

4. Recent empirical work by Benjamin Friedman (1983) has demonstrated that the facts do not justify assuming gross substitutability among all assets in savers' portfolios.

5. It should be noted that Minsky (1982) has explicitly demonstrated the inapplicability of the axiom of reals for at least one major sector of the economy. In his work Minsky has emphasized that there are at least some entrepreneurs, we call them bankers, who are guided solely by money-cash flows and maintaining increasing nominal values of net worth in balance sheets even if this means lower real values. Thus at least for this very important sector of the economy, the axiom of reals cannot be applicable.

References

Arrow, K. S. and F. H. Hahn (1971), *General Competitive Analysis* (San Francisco: Holden-Day).

Barro, R. J. and H. I. Grossman (1976), *Money, Employment, and Inflation* (Cambridge: Cambridge University Press).

Clower, R. W. (1965) 'The Keynesian Revolution: A Theoretical Appraisal', in

F. H. Hahn and F. R. R. Brechling (eds), *The Theory of Interest Rates* (London: Macmillan).

Danziger, S., J. van der Gaag, E. Smolensky and M. K. Taussig (1982–3), 'The Life-cycle Hypothesis and Consumption Behavior of the Elderly', *Journal of Post Keynesian Economics* 5(2), pp. 208–27.

Davidson, P. (1972), *Money and the Real World* (London: Macmillan).

Davidson, P. (1977), 'Money and General Equilibrium', *Economie Appliquée*, 30 (Chapter 12 in this volume).

Davidson, P. (1980), 'The Dual-faceted Nature of the Keynesian Revolution', *Journal of Post Keynesian Economics*, 2(3), pp. 291–307 (Chapter 39 in this volume).

Davidson, P. (1982–3), 'Rational Expectations: A Fallacious Foundation for Studying Crucial Decision-making Processes', *Journal of Post Keynesian Economics*, 5(2), pp. 182–98.

Friedman, B. (1983), 'The Substitutability of Debt and Equity Securities', National Bureau of Economic Research Working Paper 1130 (May).

Friedman, M. (1974), 'A Theoretical Framework for Monetary Analysis', in R. J. Gordon (ed.) *Milton Friedman's Monetary Framework: A Debate with his Critics* (Chicago: University of Chicago Press).

Hahn, F. H. (1977), 'Keynesian Economics and General Equilibrium Theory', in G. C. Harcourt (ed.), *Microfoundations of Macroeconomics* (London: Macmillan).

Hahn, F. H. (1983), *Money and Inflation* (Cambridge, Mass.: MIT Press).

Hicks, J. R. (1979), *Causality in Economics* (New York: Basic Books).

Keynes, J. M. (1930), *A Treatise on Money* (London: Macmillan).

Keynes, J. M. (1936), *The General Theory of Employment, Interest and Money* (New York: Harcourt).

Keynes, J. M. (1973), *The Collected Writings of John Maynard Keynes*, Vol. XIII, ed. by D. Moggridge (London: Macmillan).

Keynes, J. M. (1979), *The Collected Writings of John Maynard Keynes*, Vol. XXIX, ed by D. Moggridge (London: Macmillan).

Kregel, J. A. (1983), 'The Multiplier and Liquidity Preference: Two Sides of the theory of Effective Demand', (mimeo).

Lucas, R. E. (1983), *Studies in Business Cycle Theory* (Cambridge, Mass.: MIT Press).

Malinvaud, E. (1977), *The Theory of Unemployment Reconsidered* (Oxford: Blackwell).

Minsky, H. P. (1982), *Can It Happen Again?* (Armonk, N.Y.: M. E. Sharpe).

Minsky, H. P. (1984), 'Frank Hahn's *Money and Inflation*: A Review Article', *Journal of Post Keynesian Economics*, 6(3), pp. 449–57.

44 Sidney Weintraub – an Economist of the Real World*

In the view of both the general public and most professional economists, Sidney Weintraub is undoubtedly more closely associated with the concept of a tax-based incomes policy (or TIP) than with any other analytical or policy construction of economics. Yet, TIP is only one of many analytical innovations that Weintraub has developed in the more than a dozen books and a hundred articles he has authored since the 1940s.

In his first book, *Price Theory* (1949), Weintraub presented a 'systematic and reasonably complete statement of modern price theory' (p. vii). In its 'Dynamic Analysis' section (ibid., pp. 337–433) Weintraub took a monumental step forward; he moved price theory into the real world when he provided a conceptual scheme for the 'forward-looking nature of the economic process . . . [where] production and consumption take time, decisions and actions in these spheres are guided by an estimate of the future' (ibid., p. 337). Had professional economists followed Weintraub's pathbreaking analysis of time and uncertainty, imperfect equilibrium adaptions, multiperiod anticipations with their intertemporal demand and user costs relationships, and his 'clock-time sequences' analysis, instead of being diverted into the rather sterile static and dynamic general equilibrium analysis of the last few decades, microeconomics theory might have

* Earlier, shorter versions of this paper were published in *Contemporary Economics in Perspective*, ed. by H. W. Spiegel and W. J. Samuels (Greenwich: JAI Press, 1984) and *The Eastern Economic Journal*, 9, 1983. This version was first published in *Journal of Post Keynesian Economics*, 7 (1985).

Professor Davidson reminisces:

I first met Sidney Weintraub when he was the Professor of the course on microeconomics that I took as a graduate student in economics at the University of Pennsylvania in 1955. I had previously been a Ph.D. candidate and Instructor in Physiological Chemistry at Pennsylvania before being drafted into the army and classified as a scientific and professional soldier to do medical research during the Korean War. This military scientific experience convinced me to change my occupational choice and I received an M.B.A. degree from City University of New York before going to Pennsylvania in 1955.

As a refugee from the empirical research of the biological sciences with its emphasis on experimental design and statistical inference, I found Weintraub's realistic approach to economic analysis more relevant than the so-called 'scientific' empirical approach of some of my more famous professors at Pennsylvania who tried to distill the values of economic parameters from time series data. (My M.B.A. thesis had been on the use of Time Series Analysis in economics.) I was fortunate to study under Sidney during the period when he was developing his ideas for his *Approach* analysis; the lucidity of his arguments strongly affected my own choice of problems to be studied in future years.

made great strides towards providing policy guidelines which were *roughly* right rather than precisely wrong!

In his 1949 *Price Theory* volume, Weintraub distinguished between *particular equilibrium analysis*, which focuses 'attention on one market while ignoring ramifications and repercussions in other markets . . . in contrast to *general equilibrium analysis*, which adumbrates the conceptual possibility of the simultaneous equilibrium . . . in all markets besides demonstrating the interrelations between the separate markets' (ibid., p. 126). At this early stage, Weintraub specifically noted the need to study general equilibrium analysis in order to specify the necessary conditions, and to explore interdependencies of markets, despite the 'violence the idea of general equilibrium does to our sense of reality, and even if we entirely reject it as an artificial image of the economic world' (ibid., pp. 126–7).

Almost a quarter of a century later, after millions of man-hours have been spent by professional economists throughout the world on developing such an analysis, Hahn has written that at this time the one and only useful function that general equilibrium analysis has demonstrated so far is to explain why the conditions necessary to assure an optimal resource allocation can *never* be achieved in the real world. As Hahn states,

> The argument will here turn on the absence of futures markets and contingent futures markets and on the inadequate treatment of time and uncertainty. This negative role of Arrow–Debreu equilibrium I consider almost to be sufficient justification for it, since practical men and ill-trained theorists everywhere in the world do not understand what they are claiming to be the case when they claim a beneficient and coherent role for the invisible hand. *But for descriptive purposes, of course, this negative role is hardly a recommendation.* (1973, pp. 14–15, italics added)

Thus, after years of effort, Hahn's conclusion is Weintraub's intuitive starting point.

Weintraub's dynamic analysis of the relationships between pricing behaviour, innovations, and development is more in the mould of Schumpeter's conception of creative destruction than in the pseudo *welfare* constructions of modern 'ill-trained' theorists who envision deregulation in the absence of demonstrated externalities as the only policy solution to all our economic maladies. Weintraub, however, after delving deeply into real world dynamics, concluded,

> It is a spurious, and perhaps dangerous, pastime to suggest price changes as a means of improving the resource-allocating efficiency of the price mechanism without probing the effects of price changes on such dynamic phenomena as commodity innovation and commodity progress, and the impact of controls upon the spirit of business enterprise. So much of the

analysis presumes that we have an original choice of instituting one mode of pricemaking rather than another, while realistically we must always remember that the economy is a 'going' one; any change will work hardships and will be resisted by those adversely affected. Policy cannot assume this problem away by presupposing that the damages are unimportant, that the hostility is misguided, or that the ill effects fall only upon powerful 'vested interests' whose welfare can be disregarded. Animated by a bitter political philosophy, the policy will be self-defeating, inimical as it is to our institutions, ethics and concepts of freedom. (1949, pp. 437–8)

As an indication of the kind of problems he would devote most of his energies to in the following years, Weintraub wrote in his Preface to *Price Theory* that 'the theory of income division, on the other hand, is in a more chaotic state; a laborious job of reconstruction, in my opinion is necessary' (ibid., p. vii). Since then Sidney Weintraub, with characteristic goodwill and indefatigable effort, was engaged in such a reconstruction.

In 1958, his *Approach to the Theory of Income Distribution* explicitly developed the conceptual analysis of Keynes's aggregate supply function. In this classic volume, Weintraub rendered intelligible the Marshallian microfoundations of Keynes's macroanalysis. Clearly, his earlier *Price Theory* system of analysis provided Weintraub with the insights necessary to become the first economist since 1936 to develop a supply-side dimension to Keynesian macroeconomics. Thus, in one sense, Weintraub was the first 'supply-side' economist, but his system was far superior to those who, in recent years, profess a 'supply-side' analysis based on the dual misconceptions of Say's Law, which assured there were no obstacles to full employment, and Walras's Law, which assured instantaneous and simultaneous market clearings.

In personal correspondence (dated 1 November 1957) to Weintraub, Robert Clower wrote:

I have just finished reading with great interest (and therefore care) your recent *EJ* article on 'Aggregate Demand and Supply', and it seemed appropriate to let you know that I found it very good. The spate of recent articles on the topic, each of which has served to muddy more water than it has cleared, should be choked off at this stage.

Herewith my personal thanks for providing a reference to which I may refer future students of aggregate economics for *a beautifully clear statement of what Keynes 'should have meant' if we suppose that he was a rational being*. (Italics added)

Similarly, in personal correspondence (dated 14 January 1959) Dennis Robertson, writing to Weintraub from Trinity College, Cambridge, noted that he had 'been reading your [1956] *AER* article again with great appreciation of its clarification and thoroughness' in its discussion of the '*D* [aggregate demand] and *Z* [aggregate supply] curves'.

Clower and Robertson obviously recognized the clarity and importance of Weintraub's aggregate supply and demand analysis, which first appeared in the *American Economic Review*, December 1956, and the *Economic Journal* in September 1957 (and was incorporated in and subsequently developed further in Weintraub's *Approach*, 1958). Had the rest of the economics profession paid as much attention to Weintraub's *Approach* and its analysis of aggregate supply and demand interdependence for monetary production economies, with its explicit link between productivity and relative income shares, many of the false 'trade-off' prognostications of the neoclassical synthesis Keynesians could have been avoided and the popular fortunes and successes of Keynesian economics maintained.

Western governments, when faced with the growing problems of inflation and stagnation in the twenty years following Weintraub's *Approach*, would not have been advised by their 'ill-trained' economists to adopt policies which only exacerbated stagflation tendencies. Had the Weintraubian aggregate supply system been more widely adopted by Keynesians, the resulting theoretical framework would have been sufficiently strong to ward off the simplistic, faddish solutions put forth by monetarists and their rational expectations brethren in recent years to fill the vacuous gap in theory and policy left by the bastardized neoclassical synthesis Keynesian analysis. Had Weintraub's contributions been more widely recognized by leaders in the Keynesian movement, both economic theory and the inhabitants of Western economic systems would have been far better off.

It is indeed difficult, from hindsight, to comprehend why economists who pride themselves on their objectivity and complete separation from value judgements did not react more enthusiastically to Weintraub's clear, concise, and correct micro- and macroanalysis. It could not be for lack of information as to the existence of Weintraub's work. Paul Samuelson, for example, in a 1964 essay entitled 'A Brief Survey of Post Keynesian Development' (which appeared in R. Lekachman's best selling *Keynes' General Theory: Report of Three Decades*) wrote, 'Pretty much as a lone wolf, Sidney Weintraub has also been formulating macroeconomic theories of income distribution' (p. 343). Moreover, Samuelson went on to note that there was 'ample evidence' that Weintraub had been fruitfully working in this area 'for a considerable period of time'. Nevertheless, the devastating realities of Weintraub's far-sighted analysis of inflation, income distribution, and growth were continually ignored by the 'Keynesian' economics establishment who preferred to fill 'empty economic boxes' throughout the 1960s and 1970s. Sidney Weintraub was clearly an economic prophet before his time!

In 1959, Weintraub presented, in *A General Theory of the Price Level*, a simple but powerful statistical analysis to demonstrate that the price level associated with the *business gross product* produced by the entrepreneurial firms in the private sector could be viewed as related to wage costs per unit of output (i.e. money-wage rate divided by the average productivity of labour) plus a gross profit mark-up. Weintraub demonstrated that between 1929 and 1957 the aggregate profit margin or markup (which Weintraub labelled k) in business gross product showed small, *non-systematic*, annual percentage changes. Over the three decades surveyed, Weintraub concluded 'the evidence is clear: the practical constancy of k is an empirical fact' (ibid., p. 39). Through the Great Depression, the Second World War, and the post-war boom, the *facts* had dictated that secular price level movements could be mainly described via changes in money-wages relative to productivity. From this simple but clear analytical construction and its theoretical basis in the relationship between income shares and aggregate supply enveloped in his *Approach*, Weintraub was able, at that early date, to criticize the monetarist approach to controlling inflation. 'Our criticism of the Federal Reserve has been of the incompatibility between the job and the tools allotted. Man may get to the moon in a rocket, not in a rocking chair. The wage level, not the money supply, governs the price level . . . the Federal Reserve with the power to cut off or augment money supplies is a poor instrument for achieving economic stability in prices with near full employment' (ibid., p. 88).[1]

Since the mid 1950s, Weintraub laboured at picking up the shattered pieces of the Keynesian Revolution and redirecting economic theory and policy towards the practical, important problems of our times. As early as 1960, he was advocating guidelines (or what he called 'watchtower' incomes policies) – several years before the Kennedy administration adopted and successfully pursued such policies. In January 1971, Weintraub published the first version of a tax-based incomes policy in the *Lloyds Bank Review* in which he proposed using tax penalties on firms. Later in that year he collaborated with Henry Wallich, a member of the Board of Governors of the Federal Reserve System, to spell out in greater detail a tax-based incomes policy. The fruitful collaboration (apparently encouraged by Leonard Silk of the *New York Times*) provided Weintraub with sufficient public and professional attention to attract others to accept the verities that Weintraub had spent years analysing. Today, his vision still offers developed entrepreneurial economies the primary solution to the second great crisis of capitalism in the twentieth century – stagflation.

I have often heard Sidney Weintraub admiringly quote Jevon's view that 'in matters of philosophy and science authority has ever been the great opponent of truth. A despotic calm is usually the triumph of error. In the republic of the sciences sedition and even anarchy are beneficial in the long run to the greatest happiness of the greatest number.' Weintraub continually railed against the smug and complacent economics establishment who, he believed, ignored economic realities as they increased their professional prestige. Sidney had an inextinguishable faith in the ultimate victory of the truth of ideas over vested intellectual interests. With his co-founding of the *Journal of Post Keynesian Economics*, Weintraub hoped to leave a permanent medium for preventing the despotism of authority in economics from fostering intellectual games while ignoring the hard economic truths.

Notes

1. Of course, the alternative method of constraining money wages via massive unemployment, direct union bashing, forcing losses and bankruptcies on productive enterprises, and so on can also be effective – as Ronald Reagan, Paul Volker, and Mrs Thatcher have demonstrated. This approach, however, was considered an unacceptable and barbaric policy by Weintraub – especially since other, more civilized, policy options (e.g. TIP) were available.

References

Hahn, F. H. (1973), *On the Notion of Equilibrium in Economics* (Cambridge: Cambridge University Press).

Samuelson, P. A. (1964), 'A Brief Survey of Post Keynesian Developments', in R. Lekachman (ed.), *Keynes' General Theory: Reports of Three Decades* (New York: St Martin's Press).

Weintraub, S. (1949), *Price Theory* (New York: Pitman).

Weintraub, S. (1956), 'A Macroeconomic Approach to the Theory of Wages', *American Economic Review*, 46.

Weintraub, S. (1957), 'The Micro-foundations of Aggregate Demand and Supply', *Economic Journal* 67.

Weintraub, S. (1958), *An Approach to the Theory of Income Distribution* (Philadelphia: Chilton).

Weintraub, S. (1959), *A General Theory of the Price Level, Output, Income Distribution, and Economic Growth* (Philadelphia: Chilton).

45 Liquidity and Not Increasing Returns Is the Ultimate Source of Unemployment Equilibrium*

In 1982, President Reagan suggested that the unemployment problem could be solved if only each business firm in the nation immediately hired one more employee. Since there are more firms than unemployed workers, the solution is obviously statistically accurate, but unless the employment by each firm of these additional workers creates a profitable demand for all the additional output, it will not be profitable to employ the extra workers. In a Keynesian world, the lack of effective demand means that sales of this additional output produced under this Reagan proposal cannot be profitable. Nevertheless, in a recent article, M. L. Weitzman's analysis (1982) implies that the Reagan announcement, if somehow implemented, would assure profitable sales of the additional output.

Weitzman has unwittingly presented the 'foundations of unemployment theory' which provides a theoretical basis for this Reagan solution to the unemployment problem. Thus despite Weitzman's claim (ibid., p. 789) that his analysis 'is more an exercise in logical consistency than a serious attempt to derive policy conclusions', unless the logical flaws, limitations, and inapplicability of his logical 'exercise' to real world unemployment problems are demonstrated, economic advisors to conservative heads of state might use this exercise to justify a Reagan 'private sector' policy solution.

This chapter demonstrates that Weitzman's foundations of unemployment theory are neither (a) logically consistent with Keynes's unemployment theory (which Weitzman might admit) nor (b) applicable to the real world. Weitzman has implicitly conceded (b) when he suggests that he wishes to model a coordination failure in a Say's Law world, while recognizing that 'the practical macroeconomist . . . [might avoid] the issue by asserting, *quite correctly, the empirical proposition that Say's Law does not hold in a modern industrial economy*' (ibid., p. 794; italics added).

More importantly from a theoretical viewpoint, this chapter provides (c)

* *Journal of Post Keynesian Economics*, 7 (1985).

a simple refutation to Weitzman's claim that his analysis demonstrates that increasing returns is a necessary condition for, and the *ultimate source* of, a meaningful unemployment theory.

1 THE WEITZMAN MODEL

Weitzman correctly demonstrates that, given the fundamental neoclassical assumptions of optimizing agents with immediate, insatiable tastes for producible goods and a production technology of constant returns to scale, there will never be involuntary unemployment. Idle workers could always hire themselves and produce the same quantity of goods that each worker would produce (*and immediately consume* under Weitzman's assumptions) if hired by existing firms. 'When unemployed factor units are all going about their business spontaneously employing themselves or being employed, the economy will automatically break out of unemployment' (Weitzman, 1982, p. 792); i.e. Say's Law would hold and there would be no barrier to full employment.[1]

Weitzman, to his credit, recognizes that there is something wrong with this logically correct orthodox neoclassical solution to a pressing real world problem. Since he has resurrected the Say's Law notion that supply creates its own demand, Weitzman searches for a change in some fundamental supply-side neoclassical assumption which will logically result in an 'internally consistent theory of steady state involuntary unemployment [which] is possible, even plausible' (p. 787). Unfortunately, Weitzman provides a scheme which is not logically possible much less plausible, for he assumes (p. 792, n. 1) that his analysis is applicable to an economy where all products including money are producible by labour.

In Weitzman's view 'the ultimate source of unemployment is increasing returns' (p. 788), and not the existence of money, savings, or international trade (p. 792), or even a distinction between financial and real activities (p. 790). The 'basic truth', Weitzman insists, is that 'increasing returns . . . the natural enemy of pure competition and the primary cause of imperfect competition' (p. 794) is, in the final analysis, *the* cause of involuntary unemployment (p. 788).

Here then is yet another neoclassical proof that the primary cause of involuntary unemployment is the existence of monopolistic competition and fixed nominal wages (pp. 795, 797). The novelty in Weitzman's model is, however, that flexible wages and prices will *not* cure unemployment (p. 800). Since it is a coordination failure which only exists in an imperfectly competitive world which creates 'a vicious cycle of self-sustaining involuntary unemployment', Weitzman claims that unemployment 'would go away if only all firms would simultaneously expand output' (p. 788); if, for example, all firms simultaneously heeded President Reagan's clarion call.

If only the Weitzman analysis were applicable to modern-day monetary economies, then full employment could be readily achieved via (1) self-employment policies in constant returns to scale industries, and (2) government policies, à la Reagan, which encourage firms with increasing returns production processes to expand employment immediately. Such pernicious policy suggestions necessarily follow from Weitzman's system no matter what his disclaimers. Real world unemployment, unfortunately, has a more fundamental 'ultimate source' than Weitzman's special type of increasing returns.[2]

Although not denying the existence and importance of monopoly power and money-wage (or price) rigidities, Keynes argued that involuntary unemployment equilibrium was due to the interaction of conditions of aggregate demand with those of aggregate supply (Keynes, 1973, p. 179) in a monetary economy. Involuntary unemployment could persist even in the presence of constant returns to scale (Keynes, 1939), and even increasing returns. Flexible money-wages (and prices) and a purely competitive economic system would not, *ceteris paribus*, have a tendency to produce full employment if there were initially lack of effective demand (Keynes, 1936, pp. 245–54, 260–2). For Keynes (ibid., ch. 17) it was the existence of money and other non-producible liquid assets, and not the existence of monopoly power or the technical production conditions of aggregate supply, which was the ultimate cause of involuntary unemployment. Yet Weitzman (1982, p. 792, n. 1) specifically denies that the existence of 'hoarding of a non-produced asset' such as money will necessarily produce involuntary unemployment.

In his 'exercise in logical consistency' Weitzman (p. 789) employs the *deux ex machina* of monopolistic competition in combination with short-run expectations of spoiling the market (if output increases) to maintain an exogenously determined unemployment rate u which is 'parameterising the level of short run aggregate demand' (p. 796). It is the *ad hoc* assumption of 'spoiling the market' expectations (which could not exist in a competitive environment) added to the assumption of increasing returns (that assures monopolistic competition) which is the specific case 'logical mechanism' for Weitzman's coordination failure, which ultimately sustains an exogenously given unemployment.

Keynes, on the other hand, provided a *general* theory of involuntary unemployment which does not require either increasing returns, or monopolistic competition, or spoiling the market expectations, or a fixed nominal wage, or a parameterized level of aggregate demand. For Keynes (1936, pp. 30–2), there could be a lack of effective demand *even if firms were to initially hire the full employment level of workers – hence a coordination failure cannot be the cause of Keynesian involuntary unemployment*.

The ultimate source of unemployment, instead, involved the concept of liquidity and the resultant 'essential properties' of interest and money which requires that liquid assets cannot be produced by labour in the private sector (ibid., ch. 17). When, in the aggregate, people want to spend some portion of their full employment income on money or other liquid assets, '[u]nemployment develops, that is to say, because people want the moon; – men cannot be employed when the object of desire is something which cannot be produced and the demand for which cannot be readily choked off' (ibid., p. 235).

2 WEITZMAN'S AND KEYNES'S UNEMPLOYMENT THEORIES ARE LOGICALLY INCOMPATIBLE

Weitzman (1982, p. 794) claims that Say's Law is a 'first principle' upon which logically to build a consistent microfoundation for underemployment equilibrium theory. Weitzman's analysis is, therefore, logically inconsistent with Keynes's underemployment equilibrium theory, for Keynes (1936, p. 26) declared that Say's Law 'is not the true law relating the aggregate demand and supply functions . . . [hence] there is a vitally important chapter of economic theory which remains to be written and without which all discussions of the volume of aggregate employment are futile'.

In Keynes's description of Say's Law (ibid.) full employment is not automatically achieved since 'effective demand instead of having a unique equilibrium value, is an infinite range of values all equally admissible; and the amount of employment is indeterminate except in so far as the marginal disutility of labour sets an upper limit'. In Weitzman's analysis the level of employment must be exogenously determined within the constraint of full employment; otherwise employment is indeterminate. Once the exogenous rate of unemployment is specified, then

increasing returns prevents supply from creating its own demand because the unemployed are essentially blocked from producing. Either existing firms will not hire them given the current state of demand, or, even, if a group of unemployed workers can be coalesced effectively into a discrete lump of new supply; it will spoil the market before ever giving Say's Law a chance to start operating. (Weitzman, 1982, p. 801)

In Weitzman's analysis, the only barrier to full employment is that there is no automatic mechanism 'for the balanced simultaneous expansion of all markets' (ibid.). If either entrepreneurs would initially hire the full employment level of workers, or if the nation's leader called for a simultaneous expansion of all markets by each firm hiring an equal share of unemployed workers, then there would never be a lack of effective demand.

Weitzman's casual treatment of the conditions of aggregate demand is due to his Say's Law assumptions that (i) all income earned in the production of goods will be immediately spent on the production of goods (p. 798), and more specifically, (ii) the workers' marginal propensity to consume commodities produced by labour is unity so that, as far as workers are concerned, any additional supply of real output creates its own demand (p. 795). Weitzman's 'model treats as exogenously fixed: aggregate demand, the number of firms, and the nominal wage. Endogenously by profit maximization are: prices, outputs and employment' (p. 797).

Weitzman must realize that his analysis is logically inconsistent with Keynes's, although he does not specifically indicate this to the reader. If Weitzman is presenting his employment theory as preferable to Keynes's then he must be claiming:

(a) that Weitzman's analysis provides microfoundations based on the first neoclassical principle of Say's Law, while Keynes's theory is not logically consistent with this neoclassical first principle; therefore
(b) the Weitzman micro–macro analysis is internally consistent (p. 794), while
(c) Keynes's analysis has no consistent microfoundation.

Unfortunately for Weitzman, only proposition (a) is clearly correct. Keynes specifically rejects Say's Law and, therefore, his theory cannot be consistent with neoclassical 'first principles'. This does not mean that Keynes did not have any microfoundations for his unemployment theory. It does mean that Keynes's analysis was revolutionary!

Elsewhere (Davidson and Smolensky, 1964; Davidson, 1972; 1974; 1977; 1980) I have demonstrated that Keynes's macrosystem does have a logically consistent Marshallian microfoundation. Consequently, I reject proposition (c), but having developed the argument in detail elsewhere, I will not join that debate here.

More importantly, it can be demonstrated that proposition (b) is not correct. Weitzman's analysis is logically inconsistent within his own neoclassical framework and hence cannot provide the 'foundations of unemployment theory'.

3 THE LOGICAL INCONSISTENCY OF WEITZMAN'S MODEL

Without delving into a deep analysis of all the strange neoclassical 'hang-ups' in the Weitzman analysis, it is easy to demonstrate that involuntary unemployment cannot be maintained in an economy operating under either constant or increasing returns to scale *unless* there exists money and/or other liquid assets which are non-producible by labour in the private sector – a result which Weitzman's analysis specifically denies (p. 792, n. 1).

To refute the claim that increasing returns is a necessary condition for unemployment, assume that money is a producible good that grows on trees (since Weitzman claims non-producibility is not the cause of unemployment). As long as money is a producible thing, unemployed workers should individually (or in groups) go into the business of harvesting money trees, no matter what law of returns – constant, increasing, or decreasing – prevails. Starting from an initial unemployment level, real aggregate demand can always be increased as idle workers can always become self-employed to earn additional income by harvesting money trees! There can be no fears of spoiling the market in the money-tree industry as long as either the nominal wage is given or there is a coordinated fall in wages and prices. *Thus, as long as workers are free to move into and out of the money-tree-harvesting industry, as long as the marginal yield per man hour exceeds the marginal disutility of harvesting, workers can, and will, improve their satisfaction by harvesting money.*[3] Workers can always voluntarily reach full employment, if the money commodity is readily producible under increasing, constant, or diminishing returns with the use of labour in the private sector!

Of course, if money was a non-producible asset, the exogenously determined unemployment rate could be maintained in Weitzman's analysis – but he specifically denies this possibility. Weitzman's analysis, which embodies a Say's Law proposition that the supply of labour is the demand for goods produced by labour, will not permit any steady state rate of unemployment, as long as labour is permitted to produce money (under constant, diminishing, or increasing returns to scale) and the marginal disutility of harvesting money trees is less than the marginal utility of possessing money.

As Hahn has clearly shown, and Weitzman should have recognized, microfoundations that permit the existence of involuntary unemployment equilibrium require demand conditions which involve the existence of 'resting places for savings other than reproducible assets'[4] (Hahn, 1977, p. 31). As I have demonstrated (Davidson, 1972; 1980), the existence of such resting places is a fundamental building block of Keynes's and the Post Keynesians' analysis of a monetary economy, where the 'essential properties' of money are zero or negligible elasticities of production and substitution (Keynes, 1936, ch. 17).

To denote that the elasticity of production of money (as well as other liquid assets (Keynes, 1936, p. 241, n. 1) is zero is merely to recognize, in the language of economists, that 'money does not grow on trees' and hence cannot be harvested by the use of labour in the private sector whenever workers are made idle by a lack of effective demand for all other producible goods. Since the elasticity of substitution between money (and liquid assets) and producible goods is also zero (or negligible), idle economic resources cannot become employed in producing other producible (by the use of labour) assets which can (as a substitute) easily do money's work and therefore generate a demand for the products of labour.

4 CONCLUSION

In sum, Weitzman has shown that, in a neoclassical world, the orthodox assumptions used to demonstrate an automatic market process which assures full employment do not permit any analysis of unemployment equilibrium. Neoclassical theory solves the problem of unemployment by assumptions which assure it does not exist! What Weitzman has failed to do even as an exercise in logical consistency is to show that neoclassical 'first principles' which postulate some form of Say's Law as the basic condition for labour supply can provide any consistent logical foundation for unemployment theory.

Weitzman has not comprehended Keynes's revolutionary message that it is not only conditions of supply which (as even pre-Keynesians recognized) can result in monopoly and unemployment. More importantly, in an economy that organized its production processes efficiently by the use of money and contracts, there is always a threat of a lack of effective demand, independent of the existing returns to scale. Moreover, this threat is more likely to occur as the wealth of the community increases and as savings and the desire for liquidity become more important relative to the need to use current production for survival of income earners (Keynes, 1936, p. 219).

POSTSCRIPT

The existence of non-producible liquid assets is a necessary *and* sufficient condition for unemployment whenever the public desires additional liquidity out of full employment income.

The existence of non-producible (by the private sector) assets is a necessary condition for involuntary unemployment. Some have incorrectly suggested, however, that the existence of such non-producibles is not a sufficient condition due to what may be termed the 'real liquidity effect' of existing nominal financial assets.

This real liquidity effect can be described as follows. If there is a coordinated fall in money-wages and *all* prices and if there is an *unchanging* nominal stock of financial assets, then the unchanged total nominal value of these assets can provide any amount of liquidity desired. (This presumes that the nominal prices of financial assets are not included in the coordinated fall of *all* prices.) With sufficient real liquidity provided via the increased real liquidity value of nominal financial assets, the public, it is claimed, will spend its entire full employment income on producible goods. Hence full employment equilibrium can be restored even in the presence of non-producible liquid financial assets.

This real liquidity effect brought about by a coordinated fall in money-wages and prices with a fixed nominal stock of financial assets is, however, logically incorrect for it ignores the feedback effects of the coordinated fall in wages and product prices (and hence money incomes) on the nominal value of all outstanding financial assets. Whenever there is a coordinated fall in all money-wages and product prices, then *there cannot be a given stock of financial assets whose total nominal value remains unchanged*. The total nominal value of all outstanding financial assets (including bank money) will fall *pari passu* with the hypothesized coordinated drop in wages and prices of producibles.

The nominal market (present) value of all financial (equity and debt) securities depends on their expected future net (nominal) cash flows. If all product prices fall, then the future net cash inflow associated with any equity security must decline. Hence the nominal value of equity securities falls concomitantly and therefore equity assets cannot increase in real liquidity value in the face of a coordinated price fall.

Similarly for debt securities: either the debtors' nominal contractual obligations are included in the hypothesized 'coordinated fall' and therefore the market value of debt security holdings (by creditors) falls proportionately; or the debtors will be unable to meet their (unchanged) nominal contractual interest and principal repayments since the debtors' money incomes are dependent on the falling money wage and product price level. If debtors are unable to meet their unchanged nominal obligations then they will go bankrupt. With the ensuing bankruptcies the total market value of the debt securities held by creditors will decline to accompany the coordinated drop in wages and prices. In either case, the real liquidity value of outstanding debt holdings will not be enhanced with a coordinated fall in prices.

The final fallback position of those who claim the real liquidity effect of a coordinated fall in prices is the belief that there is an unchanging nominal money stock whose real liquidity value will be enhanced. If, however, the money in the economy is primarily bank money based on a fractional reserve system (as in all modern societies), then the nominal value of the outstanding money stock will not be unchanged as all prices fall.

An unchanged nominal quantity of money means an unchanged nominal liability total for the banking system. A coordinated fall in money-wages and product prices will, however, induce the collapse of nominal values on the banking system's asset side of its balance sheet so that with an unchanged nominal total liability there will be widespread bankruptcies of banks.

The nominal value of the banks' portfolio of assets depends on bank borrowers being able to meet their nominal cash flow obligations. Consequently, a coordinated fall in all prices will force private sector borrowers to default *en masse* on their obligations to the banks. The result will be a collapse of asset values on banks' balance sheets. Consequently, any significant coordinated fall in wages and prices will wipe out the banks' net worth thereby inducing massive banking system bankruptcies. As banks go 'belly up' on any significant scale, the outstanding nominal stock of bank money will, *ceteris paribus*, decline and therefore the real liquidity value of the remaining money stock will not increase (shades of the Great Depression!).

Finally, with significant bankruptcies – which are inevitable if unchanging nominal debts securities are a significant portion of liquid financial assets (and in a bank money economy this must be so) – then all full employment existence proofs are in jeopardy. Consequently, it is impossible to demonstrate that any coordinated fall in wages and prices in the presence of possible bankruptcies will ever lead to a full employment equilibrium – for no such position may exist.

In sum then, even in the face of a coordinated fall in wages and prices, *the existence of non-producible assets is a necessary and sufficient condition for unemployment equilibrium to occur whenever the public desires to place savings in resting places other than producible assets.*

Notes

1. Thus, if economic advisors of conservative governments are logically consistent in their use of orthodox (constant returns) neoclassical models to develop their policy recommendations for reducing involuntary unemployment, they should discourage heads of state from even urging existing firms to hire the unemployed. Logically consistent neoclassical advisors could provide the nation with 'proof' that idle workers are not involuntarily unemployed; they are parasites living off the dole rather than joining the productive elements of society by becoming self-employed.

2. For an analysis of why Weitzman's increasing returns is only a special (type III) case, see note 3.

3. At one point, Weitzman (1982, pp. 794–5) limits his proof to a conception of 'increasing returns' to a 'stage III large scale specialization' production function which requires a fixed 'overhead' labour input (F) before any output is achieved. Thus, Weitzman, even if he is internally consistent in his argument, has *not* provided a *general* analysis of unemployment; he has not shown for the more general case of increasing returns (independent of 'overhead labour') that increasing returns condition is a necessary condition for unemployment.

   In fact, however, at various points Weitzman implies that his analysis is applicable not only to a specific form of stage III increasing returns but to any generalized form of increasing returns. For example, Weitzman writes: 'The specific form of the production function (3) is chosen because it is easy to work with and interpret. *More general production functions showing increasing returns would give similar results*' (p. 795; italics added); 'Increasing returns, understood in its broadest sense . . .' (p. 794); and, 'In this paper I want to argue that the ultimate source of unemployment is increasing returns' (p. 788).

Thus, even if Weitzman's analysis was internally consistent, he is providing only a *special theory of unemployment*, while Keynes presented a 'general theory' of unemployment which did not rely on either any specific form of production function, coordination failures, or the existence of monopoly for its results.

Unfortunately, Weitzman's 'stage III' case claim that increasing returns is a necessary condition for unemployment is not internally consistent with his assertion (1982, p. 801) that 'even if a group of unemployed workers can be coalesced effectively into a discrete lump of new supply, it will spoil the market before ever giving Say's Law a chance to start operating'. For if money is a producible good (even if produced under Weitzman's stage III production function) then as long as 'unemployed workers can be coalesced effectively' (i.e. into a group which exceeds the minimum fixed labour input requirement of Weitzman's specific 'stage III' production function so that some money-tree harvesting can occur), then, as our analysis above shows, there can be no spoiling of the market for the fruits of the money-tree industry. Accordingly, Weitzman's own analysis is not internally consistent in his attempt to demonstrate that 'the ultimate source of unemployment equilibrium' (1982, p. 788) and a necessary condition for unemployment is a 'stage III' increasing returns production function. In the presence of producible money, there can be no involuntary unemployment.

4. Finally, for those who might try to argue that Hahn's 'resting place' argument does not deny that with a coordinated fall in wages and prices some liquidity or real balance effect could restore full employment via stimulating consumption, it should be pointed out that this argument is merely a semantic obfuscation. For a full employment equilibrium to come about, consumption (out of the full employment level of income) must rise and *real savings must fall*. Thus the hypothesized initial rate of savings would not end up finding a 'resting place' in other than producible assets.

To assert that there are 'resting places in other than producible assets' is to assume that the marginal propensity to consume *in real terms* is always less than unity, even in the face of a coordinated fall in money wages and prices. Unless words have lost their meaning, savings means 'the excess of income over what is spent on consumption' (Keynes, 1936, p. 74) and 'a resting place' means no further movement out of such places. Accordingly, any claim that a coordinated fall in money-wages and prices of producibles will move real savings out of their resting place back into the purchase of consumption goods is simply bosh!

References

Davidson, P. (1972), *Money and The Real World* (London: Macmillan).

Davidson, P. (1974), 'Disequilibrium Market Adjustment: Marshall Revisited', *Economic Inquiry*, 12, pp. 146–58. (Chapter 34 in this volume).

Davidson, P. (1977), 'Discussion of Paper by Professor Leijonhufvud', in Harcourt, pp. 313–17.

Davidson, P. (1980), 'The Dual-faceted Nature of the Keynesian Revolution:

Money and Money Wages in Unemployment and Production Flow Prices', *Journal of Post Keynesian Economics*, 2 (3), pp. 291–318 (Chapter 39 in this volume).

Davidson, P. and E. Smolensky (1964), *Aggregate Supply and Demand Analysis* (New York: Harper & Row).

Hahn, F. H. (1977), 'Keynesian Economics and General Equilibrium Theory', in Harcourt, pp. 25–40.

Harcourt, G. C. (1977), *The Microfoundations of Macroeconomics* (London: Macmillan).

Keynes, J. M. (1936), *The General Theory of Employment, Interest, and Money* (New York: Harcourt).

Keynes, J. M. (1939), 'Relative Movements of Real Wages and Output', *Economic Journal*, 49, pp. 34–51.

Keynes, J. M. (1973), *The Collected Writings of John Maynard Keynes*, Vol. XIV (London: Macmillan).

Weitzman, M. L. (1982), 'Increasing Returns and the Foundation of Unemployment Theory'. *Economic Journal*, 92, pp. 787–804.

46 The Simple Macroeconomics of a Non-ergodic Monetary Economy Versus a Share Economy: Is Weitzman's Macroeconomics Too Simple?*

Years ago, Dennis Robertson (1956, p. 81) uttered the following witticism about economic analysis: 'Now as I have often pointed out to my students, some of whom have been brought up in sporting circles, highbrow opinion is like a hunted hare: if you stand in the same place, or nearly the same place, it can be relied upon to come round to you in a circle.' Martin Weitzman's (1985) effort to demonstrate that (a) a money-wage system is *the* cause of unemployment, and (b) a cooperative (share) economy presents no obstacle to full employment is the latest example in this Robertsonian genre in several respects.

Weitzman, using a variant of the 'temporary equilibrium' system developed by Bénassy (1982) and Grandmont (1983), 'proves' once again that, in a fixed money-wage system, a short-run 'temporary competitive equilibrium' with less than full employment is possible. Of course, over forty years ago, in a less sophisticated analysis of equilibrium, Modigliani (1944) also 'proved' that unemployment was due to downward inflexible money-wages. And, again even before Keynes's *General Theory*, it was well known to orthodox economists that unemployment occurred when money-wages failed to decline in the face of unemployment. Thus, for at least the third time in a century, erudite opinion has 'demonstrated' that only labour's foolish reluctance to accept a flexible wage system cause it to be unemployed.

Weitzman's claim that his microeconomic model of monopolistic competition provides a 'natural underpinning for the standard aggregate demand specification' (1985, p. 937), however, seems to suggest that at least in this area, he has provided a scholarly innovation. Apparently, Weitzman

* *Journal of Post Keynesian Economics*, 9 (Winter 1986–7).

is unaware that in *The General Theory* Keynes assumed a given 'degree of competition' (1936, p. 245) (not necessarily pure competition) as part of his microanalytical foundations. Weintraub (1957; 1958) and later Davidson (1962) and Davidson and Smolensky (1964) have shown that this meant that Keynes's analytical Marshallian microfoundation framework assumed a constant degree of monopoly (as measured by Lerner's μ, 1935). Thus, in section 3 below, it is shown that Weitzman's micro-underpinnings represent a return to the Keynes–Weintraub aggregate supply analysis (even to the use of the symbol, μ, as a measure of the monopoly mark-up), despite Weitzman's disclaimer that he believes that the aggregate supply function is 'a dubious macroeconomic concept at best' (1985, p. 940, n. 6).

While Keynes combined this aggregate supply function with demand aspects which demonstrated that Say's Law 'is not the true law relating the aggregate demand and supply functions' (Keynes, 1936, p. 26), Weitzman has grafted Keynes's aggregate supply analysis onto a neoclassical (really pre-Keynesian) demand microfoundation based on Say's Law. That this latter hybrid analytical framework cannot be applicable as a description of real world monetary economies is evidenced by the fact that important results implied in the Weitzman model are, as explained in section 1 below, contrary to the facts of history and experience.

These incongruities between the Weitzman model and the real world experience are due to the use of some seemingly innocuous, but really very artificial, assumptions which make Weitzman's erudite framework inapplicable to real world economic phenomena.

1 WEITZMAN'S ASSUMPTIONS

Weitzman's analysis is severely biased by his selection of suppositions which logically eliminate such real world causes as variations in investment spending from affecting output levels, while requiring government policy to be the only destabilizing factor. These seemingly innocent assumptions include:

1. *All products are 'highly perishable'* (1985, p. 938). If this assumption is taken seriously, then there can be no capital goods industry, no capitalists, no existing stock of capital, no accumulation, and ultimately no behavioural analysis of investment decision-making and spending.

This fundamental perishability assumption throws out the Keynesian baby of variable investment expenditures as a possible source of employment instability with the bath water. Consequently, it is impossible to explain within the model the causes of employment instability as originating in the behavioural transactions of individual agents in the marketplace in the absence of any government action. (Thus as Weitzman's Table 1 (p. 942) implies, given the parameters of his system, *all* short-run changes in output and the price level are explained only by changes in autonomous government expenditures and/or government deficits!)

2. *The household's utility function implies an intertemporal marginal propensity to consume of unity*; that is, in the long run Say's Law holds,[1] even though households are assumed to have a parametrically determined (short-run) marginal propensity to consume out of current after-tax income of less than one. This Say's Law household utility function, combined with the previous assumption of highly perishable goods, implies that the only possible barrier to full employment in the current period is a technological one of the time incompatibility between demand and supply. The demand for goods is more durable, extending over periods, while the supply of all goods is highly perishable and lasts only one (undefined) time period.

If Weitzman permitted firms to produce *non-perishable* working capital goods, the households' current demand for future goods – as proxied by households' real balances (ibid., p. 938) – would induce firms to start up the production of work-in-process inventories immediately in order to be prepared to provide the goods for the future.

In an Arrow–Debreu type world of spot and forward markets (which is ultimately the foundation of Weitzman's 'temporary equilibrium' analysis), households would never hold any money. Instead, households would maximize utility (Weitzman's equation (1)) by allocating their entire budget to either buying goods spot or ordering goods on forward contract. *Payment for all spot and forward transactions would be made*, as Debreu (1959, pp. 32, 100) has always insisted, *at the initial (current) period*. Firms would respond to all market orders by immediately hiring workers not only to produce goods for current consumption by households and government but also to produce goods for future delivery under a technology which minimized the present value of the costs of production.

Consequently, if forward contracts and non-perishable inventories were permitted in the Weitzman model, there would not be any obstacles to full employment equilibrium – as this period's households' savings out of after-tax income would always equal this period's stock building of work-in-process future consumer goods. It is only the assumptions of a highly perishable supply interacting with an intertemporal Say's Law demand so that today's supply does not create today's demand for current goods *and* current production of inventories which permits Weitzman to have any possible barrier to full employment in his system.

In the real world where output and employment cycles are the greatest in the durable goods industries rather than in the non-durable sector, Weitzman's analysis of unemployment in a model where all goods are non-durables seems scarcely relevant!

3. *The government is the only autonomous spending sector* in the Weitzman model. All government deficits are financed by the government's

printing of money. The existing stock of money, therefore, is solely the result of past government deficits. Households are induced to hold more money any time the government decides to finance expenditures by printing money rather than via tax revenues (Weitzman, 1985, p. 939).

If, therefore, either government spending as a percentage of GNP is negligible, or if the government does not run a deficit (both of which are stylized facts describing the years just before the Great Depression), then (a) there would be no money (or at least no changes in the money stock) in the system, and (b) the level of aggregate demand would be basically unchanged. What then would have caused the Great Depression in the Weitzman model?

Furthermore, because the government is the only autonomous spender, it follows that households' savings are positively related to government deficits. If this model is a serious description of how the American economy currently operates, then we should have expected that in the years since 1980, with huge government deficits relative to both GNP and after-tax income, the US personal savings ratio should be at an all time high.[2] In fact, the personal savings–after-tax personal income ratio, in the last few years, has sunk to record lows as federal deficits grew to record highs. It would therefore appear that Weitzman's hypothetical world is quite remote from the facts of experience.

Moreover, if the government were to run a current period balanced budget continuously (as required in 1991 by the Gramm–Rudman legislation) then, as note 2 demonstrates, household savings out of after-tax income would be zero. Surely no one expects a permanent zero personal savings rate after 1990!

4. *Households hold money balances only for one reason – to buy future consumer goods* (ibid., p. 938). Even though Weitzman mentions the existence of an uncertain future (p. 938, n.4) and the unpredictability of changes in variables (p. 943), his model contains no concept of households holding money for the liquidity purposes associated with the precautionary motive. The speculative (but not the precautionary) motive is eleminated by Weitzman's assumption that no durables exist (besides money) which can be held over time and then resold in organized spot markets; hence, there is no future spot price to speculate on. But as Keynes (1936, p. 170) cogently argued, 'in the absence of an organised market, liquidity preference due to the precautionary motive would be greatly increased; whereas the existence of an organised market gives an opportunity for wide fluctuations in liquidity preference due to the speculative motive'.

In the real world, the demand for inactive precautionary (and speculative) money balances is due to human recognition that future economic outcomes cannot be predicted by the statistical analysis of existing data; that is, economic processes are non-ergodic (Davidson, 1982–3). Weitzman's elimination (by assumption) of the possibility of speculation will merely increase household demand for money for precautionary purposes, if, in his model, there is an 'uncertain future' (1985, p. 398) 'and at any time or place . . . variables are changing too rapidly and unpredictably' (p. 943).

In a non-ergodic economic system, sensible economic agents hold money – not simply for the purchase of goods either currently or in the future. Money is also held for the purposes of precautionary *liquidity*, that is, to meet either existing and/or potential future *money contractual obligations* when uncertain and statistically unpredictable future events can cause unforeseeable variations in cash flows and/or future spot purchase opportunities (Davidson, 1982–3).

Moreover, sensible agents will enter into money contracts which make them legally responsible for organizing long-lived complex and interdependent production (and durable consumption) activities, only because they are assured that, no matter how wrong future events may go, their liabilities are limited by their nominal contracts. Hence as long as they possess money, or liquid assets readily resaleable for money at an expected spot price in the future, agents 'know' they will have the funds necessary to meet these commitments as they come due. In a non-ergodic world, the institution of money contracts has evolved to permit sensible economic agents to limit, in advance, their potential cash outflows when they undertake activities the outcomes of which will only become known in the non-predictable future (Davidson and Davidson, 1984).

In an uncertain world where monetary contractual obligations span a significant period of calendar time, utility functions of all *sensible economic agents* must contain three arguments (rather than only two as proposed by Weitzman), namely (a) current goods, (b) future goods, and (3) money (and/or liquid assets readily resaleable for money on organized spot markets) to meet unforeseen and statistically unpredictable events (Davidson, 1983).

If (a) money and liquid assets have the *non-producibility properties (for the private sector)* assumed by Weitzman (1985, p. 938), *and* (b) if money and other liquid assets are *non-substitutable with producible goods* (a condition which violates Weitzman's household utility function specification but is consistent with Keynes's (1936, ch. 17) specification of the essential properties of money), then *a three-argument household utility function* involving current goods, future goods, and liquid assets (including money) *will provide the necessary and sufficient conditions to make Say's Law inapplicable in both the short run and the long run* (Davidson, 1984).

In this case, money is never neutral. Its very existence can form a barrier to full employment. For example, an increased demand for liquid money balances due to increased fears about an uncertain future can cause an increase in Keynesian unemployment (cf. Keynes, 1936, ch. 17; Davidson, 1972; 1978). Moreover, as Keynes readily demonstrated (1936, ch. 18), in such a monetary system, even if money wages were flexible, unemployment can be an equilibrium outcome in both the short run and the long run.

2   IS TECHNOLOGY INDEPENDENT OF THE COMPENSATION SYSTEM?

Because of Weitzman's assumptions of highly perishable goods and a ubiquitous technology where labour is the only fixed *and* variable input, no investment behaviour specification is possible to explain the labour intensity of the production process used by all firms. Instead, a constant marginal productivity of the variable labour input is assumed,[3] in the short as well as the long run (1985, p. 940). The same productivity of labour is also assumed in a wage system as in a profit sharing system (p. 944).

Is this *unvarying productivity of labour assumption*, independent of the labour compensation scheme, justifiable? If the gains of conversion from a wage system to a share economy involve only the real benefits of an end to unemployment and inflation and no real costs-of-productivity declines, as Weitzman claims (pp. 949–51), why has the historical development of industry tended to 'convert' the other way?

Weitzman's share economy is merely an extension of the ancient agricultural system of agreeing to share sales revenue from future farm production – known as sharecropping. The sharecropping system disappeared when it could not compete with the money-wage compensation system used by all modern large-scale agriculture firms. Sharecropping did not provide the capitalist–landowner incentives to apply labour-saving, cost-efficient technology, while it simultaneously tended to reduce the real income of sharecropping labourers to a bare subsistence. These facts suggest that identical technology (and productivity) will not occur in a share system of industry as in a wage system.

The reason is obvious. In the simple model of firms converting over from a wage system to a pure share system, where workers agree to accept a fixed proportion of total revenue independent of the existing hired labour force, there will be no incentive for managers of the firms to economize on labour use. The marginal cost of additional workers, for any given sales level, is zero.

If firms had any capital stock before they converted from a money wage system (with its incentives to seek out reduction in unit labour costs, given any demand specification) to a profit-sharing system, there would be no incentive in the share economy for rent-seeking managers to replace equipment as it wears out. Hiring more workers to replace the worn-out equipment to produce the same output would not cost the firm anything, while the cost of replacing the equipment would. Ultimately, for example, we would see a car industry where workers hand-carried frames down the assembly line, thereby increasing the rate of return on the declining capital base.

Consequently, if the marginal productivity of labour is a function of the capital–labour ratio, any conversion from an existing wage system to a pure profit-sharing system would encourage the adoption of a technology using more labour and as a result lead to a decline in the real productivity of labour. Firms would have the incentive to maximize their pure monopoly rents by eliminating all capital costs and instituting a complete labour-using technology (such as the one underlying Weitzman's equation (3)).

3 THE AGGREGATE SUPPLY FUNCTION

Keynes wrote *The General Theory* in order to show that Say's Law, where (aggregate) supply created its own (aggregate) demand, was not a 'true law' (Keynes, 1936, p. 26) applicable to a monetary, production economy. *In a Say's Law world, the aggregate demand function would be coincident with the aggregate supply function* so that 'effective demand, instead of having a unique equilibrium value, is an infinite range of values all equally admissible; and the amount of employment is indeterminate except in so far as the marginal disutility of labour sets an upper limit' (Keynes, 1936, p. 26). In other words, under Say's Law the economy is, at any employment level determined by firms' hiring decisions, in neutral equilibrium. Actual demand is constrained by actual income and employment; but there is no barrier to the economy obtaining a full employment output level (Davidson, 1984, pp. 563–5).

Keynes's revolutionary analysis stemmed from his belief that in a monetary, entrepreneurial economy *the aggregate demand function differed from, and was not coincident with, the aggregate supply function*. Weitzman, on the other hand, as shown in section 1, assumes an intertemporal Say's Law and hence his system will always be in long-run neutral equilibrium while his implicit supply and explicit demand function must be intertemporally coincident.

Weitzman's doubt about the concept of an aggregate supply function (1985, p. 940, n.6) is somewhat surprising since it is demonstrated below that his equations (30), (42), and (43) imply a Keynes aggregate supply function deeply imbedded in his framework.

Keynes's aggregate supply function is readily derived from ordinary Marshallian firm supply functions (1936, pp. 44–5). Hence, Keynes argued that the properties of the aggregate supply function 'involved few considerations which are not already familiar' (p. 89), while 'it was the part played by the aggregate demand function which has been overlooked' (p. 89). Accordingly, though Keynes briefly described the aggregate supply function (pp. 25, 44–5) and its inverse, the employment function (pp. 89, 280–1), aggregate supply was treated perfunctorily while the bulk of *The General Theory* was devoted to developing the characteristics of aggregate demand. (This may explain why many neoclassical synthesis Keynesians never explicitly developed the aggregate supply aspects of their model.)

It was left to Weintraub (1957; 1958) to elucidate Keynes's aggregate supply function which relates the aggregate number of workers (N) that profit-maximizing entrepreneurs would want to hire for each possible level of expected sales proceeds (Z) – given the money-wage rate (w), technology, and the degree of competition or monopoly (μ) (cf. Keynes, 1936, p. 245). If firms are fully integrated, aggregate sales proceeds equals GNP.

Following Keynes's argument (ibid., p. 41) that money values and quantities of employment are the only two 'fundamental units of quantity' to be used when dealing with aggregates, one should specify the aggregate supply proceeds either in money terms (Z) or in Keynes's wage unit terms (Z_w) which is money sales proceeds divided by the money-wage rate. Hence the aggregate supply function is specified as:

$$Z = f_1(N) \tag{46.1}$$

or

$$Z_w = f_2(N) \tag{46.2}$$

The Marshallian supply curve[4] for a single firm (s_f) indicates alternative price (p_f) versus quantity (q_f) profit-maximizing combinations based on the degree of monopoly facing the firm (μ) and marginal production costs (mc); i.e.

$$s_f = f_3(\mu, mc_f) \tag{46.3}$$

The value of μ depends on the market demand conditions facing the firm. Each profit-maximizing firm's mark-up over marginal costs is related to Lerner's (1935) measure of the degree of monopoly power ($\mu = 1/E$) where E is the price elasticity of demand facing the firm for any given level of effective demand (cf. Weitzman's [$\mu = E/(E - 1)$], equation (42).

In the simplest case, as aggregate demand changes, the firm faces a shifting isoelastic demand curve (cf. Weitzman, 1985, p. 942), so that employment and output varies without any change in the mark-up over marginal costs.[5]

The firm's marginal cost (mc_f), assuming labour is the only variable input in the production process, equals the money-wage (w) divided by marginal labour productivity (γ) where the latter is a function of employment (and the laws of returns involved in the technology of the firm).

Accordingly, Weitzman's equation (43) is equivalent to our equation (46.3) above.

Although output across firms in the same industry may be homogeneous and therefore can be aggregated to obtain the industry supply schedule in terms of prices (p) and quantities (q), this homogeneity of output assumption cannot be accepted as the basis for summing across industries or across firms in monopolistic competition to obtain the aggregate supply function (Keynes, 1936, ch. 4). Accordingly, each firm's Marshallian supply function must be transformed into Keynes's (1936, p. 44) microfirm supply function, which relates each firm's expected sales proceeds in money terms $(z_f = p_f \times q_f)$ with the firm's employment hirings (n_f)

Since returns, the money-wage, and the degree of monopoly are given, every point on a Marshallian supply function is associated with a unique profit-maximizing price-quantity combination whose multiple equals total expected sales proceeds, and since every firm's output level can be associated with a firm's unique hiring level, that is, $q_f = f(n_f)$, then every point of equation (46.3) (Weitzman's equation (43)) of the s-curve in p-versus-q space can be transformed to a point on a z-curve in pq-versus-n space to obtain

$$z_f = f_4(n_f) \tag{46.4}$$

Keynes's firm supply functions can then be aggregated in terms of homogeneous money and employment units together to obtain the aggregate supply function relating aggregate money sales proceeds (Z) and the aggregate quantity of employment units (N) as specified in equation (1).[6]

Weitzman, by assuming a specified law of production returns, degree of monopoly, and money-wage system, has, in effect, utilized a Keynes–Weintraub aggregate supply function in his system, in spite of his disclaimer. Unfortunately, this demand assumptions constrain his aggregate demand curve to be intertemporally coincident with aggregate supply, while Keynes permitted a more general, non-coincident demand relationship.

4 WAGE SYSTEM VERSUS SHARE SYSTEM OR ENTREPRENEURIAL ECONOMY VERSUS COOPERATIVE ECONOMY

Weitzman attempts to draw real world policy implications from his logically very restrictive and contrived Say's Law temporary equilibrium model, rather than attempting to follow the more general aggregate supply–demand analysis laid out by Keynes.

Just as Weitzman, in his limited framework, compared a money-wage economy with a share economy, Keynes, in his more general theory, juxtaposed an entrepreneurial economy with a cooperative economy. In an entrepreneurial economy, fixed money commitments (contracts) and especially money-wage contracts are used to organize production processes and hence money is never neutral. A cooperative economy, on the other hand, is a system where the 'factors of production are rewarded by dividing up in agreed proportions the actual output of their cooperative efforts' (Keynes, 1979, p. 77). In the cooperative system (Weitzman's pure share system), Keynes noted, Say's Law was applicable and money was neutral (ibid., pp. 77–8). But in the non-ergodic monetary world we live in, which Keynes labelled an entrepreneurial system, the conditions of a pure share economy are 'not satisfied in practice; with the result that there is a difference of the most fundamental importance between a cooperative economy and the type of entrepreneurial economy we actually live in' (ibid., p. 79).[7]

Weitzman, who has previously (1982, p. 794) argued that Say's Law is a 'first principle' upon which to build a consistent microfoundation of macroeconomics, cannot accept that we live in an non-ergodic entrepreneurial economy where liquidity and money contractual institutions are important and therefore Say's Law is inapplicable. Instead Weitzman, like Ricardo before him, 'offers us the extreme intellectual achievement . . . of adopting a hypothetical world remote from experience and then living in it consistently' (Keynes 1936, p. 192). Keynes, on the other hand, thought it more useful to build a hypothetical world that had the characteristics of the world we lived in and could generate proposals for improving the operation of that real world rather than *assuming* the easy transmutation of existing human economic systems.

Notes

1. What Weitzman does not seem to recognize is that Say's Law does not assure full employment as an equilibrium outcome. It only asserts that at any level of employment the economy is in neutral equilibrium and hence there is no obstacle to full employment (Keynes, 1936, p. 26). If, in a Say's Law world, firms hire less than capacity employment, then the supply produced will create exactly its own demand (and no more!), and equilibrium production will be at less then capacity. If firms then, for any reason, increase their labour hirings to full employment, then the additional supply produced creates additional demand so that all the additional output will be sold. (For a further discussion, see section 3.)
2. Aggregate nominal income is

$$PY = PC + PA \qquad (a)$$

where Y is real aggregate output, C is real consumption, A is real government expenditures, and P is the price level. Tax revenue (T) is

$$T = sPY \qquad \text{(b)}$$

where 'the government collects the fraction s of each household's current income as taxes' (Weitzman, 1985, p. 939) so that aggregate after-tax disposable income (PY_d) is:

$$PY_d = (1 - s)PY \qquad \text{(c)}$$

Government expenditure is equal to tax revenues plus new money (M) created to finance the deficit (D), where $M = D$, so that

$$PA = sPY + M = sPY + D \qquad \text{(d)}$$

If the government budget is balanced, then

$$PA = sPY \qquad \text{(e)}$$

Substituting equation (e) into (a) and rearranging terms shows that, if the government runs a balanced budget, the ratio of personal savings to after-tax income is zero as aggregate consumption on current output just equals households' aggregate disposable income; that is,

$$PC = (1 - s)PY \qquad \text{(f)}$$

If, on the other hand, the government runs a deficit, then substituting equation (d) into (a) and rearranging terms shows that, therefore, the personal savings ratio is equal to D/PY_d so that *the larger the deficit, ceteris paribus, the greater the personal savings ratio.*

3. Although, earlier, Weitzman (1982) had claimed that the existence of increasing returns was the foundation of all unemployment theory, his current analysis does not rely on increasing returns to demonstrate unemployment. In his recent model discussed herein, unemployment would occur due to the perishability of supply and the intertemporal stretch of demand whether there was increasing, decreasing, or constant returns to labour, while the price of each firm (equation (43)) as well as the price level either decreases, increases, or remains constant (via equation (43)) as employment varies under the different laws of returns.

4. For purposes of simplicity and ease of comparability with the ordinary Marshallian firm supply function, only the form of equation (1) will be developed in the following discussion. Equational form (2) of the aggregate supply function can then be derived merely by dividing all money sums expressed in equations (1), (3), and (4) by the existing money-wage rate.

5. For example, in the purely competitive case, it is always assumed that changes in aggregate demand do not affect the elasticity of the demand curve facing each firm. In more complex cases the degree of monopoly may vary as aggregate demand changes and the firm's demand curve shifts, that is, $\mu = f(N)$, as, for example, suggested by Harrod (1936).

6. Provided one reasonably assumes that corresponding to any given point of aggregate supply there is a unique distribution of proceeds and employment between the different firms in the economy (Keynes, 1936, p. 282). Weitzman's

assumption that the government and all households have the same trade-off among goods and all firms have the same production function assures this unique distribution of proceeds and employment.

7. Small closed, homogeneous communities such as a kibbutz or a monastery may be able to hammer out a social order based on a sharing concept. Weitzman postulates a homogeneous community of interests with the *same* utility function for all households (1985, p. 939). For large economic systems with production and consumption processes involving interdependencies and feedback among a large number of heterogeneous and different interest (i.e. differing utility functions) subsectors, the institution of money contracts appears to be the best civilized system yet devised by humans over centuries to encourage the undertaking and carrying out to completion of these complex economic processes.

References

Bénassy, J. P. (1982), *The Economics of Market Disequilibrium* (New York; Academic Press).

Davidson, P. (1962), 'More on the Aggregate Supply Function', *Economic Journal* (June) (Chapter 31 in this volume).

Davidson, P. (1972), 'A Keynesian View of Friedman's Theoretical Framework for Monetary Analysis', *Journal of Political Economy* (September–October) (Chapter 8 in this volume).

Davidson, P. (1978), *Money and the Real World*, 2nd edn (London: Macmillan).

Davidson, P. (1982–3), 'Rational Expectations: A Fallacious Foundation for Studying Crucial Decision-making Processes', *Journal of Post Keynesian Economics*, 5 (2), pp. 182–98.

Davidson, P. (1983), 'The Marginal Product Curve Is Not the Demand Curve For Labor and Lucas's Labor Supply Function Is Not the Supply Curve for Labor in the Real World', *Journal of Post Keynesian Economics*, 6 (1), pp. 105–17 (Chapter 42 in this volume).

Davidson, P. (1984), 'Reviving Keynes's Revolution', *Journal of Post Keynesian Economics*, 6 (4), pp. 561–75 (Chapter 43 in this volume).

Davidson, P. and G. S. Davidson (1984), 'Financial Markets and Williamson's Theory of Governance', *Quarterly Review of Economics and Business*, Spring 1984.

Davidson, P. and E. Smolensky (1964), *Aggregate Supply and Demand Analysis* (New York: Harper & Row).

Debreu, G. (1959) *Theory of Value* (New York: Wiley).

Grandmont, J. M. (1983), *Money and Value* (Cambridge: Cambridge University Press).

Harrod, R. F. (1936), *The Trade Cycle* (London: Macmillan).

Keynes, J. M. (1936), *The General Theory of Employment, Interest and Money* (New York: Harcourt).

Keynes, J. M. (1979), *The Collected Writings of John Maynard Keynes*, Vol. XXIX, ed. by D. Moggridge (London: Macmillan).

Lerner, A. P. (1935), 'The Concept of Monopoly and the Measurement of Monopoly Power', *Review of Economic Studies*.

Modigliani, F. (1944), 'Liquidity Preference and the Theory of the Interest Rate', *Econometrica*.

Robertson, D. H. (1956), *Economic Commentaries* (London: Macmillan).

Weintraub, S. (1957), 'The Micro-Foundations of Aggregate Demand and Supply', *Economic Journal* (September).

Weintraub, S. (1958), *An Approach to the Theory of Income Distribution* (Philadelphia: Chilton).

Weitzman, M. L. (1982), 'Increasing Returns and the Foundation of Unemployment Theory', *Economic Journal* (September).

Weitzman, M. L. (1983), 'The Simple Macroeconomics of Profit Sharing', *American Economic Review* (December).

Weitzman, M. L. (1985), 'The Simple Macroeconomics of Profit Sharing', *American Economic Review*, 75.

47 Financial Markets, Investment and Employment*

The concept of financial market is limited, in the following analysis, to any market where easily resaleabale debt and/or equity securities of business firms and governments are traded.[1] Financial markets, therefore, always encompass well-organised, continuous and orderly spot markets.

1 LIQUIDITY AND THE ROLE OF SPOT FINANCIAL MARKETS

Well-organised markets for financial assets are essential to the development of liquidity properties for any asset other than money. For an agent to possess liquidity one must have the ability to meet one's contractual obligations when they come due, i.e. to be liquid means that an agent has available, or can readily obtain, the means of contractual settlement. In order to provide *liquidity*, therefore, any asset other than money must be readily resaleable in a well-organized, continuous spot market in order to obtain the means of contractual settlement. (Money which, by definition, is *the* means of contractual settlement, possesses the highest degree of liquidity possible.)

A real world requirement for the existence of any well-organized spot market is a *market-maker*, i.e. an institution willing, and able, to act as the buyer and/or seller of last resort in the market.

A fully liquid asset is any durable whose resale market is dominated by a market-maker who (i) stands ready to buy or sell any quantity of the asset being traded *at a fixed announced nominal price*, and (ii) has virtually unlimited resources to maintain this market price. Fully liquid assets, therefore, can be converted into the medium of contractual settlement at the option of the holder. In modern bank-money economies, this implies that all fully liquid assets are those whose value in terms of domestic money is guaranteed via a market-maker institution which is either a division or an agent of the central bank.

A liquid asset is a durable traded in a well-organised, continuous resale market in which the market-maker is expected to intervene only to main-

* In *Barriers to Full Employment* (London: Macmillan, 1988), ed. E. Matzner, J. A. Kregel, and S. Roncaglia.

tain 'orderliness' in the spot market, whenever price movements become, in the judgement of the market maker acting under the rules of the particular organized market, too volatile to be justified by the circumstances. In liquid asset spot markets, it is expected that, in normal times, the price will change by small increments over time; most of the transactions will involve bull and bear individuals, with very few transactions involving the market-maker. The latter will be required by the rules to intervene to slow price changes only when one side of the market (either the bulls or the bears) tends to dry up – with the result of disorderly, discontinuous large changes in spot market prices in the absence of deliberate market-maker actions. The existence of market-makers in liquid asset financial markets permits most market participants to expect that they can liquidate their holdings easily whenever they desire. Most financial markets trade in liquid, rather than fully liquid, assets.

Finally, an *illiquid asset* is any durable whose spot market is poorly organised, disorderly, and/or even notional. Most real capital goods are illiquid assets. Some debt (e.g. most consumer and some business bank loans) as well as some small business equity certificates are essentially illiquid assets.

2 FINANCE, FUNDING AND NEW INVESTMENT

Financial markets play two important roles in the economy. First, via the 'new issue' segment of the financial market, money is transferred from economic agents who currently possess some wealth in the form of the medium of contractual payment to others who desire to 'fund' investment in costly, long-lived, illiquid assets. The concept of *funding* involves the selling of new issues of long-term debt and/or equity securities by buyers who use these 'funds' to pay the producers of illiquid fixed capital goods immediately for delivery – thereby permitting investors to take a position in real illiquid assets (cf. Davidson, 1982, pp. 36–7). Since fixed capital goods are not expected to generate sufficient quasi-rents to pay for themselves in the current period, buyers must fund the purchase price over a long period.

If entrepreneurs, who desire to establish profitable positions in costly illiquid real fixed capital, could not be assured of obtaining funding at acceptable costs via the new issue market by underwriting institutions, then these investors would not be willing to commit themselves contractually by ordering forward the new capital goods upon which the growth of the economy depends. The underwriting commitment for future funding permits entrepreneurial investors to commit themselves contractually today for the future (date of delivery) purchase of capital goods.

The producers of capital goods, armed with these forward contractual purchase orders, can then borrow finance from their bankers. These short-term bank loans permit capital goods producers to build up their working capital which, when completed, are the finished capital goods sold to investors who use their funding proceeds to meet their purchase obligations. The resulting sales receipts of the capital goods producers are used to pay off their working capital loans – and become a revolving fund available from the banks to finance the production of new working capital.

3   FINANCE AND LIQUIDITY

The second function of financial markets – and the most important one in modern economies – involves the spot market segment. Spot financial markets that deal in 'second-hand' assets provide various degrees of liquidity havens for those wealth owners who, facing an uncertain future, currently do not want to commit all their current claims on resources either (i) to purchase currently produced consumer goods, or (ii) to contractually order specific future produceable consumer goods at a specified future date, or (iii) to the current purchase of illiquid assets which can be expected to generate a specific dated future time stream of purchasing power via quasi-rents. The development of well-organized resale spot markets, by providing liquidity for the second-hand assets which are actively traded in such markets, makes the initial sale of these securities in the new issue market more attractive to wealth owners, facing an uncertain future, who are looking for freedom to delay decisions on the current commitment of resource claims.

Organized resale securities markets represent the continuous conflict of expectations of bulls and bears about the spot prices in the uncertain (not statistically predictable) future; they are speculative markets. 'A speculative market is *inherently restless*' as any '*constancy* of . . . price is contrary to the expectation on which it depends' (Shackle, 1972, pp. 200–1). Spot prices of liquid assets must be 'inherently restless' over time – or else there would not be groups of bulls and bears to enter the market continuously and provide the liquidity upon which the market depends.

Since second-hand liquid assets are essentially perfectly substitutable assets for new issues, the current resale spot price equals the cost of current funding. Since the funding requirement is related to the supply price of new capital, which, in turn, includes the cost of borrowing from the banks to finance working capital loans by producers (cf. Davidson, 1972, chapters 11–13), therefore, the costs of funding, liquidity, and short-term bank loans for financing production flows are inevitably interrelated.

4   WHY DO FINANCIAL MARKET SPOT PRICES CHANGE OVER TIME?

There are two fundamentally incompatible explanations regarding the observed price movements which occur in well-organized, spot markets for second-hand liquid financial assets, namely (a) the psychological account and (b) the rational expectations narrative:

The foremost exponent of the first view was Keynes who argued that the spot bond price i.e.

> the rate of interest is a highly psychological phenomenon . . . It might be more accurate. perhaps, to say that the rate of interest is a highly conventional, rather than a highly psychological, phenomenon. For its actual value is largely governed by the prevailing view as to what it is expected to be. (Keynes, 1936, pp. 203–4)

The rational expectations (hereafter ratex) approach, on the other hand, implies that all financial markets are 'efficient'. Ratex assumes (a) that relevant information regarding future events is currently available to all; and (b) that the expectations of all agents, based on the available information, are either homogeneous or else dispersions of expectations about the mean expectation do not affect future trends via false trades, bankruptcies, etc. Efficient market theorists assume that the spot price of second-hand equity financial assets is the present value (using a stable real discount factor) of optimally forecasted future real dividends over the life of the securities. In a complete general equilibrium framework, these future real dividends are determined by the marginal physical productivity of capital.

The efficient market theory implies that in the absence of government interference, regulation, and discretionary monetary policy, the economy will, in the long run, achieve the state of bliss of full employment and a rate of economic growth that is limited only by technical progress and the growth in the labour force. Using a parade of sophisticated tools, the ratex approach justifies the old classical homilies, that *informed* agents acting in their own best interests will, in the absence of discretionary government actions, reach a state of full employment.

In Keynes's alternative model of a monetary production economy, there need not currently exist any information or market signals about future events because the future may *not* exist, even in a probabilistic sense. Accordingly, current expectations are anchored only by conventions. The Keynesian psychological view of financial markets implies, therefore, that if expectations are unsecured, financial market prices can either fluctuate violently or temporarily pause at any value, thereby affecting the liquidity of the economy and interest rates and consequently the rate of investment, employment, and economic growth. Accordingly, there is an active role for

Table 47.1 Daily Volatility* of Dollar Exchange Rates, Percentage Changes

	1980–4 average	1985 to date
D-Mark	0.7	0.9
Sterling	0.6	1.1
Yen	0.7	0.5

*Standard deviation of % change.
Source: *The Economist*, 18 May 1985.

government in promoting sticky expectations regarding spot financial market prices, via a discretionary monetary and exchange rate policy, at levels which are compatible with full employment and rapid economic growth.

The efficient markets approach has driven the psychological approach from economic discussions, despite the mounting empirical evidence, of both a short-run and long-run nature, which is incompatible with the efficient market thesis. Shiller, for example, has examined the long-run relationship between real stock prices and real dividends in the United States from 1889 to 1981 and has concluded that 'the volatility of stock market price indexes appears to be too high to accord with the efficient market model given the observed variability of aggregate dividends' (Shiller, 1984, p. 3).

Recent very short-run analysis, showing increasing financial spot price volatility, is also incompatible with an efficient market view. For example, *The Economist* (1985, p. 74) indicated that during the first few months of 1985 the daily exchange rate volatility of the Deutsche Mark and sterling 'have often swung 2–3 per cent a day against the dollar. Not so the yen (because of Bank of Japan intervention) . . . In terms of daily movements, European currencies have become more volatile this year than 1980–4' (see Table 47.1).

Since there has been no obvious increase in either random shocks or the amount of daily information flows regarding the future in the first four months of 1985 *vis-à-vis* the past four years, the data in Table 47.1 appear to be inconsistent with the efficient market hypothesis! This observed increase in European currency fluctuations is compatible with unanchored expectations in the absence of any government intervention conventions; while the daily stickiness in the Japanese exchange rate can be associated with expectations secured on the active role of the Bank of Japan.

With the decline in prestige of the Keynesian psychological explanation and the ascendancy of the ratex view of financial market prices in both academic and governmental policy discussions, there has been, not coincidentally, a similar decline in the successful growth and employment in the developed countries and a return to the slower pace of international expansion, and the higher rates of unemployment associated with pre-Keynesian years when the philosophy of free market optimisation dominated our economic thinking and policies. Until we get our theories of financial markets 'right', we will not be able to re-establish the economic policies and progress associated with the earlier post-Keynesian, post-Second World War period.

5   TIME AND STRUCTURAL STABILITY

A fundamental axiom of the ratex market approach is that the future structure of the economic system is already determined in the current period, at least in a stochastic sense. Under this view, human beings can only discover the economic future, they cannot create it.

Technically this implies that all future economic events are the result of an already operating ergodic stochastic process. In an ergodic stochastic process, the probability function which governed the occurrence of past events is the same as the probability distribution which determines today's outcomes and it is also the same as the probability function out of which the future events will be drawn (see Davidson, 1982–3). The economic universe is presumed to be in a state of statistical control over time (Davidson, 1972; 1980). Thus the efficient financial market theory is a modern hi-tech analogue of the classical theory of determinism – with *the economic future being merely a stochastic reflection of the past*; actual future events determined, despite Einstein's warning to the contrary, by Nature's throw of the dice!

By contrast, in non-ergodic circumstances, statistical time averages calculated over a single time series realisation will not approach the space (fixed point of time) average calculated from a universe of realisations with a probability of unity as the realisations approach infinity. In other words, in a non-ergodic environment, the statistical probability distribution based on past observations is not relevant for determining the probabilities of either current or future outcomes.

For ratex theorists, the study of economics is similar to astronomy – a non-experimental, but empirical science, where the governing 'scientific laws' are *timeless* and hence the economic world is presumed to be ergodic. Ratex 'scientific' economists are searching for economic laws similar to the ahistorical laws that make up Newtonian physics. But as Hicks (1979, p. 3) has noted (picking up a theme developed by Keynes and more explicitly by Shackle): 'experimental science in its very nature, is out of historical time; it has to be irrelevant, for the significance of an experiment, at what *date* it is made, or repeated'.

Non-experimental natural sciences such as astronomy rely on the laws developed in the experimental sciences such as physics. Hence astronomical predictions are based on ergodic 'laws' which are assumed to be invariant with respect to calendar time. Thus for Hicks, economics is not like astronomy; in economics one cannot suppose that past evidence is sufficient for drawing inferences about the future (cf. Shackle, 1972).

For economic decisions, calendar time and history (not just age) are essential aspects of future outcomes, i.e. observations (results) are not necessarily independent of the date that crucial decisions are carried out. The economic situation may be non-ergodic. Econometrically established past 'real' relationships cannot be automatically presumed to hold in the future. The economic future can never be fully determined, even in a stochastic sense. Accordingly, sensible economic agents know that there are always some future events which cannot be captured in the existing information about the past and the present.

6   TIME AND CRUCIAL DECISIONS

Marshall, in his *Principles* (1890, p. vii), noted that the 'element of time is the centre of the chief difficulty of almost every economic problem'. And Shackle has added '[t]ime and logic are alien to each other. The one entails ignorance, the other pre-supposes a sufficient axiom system, a system embracing everything relevant. The void of future, but relevant, time destroys the possibility of logic' (Shackle, 1972, p. 254).

Shackle has identified the concept of *crucialness* in economic affairs. 'Crucialness is the real and important source of uniqueness in any occasion of choosing' (Shackle, 1955, p. 63). A crucial decision occurs when the person 'concerned cannot exclude from his mind the possibility that the very act of performing the experiment may destroy forever the circumstances in which it is performed' (ibid., p. 6). Consequently, crucial economic decision-making, by definition, assures a non-ergodic situation so that the economic variables which impinge upon the decision-makers' environment are not ahistorical. Crucial decisions create a new future. In such circumstances, rational expectations are not relevant and our choice between alternatives depends upon 'our innate urge to activity which makes the wheels go round' (Keynes, 1936, p. 163) versus our inborn needs for safety.

Many economists strongly resist the implication of Shackle's conceptualization of crucialness in economic affairs and Keynes's emphasis (ibid., ch. 12) on (non-ergodic) uncertainty dominating financial markets. Samuelson, for example, has insisted that the condition of ergodicity and the timelessness of economic models are fundamental requirements of scientific economic analysis. Samuelson notes that in neo-classical theory there is

an interesting assumption . . . I shall call it the ergodic hypothesis . . .

technically speaking we theorists hoped not to introduce *hysteresis* phenomena into our model, as the Bible does when it says 'We pass this way only once' and in so saying, takes the subject out of the realm of science into the realm of genuine history. (Samuelson, 1968, pp. 184–5)

To Samuelson, the economics discipline is unscientific if its practitioners believe that economic agents by their own crucial actions can create the future and, therefore, the economic process depends on the history of who 'passed this way only once'. If agents can create the economic future, then, according to Samuelson, economics becomes a humanistic, historical study, which by inference, makes economists second-class citizens in the scientific community.[2] Neither Samuelson nor ratex proponents want such second-class citizenship.

Even the strongest advocates of ratex, however, reluctantly admit that sometimes it is impossible to draw statistical inferences about future outcomes based on existing evidence. In so doing, they are implicitly conceding the possibility of Shackle's crucial decision-making activities impinging on future human outcomes in a non-ergodic world. For example, Lucas and Sargent state:

we observe an agent, or a collection of agents, behaving through time; we wish to use these observations to infer how this behaviour *would have* differed had the agent's environment been altered in some specified way. Stated so generally, it is clear that some inferences of this type will be impossible to draw. (How would one's life have been different had one married someone else?) The belief in the possibility of a nonexperimental empirical economics, is, however, equivalent to the belief that inferences of this kind can be made, in *some* circumstances. (Lucas and Sargent, 1981, p. xii)

Lucas and Sargent provide no criteria to indicate when these '*some* circumstances' prevail in the economy. Indeed they tend to imply that in most circumstances non-crucial decision-making pertains. But if such mundane decisions as the choice of spouse are, in Lucas's and Sargent's view, so crucial that despite the vast historical record on the outcomes of past marriages it is impossible to draw any statistical inference, then what about crucial funding decisions wedding entrepreneurs to specific illiquid investment projects or production processes, or consumers to big-ticket expenditures? Are not these economic choices *crucial* to the future outcome of most economic events? And do not these impact on, and interact with, spot financial market prices?

Accordingly, a significant difference between most leading mainstream neoclassical economists (e.g. Lucas, Sargent, Samuelson) and Keynes and many post-Keynesians is whether they believe that crucialness in a non-ergodic context is a salient characteristic of the economic decision-making process under study.

Ratex theorists explicitly presume that currently there exists sufficient information about future probability functions so that no matter what decision is made, cruciality is not involved. As the aforementioned quote from Samuelson indicates, neoclassical synthesis Keynesians had already implicitly accepted this ergodic presumption. For Keynes, and post-Keynesians, on the other hand, the economic future does not currently exist and hence there are no market signals that future agents can provide today's decision-makers. *The future does not possess an informational shadow that it can cast today.*

We should not conclude from this that everything depends on waves of irrational psychology. On the contrary, the state of long term expectation is often steady, and, even when it is not, the other factors exert compensating effects. We are merely reminding ourselves that human decisions affecting the future, whether personal or political or economic, cannot depend on strict mathematical expectation, since the basis for making such calculations does not exist. (Keynes, 1936, pp. 162–3)

For Keynes, financial expectations cannot be rationally based on an ergodic economic process. To anchor financial expectations over time therefore, required conventions which encourage the belief in stability plus deliberate policy actions to offset wild fluctuations in private sector psychology, if such swings should occur. There is thus a vast philosophical difference between those who profess a ratex view and those who hold a post-Keynesian position. For the latter, as Hicks (1979, p. 39) declared, there are 'no constants in economics' determined by 'real' forces independent of human control and actions.

It is just that economics is in time, in a way that the natural sciences are not. All economic data are dated; so that inductive evidence can never do more than establish a relation which appears to hold within a period to which the data refer. If a relation has held . . . over (say) the last fifty years . . . we can not even reasonably guess it will continue to hold for the next fifty years. In the sciences such guesses are reasonable; in economics they are not. Economics . . . is on the edge of science and on the edge of history. (Hicks, 1979, p. 38)

In a recent paper, Solow (1985, p. 330) argues that 'the end product of economic analysis [should be] . . . a collection of models contingent on society's circumstances – on the historical context'. Solow believes, therefore, that mainstream scientific economists have been misled by following the 'best and the brightest in the profession [who] proceed as if economics is the physics of society . . . [where t]here is a single universally valid model of the world' (ibid.). Thus, at least some of the leaders of orthodox economic theory have, at last, recognised the non-ergodic nature of economic science. With the apparent conversion of J. R. Hicks and R. M. Solow to the non-ergodic view of economics, can the rest of mainstream economists be far behind?

7 ARE ECONOMIC AGENTS IN FINANCIAL MARKETS ROBOTS?

7.1 A Robot World

General equilibrium theory, especially in its ratex version, attempts to develop a theory of choice which models 'a *robot* decision maker' (Lucas and Sargent, 1981, p. xiii; italics added).

If, however, the mainstream view of a stable (real? monetary?) long-term rate of interest disturbed only by random shocks were applicable, then the robot rational agents would 'know' that it would never pay to speculate against the market by holding any specific security for a period of time less than the agents optimising intertemporal consumption decision. Since the robots would recognise that the market is the most efficient forecaster of the future, they would decide that, in the long run, all bull and/or bear speculation against the average market opinion must prove fruitless. (With the existence of transactions costs, speculation against the market must, in the long run, be costly to the speculators.) Consequently, rational expectation robot decision-makers would deprive the market of any intermediate bull–bear transactions, thereby stripping bonds of the liquidity that they provide real world bondholders who may not wish to hold bonds to maturity. Accordingly, the neoclassical assumption of a long-run parametric (real) interest rate in an ergodic world is logically incompatible with a real world bond market where bondholders desire liquidity to protect themselves from unforeseen and unforeseeable events and therefore require the continuous action of the bulls to provide the liquidity for the market.

In a world of rational expectations with intertemporal gross substitution of consumer goods by optimizing robot households[3] and the existence of contingency contracts, if bonds for all maturity dates exist, every specific bond would be sold only once, in the new issues market, to robot agents whose intertemporal consumption plan called for the expected consumption of that portion of their wealth at that bond's future maturity date.

7.2 A Human World

Post-Keynesians, on the other hand, argue for an analysis of an economic system where decision-makers have choice and free will: where humans – not robots – create the future via their crucial decisions. In such a world, the spot market is a battleground for conflicting and changing expectations which may not be resolved except via death or other grave wounds.

This view of continual conflict is most clearly discerned in the battle between the bulls and the bears in financial markets. The price of liquid assets in spot markets where activity is continuous, involves the *momentary* balancing of differing expectations about future spot prices of the traded securities. Since only one spot price will exist at any moment currently or at any specified future time, the expectations of at least half of the market participants (either the bulls or the bears) will be disappointed at each point of time.

In the real world, the continuous gyrations of spot security prices are not considered by the bull and bear players as merely random movements around a parametised long-period price. These short-run price movements are, in a significant sense, 'expected' by the market 'player' participants for these movements represent potential profit-making opportunities if they can buy at a lower price than they sell. The only relevant consideration for profit-seeking spot market players is the next period's expected return (R):

$$R = P_{t+1} - P_t - T$$

where P_{t+1} is the next period's expected spot price (including accrued interest earnings), P_t is the current market price and T is the transactions cost of buying and selling. If $T=0$, then it is only the difference between the next moment's price and the current price which is important; with $T>0$, the expected difference in price (including accrued interest) must exceed transactions costs for an agent to act bullishly on his expectations. As long as transactions costs are relatively low; the long-run expected return over the life of the asset is irrelevant for market players. Only if transactions costs were inordinately high, would the purchase of a security become 'permanent and indissoluble, like marriage, except by reason of death or other grave cause' (Keynes, 1936, p. 161) and only then would the long-run expected return be relevant as the liquidity characteristics of the asset vanished.

Hence those who 'play' the real world financial markets for profit are never concerned with the long-run price. As long as there is the potential for short-run price movements which exceed transaction costs, market players searching for profit opportunities need concentrate and speculate solely on these expected short-run price movements.

Times series data of spot financial prices are merely the stringing together of momentary, hourly, daily, etc., historical price observations in speculative markets which primarily reflect the actions of those who are attempting to outguess average opinion. No wonder that despite the billions of man-hours of computations spent searching these statistical realizations for systematic repetitive patterns to be used as the basis for forecasting future spot financial prices, no one has ever succeeded.[4] These spot price movements reflect the non-ergodic ebb and flow of speculative expectations. These expectations regarding future spot prices are anchored in the convention that liquid asset market prices are supposed to be in continual flux, while extreme (disorderly) movements are limited by market-maker actions.

## 8	LIQUID ASSET PRICES AND THE MARGINAL PRODUCTIVITY OF CAPITAL

Shiller's aforementioned study (1984) is compatible with Keynes's psychological view of spot financial price movements. One implication of this approach is that, even in the long run, time series of spot prices of liquid assets do *not* reflect a technologically determined marginal productivity of capital (cf. Keynes, 1936, ch. 16).

The lack of any such link to the real productivity of capital is especially obvious once it is recognized that resale markets for many pre-existing durables, other than liquid debt and equity securities, exist in the real world. In the absence of a 'market-maker' institution which fixes market prices by acting as the buyer and/or seller of last resort at announced prices (as opposed to a market-maker who merely limits disorderly price movements), spot prices of all pre-existing durables (not only securities) which are capable of being stored and resold on well-organised, continuous markets must be inherently restless.

These other resale markets also provide liquidity and an outlet for the same inherently restless speculation found in spot markets for financial assets. Unlike debt and equity securities whose present value is often linked to a technically determined real marginal productivity of capital by neoclassical economists, resaleable durables such as gold, old postage stamps, old masters and other collectibles cannot conceivably have any future marginal productivity 'real earnings' streams associated with their possession. Nevertheless, the spot market price movements of these durables are carefully followed by many wealth holders; with movement in spot prices readily reported in various publications. Wealth owners believe that 'other' resaleable liquid durables, such as used postage stamps, are important liquid substitutes for the speculative financial assets in their portfolios.

The mere existence of spot speculative markets for liquid 'collectibles' where there cannot be any conceivable relationship between these assets and the 'real' marginal productivity of capital should be sufficient to cast doubt on the general equilibrium foundations of the efficient market hypothesis which is ultimately based on a concept of a long-run real return on capital parameter determined by 'real productivity'.

Though the organization of these various speculative 'collectibles' markets differ in detail, all have some institutional market-maker which acts to limit volatility in spot prices and thereby encourage both speculative activities of market players and the liquidity properties of the underlying asset. The market demand and supply of all such durables could not be safely assumed to be sticky over time without the specific rules for 'market-maker' institutions which operate to limit spot price movements.

Any durable goods markets without institutional market-makers involve resale difficulties which severely limit the potential liquidity of the durables involved; hence such durables cannot be important objects of speculation. It is the conventional belief in the rules under which market-maker institutions operate in specific markets, and not stochastic determinacy, which more or less anchor expectations regarding the future spot prices of both financial assets and resaleable collectibles. These anchors are as frail as the ability of those in charge to enforce the market-making rules and practices under any circumstances. Ultimately, therefore, it is the liquidity position of the market-maker institution which assures its ability to make the market. This, in turn (as is liquidity in general), is tied to the monetary policy of the central bank.

9 POLICY IMPLICATIONS

The policy implications of this non-ergodic view of speculative spot security markets, in a world where money contracts are used to organize production activities (Davidson, 1982) and hence the ability to meet contractual commitments (liquidity) is essential, is startlingly different from the ratex approach. In the latter there is no role for discretionary interest rate policy, while in the former, *an essential aspect of providing for the stability of the non-ergodic macroeconomic system is a Monetary Authority whose activities, either directly, or indirectly via other institutional market-makers, limit the otherwise inherently restless and potentially disorderly movements in the prices of financial assets and hence interest rates.*

The Monetary Authority and, by extension, the banking system must act as a balancing factor – leaning against the potential buffeting winds of irrational psychology. By operating either directly or via financial intermediaries on the spot market for liquid assets, and, by laying down the rules of the financial game either by law or custom, the Monetary Authority via the banking system can affect not only the spot prices and volume of securities available for the public to hold, but also the cost and availability of working capital loans necessary to finance production flows in a system organized via money contracts.

Since interest rates (spots prices of financial assets) are an important determinant of aggregate employment and output, a full employment goal will *require* a Monetary Authority who will undertake a deliberate, discretionary policy of creating expectations of sticky financial prices – limiting financial spot price movements to a narrow band around that level which is necessary to provide sufficient liquidity to encourage a full employment level of effective demand. The judgement as to what is the proper level of interest rates and liquidity, which may vary over time as unforeseen and unforeseeable circumstances change, is too important an economic factor to be left to the non-probabilistic vagaries of an unfettered speculative financial market. Although, in a non-ergodic world, it is impossible to assure that a Monetary Authority will not make any errors of judgement, at least, it can be hoped for that an enlightened Authority, endowed with proper tools can act (i) to create an environment where private sector swings in liquidity preference are small, and (ii) to alleviate any shortage of liquidity if it develops.

Ultimately, the power of the Monetary Authority depends on the viability (acceptability) of the Monetary System. This viability, in a non-ergodic world, depends on the conventional belief in the stability of the money-efficiency wage (i.e. the money-wage rate divided by labour productivity) and, more generally, the money costs of production of goods. In the absence of some deliberate form of incomes policy, if the efficiency wage increases rapidly, then the Monetary Authority is likely to be 'the only game in town' to protect the viability of the Monetary System from the ravages of inflation by instituting a policy of explicitly constraining liquidity to create unemployment and thereby reduce the upward pressure on efficiency wages and other monetary costs of production. In carrying out such an anti-inflation policy, the Monetary Authority is creating a shortage of liquidity rather than alleviating it. The result will be unemployment, underutilized capacity, and unnecessary and undesirable economic deprivation.

Neoclassical economic theories such as ratex, on the other hand, assume invariant relationships over time, while postulating that in the absence of short-run random shocks to the system, the prices of financial assets and therefore interest rates will settle down to an unchanging, long-run value based on the real productivity of capital (and/or real time preference). In the long run, therefore, there is no need for any discretionary monetary policy. Despite the ubiquitous lip service paid in the ratex literature to the view that expectations drive the economic system, it logically follows from their ergodic assumption that in ratex economics 'real' phenomena of productivity and time preference drive the economic system – at least in the long run (when we shall all be dead!).

10   SHOULD EXPECTATIONS BE ENDOGENOUSLY RATIONAL?

For those economist 'scientists' who ultimately believe in an ergodic economic system, expectations about the future can never be autonomous – for such expectations would admit an indeterminateness in the argument and an openness in the system so that past quantitative measures of economic affairs need not be an adequate probabilistic guide to future events.

For post-Keynesians, on the other hand, the economic system is open-ended – the economic future is to be created by human actions. Keynes's emphasis on 'animal spirits' driving investment decisions requires an autonomous role for expectations. Keynes's response to those who wish to make expectations a well-developed endogenous quantitative variable was: 'As soon as one is dealing with the influence of expectations one is, in the nature of things, outside the realm of the formally exact' (Keynes, 1973, p. 2). For Keynes, the difference between a static and dynamic economic analysis 'is not the economy under observation which is moving in the one case and stationary in the other, but our expectations of the future environment which are shifting in the one case and stationary in the other' (ibid., p. 511). Problems in the real world can be analysed only when on average 'our previous expectations are liable to disappointment and expectations concerning the future affect what we do today' (Keynes, 1936, pp. 393–4).

It is only in a world of potential disappointment regarding future events – our world – that the 'peculiar properties of money as a link between the present and the future must enter into our calculations' (ibid., p. 294). It is only in the real world that money is not neutral and hence speculative activities on financial markets have real effects on output, employment, and growth in both the short and long run!

11   UNEMPLOYMENT, EXPECTATIONS AND THE NEUTRALITY OF MONEY

In the ratex theory, markets clear at every point of time. Logically consistency requires, therefore, the absence of involuntary unemployment – even in the short run. When faced by empirical evidence, however, ratex theorists will admit that labour resources are often, in the real world, unemployed – but not involuntarily so. Short-run changes in 'voluntary' unemployment occur, in ratex models, when agents make a mistake by confusing an observed change in their nominal selling price (assumed to be due to an absolute price level increase without any change in relative prices) for a change in the relative price of their output *vis-à-vis* all other products. As Lucas and Sargent state:

> under certain conditions, agents tend temporarily to mistake a general increase in all absolute prices as an increase in the relative price of the good they are selling, leading them to increase their supply of that good over what they have previously planned. Since on the average everyone is making the same mistake, aggregate output rises above what it would have been . . . Symmetrically, aggregate output decreases whenever the aggregate price level turns out to be lower than agents had expected. (1979, p. 307)

This ratex explanation of variations in observed unemployment over the business cycle, involves a sophisticated variant of the money illusion argument, i.e. erroneous (temporary) market responses are made in response to fluctuations in nominal values rather than (real) relative prices. For a theory which is based on the neutrality of money assumption, it is surprising that ratex can only explain the recurring real world changes in observed unemployment rates over the business cycle as due to continuous erroneous money illusion which causes money to be non-neutral.

Since the business cycle and observed variations in unemployment are persistent real world phenomena, then the ratex theorists should be required to reply to the following obvious questions: (i) since there is a long historical record of business cycles, why does the processing of the past evidence not lead sellers to form rational expectations that tell them that it is erroneous to interpret inflationary rises in the absolute price level as changes in their product prices relative to others? In other words, why does history indicate that people continue to suffer from recurrent money illusion? and (ii) if, in the real world, money illusions and the non-neutrality of money persists, what is the relevance of a theory of rational expectations which assumes the continuous neutrality of money for its equilibrium results?

In a post-Keynesian monetary production economy, on the other hand, an uncertain, non-ergodic future means that money is always non-neutral, in either the long run or the short run (Keynes, 1973, pp. 411–12). Thus right from the very beginning, unemployment is not just an errant event in a 'rational' world; rather it is a fundamental potential outcome of any *laissez-faire* economy where uncertainty and liquidity aspects are important and money and financial markets are non-neutral.

Notes

1. Thus any transactions in illiquid real or financial assets (defined below) are not included. This does not mean that purchases of basically illiquid assets are not affected by financial market conditions.
2. Yet in their political activities in working for the election of specific candidates for public office, these same self-proclaimed economic 'scientists' would probably not accept the implication of their ahistorical creed, namely that, *in the long run*, it makes no difference whether a Ronald Reagan or a Mrs Thatcher *vis-à-vis* a Walter Mondale or a Neil Kinnock is elected leader of the nation. For if the economic world is ergodic and ahistoric, the long-run economic outcomes are determined by technical conditions and are as independent of the decisions of political leaders as are the eclipses of the sun!
3. Indeed, Danziger *et al.* (1982–3) have shown that the facts regarding consumption spending by the elderly are incompatible with the notion of intertemporal gross substitution in consumption plans. Instead the facts are compatible with consumer behaviour under non-ergodic uncertainty.
4. Instant riches awaits anyone who can identify a systematic pattern.

References

Clower, R. W. (1969), *Monetary Theory* (Harmondsworth: Penguin).

Danziger, S., J. Van der Gaag, E. Smolensky, M. Taussig (1982–3), 'The Life Cycle Hypotheses and the Consumption Behaviour of the Elderly', *Journal of Post Keynesian Economics*, 5.

Davidson, P. (1967), 'A Keynesian View of Patinkin's Theory of Employment', *Economic Journal*, 77 (chapter 36 in this volume).

Davidson, P. (1972), *Money and the Real World* (London: Macmillan).

Davidson, P. (1980), 'Post Keynesian Economics: Solving the Crisis in Economic Theory', *The Public Interest*, 1980; reprinted in I. Kristol and D. Bell (eds), *The Crisis in Economic Theory* (New York: Basic Books) (chapter 17 in this volume).

Davidson, P. (1982), *International Money and the Real World* (London: Macmillan).

Davidson, P. (1982–3), 'Rational Expectations: A Fallacious Foundation for Crucial Decision Making', *Journal of Post Keynesian Economics*, 5.

Hicks, J. R. (1979), *Causality in Economics* (New York: Basic Books).

Keynes, J. M. (1936), *The General Theory of Employment, Interest, and Money* (London: Macmillan).

Keynes, J. M. (1973), *The Collected Writings of John Maynard Keynes*, Vol. XIV, edited by D. Moggridge (London: Macmillan).

Lucas, R. E. and T. J. Sargent (1979), 'After Keynesian Macroeconomics', *Federal Reserve Bank of Minneapolis Quarterly Review*, 3; reprinted in Lucas and Sargent (1981). All page references are to reprinted version.

Lucas, R. E. and T. J. Sargent (1981), *Rational Expectations and Econometric Practice* (Minneapolis: University of Minnesota Press).

Marshall, A. (1890), *Principles of Economics*, (London: Macmillan).

Samuelson, P. A. (1968), 'What Classical and Neoclassical Monetary Theory Really Was', *Canadian Journal Of Economics*, 1; reprinted in Clower, 1969. All page references are to the reprinted version.

Shackle, G. L. S. (1955), *Uncertainty in Economics* (Cambridge: Cambridge University Press).

Shackle, G. L. S. (1972), *Epistemics and Economics* (Cambridge: Cambridge University Press).

Shackle, G. L. S. (1980), 'Imagination, Unknowledge, and Choice', *Greek Economic Review*, 2.

Shiller, R. J. (1984), 'Financial Markets and Macroeconomics Fluctuations' (mimeo).

Solow, R. M. (1985), 'Economic History and Economics', *American Economic Review Papers and Proceedings*, 75.

The Economist, 295, no. 7394, May 18–24 1985.

Index